Federal Reserve System

by

Benjamin Haggott Beckhart

Professor Emeritus,
Banking
Columbia University

Distributed by Columbia University Press

AMERICAN INSTITUTE OF BANKING

THE AMERICAN BANKERS ASSOCIATION

Library of Congress Catalog No. 70-184746
ISBN 0-231-03536-5

0544
Printed in the United States of America

Preface

In 1913, when the Federal Reserve Act was enacted, the economic problems of the world seemed relatively simple and economic systems relatively stable. Economic policies were guided by a few simple maxims: balanced government budgets, gold redemption of currencies, fixed exchange rates, and freedom of trade capital movements and travel.

Government intervention in economic life was minimal. In the United States, this took the form mainly of tariff enactments. Tariffs designed to protect industrial products escalated steadily in the post-Civil War period, reaching a peak in the provisions of the Payne-Aldrich enactment of 1909. Agricultural products were sold at competitive prices in world markets.

Prior to World War I, the Federal government took little action to mitigate cyclical fluctuations or to relieve the hardships of depression. In fact, only a minority of the electorate advocated a positive policy. Their proposals envisaged the reform of the monetary standard and looked toward the substitution of bimetallism for the gold standard. Discussions of monetary issues concentrated on the merits and defects of these two standards.

Not until after the panic of 1907 was discussion centered on credit problems and on the need for a central bank. As bankers and economists began to devote their attention to the role of credit in the economy, they came to the conclusion that a central bank of some type was indispensable. One had not existed since the demise of the second United States Bank in 1836.

The conviction that another central bank should be established fostered the creation of the National Monetary Commission (1908), which issued a voluminous series of reports on central and commercial banking systems at home and abroad. These publications alerted the country to the seriousness of the problem and led to the establishment of the Federal Reserve System.

In this study, Professor Beckhart traces the operations and policies of the Federal Reserve System in the rapidly changing environment of the past sixty years. The opening chapter sets forth the origins of the System. The next four chapters discuss its administrative structure, a knowledge of which is essential to an understanding of policy actions.

Chapters 6 to 11, which cover the years from 1913 to 1960, discuss certain crucial periods in the history of the Federal Reserve System. These include the policies followed during World Wars I and II, attempts to curb post-war inflation, efforts to promote economic stability, action followed in depressions, and the adjustments which were necessitated by changes in the international gold standard. It was during these years that the techniques and objectives of Federal Reserve policy were formulated and developed.

Chapters 12 to 15 are devoted to the problems of the sixties. These years were dominated by a unique and unexpected development in American economic history: heavy deficits in the balance of payments, accompanied by massive flows of short- and long-term capital.

The developments described in this part form the basis of the discussion in Chapters 16 and 17, which deal with international monetary relations following the end of World War II. These include the work of the International Monetary Fund, swap agreements among central banks, the creation of paper gold (i.e., the special drawing rights), and Bretton Woods Revisited.

The study concludes with a review and analysis of monetary instruments (Chapter 18) and of the goals of monetary policy (Chapter 19).

Initiated and published by the American Institute of Banking, this study is also being distributed by the Columbia University Press. Representing a unique departure in its publication policies, AIB welcomes the collaboration of the Columbia University Press. This assures a wider audience—among libraries, businessmen, economists, and students. All can have access to and profit from studies sponsored by AIB.

As in the case of all of its publications, the American Institute of Banking appointed at the outset a Committee of Review. Besides the author, the members of the initial Committee included: David M. Kennedy, ex-Chairman of the Board, Continental Illinois National Bank and Trust Company, Chicago, Illinois (former Secretary of the Treasury); Dr. E. Sherman Adams, Senior Vice President, First

National City Bank, New York (subsequently Senior Vice President and Economist, The Fidelity Bank, Philadelphia, Pennsylvania); Dr. Karl R. Bopp, ex-President, Federal Reserve Bank of Philadelphia; Alan R. Holmes, Senior Vice President, Federal Reserve Bank of New York; Dr. Murray G. Lee, Deputy Manager, The American Bankers Association (deceased July 3, 1965); Dr. Donald C. Miller, former Senior Vice President, Continental Illinois National Bank and Trust Company; Dr. Weldon Welfling, Chairman, Banking and Finance Department, School of Management, Case Western Reserve University, Cleveland, Ohio.

Subsequently, the Committee was enlarged to include: Dr. David P. Eastburn, who succeeded Karl R. Bopp as President of the Federal Reserve Bank of Philadelphia; Dr. Robert G. Link, Senior Vice President, Federal Reserve Bank of New York; Dr. George W. McKinney, Jr., Senior Vice President, Irving Trust Company, New York City. In addition, Dr. Arthur I. Bloomfield, Professor of Economics, Wharton School of Finance and Commerce, Pennsylvania University, reviewed the original manuscript and made helpful suggestions.

The Institute wishes to acknowledge its indebtedness to the members of the Review Committee, who devoted themselves assiduously to a review and analysis of the chapters through many revisions, and who by their suggestions made substantial improvements in the manuscript through the elimination of errors of omission and commission. They, as well as other critics, are not to be held responsible for errors of fact or to be deemed to support the author's analysis and interpretations.

Many others from American banking circles participated in a review and appraisal of the chapters: Dr. Clay J. Anderson, former Economic Adviser, Federal Reserve Bank of Philadelphia; Edward H. Boss, Jr., Associate Economist, Continental Illinois National Bank and Trust Company, Chicago; Dr. Harry Brandt, Vice President, Research, Federal Reserve Bank of Atlanta; A. Harold Cameron, Investment Analyst, Dobbs Ferry, New York; Gerald T. Dunne, Vice President, Federal Reserve Bank of St. Louis; Howard H. Hackley, General Counsel, Board of Governors of the Federal Reserve System; Robert C. Holland, Executive Director, Board of Governors of the Federal Reserve System; Wesley Lindow, Executive Vice President and Secretary, Irving Trust Company, New York City; The Hon. William McC. Martin, Jr., ex-Chairman, Board of Governors of the Federal Reserve System; Dr. Herbert V. Prochnow, retired President, First National Bank of Chicago; Dr. William F. Staats, Secretary and Senior Economist, Federal Reserve Bank of Philadelphia; Dr. Parker B. Willis, Vice President and

Economic Adviser, Federal Reserve Bank of Boston; Albert M. Wojnilower, Economist and Vice President, The First Boston Corporation, New York City.

Among foreign and international bankers who assisted in the study, the author wishes to acknowledge his indebtedness to: Antonio d'Aroma, The Secretary General, Bank for International Settlements, Basle, Switzerland; Gabriel Ferras, late General Manager, The Bank for International Settlements; W. Lawrence Hebbard, Secretary, International Monetary Fund; the Hon. Ivar Rooth, former Governor of the Sveriges Riksbank and former Managing Director of the International Monetary Fund; the Hon. Pierre-Paul Schweitzer, Managing Director, The International Monetary Fund.

Miss Mathilde C. Stralucke and Mrs. Mildred S. Tubby, with great patience and perseverance, typed the manuscript from the author's handwriting.

A debt of gratitude is owed the author's wife, Dr. Margaret G. Myers, Professor Emeritus of Economics at Vassar College, who carefully reviewed the manuscript, thereby greatly improving the exposition and the logical sequence of thought. The author also wishes to acknowledge the generosity of Vassar College in permitting him to use its excellent library facilities.

The Institute hopes that the work may prove serviceable in an understanding of the difficult problems challenging the Reserve System through these many years. To understand the vicissitudes of the period is to appreciate the cyclopean tasks of the System.

> Robert P. Cavalier, Ph.D.
> Director of Education
> American Institute of Banking

Contents

Background of the Federal Reserve System

CHAPTER 1

CENTRAL BANKING FUNCTIONS

A prominent economist once said that money is as money does. By this he meant that anything is money that performs the functions of money; anything is money which serves as a medium of exchange, a storehouse of value, a standard of value, and a standard of deferred payments.

If in like manner it can be said that a central bank is as a central bank does, what then does a central bank do? Sir Ernest Harvey, then Comptroller of the Bank of England, noted some years ago in a lecture in Australia that a central bank should have the sole right of note issue; should serve the needs of commercial banks and other financial institutions; should be the principal fiscal agent of its government; should have the main responsibility for the maintenance of the gold and foreign-exchange reserves of the nation; and should have principal responsibility for the control of the volume and use of money in the interests of economic stability and growth.[1] It has a distinctly public purpose. It is not primarily a profit-making institution, although its profits may at times be large. It is above all a guardian of the national interest.

Only since World War I has the term "central bank," a term descriptive of the functions of such institutions, come into common usage. Previously, institutions now known as central banks had been referred to either individually—the Bank of England, the Banque de France, the Reichsbank—or collectively as note issuing banks, the common expression on the European continent. Bray Hammond pointed out, in his classic study, that the term had actually been used as early as 1834 by a French traveller to the United States, Michel Chevalier, who had referred to the Bank of the United States as a *banque centrale*.[2]

Today nearly all nations have central banks. The worldwide movement toward central banking was furthered by a resolution at the International Financial Conference held in Brussels in 1920, which advocated the establishment of a central bank in every nation that did not have one. The establishment of such banks, so the resolution read, would not only facilitate the restoration of stable banking and monetary systems but would also promote international monetary cooperation. (This movement was greatly encouraged throughout the British Commonwealth by Montagu Norman, Governor of the Bank of England during the 1920s.) Even if a country has little need today for a central bank, it must possess one. A central bank, housed in an imposing chrome-and-glass structure, is as much a status symbol for a developing nation as a steel mill.

THE BANK OF ENGLAND

The progenitor of this vast brood was the Bank of England—known as the Old Lady of Threadneedle Street. It was founded in 1694 from plans prepared by a Scot, William Patterson, who had traveled extensively on the Continent and who was familiar with the work of the Bank of Amsterdam and may even have heard of the issuance of bank notes by the Bank of Sweden as early as 1661. In his travels, he had seen the virtues of transferable funds of interest,[3] that is, perpetual interest-bearing loans. On the basis of such a loan to the British government, he founded the Bank of England.[4]

In 1691, in association with some London merchants, Patterson first proposed the establishment of the Bank, but nothing came of the proposal for three years. And even then, the Bank might not have been established had England not been at war and had Charles Montagu, a Lord of the Treasury and from 1694 Chancellor of the Exchequer, not found it the most promising of a score of suggested financial plans.

The act chartering the Bank of England was called the Tunnage Act. It permitted their Majesties several rates and duties upon the tunnages of ships and vessels, and upon beer, ale, and other liquors. Besides such taxes, the act authorized the raising of £1.2 million by subscription, the subscribers forming a corporation to be known as The Governor and Company of the Bank of England, a title by which the Bank is still well-known.

Winning a Unique Position

The Bank of England early attained a unique position in the British financial structure, as a result of its close relations with the government, the evolving use of its bullion holdings as the central monetary reserves of England, the exclusive use of its bank notes in the London area, and the tendency of provincial banks to hold deposits with London banks and they in turn with the Bank of England. Note and deposit liabilities of the Bank of England were gradually becoming the basis of British bank credit.

Even while its central-banking functions were gradually coming into flower, the Bank of England has through much of its history looked upon itself as a commercial bank, in competition with other banks for deposit and borrowing customers. It was not until the crisis of 1847 that the Bank clearly recognized that it was indeed a special type of institution and not merely one of many commercial banks. Old beliefs lingered on, however, and as late as the 1890s some Bank officials were still debating the desirability of permitting branches to compete for commercial discounts.

These views represented the attitude of a small minority, however. The crisis of 1847 had demonstrated that the Bank, as the holder of the nation's monetary reserves had special responsibilities. As John Stuart Mill pointed out in testimony before a parliamentary committee in 1857:

> Since 1847 the Bank have been quite aware, and the public have been aware . . . that an establishment like the Bank is not like other bankers, who are at liberty to think that their single transactions cannot affect the commercial world generally, and that they have only their own position to consider. The transactions of the Bank necessarily affect the whole transactions of the country, and it is incumbent upon them to do all that a bank can to prevent or mitigate a commercial crisis.[5]

Its experience through those years taught the Bank of England that it could not be operated as an ordinary commercial bank, that it should endeavor to anticipate and to curb inflationary and speculative trends, but that, once a crisis had occurred, it should lend liberally but at a high rate to prevent panic and to provide needed liquidity to the financial system. As Walter Bagehot later pointed out, it was the lender of last resort.[6] The basis of central banking had been laid.

The Bank of England served as a prototype for many central banks over the world, including the first and second Banks of the United States.

THE FIRST BANK OF THE UNITED STATES

It was very fortunate for this country that George Washington appointed Alexander Hamilton as the first Secretary of the Treasury. Brilliant, imaginative, well read, Hamilton brought to his office high standards of competence and rectitude in fiscal and monetary policy. He laid the basis for a federal tax system that yielded sufficient revenues to balance the budget during the whole of Washington's administration. He proposed the establishment of a mint and the adoption of bimetallism at the rate of 15 to 1.* He insisted that the monies borrowed from foreign governments during the Revolution be paid in full as soon as possible. He proposed that the heavily depreciated obligations, issued under the Articles of Confederation, be exchanged for new federal securities at the ratio of 100 to 1. He proposed, too, that the federal government assume the outstanding state debts. This the federal government did to the tune of $18.2 million.[7] These measures successfully established the credit of the new government at home and abroad and thus laid the basis for rapid economic growth.

Among the most important of Hamilton's recommendations was the proposal for a national bank, to be modeled after the Bank of England as it then existed. In a report submitted to Congress on December 14, 1790, he explained that "A National Bank is an institution of primary importance to the prosperous administration of the finances." [8] According to Hamilton the advantages of such a bank would be several:

1. A bank in good credit standing may augment the active capital of a country by receiving deposits and expanding bank credit, in the form of notes or deposits, upon a given base of gold and silver.

---

* The bimetallic standard is one in which both gold and silver coins of standard weight and fineness have the full legal tender power. It existed legally, in various forms, in the United States, from 1791 to 1873. A ratio of fifteen to one means that the weight of pure silver in the standard silver dollar was fifteen times the weight of pure gold in the standard gold dollar. This ratio must necessarily conform to the market price of one in terms of the other.

2. A bank is in a position to make loans to a government con-
    fronted by sudden emergencies.
3. A bank may facilitate the collection and payment of taxes.[9]

To be sure, as Hamilton also noted, there were arguments against the establishment of a national bank.* Opponents feared that it would increase usury, prevent other kinds of lending, furnish temptations to overtrading, afford aid to
ignorant adventurers, give bankrupt and fraudulent traders fictitious credit, and
banish gold and silver from the country. But these arguments, Hamilton declared,
were either false or based on the premise that the management of the bank would
be incompetent and imprudent. As a matter of fact, the Secretary declared, a national bank would make significant contributions to the economy by forcing traders
to be punctual in their payments. It would reduce interest rates by increasing the
quantity and quickening the circulation of money. It would draw gold and silver
into the country by stimulating the production of goods for export markets.

Hamilton also pointed out that the deficiency of money in the United States
could best be met by bank notes. The Constitution wisely forbade the states to issue
paper money, and the federal government should not disregard the spirit of that
prohibition. Governments are prone to issue paper money to excess, whereas if
banks were to do so, the bank notes would be returned for redemption in specie,
that is, in silver or gold. The amounts issued would thus be limited to the amounts
which the banks would be able to redeem.

Hamilton declared that none of the three commercial banks then in existence
in the United States would lend itself to conversion into a national bank. A new
bank had to be established, and he furnished Congress with a detailed outline of
an appropriate institution.

Charter of the First Bank

The act chartering the first Bank of the United States for a twenty-year period was signed by President Washington on February 25, 1791. The preamble
declared that the Bank would be conducive to the successful conducting of the national finances and would be productive of considerable advantages to trade and
industry.

The Bank was established with a capital of $10 million divided into 25,000

---

*It should be noted that a national bank, as proposed by Hamilton, was simply a commercial bank
operating on a nation-wide basis. As initially conceived it was not a central bank, though it might, and
would probably inevitably, develop into such.

shares, one-fifth to be subscribed by the U.S. government and four-fifths by individuals, partnerships, and corporations. The government borrowed from the bank an amount equal to its own subscription, $2 million, "borrowing with the one hand," as Hamilton said, "what is lent with the other."[10] Other shareholders were to pay for their stock, $8 million in all, one-quarter in gold and silver and three-quarters in Federal obligations. The Bank was permitted to organize as soon as it received $400,000 in specie from its subscribers. That it had received more at its inception is open to doubt.[11] If these transactions had been carried out, and carried out simultaneously, the balance sheet of the bank at its inception might have appeared as in Table 1.1.

Table 1.1
Hypothetical Balance Sheet, Bank of the United States, 1791
(Millions of Dollars)

Assets		Liabilities	
U.S. obligations	8	Capital	10
Gold and silver	2		–
Total	10	Total	10

The stockholders elected twenty-five directors, each of whom had to be an American citizen. The directors served without pay, were elected for one year, and only three-quarters of them, exclusive of the president of the Bank, were eligible for reelection. The directors were to appoint the necessary officers and clerks. The voting rights of shareholders diminished proportionally as their stock holdings increased. Each shareholder was entitled to at least one vote but no more than thirty. Only those stockholders actually residing in the United States could vote by proxy.

The Bank's operations were confined to the purchase and sale of gold and silver bullion, of bills of exchange, and of goods "really and truly pledged for money lent and not redeemed in due time." [12] It could sell its holdings of the public debt (U.S. obligations) and actually reduced them sharply over time. It could not purchase the public debt, except for the amount acquired at the time of its establishment, and could not lend the U.S. government in excess of $100,000, or any particular state in excess of $50,000. It was forbidden to deal or trade in goods on its own account. Interest on loans and discounts was limited to 6 percent per annum.

The head office of the Bank was located in Philadelphia, then the commercial and financial center of the country. The Bank was permitted to establish branches and did so in New York, Boston, Baltimore, Charleston, Norfolk, Savannah, the District of Columbia, and New Orleans—eight in all. The parent bank assigned a definite capital sum to each branch, appointed the directors and cashiers, fixed their salaries, and prescribed the method of keeping accounts and records. All notes issued at the branches were signed and countersigned by the president and cashier of the head office but were payable at the issuing branches. The time required for communication and travel in those days, however, gave the branches a great deal of actual autonomy.

The directors of the Bank of the United States chose Thomas Willing as the first president; he served from 1791 to 1807, when age and ill health brought about his resignation. He was succeeded by David Lennox, who served as president for the remaining four years of the Bank's existence.

Evaluation of the Bank

Discussion of the rechartering of the Bank arose as early as January 1808, when the stockholders first petitioned for its renewal. Over the years the Bank had become a very important financial institution, as one of the few balance sheets still in existence reveals (see Table 1.2). It was in a solvent and highly liquid condition. Its capital funds were equal to 77 percent of its deposit and note liabilities. Deposits greatly exceeded the volume of outstanding bank notes. The specie reserve equaled 38 percent of total deposit and note liabilities. Loans, consisting primarily of self-liquidating paper (short-term loans arising mainly from the sale of goods), were about seven times as large as holdings of U.S. government obligations.

Table 1.2
Balance Sheet, Bank of the United States, 1809*
(Millions of Dollars)

Assets		Liabilities	
U.S. government obligations	2.2	Bank notes	4.5
Loans, primarily sixty-day		Deposits by the government,	
discounted notes	15.0	other banks, and individuals	8.5
Balances due from state banks	.8	Capital	10.0
Specie	5.0	Undivided profits	.5
Cost of grounds and buildings	.5		
Total	23.5	Total	23.5

* A statement submitted by Albert Gallatin to the U.S. Senate on March 3, 1809.

In advocating rechartering, Secretary of the Treasury Albert Gallatin declared, "The affairs of the Bank of the United States, considered as a moneyed institution, have been wisely and skillfully managed." [13] He pointed out that the bank had provided a safe depository for public funds, had distributed monies around the country, had collected public revenues, and had occasionally made loans to the Federal government. In addition, it had issued a safe and elastic currency, financed commerce and industry, and provided foreign-exchange facilities.

It had exercised control over the note issues of the state banks by sending their notes promptly back for redemption. In thus curbing the tendency of state banks to overextend their note issues, the Bank had, however, generated powerful political opposition, which was further augmented by those who believed the original act to be unconstitutional and who were convinced that the Bank was controlled by hostile British interests (foreign stockholders, however, could vote their stock only in person, which meant that they had to come to the United States). Others looked upon the Bank simply as an avaricious monopoly. The charter was allowed to expire on February 25, 1811. By 1815 it had returned 100 percent of its capital to the stockholders and when it was finally liquidated in 1852 it had returned 109 percent. Its branches were sold to local interests. On June 23, 1812, the City Bank (now the First National City Bank) purchased the property of the New York branch—which consisted of a banking house on Wall Street, a dwelling for the cashier on Pine Street, a banking house at Greenwich (presumably the present Greenwich Village), and sixteen lots—for $100,000. The head office in Philadelphia became the Bank of Stephen Girard.

Had the charter of the first Bank been renewed, it would probably have continued as the central bank of United States and through the years would have provided the country with an elastic currency, prevented wildcat and red-dog banking orgies* and rendered unnecessary the National Currency Act and the Federal Reserve Act. The nation's growth would have been at least as rapid as it was and doubtless also would have been much less volatile.

THE SECOND BANK OF THE UNITED STATES

The charter of the first Bank could not have been terminated at a more inopportune time, for within a year the country was involved in the War of 1812, and ineptitude of American military leadership was matched only by the deterioration

---

* Wildcat and red-dog banks, so-called, were purposely located in remote areas, which made it difficult for holders of the banknotes issued by these banks to redeem the notes.

of federal finances and the currency. Secretary of the Treasury Alexander James Dallas reported in 1814 that public credit was depressed, that there was no adequate circulating medium common to all citizens of the United States, and that private money transactions were at a standstill. It was impossible, he added, that such a state of things could be long endured. The remedy lay in "the establishment of a national institution, operating upon credit combined with capital, and regulated by prudence and good faith. . . ."[14]

Secretary Dallas prepared a plan for a new national bank, which was enacted by Congress but vetoed by President James Madison. The veto message criticized the bill on the grounds that the proposed bank's capital would be insufficient, that the bank could not be relied upon during the war to provide a circulating medium or indeed even to furnish loans in anticipation of public revenues, and that the government would be insufficiently compensated for the monopolistic privileges conferred upon the bank.[15]

After several unsuccessful efforts, a proposal did finally receive the approval of President Madison and became law on April 10, 1816. The act provided for the establishment of a bank with a capital of $35 million, one-fifth of which was to be subscribed by the federal government and four-fifths by individuals, partnerships, and corporations. The government was permitted to pay for its stock in coin or in its own obligations. Other shareholders were required to pay for their stock one-fourth in coin and three-fourths in coin or federal government obligations. The Bank had twenty-five directors, five appointed by the President from among the shareholders and twenty elected by the shareholders themselves. The directors were empowered to elect the President of the Bank from among their own number. All directors had to be resident American citizens.

The Bank was empowered to issue bank notes up to the amount of its capital, to receive deposits, and to deal in bills of exchange and gold and silver bullion. Its main office was again in Philadelphia; it was authorized to establish branches and at one time had as many as twenty-five, from Portland, Maine, to New Orleans.[16] It was the sole depository of federal funds unless the Secretary of the Treasury should direct otherwise and was required to transfer public funds from branch to branch, according to need, without charge. The Bank's charter was limited to twenty years, and for its privileges it was to pay the United States $1.5 million in three annual instalments.

The second Bank which opened for business on January 7, 1817, was at the outset under the control of directors whom Stephen Girard declared had been elected by "intrigue and corruption." There were several men on the board, he continued, "whose occupations, moral characters, or pecuniary situation will not inspire that indispensable confidence which is absolutely necessary to establish and consolidate the credit of that institution." [17]

The Bank shortly began to overextend itself. Trade was active, prices were rising, and loans were granted with great liberality. President William Jones, who had few qualifications for his position, exercised no restraint over the branches. There was a "perfect want of system." [18] The branches renewed loans again and again and extended loans on mortgages* and on the bank's own stock.[19] Lacking restraint itself, the Bank placed no restraint on the state banks.

To mismanagement were added speculation and fraud. Stock speculators gained control of the Baltimore branch, borrowed on the stock of the parent bank, overdrew their accounts, engaged in fraudulent transactions, and caused a loss to the branch of $1.5 million.[20]

Jones resigned under pressure, and Langdon Cheves was elected president in March 1819. The Bank had been on the brink of bankruptcy, or, to use a contemporary expression, was "crippled." The new president cut expenses, obtained the appointment of new officers and directors, curtailed business at the southern and western offices, initiated prosecutions against guilty parties, began collecting the amounts due from state banks, and made it clear that no branch was to draw on any other branch unless it had deposit funds to draw against. Cheves saved the Bank—which act earned him little praise. Debtors were furious at being called upon to pay their debts, employees were disgruntled at cuts in salaries and other expenses, and stockholders complained of niggardly dividends.

Wearied by his struggles, Cheves resigned, and Nicholas Biddle—a graduate of Princeton College who had traveled extensively abroad, was versed in the writings of the British and French economists, had practiced law, and had written poetry—was elected president on January 6, 1823. The Bank was in terms of its capital the largest corporation in the United States and one of the largest in the world. Biddle's management of the Bank fell into two periods: 1823–1830, the period of central banking, and 1830–1836, the period of central banking frustrated by politics.

Cheves' policies had necessarily been more negative than positive. He had been the conservator of the Bank. Biddle had the opportunity and the ability to initiate constructive policies, converting the Bank into a dynamic and progressive

---

* It is not considered good banking practice for a bank such as the Bank of the United States, with its liabilities mainly in the form of demand liabilities, to place its funds in mortgages.

force in American economic development. The second Bank was primarily a commercial bank that, under Biddle's guidance, gradually assumed central-banking functions.[21]

Biddle wanted to develop the "power and usefulness" of the Bank. To do so he first restored its capital by selling the stock that had been forfeited to it as collateral.[22] He enlarged the Bank's holdings of business paper, emphasizing short-term commercial loans and the discounting of bills of exchange, arising from domestic and foreign trade. The Bank actively bought and sold foreign exchange, keeping its London balances mainly with the Barings, the most influential British private banking firm. The large increase in its holdings of business paper in the 1820s was paralleled by an equally large increase in its note and deposit liabilities. The bank was rapidly becoming the most important note-issuing bank in the country. In time, had its charter been renewed, it undoubtedly would have emerged as the sole bank of issue.

Biddle as Central Banker

It is as a central banker that Nicholas Biddle is justly honored today. In his era he had no peer, and in fact he has been called "the world's first conscious central banker."[23] He was thoroughly familiar with British books, articles, and parliamentary papers on the Bank of England. In all probability he was equally familiar with comparable French treatises.

By 1826 Biddle had recognized the Bank's role as holder of the country's specie and protector of its specie reserves. He maintained these reserves in adequate ratio to the Bank's liabilities and shifted them from branch to branch in response to need. He operated in the domestic exchange market and thus reduced domestic exchange rates to a minimum. He operated in the foreign-exchange market in order to conserve, as much as possible, the nation's supply of specie and to eliminate seasonal fluctuations in exchange rates. He returned for redemption the notes of state banks, which came into the Bank's possession usually through the deposit of U.S. government funds, thus bringing pressure upon those banks to follow prudent policies. On occasion he abstained from returning such notes if such a course seemed in the best interests of the nation as a whole. Finally he endeavored to prevent Treasury operations from disturbing the money market. In general he pursued counterseasonal and countercyclical policies in order to promote orderly economic and financial development.

Biases of President Jackson

Nevertheless, despite its great contributions, the second Bank was also al-lowed to die. It had incited the antipathy of President Andrew Jackson, who, ever since reading of the South Sea Bubble (a speculation centered around the South Sea Company and similar enterprises from 1711 to 1720, a period in England somewhat similar to that of 1928–1929 in the United States; the Bubble had burst in a rash of bank failures), had been opposed to banks in general and to the Bank of the United States in particular. In his first annual message to Con-gress, on December 8, 1829, President Jackson questioned the constitutionality of the Bank's charter and made the absurd charge that it had "failed in the great end of establishing a uniform and sound currency." [24] These statements came as a bolt from the blue. The question of rechartering the Bank had not been an issue in the 1828 campaign. Biddle had actually voted for Jackson, and Jackson kept his own deposits in the Bank's Nashville branch.

Once he had declared himself an opponent of the Bank, Jackson was quickly joined by the state banks, which would once again be able to issue notes without restraint, if freed of controls by the second Bank. Other opponents included Wall Street financiers, who were determined to replace Chestnut Street (Philadelphia) as the financial center of the country, and groups that nurtured grievances against all banks and especially against the Bank of the United States. They were joined by those who merely wanted Jacksonians to staff the bank. [25]

That part of President Jackson's message to Congress having to do with the second Bank was referred to the Committee on Ways and Means of the House of Representatives. In a report dated April 13, 1830, the majority of the committee declared that Congress had the constitutional power to incorporate a bank, that the Bank had given the nation a sound and safe currency, that it had actually fur-nished a circulating medium more uniform than specie, and that it had enforced specie payments on the state banks. It concluded that no one institution in the country, not even the army or navy, was more vital than a national bank. The Bank not only cost the nation nothing but actually yielded a financial return, either in the initial payments for its charter or in dividends received on the stock owned by the U.S. government. Finally, according to the committee, the Bank had not used its great power in a partisan fashion. [26]

A bill to recharter the Bank was passed by Congress but vetoed by Jackson on July 10, 1832, and the Senate failed to override the veto. In his veto message Jackson decried the ownership of much of the Bank's stock by stockholders in the eastern states and abroad, especially in Great Britain, and argued that to pay dividends on this stock, specie was drawn from branches in the western and southern states, which enjoyed the highest earnings. In its extreme nationalism this argument showed no insight into the various factors constituting a nation's internal or external balance of payments. Jackson feared that the management might become self-perpetuating, and might fall under the influence of those whose primary loyalties would be not to the United States but to foreign powers, perhaps even to hostile powers: "All of its operations within would be in aid of the hostile armies and fleets without." He entertained grave suspicions that the Bank had abused and violated its charter and that it had conferred special privileges on the rich. And, above all, he deemed the enabling act "unconstitutional." [27]

The United States Bank of Pennsylvania

In 1832 Jackson was overwhelmingly reelected, and the fate of the Bank was sealed. When its federal charter expired in February 1836, it received a state charter from Pennsylvania. Biddle, embittered by the long struggle with Jackson, became erratic and imprudent and began to engage in empire building on a gigantic scale. The United States Bank of Pennsylvania began buying shares in banks, railways, toll bridges, turnpikes, and canals. Biddle also tried to corner the cotton market and for about two years succeeded in doing so. But the inevitable happened: The Bank failed on February 4, 1841. Depositors and note holders were eventually paid in full, but private stockholders lost all.[28]

The failure of the United States Bank of Pennsylvania cannot, however, efface the great contributions of the second Bank of the United States or the brilliant direction of its affairs by Nicholas Biddle. In his *History of the American People* Woodrow Wilson wrote that the Bank "had not only served its purpose as a fiscal agent of the government to the satisfaction of the Treasury, but had also steadied and facilitated every legitimate business transaction and rid the money market of its worst dangers." [29] Such was the appraisal of the scholar who was one day to sign the Federal Reserve Act into law.

THE INDEPENDENT TREASURY

The large flow of funds through the finance departments of modern governments requires expert handling if financial institutions and money and capital markets are not to be subject to disruptive and disorganizing pressures. The problem is complicated not only by the size of Treasury funds but also by variability in the time and place of receipts and expenditures.*

From 1791 to 1811 and again from 1817 to 1833 (Secretary of the Treasury R. B. Taney directed on December 3, 1833, that deposits of United States funds were not to be made thereafter in the Bank of the United States),[30] Treasury receipts were deposited mainly with the first and second Banks, which managed them with an expertise that could well excite the envy of modern central banks. From 1811 to 1817, the U.S. Treasury placed its money with state banks, suffering considerable losses in the process. Again from 1833 to 1846 the state banks served as depositories and fiscal agents.

Political considerations often prevailed in the selection of depository banks. Capricious action on the part of the Secretary of the Treasury could make or break banks. Government funds were often placed in too many banks and too widely separated. There were difficulties in transferring government moneys from where they were collected to where they were to be disbursed. Banks failed, and the U.S. Treasury suffered losses. If, to avoid losses, the Secretary of the Treasury set high standards for the depository banks, he could find few to meet the requirements.[31]

The Whig Party would have solved these difficult problems by establishing a third Bank of the United States, but this suggestion was adamantly opposed by the Democrats. In his message to Congress of September 4, 1837, Democratic President Martin Van Buren rejected the suggestion that a third Bank be established, pointing out that the people had declared against it in two elections. He advocated that the government receive, maintain, and disburse its own funds and that its fiscal operations be completely severed from those of commercial banks. To this end he recommended the establishment of the Independent Treasury System, sometimes called the Sub-Treasury or the Constitutional Treasury.[32]

In effect, Van Buren envisaged the establishment of strongboxes around the country, into which government funds would flow in the form of specie and from which disbursements would be made in the same form. Daniel Webster vigorously opposed this plan, for it would have moved the country back from a credit to a purely cash economy.

The Independent Treasury Act was adopted in 1840, but, with a change in the political composition of Congress, it was repealed in 1841. Owing to another change in political fortunes, it was reenacted in 1846, and the Sub-Treasury System went into operation on January 1, 1847. Although it was superseded by the

---

* As indicated in Chap 5, Treasury funds are now skillfully handled by means of techniques that have developed over many decades.

establishment of the Federal Reserve System in 1914, it continued in legal form until 1921.

The act received support from the antibank and anticredit Democrats. Its passage constituted a victory for the hard-money adherents, those who disapproved of all paper money and the banks which issued it, including the redoubtable Senator Thomas Hart Benton of Missouri. It received support also from Senator John C. Calhoun of South Carolina, who was convinced that an independent treasury would shift funds from the North to the South to latter's advantage.[33]

The establishment of the Independent Treasury was a victory for states' rights and represented an abdication of federal control of banking and credit. The establishment of strongboxes resulted in purposeless hoarding of cash by the government, the "haphazard contraction and expansion of bank reserves without reason, intent or policy." [34] Reserves contracted when government receipts exceeded expenditures and expanded under reverse circumstances. These fluctuations occurred without reference to economic conditions or need.

As David Kinley has pointed out, the Independent Treasury had many disadvantages. It introduced short-term money-market disturbances through seasonal irregularities in the inflow and outflow of Treasury funds. It tended in capricious manner to function in a pro- or countercyclical fashion. Whether it functioned in the one direction or the other depended upon the relation of government receipts to expenditures. Should receipts exceed expenditures over a long period, the pressures could become catastrophic.

These disadvantages persisted as long as the original act remained unchanged. In the course of time, however, circumstances did force many changes, with the result that the Independent Treasury System was dead long before it was interred. Only in its early history, from 1846 to 1847, were banks not used as depositories for public funds. Even then the federal government was occasionally forced to buy silver bullion for new coinage or to prepay the public debt, in order to relieve stringencies in the money market.

Attrition of the original act took place rapidly during the Civil War. In 1861 an act permitted the proceeds of bond purchases to be left with the purchasing banks; in 1864 Congress decided that national banks, after depositing "United States bonds and otherwise" as security, could serve as depositories of any public funds except customs receipts. A third law of the Civil War period made U.S. notes (the Greenbacks) legal tender in payment of all obligations save customs duties and interest on the public debt and thus further undermined the Independent Treasury. A flood of paper money flowed through the Treasury compared with a mere trickle of gold.

As time went on, successive Secretaries of the Treasury made administrative changes, in an effort to make a basically unworkable system function.[35] Many actions, some legal, some extralegal, were taken to prevent the Sub-Treasury System from completely disrupting the economy. When public demand caused an increase in the market price of gold before the resumption of specie payments in 1879, the Treasury purchased the public debt with gold or exchanged gold for Greenbacks in order to make gold available. When the Treasury experienced a budgetary surplus, as it did from 1879 to 1890, it purchased government bonds at a premium and relaxed the stringent rules governing the collateral with which national banks secured government deposits in order to release its hoards of cash. After 1900 Secretaries of the Treasury operated the Sub-Treasury System increasingly as if it were a central bank. They purchased bonds with Sub-Treasury cash, accepted securities other than government obligations as collateral for government deposits, exempted government deposits with federal securities from the reserve requirements of national banks as collateral, and granted interest-free loans against gold imports. In 1907 Congress repealed that portion of the Independent Treasury Act requiring customs receipts to be placed with the Sub-Treasury. For the first time since 1846 they could be placed in banks, that is, in national banks. After 1911 customs duties could be paid in certified checks.[36]

Although it had originally been established to obviate the need for a central bank, the Independent Treasury was so managed by various Secretaries that it gradually assumed central banking functions. Designed as a substitute for the second Bank, it had itself become a central bank, functioning imperfectly to be sure, but still exercising in primitive fashion central banking functions.

THE NATIONAL BANKING SYSTEM

In his annual report for 1865, Secretary of the Treasury Hugh McCulloch stated:

> The establishment of the National Banking System is one of the great compensations of the war—one of the great achievements of this remarkable period. In about two years and a half from the organization of the first national bank, the whole system of banking under state laws has been superseded, and the people of the United States have been furnished with a circulation bearing

upon it the seal of the Treasury Department as a guarantee of its solvency.[37]

This encomium to the new banking system established under the National Currency Act of February 25, 1863, was delivered by a gentleman who had originally traveled from Indiana to Washington, D.C. expressly to oppose passage of the act. He had regarded the proposal as a wildcat measure, prejudicial to state banks. The incumbent Secretary of the Treasury at that time, Salmon P. Chase, convinced McCulloch that the new system was necessary and offered him the post of first Comptroller of the Currency. McCulloch accepted and served with great distinction.[38]

Although the national banking system did not actually supersede state banking systems, it expanded vigorously and played an important role in the economic development of the United States. From the Civil War to the passage of the Federal Reserve Act, it provided the country with stable currency; relatively safe depositories for the funds of individuals, firms, and government units; and banking institutions equipped to finance the credit needs of agriculture and business.

The national banks were, of course, national only in the sense that their charters were granted by the central government, not in the sense that they could operate on a national scale. It was true that the 1863 measure permitted the business of a national bank to be transacted at "offices" located at various places specified in the articles of association. The use of the plural was consistent with the existing branch systems, and apparently there was no intention on the part of Congress to eliminate branch banking, which existed in many states, particularly in the South. In the 1864 version, however, the plural word "offices" was changed to the singular, possibly through a typographical error.[39] As a consequence, Comptrollers of the Currency interpreted the law strictly and ceased to permit branch banking. Former branch banking systems came into the national banking system as single units, and state laws were often modified to ease conversion from state to national status.

Reasons for the Strength of the System

Among the features that contributed to the strength of the national banking system were the supervision exercised by the Comptroller of the Currency, stringent capital requirements, and restrictions on loans. The Comptroller of the Currency, appointed for a five-year term by the President of the United States with the advice and consent of the Senate, was charged with the responsibility for administering the system. From 1914 to 1935 he was also a member of the Federal Reserve Board.

Supervisory Procedures • Supervision by the Comptroller of the Currency took the form mainly of examinations of national banks and of calling for periodic condition reports. The first state to require examinations of banks was New York, in 1829. State examinations varied greatly in quality, a point frequently reiterated by John Jay Knox when he served as Comptroller of the Currency (1872–1884).[40] Even today the variation in the quality of state bank examinations has induced the Federal Reserve System itself to examine all state member banks, although it relies upon the reports of the Comptroller of the Currency for national banks.

Examinations by the office of the Comptroller of the Currency, though they have occasionally left much to be desired, were nevertheless one of the factors accounting for fewer failures among national banks. In his report for 1892 Alonzo Barton Hepburn, then Comptroller of the Currency declared that the examination staff constituted the mainstay of the Comptroller's office.[41] The examiners, he continued, had to be fearless, competent, conscientious, and painstaking; their work was not espionage, but they had to be able to aid banks by suggesting better operating methods.

The condition reports required of the national banks were another important factor in the relative stability of the system. Secretary Chase was convinced that publicity was essential to a well-functioning banking system. Reports had been required of the first and second United States Banks, of state banks in Massachusetts since 1803, and of New York banks since 1834. Banks that held federal deposits were required by an act of June 23, 1836, to submit financial statements to the Secretary of the Treasury. Initially national banks were required to submit two statements of condition a year. Today at least four are required and additional and special reports may be demanded from all banks or particular banks. This requirement has exerted a constructive influence on the national banking system and also on state banking systems, which frequently have emulated the practices of the Comptroller of the Currency.[42]

Capital Requirements • Still other provisions of the early national-banking statutes that contributed to the success of the system were the capital requirements and the restrictions on loans extended and funds borrowed. Each national bank was required to have a minimum capital, based on the population of the city in which it was located. Until 1937 bank capital bore double liability; that is, in the event of a bank's failure, a shareholder ran the risk not only of losing his original investment but also of being called upon by the receivers to contribute an additional amount equal to the par value of the stock. The capital had to be paid in cash upon the organization of the bank or soon after. A national bank was not permitted to lend against its own stock or to purchase its own stock except to ensure the repayment of a debt, and in this case it had to sell the stock within six months. These provisions were intended to eliminate practices that had been all too common among pre-Civil War state banks, permitting the organizers to borrow from the bank the amounts needed to pay for their own stock subscriptions.

Lending Provisions • The 1864 act limited the loans that could be extended to any one party to 10 percent of the capital stock; save that the discounting of bona fide bills of exchange drawn against actually existing values and the discounting of commercial or business paper actually owned by the negotiator were not, however, to be considered money borrowed. This provision has been greatly modified since 1864, but it did force national banks to distribute their loan risks. During the first fifty years of the national banking system, loans were extended mainly to businessmen, farmers, and stockbrokers. Loans against real-estate mortgages were subject to severe restrictions, and consumer-instalment credit was virtually unknown. The bonds held by national banks consisted principally of government obligations to secure the note issue.

The loan-and-investment totals of national banks on April 28, 1909, compiled by the National Monetary Commission from special reports, are shown in Table 1.3, which is included here for historical interest.

State Banks Overtake the National System

By 1870 national banks were about five times as numerous as state banks and, in terms of total assets, the national banking system was more than seven times as large. But by 1890 state banks had overtaken the national banking system, both in numbers and in total assets. Although national banks increased sharply in number in the first decade of the twentieth century, state banks still outranked them in 1913, as shown in Table 1.4. The reasons for the decline in relative importance of national banks were, first, the growing use of deposits as money; second, the lower reserve requirements to which the deposits of state banks were subject; third, the greater latitude state banks enjoyed in extending loans and in purchasing securities; fourth, smaller capital requirements of state banks; and, fifth, the greater ease, particularly in the latter part of the period, in obtaining state rather than national charters. It was largely because of the increasing importance of deposits as

Table 1.3
Loan-and-Investment Account of All National Banks,
April 28, 1909
(Millions of Dollars)

Loans		Bonds and Stocks	
On demand, unsecured	432	Federal bonds	740
On demand, secured	977	State, county, and municipal	
On time, two or more		bonds	157
names, unsecured	1,635	Railroad bonds	351
On time, single-name,		Street-railway, interurban-railway,	
unsecured	899	and public-utility bonds	149
On time, secured by collateral	961	Other bonds	152
Secured by real estate	57	Stocks	35
Overdrafts	25	Foreign bonds	
		Government	13
		Other	9
Total	4,986	Total	1,606

Source: National Monetary Commission, Special Report from the Banks of the United States, April 28, 1909, 61st Cong., 2nd sess., Senate Document No. 225 (Washington, D.C.: Government Printing Office, 1909), p. 11.

Table 1.4
Growth of the Commercial Banking System
(Millions of Dollars)

	National Banks		Non-National Banks	
Year	Number	Total Assets	Number	Total Assets
1863	66	$ 17	1,466	$ 1,192
1865	1,294	1,127	349	231
1870	1,612	1,566	325	215
1880	2,076	2,036	1,279	1,364
1890	3,484	3,062	4,717	3,296
1900	3,731	4,944	9,322	6,444
1910	7,138	9,892	18,013	13,030
1913	7,467	11,032	19,818	15,071

Source: Historical Statistics of the United States, 1789–1945, United States Department of Commerce, Bureau of the Census (Washington, D.C.: Government Printing Office, 1949), pp. 263–265; and The Statistical History of the United States from Colonial Times to the Present (Stamford, Conn.: Fairfield Publishers, Inc., 1965), pp. 626–628.

money that the confiscatory tax of 10 percent per annum, which had been levied upon the notes of state banks since July 1, 1866, did not destroy the state banking system.

Despite its many contributions, there were two basic defects in the national banking system that demanded reform: the inelastic note issue and the absence of a "lender of last resort," to use Bagehot's expression.

The Note Issue • Had national banks been given the right to circulate asset bank notes similar to those issued by Canadian banks, national-bank notes would have responded to seasonal and cyclical demands for currency. As it was, national-bank notes were issued against a specific asset, United States obligations, the amount of which fell sharply after the Civil War from $2,755 million in 1866 to $961 million in 1893.

Until 1900 national banks were permitted to issue notes up to 90 percent of the par or market value of the bonds, whichever sum was smaller and, beginning in 1900, up to 100 percent of the par value. As Table 1.5 shows, the total circula-

Table 1.5
Types of Currency in Circulation
(Millions of Dollars)

Year	Gold Coin and Certificates	Silver Dollars and Certificates, Treasury Notes of 1890	Subsidiary Silver, Fractional Currency	U.S. Notes	State- Bank Notes	National- Bank Notes
1860	$ 207	–	$ 21	–	$207	–
1870	113	–	46	$325	2	$289
1880	234	$ 26	49	328	–	337
1890	505	354	54	335	–	182
1900	812	549	103	318	–	300
1910	1,394	555	182	335	–	684
1913	1,612	544	209	337	–	716

Source: *The Statistical History of the United States from Colonial Times to the Present* (Stamford, Conn.: Fairfield Publishers, Inc., 1965), pp. 648–649.

tion of national-bank notes was smaller in 1890 than it had been in 1870. There were two reasons: the decline in the public debt and an increase in government bond prices, which had reduced the profits to be derived from note issues. Gold coins and gold certificates, silver dollars, silver certificates, and, later, the Treasury notes of 1890 were increased to meet monetary needs.

After 1900 the amount of national-bank notes in circulation increased rapidly. The reasons were the permission granted to national banks to issue notes up to 100 percent of the par value of government bonds; the decline in bond prices, which increased the profits of note circulation; the rise in the public debt following the Spanish-American War and the building of the Panama Canal.

Because they were based specifically upon the public debt, which was declining over the entire period, issues of national-bank notes possessed very little elasticity. The notes did not increase to meet seasonal currency demands in the autumn of each year and did not rise during periods of panic or crisis when depositors sought to convert their deposits into cash. The lack of seasonal elasticity engendered pronounced seasonal swings in interest rates that were not to be found in the Canadian economy, with its asset bank note currency. The inability of national-bank notes to meet panic demands for currency led to suspensions of cash payments in 1873, 1893, and 1907 and to payments of heavy premiums for currency.[43] To meet the monetary demands in those years, clearinghouses, business firms, and even individuals issued currency. A similar phenomenon occurred in 1933, but as a result not of inelastic currency (Federal Reserve notes had ample elasticity) but rather of the disappearance of banks in many sections of the country.

Reserve Requirements • The second important defect developed from the legal reserve provisions of the National Bank Act and the resulting absence of a lender of last resort. For the purpose of determining reserve requirements, national banks were divided into three classes: those in the so-called "country towns," those in the reserve cities, and those in the central reserve cities. This classification has a familiar ring, for it was continued under the Federal Reserve System.

There were three central reserve cities in 1913—New York, Chicago, and St. Louis. National banks in those centers had to maintain reserves in lawful money or in clearinghouse gold certificates (receipts issued by clearinghouses against deposits of gold by member banks) equal to 25 percent of all deposits. National banks in the forty-seven reserve cities had to maintain 25 percent reserves, but half could be in the form of deposits with a national bank in one of the central reserve cities. National banks in the country towns had to maintain 15 percent reserves of which three-fifths could be on deposit with national banks in either reserve or central reserve cities. (The redemption fund equal to 5 percent of circulating bank notes that national banks were required by the Act of June 20, 1874, to hold with the Treasury was counted as part of the legal reserves.) Reserves not held in the form of deposits by reserve-city and country banks had to be held in lawful money or clearinghouse gold certificates. There was at that time no distinction between demand and time accounts; the same reserve was held against all deposits. (Federal government deposits were exempted from reserve requirements by the Aldrich-Vreeland Act of May 30, 1908.)

The system existing then has been likened to an inverted pyramid, with its apex resting in New York City. Funds flowed to New York from the reserve-city and country-town national banks, and these funds were to a large extent invested in "street loans," that is, loans to stock-exchange brokers. These loans were by no stretch of the imagination self-liquidating and could be called in only if the borrowers could find other lenders to take over the burden—which they could not do in time of panic. If the stock exchange closed, the loans were frozen, and New York City banks were unable to remit funds to the interior banks clamoring for their deposits. As many students of the subject, Paul Warburg and Andrew Carnegie among others, have pointed out, the use of reserve funds to finance stock-market operations gave the United States one of the worst banking systems in the world.

Even so the system might have worked better had the New York central reserve city banks, which were really functioning as central banks, maintained reserves much above the legal minimum. But, of course, they did not, motivated as they were by considerations of profit to expand their own loans and investments to a maximum. In consequence, they had no spare lawful money with which they could meet the demands of inland banks or on which they could expand loans to meet emergency needs. They tried as best they could to remedy the situation either by calling upon London for gold or by pooling their reserves through the local clearinghouse.

Defective Exchange and Transfer System

Still another defect in the American banking system before 1913, a defect of both national and state systems, was the expensive, awkward, and cumbersome method of collecting out-of-town checks, resulting from the desire to reduce exchange and collection charges to a minimum. In the process, out-of-town checks crossed and crisscrossed the United States, following devious routes to the drawee banks. Local checks were, it is true, cleared with great dispatch through local clearinghouses, but the expense of collecting out-of-town checks imposed a heavy toll on American commerce.

The fact that nationwide transfers of funds frequently required the shipment of currency led to the emergence of currency-shipping points similar to gold-import and -export points for foreign transactions. The San Francisco dollar might be at a discount in terms of the New York dollar, the discount determined by the cost of shipping currency. This variation, too, levied a toll on domestic commerce. Domestic exchange rates continued until the establishment of the Gold Settlement Fund under the Federal Reserve System.

It finally came to be generally recognized that only a central bank, possessing the note-issue privilege and holding the reserves of commercial banks, could impart the elasticity in money and credit that was essential to the smooth functioning of the American banking system. Only a central bank could eliminate the defects in our domestic exchange-and-transfer system. Only a well-managed central bank could help reduce financial and industrial instability in American economic life.

THE FEDERAL RESERVE ACT

In the fall of 1912 Democratic leaders in Congress, anticipating a presidential victory, concluded that an early investigation of the banking and currency situation in the United States should be undertaken as a basis for formulating remedial measures. The House of Representatives, in a resolution adopted on February 24, 1912, directed its Banking and Currency Committee to make such a study. On April 25 the committee was further instructed to investigate the degree of financial concentration in the United States and the possible existence of a "money trust." To facilitate these two investigations of quite different import, the committee was divided into two sections: One, under the chairmanship of Representative Carter Glass of Virginia, was to propose banking reforms, and the other under the chairmanship of Representative Arsène Pujo of Louisiana, was to propose means of curbing the money trust. The latter inquiry resulted in passage of the Clayton Act and the Federal Trade Commission Act. The former began its active work during the first part of April 1912, engaging the services of H. Parker Willis, then Dean of the College of Political Science of George Washington University, as expert adviser.

After a series of discussions, the Glass subcommittee concluded that a monolithic central bank was not suitable to American conditions and that a district organization was to be preferred. This conclusion was in accordance with the Democratic platform of 1912. A bill was drafted during the summer and early fall of 1912 and presented to President-elect Wilson at his home in Princeton, New Jersey. He gave the bill his tentative approval, expressing his opinion that it should provide for a complete reform of the American banking system and for a permanent type of banking organization under central control but organized in local units. Following committee hearings and floor debates, the Glass bill, somewhat altered, was passed by the House of Representatives on September 18, 1913. The Senate then began its lengthy considerations and enacted its own version on December 19. The House and Senate versions of the measure were reconciled and signed by President Wilson on December 23. The final measure resembled the original House measure in all important particulars.[44]

The history of banking reform from 1791, when the United States Bank was established, to 1913, when the Federal Reserve Act was passed, was long and tortuous. But no economic measure, however well conceived, can long endure unchanged. Either it falls prey to political onslaughts, or adaptations must be made because of changing conditions. The Federal Reserve Act has been amended many times since its initial enactment and doubtless will be amended many times more in the future. The principal changes so far have resulted from two world wars and the Great Depression. Possibly no other central bank has survived such turbulent early years as has the Federal Reserve System.

Notes

1. Ernest Harvey, *Central Banks* (London: General Press, 1928), pp. 16–23.

2. Bray Hammond, *Banks and Politics in America* (Princeton: Princeton University Press, 1957), p. 306.

3. J. Keith Horsefield, *British Monetary Experiments 1650–1710* (Cambridge, Mass.: Harvard University Press, 1960), p. 125.

4. For histories of the Bank of England, see A. Andréadès, *History of the Bank of England* (London: King, 1909); John Clapham, *The Bank of England*, 2 vols. (New York: Macmillan, 1945); and Albert Feavearyear, *The Pound Sterling*, 2nd ed., rev. by E. Victor Morgan (Oxford: Clarendon, 1963).

5. *Report from the Select Committee on Bank Acts; Together with the Proceedings of the Committee, Minutes of Evidence, Appendix, and Index* (London: ordered by the House of Commons to be printed, July 30, 1857), Question 4010.

6. Walter Bagehot, *Lombard Street* (New York: Scribner, 1873), pp. 187–207.

7. Margaret G. Myers, *A Financial History of the United States* (New York: Columbia University Press, 1970), pp. 60–63.

8. *Federal Banking Laws and Reports, 1780–1912*, Committee on Banking and Currency, United States Senate, 88th Cong., 1st sess., March 15, 1963 (Washington, D.C.: Government Printing Office, 1963), p. 7.

9. *Ibid.*, pp. 8–10.

10. *Ibid.*, p. 32.

11. Hammond, *op. cit.*, p. 123.

12. *Federal Banking Laws and Reports, 1780–1912*, *op. cit.*, p. 70.

13. *Ibid.*, p. 76.

14. Letter to the House of Representatives, *Federal Banking Laws and Reports, 1780–1912*, *op. cit.*, pp. 91–92.

15. *Ibid.*, pp. 99–101.

16. An excellent discussion of the work of these branches can be found in Ralph C. H. Catterall, *The Second Bank of the United States* (Chicago: University of Chicago Press, 1903), chap. 16.

17. Hammond, *op. cit.,* p. 252. Chaps. 10–16 give a vivid scholarly account of the second Bank of the United States.

18. Catterall, *op. cit.,* p. 32.

19. *Ibid.,* pp. 32–33.

20. Hammond, *op. cit.,* p. 262.

21. Fritz Redlich, *The Molding of American Banking, Men and Ideas* (New York: Hafner, 1947), chap. 6.

22. Hammond, *op. cit.,* p. 302.

23. Redlich, *op. cit.,* p. 128.

24. *Federal Banking Laws and Reports, 1780–1912, op. cit.,* p. 144.

25. Hammond, *op. cit.,* pp. 443–444.

26. *Federal Banking Laws and Reports, 1780–1912, op. cit.,* pp. 154–186.

27. *Ibid.,* pp. 214–228.

28. Hammond, *op. cit.,* chap. 16; and *Federal Banking Laws and Reports, 1780–1912, op. cit.,* p. 422.

29. Woodrow Wilson, *A History of the American People,* IV (New York: Harper, 1906), p. 47.

30. *Federal Banking Laws and Reports, 1780–1912, op. cit.,* p. 243.

31. David Kinley, *The Independent Treasury of the United States and Its Relations to the Banks of the Country* (Washington, D.C.: Government Printing Office, 1910), chaps. 1 and 2.

32. Margaret G. Myers, *The New York Money Market: I. Origins and Development* (New York: Columbia University Press, 1931), chaps. 9 and 17.

33. Hammond, *op. cit.,* pp. 542–544. Also see Myers, *A Financial History of the United States, op. cit.,* pp. 90 and 132.

34. Hammond, *op. cit.,* p. 544.

35. Esther Rogoff Taus, *Central Banking Functions of the United States Treasury, 1789–1941* (New York: Columbia University Press, 1943).

36. Myers, *The New York Money Market, op. cit.,* chap. 17.

37. *Report of the Secretary of the Treasury on the State of the Finances for the Year 1865* (Washington, D.C.: Government Printing Office, 1865), p. 35.

38. Hammond, *op. cit.,* p. 731.

39. Myers, *The New York Money Market, op. cit.,* p. 231.

40. See for example *Annual Report of the Comptroller of the Currency* to the 3rd sess. of the 45th Cong. of the United States, December 2, 1878 (Washington, D.C.: Government Printing Office, 1878), pp. 17–18.

41. *Annual Report of the Comptroller of the Currency* to the 2nd sess. of the 52nd Cong. of the United States, December 5, 1892 (Washington, D.C.: Government Printing Office, 1892), p. 43.

42. Comptroller of the Currency, *National Banks and the Future: Report of the Advisory Committee on Banking to the Comptroller of the Currency*, Part V, U.S. Treasury Department, September 17 (Washington, D.C.: Government Printing Office, 1962); and *Federal Reserve Bulletin*, (October 1963), pp. 1380–1385.

43. See O. M. W. Sprague, *History of Crises Under the National Banking System* (Washington, D.C.: Government Printing Office, 1910).

44. For a history of the Federal Reserve Act, see the classic study by H. Parker Willis, *The Federal Reserve System* (New York: Ronald, 1923). Also, see Paul M. Warburg, *The Federal Reserve System: Its Origin and Growth*, 2 vols. (New York: Macmillan, 1930); Carter Glass, *An Adventure in Constructive Finance* (New York: Doubleday, Page and Company, 1927); and Gerald T. Dunne, *A Christmas Present for the President* (St. Louis: Federal Reserve Bank, 1964).

Organization and Administration of the Federal Reserve System*

CHAPTER 2

ORGANIZATION OF THE FEDERAL RESERVE SYSTEM

The passage of the Federal Reserve Act was only the initial step toward the establishment of a central banking system. The system had yet to be organized, a task that Congress had delegated to the Secretary of the Treasury, the Secretary of Agriculture, and the Comptroller of the Currency. These officials, constituting the Reserve Bank Organization Committee, had been empowered to designate not less than eight nor more than twelve cities to be known as Federal Reserve cities and to divide the continental United States, excluding Alaska, into Federal Reserve districts, each district to contain one Federal Reserve city. The districts were to be apportioned with regard for the convenience and customary patterns of business and

---

* Howard H. Hackley, Assistant to the Board of Governors of the Federal Reserve System, kindly read this chapter in preliminary form and offered many helpful suggestions for changes. He must not, however, be held responsible for any remaining errors of omission or commission or for value judgments, which are the author's own.

were not necessarily to be coterminous with any state or group of states. The Federal Reserve Board itself was given the power to readjust these districts and to create new districts at will, as long as the total number did not exceed twelve.[1]

In proceeding with its work, the organization committee decided to select the cities in which the Federal Reserve banks were to be located and then to group the districts around them.[2] The present twelve cities were selected—Boston, New York, Philadelphia, Cleveland, Richmond, Atlanta, Chicago, St. Louis, Minneapolis, Kansas City, Dallas, and San Francisco. The wisdom of putting Reserve banks at that time in Richmond, Cleveland, and Minneapolis may be questioned, as well as that of selecting Atlanta over New Orleans. It was recognized, however, that whatever mistakes had been made could be rectified to some extent through the later establishment of branches.

The majority of the cities selected were logical choices considering the existing concentration of mercantile, industrial, and financial transactions; railway connections; and prevalent business patterns. The districts had to be so delineated that each Reserve bank would have the requisite number of member banks to supply the minimum capital, $4 million. The Federal Reserve Board has occasionally exercised its power to change district lines. The New Jersey shore opposite Manhattan, for example, was originally assigned to the Philadelphia district but was subsequently transferred to New York, as was the southern part of Connecticut. The new states of Alaska and Hawaii were designated as part of the San Francisco Reserve district.

Once the Reserve cities had been selected and the district lines drawn, the next question concerned the internal organization of the Reserve banks. Many problems arose: for example, the establishment of uniform accounting systems and the use, in connection with these systems, of accounting machines to the maximum extent possible; arrangements for the publication of weekly condition reports by the Reserve banks and for the examination of the Reserve banks; organization of a clearance system, including the Gold Settlement Fund now the Interdistrict Settlement Fund; and establishment of rules and regulations for discount operations.

The Secretary of the Treasury, whose responsibility it was, decided that the Reserve banks should open for business on November 16, 1914, only eleven months after passage of the act. In this remarkably short time span all the organizational details were completed, premises for the Federal Reserve banks selected, and staffs assembled. In view of the outbreak of the European war in August, which initially had significant disruptive effects on the American economy,[3] this decision on the part of Secretary William G. McAdoo took considerable courage.

LEGAL STATUS OF THE FEDERAL RESERVE BOARD

Independent Status

In an important opinion rendered by the Attorney General of the United States on December 19, 1914, the Federal Reserve Board was described as an independent bureau, or establishment, of the government and as such not under the jurisdiction of the Treasury Department.[4] This early opinion was repeated years later by the Board of Governors of the Federal Reserve System in its reply to the Patman inquiry of 1952, in which it reminded the country that it had been recognized as an independent establishment of the government.[5] The title of the Federal Reserve Board was changed in 1935 to the Board of Governors of the Federal Reserve System. It sends its annual report to the Speaker of the House of Representatives, who has it published for the information of Congress.

The Federal Reserve Act empowers the Board to act in accordance with its best judgment but subject to such guiding principles and restrictions as Congress may prescribe. In essence, the Reserve System is independent within but not independent *of* government. This distinction may seem illusory, but what it means is that, while the System must endeavor to attain the general economic goals of Congress, it is free to use its own means to achieve them, subject of course, to various statutory limitations.

Funds to meet the expenses of the Board of Governors are levied upon and paid by the Reserve banks, a procedure that enhances the independence of the Reserve System. Such expenditures are not part of the budget of the U.S. government and are not voted upon by Congress; they are not construed as government funds or appropriated monies.[6] Until 1933 the expenditures of the Board of Governors—but not those of the Reserve banks—were audited by the General Accounting Office. In that year Congress freed the Board from this audit, in order to give it leeway in the determination of its internal management policies.[7]

The Board was the only part of the Reserve System ever subject to a Federal audit. Its income and expenditures are now audited annually by independent certified public accounting firms, and the reports are submitted to the two Banking and Currency committees of Congress. Examiners from the Board of Governors examine each of the Reserve banks and, on occasion, are accompanied by outside commercial auditors. In addition, each Reserve bank has its own resident auditor, who reports directly to its board of directors.

The provision of the Federal Reserve Act permitting the Federal Reserve Board to levy semiannual assessments upon the Reserve banks sufficient to pay its estimated expenses was inserted in order to free the Board from possible congressional domination.[8] The drafters of this provision had an important precedent in mind: The Payne Aldrich Tariff Act of 1909 had established a Tariff Board, which was presumably to be wholly scientific in its study of tariff rates and comparative production costs at home and abroad. Despite the excellence of the Board's studies, however, Democrats in the House of Representatives, convinced that the purpose of these studies was to postpone effective action, refused in 1912 to appropriate further funds, in effect terminating the life of the Board. The framers of the Federal Reserve Act feared that a hostile Congress might similarly terminate the life of the Federal Reserve Board by simply refusing to vote appropriations. And if the purpose were not to terminate its life, the aim might be that of influencing Federal Reserve policy.

The Federal Reserve System has always endeavored to conduct its operations in the most efficient fashion and at the lowest possible cost. The various Federal Reserve banks vie with one another in reducing operating unit costs to a minimum. As it is not subject to the restrictive standards inevitable in the Federal Civil Service, the System has been able to attract highly competent and technically trained personnel. Political influence in the selection of such personnel has been virtually nonexistent. Should the expenses of the Board of Governors ever become subject to congressional appropriation, the System would lose whatever degree of independence it has enjoyed and would surely be buffeted by the whims of Congress and the administration.

Membership and Organization

The Glass Bill • The first draft of the Glass Bill (which laid the basis of the Federal Reserve Act) provided for banker representation on the Federal Reserve Board. This provision was included to ensure a role for men with banking experience, to reduce the dangers of political influence, and to enlist the support of the banking community for the new legislation. President Wilson was convinced by Secretary of State William Jennings Bryan, however, that this provision should be eliminated and that the Board should be an active government body.[9]

In explaining his stand to the Currency Commission of The American Bankers Association, President Wilson declared it would be quite as wrong to allow bankers to select members of the Federal Reserve Board, even if they were in a minority, as it would be to permit the railroads to select members of the Interstate Commerce Commission.[10] Provision for such banker representation would, in Wilson's opinion, have subjected the Federal Reserve Board to undesirable pressures from narrow vested interests. Representative Glass was convinced, on the other hand, that there was sufficient government representation to ensure freedom from undue control or influence by the banking community.[11] The President's view prevailed, and the Federal Reserve Board has from the outset consisted solely of presidential appointees.

Section 10 of the original Federal Reserve Act established a Federal Reserve Board of seven members, including the Secretary of the Treasury and the Comptroller of the Currency as ex officio members, and five others, to be appointed by the President of the United States for a term of ten years each with the advice and consent of the Senate.[12] The President was to appoint no more than one member from any single Federal Reserve district and was to select members with due regard to a fair representation of the different commercial, industrial, and geographical divisions of the country. At least two of the appointed members were to be experienced in banking and finance.

The Secretary of the Treasury was to serve as ex officio chairman. One of the five appointed members was to be designated by the President as governor, the active executive officer, and another as vice-governor. As the law was silent on the terms of service for both governor and vice-governor, it became customary to appoint each for one year.

In 1922 the appointive membership of the Board was increased to six so that President Warren G. Harding might appoint an "agriculturist," or in the language of some Senators "a dirt farmer," to the Board. This action by Congress represented a concession to the farm bloc, which had attained considerable political power in the depression years following World War I. The amendment also eliminated the provision that two members had to be experienced in banking and finance. In stipulating that one member of the Federal Reserve Board should represent a definite interest, this change in the act tended to undermine its original concept, which was that the members of the Board were not to represent particular groups but were to evolve policies in the best interests of the entire country. In appointing members to the Federal Reserve Board today, the President is expected to pay due regard to a fair representation of the nation's financial, agricultural, industrial, and commercial interests and to its geographical divisions; he may appoint no more than one member from any one Federal Reserve district.[13]

The Banking Act of 1935 • The next change (except for an amendment in 1933 that increased the term of office to twelve years) occurred in 1935, when, in order to create what some called "a supreme court of finance" free of political influence, the ex officio positions on the Board were eliminated and the number of appointive members, to serve fourteen-year terms, was increased to seven. The President was empowered to designate one appointive member as chairman and one as a vice-chairman, each to serve for four years.

In reconstituting the Federal Reserve Board, the Banking Act of 1935 endeavored to enhance its independence and prestige. The framers of the act believed that removing the Secretary of the Treasury would render the Board less subservient to his department, which, as a large borrower itself, tended to have a bias toward low interest rates. Indeed, Glass, by then a senator, declared that the Secretary's influence had always been pernicious. It was assumed, too, that lengthening the members' terms of office would render the Board more independent of the appointive power of the Chief Executive. With greater independence, the Board of Governors would, it was hoped, be able to safeguard more effectively the purchasing power of the dollar. It was regarded as the one government agency most directly concerned in that task.

Various Proposals for Change • Over the years a number of proposals have been made for altering the structure of the Board of Governors. One, advanced by E. A. Goldenweiser, would have replaced it with a single executive of Cabinet rank, on the ground that the principal shortcoming of the System was not precipitate action but tardiness. A single executive could, so Goldenweiser claimed, make quick and timely decisions.[14] His proposal never evoked enthusiasm, however, positing as it did the concentration of enormous power in one person, who might indeed make quick, but not necessarily well-considered, decisions.

Apropos of suggestions that the decision-making processes be concentrated, Karl R. Bopp, for many years President of the Federal Reserve Bank of Philadelphia has stated:

> . . . The Federal Reserve System relies heavily on a pluralistic decision-making process. We are convinced that all truth does not reside in one place or in one man. Judgments are based on a free interplay of ideas flowing from the member banks, the boards of directors and staffs at the Reserve banks, and the Board of Governors in Washington. I have seen this work; and it works well —not perfectly, but well. One advantage of the process, of course, is that it adds stability. Ideas are cross-checked, balanced against other ideas, and compromised. The chances of the Fed going off half-cocked are remote.[15]

Congressman Wright Patman has several times introduced in the House of Representatives bills that would in effect place the Federal Reserve System under the control of the Secretary of the Treasury.[16] The membership of the Board would be increased to twelve, one of whom would be the Secretary of the Treasury, who would serve as chairman. The President would be given the power to select the other eleven members for four-year terms and would have explicit power to remove any appointed member from office.

In testifying on one of these bills, Chairman William McChesney Martin of the Federal Reserve Board declared that monetary policy has to be geared to the needs of the whole economy and not simply to the particular needs of the Treasury. Not, he added, that the System should operate in isolation from the Treasury. On the contrary, the System enjoys close and cordial relations with the Treasury; both work in harmony to meet their separate responsibilities. Later C. Douglas Dillon, then Secretary of the Treasury, testified that he did not wish to act as Chairman of the Federal Reserve Board and that he had sufficient responsibility without assuming the onerous duties of monetary management. He noted that during the years 1914–1935, when Secretaries of the Treasury had served as members and chairmen of the Board, they had seldom attended its meetings.

A number of studies, including those of the New York Clearing House and the Commission on Money and Credit have proposed that the membership of the Board be reduced from seven to five, a suggestion that grew out of a collateral proposal that the terms of office be reduced from fourteen to ten years.[17] It was recognized that long terms of office permit members to acquire specialized knowledge of the complex problems of credit and monetary control. On the other hand, long tenure may cause members to lose their initial enthusiasm and to discharge their duties with less effectiveness. Repeal of the present prohibition against reappointment of those who have served full terms would, it has been suggested, permit the country to keep members who have rendered distinguished service.

The Commission on Money and Credit also proposed that the President of the United States continue to choose the Chairman and Vice-Chairman of the Board but that their terms be coterminous with his own. This proposal has received support from the officials of the System who argue that it would permit better coordination of its policies with those of the Chief Executive. The question has arisen, however, whether or not this change might weaken the Board's independence—as indeed it might.

Another proposal by the Commission on Money and Credit would make the chairman the chief executive officer, with power to delegate to Board members or senior staff officials some of his supervisory functions and powers. This suggestion was partly incorporated into legislation approved on November 5, 1966, by which the Board of Governors is authorized to delegate certain of its functions to hearing examiners, to members or employees of the Board, or to the Federal Reserve banks. The assignment of such responsibilities is a task of the chairman. No Board function relating to monetary or credit policies may be delegated, however.[18]

In reviewing these different suggestions, one must bear in mind that changes in structure do not alone ensure a well-managed central banking system. To be sure, the System should not be handicapped by having the Secretary of the Treasury on the Board; the members should not be subject to removal by the Chief Executive or handicapped by very short terms. But it does not really matter whether the Board consists of five or seven members or whether their terms of office are for ten or fourteen years. What is of paramount importance is that the President appoint the best available men to the Board. He should be interested only in the intellectual qualifications, abilities, and experience of potential Board members and should not endeavor to provide a so-called "balanced Board," Republican matched with Democrat, liberal with conservative, agriculturalist with industrialist. Changes in the structure are far less important than the types of people selected to serve. In recent years Presidents have appointed several members to the Board of Governors who had previous employment in the Reserve System. Promotion from within has the advantage of placing on the Board men with central banking experience and knowledge.

Supervisory Powers

The powers of the Board of Governors, set forth in various sections of the Federal Reserve Act, can be grouped into two main classifications, those of a supervisory character and those that deal with the control of the volume and the use of bank credit. This section will concentrate on the first, reserving until later discussion of its monetary powers. The supervisory powers themselves may be subdivided into those related to the Federal Reserve banks and those related to member banks and other financial institutions.

Supervision of Federal Reserve banks includes the right to examine the banks, to readjust the district boundaries, and to suspend or remove officers and directors (the Board also had the power to suspend reserve requirements for Federal Reserve banks when such requirements were still in force). Furthermore, the Board may permit or require any Federal Reserve bank to establish branch banks and to maintain accounts in foreign countries.

The Board of Governors appoints the class C directors of each Federal Reserve bank (see pp. 45–46), exercises special control over all relations and transactions of any kind between any Federal Reserve bank and foreign banks or bankers, supervises and regulates the issue and retirement of Federal Reserve notes, and issues regulations governing the transfer of funds among Federal Reserve banks. In a blanket clause the Board of Governors is given the power to exercise general supervision over the Reserve banks.

The more important supervisory powers which the Board of Governors exercises over member banks include power to examine member banks (in practice this power is delegated to the Federal Reserve banks), to receive state banks into the Federal Reserve System, to remove (subject to various legal safeguards) the officers and directors of member banks, and to permit (subject to the limitations of the Clayton Act) a director, officer, or employee of a member bank to act in a similar capacity in another bank. The Board is to obtain financial reports from the affiliates of state member banks, may require reports from and examine bank holding companies, must approve mergers between two commercial banks if any party is a state member bank, must approve the establishment of branches by any state member bank, and must approve the establishment of foreign branches by national and state member banks and investments by such banks in overseas banking corporations. Furthermore, it defines and regulates interest payments on deposits by national and state member banks.

Suggestions have been made from time to time that the supervision which the Board of Governors exercises over member banks and other financial institutions be transferred to some other existing agency of government or to a newly created Federal banking board. This change would, according to its proponents, allow the Board to devote its full attention to its most important function, monetary and credit control.

Certain supervisory functions are, however, closely related to questions concerning the control and use of credit: the powers to examine member banks, to remove officers and directors of such banks for continued violations of the law or unsound banking practices, to obtain condition reports from the affiliates of state member banks, to approve the establishment of bank holding companies and to examine their operation, to reclassify Reserve cities, to regulate the payment of interest on deposits, and to admit state banks to membership. Conceivably certain other supervisory functions could be taken away from the Board without impairing its ability to exercise credit control. They include the power to permit national banks to establish foreign branches and state member banks to establish domestic branches. These powers do not have the same relevance to the control of credit as do the others.

To exercise effective credit control, the Board must be familiar with the operations of member banks, of state member bank affiliates, and of bank holding companies. It must be permitted to regulate interest on savings and time accounts of member banks and, obviously, to pass on the application of state banks for membership.

THE FEDERAL ADVISORY COUNCIL

Carter Glass pointed out that Woodrow Wilson himself had suggested organization of the Federal Advisory Council.[19] He did so as a concession to the banking community for denial of banker representation on the Federal Reserve Board. The Council, to be composed of as many members as there were Federal Reserve districts, was established by Section 12 of the Federal Reserve Act. The board of directors of each Federal Reserve bank annually selects one member from its own district. The Council must meet at least four times a year in Washington, D.C., and may meet more often if summoned by the Board of Governors. In addition, the Council on its own initiative may hold such other meetings in Washington, D.C., or elsewhere as it deems necessary. It selects its own officers and determines its own procedures. The officers consist of a president, a vice-president, a secretary (customarily but not necessarily an official of the First National Bank of Chicago), and a five-man executive committee.

As its name implies, the Council is purely advisory. It has the power to confer directly with the Board of Governors of the Federal Reserve System on general business conditions; to make oral or written representations on matters within the jurisdiction of the Board of Governors; and to call for information and make recommendations related to discount rates, rediscount business, note issues, reserve conditions, the purchase and sale of gold or securities by Reserve banks, open-market operations, and general affairs of the reserve banking system. The Federal Advisory Council is one of the links between the Board of Governors and the banking community. Those elected to membership are prominent member bankers: leaders and spokesmen of the banking community.

The membership of the Federal Advisory Council, the dates of its meetings, and any public statements that it has issued are published in the annual reports of the Board of Governors. Public statements include replies by the Council to questions put by the Board, as well as recommendations on its own initiative.

During World War I the Council considered numerous questions raised by the Federal Reserve Board. In the 1920s it began to make recommendations on its own. In the spring of 1929, when brokers' loans were increasing rapidly, it urged that the discount rates of the Federal Reserve banks be raised to 6 percent. During the Great Depression it made numerous comments on banking and monetary legislation and on banking and credit policy. In 1934 it criticized the monetary policy of the administration and, for doing so, was rebuked by the Board. In 1936 it recommended a substantial increase in member-bank reserve requirements in order to prevent the increase in the gold stock, which might be of a temporary character, from being used as the basis for credit expansion. In 1939 it inveighed again and again against the easy-money policy of the Reserve System. At the end of 1940 it joined the Board of Governors and the presidents of the Federal Reserve banks in an unprecedented report to Congress, which urged *inter alia* that action be taken to reduce member banks' excess reserves, to eliminate the President's power to issue Greenbacks and additional silver certificates, to sterilize further gold imports, to finance government requirements with existing bank deposits instead of creating new deposits and to cover a larger proportion of defense expenditures by tax revenues. In 1947 it opposed the imposition of secondary reserve requirements, and in 1948 it made a weak statement opposing any change in reserve requirements, in the discount rate, and in the support prices of government obligations. No public statement has been published since 1948, although the Council frequently submits comments and suggestions on monetary policy to the Board.

The role of the Council was clearly much more important in the early years of the Federal Reserve System than it has been in the past twenty years. In the earlier period its comments and recommendations were published and received wide press coverage. In recent years its potentiality has not been fully used, as it can be only if the Council's comments and recommendations are made public and its membership expanded to include leading academicians and industrialists, as well as bankers.

THE FEDERAL OPEN MARKET COMMITTEE

Glass credited H. Parker Willis with the authorship of Section 14 of the Federal Reserve Act, which permits the Federal Reserve banks, under rules and regulations prescribed by the Board of Governors, to engage in open-market operations.[20] Willis proposed this section to enable the Reserve banks to increase their operating earnings, to make their discount rates effective, to promote the use of trade and bankers' acceptances, to stimulate the establishment of discount markets, and to force the reduction of interest rates in localities where competition among lending institutions seemed weak. A review of the 1913 hearings and debates on the Federal Reserve Act affords convincing evidence that the framers of the act were aware of the credit-control implications of this section.

Before the United States entered World War I (April 7, 1917) open-market purchases by the Federal Reserve banks were considerably more important than discount operations (see also Chapter 6). The large gold inflow from Europe through 1915 and 1916, resulting from military purchases by the allied powers, made it unnecessary for the great majority of member banks to borrow. Except in the southern districts discount operations were slight. To meet their operating expenses the Reserve banks purchased municipal warrants; to meet operating expenses and to create broader discount markets, they purchased acceptances; to meet operating expenses and to aid in the retirement of national bank notes, they purchased government bonds. Purchases were made by each Reserve bank on its own initiative, to cover operating expenses. The Reserve Board held that Reserve banks should not enlarge their investments beyond that point, for to do so would simply increase member-bank reserves already swollen by gold imports.

Because of the absence of organized money markets in other districts, the Federal Reserve Bank of New York early began to act as agent for all the Reserve banks in the purchase and sale of municipal warrants. Governor Benjamin Strong of the New York bank proposed in 1915 that the Reserve banks cease buying and selling government obligations for their own accounts and entrust all such operations to a committee of the governors of the Reserve banks, which would handle transactions for the System as a whole.[21] That there was one centralized money market led logically to the centralization of open-market operations.

During World War I, Federal Reserve credit expanded, in the form of loans to member banks. Open-market operations were of negligible importance. Income to pay operating expenses and current and past dividends, and to build up sizable surpluses was assured by the rapidly rising interest return on discounts. With war financing terminated, member banks were able to reduce borrowings rapidly through 1920 and 1921, thanks to funds made available from the cyclical decline of the currency and from gold imports.

The decline in borrowing, accompanied by a reduction in income, prompted the Reserve banks to enter the open market in 1921 and to begin purchasing acceptances and U.S. obligations. Once again each bank did so separately, on its own initiative. Before long it came to be recognized that a centralized body for formulating and carrying out open-market policy was necessary to coordinated central banking policy.

In May 1922 the Committee on the Centralized Execution of Purchases and Sales of Government Securities was organized at a Conference of the governors (now presidents) of the Federal Reserve banks. This committee included the governors of the Federal Reserve banks of Boston, New York, Philadelphia, and Chicago (and, after October, Cleveland) and was established initially to execute decisions by individual banks and thus to avoid the disruptive effects of large competitive orders on the government securities market. In October the committee's duties were extended to include occasional recommendations on the advisability of purchasing or selling securities. Such recommendations, however, were not binding on the Reserve banks.

As open-market operations continued, it was discovered that purchases by the Reserve banks undertaken to increase their earnings actually reduced borrowing by member banks and consequently had little effect on their income. The funds going out the open-market window were used to pay off borrowings at the discount window. Growing awareness of this inverse relationship caused the Board to put more emphasis on the credit-control aspects of open-market operations.

Federal Open Market Investment Committee

Emphasis on the credit-control aspects of open-market operations induced the Federal Reserve Board to create the Federal Open Market Investment Committee on March 22, 1923. The purpose of the new committee, which had the same membership as the old one, was not simply that of coordinating open-market operations; its objectives were broadened to include directing, supervising, and controlling these operations, with primary regard to their effect on the use and quantity of credit.

The official purpose of the Federal Reserve System in reconstituting the Open Market Committee was announced as follows: "that the time, manner, character, and volume of open market investments purchased by Federal Reserve banks be governed with primary regard to the accommodation of commerce and business and to the effect of such purchases or sales on the general credit situation." The adoption of this principle by the Board placed open-market policy on the same basis as discount policy.

The recommendations made by the Committee were to be submitted to the Board for its approval. Although the Federal Reserve banks were not compelled to follow these recommendations, they generally did so. A System open-market account was established, participation in which was allocated among the various Federal Reserve banks. In addition the individual Reserve banks continued to maintain separate investment accounts of their own.

Open Market Policy Conference

A further change in open-market procedures was made on March 25, 1930, when the Open Market Policy Conference was created to replace the former committee. The new conference included a representative of each of the twelve Reserve banks. An executive committee, consisting of the representatives of the five banks that had composed the Federal Open Market Investment Committee, was authorized to handle much of the detailed work. The Federal Reserve Board was authorized to call committee meetings and to participate in its discussions. Each Reserve bank, however, still retained the right to decide whether or not it would participate in conference transactions.

The reason for this change was a conviction on the part of many Federal Reserve officials that the dominant role of the Federal Reserve Bank of New York in the deliberations of the former committee had not been wholly constructive. Inclusion of all the Reserve banks diluted the power of the New York bank.

Banking Act of 1933

The Banking Act of 1933, one of a long series of important pieces of monetary legislation during the Roosevelt administrations, provided the first explicit statutory basis for an open-market committee. It established the Federal Open Market Committee, to consist of one representative from each Reserve bank. Meetings could be called upon the initiative of the Governor of the Federal Reserve Board or of any three members of the committee itself. Board members were empowered to attend committee meetings and to issue regulations governing open-market operations. Although somewhat restricted in their independence, individual Reserve banks still retained authority to decide whether or not to participate in System operations, as well as to carry on operations themselves.

Banking Act of 1935

The Banking Act of 1935 eliminated the 1933 committee and established the present Federal Open Market Committee, which consists of the seven members of the Board of Governors (the Chairman of the Board serving as chairman of the committee) and five representatives of the twelve Federal Reserve banks. The five representatives of the Federal Reserve banks, either the presidents or first vice-presidents, are elected annually from the following groups of banks (as amended by the act of July 7, 1942):

1 from New York
1 from Boston, Philadelphia, and Richmond
1 from Chicago and Cleveland
1 from Atlanta, Dallas, and St. Louis
1 from Kansas City, Minneapolis, and San Francisco

The New York Federal Reserve Bank is always represented, and its president is by custom vice-chairman of the committee. The committee must meet at least four times a year in Washington, D.C., at the summons of the Chairman of the Board of Governors or at the request of any three members of the committee itself. Actually it usually meets every third or fourth week. The Federal Reserve Bank of New York executes all transactions.

The Federal Open Market Committee has complete control of all open-market operations for the entire System. No Federal Reserve bank can individually engage or decline to engage in open-market operations (as defined in Section 14 of the Federal Reserve Act) except in accordance with the direction and regulations of the committee. The time, character, and volume of all purchases and sales are to be managed with a view to accommodating commerce and business and with regard to their bearing upon the general credit situation of the country.

The great merit of the present organization of the Federal Open Market Committee is that the Board of Governors brings a national point of view to bear on credit problems while the individual Reserve banks represent regional points of view. The Commission on Money and Credit recommended that the determination of open-market policies be vested solely in the Board of Governors. The adoption of this proposal, as Allan Sproul, former President of the Federal Reserve Bank of New York has pointed out, would cut the heart out of the Reserve System. If the presidents of the Reserve banks were not to participate in the formulation of these policies, their responsibilities would be relegated to certain routine functions, and men of stature, vision, and perception could no longer be persuaded to head the Reserve banks. Open-market policy would lack the wisdom and judgment of competent men familiar with business and credit conditions in the various districts.

THE FEDERAL RESERVE BANKS

Federal Reserve banks, whose stock is owned by member banks, have been defined as "instrumentalities" of government, a broad and ambiguous term that also covers the numerous corporations owned by the government, independent government contractors, and national banks. When asked whether Federal Reserve banks were part of the U.S. government or the private economy, Sproul replied that in their fiscal responsibilities and their monetary and credit policies they function as part of government and that as a clearinghouse for checks they function as part of the private economy. They are thus somewhere between government and private enterprise, allied to, but not part of, government.[22] Sproul saw wisdom in this segregation. According to him, it has enabled the Federal Reserve banks to resist the pressure of private interests, has provided the country with career central bankers, and has ensured high standards of efficiency and service in operations.

The original Federal Reserve Act provided that no Federal Reserve bank was to commence business with a subscribed capital of less than $4 million. If subscriptions by member banks were insufficient to provide the amount of capital required, stock was to be offered first to the public and then to the Federal government. Stock not owned by member banks was to carry no voting rights. In accordance with the then prevailing practice, it bore and still bears double liability. Stockholders were entitled to receive an annual cumulative dividend of 6 percent on their capital stock; dividends on stock issued before March 1942 are tax free.

Each member bank subscribes to an amount of stock in its own Federal Reserve bank equal to 6 percent of its capital and surplus, actually paying in an amount equal to 3 percent. The balance is subject to call by the Board of Governors, but the prospect that it will ever be demanded is very remote because the Reserve banks have little need of the money. Stock ownership by a member bank is increased or decreased from time to time as the bank augments or reduces its own capital and surplus. This stock may not be transferred or used as collateral for loans.

As of December 31, 1970, the twelve Federal Reserve banks had a total capital of $702 million owned by 5,767 member banks. It has occasionally been suggested that the stock be retired and that member banks receive in payment a credit to their reserve accounts. The Commission on Money and Credit suggested that membership in the Federal Reserve System be evinced not by stock ownership but by nonearning certificates of perhaps $500 for each member bank. A bill introduced in the House of Representatives by Congressman Patman would substitute a

$10 membership fee for the stock subscription. The arguments advanced for retirement of stock are that stock is not necessary to provide Reserve banks with working capital, that stock ownership by member banks may cause the Reserve banks to lay emphasis on profits rather than public service and that the government could use the $30 million now paid out as dividends.

In their comments on this proposal, Federal Reserve officials have observed that stock ownership serves to integrate member banks and bankers under the guiding principles of American central banking and that it enables member banks, which receive no interest on their reserve deposits, to share in the earnings of the Federal Reserve System. These officials point out that stock ownership has important psychological advantages: It stimulates interest in the affairs of the System and helps to secure effective cooperation between private interests and the government. Ownership of stock does not imply proprietary interest in or control over the policies or operations of the Reserve banks.

Selection of Board of Directors

Each of the twelve Federal Reserve banks has nine directors, divided into three classes: A, B, and C. The directors serve for three-year terms, with one-third of each class retiring each year; but those retiring are eligible for reelection or reappointment. Class A and B directors are elected by the member banks which for the purpose of election are divided by size of capital funds into three groups. Each group of banks elects one class A and one class B director. Class A directors are representatives of stock-holding banks, i.e., bankers; class B directors are actively engaged in commerce, agriculture, or industry, but they may not be officers, directors, or employees of any bank. Class A directors are expected to be familiar with the problems of lenders and class B directors with those of borrowers.

Class C directors are appointed by the Board of Governors and represent the public; none may be an officer, director, employee, or stockholder of any bank. Most are public-spirited individuals, serving by reason of a sense of community responsibility. Often a class C director is actively engaged in academic work. The Board of Governors designates one class C director as chairman of the local board and another as deputy chairman. The chairman serves also as Federal Reserve agent, exercising certain administrative duties connected with the issue of Federal Reserve notes.

The board of directors of a local Reserve bank or its executive committee meets at least fortnightly. The chairman, or in his absence the deputy chairman, presides at the meetings (in the event that both are absent the third class C director presides). The directors share a broad public responsibility and must administer the Federal Reserve bank without discrimination for or against any member bank. They formulate bylaws under which the Reserve bank's general business is conducted and its privileges exercised. They are responsible, subject to the rules and regulations of the Board of Governors, for the management policies of the bank. They have a special responsibility for internal auditing, appointing the auditors who report directly to them. They also appoint the president and first vice-president, with the approval of the Board of Governors, for terms of five years. The president is the chief executive officer of the bank, to whom all other officers and employees are responsible.

It has been suggested—and the suggestion seems to have merit—that the president and first vice-president of each Reserve bank be given indefinite rather than five-year appointments. They might thus feel freer to express dissent from decisions by the Board of Governors should the occasion arise. The proposal occasionally advanced that the president of each Reserve bank be appointed by the President of the United States, with the advice and consent of the Senate, would thrust the whole Reserve System into the political maelstrom, might deny the position of president to executives of ability, and would disrupt the harmonious and effective functioning of the System.

Among its other powers, the board of directors of each Reserve bank can establish discount rates, subject to the review and determination of the Board of Governors; can determine whether or not a member bank is making undue use of Federal Reserve credit and whether accommodation should be extended or refused; can appoint three of the five, or four of the seven, directors at each branch bank and can designate one as chairman; can elect one member of the Federal Open Market Committee and one alternate; and can appoint a representative to the Federal Advisory Council.

Subject to the rules and regulations established by the Board of Governors, the twenty-four branches of the Federal Reserve banks are each managed by a board of directors of from five to seven members, three or four of whom are appointed by the parent Reserve bank and two or three by the Board of Governors. A definite geographical area is assigned to each branch, and the member banks within that area deal with the branch rather than with the head office. (The Federal Reserve Board at first authorized branches only reluctantly. Gradually their number increased, and by 1920 the branch structure was nearly complete. Beginning in 1942 the Board of Governors increased the responsibilities of the branches and strengthened their personnel.) [23]

It has become customary in some Federal Reserve districts for representatives of member banks to meet occasionally with Federal Reserve officials. These meetings may be devoted to broad questions of credit policy or to specific technical problems and have been found to be very useful in promoting an exchange of views and a better understanding of the purpose and functions of the Federal Reserve System.

"A special strength of the System," President Alfred Hayes of the Federal Reserve Bank of New York insisted, "is its regional structure that brings it close to the day-to-day life of the whole country." [24] So great are the advantages of such a regional structure that it has been copied rather closely in Australia. The member banks have a fine record of electing outstanding businessmen and bankers as directors; they have contributed both sound judgment and intimate knowledge of the current state of the economy to the formulation of monetary policy.

CENTRAL COORDINATING MECHANISMS

Early in the history of the Federal Reserve System it became apparent that the Board alone could not provide the coordination necessary to the unified and harmonious operation of the twelve Federal Reserve banks. This imperfection in the machinery led to the organization in 1914 of a conference of the governors of the Reserve banks. At about the same time the Board began arranging periodic meetings of the chairmen of the twelve banks, or as they were then called, "the Federal Reserve agents." These sessions proved of great value in permitting interchange of information.

At present there are numerous conferences among the officials of the Federal Reserve System. The presidents of the Reserve banks gather at the meetings of the Federal Open Market Committee; the chairmen and deputy chairmen of the Reserve banks meet periodically with the Board of Governors; operating officers and those engaged in research and legal activities convene frequently. Various means are employed to coordinate policies and action. Conferences are facilitated by modern methods of communication and travel.

CONCLUDING REMARKS

In a recent study the New York Clearing House declared that the Federal Reserve System

> . . . cannot serve the high purposes for which it was established unless the members of the Board of Governors are men fully qualified for their authority and responsibility and unless the decision-making responsibilities within the System are clearly defined. Moreover, the aims of credit policy cannot be achieved unless the powers and functions of the System, in relationship to those of other government agencies, are clearly delineated and unless the activities of these other government agencies are also geared to assist in promoting stable economic progress.[25]

Lines of demarcation cannot be so clearly drawn that conflicts between the Federal Reserve System, on the one hand, and the Treasury, on the other, will not occur or that the Treasury will not, on occasion, control Federal Reserve policy, as it did from April 1917 to December 1919 and from December 1941 to 1951. At other times its influence has also been very powerful.

In Australia and Canada, the central bank statutes provides that in a conflict between the central bank and the state, when no agreement can be reached, the state is to determine the policy to be followed by the bank. In the United Kingdom, the Treasury is empowered to give directions to the Bank of England as often as it thinks necessary, following consultations with the governor of the bank. In France and Italy, attempts have been made to effect coordination through interministerial committees. The committee in France has only advisory powers; that in Italy has powers of compulsion as well. The Reserve System has not favored the establishment of such a committee in the United States, for its officers have recognized that it would then be a subordinate, not a coordinate, cog in the administrative machinery. The Chairman of the Reserve Board would be subordinate to the Secretary of the Treasury, who is a Cabinet minister and a spokesman for the President.

In order to induce the Treasury to conform to the policies of the Federal Reserve System, a subcommittee of the joint Committee on the Economic Report recommended in 1950 that the two houses of Congress declare by joint resolution that

> . . . primary power and responsibility for regulating the supply, availability, and cost of credit in general shall be vested in the duly constituted authorities of the Federal Reserve System, and that Treasury actions relative to money, credit and transactions in the Federal debt shall be made consistent with the policies of the Federal Reserve.[26]

The New York Clearing House pointed out that the great merit of this proposal was that it would force the Treasury to make debt-management decisions in the light of the credit objectives of the System.[27]

The resolution was not adopted, and the Board in its efforts to achieve such coordination relies, at times successfully, at times unsuccessfully, on informal consultations with the Treasury Department, the Council of Economic Advisers, and other government agencies.

The ability of the Reserve System to follow a course of action that it deems in the best interests of the nation, even though this course is opposed by the administration, depends upon the respect and prestige that the officials of the Reserve System command in the community. If they are regarded as sincerely concerned with the nation's welfare and if they are articulate in explaining their actions, they are likely to command the support of an alert and vocal segment of public opinion. An intelligent and watchful public is perhaps the best defense of Federal Reserve independence.

The desirability of securing the best available talent for the Board of Governors is self-evident; the task is primarily the President's responsibility. Throughout the history of the System the men named to the Board have ranged in caliber from poor to excellent. The nadir was probably reached in the 1920s, paving the way for Benjamin Strong, then Governor of the Federal Reserve Bank of New York, to assume a commanding position.

Independent-minded and able persons will not be willing to serve on the Board if it is made subservient to any other agency of the government, including the Treasury Department. Nor will they be willing if certain recent proposals are adopted: appointing the Secretary of the Treasury as Chairman of the Board, forcing the Board to rely on congressional appropriations for its funds, or limiting the members' terms of office to four years. Membership must carry dignity and prestige. Once this is assured, the President can exercise his obligation to select regardless of party affiliation, able men versed in banking and finance, and to select men who are willing to bring their abilities to bear objectively on credit and monetary problems.

Notes

1. This discussion is based largely on H. Parker Willis, *The Federal Reserve System* (New York: Ronald, 1923).

2. *Ibid.*, p. 587.

3. For a series of historical vignettes, entitled "Fiftieth Anniversary of the Federal Reserve System," see issues of the *Monthly Review* of the Federal Reserve Bank of New York, 1964.

4. Willis, *op. cit.*, pp. 672–673.

5. *Monetary Policy and the Management of the Public Debt*, Joint Committee on the Economic Report, 82nd Cong., 2nd sess. (Washington, D.C.: Government Printing Office, 1952), Part 1, pp. 239–240.

6. *Ibid.*, p. 307.

7. William McChesney Martin, Jr., "Statement on Proposed Changes in Federal Reserve Act," *Federal Reserve Bulletin* (Board of Governors, February 1964) p. 153.

8. *Federal Reserve Act,* as amended through November 6, 1966 (Section 10, paragraph 3).

9. Willis, *op. cit.*, pp. 250–251 and 1538–1541.

10. Carter Glass, *An Adventure in Constructive Finance* (New York: Doubleday, 1927), p. 116.

11. Willis, *op. cit.*, p. 250.

12. For a detailed discussion of the administrative framework of the Federal Reserve System, see Karl R. Bopp, *The Agencies of Federal Reserve Policy* ("The University of Missouri Studies," Vol. X, 1935). For a list of the members of the Federal Reserve Board from 1913–1970, see *Federal Reserve Bulletin,* (February 1970), pp. 129–130.

13. *Federal Reserve Act* (Section 10, paragraph 1).

14. E. A. Goldenweiser, *American Monetary Policy* (New York: McGraw-Hill, 1951), p. 301.

15. Karl R. Bopp, "The Human Side of the Federal Reserve—Observations in Retrospect," *Business Review* (Federal Reserve Bank of Philadelphia, May 1969) p. 5.

16. For example, 88th Cong., 2nd Sess., H.R. 9631. See *Federal Reserve Bulletin* (February 1964), p. 151.

17. *The Federal Reserve Re-Examined* (New York: New York Clearing House, 1953), pp. 138–139 and *Money and Credit: Their Influence on Jobs, Prices and Growth* (Englewood Cliffs, N.J.: Prentice-Hall, 1961), p. 87.

18. See *Rules Regarding Delegation of Authority*, as amended April 2, 1970 (Board of Governors of the Federal Reserve System, 1970).

19. Glass, *op. cit.*, p. 116.

20. Glass, *op. cit.*, p. 90.

21. Lester V. Chandler, *Benjamin Strong Central Banker* (Washington, D.C.: The Brookings Institution, 1958), pp. 77–78.

22. *Monetary Policy and the Management of the Public Debt, op. cit.*, Part 2, p. 649.

23. See *Monthly Review*, 38, Federal Reserve Bank of St. Louis (August 1956), pp. 90–97. For a discussion of the work of the Board of Directors, see the Annual Report of the Federal Reserve Bank of Richmond, 1961.

24. Alfred Hayes, address entitled: "Central Banking in a Time of Stress" before the New York State Bankers Association, January 20, 1969.

25. *The Federal Reserve Re-Examined, op. cit.*, p. 137.

26. *Monetary, Credit and Fiscal Policies: Report of the Subcommittee on Monetary, Credit, and Fiscal Policies of the Joint Committee on the Economic Report, Congress of the United States* (Washington, D.C.: Government Printing Office, 1950), p. 18. See also Chapter 5 of this book.

27. *The Federal Reserve Re-Examined, op. cit.*, p. 143.

The Federal Reserve Banks as Bankers' Banks*

CHAPTER 3

Modern central banks limit their clientele mainly to domestic commercial banks and other financial institutions, to the government and to government agencies of the country in which the central bank is located, to foreign central banks and governments, and to international financial institutions such as the International Monetary Fund and the Bank for International Settlements. They are bankers to banks and to governments. Because the bulk of their deposits is owed to banks, they are called "bankers' banks."

Older central banks were initially commercial banks and held the accounts of individuals and business firms. Even today the Bank of England has a few private customers, vestiges of earlier relationships. The new central banks, like the Federal Reserve banks and the Bank of Canada, have, however, from the beginning lim-

---

* In addition to the members of the review committee, who read all the chapters and whose names are listed in the Preface, Parker B. Willis, Vice-President and Economist of the Federal Reserve Bank of Boston, reviewed this chapter with meticulous care. His suggestions were of great value in the revision of the manuscript.

ited their clientele to commercial banks, other types of financial institutions, and governments.

In Western economies there is a sharp demarcation between commercial and central banks and their respective functions. The former operate in the private sectors of the economy; the latter serve the needs of commercial banks and government, helping to bridge the gap between private and public sectors. In communist nations the two are merged in a single gigantic institution that is part of the planning apparatus of the state. Central banks serve the needs of their clients in many ways: as depositories of funds, as suppliers of coin and currency, as lenders, as supervisors of bank operations, as advisers on bank-management policies, and as sources of economic and financial information.

DEPOSITORY OF BANKERS' FUNDS

Member-Bank Reserves

Early in their history, institutions that subsequently were to develop into central banks began holding deposit balances of other banks, a logical result of size, prestige, and location. These balances enabled the depositing institutions to settle clearinghouse transactions, to redeem bank notes, to purchase foreign exchange, and to borrow monies when required. The depositing banks were expected to maintain balances sufficiently large to compensate the correspondent bank for its many services. As time went on, the depositing banks began holding balances equal to certain proportions of their own note and deposit liabilities. These balances, which were large enough to meet customary note redemptions and deposit withdrawals but not so large as to impair seriously their earning power, evolved into the reserves of commercial banks.

This development may be illustrated from American banking history. The acts of 1863 and 1864 establishing the national banking system set the reserve requirements for national banks in the central reserve cities, reserve cities, and country towns at the levels which, on the basis of the trial and error of long experience, were customarily maintained by banks in those localities. The Federal Reserve Act of 1913 continued these reserve requirements, with important modifications. The balances that banks held with one another in informal fashion prior to the Civil War constitute the background of present requirements.*

The reserves of member banks, consisting now of cash on hand and deposits

---

* At the time the Reserve System was established (1914), national banks were compelled to join the Reserve System; state banks and trust companies (if eligible) were invited to become members. For reserve requirements under the national banking system, see Chapter 1, p. 22.

with the Reserve banks, must be maintained at certain stipulated percentages of member-bank deposit liabilities. The amounts to be maintained depend not only on these percentages, which have been changed from time to time, but also upon the size, nature, and definition of deposit liabilities. Since the end of World War II total deposits have soared. Time and savings deposits have increased more rapidly than demand deposits (see Chapter 13). Definitions of deposit liabilities were on occasion altered as a means of increasing the effectiveness of Federal Reserve policy (see Chapter 15).†

Reserves as a Credit Control Device

Member-bank reserves underlie the credit superstructure of loans, investments, and deposits. Any increase over the required minimum permits member banks to increase their loans and investments and thus to enlarge their deposit liabilities. The smaller the percentage of required reserves, the greater is the potential credit expansion and, of course, the potential contraction.

Reserve requirements determine the potential leverage of increases in excess reserves. Requirements should not be set so low that increases induce multiple changes in bank credit of such size that they may be difficult to control without inducing the risk of sharp deflation. Although no percentage is sacrosanct, a reserve of 10 percent against total deposit liabilities seems a desirable minimum; it permits flexibility without necessarily inducing extremely wide swings in the credit volume. At the end of 1970 total member-bank reserves as a percentage of deposits subject to reserve requirements equaled the recommended minimum.

In establishing minimum reserve percentages, it must be remembered that American banks have customarily expanded credit to the maximum extent possible. Minimum reserve percentages have nearly always tended to become the actual percentages.

Reserves are an instrument of credit control and the principal medium through which the Reserve System "exercises its policies to accelerate or retard credit expansion."[1] They do not contribute to a bank's liquidity. Indeed they provide liquidity only for failed, not for operating, banks. The latter obtain liquidity through holdings of short-term loans (including current repayments on longer loans) and holdings of such financially shiftable assets as short-term government obligations and other securities. In the 1960s American commercial banks, because of a decline in their short-term shiftable assets, began to rely on liability rather than on

---

† Current definitions are to be found in Regulation D, as amended effective February 12, 1970, issued by the Board of Governors of the Federal Reserve System.

asset management to provide liquidity. They purchased Federal funds, issued negotiable certificates of deposit and noneligible bankers' acceptances, sold loan participations, sold commercial paper through one-bank holding companies, and borrowed in the Eurodollar market. Heavy reliance on increased liabilities to provide liquidity represented a new departure in American banking practice. It is questionable, however, whether liability management as opposed to asset management can prove a satisfactory source of liquidity for commercial banks (see Chapter 13 for further discussion).

Because reserve requirements are an instrument of credit control, it has been suggested from time to time that all insured commercial banks, rather than simply member banks, be subject to the provisions of the Federal Reserve Act. This requirement was incorporated in the Banking Act of 1933, but was never implemented and was finally repealed in 1939. The proposal was revived after World War II by various congressional committees and by the Commission on Money and Credit. Advocates of compulsory membership point out that not only would monetary control be strengthened but that considerations of equity dictate this course of action.

It has also been suggested from time to time that financial intermediaries (such as mutual savings banks) be subjected to reserve requirements similar to those imposed upon commercial banks. It should be remembered that the reserve requirements imposed on commercial banks in the United States and other nations are a means of regulating the money supply, that is, demand deposits. Only those credit institutions that offer checking accounts can create money, that is, can create liabilities against themselves. As long as financial intermediaries do not offer checking accounts they can lend only the funds that they receive. Their existence may increase the velocity of money movement but not its volume.

Initial Reserve Requirements

The framers of the Federal Reserve Act believed that the 1913 reserve requirements for national banks could be safely lowered, as reserves would be concentrated with the Reserve banks, which could in turn satisfy member banks' needs for additional reserves through lending and open-market operations. The act not only lowered reserve requirements but also differentiated for the first time between demand and time accounts (which included savings deposits) and reduced required reserves against time accounts below those against demand deposits.

Table 3.1
Initial Reserve Requirements
for Member Banks, in Required Percentages

	Against Demand Deposits	Against Time Deposits
Country banks	12%	5%
Reserve-city banks	15	5
Central reserve-city banks[a]	18	5

a. In 1913 those banks were in New York, Chicago, and St. Louis. St. Louis was reclassified as a reserve city on July 1, 1922.

After a transition period of thirty-six months the initial reserves required to be maintained by member banks could be held, in certain designated proportions, either as cash in vault or as a deposit account with a Reserve bank. Meanwhile, member banks in country towns and reserve cities could hold part of their reserves with national banks in reserve or central reserve cities. This provision, which was designed to prevent a sudden disruption of correspondent-bank relations, was superseded by an amendment to the Federal Reserve Act in 1917.

Lower reserves against time deposits were defended on the ground that they were actually savings funds akin to deposits in mutual-savings banks. As time went on it came to be realized that a large part were simply slow-demand accounts; which, in being transferred to the time category, particularly through the 1920s, lowered the volume of required reserves, thereby influencing the portfolio policies of banks, and introducing a new unstabilizing factor in American banking.

This unsatisfactory situation led a committee of the Reserve System to propose in 1932 a plan which tried in automatic fashion to relate reserve requirements to the actual nature of deposit liabilities and did so by relating reserve requirements, in part, to deposit activity.[2] Deposits that circulated more rapidly carried higher reserves. Although never adopted, this change, the committee concluded, would "act as a brake on the unsound use of credit," which might arise from an increase in either bank credit or deposit turnover. The automatic increase of reserve requirements as velocity rose during a boom and the automatic decline in a recession would, it was thought, supplement Federal Reserve open-market operations and constitute a built-in stabilizer.

In view of the special consideration given to savings deposits, the Glass Bill, as it passed the House of Representatives in 1913, required that national banks accepting such deposits establish distinct departments with separate capital and segregated assets. In other words, the savings department was to be a separate institution and was in no event to commingle its assets to pay the deposit liabilities of any other department. This section was dropped from the Senate version and from the initial Federal Reserve Act. Its elimination was regarded as a mistake by many people, who looked upon the savings departments of commercial banks as having distinct and separate functions, akin to those of mutual savings banks in the eastern states.

The rapid increase in commodity prices through 1916, induced by sharp demand for war materials by the allied powers and further stimulated by dramatic increases in demand by American consumers and businessmen, caused great concern to Federal Reserve officials. The gold inflow, along with the reduction in reserve requirements, enabled national and other member banks to increase their loans rapidly without having to borrow from the Reserve banks. In an atmosphere of expanding business activity the resulting deposits circulated at a more rapid rate. The open-market portfolio of the Reserve System was small, large enough only to cover its modest operating expenses. The Reserve banks were helpless to counteract inflationary pressures.

In an effort to check credit expansion the Federal Reserve Board advanced the then original suggestion that it be given the power to make small temporary increases in the reserve requirements of member banks.[3] Although the modest changes proposed probably would not have checked inflationary trends, the importance of the proposal lay less in its potential effectiveness than in the fact that this was the first time that a central bank had requested such powers. Authority to change commercial bank reserve requirements is now generally held by central banks.

Amendments to the Federal Reserve Act

An amendment to the Federal Reserve Act on June 21, 1917 lowered reserve requirements for member banks still further (see Table 3.2) and required that all reserves be held as realized deposit balances with the Reserve banks. The reduction was not as large as the change would imply for vault cash was no longer included in required reserves, a change that affected the country banks more than it affected the reserve- or central reserve-city banks. These new requirements continued in effect to August 16, 1936.

Table 3.2
Percentages of Member-Bank Required Reserves
June 21, 1917–August 16, 1936

	Against Demand Deposits	Against Time Deposits
Country banks	7%	3%
Reserve-city banks	10	3
Central reserve-city banks	13	3

This amendment had been foreshadowed by one enacted on September 7, 1916, which authorized the Federal Reserve Board, upon the affirmative vote of no fewer than five of its members, to permit member banks to carry with the Reserve banks any portion of their reserves then required to be held in their own vaults. The Federal Reserve Board voted the permission, but member banks failed to respond and subsequently were compelled by the 1917 amendment to place all their reserves with the Reserve banks.

The purpose of the 1917 amendment, according to Carter Glass, was to bring about a transfer of gold coin and bullion from member banks to Reserve banks. Concentrating the gold stock of the nation with the Reserve banks greatly increased the expansibility of Federal Reserve credit and, in turn, the expansibility of member-bank credit. This was deemed necessary in view of the impending requirements of war finance. World War I brought about a concentration of the gold stock with the Reserve banks; the Great Depression led to its concentration with the Treasury Department. The first severed the direct relation of gold to member-bank credit and the second the direct relation of gold to central-bank credit.

It was not until 1933 that the request of the Federal Reserve Board for authority to make discretionary increases in reserve requirements was enacted into law. The Thomas Amendment (to the Agricultural Adjustment Act) of May 12, 1933, permitted the Federal Reserve Board, upon the affirmative vote of no fewer than five of its eight members and with the approval of the President of the United States, to declare that an emergency existed by reason of credit expansion and to increase or decrease during such an emergency the required reserve balances against either demand or time accounts. No limit was placed on increases or decreases in the requirements. Although this authority was never used, it was granted because Congress feared that certain other provisions of the Thomas Amendment (those permitting the President to issue $3 billion in greenbacks, to double the price of gold, and to adopt bimetallism at any ratio thought appropriate) might through their effect on member-bank reserves give rise to an inflationary expansion in credit.

The Banking Act of 1935 permitted the Board of Governors itself, upon the affirmative vote of at least four of its seven members, to increase or decrease the reserve requirements of member banks in central reserve and reserve cities, or of member banks in country towns, or of all member banks. Reductions were not to lower reserve requirements below those established in 1917, and increases were not to raise them more than 100 percent.

By an Act of July 7, 1942, the Board of Governors was empowered to change the reserve requirements of member banks in central reserve cities without changing those in reserve cities. The two, which had been bound together in the 1935 legislation, were thus separated. New York City banks had been losing reserves to the rest of the country; government obligations were being sold in large amount in the money market, and funds were moving rapidly out to centers of war production. In 1943 war-loan accounts (U.S. deposits resulting solely from subscriptions to Federal government obligations) were exempted from existing requirements, and they remained exempt until 1947. (By a joint resolution of Congress in August 1948 maximum permissible reserve requirements were temporarily raised to 30, 24, and 18 percent in central reserve-city, reserve-city, and country banks respectively. Maximum permissible reserve requirements against time deposits were raised to 7.5 percent. This temporary authority expired on June 30, 1949. See Chapter 8.)

The next important change was adopted in 1959: member banks were permitted to include vault cash in their reserves. As the Board explained, this action was taken "to remedy inequities that had arisen because many banks, particularly smaller country banks, had found it necessary to hold relatively larger amounts of vault cash than other banks did for operating purposes." [4] At first only limited amounts could be counted as reserve, but since November 24, 1960, all vault cash has been included, a change similar to the requirements in the initial Reserve Act. The important difference was that in the 1913 enactment only legal tender money, which did not include Federal Reserve notes, could be counted as vault cash. Once the 1933 legislation had given Federal Reserve notes full legal tender power, they, along with other types of currency and coin, could be included.

The classification of central reserve cities, which had existed since the 1864 revision of the National Banking Act, was terminated on July 28, 1962. Since then all cities have been classified as either reserve cities or country towns. The 1970 legal requirements are shown in Table 3.3

Table 3.3
Percentage of Reserve Required

	Against Net Demand Deposits Reserve-City Banks	Country Banks	Against Savings and Time Deposits All Member Banks
Minimum	10%	7%	3%
Maximum	22	14	10

The changes ordered in member-bank reserve requirements by the Board of Governors since the passage of the Banking Act of 1935 are shown in Table 3.4.

Table 3.4
Member-Bank Reserve Requirements
(Percentage of Deposits)

Through July 13, 1966 Effective Date [a]	Net Demand Deposits [b]			Time Deposits	
	Central Reserve-City Banks [c]	Reserve-City Banks	Country Banks	Central Reserve and Reserve-City Banks [c]	Country Banks
1917–June 21	13	10	7	3	3
1936–Aug. 16	19½	15	10½	4½	4½
1937–Mar. 1	22¾	17½	12¼	5¼	5¼
May 1	26	20	14	6	6
1938–Apr. 16	22¾	17½	12	5	5
1941–Nov. 1	26	20	14	6	6
1942–Aug. 20	24	–	–	–	–
Sept. 14	22	–	–	–	–
Oct. 3	20	–	–	–	–
1948–Feb. 27	22	–	–	–	–
June 11	24	–	–	–	–
Sept. 24, 16	26	22	16	7½	7½
1949–May 5, 1	24	21	15	7	7
June 30, July 1	–	20	14	6	6
Aug. 1	–	–	13	–	–
Aug. 11, 16	23½	19½	12	5	5
Aug. 18	23	19	–	–	–
Aug. 25	22½	18½	–	–	–
Sept. 1	22	18	–	–	–
1951–Jan. 11, 16	23	19	13	6	6
Jan. 25, Feb. 1	24	20	14	–	–
1953–July 9, 1	22	19	13	–	–
1954–June 24, 16	21	–	–	5	5
July 29, Aug. 1	20	18	12	–	–
1958–Feb. 27, Mar. 1	19½	17½	11½	–	–
Mar. 20, Apr. 1	19	17	11	–	–

Effective Date	Net Demand Deposits [b,d]				Time Deposits [d,e] (All Classes of Banks)		
	Reserve-City Bank (Under $5 Million)	Reserve-City Bank (Over $5 Million)	Country Banks (Under $5 Million)	Country Banks (Over $5 Million)	Savings Deposits	Other Time Deposits (Under $5 Million)	Other Time Deposits (Over $5 Million)
Apr. 17	18½	—					—
Apr. 24	18	16½					—
1960—Sept. 1	17½	—					—
Nov. 24	—	—					12
Dec. 1	16½	—					—
1962—July 28	(c)	—			(c)		—
Oct. 25, Nov. 1	—	—			4		4
Beginning July 14, 1966							
1966—July 14, 21	16½[e]	—	12[e]	—	4[e]	4[e]	5
Sept. 8, 15	—	—	—	—	—	—	6
1967—Mar. 2	—	—	—	—	3½	3½	—
Mar. 16	—	—	—	—	3	3	—
1968—Jan. 11, 18	16½	17	12	12½	—	—	—
1969—Apr. 17	17	17½	12½	13	—	—	—
1970—Oct. 1	—	—	—	—	—	—	5
Present legal requirement:							
Minimum	10		7		3	3	3
Maximum	22		14		10	10	10

a. When two dates are shown, the first applies to the change at central reserve-city or reserve-city banks and the second to the change at country banks.
b. Demand deposits subject to reserve requirements, which, beginning with August 23, 1935, have been total demand deposits minus cash items in process of collection and demand balances due from domestic banks (also minus war-loan and Series E bond accounts during the period April 13, 1943–June 30, 1947).
c. Authority of the Board of Governors to classify or reclassify cities as central reserve cities was terminated effective July 28, 1962.
d. Effective January 5, 1967 such time deposits as Christmas- and vacation-club accounts became subject to the same requirements as are savings deposits.
e. See columns above for earliest effective date of this rate.

Source: Fifty-Fourth Annual Report Board of Governors of the Federal Reserve System Covering Operations for the Year 1967 (Washington, D.C.: May 22, 1968) p. 364 and Federal Reserve Bulletin (August 1970), p. A 10.

Later, in a discussion of the credit policies of the Reserve System, the occasion will arise to revert to this table and relate, as far as possible, the changes taking place to policy action on the part of the Reserve System.

Over the years a number of proposals for substantially altering member-bank reserve requirements, aside from that relating reserve requirements to deposit turnover, have been advanced. Space does not permit discussion of these proposals, many of which have raised intriguing questions of monetary management and banking theory.[5]

One proposal that the Board of Governors has favored for several years would permit it to fix progressive reserve percentages, graduated according to the amount of a bank's deposits, and to apply such requirements to all Federally insured banks rather than to member banks alone. It represents an attempt, as did the velocity proposal, to relate reserve requirements automatically to the character of a bank's deposits.

The arguments for the proposal are that the division of member banks between reserve-city and country banks is wholly arbitrary and in no way reflects the type of business or the deposit liabilities of the member bank and that the deposits of nonmember banks should, as part of the money supply, be subject to the same requirements as are those of member banks.* The proposed legislation would at the same time grant nonmember insured banks access to the discount window.

A smoothly graduated system would require each bank to maintain a relatively low reserve against the first few millions of its demand deposits and higher reserves against increments above this minimum. All banks of the same size would maintain equal reserves. As a bank grew, its reserve requirements would rise smoothly and gradually. The new proposal would give preferential treatment to small banks, as do present requirements: in effect a subsidy for the unit banking system. The Board has concluded that it has the power under existing law to establish graduated reserve requirements for member banks subject to existing minimum and maximum requirements but maintains that it is essential that all insured banks fall subject to reserve requirements.

In recent years the Board of Governors has shown great flexibility in the use of reserve requirements. Beginning in 1966 it began to differentiate between the time deposits of large and small banks, and in 1968 between the net demand deposits of large and small banks (see Table 3.4). Through 1969 and 1970

---

* The reserve requirements imposed by state law on nonmember banks are less onerous than those imposed by the Federal Reserve Act giving nonmember banks a competitive advantage and inducing member banks to leave the Reserve System.

it extended requirements to a wide range of banking transactions. The purpose of these changes (see Chapter 15) was to check credit expansion, particularly on the part of large banks.[6]

Reserve Computation Periods

From the early days of the Federal Reserve System, regulations have given member banks some leeway in meeting reserve requirements, with penalties imposed on member banks that do not comply. Under regulations dating from the 1920s and still in effect, member banks meet their legal requirements not on a daily basis but on a daily average basis over a stated period.

The precise requirements are important because of their possible effects on money-market fluctuations and on necessary counteraction by the Reserve System. Under regulations that became effective on September 12, 1968:

1. Reserve computation periods, ending at the close of business on Wednesday of each week, are made uniform for all member banks;

2. Required reserves for a particular week are based on average daily net deposit balances held by a member bank for the reserve period two weeks earlier;

3. The reserve balance of each member bank consists of its average daily balance with its Reserve bank during the computation period for which the computation is made and the average daily currency and coin held by the member bank during the second computation period prior to the computation period for which the computation is made;

4. Any excess or deficiency of reserves, but not more than two percent of required reserves, may be carried forward to the next following computation period.

The new regulations were devised in order to make the calculation of required reserves easier for member banks, particularly for those with deposits and vault cash scattered among many branches; to enable member banks to manage their reserve positions with greater precision; to smooth out intra-monthly fluctuations in total reserves with less assistance from Federal Reserve open-market operations; and in general to aid Reserve officials in their conduct of open-market operations. These expectations may not have been fully realized.[7]

Creation of Member-Bank Reserves

To comply with the reserve provisions of the original Federal Reserve Act and the 1917 amendment, member banks shifted gold and gold coin, legal tender notes, and silver certificates from their own vaults to the Reserve banks. Since this initial transfer of funds, total reserve deposits of member banks have increased or decreased in response to factors which, for the most part, are outside their immediate control.

Increases or decreases in the reserve deposits of member banks reflect in the main shifts in the following important factors:

1. Changes in gold stock that respond principally to shifts in America's balance of payments (until 1933 member banks could buy and sell, hold, import or export gold, and transfer this gold to Reserve banks);

2. Changes in Federal Reserve holdings of Special Drawing Rights (see Chapter 16);

3. Transactions in foreign exchange held by the Federal Reserve banks that may result from direct purchases by the Reserve banks and from an activation of swap agreements (see Chapter 16 for further discussion); [8]

4. Changes in the open-market portfolios of the Federal Reserve banks that fluctuate in response to Federal Reserve policy;

5. Fluctuations in the volume of money in circulation that reflect changes in wages, retail prices, and currency hoarding, income tax evasion, the emergence of black markets as in World War II, and large amounts of currency carried by the troops in the two world wars;

6. Changes in member-bank borrowings that respond to the factors already listed and which may rise as member banks borrow to obtain reserves needed to support a growing volume of deposits.

Member-bank reserves, a liability on the books of the Federal Reserve banks, can fluctuate only as other liabilities or assets change. Member banks have little power to influence the assets or liabilities of the Reserve banks, save as they borrow from the Reserve System, and they usually borrow because the Reserve System forces them into debt through open-market sales of securities or because it has ordered an increase in member-bank required reserves.

These points can best be illustrated by the dramatic developments occurring during World War II. Total member-bank reserves increased from $12.5 to $15.9 billion. This rise was necessitated by the rapid wartime increase in demand deposits and resulted principally from interplay of items in the Federal Reserve statements of condition as shown in Table 3.5.

Table 3.5

Changes in Federal Reserve Condition Statements Between the End of 1941 and the End of 1945 (Millions of Dollars)

Factors Causing Member-Bank Reserves to Decrease	
Decline in gold certificates	$ 2,637
Increase in Federal Reserve notes	16,457
Increase in the capital account of the Federal Reserve banks	221
	$19,315
Factors Causing Member-Bank Reserves to Increase	
Increase in U.S. securities owned by Federal Reserve banks	$22,008
Increase in other Federal Reserve credit	484
Increase in discounts and advances	246
	$22,738
Increase in member-bank reserves	$ 3,423

The only item in Table 3.5 that changed as a result of the initiative of member banks themselves was the small increase in discounts and advances. All other changes resulted from developments outside their control. The huge expansion in the security portfolios of the Reserve banks occurred on their own initiative and was large enough not only to offset the effects of the decline in the gold stock and the rise in Federal Reserve notes on member-bank reserves but also to bring about an actual increase in reserves.

Reserves: Total, Required, Excess, Net Free, and Net Borrowed

In order to understand what the Reserve banks are doing at any particular time, it is important to follow not only changes in total reserves but also changes in required reserves against demand, savings, and time accounts, changes in non-borrowed reserves and changes in net free and net borrowed reserves.

Total reserves are the sum of member-bank deposits with the Reserve banks plus member-bank's vault cash. Required reserves are, of course, those required to be maintained. In October 1971, these were 3–5 percent of savings and time deposits and 12.5–17.5 percent of net demand deposits. Moreover, the total of reserves may be further subdivided into borrowed and nonborrowed reserves. An increase in the proportion of borrowed reserves (seasonally adjusted) warrants the conclusion that the Reserve System is following a tighter money policy, which sooner or later will affect bank-credit expansion. Required reserves may also be subdivided into those against private demand deposits, the demand deposits of the U.S. government, and time and savings accounts. The purpose of this classification is to single out the reserves that are required against the actively used demand deposits of the private sector of the economy.

Excess reserves are simply total reserves minus required reserves. Excess reserves minus member-bank borrowing equal net free or net borrowed reserves. If excess reserves are greater than member-bank borrowings, the banking system possesses net free reserves, on the basis of which it may expand loans and investments. Interest rates will then be relatively low. If, on the other hand, excess reserves are less than member-bank borrowing, the banking system is a net debtor to the Reserve System, and interest rates will be relatively high.

Although all these different concepts and definitions of reserves are in combination useful in understanding Federal Reserve policy, appraising credit trends and following developments in the money market, they must be used with considerable caution. The actual effects of changes in any one of these series is dependent upon many attendant circumstances, such as the intensity of the loan and investment demand, the size of the secondary reserves held by commercial banks, and the growing dependence on liability as opposed to asset management in the quest for liquidity. Other factors include the distribution of excess reserves and of member-bank borrowings within the banking system, the varying proportions of demand and time accounts and, finally, but by no means least, the degree of restraint on member-bank borrowings exercised by the Reserve banks at the discount windows.[9]

Basic Reserve Position

To reflect the increasing reliance of commercial banks upon the Federal-funds market (see pp. 71–74), the Reserve System has since September 2, 1959, computed weekly the "basic reserve positions" of large city banks. This equals excess reserves less borrowing at the Reserve banks and less net interbank Federal-funds transactions. For example, on August 25, 1971, the basic reserve position of forty-six large banks was $5,976 million, computed as follows: [10]

Excess reserves	$ – 4 million
Less borrowing at Federal Reserve banks	– 326 million
Less net interbank Federal-funds transactions	– 5,646 million
Net Deficit	$ – 5,976 million

This deficit, which was equal to 47.1 percent of the average required reserves of these banks, reflected a much tighter credit position than was recorded in the simply global data of net excess and net borrowed reserves. The deficit in the case of five Chicago banks had soared as of that date to 114.1 percent of average required reserves.*

Concentration of Excess Reserves

For many years the New York City and other reserve-city banks have kept fully invested, eliminating their excess reserves in the process. The excess reserves of the banking system have been held largely by country banks, which until recently have lacked the specialized talent or aid from correspondent banks to control their cash positions with greater precision. As interest rates and costs began to rise and the profits squeeze became increasingly effective, country banks sought to increase earnings by placing excess reserves in money-market paper or in the Federal-funds market. Their sophistication increased.

Reserve Management

Each large city bank has one or more departments responsible for maintaining and supervising its reserve position. The officers in charge often receive hourly reports on the inflow and outflow of funds, which may result from large transfers of corporate funds; from receipts and withdrawals of government deposits; from purchases, sales, and maturities of securities; from extensions and retirements of loans; and from cash transactions. The officials must also be able to predict, as closely as they can, future changes in the levels of loans and deposits. Should a bank be faced with a reserve deficiency, it must decide whether to borrow from its Reserve bank or from other sources or to liquidate assets. The method chosen will depend upon the bank's analysis of relative costs and its forecast of the permanence of the deficiency.

---

* A discussion of "monetary aggregates" as a goal of Federal Reserve policy is to be found in Chapter 19.

Reserve Absorption

Increases in deposit liabilities (while reserve requirements remain the same), as well as shifts of deposits from the time to the demand category or from centers of lower reserve requirements to those of higher reserve requirements absorb reserves, that is, force increases in required reserves. Changes in the opposite direction release reserves. Over a period of time, demand deposits adjusted would be expected to rise in response to community needs for a larger volume of money. Time deposits would also rise, and indeed have risen sharply, as money savings are placed with commercial banks.

The additional reserves required to support a growing volume of deposit totals (if reserve requirements are not lowered) can be supplied only in one of the following important ways: gold imports, the acquisition of foreign exchange and Special Drawing Rights by the Reserve banks, open-market purchases by the Reserve banks, or member-bank borrowings. The last method causes a rise in interest rates; the others help to maintain rate levels.

In the postwar period, as Table 3.4 indicates, substantial reductions in reserve requirements were ordered. These reductions—plus the decrease in excess reserves, inclusion of vault cash in required reserves, and the rapid increase in time deposits —have held increases in required reserves to a relatively modest total despite an enormous rise in deposit totals. That is, reserve absorption has been much less than it would have been in the absence of these factors.

The reduction in reserve requirements has increased the potential expansibility of the banking system and, it might be added, its potential contractability as well. Federal Reserve credit, always high-powered money, possesses still greater power.

THE CLEARING FUNCTION OF MEMBER-BANK RESERVES

Before the Federal Reserve System was instituted, out-of-town checks were routed in a highly circuitous fashion, often taking an inordinately long time to arrive at the banks on which they were drawn. This procedure was necessary to avoid or reduce exchange charges, which represented in fact a toll on the commerce of the nation. Correspondent banks, engaged in avid competition for bankers' balances, often absorbed these charges, granted credit before collection of the checks, and thus paid interest on uncollected funds. Consequently part—some people think a large part—of the deposited reserves were fictitious. As will be seen later, this defect has not yet been wholly eliminated, but procedures today are nonetheless superior in speed and simplicity to those in effect before World War I.

The committee charged with setting up the Federal Reserve System went to work even before the Reserve banks were established to institute clearance procedures. The Gold Settlement Fund (now the Inter-District Settlement Fund) was established, permitting quick clearance and transfer of funds among Reserve banks. As time went on, it was decided to accept clearing deposits from nonmember banks, to collect checks from drawee banks only at par, to settle clearinghouse balances on the books of the Reserve banks, and to promote the establishment of regional or district clearinghouses. (Stymied by court decisions and hostile legislation, the Federal Reserve banks finally decided to refuse to handle checks drawn on the non-par banks, those banks that refused to remit at par for checks sent to them by the Reserve System. At the end of 1970, there were 501 such institutions, mostly small banks located in the Atlanta, Dallas, Richmond, St.Louis, and Minneapolis Federal Reserve districts.)

For a unit banking system the clearance mechanism that has evolved is highly efficient. About 8 billion checks, involving over $3 trillion are collected annually. Local checks are collected now as they were before 1913, through local clearinghouses, with the net balances settled on the books of the Reserve banks. Intradistrict items, in case the drawee is not a party to local or regional clearinghouse arrangements, are sent directly by the Reserve banks to the drawee banks, which remit authorizations to debit their accounts or send drafts on their correspondent banks. Interdistrict checks are usually sent to local Federal Reserve banks, and settlement is made through the Inter-District Settlement Fund. Many large commercial banks, however, send checks drawn on member banks in other Federal Reserve districts directly to the Reserve banks concerned. Every effort is made to expedite the collection of checks and the remittance of funds.

Collection Time Schedule

The Reserve System early established a time schedule for the collection of checks which in the course of time has been modified as circumstances have warranted.* The Federal Reserve Bank of New York thus gives immediate credit for clearinghouse items received in time for presentation through the clearinghouse the same day, for checks signed by the Treasurer of the United States received before 10:00 A.M., and for checks on the Reserve bank itself received before 3:00

---

* The time schedule found its legal basis in the requirement that funds on deposit with the Reserve banks are expected to represent realized deposit balances.

P.M. A deferred credit of one to two days is given to all other items, provided they are received by a specified time.

Often it is impossible to collect items within the time allotted, which means that the proceeds of checks are frequently credited to the accounts of member banks before they are collected. At the end of 1970, the total of such credits amounted to $4,150 million, which is the difference between "uncollected items" on the asset side of the consolidated statement of all Federal Reserve statements and "deferred availability items" on the liability side. This difference is called "the float" and represents fictitious reserves, in that credit has been given before collection.

Throughout the history of the Reserve System, the time schedule has been greatly reduced. In the days of steam locomotives, San Francisco in relation to New York City was an eight-day point. That is, it took eight days to send a check to the Federal Reserve Bank of San Francisco, pass it through the local clearinghouse, and remit the proceeds east by telegraph. The advent of jet transport has cut the time schedule to two days. It is not always possible, however, even under the most favorable conditions, to adhere to the present time schedule (time-schedule float). In fact, some officials in the Reserve System opposed reducing the collection time to that now in effect, pointing out that such a reduction would increase the float, as indeed it did. In addition to the time-schedule float, there is the "holdover float," resulting from a large volume of incoming checks that cannot be processed in time to meet plane or rail schedules. Weather condition and strikes may also delay the collection of checks (transit float). Holdover and transit floats would, of course, occur under any time schedule. It is the time-schedule float that has caused the volume to soar.

Since the end of World War II the daily average float has ranged from $578 million to $4.3 billion. These variations have a direct effect on member-bank reserves, other factors remaining the same. Consequently it is essential that the Reserve System endeavor to estimate probable fluctuations and be prepared to take counter action, otherwise the money market would be subject to wide and damaging variations.

There are several types of variations in the float. First, there is the secular trend, the daily average of which has risen from about $1.4 billion in 1950 to $4.3 billion in 1970. This increase resulted from a sharp rise in the volume of checks to be processed, which, despite many technological improvements, has tended to tax the clearing facilities of the Reserve System.

Fluctuating around the annual average are important seasonal variations. The float is at the lowest level in August, a time of seasonal lull in business. It reaches a maximum in December, about 40 percent above the average. It falls in January and rises again in June and September, when clearing facilities are strained by individual and corporate income-tax payments. It remains high in July, the beginning of the vacation season. Within each month the float follows a bell-shaped curve, with the peak around the middle of the month, indicating perhaps that most bills are paid before the 10th. Each month is, of course, subject to special factors caused by holidays and the influence of local tax collections. Even within a week the float shows considerable variation. The high is reached on Thursdays, when the float is about 8 percent above the average for the week. The reason is that banks receive the largest volume of incoming checks on Monday, which they process and send to the Reserve banks on Tuesday; the Reserve banks, in turn, process them and give credit for many interdistrict items two days later, frequently before actual collection. The large Thursday float is thus a time-schedule float.

The Reserve banks forecast these fluctuations with considerable accuracy and offset them, when necessary, by increasing or decreasing their open-market portfolio.[11] The ideal would be a total absence of float, and it may come about when member banks and Federal Reserve banks become so fully interconnected by electronic circuits that immediate credit may be given for all checks and immediate debit will follow immediate credit.

THE FEDERAL-FUNDS MARKET

Federal funds are simply excess credit balances of member banks on the books of a Reserve bank, and the Federal-funds market involves the borrowing and lending of these balances at specified rates of interest. The continuous flow of funds among the 5,767 (December 31, 1970) member banks and other participating institutions, resulting from numerous transactions, leaves some with excess reserves and others with deficiencies. The larger banks in the financial centers are especially subject to wide daily swings in their reserve positions, and they are the ones that participate most actively in the Federal-funds market. Among the reasons for these swings are the fluctuations occurring in the float.

The Federal-funds market,[12] developed in the 1920s, became moribund during the banking difficulties and the excessively low money rates of the 1930s, continued moribund during the era of pegged interest rates of the 1940s, and finally revived vigorously after the Treasury-Federal Reserve Accord of 1951 (see Chapter 8), which permitted greater flexibility in the credit policy of the Reserve banks. In the 1920s banks used the market to adjust their reserve positions. In the 1950s and 1960s they used the market not only for that purpose but also as an outlet for short-term funds, as a means of financing securities dealers in U.S. obligations, and as a basis for increasing their loans and investments.

The market, which throughout its life has expanded from local and regional to national scope, is quite informal, with no trading center and no group of organized traders. Interest rates are arrived at by direct negotiation. Several stock-brokerage firms and banks serve as intermediaries, bringing buyers and sellers together. The market finds its origins in the legal reserve requirements to which member banks are subject; in the fact that checks drawn on a Federal Reserve bank are given immediate credit by the Reserve bank, whereas checks drawn on commercial banks are given delayed credit, in accordance with the collection time schedule; and in the fact that the excess reserves that member banks maintain with Reserve banks earn no interest, whereas reserve deficiencies are subject to penalties.

If checks drawn on commercial banks resulted in immediate credit and debit at the Reserve banks, the Federal-funds market would decline greatly in importance. The float would disappear. Contrarily, any change that enlarges the float (as did the reduction in the time schedule in 1951) increases the importance of the Federal-funds market. Besides fluctuations in the float, other factors that influence the size of the Federal-funds market are longer reserve-averaging periods, improvements in the wire-transfer facilities of the Reserve System, the establishment of direct wire communications among approximately 250 large banks in 69 principal cities, swings in Treasury and foreign deposits at the Reserve banks, interbank competition for correspondent balances and growing awareness among smaller banks of the advantages accruing from use of the market. Increases in the breadth and activity of the government securities markets, in which about two-thirds of purchases and sales are in Federal funds, has also had a significant impact on the Federal-funds market. Finally, the growing volume of negotiable time certificates of deposit issued by the commercial banks are often sold for Federal funds and repaid in Federal funds.

The market for Federal funds is used not only by large banks but also increasingly by small banks for short-term adjustments or turnabouts in their reserve positions. It is employed also by agencies of foreign banks, savings banks, government securities dealers, and a few nonfinancial corporations. About 3,500 banks now participate in the market, about 350 regularly; perhaps 70 banks account for the bulk of all transactions. Daily average gross purchases amount to about $9 billion.[13]

Although the Federal-funds market is national in scope, transactions are concentrated in three Federal Reserve districts: New York, Chicago, and San Francisco. New York City, as the Board of Governors pointed out in its study, is the hub of the market.[14] For long periods of time New York and Chicago have been net buyers and San Francisco a net seller. Whether a district is a net user or supplier depends upon the ebb and flow of funds arising from seasonal forces and other factors. The typical movement is from small country banks to smaller city banks to larger city banks.

Various trading techniques have developed, reflecting different legal arrangements and the desire to minimize risk and keep bookkeeping transactions to a minimum. In local transactions in New York City, for example, the lending bank gives to the borrowing bank a check on the Federal Reserve bank and receives a cashier's check, which, as a one-day item, is larger than the Federal Reserve check by the amount of interest. Local transactions outside New York City are often handled by telephone requests to the Federal Reserve bank, followed by written confirmation. Interest payments are handled separately. If the two banks are in different reserve districts, they arrange details by wire or telephone, followed by formal confirmation. The transfer is effected through the leased wire facilities of the Federal Reserve banks.

Aside from straight or unsecured transactions, the lender of Federal funds may transfer the funds by buying government securities from the borrower, which becomes a commitment to repurchase the same securities with Federal funds at a specified future date at a definite price. The repurchase price includes interest. A variant is the so-called "buy back," in which the borrowing bank agrees to sell perhaps $5 million of Treasury bills against Federal funds. It buys them back the next day, paying in Federal funds. The bulk of Federal-funds transactions are straight overnight unsecured transactions, which are convenient, flexible, and free from the troublesome accounting details of secured transactions. Not more than 5 percent of total purchases and sales have maturities longer than one day.

Commercial Bank Use of the Market

Commercial banks using the market may be divided into several groups: small banks that usually have excess reserves and are typically sellers, using the market as an investment outlet for their excess funds; banks that use the market to adjust their own reserve positions; banks, about seventy in number, which use the market to accommodate the demands of their correspondent banks; and a few banks that rely upon the market as a fairly constant source of reserve funds. (Banks that make continual use of the market to cover reserve deficiencies could be subject to disciplinary pressures by the Reserve banks and would, in time, find their credit ratings lowered in the market.)

Trading in Federal funds has risen substantially over the past ten years. Although participation in the market declines with bank size, increasing numbers of smaller banks are participating. The rise in interest rates has induced smaller banks to pare their cash reserves and correspondent balances to a minimum. Among other incentives is the decline in the dollar unit of trading and the spreading knowledge of the market among brokers and banks. The Federal-funds market has proved a convenient and risk-free outlet for temporary surplus funds. It involves few bookkeeping transactions and low bookkeeping costs.

Net income from the sale of Federal funds is frequently impressively high. One bank in the Philadelphia Reserve District, with deposits between $25 million and $50 million received almost 75 percent of its net current operating income in 1966 from the sale of the Federal funds. Although this example is extreme, the average proportion of net current operating income for country member banks that year was more than 8 percent. Operating costs are negligible.[15]

An increasing number of banks, particularly large ones, prefer to adjust their reserve positions by buying Federal funds rather than by borrowing from their Reserve bank.* Borrowings from a Reserve bank are subject to surveillance, must be collateraled and may be taken as a sign of weakness. Continual borrowing is not regarded as appropriate. Smaller banks, on the other hand, do not hesitate to borrow from their Reserve banks and rely on the Federal-funds market as a source of funds less than do the large banks. Although the purchase of Federal funds relieves the individual bank of the need to borrow, it does not relieve the banking system from reliance on the Federal Reserve System.

The Federal-Funds Rate

As a competitor with the discount window, the rate on Federal funds is not likely to rise above the discount rate save in periods, like 1928 and 1929 and the latter half of the 1960s, when member banks were running short of eligible paper or Reserve banks were exerting pressure to dissuade them from using discount facilities. In periods of easy money, the Federal-funds rate moves in harmony with

---

* In the condition reports issued by the Comptroller of the Currency since September 1963, national banks must report "Federal funds purchased" and "Federal funds sold" separately. The Comptroller ruled that these funds are no longer subject to the borrowing and lending limits applicable to national banks.

other short-term rates, but with the discount rate as an upper limit. In tight-money periods, the Federal-funds rate rises above the discount rate, at times substantially. Banks may wish to hold their discount privileges in reserve for "emergencies," to circumvent what is termed the "red tape" associated with borrowing and to avoid becoming permanent borrowers at the Reserve bank. Often banks that are heavy buyers of Federal funds are also frequent borrowers at the Reserve banks. They have chronic reserve deficiencies.

The administration of the discount window was reputedly more severe in the 1950s and 1960s then it had been in the 1920s. Consequently the Federal-funds rate ranged above the discount rate and, in a way, acted as a substitute for a higher discount rate.[16] Toward the end of June 1969 it reached 10.5 percent, in contrast to a discount rate of 6 percent.

Unifying Force of the Market

The Federal-funds market tends to bring the commercial banks of the country into greater unity, enabling member banks to hew close to minimum legal reserve requirements. It was for this reason that the Reserve System once expressed opposition to it, believing that, in the absence of such a market, member banks would maintain larger excess reserves. The existence of the market, however, does not interfere with Federal Reserve policy—instead, it actually increases its effectiveness. The impact of policy changes is quickly transmitted across the nation.

CONCLUDING OBSERVATIONS

Except for member-bank borrowing from the Reserve banks, total member-bank reserves fluctuate in response to factors over which member banks have little control. The most important of these factors are changes in the volume of money in circulation, in holdings of gold certificates, foreign exchange and SDR's by the Reserve banks and in their open-market portfolios. The net increase in the total volume of member-bank reserves since the end of World War II has resulted mainly from Federal Reserve credit operations.

Those who drafted the Federal Reserve Act accepted without question the need to impose reserve requirements on member banks. The requirements which were adopted represented a continuation of those that had been imposed by the National Currency Act, which had itself frozen into law the percentages maintained by state banks prior to the Civil War.

Average reserves of national banks were much higher than those now maintained by member banks. A few years prior to the enactment of the Reserve Act (April 28, 1909), the reserves of cash and deposits of all national banks equaled 33 percent of their total deposit liabilities, as contrasted with about 9.5 percent on the part of all member banks in July 1970.[17] There were, of course, many important intermediate fluctuations, but the long-time trend has declined. The potential expansibility of the banking system, as well as its contractibility, has greatly increased. The basic reason for the sharp decline in the ratio of bank reserves between these two dates was the establishment by the Reserve Act of lower and different reserve requirements against demand and time accounts and later against demand, time, and savings accounts. The differences rested on the conviction that the nature of these various deposits differed. This belief was shaken in the 1920s when slow demand accounts were shifted into the time category to make possible a still larger expansion in credit, and again the 1960s with a shift into time and savings accounts for the same reason.

It would be expected that over a period of time, member-bank deposit liabilities would rise and that this would force an increase in total member-bank reserves. And so it would, unless the Board of Governors ordered, reductions in reserve requirements, as it often has.

Whether the Reserve System at a given moment is following an expansionist or restrictive policy can be detected by changes in member-bank net free or borrowed reserves. Net free reserves connote an easy-money policy; net borrowed reserves, a tight-money policy. The precise effect will depend on many attendant circumstances. The data need to be supplemented by various other series and by an appraisal of psychological currents in the money and capital markets.

Changes in the float give rise to wide fluctuations in member-bank reserves which, in the interests of a stable money market, must be offset by Federal Reserve operations. Trading in Federal funds leads to an intensive utilization of member bank excess reserves. It helps to reduce geographical differences in interest rates and to increase the effectiveness of Federal Reserve policy.

Notes

1. *Twenty-Third Annual Report of the Board of Governors of the Federal Reserve System Covering Operations for the Year 1936* (Washington, D.C.: Government Printing Office, 1937), p. 19.

2. *Nineteenth Annual Report of the Federal Reserve Board, 1932* (Washington, D.C.: Government Printing Office, 1933), pp. 260–285.

3. *Federal Reserve Bulletin* (February 1917), pp. 102, 108. See also John Maynard Keynes, *A Treatise on Money*, II (New York: Harcourt, 1930), pp. 260–261.

4. *Forty-Sixth Annual Report of the Board of Governors of the Federal Reserve System Covering Operations for the Year 1959* (Washington, D.C.: Government Printing Office, 1960) p. 5.

5. A discussion of these proposals can be found in Irving M. Auerbach, "Reserve Requirements of Commercial Banks," *Bank Reserves: Some Major Factors Affecting Them* (Federal Reserve Bank of New York, November 1953). Also see Lucille Stringer Mayne, *The Cost of Federal Reserve Membership*. A research paper prepared for the Department of Economics and Research (The American Bankers Association, 1967).

6. See remarks by Andrew F. Brimmer, "The Banking Structure and Monetary Management," before the San Francisco Bank Club. Mimeograph release, Board of Governors of the Federal Reserve System, April 1, 1970.

7. See "Reserve Management Made Easier," *Business Conditions* (Federal Reserve Bank of Chicago, March 1968); and Parker B. Willis, *The Federal Funds Market, Origin and Development*, 4th ed. (Federal Reserve Bank of Boston, 1970), pp. 70–72.

8. "A New Swinger in Reserve Figures," *The Morgan Guaranty Survey* (July 1968), pp. 3–8.

9. See *Weekly Money-Market Bulletin* (Morgan Guaranty Trust Company, August 7, 1970).

10. *Federal Reserve Bulletin* (October 1971), p. A 8.

11. "Forecasting Float," *Monthly Review* (Federal Reserve Bank of New York, February 1963), pp. 30–35.

12. For detailed discussions of the Federal funds market see Parker B. Willis, *The Federal Funds Market, Origin and Development*, 4th ed. (Federal Reserve Bank of Boston, 1970); Parker B. Willis, *Fundamental Reappraisal of the Discount Mechanism: A Study of the Market for Federal Funds* (Washington, D.C.: Board of Governors of the Federal Reserve System, March 28, 1967); and Dorothy M. Nichols, *Trading in Federal Funds* (Washington, D.C.: Board of Governors of the Federal Reserve System, 1965). Also see *Business Review* (Federal Reserve Bank of Philadelphia, April and November, 1967, and September 1968); *Business Conditions* (Federal Reserve Bank of Chicago, October 1967); and *Monthly Review* (Federal Reserve Bank of Atlanta, January 1968). Earlier studies are B. H. Beckhart and James G. Smith, *The New York Money Market*, Vol. II, *Sources and Movements of Funds* (New York: Columbia University Press, 1932), pp. 40–48; and B. C. Turner, *The Federal Funds Market* (New York: Prentice-Hall, Inc., 1931).

13. *Business Conditions* (Federal Reserve Bank of Chicago, October 1967), p. 2; Harry Brandt and Paul A. Crowe, *Trading in Federal Funds by Banks in the Southeast* (Federal Reserve Bank of Atlanta, 1967); Willis, *The Federal Funds Market, op. cit.*, pp. 51–54.

14. *The Federal Funds Market.* A study by a Federal Reserve System Committee (Washington, D.C.: Board of Governors, December 1959).

15. *Business Review* (Federal Reserve Bank of Philadelphia, November 1967), p. 7.

16. Willis, *Fundamental Reappraisal of the Discount Mechanism, op. cit.*, p. 35.

17. National Monetary Commission, *Special Report from the Banks of the United States,* April 28, 1909. Senate. 61st Congress. 2d Session. Document No. 225 (Washington, D.C.: Government Printing Office, 1909), p. 11. Also *Federal Reserve Bulletin* (August 1970), p. A 17.

The Federal Reserve Banks as Lenders and Supervisors*

CHAPTER 4

LENDERS OF LAST RESORT

Central banks are often described as lenders of last resort .They are the lenders to which commercial banks and, in certain cases other financial institutions, may have recourse when all other avenues have been explored. These other avenues include domestic and foreign borrowing and the liquidation of loans and investments.

Central banks are able to serve as lenders of last resort because they are usually the only lenders with the right to issue bank notes and to create reserves on the basis of which the loan and investment structure of commercial banks rests —and often are the only lenders with actual holdings of gold and foreign exchange. They are therefore in a position to lend when other institutions have exhausted

* In addition to the members of the committee of review, whose names are listed in the Preface, this chapter was very carefully reviewed by Dr. Harry Brandt, Vice President of Research, Federal Reserve Bank of Atlanta. His comments and suggestions were of great value in the final rewriting of the chapter. Needless to say he is not to be held responsible for errors of commission or omission or value judgments.

their liquidity. The power to issue legal tender means that central banks never exhaust their financial liquidity, at least domestically, although they may do so in their relations with foreign central banks. Even though financial liquidity is not exhausted domestically, an excess resulting from sharp increases in money and credit is reflected in a decline in the purchasing power of a currency. In international monetary relations a decline in liquidity is reflected in a loss of gold, SDR's, and foreign-exchange reserves and in increased borrowing from foreign nations or from the International Monetary Fund.

Commercial banks in the United States and other nations borrow from their central banks for a variety of reasons. First, they may wish to relieve seasonal pressures that arise from changes in the public's demand for currency, from seasonal drains of funds from one area to another, and from seasonal increases in the demand for credit. Discounts and loans extended by a central bank help to eliminate seasonal stringencies in the money market. More frequently than not, however, seasonal requirements in the United States are met through open-market operations by the Reserve System, rather than through member-bank borrowing. At times, too, reserve requirements of member banks have been reduced to permit them to meet seasonal increases in required reserves. Member banks in the United States are not expected to meet all their seasonal needs by obtaining funds from their Reserve banks, only those amounts that cannot reasonably be met from their own resources (see pp. 88–92 for proposed changes in the administration of the discount window).

Second, banks borrow to meet cyclical increases in loan demands as well as cyclical withdrawals of deposit liabilities. An example of the first occurred in 1919 when banks were called upon to meet a sharp cyclical increase in bank loans resulting largely from a rapid build up of inventories. An example of the second occurred during the Great Depression when centers of durable goods production like Detroit and Pittsburgh, subject to heavy unemployment and acute economic distress, lost funds to other regions. Funds were moved out either to obtain greater security than was afforded by local banks or to repay loans incurred elsewhere. Banks experiencing a loss of deposits were forced to liquidate assets, or to borrow from their Reserve bank and on occasion from such emergency institutions as the Reconstruction Finance Corporation. A unit banking system is particularly affected by cyclical movements of funds. A branch system covering an entire nation is usually able to make adjustments within the system.

Third, banks may be forced to borrow to obtain currency at the time of a panic. A currency panic, such as that experienced early in 1933, occurs on the downward sweep of a business cycle and results from a general loss of confidence in commercial banks and by the resultant desire of depositors to convert their deposits into currency. The only type of American currency that may expand to meet this demand is Federal Reserve notes. During the course of the 1933 panic, banks within a few weeks increased their borrowings from the Reserve banks by $1.2 billion (see Chapter 10).

Fourth, banks may borrow, other factors remaining the same, by reason of the withdrawal of deposits by Federal, state, and local governments. An example, which is cited in a later chapter, was the continuous loss of Federal funds by the New York City banks in World War II. Member banks were then relieved of the need to borrow by reason of the reduction in reserve requirements (see Chapter 7, p. 168).

Fifth, banks may borrow to build up reserves necessary to support deposit expansion resulting from war finance or secular (long-term) increases in monetary needs. Borrowing for war purposes rose to the unprecedented height of $2.5 billion in World War I. Member banks borrowed not only to acquire additional reserves but also to offset the effects on their reserves of gold exports and currency increases. In World War II, reserves were provided through Federal Reserve open-market operations. In the United States member banks have not been obliged to borrow to obtain reserves required for secular increases in deposit needs. Funds for this purpose have been provided through Federal Reserve open-market operations and through reductions in member-bank reserve requirements. In fact, continual borrowing by individual banks to support increases in the monetary supply would be contrary to Regulation A issued by the Federal Reserve Board (see pp. 82 ff.).[1]

Sixth, banks may wish to obtain funds to relend at a profit. As will be noted in subsequent discussions of the provisions of Regulation A, Federal Reserve banks do not look with favor on borrowing by member banks for the purpose of relending at a profit. The willingness of member banks to incur debt for this purpose varies among different banks and at different times. Reserve banks' policies on this point are reputed to have differed, but on the whole they have tried to discourage such borrowing.[2]

So far, in citing the reasons causing member banks to borrow, we have concentrated on factors arising primarily within the domestic economy. In addition, there are international developments, reflected in a loss of gold and other international reserves, which could force not only member banks to borrow but also the Reserve banks and the U. S. Treasury itself to seek accommodation from foreign central banks or the I.M.F. Of course, it must be kept in mind that domestic and international developments are closely intertwined so that it is difficult, if not impossible, to separate the one from the other.

Also, Federal Reserve policy itself, exemplified by the sale of securities, by increases in member-bank reserve requirements, and by the shifting of Treasury deposits from commercial banks to the Reserve banks, forces an increase in borrowing.

There are many reasons for fluctuations in member-bank borrowing. The various factors involved can be detected by examining the Federal Reserve statement and by keeping in mind that member-bank borrowings are an asset item. An increase could result from a decrease in other assets or from an increase in other liabilities. Thus a decline in the gold certificate account, in holdings of S.D.R. certificates, of foreign exchange, of acceptances, of government securities or in the amount of the float would cause, other factors remaining the same, an increase in member-bank borrowing. On the liability side of the statement, an increase in Federal Reserve notes (currency), an increase in member-bank reserve deposits, or an increase in Treasury or foreign deposits, would, separately or in combination, force an increase in member-bank borrowing. An increase in capital accounts (although the amount is small) would have a similar effect.

Changes in the Federal Reserve statement reflect the effects of domestic and foreign monetary developments and enable us to group those changes which cause borrowing to rise or to fall. This we shall endeavor to do in the chapters which follow.

Discounts and Advances

Access to Federal Reserve discount facilities, according to Regulation A issued by the Board of Governors (as amended April 16, 1970) is granted, on the basis of certain guiding principles, as a privilege of membership. Credit is generally extended on a short-term basis to enable a member bank to adjust its asset position when sudden withdrawals of deposits or seasonal requirements for credit beyond those that can reasonably be met from the bank's own resources occur. Federal Reserve credit is also available for longer periods in order to assist member banks in meeting unusual situations that may result from national, regional, or local difficulties or from exceptional circumstances involving particular member banks. There is no prescribed limit on the amount of credit which a member bank may obtain from its Reserve bank. It is not, however, expected to make continual use of Federal Reserve credit, and, in addition, there are various qualitative limitations. The latter are summarized in the following pages.

The authority of the Federal Reserve banks to discount paper or to make advances to member banks is permissive. The Act repeatedly employs the word "may" in connection with credit extensions to a member bank. Only as much credit may be extended as can safely and reasonably be granted with due regard for the maintenance of sound credit conditions. Even when the paper is intrinsically sound, the Reserve bank must be assured that the credit is extended with due regard to the claims and demands of other member banks. The Reserve banks are expected to consider not only the quality of the paper but also the desirability, from the point of view of the public interest, of placing additional funds at the disposal of a particular member bank.

The Reserve banks are under no compulsion to extend loans or to grant rediscounts. Rediscounting is a privilege, not a right (see pp. 89–92 for proposed changes). Foreign central banks have similar discretionary authority to grant or refuse accommodation to commercial banks. They are often empowered to establish rediscount ceilings, to discriminate against types of paper that may provoke inflationary price movements, and to discriminate against paper of industries that are believed to be overextended.

A Federal Reserve bank is required to keep itself informed of the general character and the amount of loans and investments by its member banks with a view to ascertaining whether or not "undue" use ("undue" is not specifically defined) is being made of bank credit for speculative trading in securities, real estate, or commodities—or for any other purposes inconsistent with the maintenance of sound credit conditions. It must determine, too, whether a bank is borrowing principally for the purpose of obtaining a tax advantage or to profit from rate differentials in the money market. In determining whether to grant or to refuse discounts and advances to a member bank, a Reserve bank may require from the member bank whatever information it deems necessary.

For any advance or discount a Reserve bank may require such excess collateral as it deems advisable or necessary. It is expected that, in determining the amount of excess collateral, the Reserve bank will give "due" regard to the public welfare and to the general effects that its actions may have upon the position of the member bank, its depositors, and the community as a whole. In general, a Reserve bank is expected to limit the amount of collateral that it requires to the minimum consistent with safety. In the early post-World War I period, excess or additional collateral was frequently required by the Federal Reserve banks for purposes of safety, to reduce what was regarded as excessive borrowing, or to reduce member banks' holdings of eligible paper and thus their ability to borrow.[3]

How Credit Is Obtained

Member banks may obtain funds from their Reserve bank or its branch in any one of the following three ways:

1. By discounting eligible paper at the bank rate.

2. By borrowing at the bank rate, for periods not exceeding ninety days, against promissory notes secured by obligations or other paper eligible under the Federal Reserve Act for discount or purchase by the Reserve banks. The maturity on such advances is customarily limited to fifteen days.

3. By borrowing at a rate at least .5 percent higher than the highest rate applicable to discounts, against promissory notes secured to the satisfaction of the lending Reserve bank, regardless of whether or not the collateral offered conforms to eligibility requirements. The promissory notes offered by a member-bank under this provision must have a maximum maturity of four months.

Eligible Commercial Paper • Under the authority of Sections 13 and 13a of the Federal Reserve Act,[4] any Federal Reserve bank may discount for a member-bank any note, draft, or bill of exchange that meets the following requirements:

1. It must bear the endorsement of a member-bank.

2. It must have been issued or drawn, or the proceeds must have been used or are to be used in producing, purchasing, carrying, or marketing goods in one or more of the steps of the process of production, manufacture, or distribution, or in meeting current operating expenses of a commercial, agricultural, or industrial business, or for the purpose of carrying or trading in direct obligations of the United States.

3. It must have a maturity at the time of discount of not more than ninety days, exclusive of days of grace, except that agricultural

paper may have a maturity not exceeding nine months, exclusive of days of grace; this requirement is not applicable to bills of exchange payable at sight or on demand.

There are also certain negative requirements that may be summarized as follows:

1. It must not be a note, draft, or bill of exchange the proceeds of which are to be used for permanent or fixed investments of any kind, such as investments in land, buildings, or machinery, or any other fixed capital purpose.

2. It must not be a note, draft, or bill of exchange the proceeds of which have been used or are to be used for purely speculative transactions or for trading in stocks, bonds, or other investment securities except direct obligations of the United States.

A Federal Reserve bank may take whatever steps are necessary to satisfy itself as to the eligibility of paper offered for discount.

Eligibility Requirements in Other Nations • It is a general practice among central banks to stipulate in detail the type of paper eligible for discount. For example, the Deutsche Bundesbank (the central bank of West Germany) requires that the bills which it purchases arise from specific transactions. The period to maturity must not exceed the time necessary for the underlying transaction in goods, and in no case is it to exceed three months. Although there are exceptions to these general principles, the Deutsche Bundesbank does endeavor to limit its purchases of bills to self-liquidating paper. The Netherlands Bank (the central bank of the Netherlands) restricts its purchases of bills to those that run for periods no longer than customary trade practices. Similarly the National Bank of Belgium (the central bank of Belgium) extends credit to commercial banks, principally by rediscounting commercial bills and bankers' acceptances that arise from bona fide commercial transactions.

Advances • Permission to lend to member banks against the pledge of government obligations and eligible paper was initially incorporated into the Federal Reserve Act in 1916. The amendment was requested by the New York Clearing House banks in order that they might gain access to Federal Reserve credit with less formality than through rediscounting eligible paper. An additional motive was the desire to borrow against eligible paper without the endorsement that would be required if it were to be discounted, a procedure that revealed to the banks' borrowing customers that their paper had been so used.

Granting to Reserve banks the privilege of lending against government securities was not regarded as a significant departure from the provisions of the original Reserve Act, with their emphasis on self-liquidating paper. The amount of "free" public debt not tied up as collateral for national-bank notes was then very small. Shortly after the amendment was enacted, however, the United States entered World War I, and this provision enabled member banks to borrow heavily from the Reserve banks, thereby permitting a huge expansion in Federal Reserve and commercial-bank credit. Since that time it has afforded the principal means of access to Federal Reserve credit, and discounts of eligible paper have been negligible.

A Federal Reserve bank also has the authority to make advances not exceeding ninety days to individuals, partnerships, and corporations (including member and nonmember banks) on promissory notes secured by direct obligations of the United States or by any of its agencies. Such advances are granted only in unusual or exigent circumstances.

Under Section 10b of the Federal Reserve Act,[5] any Reserve bank may make advances to a member bank upon its promissory note secured to the satisfaction of the Federal Reserve bank, even if the collateral does not conform to the eligibility requirements of the Act. This provision was inserted as a temporary measure in the Federal Reserve Act on February 27, 1932, and was made permanent in the Banking Act of August 23, 1935. Its purpose was to give member banks access to Federal Reserve credit even if they lacked sufficient eligible paper and government obligations.

Other central banks usually have the power to grant advances against collateral or to make "Lombard loans" (the collateral loans) as they were once called. The Deutsche Bundesbank may grant advances to credit institutions against eligible assets for short periods to cover a temporary need for liquidity. They are subject to rediscount quotas and to a penalty interest rate 1 percent above the discount rate. The Bank of France may make advances to any person against French government and certain other securities for periods of five to ten days. The interest rate is customarily higher than the discount rate. The Bank of France also makes advances to credit institutions, subject to a ceiling, for periods of five to thirty days. The rate charged may be lower than the discount rate.

Lombard loans granted by foreign central banks are usually extended at rates higher than the discount rate, are extended only against acceptable and eligible collateral, and are often subject to discount quotas or ceilings. The reason for these restrictions is the fear that the proceeds of such loans may be used for speculative purposes unrelated to production and distribution. If renewals were permitted, they might come to be considered by the borrowing banks as a form of capital funds.

Proposals by the Board of Governors to Expand Eligibility Rules • In letters to the chairmen of the Banking and Currency committees of Congress on August 21, 1963, the Board of Governors recommended legislation that would permit Reserve banks to lend to member banks against any acceptable collateral at the basic rate instead of at a penalty rate. Loans were to be based primarily on the soundness of the paper offered for discount and the appropriateness of the purpose for which the credit was sought. This change would, according to the Board, do away with the "outmoded technical requirements governing the eligibility of collateral." These requirements were based on the premise that the liquidity of commercial banks was related to short-term, self-liquidating paper and that the pledge of such paper served as an elastic base for Federal Reserve notes. The provisions had been found to be too limiting, the Board continued, and various departures had been made. In large part departures have resulted from changes in banking practices and in the credit needs of the economy. Such restrictions were of little importance, the Board emphasized, as long as member banks held large quantities of governmental obligations. A substantial increase in economic activity might, however, compel member banks to reduce their holdings of government obligations, and they would then be forced to offer other types of collateral at penalty rates. In appraising this collateral, the Reserve banks might have to resort to cumbersome differentiation of eligible and ineligible paper. Even current holdings of government obligations were inadequate for some member banks, the Board argued, because of their use as collateral for government deposits, trust accounts, and other purposes.

A central bank must necessarily adjust its procedures to the types of credit organization and trade finance of the particular nation that it serves. It may, however, exert influence on the portfolio policies of commercial banks and on credit usage through its own regulations respecting the type of paper that it discounts and the loans that it extends. The evolution of a credit system reflects not only what we may call "indigenous" factors but also the particular credit policies of a central bank.

A central bank that lends at the minimum discount rate (and most do not) against all the earning assets of commercial banks may find itself beset by a host of problems. At the moment (1972), for example, the Reserve banks lend against Federal obligations at par. Should they follow the same course of action with municipal obligations, which would doubtless be defined as an acceptable asset? Or should they lend at varying proportions of market value, depending upon the credit standing of the municipality? And, if they discriminate against one municipality and in favor of another, might not political repercussions result? Similarly, should Reserve banks lend against urban mortgages? If they refused to do so, would they hear from clamorous congressmen who look upon home ownership as an inalienable right? Would they regard instalment paper as sound and appropriate? Would the separate Federal Reserve banks accept the paper of national finance companies on a uniform basis?[6]

Differentiating among various types of acceptable collateral, the Reserve banks would in effect be exercising a type of selective credit control and the Reserve banks might find themselves enmeshed in questions quite as perplexing as those involved in distinguishing between eligible and ineligible paper.

A Proposed Basic Change

Regulation A, to which we have devoted considerable attention, was issued, largely in its present form, in 1955, following a reactivation of monetary policy that resulted from the 1951 accord between the Treasury and the Federal Reserve System (see pp. 199–202). Member-bank borrowings from the Reserve banks had been minimal for the preceding eighteen years. Reserves had been supplied by gold imports and Federal Reserve open-market operations. Once Reserve banks were freed of the mandate to support government bond yields and prices, member banks were no longer able to obtain reserves through the sale of their holdings of government securities at pegged rates and prices. As credit policy turned restrictive, they began to use the discount window, which to many banks was a new experience. Borrowing rose very rapidly, reaching an average of $1.2 billion in the first quarter of 1952, the highest since early 1921. The upsurge, which came during the Korean war, was abetted by an excess-profits tax that was drafted so that the tax liability of banks would be reduced as their borrowing increased. The skyrocketing of borrowings at a time when interest rates, although rising, were relatively low, and member banks held a relatively large volume of shiftable assets, came as a distinct surprise to Federal Reserve officials. This development indicated that the so-called "tradition against borrowing" was not particularly inhibiting and that the Reserve System would have to formulate rules for appropriate use of the discount window. A committee of Federal Reserve officials, supported by a working group of System economists, drafted Regulation A, which set forth the System's basic philosophy on access to the discount window.[7]

Emphasizing that borrowing is a privilege and not a right, Regulation A endeavored to restrict it to what were deemed appropriate uses. The principles set forth, as Clay Anderson has pointed out, had evolved in the 1920s.[8] The discount facilities of the Federal Reserve System would serve, through appropriate policing at the discount window, as a temporary "safety valve" and play only a marginal role in supplying member-bank reserves.

With the idea that the principles set forth in Regulation A were outmoded, that a "helping hand" concept of borrowing should be substituted for the "safety valve" concept, a fundamental reappraisal of the discount mechanism was launched by the Federal Reserve System in mid-1965, under the overall direction of a steering committee composed of three members of the Board of Governors and the presidents of four of the Federal Reserve banks. A secretariat was responsible for developing about twenty separate research studies.

There are several principal reasons for this investigation. First, it was believed that the discount window should play a more important role in Federal Reserve credit operations. The original Federal Reserve Act was based on the assumption that discount operations would serve as the principal means for injecting Federal Reserve credit into the credit system, which proved to be correct from 1917 until 1922, when open-market operations came to the fore (see Chapters 2 and 9). The original act was predicated on the belief not only that discount operations would prove important but also that Reserve banks should limit their discounts, as did other central banks of the period, to self-liquidating paper. To ensure an adequate volume of such paper, the System undertook, unsuccessfully as it turned out, to encourage the use of domestic trade and bankers' acceptances. Confining discounting operations to self-liquidating paper would, it was believed, provide Reserve banks with truly liquid portfolios and would induce member banks to direct their credit extensions toward short-term commercial and agricultural needs. Central banks' definitions of paper eligible for discount have had an important influence on the lending policies of commercial banks.[9]

Second, it was argued that more active use of the discount window would lead to better distribution of bank credit in the United States, particularly through small banks. Large banks were able to offset losses of funds or to increase their ability to extend credit by drawing funds from domestic and foreign capital markets. Small banks did not have equal access to these markets and were thought to be particularly vulnerable to restrictive credit policies.[10]

Third, some experts believed that Federal Reserve officials had failed to "communicate clearly, consistently and unambiguously" with member banks about the availability of discount window accommodations.[11] According to some students of the subject, this failure forced some banks to seek money through the issue of marketable certificates of deposit and debentures and from the Federal-funds and Eurodollar markets. According to others, the avid search for funds in the 1960s reflected greater sophistication among managers of the money positions of large banks.[12] These new developments permitted such banks to adjust their positions through liability management, whereas small banks were still confined to asset management.

Fourth, the administration of the discount windows at the twelve Federal Reserve banks and their twenty-four branches varied greatly, despite efforts to achieve uniformity.[13] Absence of uniformity is difficult to document. Ordinarily, an initial extension of credit is made automatically and is initiated by means of a telephone call from a borrowing member bank.[14] If the loan is renewed and has been outstanding for some time, administrative pressures of increasing severity are applied to force repayment. According to an American Bankers Association study, dissatisfaction with the administration of the discount windows was fairly general, and was particularly pronounced in the Dallas and San Francisco Federal Reserve districts.[15]

Fifth, changes in the portfolios of member banks over the past twenty years, resulting from a decline in readily salable United States obligations and an increase in less readily shiftable municipal obligations and in consumer and mortgage loans, may have to be offset by increased availability of Federal Reserve credit.

Finally, greater flexibility in discount operations may be needed to enable those banks that are particularly affected to cushion the effects of open-market operations. The Reserve banks, so the argument goes, would be able to carry on their open-market operations more aggressively.

These various developments convinced the steering committee that drastic changes at the discount window were required in order to increase the use of Federal Reserve lending facilities. Low member-bank borrowing was not looked upon as consistent with "optimum performance of the banking system." The safety-valve concept of Federal Reserve operations that had displaced the initial self-liquidating concept was itself to be replaced by the helping-hand concept. The New Plan, which was to enhance the advantages of membership (but would not itself change existing eligibility requirements), proposed the establishment of three discount windows, at two of which borrowing would be a "right" and not simply a "privilege." (The steering committee continued to refer to rediscounting by member banks as a privilege. Inferentially, discounting would be a right at discount windows 1 and 2. Otherwise the New Plan has no meaning.) [16]

The First Discount Window • At the first discount window, a member bank would have a virtually automatic borrowing "privilege" or "right" up to a specified maximum amount of Federal Reserve credit for a specified period of time. In order to prevent continual use of Federal Reserve credit, the steering committee suggested that duration and amount of borrowing be fixed according to a formula. A qualified member bank would be entitled to borrow up to a certain amount in relation to its capital and surplus in half the weeks of a given period. A qualified member bank was defined as one in satisfactory internal condition and not borrowing to relend in the Federal-funds market. The American Bankers Association would have the borrowing "right" related to required reserves rather than to capital and surplus. It has proposed that the refusal to permit borrowed funds to be resold in the Federal-funds market be reconsidered. The amounts that could be borrowed were skewed in favor of small banks not only as a concession to the unit banking system but also in recognition of the greater ability of larger banks to borrow at home and abroad.

The establishment of a basic borrowing "right," exclusive of the seasonal right to be discussed next, would, according to the steering committee, ensure for each member bank unqualified access to Federal Reserve credit and uniform administration of the discount window. It was estimated that, in accordance with the preliminary proposals, member banks in the aggregate could borrow a maximum between $2.5 and $3.8 billion.[17]

The Second Discount Window • The purpose of the second discount window was to help meet needs for funds resulting from seasonal swings in loans and deposits. To be eligible for such loans, a borrowing bank would have to demonstrate recurrent swings in its demand for funds, continuing more than four weeks and in excess of 5 to 10 percent of its average annual deposits subject to reserve requirements. Any part of the seasonal need in excess of this limit would be eligible for financing through the seasonal discount window for as long as nine months. The deductible principle was designed to encourage individual banks to maintain minimum liquidity. Branch-banking systems covering wide areas are themselves often able to handle seasonal fluctuations in loans and deposits without recourse to the central bank. This discount window, it was thought, would appeal particularly to the small bank, which is currently expected under Regulation A through appropriate asset management to anticipate seasonal swings. It might also increase attractiveness of membership for small nonmember banks.

The Third Discount Window • The purpose of the third discount window was to extend loans to troubled but solvent member banks. A bank might need funds by reason of economic distress in a particular locality, a collapse of security values, or a liquidity crisis. The troubled bank would be under extensive administrative review, including a coordinated program with relevant supervisory and chartering authorities.

The "Right" to Credit • A fundamental premise of a free market economy is that no borrower—individual, corporation, or bank—has a "right" to credit. In emphasizing that discounting is a privilege, Regulation A is based on this basic premise. Should it ever become a "right," a commercial bank might, in its effort to maximize immediate profits, be tempted to lower qualitative lending or investing standards and neglect to maintain an appropriate volume of financially liquid assets. Member banks might also exert pressure to enlarge this right beyond the limits initially imposed. If member banks themselves did not urge a broadening of the "right," Congress or its committees might insist that this be done in order to promote particular sectors of the economy, like the construction industry.[18] Once access to credit became a "right," the Reserve banks might find it necessary, in order to defend themselves against possible abuse of that "right," to exercise close surveillance over all credit operations of member banks.

Provision for three discount windows, each with separate rules, seems cumbersome. Customers of commercial banks have only one discount window, which seems a logical arrangement for central banks as well. The suggestion that one window grant basic loans and the other grant emergency credits has already proved confusing. Bankers want to be assured that use of one will not militate against use of the other. They are confused, too, about the purpose of the proposed emergency window. Is it to shore up embarrassed institutions, performing, in this respect, functions similar to those of the Reconstruction Finance Corporation in the Great Depression? Should a central bank itself be involved in such activities, which usually entail the investment of equity funds and direct management responsibilities? Or is window three intended simply to supplement credits granted at window one?

The steering committee recognized that if its proposals, which are still under discussion, were accepted, the discount rate would have to be altered more frequently and be more closely related to market rates.* It is to this aspect of Federal Reserve credit powers that we now turn our attention.

---

* It also indicated that use of the discount rate would have to be supplemented by various quantitative controls and administrative action.

Establishment of Discount Rates

The Federal Reserve Act empowers the board of directors of each Federal Reserve bank to establish from time to time, subject to the review and determination of the Board of Governors, the discount rates to be charged for each class of paper. Rates are to be fixed with a view to accommodating commerce and business. Each Reserve bank is to establish such rates every fourteen days or oftener if deemed necessary by the Board of Governors. Emergency advances to member banks secured to the satisfaction of a Reserve bank are, as previously indicated, made at a penalty rate "not less than one-half of 1 per centum per annum higher than the highest discount rate in effect at such Federal Reserve bank." This wording has been construed to mean the highest discount rate applicable to member-bank discounts of eligible paper. Rates on bankers' acceptances and on government securities purchased under resale agreements are also under the control of the Board of Governors.

Control over Rates • One of the early drafts of the Federal Reserve Act provided that the Board itself was to fix discount rates for each Reserve bank and each class of paper. Considerable opposition developed, however. Conservative bankers believed that each regional bank should have full control over its discount rates, free of influence from Washington. A compromise was reached; discount rates were to be initiated by the Reserve banks subject to the review and determination of the Board.

After the System had been organized and discount rates had been initially fixed it was found that the Board could, in fact, exercise little control over the rate structure. If a Reserve bank did not want to make a change, it did not file its rate with the Board, and consequently there was nothing for the latter to veto. The procedure was changed so that the Reserve banks were required to submit their recommendations for changes in discount rates in time to be considered by the Reserve Board's discount committee at its weekly meeting. The Board prescribed a form for use by the Reserve banks in submitting weekly recommendations, first by mail and later by code telegram. Even if no change were contemplated by a Reserve bank, the telegram had to be dispatched.

Only rarely in the early days of the System were rates proposed by the Reserve banks disapproved by the Board. One such occasion came late in 1919. Governor Benjamin Strong of the Federal Reserve Bank of New York sought to increase the bank's discount rate and claimed that the power of review conferred on the Board by the Federal Reserve Act meant that the Board could not immediately disapprove a change in rate. Carter Glass, then Secretary of the Treasury and a member ex officio of the Board, concluding that an increase in the discount rate at the New York bank would not only interfere with the flotation of government securities but also constituted an unlawful exercise of authority, requested a ruling from the U.S. Attorney General's office.

In his letter of inquiry Glass indicated that he believed that the Reserve Board possessed the implied power, as suggested in the report to Congress on the Glass Bill by the House Committee on Banking and Currency, to initiate changes in rates when a Reserve bank persisted in establishing a dangerously low rate for "sinister purposes" or a rate so high that it would contravene that provision of the Reserve Act requiring rates to be fixed with a view to accommodating commerce and business. At that time the members of the Board did not share Glass's judgment on the implied powers of the Act. But in an opinion dated December 9, 1919, the acting Attorney General of the United States went far beyond even Glass's interpretation and ruled that the Board, under its power of review, might establish discount rates that had been in effect at any time in the past at any one Reserve bank.[19]

It was not until 1927, eight years later, that the Board actually exercised its authority over discount rates. Under the leadership of Governor Strong the System decided to bring about a lowering of interest rates in the United States in order to strengthen sterling exchange and to induce France to take the gold she desired from the American rather than from the British stock. The open-market portfolios of the Reserve banks were to be enlarged and discount rates lowered. Not all the Reserve banks were convinced of the desirability of this policy, fearful as they were that it might give rise to renewed stock-market speculation. Among the opponents was the Federal Reserve Bank of Chicago. Impatient with its refusal to apply for a lower rate, which would have received pro forma approval, the Board, on September 6, 1927, took control of the Federal Reserve Bank of Chicago out of the hands of its directors and announced a rate reduction without the directors' consent.

This action led to a vigorous protest by its directors, who traveled to Washington, D.C., to complain to Secretary of the Treasury Andrew William Mellon. The result was that Governor D.R. Crissinger of the Federal Reserve Board resigned and Roy A. Young, who had been Governor of the Federal Reserve Bank of Minneapolis, took his place.[20]

At present the desirability of any prospective change in discount rates is often considered in advance by the Board and the presidents of the Federal Reserve banks during meetings of the Open Market Committee. When it is decided that there should be a change in rates, action is usually taken uniformly by the boards of directors of the regional banks and approved pro forma by the Board. This statement must not be taken to mean that the Board and the Reserve banks have always been in complete agreement on the matter of changing discount rates. Many disputes have arisen, as we shall have occasion to note later.

The Board of Governors is convinced that it does have the legal power to change discount rates on its own initiative, although the 1919 ruling by the Attorney General has never been subjected to a court test. The presidents of the twelve Federal Reserve banks appear, as the New York Clearing House Association stated in its report,[21] to have some reservation about the Board's authority. Their joint answer to a questionnaire from the Patman subcommittee suggests that greater coordination in the use of credit instruments in the future could be achieved by placing approval of the discount rates in the hands of the Federal Open Market Committee.[22]

Several times in the early 1920s some Reserve banks publicized rate changes before the dates on which the changes were to become effective. Consequently, on August 22, 1924, the Board adopted regulations designed to ensure the confidential nature of information on prospective changes; announcements of rate changes were to be made simultaneously by the Federal Reserve banks and the Board of Governors immediately after the close of business on the day on which the rate was approved.

In the early days of the System, Reserve banks had complex rate structures. Rates varied greatly according to the maturities and types of paper eligible for discount and among different Reserve districts. Preferential rates were frequently granted on short-term paper and on trade and bankers' acceptances. During both world wars preferential rates were established on member-bank promissory notes secured by government obligations. Discount rates were often higher in certain Reserve districts than in others. Indeed, Professor O.M.W. Sprague of Harvard University declared that it was one of the advantages of the Reserve System that discount rates could vary geographically and thus be related to differences in economic development. This feature of the Federal Reserve Act, he added, made it superior to the Aldrich plan, which would have required uniform discount rates for the entire nation.[23]

Not for many years have different discount rates been set for different types of eligible paper or (except for temporary periods) varied among Reserve districts. The first type of rate structure was abandoned as member banks increasingly obtained the accommodations that they desired on the basis of promissory notes secured by government obligations. The second type of rate structure gave way before the evolution of closely knit national money markets.

Foreign Rate Structure • Foreign central banks generally retain more complex rate structures. The National Bank of Belgium applies four discount rates, depending upon the quality of the paper offered; the spread between the lowest and highest rates is usually 1.5 percent. The Swiss National Bank has only one official discount rate, although it does apply special rates to the discounting of bills resulting from the financing of officially prescribed compulsory stocks of commodities, which are accumulated at the request of the government in order to enable Switzerland to weather a war emergency. In recent years the Bank of France has applied as many as seven discount rates, with a spread as high as 2 percent.

The discount rate of the Bank of England is a minimum rate applicable to the finest bills, those which arise from foreign trade and are in consequence known as "salt-water bills." Rates on other bills may range above the minimum rate. The Bank is not called upon to extend accommodation directly to the commercial banks, as it lends indirectly through bill brokers.

The rates established by foreign central banks, although uniform throughout each country, generally vary considerably among different types of paper offered for discount. They thus grant preferential treatment to export bills and short-term self-liquidating paper and discriminate against paper related to speculative investment, and long-term transactions.

Progressive Rates • Immediately after World War I the Reserve System experimented with progressive discount rates. During 1919 a few member banks began to borrow from the Reserve banks on an excessive scale, violating Section 4 of the Federal Reserve Act, which directs the board of governors of each Reserve bank to administer its affairs fairly and impartially and without discrimination in favor of or against any member bank and to extend to each member bank such discounts, advances, and accommodations as can safely and reasonably be made, with "due" regard to the claims of other member banks. To correct this situation, an amendment (the Phelan Act) to the Federal Reserve Act was enacted in April 1920; it permitted Reserve banks, with the approval of the Board, to determine the normal maximum rediscount line of each member bank and to fix graduated rates on an ascending scale applicable equally and ratably to all member banks rediscounting on a scale in excess of the normal line.

These provisions were permissive and were actually applied in only four Reserve districts: Atlanta, St. Louis, Kansas City, and Dallas. Methods of determining the maximum basic line and of fixing discount rates varied among the Reserve districts. Generally speaking, the more a member-bank borrowed in relation to its reserve balance plus its paid-in subscription to the capital stock of the Reserve bank, the higher the rate it paid on its borrowing. Member banks' promissory notes for which government obligations were collateral were generally exempt from progressive rates.

The progressive rate structure was inaugurated in April and May 1920 and was abandoned by the different Reserve banks after trial periods varying from a few weeks to nine months. Local political opposition soon developed. The rates were instituted in mainly agricultural districts, which were then suffering losses of funds to industrial areas. The adverse balance of payments compelled member banks to borrow heavily, and some were forced under the progressive rate schedule to pay very high rates on their excess borrowing.[24]

Those who favored progressive discount rates pointed out that before the passage of the Federal Reserve Act no national bank could incur indebtedness beyond the amount of its capital stock. Liabilities incurred under the provisions of the Federal Reserve Act were exempt from this requirement. Some member banks had taken advantage of this provision to borrow several times their capital and surplus. A progressive discount rate, it was claimed, would penalize culprit banks, without the need to raise interest charges for all banks and would bring about better allocation of Federal Reserve credit.

Those who opposed the introduction of progressive rates, including Governor Strong of the New York Reserve Bank, cast doubt upon a purely automatic mathematical method of credit control and declared that it might penalize those banks that had the courage to extend loans in times of emergency. Once abandoned the progressive rates were never reapplied.

Relation to Market Rates • The appropriate relation between the discount rate and market interest rates was still another problem that caused considerable discussion during the early years of the System. The Bank of England kept its own discount rate above the rates prevailing for the type of paper that it discounted—bankers' bills—and some people thought that the Reserve System should also keep its rate above the market rates. The definition of market rates was fairly simple for the Bank of England, but it was much more difficult in the United States.

Several definitions of market rates were offered. Some people advocated defining the market rate as the prime rate charged by commercial banks and argued that the discount rate would be above the market only when it exceeded the prime rate. Others wanted to use the rate prevailing on prime open-market commercial paper, which was, of course, very close to the prime commercial bank-lending rate. Others suggested the yields on bankers' acceptances as the measure of market rates. When the U.S. Treasury began to issue Treasury bills, many favored the yield on this paper as a measure of the market rate. They argued that member banks ordinarily adjusted their reserve positions by buying and selling Treasury bills and that consequently the rate on such bills could appropriately represent market rates. In other words, discount rates could be considered above the market if they exceeded the yields on the type of paper employed to adjust the reserve positions of member banks.

If discount rates were fixed with reference to the Treasury bill rate, they would necessarily be lower than the interest return received by commercial banks on the bulk of their earning assets. This difference has tempted some commercial banks to borrow from the Reserve Banks in order to relend at a profit. To discourage this practice, the Reserve Banks have used gentle and not such gentle persuasion. In some districts, the Reserve banks have resorted to what is termed the telephone policy. Officials phone culprit banks to urge the discontinuation of objectionable practices. In other districts admonitions are sent by mail. The degree of pressure brought to bear on member banks has varied among different districts, reflecting the management policies of the various Reserve banks.[25] The ultimate weapon is refusal to lend. As we have already pointed out, no Reserve bank is currently compelled to lend to any member bank.

Changes in discount rates usually follow changes in market rates that are brought about by the Reserve System's operations. Thus if the System decides to influence money-market conditions, it might buy or sell securities or alter reserve requirements. When market rates have changed, the System then adjusts the discount rates to the changed market rates.

In contrast with the pre-1914 policy of the Bank of England, which used open-market operations to make the discount rate effective, today open-market operations in the United States are usually the initiating factor. The rates charged by Reserve banks are then adjusted to market rates brought about by open-market policy.

The Revival of the Discount Rate • For about twenty years through the Great Depression and World War II the discount rates at central banks throughout the world remained .unchanged or were altered only at very infrequent intervals. The British bank rate, which had stood at 1.5 percent for a number of years, was often characterized as a "museum piece." Beginning in the early 1950s central banks again began to turn to discount policy and to make frequent changes in discount rates. Since then the Bank of England has raised its rate as high as 8 percent. Wider recourse to discount-rate policy has been called a "revival of monetary policy," a revival that was deemed essential if nations were to be able to combat inflationary trends.

EXAMINERS AND SUPERVISORS

In the original Federal Reserve Act, Federal Reserve banks were given power to examine member banks. Central banks have this power in most nations, properly so according to many observers. Otherwise a central banker would find himself in a predicament similar to that in which the Governor of the Austrian national bank found himself in 1931, when the Credit Anstalt, Austria's largest commercial bank, failed. When asked why he had not been acquainted with the condition of the bank's portfolio that had led to this failure, he replied that he could have had no such knowledge as the Credit Anstalt had not borrowed from the central bank. Periodic examinations keep a central bank informed so that it can take remedial measure before bankruptcy or other serious crises occur.

Although they have power to examine all member banks, Reserve banks do not customarily examine national banks. They rely for information upon the reports of the U.S. Comptroller of the Currency. Reserve banks examine some state member banks jointly with state examiners; they examine others separately. The Federal Deposit Insurance Corporation, jointly with state authorities, examines the banks that are members of the Corporation but not members of the Federal Reserve System. State authorities alone examine state banks that are members neither of the Reserve System nor of the Corporation. Representatives of the Reserve System, the Comptroller of the Currency, the Federal Deposit Insurance Corporation, and state banking departments meet regularly to unify examination procedures and to eliminate jurisdictional overlapping and duplication.

A bank examination is not an audit, although examiners endeavor to determine whether or not auditing procedures are adequate and satisfactory controls on both asset and liability accounts are maintained. If auditing procedures are not satisfactory, the Reserve bank stands ready to assist the member bank to establish a better system. The purpose of a bank examination is basically to enforce the banking laws, rules, and regulations and to ensure solvent and effective banking institutions.

In the course of his duties, the examiner tries to analyze a bank's assets and liabilities, to appraise the capabilities of its management, to review its capital and liquidity positions, and to evaluate its performance in the light of business conditions in its particular locality and of various statutes and regulations affecting its operations.

In evaluating the soundness of the bank's loans, the examiner appraises lending policies, procedures for obtaining and maintaining credit information, and efficiency in servicing loans. He also appraises the investment portfolio for quality and distribution of maturities. Appraisal of the bank's capital position includes evaluation of its earning capacity. Satisfactory earnings are essential if a bank is to offset losses on assets and if it is to remain in business.

Copies of examiners' reports are sent to each director of the examined bank, to the Reserve bank of the district, and to the Board of Governors. Reports are designed to be helpful to the bank's management. When criticisms of a bank's policies are made, suggestions for correction are also advanced. An examiner's knowledge of other banks of comparable size enables him to pass expert judgment on a particular institution.

The precise type of examination depends upon the caliber of the bank's management. In well-managed banks, examination is often confined to a survey of asset and liability accounts. In banks that are not so well managed, the examiner may perform some of the functions usually assigned to an auditor. Generally speaking, the examination is not intended to substitute for an audit or to usurp the responsibilities of management. In the event that management, despite an examiner's warnings, continues to violate banking laws or persists in unsafe or unsound practices, the Comptroller of the Currency or the Federal Reserve agent, as the case may be, certifies the fact to the Board of Governors of the Federal Reserve System. The Board may then serve notice upon the directors or officers of the bank to show cause why they should not be removed from office.

A number of suggestions for unifying the examining powers of various Federal agencies under one administration have been advanced. However much such suggestions may appeal to those who like to display the powers and interrelations of banking agencies in neat and orderly organization charts, they often neglect the essential point that a central bank must know the condition of commercial banks and can have such knowledge only if they are given the power of bank examination.

INFORMATIONAL AND EDUCATIONAL SERVICES

Closely allied to the bank-examination function is that of maintaining member-bank relations. These services are highly important, involving as they do periodic visits by Federal Reserve officials to each member bank, the scheduling of conferences of member banks, and visits by member bankers to the Reserve banks. The purpose of visiting member banks is to acquaint their staffs directly with the policies and services of the Reserve bank and to hear and answer complaints and questions. The visitors assist member banks with management problems, for example, helping them to reduce unit costs of production, to plan for automation, to improve credit files and information, to establish procedures for handling consumer credit, and to simplify auditing procedures and job-evaluation plans.

The purpose of conferences, scheduled for all member banks of a district or for groups of member banks, is to discuss problems of mutual interest and to acquaint member bankers with recent financial and economic trends and Federal Reserve policies. Frequently the proceedings of these conferences are published.

Early in the history of the System the Board of Governors and the separate Reserve banks established research departments. The initial purpose was to obtain quantitative assessments, as accurate as possible, on business and financial conditions. Fifty years ago people spoke in qualitative terms of business conditions, reporting that they were "good," "fair," or "poor," without being able to express these terms quantitatively.

Toward the close of World War I the Federal Reserve Board established a research section under the supervision of H. Parker Willis. Originally located in New York City, it was moved to Washington, D.C., in the early 1920s and placed under the supervision of Walter W. Stewart, who had been a prefessor of economics at Amherst College. Since those days the Board's research activities have grown vigorously, as the staff has compiled and analyzed facts about the American economy. Among the data first gathered were those on retail sales and production; both eventually were expressed in index numbers. Later the Board instituted studies in such fields as brokers' loans, consumer credit, financial requirements of business and agriculture, and the flow of funds. It has continued to gather banking data, adding greatly to our knowledge of domestic and foreign developments as they impinge upon the American economy.

The Reserve banks were not slow in following the example of the Board. Before the end of World War I, the Federal Reserve Bank of New York established a research department, with Carl Snyder in immediate charge under the general administration of Federal Reserve agent Pierre Jay, a scholar keenly interested in economic research. In its early days the department enjoyed the counsel of Wesley Clair Mitchell of Columbia University, E.W. Kemmerer of Princeton University, and Irving Fisher of Yale University.

The pivotal location of the Federal Reserve Bank of New York led the department to study international as well as domestic problems. It is now organized in five divisions: domestic research, financial statistics, foreign research, the balance of payments, and the library, with approximately 125 employees in the aggregate. The department issues a monthly review, helps with the Bank's annual report, issues innumerable memoranda for use within the System, and publishes a number of special studies.

The research departments of the other Federal banks are similarly constructive. They gather statistics, issue monthly reviews that concentrate largely on district developments, and publish special studies that elicit widespread interest. Members of the various research staffs often publish studies in professional journals as well. These activities are wisely encouraged by Reserve officials. From time to time members of the research staffs are lent to various international organizations or to foreign central banks, where they assist in solving pressing problems.

The research of each Reserve bank is closely coordinated with that of the others and of the Board itself. The purpose of these activities is, of course, to provide the necessary factual and analytical background for policy decisions by the Reserve System.

ADVANTAGES OF MEMBERSHIP

Of the 13,686 commercial banks in the United States on December 31, 1970, 5,766, or slightly over 42 percent, were members of the Federal Reserve System. Although member banks are outnumbered by nonmember banks, they claim more than 80 percent of the total assets of all commercial banks.

Membership confers both tangible and intangible benefits upon commercial banks. The tangible advantages are the services that a member-bank may expect to receive, such as the ability to borrow from its Reserve bank, to keep securities with its Reserve bank without charge, to avail itself of collection services, to obtain currency and coin free of shipping charges, and to receive advice on management problems. The intangible advantages of membership include those that accrue to the banking community and to the public at large from having a central bank with the largest possible base. Commercial banks whose operations add to the total money supply and enjoy the fruits of a central banking system should participate actively as member institutions.

The cost of membership is compliance with the reserve requirements of the Federal Reserve Act, which are often higher than those required by the states, and the further requirement of par remittance. Offsetting these costs are the free services of the System and the dividends paid on Federal Reserve stock.

From time to time it has been suggested, as it was by the Commission on Money and Credit, that membership be made compulsory for all commercial banks. On the other hand, as branch banking spreads through the country, total membership may come about without legislation, for large branch systems will almost certainly be members.

CONCLUDING OBSERVATIONS

Many reasons impel a member-bank to seek accomodation from its Reserve bank, which is itself under no compulsion to lend but may grant or refuse the request without explanation. Basically member banks borrow to *replenish* or to *increase* their reserve balances. Reserve balances may have been depleted by such factors as currency increases (seasonal or cyclical), open-market sales of securities by the Reserve System, loss of deposits, and gold exports. Or banks may require a larger credit base for their rising deposit liabilities.

Borrowing by member banks rises and falls in response to factors largely outside their control. Nevertheless, an individual member bank may reduce its own indebtedness by drawing upon its deposits with other banks or by selling securities, which may have the effect of forcing some other bank into debt. The indebtedness of individual banks is often tossed about as if it were a basketball, resting momentarily here and there, while the total indebtedness of the banking system remains the same. This shifting disseminates the effects of Federal Reserve policy, subjecting all banks to its impact and forcing them to make changes in their assets.

The Federal Reserve System endeavors to prevent a single member bank from remaining indefinitely in debt. If such a bank were to remain in debt for a long period it in effect would have obtained part of its capital from the Reserve bank. Again, if individual banks were to remain in debt for prolonged periods, they would prevent the effects of restrictive action on the part of the Reserve System from being disseminated over the whole banking system.

In considering the loan application of an individual bank, the Reserve bank must be acquainted with its loan and investment policies so that it can decide whether or not an extension of credit to the bank in question is consistent with sound credit policy and compatible with the needs of other banks. By refusing to lend or lending only reluctantly, the Reserve bank can force individual banks to face the implications of a restrictive policy and to make necessary readjustments in their earning assets. If the Reserve System is to exercise effective control over the volume and quality of credit, discounting must remain a privilege and not become a right.

In a unit banking system the individual bank can repay its debt to its Reserve bank only by liquidating assets and shifting the burden to some other bank. The entire banking system can repay debts if the Reserve banks enlarge their open-market portfolios, if the gold stock or other U.S. international reserve assets are increased, or if currency in circulation is reduced. It has been suggested that the commercial banking system may reduce debt by reducing its own loans and investments *pari passu*. Actually it would have to reduce its own loans and investments by about ten times the reduction that it wished to effect in its borrowing at the Reserve banks. In other words, it would take a sharp deflation in member-bank credit to effect even a modest reduction in member-bank borrowing at the central bank.

Notes

1. *Advances and Discounts by Federal Reserve Banks,* Regulation A. As amended effective April 16, 1970 (Washington, D.C.: Board of Governors of the Federal Reserve System).

2. See *The Discount Function* (New York: The American Bankers Association, 1968).

3. Clay J. Anderson, *Evolution of the Role and Functioning of the Discount Mechanism* (Federal Reserve Bank of Philadelphia, 1966), pp. 35–46.

4. *The Federal Reserve Act* (Washington, D.C.: Board of Governors of the Federal Reserve System).

5. *Ibid.*

6. A bill to implement these changes (Senate Bill 966) was referred to the Banking and Currency Committee of the House of Representatives, but died in Committee at the end of the 90th Congress. In anticipation of its possible passage, however, the Reserve System established a school to train Federal Reserve discount personnel in collateral appraisal. U.S. Treasury rules for the appraisal of collateral used to secure "special deposits of public monies under the Act of Congress approved September 24, 1917," can be found in Treausry Department Circular No. 92, Fiscal Service, Bureau of Accounts.

7. George Garvy, "The Discount Mechanism in the United States," *Quarterly Review* (Rome: Banca Nazionale del Lavoro), December 1968, 87: pp. 318–322.

8. Anderson, *op. cit.* See also George Garvy, *The Discount Mechanism in Leading Industrial Countries Since World War II* (Federal Reserve Bank of New York, undated); Robert C. Holland and George Garvy, *The Redesigned Discount Mechanism and the Money Market* (Federal Reserve Bank of New York, July 1968); David M. Jones, *A Review of Recent Academic Literature on the Discount Mechanism* (Board of Governors of the Federal Reserve System, February 20, 1968). Also see *The Discount Function,* Banking and Financial Research Committee (The American Bankers Association, 1968).

9. Garvy, *The Discount Mechanism in Leading Industrial Countries Since World War II, op. cit.,* pp. 10–11.

10. *Reappraisal of the Federal Reserve Discount Mechanism.* Report of a System Committee (Board of Governors, July 1968).

11. *Ibid.,* p. 7.

12. *The Discount Function, op. cit.,* p. 25.

13. *Ibid.,* p. 50.

14. Garvy, "The Discount Mechanism in the United States," *op. cit.,* p. 320.

15. *The Discount Function, op. cit.,* p. 50.

16. *Reappraisal of the Federal Reserve Discount Mechanism, op. cit.,*

17. For discussions of the details of the initial proposal, see *Reappraisal of the Federal Reserve Discount Mechanism, op. cit.,* p. 10; and Garvy, "The Discount Mechanism in the United States," *op. cit.,* pp. 324–331.

18. See *Federal Reserve Discount Mechanisms: System Proposal for Change.* Report of the Joint Economic Committee, Congress of the United States, together with Supplementary Views, 91st Congress, 1st Session (Washington, D.C.: Government Printing Office, 1969), p. 5.

19. For a discussion of this episode see Harold Barger, *The Management of Money* (Chicago: Rand McNally and Company, 1964), p. 57; Lester V. Chandler, *Benjamin Strong Central Banker* (Washington, D.C.: The Brookings Institution, 1958), Chapter 5; Elmus R. Wicker, *Federal Reserve Monetary Policy 1917–1933* (New York: Random House, 1966), pp. 37–45; and H. Parker Willis, *The Federal Reserve System,* New York: Ronald, 1923), chapter 57.

20. Chandler, *Benjamin Strong Central Banker, op. cit.,* pp. 435–450.

21. *The Federal Reserve Re-Examined* (New York: New York Clearing House, 1953), pp. 80–81.

22. *Ibid.,* p. 81; and *Monetary Policy and the Management of Public Debt,* Part II. Joint Committee Report, 82d Congress, 2d Session (Washington, D.C.: Government Printing Office, 1952) p. 673.

23. For a discussion of the Aldrich plan, see Paul M. Warburg, *The Federal Reserve System: Its Origin and Growth,* vol. I (New York: Macmillan, 1930), pp. 56–81.

24. B. H. Beckhart, *The Discount Policy of the Federal Reserve System* (New York: Holt, 1925), pp. 367–377.

25. See George W. McKinney, Jr., *The Federal Reserve Discount Window* (New Brunswick, N.J.: Rutgers University Press, 1960).

26. John J. Balles, *The Discount Function: Another Look* (New York: The American Bankers Association, 1969), pp. 32–33.

*Monetary and Fiscal Services**

CHAPTER 5

FLASHBACK TO 1914

An affluent banker strolling down Fifth Avenue in the summer of 1914, intent upon buying an anniversary present for his wife, would probably have been jingling gold and silver coins in his pocket and carrying gold certificates, silver certificates, U.S. notes, and national bank notes in his wallet. His silver coins and paper money would have been the equivalent of gold. The banker would have been at peace with himself and the world. The new Federal Reserve Act was going to provide the nation with an elastic currency. It would concentrate and thereby make more usable the national gold stock. Many bankers had opposed the act, but opposition had subsided. Only a handful of national banks had taken out state charters in order to evade the obligations of membership.

The new administration of Woodrow Wilson was not as hostile to business as had been feared. The United States was becoming a capital-exporting nation and had to be ready to accept goods in payment of interest and principal on foreign loans. The Underwood Tariff, which had sharply reduced tariff rates, would make this possible. In time New York might rival London as a world money market, and the bank of the affluent banker would benefit.

_____

* Besides the help of the committee of review, whose names are included in the Preface, the author was fortunate enough to have the advice of Howard H. Hackley, Assistant to the Board of Governors of the Federal Reserve System and Albert M. Wojnilower, Economist, First Boston Corporation, in preparing this chapter.

As the banker engaged in such pleasant reveries he would not have been unaware of the storm clouds over the Balkans. But he would have quickly dismissed them as reflecting the volatile temperaments of faraway people. Surely there would be no general war; had not economists warned that even a short war would bankrupt all nations?

A banker taking the same stroll in the late 1960s would not have been jingling gold coins, for they had long since been removed from circulation; nor would he have been carrying gold certificates, for they too had disappeared. Silver coins had been debased, to use an old-fashioned expression. There was no longer any silver in dimes and quarters, and the silver content of half-dollars had been substantially reduced. Silver certificates, promising to pay in certain quantities of silver, were no longer circulating. The only money that had remained unchanged between 1914 and 1969 was pennies, nickels, and the U.S. notes, which had been introduced during the Civil War.

The principal forms of currency carried by the banker in the 1960s would have been Federal Reserve notes, which are printed under the direction of the Comptroller of the Currency and the Secretary of the Treasury. These notes are issued in denominations ranging from $1 to $100 and bear upon their faces distinctive letters and serial numbers, which are assigned by the Federal Reserve Board to each Reserve bank. The original act made Reserve notes receivable for all taxes, customs, and public dues; beginning June 15, 1933, they attained full status as legal tender. Until 1964, when the "exchange legend" was removed, they carried the promise of gold redemption. The promise had not in fact been honored since 1933, when the United States had adopted a whole series of measures intended to reconstitute and "reform" the gold standard.

The Federal Reserve note is, in effect, a circulating government obligation, and it is for this reason that we are treating monetary and fiscal services of the Federal Reserve System in one chapter.

MONETARY SERVICES

Federal Reserve Notes

Federal Reserve notes authorized in the 1913 enactment were intended to provide the nation with a "safe, sound and elastic currency," which it had not enjoyed since the demise of the Second Bank in 1836. The amount in circulation would expand to meet seasonal needs and would contract once these needs had been satisfied. It would expand to meet crisis demands for currency, like that experienced in 1907, and would contract once such demands had been met. Federal Reserve notes would supplement the currency which the banker was carrying in his wallet and which met ordinary basic currency needs.*

According to doctrines of the time, the Federal Reserve note was expected to be elastic because it was to be based on good commercial paper that itself would respond to seasonal and cyclical demands. Initially redeemable on demand in gold at the Treasury Department or in gold or other legal tender at any Federal Reserve bank, it was "as good as gold." To enable the Treasury to redeem such Federal Reserve notes as were presented to it, each Reserve bank was required to maintain with the Treasury a redemption fund in gold amounting to not less than 5 percent of the notes issued to it. This fund could be counted as part of the gold reserve that was then required to be held against Federal Reserve notes.

Federal Reserve notes are issued by the Board of Governors to a Federal Reserve bank through the Federal Reserve Agent. It will be recalled from Chapter 2 that the Chairman of the Board of Directors of a local Reserve bank, who is appointed by the Board of Governors from among the class C directors, also serves as the Federal Reserve agent (see Chapter 2, p. 45). As a Federal Reserve agent, he maintains a local office of the Board on the premises of the Bank, making regular reports to the Board, and holds the collateral against which Federal Reserve notes are issued. The collateral, consisting of gold certificates, eligible paper, and U.S. government securities must be equal to at least 100 percent of the notes issued.

As will be noted from the consolidated statement of all Federal Reserve banks in Table 5.1, collateral placed with Federal Reserve agents at the end of December 1970 exceeded the amount of notes issued.

Table 5.1
Federal Reserve Notes in
Federal Reserve Agents' Accounts, December 31, 1970
(Millions of Dollars)

Federal Reserve notes outstanding	$53,745
Collateral for Federal Reserve notes:	
Gold certificate account	$ 3,330
Eligible paper	0
U.S. government securities	51,415
Total collateral	$54,745

Source: *57th Annual Report 1970*. Board of Governors of the Federal Reserve System (Washington, May 21, 1971), p. 217.

---

* Space does not permit a discussion of Federal Reserve bank notes, whose issue was discontinued on June 12, 1945.

Prior to 1954 no Reserve bank was permitted to pay out the notes issued by another Reserve bank except upon payment of a 10 percent penalty tax. The purpose of this tax was to force Reserve notes back "home" for gold redemption and to prevent single Federal Reserve banks from following policies opposed by the others. As credit policies are now fully coordinated, this provision is no longer necessary and has been eliminated.

Table 5.1 indicates that the collateral held by Reserve agents, as of the date in question, included no eligible paper. Yet, despite its absence, Federal Reserve notes are perfectly elastic. The collateral against which they are issued—government securities—is sufficient in amount to form an elastic base.

The banking system has come full circle. The old national bank note was backed by government obligations, and the Federal Reserve note is backed mainly by government obligations. The national bank note was, however, inelastic, for the amount that could be issued by each bank was limited; the public debt on which it was based had declined substantially since the Civil War, interest yields had fallen and the profits from note issues were frequently meager. Today an ample amount of government obligations is available. The "profits" from note issues which are of little consequence to a nonprofit institution like a central bank, are remitted to the Federal government (see pp. 113–114). The currency in circulation under the pre-1914 banking system was closely associated with the public debt resulting mainly from the Civil War; today's currency is similarly associated with the public debt resulting mainly from World Wars I and II and their aftermath.

The Original Act • The original Federal Reserve Act provided that a Reserve bank could obtain Federal Reserve notes from its agent upon the deposit of paper discounted for member banks under the provisions of Section 13. Such paper included notes and bills of exchange issued or drawn for agricultural, industrial, or commercial purposes; bearing the endorsement of a member bank; and having a maturity of not more than ninety days. Under certain limited conditions agricultural paper with a maturity of six months could also serve as collateral.

Upon receiving Federal Reserve notes from the agent, a Reserve bank could put them into circulation, provided that it set aside a reserve in gold or gold certificates equal to at least 40 percent of the notes circulated. The collateral requirement was 100 percent and the reserve requirement an additional 40 percent.

Subsequent Amendments • Since the passage of the original act, the provisions affecting the issue of Federal Reserve notes have been amended many times.

An amendment adopted on September 7, 1916, broadened the collateral to include bankers' acceptances purchased under the provisions of Section 14 and also the promissory notes of member banks secured by eligible paper or by bonds and notes of the Federal government. At the time that it was enacted, this amendment was regarded as simply a technical alteration of no great importance, for the free public debt (the amount not tied up as collateral for national bank notes) was then only $300 million. There were few who foresaw America's entrance into World War I and the resulting effect of this action on the public debt and the parallel use of a sharply rising debt to finance a rapidly expanding volume of Federal Reserve notes.

A wartime amendment on June 21, 1917, changed the Federal Reserve Act to permit the gold and gold certificates held by the Federal Reserve agent to be included in the gold reserves required to be held against Federal Reserve notes. The effect of this amendment was to reduce the combined collateral and reserve requirements from 140 to 100 percent. Previously the Reserve banks had not been able to obtain additional Federal Reserve notes unless they possessed eligible paper. In order to obtain eligible paper at a time when member-bank discounts were low, they had used a provision of the act permitting them to discharge their liabilities to the agents for notes received by placing gold and gold certificates with them. In return for the gold and gold certificates, the agents surrendered equal amounts of eligible paper to the Reserve bank; this paper could be used in turn to obtain additional Federal Reserve notes. Through repeated use of this process, the gold holdings of the nation, resulting from sharply rising gold imports, could be placed with the agents, and the Federal Reserve note became virtually a gold certificate. With the adoption of the 1917 amendment, gold and gold certificates could be placed directly with the agents and thus concentrated in the vaults of the Federal Reserve banks without resorting to this subterfuge.

An amendment of February 27, 1932 (the Glass-Steagall Act), broadened the acceptable collateral for Federal Reserve notes once again, to include direct U.S. obligations owned by the Reserve banks. The way was thus cleared for the issue of Federal Reserve notes directly against the public debt, limited only by the requirement of a 40 percent gold and gold-certificate reserve. The framers of this amendment looked upon it as a temporary measure to meet depression needs and stipulated that it expire after three years. It was, however, periodically renewed and finally made permanent on June 12, 1945. The basic purpose of the amendment was to permit Reserve banks to engage in huge open-market operations (see pp. 42–43). Before this change, open-market purchases of government securities by the Reserve banks (other factors remaining the same) in reducing member-bank borrowings also reduced the volume of eligible paper held by the Federal Reserve banks and available as security for Federal Reserve notes. The reduction in holdings of eligible paper forced the Reserve banks to place additional quantities of gold and gold certificates with the agent. The decline in eligible paper as collateral had to be compensated for by gold. The amount of "free gold"—the supply over and above all reserve requirements—declined, thus limiting potential credit expansion. Following the passage of the amendment, Reserve banks could use their holdings of government securities, along with discounts and advances, of course, as collateral for Federal Reserve notes. The amount of free gold would be limited only by the 40 percent requirement of gold and gold certificates against notes and the 35 percent requirement of gold, gold certificates and lawful money requirement against deposits. Within a few weeks after the passage of this amendment the Reserve banks began to engage in vast open-market operations (see Chapter 10).

The amendments to the Federal Reserve Act liberalizing the collateral to be placed behind Federal Reserve notes were never extended to include emergency advances to groups of member banks (Section 10a), advances to individual member banks secured to the satisfaction of each Reserve bank (Section 10b), and agricultural paper with maturities longer than six months unless specially secured (Section 13a, paragraph 1). These exceptions apparently reflect legislators' belief that Federal Reserve notes should be secured only by those obligations that arise from the short-term credit needs of business and agriculture or from the borrowing of the Federal government. Nor have the reserve provisions been extended to include the convertible foreign-exchange holdings of the Reserve System, which on December 31, 1969, amounted to nearly $2 billion. Including them would seem a logical recognition of existing international monetary arrangements.

The rapid increase in Federal Reserve notes and deposit liabilities during World War II carried reserve requirements close to the legal minimum and on June 12, 1945, led to a reduction of reserve requirements for Federal Reserve notes and deposit liabilities to 25 percent, to be held in gold and gold certificates. The huge gold exports of the late 1950s and early 1960s led to the elimination on March 3, 1965, of reserve requirements against deposits and, on March 18, 1968, of those against Federal Reserve notes. The change was adopted in order to release gold for export, although not long after its adoption the Treasury ceased exchanging gold for dollar balances owned by foreign holders other than central banks or official monetary authorities (see Chapter 16).

Reserves • The requirement that gold reserves in minimum percentage amount be held against Federal Reserve notes was a provision to be found in most central-banking statutes at the time of the enactment of the Federal Reserve Act. Its function was to act as a check on increases in central-bank credit and thus indirectly on increases in commercial-bank credit.

These checks were reinforced in the United States by the stipulation that, as gold and gold-certificate reserves fell below minimum reserve requirements against notes (first 40 percent and later 25 percent), a graduated tax was to be imposed on the amount of deficiency that would be added to and so increase rates of interest and discount fixed by the Board of Governors. This additional check has been eliminated.

Gold reserve requirements are, of course, quickly modified or abandoned by nations involved in major wars or serious depressions. They have not been allowed to stand in the way of military operations or the policies deemed necessary to stimulate recovery. In "normal" times, however, mechanical checks of this type often serve to mobilize public opinion in favor of restrictive credit policies. With their removal, a community must be sufficiently informed and enlightened so that it will itself support prudent credit and fiscal policies on the part of central banks and ministers of finance. The willingness of a community to do so reflects enlightened democratic action.

"Tax" on Federal Reserve Notes • Increases in holdings of the public debt by the Reserve banks have provided a cheap means of financing the Federal deficit. Since 1959 Reserve banks have remitted to the U.S. Treasury 100 percent of their net earnings after the payment of dividends and the amount necessary to bring surplus to the level of paid-in capital. They do so in the guise of a "tax" on Federal Reserve notes. At the end of each calendar year the Board of Governors computes the net earnings of the Reserve banks and then to recoup this amount, levies a "tax" upon the notes issued to each bank, less the amount of gold-certificate reserves, at a rate sufficiently high to obtain the computed sum.[1]

This tax is levied under the provision of paragraph 4 of Section 16 of the act which authorizes the Board to levy interest charges upon notes not covered by gold or gold certificates. The original intent of this provision was to give the Board a further instrument of credit control, one that could, if necessary, be used to restrict the quantity of Federal Reserve notes issued by any Federal Reserve bank. It has never been used for that purpose, however; instead it has been used to divert the bulk of Reserve banks' earnings, derived mainly from government securities, to the Treasury.

The Board began to levy the "tax" on Federal Reserve notes in 1947—then at a rate of 90 percent—in order to obtain the consent of the Treasury to unpegging the Treasury bill rate, which the Reserve System was convinced was necessary to check inflation (see Chapter 8). The Treasury was not willing to do so unless it was somehow reimbursed for possible increases in borrowing costs. It was so reimbursed by the tax on Reserve notes, which from 1947 through 1970 yielded the Treasury about $23.1 billion.[2]

The Ratio of Currency to the Total Money Supply

Writing in the *Monthly Review* of the Federal Reserve Bank of New York for February 1964, Irving Auerbach stated that "Currency in circulation is one of the most important factors that absorb or supply member bank reserves."[3] The Federal Reserve System, he added, tries to offset the effect of currency changes on member-bank reserves by appropriate open-market operations. In order to assist the manager of the System Open Market Account in determining and anticipating the need for such operations, the Federal Reserve Bank of New York has for many years prepared forecasts of possible currency fluctuations. Increased demand for Federal Reserve notes draws down member-bank reserves by an equal amount. An increase in member-banks' deposit liabilities causes an increase in required reserves by about 10 percent of the amount involved. Obviously, the first forces a much larger increase in the open-market portfolio of the Federal Reserve System than does the second.

Currency fluctuations would not affect member-bank reserves if commercial banks were still issuing notes as they did before the Civil War. An increase in currency demand would then lead to an increase in bank-note liability and a decrease in deposit liability. One liability would simply be substituted for another. It is the concentration of the note-issuing power with the central bank that permits currency fluctuations to affect member-bank reserves.

At the time when the United States resumed gold payments in 1879, according to data from the National Bureau of Economic Research, the ratio of currency to the total money supply, as then defined, was about 30 percent. That is, there were $30 of circulating notes and coins to $70 of demand and time deposits held by nonbank depositors in all commercial banks.[4] Except for a brief rise during World War I, the ratio, computed in this fashion, declined to 8 percent by 1930. Meanwhile the total volume of currency increased in this half century nearly sevenfold, rising from $547 to $3,700 million. The factors responsible were population growth, increased sales of goods and services, and increased travel within the United States. This increase was much less rapid, however, than that in demand and time accounts, a disparity that brought about the lower ratio of currency to deposits. The long relative decline in the amount of circulating money has been ascribed more immediately to such developments as the spread of the banking habit (itself a consequence of the growth of urban and the corresponding decline of rural America), the rise in per capita real income, and consequently in the number of those making use of banks.

Beginning in 1930 the volume of currency in circulation began to rise, accelerating very rapidly during World War II. Save for a dip in the late 1940s, the volume has continued to increase. The ratio rose from 8 percent in 1930 to about 12 percent in December 1969. The huge increase ($42 billion) in the volume of currency between 1930 and 1969 caused Reserve banks to add an approximately equivalent volume of government securities to their open-market portfolio. (Had the former ratio of currency to the total money supply, 8 percent, prevailed, circulating currency would have increased only $28 billion.) The change in ratio, over which the Reserve System has no control, obviously was of assistance to the Federal government in financing its deficit.

The rapid rise in the volume of currency during World War II can be ascribed to the sharp increase in total payrolls, increased mobility of the population and especially of the labor force, the use of currency by the armed forces, currency hoarding at home and abroad, the growth of black markets, and tax evasion. The importance of black markets and tax evasion in currency demand is indicated by the increase in bills of large denominations.

Beginning in 1962, the increase in circulating currency began to accelerate. Explanations include a phenomenal growth in vending machines, an increase in the relative number of teenagers who earn and spend money though few have checking accounts, renewed hoarding to evade payment of income taxes, and increases in the vault cash of commercial banks to meet reserve requirements and customers' needs for currency.

Seasonal and Monthly Currency Fluctuations

Seasonal fluctuations in circulating currency reflect the effects of climatic changes in retail trade, travel, employment, and agriculture, as well as in certain religious and social customs.

Immediately after Christmas the volume of currency drops sharply, as cash spent by holiday shoppers and vacationers flows back into the banks. It declines more modestly in March but rises through April and May, as a result of seasonal increases in retail trade at the Easter season and in factory payrolls. The demand for currency continues to rise in June and July because of the summer vacation season and the Fourth of July holiday. Following a lull in August, currency demand increases sharply, responding to the autumn rise in retail sales and factory payrolls, until it reaches a peak at Christmas.

Seasonal swings in currency, averaging as much as $2 billion within a single year, would cause sharp seasonal swings in the money market were they not customarily offset by Federal Reserve open-market operations.

Within any given month, the primary factors affecting currency volume are the meeting of payrolls and the payment of bills. Currency begins to flow out of the Federal Reserve banks around the eighteenth working day of one month and reaches a peak by the eighth working day of the following month. The average net outflow amounts to about $220 million. The demand for currency within a given month is also influenced by holiday and seasonal requirements.

The Derived Character of the Currency Demand

Deposit increases are immediate results of the credit operations of commercial banks. As deposits are generated and circulated through the economy from lending bank to retailer, to manufacturer, to purchaser of raw materials, they come into the possession of those wage earners, retailers, and others who require currency. To obtain this currency, individuals and firms draw upon their deposit balances, causing member banks in turn to draw upon their own deposits at the Reserve banks to obtain Federal Reserve notes. If member banks do not possess excess reserves, they must then borrow from their Reserve banks, unless the latter engage in open-market or other offsetting operations in order to forestall increased interest rates. An operation that at the outset has nothing to do with government fiscal operations thus ends by helping to finance the Federal deficit.

The fact that the demand for currency is, so to speak, a derivative one, does not mean that there is no "feedback." Controls exercised over the issue of currency will themselves affect the credit policy and operations of the banking system. The Board of Governors has the legal power to reject partly or entirely the application of any Federal Reserve bank for Federal Reserve notes, although it has never exercised this power. Applications have always been granted in full. The Board, acting through its agent, may also call upon a Federal Reserve bank for additional security to protect the Reserve notes issued to it, but again it has never done so.

The partial or total rejection of an application for Federal Reserve notes might generate currency crises similar to those experienced before 1914 when individuals and firms might offer a check for $105 for $100 of currency. A currency crisis would probably induce drastic reductions in the volume of credit. Although increases in deposit volume are the initiating factor in currency increases, limitations imposed on the issue of currency, if resorted to, will themselves react on credit policy and thus on the volume of deposits.

FISCAL SERVICES

The fiscal services of central banks were among the earliest services and continue among the most important. They include the handling and transfer of government funds, the payment of interest and principal on the public debt, the marketing of government obligations, and assistance in managing the public debt.

These various functions are closely interrelated with monetary functions and credit policy. Bank notes issued by a central bank are often backed by government obligations. Ineptitude in handling government funds causes marked disturbances in the money and capital markets, and government mismanagement of its debt may undermine and even nullify efforts by the central bank to dampen inflationary tendencies and to rectify the imbalance in the balance of payments.

Handling and Transfer of Government Funds

At the time when the Federal Reserve Act was passed, Federal government funds were held by the country's nine subtreasuries and those national banks that qualified as depositories. This system led to the hoarding of money in Treasury vaults, withdrawal of funds from the money market when the inflow of Federal tax revenues exceeded Federal disbursements, and pumping in of funds at other periods, causing marked disturbances in interest rates and security prices. It gave rise to charges of favoritism, as the Secretary of Treasury placed funds with one bank instead of another and caused the depository banks to rely on the paternalism of the Secretary in times of crisis.

To remedy these defects, the Glass bill, as passed by the House of Representatives, designated the Reserve banks as fiscal agents of the government and provided that all government funds be equitably distributed among the Reserve banks.

The Senate bill wisely eliminated this mandatory provision, leaving it to the discretion of the Secretary of the Treasury whether or not he placed government funds exclusively with the Reserve banks. This discretionary power was retained in the final bill, which specified that nothing in the act was to be construed as denying to the Secretary of the Treasury the power to use member banks as depositories.

In fiscal 1971 the inflow of funds to the Treasury (unified budget) amounted to $188.3 billion and expenditures to $210.7 billion. These huge operations, involving large monthly imbalances, would have had a very unsettling effect on the money and capital markets had it not been for the very efficient mechanism—tax-and-loan accounts—developed jointly by the Treasury and the Federal Reserve System.

Tax-and-Loan Accounts • The Treasury keeps a minimum working balance with Federal Reserve banks by allowing its deposits with commercial banks to bear the brunt of major fluctuations in cash balances. Fluctuations in the cash balances at commercial banks have little or negligible effect on member-bank reserves as long as reserve requirements are the same for government and private accounts, which has been the case since 1947. Changes in Treasury balances at Reserve banks, on the other hand, cause member-bank reserves to fluctuate by equivalent amounts.

In fiscal 1967 Treasury balances with the Federal Reserve banks fluctuated between $300 and $1,600 million (end-of-month figures), whereas the tax-and-loan accounts in special depositories fluctuated between $3 and $10 billion. Special depositories are commercial banks that have met Treasury qualifications for tax-and-loan balances. They are to be distinguished from general depositories, which in the aggregate hold Treasury deposits of only around $200 million. Accounts are placed with general depositories only when they are necessary to meet specific cash requirements for government payrolls or other expenditures or to receive cash from depositors of public monies. General depositories are permitted stated maximum balances fixed in relation to the volume of business in the Treasury accounts. All receipts in excess must be remitted to the Federal Reserve bank of the district.

The system of special depositories originated during World War I. The first Liberty Loan Act of 1917, profiting by Secretary Chase's mistakes in the Civil War, provided that banks purchasing securities for their own accounts or for their customers could deposit the proceeds in special "war-loan accounts." Until 1935 such deposits were not subject to reserve requirements.

The Treasury's need to borrow heavily during World War II reactivated the war-loan accounts, which had been dormant during the 1930s. On April 13, 1943, to make these accounts particularly attractive Congress exempted them from reserve requirements and Federal Deposit Insurance assessments for the duration of hostilities plus six months. This exemption ended June 30, 1947. After World War II Congress authorized wider use of these accounts. They were renamed "tax-and-loan accounts" on January 1, 1950.

Tax-and-loan balances, held by about 12,000 banks, are increased through such operations as purchases of government securities by banks and their customers, when permitted by the treasury; receipts of withheld income taxes; deposits of payroll taxes from the old-age insurance program; large quarterly payments of income and profit taxes; and deposits of railroad retirement taxes and certain excise taxes. Deposits are not made directly by the Treasury in these accounts but occur in the normal course of business through a uniform procedure applicable to all banks. The transaction involves merely the transfer of funds from a customer's account to the government's account at the same bank.

As the working balances that the Treasury holds with the Federal Reserve banks become depleted, the Treasury restores them by calling in funds from the tax-and-loan accounts. To simplify the process, it has classified the special depositories into groups, A, B, and C, whose members are reclassified once a year. Group A includes the smaller banks, on which calls for funds are usually made once a month. Group B includes those with larger balances; if deposits exceed the established limitations, they are redeposited with group C banks. Group C banks are those with balances of $500 million or more. Calls on group B and C banks are usually announced twice a week, with payment made a few days later. Calls on group C banks are, however, subject to withdrawal the same day if funds are urgently required. Calls on group A and B banks are made on a pro rata basis; calls on group C banks are geared to the funds needed.[5] The funds that are withdrawn to meet Treasury needs are routed quickly through the Reserve banks in order to reduce to a minimum the effect on member-bank reserves.

The specific terms on which banks accept Treasury deposits are spelled out in various Treasury circulars. The more important are first, that the banks must be designated by the Treasury; second, that they must pledge collateral equal to Treasury deposits; third, that Treasury deposits may not exceed certain limitations set by the Treasury; fourth, that Treasury deposits are subject to reserve requirements and Federal Deposit Insurance assessments; and fifth, that the banks must perform the services stipulated in the designation and submit prescribed reports.

The ability of banks to pay for government obligations by crediting Federal tax-and-loan accounts means that the Treasury can sell its obligations at lower interest than it otherwise could. Commercial banks begin receiving interest on these obligations when they are allotted and do not begin to lose deposits until the Treasury makes its calls. They can thus outbid nonbank buyers, in effect underwriting the securities. As calls are made, commercial banks can begin feeding securities into the market.[6]

So advantageous have the tax-and-loan accounts proved that they have been introduced in other countries where government expenditures and receipts have vastly increased. The United Kingdom is an exception, in that the Treasury keeps all its funds with the Bank of England. The British Treasury manages its accounts so expertly that no more than a minimum working balance is left with the Bank of England at the end of each day. If the balance is larger, the surplus is used to buy Treasury bills; if the account is in the red, the deficit is covered by Ways and Means Advances to the British government. The effects on the money and capital markets of the flow of government funds into and out of the Bank of England are thus held to a minimum.

Interest on Federal Deposits • Recently proposals have been made in Congress that required commercial banks to pay interest on Federal demand deposits. The Treasury has pointed out that, if such interest were required, commercial banks would be less willing to purchase, underwrite, and distribute government securities. In its opposition to this proposal, the Treasury has also called attention to the many free services that commercial banks render the government, including the cashing of government checks, the sale of U.S. savings bonds, the receipt of subscriptions for marketable issues, the sale and distribution of Treasury bills, the redemption of matured marketable issues, and the handling of income and social security taxes withheld by employers. In only a few instances—for example, the redemption of savings bonds and the servicing of Commodity Credit Corporation crop loans—do commercial banks receive fees for these services.

After a careful study of the income derived by banks from the tax-and-loan accounts and the cost incurred in rendering free services to the government, the Treasury concluded that the cost to the banks exceeds income. There were, however, as the Treasury pointed out, certain additional intangible benefits to the banks, like improved customer and correspondent relations. If commercial banks were compelled to pay interest on these accounts, the Treasury is convinced that they would be less willing to handle them and to act as underwriter of new issues. Treasury funds would, to a greater extent than at present, be channeled to the Federal Reserve banks, with disruptive effects on the money market.

Public-Debt Operations

Handling the cash balances of governments is the first important fiscal service of central banks; the second is related to public-debt operations. "Public debt" is not easily defined. It may include not only the obligations of the central government but also those of state and local units. It may include or exclude obligations that are insured or guaranteed by government bodies, portions of the debt (often very large) held by the government itself, cash assets held by the borrowing government, loans that it has extended or investments that it has made, and the non-interest-bearing debt exemplified by issues of fiat money. It may include only the marketable debt or all types. The objectives or purposes of a particular study will govern the definition used, and definitions will alter as these purposes change.

In this and other nations, public debts, however they are defined, may be held at home or abroad; may be denominated in domestic or foreign currencies; may be secured or unsecured; may have very short or very long, even perpetual, lives; may be issued on a discount basis or carry coupons; may be issued above or below par; may be issued in the form of annuities; may have such special attributes as exemption from taxation, redemption in foreign exchange or gold, and payment of interest and principal in accordance with a price index; and as in England, the debt may carry lottery privileges. The types of obligations issued by governments are as numerous as the fertile imagination of man can contrive.

On December 31, 1970, the total interest-bearing direct public debt of the United States totaled $387 billion, divided into the categories shown in Table 5.2.

Table 5.2
Total Interest-Bearing Direct Public Debt, December 31, 1970
(Billions of Dollars)

Public Issues	
Marketable	
Treasury bills	$ 87.9
Treasury notes	101.2
Treasury bonds	58.6
	$247.7
Nonmarketable	
Convertible bonds	$ 2.4
Savings bonds and notes	51.8
Other	7.2
	$ 61.4
Special Issues	$ 78.1
Total	$387.2

Source: *Treasury Bulletin* (July 1971), p. 21.

The marketable debt, which amounted to $247.7 billion, is a short-term debt, shorter than the public debts of Britain and Canada. The average maturity on December 31, 1970, was three years and four months having fallen sharply since the end of World War II; it would have fallen even more had action to refinance long-term obligations before maturity not been taken in 1960.[7] Advance refunding, as important as it is, tends to maintain average maturity. A significant lengthening of average maturity can occur only through very large refunding operations.

Average maturity is a concept that must be used with considerable caution. An identical average may result from a debt evenly distributed through time or from a large volume of debt concentrated in both short- and long-term maturities. Average maturity, computed on the basis of first call dates will differ from that computed on the basis of final maturity dates. Finally, average maturity has little significance when the yields of government obligations are pegged, as they were from 1941 to 1951. During those years all securities were, in effect, demand obligations.[8]

Data on average maturity have to be supplemented by statistics on the maturity distribution of debt by various time intervals. As Table 5.3 shows, a rapid increase in the short- and intermediate-term debt and a rapid decline in the long-term debt occurred between 1946 and 1970. In the absence of vigorous countermeasures, the aging of debt rapidly shortens its maturity distribution. During those years the time never seemed opportune to issue large amounts of long-term securities, as Canada did, for example, in 1958. It was feared that such an issue in a boom period might curb growth and in a depression might prevent recovery.

Table 5.3
Maturity Distribution of Interest-Bearing
Public Marketable Securities
(Billions of Dollars)

Date	Amount Outstanding	Within 1 Year	1–5 Years	5–10 Years	10–20 Years	20 Years and More
December 31, 1946	$176	$ 54	$ 27	$ 32	$ 19	$ 45
December 31, 1970	248	123	82	23	9	11

Source: *Treasury Bulletin* (February 1971), p. 21.

The decline in average maturity was accompanied by a significant change in ownership distribution. Securities moved rapidly into the hands of liquidity holders (corporations, state and local governments, and foreign buyers). The only investment holders to acquire sizable amounts of securities were the investment accounts of the Federal government and the pension funds of state and local governments.

On December 31, 1970, the floating debt (that maturing in less than a year) of the U.S. government totaled $123 billion (Table 5.3), making an average monthly maturity of about $10 billion. The magnitude of this debt compels the Treasury to engage in continual refinancing operations, which have played an important inhibiting role in Federal Reserve credit policy. The Federal Reserve may simply refrain from instituting restrictive credit policies during periods when government obligations are being sold or exchanged for other obligations, or it may adopt policies of active support. The more often the Treasury comes into the market the more the central bank is restricted in its freedom of action.

Even Keel • Maintenance of a favorable climate in the money market or at least avoidance of an unfavorable climate during Treasury financing operations is called "even keel."[9] With the decline in the average maturity of the debt and with the continuing fiscal deficits of the 1960s, even keel assumed increasing importance and often stymied efforts by the Reserve System to check inflationary pressures. Although even keel is an elusive concept, it usually implies no change in the discount rate or in member-bank reserve requirements, and that the Federal Open Market Committee will not follow a more or a less restrictive policy than that already in force.

The policy of even keel begins a few days before an announcement of Treasury financing and continues for a few days after the payment and delivery of the securities. Not only the Treasury but also government-securities dealers have come "to expect and depend on even keel."[10] Between 1959 and 1968 a few even-keel periods were as short as nineteen working days and a few longer then thirty days. Most were between twenty-two days and twenty-four days. The maintenance of even keel in the money market during Treasury financing periods, which was made possible by the abandonment of operating policies established in 1953, undoubtedly contributed to inflationary developments in the 1960s. (On September 24, 1953, the Federal Open Market Committee had decided that during Treasury financing periods the Reserve System would not purchase maturing issues for which an exchange was offered, when issued securities or outstanding issues of maturities comparable to those being offered for exchange.) These operating policies were abandoned in 1961. With their abandonment, even keel became a customary operating procedure. In 1968, for example, eight of the twelve months included even-keel periods.

Degrees of Independence • The structure of the public debt, its ownership, and maturity distribution promote or restrict the free functioning of a central banking system. If the debt is relatively short and is placed with liquidity holders, as it has been recently in the United States, a central banking system may have difficulty in asserting its independence. If, on the other hand, it takes a long-term form and is placed with investment holders, as in France before World War I, the central bank is apt to have a high degree of freedom, even if the budget is in deficit. Such freedom generally declines as the budget becomes unbalanced and the debt becomes shorter and is placed with liquidity holders.

Table 5.4
Central-Bank
Autonomy, the Budget, and Debt Structure

Central-Banking Autonomy	State of the Budget	Debt Structure
Relatively complete	In balance	Long-term with investment holders
Less	In deficit	Long-term with investment holders
Still less	In balance	Short-term with liquidity holders
Very little	In deficit	Short-term with liquidity holders

Selling the Public Debt

The Federal government offers its securities for subscription and allotment through the Federal Reserve banks. Treasury bills are sold on a variable auction basis, other obligations are sold at fixed prices. The sale of Treasury bills is routine; the Treasury decides the amount and maturity, and the market determines the discount. Before deciding on other securities to be issued, whether certificates, notes, or bonds, the Treasury consults with officials of the Reserve System and various money-market experts on rates and terms. The principal function of these advisory groups is to assist the Treasury in interpreting potential market demand for securities of various types, maturities, and rates.

Once having decided on the issues to be offered and the terms that they are to carry, the Treasury opens the issues for subscription and allotment through the Federal Reserve banks. Subscriptions are made on a fixed-price basis by thousands of banks, corporations, associations, and individuals. Subscriptions from commercial banks to medium- and long-term bonds are typically limited to a certain percentage of capital and surplus, and on occasion subscription limitations have been imposed on other investors. Substantial down payments are often required to minimize speculation.

From time to time it has been suggested that the Treasury make use of the auction technique in the sale of bonds. Yielding to these suggestions, the Treasury decided in 1962 to sell $250 million of 1988–1993 bonds, carrying a coupon of 4 percent, to the underwriting syndicate offering the highest bid. The date of financing was January 17, 1963, and the issue was sold on a net yield basis of 4.008210. The auction resembled those at which state and local government securities are sold, a single-price rather than a variable-price auction. Competition was keen because of the prestige that would accrue to the winning syndicate. The yield spread between a comparable security in the secondary market and the auctioned security was very narrow. Investor response was excellent; the whole issue was sold within two hours.

Again in April 1963 the Treasury offered at auction $300 million of 1989–1994 bonds, carrying a coupon of 4⅛ percent. The bond market had weakened since the first auction, investor response was unenthusiastic, and the syndicate sold only 50 percent of the bonds within ten days.

For the time being the Treasury shows no inclination to revive the auction technique in the sale of long-term bonds. It continues to use and is well satisfied with the variable auction technique used in the sale of Treasury bills. In this market dealers not only compete among themselves but also with a large number of professional buyers who purchase for their own and their customers' portfolios. On the basis of experience gained in the auctioning of longer-term government securities in 1963 (and in the 1930s), the Treasury is convinced that the present method of subscription and allotment is superior to the auction technique and results in more effective distribution of new Treasury issues at minimum cost to the taxpayer.[11]

THE GOVERNMENT-SECURITIES MARKET

The organization of the market for United States Government securities, as it stands today has been an evolutionary process that has grown out of the enormous changes over the years in the volume of the public marketable debt, out of the changing patterns of debt management and monetary policy followed by the country's fiscal and monetary authorities.[12]

Trading in government securities takes place in the over-the-counter market consisting of twenty dealers (nine bank and eleven nonbank) linked with one another and with several thousand securities dealers, banks, and important customers by telephone and teletype. The market has no organized place of trading; it is a negotiated market, buyers and sellers negotiating the terms of sale or purchase before a transaction takes place. The principal market is located in New York, a much smaller one in Chicago. Other cities are served by the branch offices of the nonbank securities dealers.[13]

A potential buyer or seller can enter the market through a government-securities dealer, a commercial bank, or a securities broker. Commercial banks and securities brokers act as agents for their customers, turning to one of the securities dealers to execute orders. Government securities dealers not only bring buyers and sellers together facilitating ownership change, but they also help make markets by buying and selling as principals, negotiating transactions, and maintaining large inventories in a variety of issues.

Dealers

The primary function of dealers in government obligations, as of dealers in any type of security or indeed in any commodity, is to try to make and maintain a market. A dealer makes a market when he is prepared both to buy and sell at quoted prices in reasonable amounts; he maintains a market when, over a period of time, he states prices at which he is ready and willing to buy and sell. The size of the transaction that he is willing to undertake is determined by such factors as his total inventory of securities, his capital and borrowing capacity, the condition of the market, the type of customer involved, and the terms of the issue being sold.

The dealer promotes markets in government obligations by bringing buyers and sellers together, by advising and assisting institutions in arranging their portfolios, by assisting in distributing new Federal securities over the country, by furnishing market quotations, and by distributing quotation sheets and other information on the government-securities market. Dealers' transactions in U.S. government securities, both purchases and sales, have averaged about $2 billion a working day in recent years.

In selling securities, the dealer may draw upon his own inventory, or he may "sell short," borrowing the securities from someone in the market. When buying securities the dealer must rely upon his own capital or upon borrowed funds. Bank dealers supplement their own funds by borrowing from the Reserve banks or from the Federal-funds market. The need to borrow is related, however, to the entire operations of the bank and not specifically to its functions as a dealer.

Aside from their own capital, which is small relative to their operations and is fully employed, nonbank dealers finance their operations predominantly from borrowed funds. These funds may be borrowed from New York City banks, from outside New York City, from foreign banks, from financial intermediaries, from nonfinancial corporations, from the Federal Reserve bank under repurchase agreements, and at times from state and local governments and agencies. The relative amounts of funds borrowed from these different sources vary at any given time. In periods of restrictive monetary policy more might be borrowed from nonfinancial corporations, at other periods more from commercial banks. Average daily borrowings in 1970 totaled about $4.0 billion. Heavy dependence on borrowed funds helps to transmit the effects of monetary policy to other markets.

In making and maintaining a market a dealer does not rigidly maintain his own position. He may vary the total amount of government obligations that he holds, may vary their maturities, and may increase his "long" or "short" position, depending upon his appraisal of the future course of interest rates. The dealer cannot be expected to peg government securities prices, although his existence may help to lend very short-run stability to the market. The dealer's function is to find a price, not to stabilize it. In doing so he must react promptly to change in monetary policy and to buyers' and sellers' assessments of security values.

In acute crises brought on by threats of war or economic collapse, the dealer ceases to act as a dealer and necessarily becomes a broker, bringing buyers and sellers together without taking a substantial position of his own. Under such circumstances the Federal Reserve System may step into the market to stabilize prices and to keep an orderly market.

Orderly Markets

An orderly market in government obligations is not necessarily one in which prices are pegged, although on occasion it has been so defined by Secretaries of the Treasury. It was once well defined by a chairman of the Federal Reserve Board of Governors, William McC. Martin, as one in which there is a degree of continuity between demand and supply at going or moderately changed prices.[14] Orderly markets preclude erratic movements of prices and yields that have no justification in terms of general economic and credit conditions. They do not preclude broad movements in prices that reflect underlying forces.

A government securities market that fulfills the needs of buyers and sellers and meets the needs of the Treasury and the Federal Reserve banks is one which possesses depth, breadth, and resilience.[15] Trading volume must be high enough to absorb or provide offerings of securities of the size that investors wish to sell or buy. It must generate a good range of offers and bids so that new purchasers will come forth at successively lower prices and new sellers at successively higher prices. There must be widespread and active participation in the market by many investors representing diverse investment needs.

A good market responds flexibly to changing economic and monetary conditions. It absorbs new offerings of substantial size with minimum disturbance. It effectively reflects monetary policy. A good market is serviced by dealers who are reliable, have high regard for the public interest, and execute orders efficiently and promptly.

A disorderly market is one in which securities may be offered without invoking bids except at greatly reduced prices. Prices fall sharply, the market is erratic, the spread between bid and asked prices is wide. Such a market occurred in 1939 at the outbreak of World War II. The Federal Reserve banks intervened and restored orderly conditions by purchasing $300 million in government obligations. The Board of Governors commented on this episode as follows:

> On September 1, when the war in Europe actually began, prices of the United States Government and high-grade corporate bonds declined sharply. . . . In the circumstances, the Federal Reserve System deemed it to be in the public interest to exert its influence in a positive way towards maintaining orderly conditions in the market for United States Government securities. While the System has neither the obligation nor the power to assure any given level of prices or yields for Government securities, it has been its policy insofar as its powers permit to protect the market for these securities from violent fluctuations of a speculative, or panicky nature. Prices of fixed-interest rate securities, including those of the Government, inevitably adjust to changes in long-time interest rates. Consequently, an orderly rise or fall in United States bond prices in response to changes in underlying credit conditions, as expressed in interest rates, does not call for action by the System. Violent temporary movements, however, caused by such circumstances as the shock of the outbreak of European hostilities, make it in the public interest for the System to use its influence toward preventing a disorganized condition in the market.[16]

Despite this disclaimer of obligation or power to ensure given levels of yields, the Federal Reserve banks, along with other central banks, were saddled with the task of pegging yields on Treasury obligations during World War II and the early postwar years. They engaged in vast open-market operations, purchasing securities of various types in amounts required to keep yields at predetermined levels. All government obligations, regardless of maturity, became demand obligations. Control over the credit volume was lost, and commodity prices eventually soared.

The Dealer and Open-Market Operations

Dealer services, reports the Federal Reserve Bank of Cleveland, are essential in implementing open-market operations.[17] The dealer is the first link in the chain that transforms action by the trading desk at the Federal Reserve Bank of New York into its financial and economic effects. (The manager of the Federal open-market account, who is an officer of the Federal Reserve Bank of New York, acts under the instructions of the Federal Open Market Committee.) Securities sold to bank dealers are paid for in debits to their reserve accounts; securities sold to nonbank dealers are paid for in Federal funds, thus debiting the reserve accounts of certain member banks. Purchases have the opposite effects.

Besides buying and selling securities with no conditions attached, the trading desk may withdraw or inject reserves for limited periods by selling or buying while simultaneously contracting to repurchase or resell. In 1970 gross purchases of U.S. Government securities by the Federal Reserve System open-market account totaled $22.5 billion, and gross sales $17.4 billion, making a net increase of $5.1 billion. Purchases took place mainly in Treasury bills and sales were exclusively concentrated in such bills. Repurchase agreements and sales each totaled $33.9 billion. There were no net purchases or sales of Federal agency obligations.

CONCLUDING OBSERVATIONS

The fiscal responsibilities of the Federal Reserve System include not only various routine functions but also very important public-debt operations. Efficient techniques have been developed to handle the huge cash resources of the Treasury, permitting Treasury funds to flow in and out of the Federal Reserve banks with minimum disturbance to the money and capital markets. The techniques developed for the sale of government obligations enable the Treasury to obtain funds readily without friction and at minimum underwriting costs.

Proceeding from consideration of techniques to an analysis of the many intricate problems involved in management of the debt and in the relation of policies of public-debt management to the Federal Reserve System, one finds oneself in an area of acute controversy. The American Federal debt is a short-term debt, causing the Treasury to make frequent trips to the market as it engages in current or advance refunding operations. Along with the refinancing of maturing issues, the Treasury is forced to borrow new money whenever the cash budget is in deficit. These frequent forays have imposed severe restrictions upon the freedom of the Reserve System.

American policies of public-debt management are to be contrasted with those of the British authorities, who since World War II have taken energetic steps to fund the debt, that is, to lengthen average maturity. The purpose of this change was to protect the Treasury from claims maturing at inconvenient and expensive moments. To lengthen the debt, the Bank of England continually feeds into the market the long-term government obligations that it holds in the Issue Department. The Bank thus not only increases the average maturity of the publicly owned debt but also influences the structure of interest rates, helping to integrate debt management and monetary policy.

Closely associated with problems of debt management is the issue of Federal Reserve notes. Over a long period of time, from 1875 to 1930, the ratio of money in circulation to deposits declined. This decline permitted greater expansion of bank deposits upon a given increase in reserves than would have been possible had the ratio remained high. The decline in the currency-deposit ratio, which was considered an "immutable law" in economics, halted in the 1930s, and the ratio now stands at twice the 1920s level. The actual volume of money in circulation has been rising recently—about $2 billion a year. Present indications are that this rise will continue, making it possible for the government to finance part of its borrowing at relatively low cost.

Notes

1. *Annual Report of the Board of Governors of the Federal Reserve System* (Washington, D.C.: 1947), pp. 83–84; *Annual Report of the Board of Governors of the Federal Reserve System* (Washington, D.C.: 1959), pp. 83–85; and *Annual Report of the Board of Governors of the Federal Reserve System* (Washington, D.C.: 1964), pp. 48–50.

2. *Annual Report of the Board of Governors of the Federal Reserve System* (Washington, D.C.: May 21, 1971), p. 277.

3. Irving Auerbach, *Monthly Review of Credit and Business Conditions* (Federal Reserve Bank of New York, February 1964), pp. 36–41.

4. Philip Cagan, *The Demand for Currency Relative to Total Money Supply,* Occasional Paper No. 62 (New York: National Bureau of Economic Research, 1968).

5. *Annual Report of the Secretary of the Treasury on the State of the Finances for the Fiscal Year Ended June 30, 1955* (Washington, D.C.: Government Printing Office, 1955), pp. 275–289; *Report on Treasury Tax and Loan Accounts Services Rendered by Banks for the Federal Government and Other Related Matters* (Washington, D.C.: Government Printing Office, June 15, 1960); and *Handbook of Securities of the United States Government and Federal Agencies* (New York: First Boston Corporation, 1968).

6. For a discussion of this aspect of the tax-and-loan accounts see *Monthly Review of Credit and Business Conditions* (Federal Reserve Bank of New York, April 1958), pp. 51–56. Also *The Treasury and the Money Market* (Federal Reserve Bank of New York, May 1954).

7. See *Federal Reserve Bulletin* (March 1963), pp. 301–310.

8. See Michael E. Levy, *Cycles in Government Securities I. Federal Debt and Its Ownership* (New York: Conference Board Studies in Business Economics, No. 78).

9. Warren J. Gustus, "Monetary Policy, Debt Management, and Even Keel," *Business Review* (Federal Reserve Bank of Philadelphia, January 1969), pp. 3–10. Also see address by Alfred Hayes, President of the Federal Reserve Bank of New York before the 42nd Mid-Winter Meeting of the New York State Bankers Association, Mimeographed Release, January 26, 1970.

10. Gustus, *op. cit.,* p. 6.

11. See Robert E. Berney, "The Auction of Long-Term Government Securities," *The Journal of Finance* (September 1964), Vol. XIX, No. 3.

12. *Treasury-Federal Reserve Study of the Government Securities Market,* Part I (Washington, D.C.: July 27, 1959). This section is based upon this study as well as upon Federal Reserve Bank of New York, background material regarding size and nature of public debt, government securities market and Federal Reserve open-market operations

for use of participants in Central Banking Seminar in connection with discussions of open-market operations at the Federal Reserve Bank of St. Louis, February 11, 1954, issued January 8, 1954; Robert V. Roosa, *Federal Reserve Operations in the Money and Government Securities Markets* (Federal Reserve Bank of New York, 1956); and *Hearings before the Joint Economic Committee,* 86th Cong., 1st sess. (Washington, D.C.: Government Printing Office, 1959).

13. Excellent descriptions of the market are to be found in the *Economic Review* (Federal Reserve Bank of Cleveland, December 1967), pp. 3–13 and (November-December, 1969), pp. 3–16.

14. *Monetary Policy and the Management of the Public Debt,* Part I, Joint Committee on the Economic Report, 82nd Cong., 2nd Sess. (Washington, D.C.: Government Printing Office, 1952), p. 296.

15. *Employment Growth and Price Levels,* Joint Economic Committee, 86th Cong., 1st Sess. (Washington, D.C.: Government Printing Office, 1959), pp. 1757–1758.

16. *Annual Report of the Board of Governors of the Federal Reserve System* (Washington, D.C.: 1939), pp. 4–5.

17. *Economic Review* (Federal Reserve Bank of Cleveland, December 1967), pp. 7–10.

Origins of Federal Reserve Policy 1914-1917

CHAPTER 6

ORGANIZATION OF THE FEDERAL RESERVE SYSTEM

On Monday morning, August 10, 1914, a group of distinguished men gathered in the office of the U.S. Secretary of the Treasury to witness the swearing-in of the new Federal Reserve Board. The members were Charles S. Hamlin, a Boston attorney renowned for his diplomacy, who was designated as the first Governor. He served in this capacity for two years and was subsequently reappointed as a member of the Board, on which he served for nearly twenty-two years. He believed in a decentralized Reserve System, and through his terms of office he kept a diary containing critical evaluations of men and events. Frederick A. Delano, a railroad executive from Chicago, was the first Vice-Governor. The appointed members included Paul M. Warburg, who had received his banking training in Germany and was a partner in Kuhn, Loeb and Company of New York; he had written extensively on central banking. Another member was W. P. G. Harding, who had been President of the First National Bank of Birmingham, Alabama, and who was to serve as Governor from 1916 to 1922. The fifth member was A. C. Miller, former Professor of Economics at the University of California; he remained on the Board until 1936.

The exofficio members were Chairman William G. McAdoo, Secretary of the Treasury, and John Skelton Williams, Comptroller of the Currency. The Chairman presided at Board meetings, whereas the Governor was the active operating officer. Since the elimination of the exofficio members by the Banking Act of 1935 (effective February 1936), the Chairman, chosen by the President from among the appointed members, for a four-year term, has fulfilled both functions.

The incorporation of the Reserve banks required a number of preliminary actions. The organization committee, which, it will be recalled, was established by the Reserve Act and consisted of the Secretary of the Treasury, the Secretary of Agriculture, and the Comptroller of the Currency, had to complete its work of delineating the Federal Reserve districts and of locating the Reserve banks within those districts (see Chapter 2). National banks were given sixty days from the passage of the act to signify their acceptance of its terms and provisions. The minimum subscription requirement ($4 million for each Reserve bank) had to be satisfied. Once this was done the organization committee designated as incorporators five of the commercial banks that had submitted applications for membership. On May 18, 1914, the incorporators filed a certificate of organization with the Comptroller of the Currency; incorporation was automatic upon filing. The directors of the Reserve banks were then chosen, bylaws adopted, and accounting procedures established. After these preliminaries, the Reserve banks opened for business on November 16, 1914. On that occasion President Woodrow Wilson, in a letter to Secretary McAdoo, enthusiastically exclaimed, "A new day has dawned for the beloved country whose lasting prosperity and happiness we so earnestly desire."[1]

THE INITIAL ECONOMIC IMPACT OF WAR

The outbreak of war in Europe in August 1914 initiated a series of political and economic developments that caused the fall of dynasties, changed the map of Europe, weakened the economic power of Western Europe, strengthened that of the United States, and replaced private with state capitalism in a large part of the world. It brought about political and economic upheavals that continue to shake the world. It was the beginning of a long struggle of which World War II was a continuation and of which the cold war was an extension.

In the summer of 1914, in accordance with their usual practice, American bankers had become indebted to British bankers to the extent of about $500 million. Funds were customarily borrowed in the spring to pay for the seasonal rise in imports and were repaid in the fall thanks to the seasonal outflow of cotton and wheat. This practice enabled American banks to sell sterling at its seasonal high and to buy it at its seasonal low. It had the important secondary consequence of reducing seasonal fluctuations in sterling exchange.

On July 27, 1914, when war seemed inevitable, the English banks discontinued the acceptance of time bills of exchange, in order to avoid potential losses on bills from individuals or firms in hostile nations.

The discontinuation of the acceptance business in London meant that the deposit balances of American banks could not be replenished through the purchase of sterling bills and their sale on the London discount market. The scramble for sterling that ensued sent the rate from $4.8820 on July 25 to $4.9200 on July 27, and to $5.5000 on the 1st of August. The rise of sterling above the gold-export point led to the export from United States of $36 million in gold. This outflow would have assisted in bringing sterling back to par had not Europe begun heavy sales of its holdings of American securities. This development caused the closing of the New York Stock Exchange on July 30; it was not reopened with all restrictions removed until April 1, 1915.[2] Meanwhile the activities of the German fleet in the North Atlantic checked further shipments of gold and commodities until the British succeeded in regaining control of the seas.

To enable American debtors to discharge their British debts, the Bank of England established a branch in Ottawa, Canada, permitting American banks to draw sterling bills against gold shipped there. In order to assemble a gold stock to send to Ottawa, the newly appointed Federal Reserve Board, together with the Secretary of the Treasury, called a meeting of representatives of the clearinghouses located in reserve and central reserve cities for September 4, 1914. A committee appointed at the conference recommended the establishment of a $100 million gold fund, to be underwritten by state and national banks. Sterling bills were to be sold at the rate of $4.96 to the pound (the new gold-export point) against the credits established. The administration of the fund was placed in the hands of a group of New York City banks.

Actually only $10 million in gold had to be shipped. By November the premium on sterling had disappeared. With the reopening of the North Atlantic to commerce, sterling began to weaken. The decline was so rapid that by the spring of 1915 action had to be taken to peg sterling at $4.76⁷⁄₁₆, the new British gold-export point, through J. P. Morgan & Company. There the rate remained until March 21, 1919, when the peg was removed. Dollars to peg the rate were borrowed from private sources by the British government before the United States' entrance into the war and thereafter from the American government.

Before World War I about 65 percent of the cotton grown in the United States had been exported. Shipments ceased at the outbreak of war and could not be resumed until the North Atlantic had been reopened to commerce. This block to cotton exports, coupled with an exceptionally large crop, paralzyed the industry, caused a sharp decline in price, and led to the closing of the cotton exchanges in England and the United States.

The cotton planter, growing his crop on borrowed money and normally liqui-dating his indebtedness by selling it abroad, was in desperate need of relief. A plan was proposed by a group of banks and approved by the Federal Reserve Board for a cotton loan fund of $135 million. Its purpose was to assist the planter to hold his crop until it could be marketed at a fair price. Actually very little such money was lent. The price of cotton began to rise in November 1914, and by the time the United States entered the war it had reached a level almost twice that of 1914. The decrease in reserve requirements of national banks had en-abled southern banks to finance the storage of cotton without outside assistance (see Chapters 1 and 2).

The crisis of 1914, which led to the closing of the stock and cotton ex-changes, caused widespread (though temporary) loss of confidence in the banks. Memories of the bank failures of 1907 were still vivid. The loss of confidence was expressed in currency hoarding, necessitating the temporary circulation of $383 million of emergency currency (issued under the terms of the amended Aldrich-Vreeland Act) and $211 million of clearinghouse loan certificates to be used in the settlement of clearinghouse balances.[3]

BUSINESS AND FINANCIAL DEVELOPMENTS

The heavy demand by the Allied powers for foodstuffs, chemicals, explosives, iron, and industrial products—that is, for war material—caused a sharp increase in American production and, once the economy had reached the limits of its produc-tive capacity, a very sharp increase in prices. Indexes of production and prices are set forth in Table 6.1.

Exports rose from $2.4 billion in 1913 to $6.2 billion in 1917 and imports from $1.8 to $3.0 billion. The Allies resorted to various means to pay for the vast

Table 6.1
Production and Price Indexes

Year	Production [a] (1913 = 100)	Wholesale Prices [b] (July 1913 to July 1914 = 100)
1914	99	98
1915	107	101
1916	111	127
1917	114	177

a. Computed by Professor Wesley Clair Mitchell. The Index records the production of basic commodities.
b. Computed by the U.S. Bureau of Labor Statistics.
Source: Wesley Clair Mitchell. *History of Prices during the War, War Industries Board* (Washington, D.C.: Government Printing Office, 1919), pp. 44–45; and *Historical Statistics of the United States 1789–1945*, United States Department of Commerce (Washington, D.C.: Government Printing Office, 1949), p. 233. Index converted to 1913 base.

flow of goods from the United States. During the early days of the war they paid for imports by cancelling the short-term debts of American bankers and businessmen, which totalled about $400 million.[4]

Later they exported gold, floated loans and requisitioned part of their nationals' holdings of American securities which were either sold or used as collateral for additional loans. The American gold stock increased about $1 billion (at $20.67 an ounce) from the outbreak of war to April 1917, increasing the proportion held by the United States to one-third of the world's total. In addition, the Allied powers borrowed $2.4 billion in the American market before the United States entered into the war, and sold nearly $2 billion of American securities previously held by their citizens. These actions were rapidly converting the United States from a debtor to a creditor nation.

The influx of gold, coupled with the reduction in reserve requirements of member banks under the Federal Reserve Act, provided the basis for a rapid expansion in American bank credit. This expansion in turn caused a sharp expansion in the money supply, which by reason of increases in volume and turnover, induced price inflation. The price rise, along with expanding production and trade, was responsible for avid borrowing by agriculture and business.

EARLY POLICY

Conservative Philosophy

Even before the Reserve banks were officially opened the members of the Federal Reserve Board, in conjunction with the directors and officers of the new institutions, were discussing credit policy. The decision was that conservatism should guide the establishment of discount rates.[5] Th reasons were the war itself, which, it was believed, would lead to higher interest rates through destruction of capital; a fear that large amounts of American securities might be dumped on the American market; the fact that more than $300 million in emergency currency was in circulation; and the fact that American businessmen and banks had incurred large seasonal short-term debts abroad.

It was also decided that the Reserve banks were not to function simply as emergency institutions, that the act had created a permanent organization that should function continuously in the interests of the common good, adapting itself to "the needs of industry, commerce, and agriculture—with all their seasonal fluctuations and contingencies."[6] Its purpose was not to wait for emergencies but to anticipate and prevent them as far as possible. The Federal Reserve banks were to be bankers' banks—not in the sense that they were to operate only in emergencies or solely in the pecuniary interest of the banking community, but in the larger meaning of the term, that they were to act through the banks and on their own initiative in the public interest.

Specific Decisions

In conformity with this conservative policy, the initial discount rates on eligible paper with maturities of sixty to ninety days ranged from 6 to 6.5 percent. At five of the Reserve banks the same rate was established for all maturities of paper; at the other seven, rates increased with the lengths of maturity. The rates established were above open-market rates in the financial centers but below credit rates charged throughout the West and South.

In the final months of 1914 and through 1915 open-market interest rates fell sharply. This decline reflected the increase in lending power of commercial banks resulting from the influx of gold and the reduction of reserve requirements. Concomitant with the rapid decline in open-market rates, the bank rate on sixty-to-ninety-day paper at the New York Federal Reserve Bank fell with equal rapidity —to 4 percent early in 1915, where it remained until after United States entry into the war.

In American financial centers the bank rate stood above market rates, defined as the rates prevailing on four-to-six-month commercial paper. It was the policy of the Reserve banks throughout this period not only to maintain the bank rate above market rates in the financial centers but also to grant preferential rates on paper of shorter maturities and on trade and bankers' acceptances. Preferential rates on trade acceptances were granted in the hope (which was not realized) that they would encourage use of this type of paper. A preferential rate was granted on bankers' acceptances in order to develop a discount market. Although this action met with quantitative success, the growth in bankers' acceptances was accompanied by a deterioration in quality, as we shall see shortly.

The practice of establishing different rates for various maturities and types of paper had proceeded so far by January 1917 that there were no fewer than thirteen separate classifications. In the spring of 1917 the Board took steps to revise and standardize discount rates. The following schedule of eight classifications was proposed:

1. Paper maturing within fifteen days, including collateral notes
2. Paper maturing within sixteen to sixty days
3. Paper maturing within sixty-one to ninety days
4. Trade acceptances maturing within sixty days
5. Trade acceptances maturing within sixty-one to ninety days
6. Bankers' acceptances maturing within ninety days
7. Commodity paper maturing within ninety days
8. Agricultural paper maturing within ninety to one hundred and eighty days.

By April 1917 all the Reserve banks had adopted this classification. Along with the simplification of the rate schedule, the Reserve banks began to equalize discount rates for the same types of paper in all Reserve districts.

At the present time (1971) the rate schedule of the reserve banks is a very simple one. One reason is that member banks, with few exceptions, obtain the funds they need by borrowing against their fifteen-day notes collateralled by government obligations. Another reason is that the Reserve banks have abandoned attempts to promote certain types of paper, for example trade acceptances, through preferential rates. Had their campaign succeeded and trade acceptances partly displaced the open-book cash-discount system, the domestic financial system doubtless would have been strengthened. The trade acceptance is not as prone to qualitative deterioration as is the open-book system. Legal safeguards tend to maintain the quality of the trade acceptance.

A final reason for the present rate schedule is a belief that the Reserve banks cannot control the use of funds by granting preferential treatment to certain types of paper. A member-bank, the argument runs, borrows because of a deficiency in its reserves caused by lending operations that have already occurred. A member bank thus should be able to borrow in the simplest fashion possible, as it does when it borrows against its collateralled note. The Board has proposed, as has been noted, that member banks be permitted to borrow against all earning assets at the minimum bank rate. (See Chapter 4.)

Advantage of Restrictive Access

Restrictive access to Reserve-bank credit, which existed in the very early days of the system, offers some distinct advantages. It forces commercial banks to assume at least partial responsibility for their own liquidity, to confine lending operations to commercial transactions, and to emphasize loan quality. When all assets are "eligible," the temptation to extend credit with undue liberality may become strong. It is perhaps no accident that the decline in the quality of commercial-bank assets in the late 1920s occurred once access to Reserve-bank credit had been facilitated by large holdings of government obligations, which served as loan collateral.

Discounts before 1917

Rediscounting was light before the entrance of the United States into World War I. The excess reserves of member banks were large and did not begin to decline, if we may judge from the course of interest rates, until the second half of 1916.

Rediscounting was resorted to for the most part by small country institutions. The large banks that rediscounted did so either as a matter of courtesy, to support the new Reserve system, or occasionally to realize profits. In both 1915 and 1916 the Dallas Federal Reserve Bank led in the number of banks accommodated.

The inability of the Reserve banks (except for those in the South) to meet their expenses by earnings on bills discounted through 1915 and 1916, forced them to invest in open-market paper: municipal warrants, government bonds, and bankers' acceptances. The Board cautioned the Reserve banks not to invest in open-market paper amounts greater than those needed to meet expenses, for to do otherwise would swell the already abundant funds in the market.

At the end of 1916 bankers' acceptances were the largest single earning asset (see Table 6.2). The bulk of the acceptances had been purchased by the Boston,

New York, Philadelphia, and Chicago Reserve Banks. The total acceptance liability of American banks by the end of 1916 had reached $250 million.

Table 6.2
Earning Assets, End of 1916
(Millions of Dollars)

Bills discounted	$ 30
Bankers' acceptances	127
Government obligations	55
Other securities	9
	$221

Abuses in Use of Acceptances

The framers of the Federal Reserve Act had believed that acceptances should be limited mainly to specific transactions involving imports and exports. The acceptance was not intended for use in speculative or investment transactions or to assist the customers of member banks to obtain a larger amount of accommodation than they could through other types of paper. The acceptance was meant to be retired by completion of the underlying transaction.

The Federal Reserve Board, in its rulings and regulations, interpreted the provisions of the act so broadly, however, that many acceptances became finance bills. They were drawn for periods longer than the underlying transactions. They were also drawn under revolving-credit arrangements, especially with the French government and French merchants—a means of war finance. Banks began discounting their own acceptances and using acceptances as means of extending additional credit to borrowers to whom they had already granted the maximum loan credits permitted by law. The practice of pyramiding acceptances also developed. Several acceptances might be drawn against the same transaction or outstanding acceptances might be used as collateral for other acceptances. These abuses in acceptance practices continued to plague the banking system during the 1920s and led to serious losses in the early 1930s.

CONCLUDING OBSERVATIONS

The Federal Reserve System devoted the period from November 1914 to April 1917 to the important tasks of completing its organizational structure, initiating fiscal services, establishing the basis for its credit policies, drafting regulations interpreting the Federal Reserve Act, and initiating research activities. It was a period of incubation.

The system did not have the means to influence economic developments or to contain the forces of inflation. It had no open-market portfolio to use as a counterweapon, and it lacked power to raise member-bank reserve requirements. It took care, however, not to intensify inflationary pressures, and it followed a commendably conservative policy in discount and open-market operations.

No one suggested at the time that Federal tax rates should be raised as a counterinflationary device. The Federal government enjoyed a small surplus in 1916, even though total expenditures were rising. To have raised tax rates under such circumstances and to have deposited the proceeds in the Federal Reserve banks, thus effectively "sterilizing" gold imports (see Chapter 7), would have been quiet alien to the prevailing attitudes of government and people.

Early in 1917, when it appeared that the United States would enter the war, the Reserve banks began to reduce their holdings of those investments (municipal warrants) that had been acquired primarily for income. They did so in order to maintain the liquidity of their assets and to discourage any unnecessary expansion of bank credit. During January and February they placed additional orders with the Bureau of Engraving and Printing for $900 million in Federal Reserve notes.[7] The war effort was not to be handicapped by lack of currency!

Notes

1. This section is based largely on a very interesting brochure entitled *1914–1964* (New York: Federal Reserve Bank, 1964).

2. See B. H. Beckhart, *The Discount Policy of the Federal Reserve System* (New York: Holt, 1924) and William Adams Brown, Jr., *The International Gold Standard Reinterpreted 1914–1934*, I (New York: National Bureau of Economic Research, Inc., 1940), chapter 1.

3. For a discussion of clearing house loan certificates, see James Graham Cannon, *Clearing Houses*, National Monetary Commission, 61st Cong., 2nd sess., Document No. 491 (Washington, D.C.: Government Printing Office, 1910), chapters 10 and 11.

4. *Yearbook of the United States Department of Agriculture, 1915* (Washington, D.C.: Government Printing Office, 1916), p. 10.

5. Henry Parker Willis, *The Federal Reserve* (New York: Doubleday, Page and Company, 1915), p. 117.

6. *First Annual Report of the Federal Reserve Board* (Washington, D.C.: Government Printing Office, 1915), p. 17.

7. *Fourth Annual Report of the Federal Reserve Board* (Washington, D.C.: Government Printing Office, 1918), p. 2.

War Finance and the Federal Reserve System*

CHAPTER 7

THE BACKGROUND

Through much of its life, Federal Reserve policies have been influenced and dominated by world wars, by regional wars, and by preparations for wars. The period has been one of conflict and destruction in which central and commercial banks have become instruments of government—an age of inflation.

On April 2, 1917, President Woodrow Wilson requested a declaration of war against Germany. "It is," he declared to Congress, "a fearful thing to lead this great peaceful people into war, into the most terrible and disastrous of all wars, civilization itself seeming to be in the balance."[1]

In contributing to the defeat of the Central Powers, the United States in-

---

* Besides the comments and suggestions received from the committee of review, those offered by Edward H. Boss, Jr., Assistant Economist, Continental Illinois National Bank and Trust Company of Chicago, and Mr. W. F. Staats, Economics Department, Federal Reserve Bank of Philadelphia, proved particularly helpful.

creased its armed forces from about 200,000 to nearly 5 million and increased its budget expenditures on national security from $305 million in fiscal 1916 to $13.5 billion in fiscal 1919. After World War I defense expenditures dropped sharply to an annual average of $675 million from fiscal 1922 to fiscal 1935.

Twenty-four years after Wilson's address to Congress, President Franklin Delano Roosevelt, on December 8, 1941, requested a declaration of war against Japan. Within a few days Germany and Italy declared war on the United States. Before World War II had run its course the United States had increased its armed forces to 12.5 million men and women, of whom 8.3 million were in the army, 3.5 million in the Navy, 486,000 in the marine corps, and 180,000 in the coast guard. Several years before its entry into World War II, the nation had begun to increase defense expenditures, which, as the conflict mounted, reached a peak of $81.2 billion in fiscal 1945.

When World War II ended, Germany and Japan were in ruins and Soviet influence had spread over the vast territory reaching to the Oder River and to the gates of Vienna. Western European influence was rapidly diminishing in Asia, where the fires of independence and self-determination were burning brightly. The United States emerged as the most powerful industrial nation and the only country capable of rendering significant aid in reconstructing the Western world.

Once again national-security expenditures fell rapidly, reaching a low of $11.8 billion in fiscal 1948. This decline, sharp though it was, was more than offset by an increase in private demand and therefore did not precipitate a recession. The amount spent on defense in 1948, even when corrected for the loss of dollar purchasing power, was nevertheless ten times as large as the average amount spent in the late 1920s and early 1930s. This is customary after a war experience; defense expenditures do not return to prewar levels.

The Undeclared Wars

Under the direction of the Security Council of the United Nations, the United States participated in a conflict in Korea which began on June 27, 1950, and ended in an uneasy armistice on July 27, 1953. Shortly after his inauguration on January 20, 1965, President Lyndon B. Johnson began to build American forces in Vietnam, whose numbers eventually exceeded 500,000. In neither instance did Congress declare war. The decision in both instances represented action by the President.

At the outbreak of the Korean war security expenditures again rose sharply to $50.4 billion in 1953. Following cessation of hostilities they fell to an annual average of $48 billion from 1954 to 1965. With the buildup of American forces in Vietnam they again increased, reaching $81 billion in fiscal 1969. If to this sum we add expenditures closely related to present, past, and future wars—such as international affairs and finance, space research and technology, veterans' benefits, and interest on the public debt—a grand total of $114 billion emerges, about 60 percent of all budget outlays.[2]

The concentration of defense expenditures in certain periods, and its effects on the Federal deficit and the public debt have often prevented the Reserve System from instituting and following those credit policies that it favored. Obviously in wartime a central bank must try to do what it can to further the efforts of government. The financial methods used by government to achieve these aims, however, may not only impede the war effort but may also increase the difficulties in transition to a peacetime economy.

In its task of protecting the stability of the currency, a central bank has the responsibility of opposing government policies that it deems detrimental to the national interest and of suggesting alternative measures. Reserve officials have occasionally done so, but unfortunately have had little influence on Treasury policies. These have invariably emphasized the desirability of keeping borrowing costs low, at the risk if need be of huge expansions in credit. The Treasury prided itself on the fact that World War II was a "2 percent war," (the average rate of interest on the public debt on December 31, 1946 was 2.06 percent).[3] A 2 percent war may, however, in the course of time bring a 100 percent increase in prices. It is not necessarily a cheap war.

During both world wars the Reserve System confronted Secretaries of the Treasury who were doctrinaire in their insistence on easy money and were little inclined to share their decision-making powers with Reserve officials.

THE NATURE OF A WAR ECONOMY

In peacetime the price mechanism generally determines the quantity and character of goods to be produced. The demands of consumers, business firms and government units affect prices, and prices in turn affect production. Private enterprise, motivated by the lure of profits, endeavors to meet demand, and, if it judges the market successfully, it profits; otherwise losses are incurred.

In wartime, when demand tends to become inelastic, the market economy gives way to one in which the state, through an elaborate system of controls, directs productive processes, allocates goods to essential uses, and denies or rations the demand of other market participants, including consumers. The state must plan for war. Complex though this planning is, it is probably the only type that can achieve even a modicum of success. The purpose of the economic controls is not only to satisfy military requirements but also, as far as possible, to hold down war costs, to meet essential civilian needs, and to equalize war sacrifices. Enforcement of controls is enhanced by (in fact, the controls can hardly function without) appropriate fiscal and monetary policies.

A beginning in the use of controls was made during World War I, which drained off about 25 percent of Gross National Product, but it was in World War II, when war demands drained off 50 percent of GNP, that direct controls penetrated the whole economy. The real cost of the two regional conflicts, the Korean war and the war in Vietnam, could be handled without need to severely regiment consumer and business demand.

The transformation of the American economic system during World War II is illustrated by changes in GNP (see Table 7.1).

Table 7.1
Gross National Product in 1958 Prices
(Billions of Dollars)

	1940	1944
Federal expenditures	$ 15.0	$165.4
State and local expenditures	21.4	16.3
Personal expenditures		
Durable goods	16.7	9.4
Nondurable goods	84.6	97.3
Services	54.4	64.7
Gross private domestic investment	33.0	14.0
Net exports of goods and services	2.1	−5.8
Total	$227.2	$361.3

Source: *Economic Report of the President* (Washington, D.C.: Government Printing Office, 1966), pp. 210–211.

The enormous sums spent on the war effort were made possible by an overall increase in production and by a diversion of production. Production increases resulted from full use of old equipment, provision of new equipment, increases in the labor force (despite the huge numbers drafted into the armed forces), and from increased labor productivity. A diversion of production resulted from declines occurring in governmental nondefense expenditures on roads, schools, and the like; consumer expenditures on durable goods; domestic construction; and investment in producers' durable equipment.

Equipment not connected with the war effort was allowed to depreciate, housing was permitted to deteriorate, and the fertility of farm lands was not maintained. Civilian demand was reduced by taxation, and was rationed. And wherever possible the productive power of foreign nations was called upon.

Soon after the attack on Pearl Harbor the War Production Board, which was responsible for controlling productive forces, stopped the manufacture of automobiles. Shortly thereafter it began controlling the use of steel, copper, and aluminum. It shifted factory production from toy trains to bomb fuses, from watches to fire-control equipment, from typewriters to machine guns, and from tombstones to armor plate.

The result was an economy far different from the one that had existed before the war. Personal consumption expenditures, which had accounted for about 68 percent of GNP in 1940, fell to about 48 percent in 1945, leaving a huge gap to be satisfied in the postwar period.

A New Kind of Money

A rapid rise in consumer income at a time when the quantity of products destined for consumer use suffers an absolute or relative decline causes nations to introduce wage and price controls and consumer rationing.

During World War I, price fixing was initiated about the middle of 1917 and ended immediately after the armistice. The most important agencies involved in this task were the Food Administration, the Fuel Administration, and the Price-Fixing Committee of the War Industries Board. Congress also fixed the minimum price of wheat; the President fixed the prices of anthracite and bituminous coal; the army, navy, Emergency Fleet Corporation, Sugar Equalization Board, Federal Trade Commission, and International Nitrate Executive Committee fixed other prices. It was the existence of so many agencies, whose policies were not always harmonious, that finally led to the centralization of most of their activities in the Price-Fixing Committee of the War Industries Board. The prices of 573 commoddities came under control. Price controls were not accompanied by formal consumer rationing. There was a certain amount of informal rationing by retailers, and efforts were made to reduce meat consumption by setting aside certain days as meatless. Had the war continued, formal consumer rationing would doubtless have been introduced.[4]

Until the spring of 1942 the U.S. government in World War II relied on selective price controls and informal agreements. These were then superseded by General Maximum Price Regulation, issued on April 28, 1942, which, with exceptions, froze the prices prevailing in March 1942. This price freeze proved unworkable, for it froze abnormal price relationships, made no provision for a "retail lag," and did not include farm products or wages. The Stabilization Act of October 1942 extended price control to both wages and farm products. But prices continued to advance, leading to the issuance, on April 8, 1943, of the "hold-the-line" order by President Roosevelt which directed government agencies to permit no increases in prices and wages that would contribute to further rises in the cost of living.[5] Subsidies were used extensively in the effort to "hold the line," and they led, of course, to further increases in the public debt.

To further stabilization, President Roosevelt in October 1942 issued an executive order placing a ceiling on all wages. Adjustments were permitted to correct maladjustments, inequalities, and gross inequities; to eliminate sub-substandard living; and to aid in effective prosecution of the war. Overall wage increases were permitted under the "Little Steel" formula, which permitted general wage increases, not to exceed 15 percent, in order to compensate for the rise in living costs between January 1941 and May 1942.

Even if rigid controls had been imposed on all wages, total individual income would have increased, due to the elimination of unemployment, longer working hours, overtime pay, labor shifts from positions or areas of lower pay to those of higher pay, adoption of various forms of incentive payments, and payments to the military. The income of unincorporated enterprises also rose, as did farm and rental income. Corporate profits before taxes soared; after taxes the increase was much more modest. Only interest income is apt to decline in wartime.

Total personal income in the United States rose from $73 billion in 1939 to $171 billion in 1945. The compensation of employees increased from $46 to $118 billion (average weekly earnings in manufacturing increased by almost identical percentages in World Wars I and II—100.5 and 93.1).[6]

Price controls without rationing would have left the task of apportioning scarce goods to retailers and other distributors, who would doubtless have given preference to their best customers. Or if this were not done, allocation, on the basis of "first come, first served," would have been characterized by long queues.

Producers would have been inclined to sell goods locally in order to avoid transportation costs. Scarce commodities would have been distributed through the black market. Many people, particularly those on fixed incomes, would have been denied food, shelter, and clothing.

Rationing Technique

Consumer rationing began in 1942. The staff of the Office of Price Administration was inexperienced and not really prepared for the colossal administrative tasks that it faced. Sugar rationing, for example, required the registration of every citizen in the country, a half-million retailers, another half-million institutional and industrial users, and all wholesalers and refiners. Tires were sold against ration certificates issued by 7,000 local boards. One hundred ninety million copies of War Ration Book 1, each with twenty-eight consecutively numbered stamps, were printed and distributed through public schools early in 1942. This was followed in due course by War Ration Books 2, 3, and 4.[7]

For some goods—like tires, typewriters, bicycles, rubber footwear and stoves —certificates were issued by local boards. Typewriter certificates were good only for secondhand machines. Other commodities—like food, fuel, oil, gasoline, and shoes were rationed by stamps. A "ration banking system," in which commercial banks established ration-book accounts and cleared ration coupons, evolved. Stamps and certificates were nontransferable.

To purchase goods and services civilians had to pay with both conventional money and the new ration certificates or stamps. This requirement persuaded many people that conventional money had outlived its usefulness and that the particular method used in financing war costs was of minor importance. The inflationary effects of issuing conventional money could, it was argued, be nullified by extension of controls and continued use of the new money.

American public attitudes toward rationing violations were tolerant. Many consumers entered black markets, purchasing meat, butter, and gasoline without benefit of coupons. Coupons were stolen and counterfeited. Organized pressure groups conducted concerted attacks on the regulations. As World War II approached its end, the public was in no mood to continue rationing into the period of peace. The day following the end of the Japanese War, the rationing of gasoline, processed foods, and stoves ended. By the end of 1945 only sugar was still rationed.[8]

Hidden Price Increases

In the long run price controls and rationing could not halt underlying inflationary pressures resulting from increased amounts of conventional money. The enforcement of price regulation became difficult and finally impossible. Price controls had to be based on goods of known specifications, but for many articles standardization was not possible. Hidden price increases became common. They took the form of the elimination of discounts, deteriorations in quality, and discontinuation of cheaper lines and of special services. Extra charges were imposed in the form of fictitious bets, bribes, tips, gifts, and kickbacks. Charges were imposed for delivery, for fictitious brokerage or legal fees, and for goods not delivered. Purchases of unwanted goods were forced as a means of obtaining scarce materials. Quality deterioration included short-weighting, use of inferior materials, and defective workmanship.

Inflationary forces may thus be temporarily suppressed by price and wage controls and rationing. Once they are removed in order to restore a free market economy, prices will quickly rise to the level necessary to equate supply and demand. If controls are continued beyond the end of a war, when they no longer command popular support, black markets take over, and the will to cooperate in rebuilding the economy disappears as people witness the growing corruption of society. Labor productivity declines unless workers can begin to enjoy some of the amenities denied them during the war. Restoration of economic health requires removal of controls and reintroduction of a free market.

The transition from a controlled to a market economy is greatly eased if the costs of war are financed in such a way that increases in the money supply are minimized. War costs should thus be financed from taxes and the sale of government obligations to investors and investing institutions. The basic financial problem in wartime is to curb increases in the conventional money supply.

MEETING WAR COSTS

Tax money is the cheapest money a government can obtain. It requires no payment of interest, and it leaves no postwar overhang of debt. The objectives of wartime tax legislation are to raise revenue, to reduce consumer demand (by reducing the gap between consumer income and the goods and services available for consumer purchase), and to check increases in the quantity of conventional money.

The most useful taxes to achieve these three goals simultaneously are the individual income tax (collected at the source), employment taxes (social security levies), sales and excise taxes.

About 32 percent of total expenditures in the fiscal years of World War I, 45 percent of those in World War II, and 94 percent of those in the Korean war were covered by taxation (see Table 7.2).

Table 7.2

Federal Expenditures, Receipts, and Debt
(Fiscal Years;[a] Millions of Dollars)

	World War I 1916–1919	World War II 1940–1946	Korean War 1950–1953
Total expenditures	$33,923	$389,700	$223,357
Total receipts	10,724	174,670	210,279
Increase in debt	24,249	226,284	8,681
Interest-bearing	24,265	225,735	8,737
Noninterest-bearing	−16	549	−56
Ratio of total receipts to total expenditures	32%	45%	94%

a. The fiscal years selected cover the whole period of war expenditures, including time required for demobilization. The increase in debt took place between the beginning of the initial fiscal year and the end of the final fiscal year. The data for tax receipts in World War II and the Korean war are net receipts.

Source: *The Statistical History of the United States from Colonial Times to the Present, op. cit.,* pp. 711–712, 718, 720–721.

World War I

The United States entered World War I in an exceedingly favorable financial condition. Not only was the public debt small, but also the budget was in balance, and the tax structure was highly elastic. Individual and corporate income tax rates were raised, and an excess-profits tax was imposed; the bulk of tax revenues was derived from these sources. However, tax revenues lagged behind rising expenditures, partly by reason of the tardiness in increasing rates, partly by reason of relatively low rates, and partly because tax payments were not on a current basis.

Despite public willingness to accept a heavier tax load, income-tax rates were tardily raised in World War I. This may have reflected an unfamiliarity with a new source of tax revenue and an unwillingness to engage in experimentation. Personal income-tax rates were relatively low; for example, in 1918 the personal exemption for a married couple with no dependents was $2,000, the tax rate on the first bracket of income was 6 percent, on the top bracket 77 percent. In 1944–1945 the personal exemption for a married couple with no dependents was

$1,000, the tax rate on the first bracket of income was 23 percent, on the top bracket 94 percent. In 1918 the effective rate on a $15,000 income with four exemptions was 10.8 percent, in 1944–1945 it was 28.4 percent. Obviously the tax system could have been used more effectively in World War I, especially by imposing higher rates on smaller incomes.[9]

World War II

The United States entered World War II with a relatively large debt, an unbalanced budget, and a tax structure not nearly as elastic as that of 1917. Even so, a larger proportion of war costs, in the years included in Table 7.2, was covered by tax revenues than had been covered in World War I. Faced with similar disadvantages, Canada and the United Kingdom, in World War II covered even larger proportions of their expenditures by tax revenues than did the United States. The United States would have had a better fiscal record if income-tax rates had been raised to high levels sooner; if tax exemptions had been withdrawn from state and municipal issues; if the Federal administration had accepted, at an earlier date, the principle of "pay as one earns," and had been willing to tax increases in the earnings of individuals at a higher rate than constant earnings; and above all if it had brought war costs, particularly wages, under tighter controls.

The Federal income tax discriminated in favor not only of owners of tax-exempt obligations but also of farmers, since home-produced and -consumed products were and still are not counted as income. It discriminated also in favor of homeowners, as opposed to renters, for the former were and are not required to declare the imputed rental values of their homes as income.

As it was, individual income taxes during World War II (fiscal years 1940–1946) produced $69 billion in revenue. In addition, corporate income and excess-profits taxes produced $61 billion, miscellaneous internal revenue $28 billion, employment taxes $9.7 billion, customs $2 billion, and other sources (including estate and gift taxes and the capital stock tax) about $5 billion. The taxes that are particularly effective in checking inflation (individual income taxes, miscellaneous internal revenue, and employment taxes) produced $107 billion out of total revenues of about $175 billion.

Corporate income and excess-profits taxes are not particularly effective in suppressing inflationary trends. High rates are apt to lead to extravagance, stimulate dubious expenditures, reduce resistance to demands for wage increases, and cause corporations to spend maximum amounts on maintenance and repairs. These taxes must be accompanied, as they were in Canada, by strict controls on corporate expenses, especially those relating to advertising, expense accounts, depreciation reserves, and maintenance. Canada granted depreciation allowances only to companies with war contracts.

Although corporate income and excess-profits taxes are not particularly anti-inflationary—indeed they may be inflationary—corporate income tax rates are raised and an excess profits tax is adopted in wartime. They are regarded as morale builders and are looked upon as giving assurance to the public that the "profits are being taken out of war." The U.S. government hoped that some "excess profits" could be recouped through renegotiation of war contracts. Actually such renegotiations brought a relatively small sum into the Treasury—about $6 billion.

Miscellaneous internal revenue in World War II was derived largely from specific taxes on liquor, tobacco, gasoline, automobile accessories, jewelry, communication, transportation, and theater admissions. A Federal retail-sales tax would have been much more effective in combating inflation. It would not only have reduced consumption but would also have shifted some of the tax burden to those who avoided or evaded the income tax.

The Treasury opposed a sales tax, however, on the grounds that it would increase living costs, make price ceilings difficult to maintain, disturb the parity-price structure in agriculture, and cause a rapid increase in government employment at a time when manpower was scarce. These reasons do not seem to counterbalance the great advantages that would have been obtained from a general Federal retail-sales tax.

Employment taxes, which yielded small revenues during World War II, can be very effective as an anti-inflationary device. They are so effective that it was a pity that rates were not increased and coverage was not extended in accordance with the recommendations of the Treasury. Had the recommendations been adopted, an annual increase of $5.3 billion in social security tax revenues would have resulted.[10]

The Korean War

Tax rates were raised quickly during the Korean war. The Revenue Act of 1950 increased individual and corporate income-tax rates and made a number of other revisions in the income tax, estate tax, and excise taxes. It also provided for acceleration of tax payments by corporations, provided for special amortization of emergency facilities, and extended various excise taxes. A second revenue measure, the

Excess Profits Tax Act of 1950, approved January 3, 1951, reinstated an excess-profits tax. Amendments to the Social Security Act extended the coverage of the program to about 10 million additional persons, increased the maximum amount of annual earnings subject to the tax, and also increased benefits. The Revenue Act of 1951, approved on October 20, increased individual income-tax rates still more, raised the normal corporate tax rate from 25 to 30 percent, increased old excise taxes, and imposed many new levies.

The result was that on a budgetary basis, 94 percent of Federal expenditures were covered by tax income. On a cash basis, the budget was in balance. The increase in the Federal debt, reflecting the budgetary deficit, was financed mainly through the increase in social-security investments. Except for initial price increases of about 10 percent through 1950, the wholesale-price index was not only stable during the Korean war but also actually declined. This fact can be attributed to the fiscal policies adopted and to the nation's ability to meet civilian and military demands with little strain on the economy. (Fiscal policy during the Vietnam war is discussed in Chapter 14.)

Taxable Capacity

Even though taxation is the most effective means to counteract inflationary price pressures, there are certain ill-defined and imprecise limits to taxable capacity. They involve a mixture of economic, psychological, and political considerations. Economic limits are set by the volume, composition, and distribution of national income. Psychological limits are set by the willingness of taxpayers to submit to heavy tax burdens; the willingness in turn rests on popular support for the war and belief that all are sharing equitably in a common sacrifice. Political limits are set by the adequacy of the tax-collection machinery and by taxpayers' belief that the tax system is equitable. If political support is lacking, a tax system will collapse. In neither World War I nor World War II were the limits of taxable capacity reached.

BORROWING IN WARTIME

The funds not secured from tax levies must be obtained from the sale of government obligations or the issue of fiat money. The latter method had not been used since the Civil War, unless one classifies Federal Reserve notes, backed largely by government obligations, as fiat money.

In wartime government obligations should be sold in such manner that their sale does not increase the demand deposits of commercial banks. This represents an ideal goal, only approximated in American war finance.

If heavy reliance is placed on the banking system, transition to a peacetime economy becomes very difficult. Either prices must be permitted to rise to absorb the excess money or a portion must be destroyed. After World War II the first method was used in France and the United States, the second method in Belgium and the USSR.

The sale of government obligations will not increase total demand deposits if they are sold: First, to consumers who make payment from current income. The sale of government obligations against current income represents the best noninflationary source of borrowed funds. There are great disparities in increase in consumer income in wartime. Unless the increases are subject to special surtax rates, they will not be absorbed by taxation and must be absorbed by sales of government obligations. Second, to consumers who make payment by drawing upon their bank balances. The use of idle balances by consumers to purchase government obligations does not reduce demand based on current income but does limit ability to use existing deposits to bid for goods and services. This method tends to increase deposit velocity though not deposit volume. Third, to savings institutions and financial intermediates which purchase obligations from cash inflow resulting from new savings or the repayment of existing debts. Fourth, to state and local governments which purchase the obligations from tax receipts which at the moment cannot be used by reason of shortages of materials and personnel. Fifth, to business firms, which, by reasons of their inability to replace depleted inventories or to spend funds in the maintenance and enlargement of plant and equipment, have idle funds to invest. Sixth, to commercial banks which acquire obligations to replace loans that are being repaid or investments that are being retired. Finally, to the Federal Reserve banks which purchase the public debt for the sole purpose of financing increased currency demand. Purchases for this purpose do not provide reserves against which commercial banks can expand credit.

State and local governments, business firms, and commercial banks cannot be considered permanent holders of the debt. Particularly interested in short-term obligations, they tend to reduce their holdings as soon as the war ends, in order to meet long-deferred expenditures and increases in the demand for credit on the part of private borrowers. Other investors may prefer longer-term obligations.

It is essential that the purchase terms on government obligations issued during wartime be such that investors, especially individuals and financial intermediaries, will be induced to buy long-term obligations and to hold them in the postwar period. The terms of the obligations, in the form of interest rates, conversion privileges, purchasing power and lottery attributes, and annuity provisions—should thus be sufficiently attractive to warrant retention.

DEBT ISSUES AND MANAGEMENT

Patterns of Debt Management

During major wars the United States has issued a great variety of obligations, reflecting in their diversity the ingenuity of the different Secretaries of the Treasury. Obligations have included demand notes, negotiable and nonnegotiable securities, appreciation and coupon bonds, bank-restricted* and unrestricted debt. They have been issued at discount or at par, have had maturities ranging up to forty years, have carried an intricate variety of tax-exempt privileges and receivability†, exchangeability, and conversion options. The obligations have included those whose interest and principal have been payable in coin or currency, and have carried a variety of sinking-fund provisions.‡ Simplicity of debt issues has not been a characteristic feature of American war finance.

The obligations issued during the Civil War bore the shortest and longest maturities of those in any war, ranging from demand notes to forty-year bonds (Table 7.3).§ In the early part of the conflict, the country was flooded with short-term paper; as the war progressed more emphasis was placed on long-term issues. The deficit of World War I was financed to a greater extent than were those of other wars through the sale of relatively long-term obligations. In World War II the Treasury relied heavily on short-term issues, with the result that the floating debt in 1946 was relatively larger than it had been in 1865 or 1919. The average maturity of the marketable debt fell during the Korean war, not as a result of the sale of obligations to meet new financial needs but of the policy of refinancing maturing debt by issuing short-term and redemption obligations. Budgetary deficits arising from the Vietnam war have mainly been financed by increases in obligations with maturities of five years or less; consequently obligations with

---

* Not eligible for commercial bank purchase except under certain conditions.
† Eligibility for use in the payment of taxes, usually state taxes.
‡ A fund set aside by a government or business from its income in order to pay debts as they fall due.
§ In this context demand notes are defined as "greenbacks." Redemption obligations issued in World Wars I and II were, in effect, demand notes. Data for the Civil War are included for the sake of comparison.

longer maturities now form a smaller proportion (partly also reflecting arbitrary interest-rate limitations imposed on the Federal debt) than on any of the dates given in Table 7.3, save for 1865.

Table 7.3
Maturity Distribution of Interest-Bearing, Direct Marketable Federal Debt (1865, 1919, 1946, 1953 and 1971)[a]

Term to Maturity	1865	1919	1946[b]	1953	1971
Less than 1 year and past due	10%	15%	32%	51%	46%
1 to 5 years	74	14	11	20	37
and over	16	71	57	28	18
Total interest-bearing marketable debt (millions of dollars)	$2,145	$25,234	$189,606	$147,335	$245,473

a. All figures as of June 30. Demand notes, redemption obligations, and special issues are not included in any of the data; bank-restricted obligations are included.

b. See Table 7.5.

Source: *Annual Report of the Secretary of the Treasury on the State of the Finances for the Year Ended 1865* (Washington, D.C.: Government Printing Office, 1866), pp. 50–55; *Annual Report of the Treasury on the State of the Finances for the Fiscal Year Ended June 30, 1919* (Washington, D.C.: Government Printing Office, 1920), pp. 221–222; *Annual Report of the Secretary of the Treasury on the State of the Finances for the Fiscal Year Ended June 30, 1965* (Washington, D.C.; Government Printing Office, 1966), p. 562; and *Treasury Bulletin* (Washington, D.C.: U.S. Treasury Department, January 1972), p. 21.

World War I

In World War I, in order to encourage thrift and to enable members of all income groups to participate in financing the war, the government continuously offered for sale war savings stamps and certificates. By June 30, 1919, about $954 million were outstanding. The funds obtained thus were small, however, and other methods had to be employed.

From May 14, 1917, to April 21, 1919, the United States floated four Liberty Loans and one Victory Loan. All were issued at par in denominations as low as $50 and could be purchased in instalments over periods of four months in the first two instances and six months in the last three. Purchasers were encouraged to borrow from their banks in order to buy the obligations. Maturities ranged from five to thirty years, and all were callable within fifteen years. The principal differences in the obligations concerned tax exemption, interest rates, and conversion privileges. Total subscriptions amounted to about $24 billion, allotments to $21 billion, and the total number of individual subscribers in all loans totaled 66 million.

The Liberty Loan drives, lasting about four weeks and spaced at intervals of five to seven months, were each preceded by issues of certificates of indebtedness. They had maturities up to one year and were issued as an integral part of the Treasury's borrowing program, rather than as a temporary emergency measure. The Treasury hoped to be able to retire those certificates, which had been sold to commercial banks (often under duress), from funds received from tax payments and the sale of bonds. From the entry of the United States into the war until October 31, 1919, the Treasury issued $6 billion in certificates in anticipation of tax payments and $19 billion in anticipation of sales of bonds and notes. Its goal of retiring the certificates from tax and bond proceeds could not be realized. Rising war expenditures exceeded the funds from tax collections and bond sales.

The increase in Federal debt (adjusted for the increase in cash assets of the Treasury) amounted to $24.1 billion between April 6, 1917, and October 31, 1919. The debt on October 31, 1919, classified by issues, is shown in Table 7.4.

Table 7.4
The Federal Debt, October 31, 1919
(Millions of Dollars)

Prewar bonds	$ 883
War-savings certificates	911
Certificates of indebtedness	3,736
Victory Loan	4,414
Liberty Loans	16,029
All debts on which interest had ceased	2
	$25,975
Noninterest bearing debt	235
Total	$26,210

Source: *Annual Report of the Secretary of the Treasury on the State of the Finances for the Fiscal Year Ended June 30, 1919* (Washington, D.C.: Government Printing Office, 1920), p. 30.

World War II

In World War II the United States sold a great variety of obligations in an effort to meet the needs of all purchasers. In order to absorb current income, to reduce consumer demand, and to finance expenditures as much as possible outside the banking system, the Treasury sold various nonmarketable redemption issues: Series E, F, and G savings bonds and Series C tax-savings notes. Series E bonds, designed for the small purchaser, were sold under payroll-deduction plans. Issued at 75 percent of par value, they matured in ten years but were redeemable sixty days after issue at stated redemption values; if held to maturity, they yielded 2.9 percent. The payroll-deduction plan proved to be an excellent method of war finance, draining off some of the large increases in income.

During 1941 and 1942, besides continuing sales of nonmarketable securities, the Treasury periodically sold Treasury bills, certificates, notes, and bonds in the open market. As time went on an increasing proportion of the deficit was financed through the commercial-banking system. In the autumn of 1942 approximately 55 percent of Treasury borrowing was absorbed by commercial banks, and the Treasury then decided to change its borrowing methods. War-loan drives modeled after those of World War I were instituted. The first drive took place between November 30 and December 23, 1942, and the final one (the eighth) between October 29 and December 8, 1945. Total Federal debt rose from $40.4 billion on June 30, 1939, to $269.9 billion on June 30, 1946 (see Table 7.3, Footnote a). The composition of the 1946 debt is shown in Table 7.5.

Table 7.5
The Federal Debt, June 30, 1946 [a]
(Billions of Dollars)

Marketable Issues	
Treasury bills	$ 17
Certificates of indebtedness	35
Treasury notes	18
Treasury bonds	119
	$ 190
Nonmarketable Issues	
U.S. savings bonds	$ 49
Special issues	22
Treasury notes (tax and savings series)	7
	$ 78
Noninterest-bearing issues	1
Total	$ 269

a. The total is dissimilar to the one in the text due to rounding.
Source: *Treasury Bulletin* (Washington, D.C.: U.S. Treasury Department, August 1947), p. 20.

Postwar Debt Management

At the end of the Civil War Secretary of the Treasury Hugh McCulloch sought to retire the greenbacks, to effect a speedy resumption of specie payments, and to fund the floating debt. He was unsuccessful in the first two objectives but did institute policies that, once embodied in congressional legislation, permitted rapid funding of the debt in his and succeeding administrations. This task was fa-cilitated by growing confidence in the credit standing of the U.S. government, by a demand for bonds to serve as collateral for national bank notes, and by budget surpluses in the 1880s.

After World War I Andrew W. Mellon, Secretary of the Treasury in the Harding, Coolidge, and Hoover administrations, also sought to fund and retire the debt. By mid-1923 the floating debt had been funded into more manageable matur-ities. Mellon then began to direct his attention to funding the Liberty Loans. Assist-ing those operations were the budget surpluses and payments received on Allied war debts, which together permitted a reduction in the total debt from $25 billion on June 30, 1919, to $16 billion on June 30, 1930. Debt operations in this period also brought about a substantial increase in the average maturity of the debt.

In contrast to the fiscal and debt-management policies after the Civil War and World War I, when the debt was funded and retired, total Federal debt was substantially increased after World War II. The increase was accompanied by a marked increase in the floating debt and a sharp reduction in the average length of the debt, developments that are apt, as we have indicated, to impair the inde-pendence of a central banking system.[11]

INTEREST-RATE POLICY

Whatever their differences on fiscal policy, Secretaries of the Treasury Salmon P. Chase, William G. McAdoo, Henry Morgenthau, Jr., and John W. Snyder (serving during the Civil War, World War I, World War II, and the Korean war, respectively) were united in their desire to hold down interest rates on the public debt. Among the reasons that led Secretary Chase to favor the issue of greenbacks was that it would help to reduce average interest costs on the total debt. Actually, interest rates on Civil War obligations were higher than those in other wars, rang-ing from 4 to 7.3 percent: 6 percent was a typical rate. These interest rates ap-plied to obligations the income from which was taxed at very low rates, with both interest and principal customarily paid in specie. Little wonder that Jay Cooke was so successful in creating a government securities market and in selling obligations to individual investors! His success in doing so probably accounted for the fact that wholesale prices rose less in the Civil War than in the two world wars de-spite the issue of greenbacks, the sharp decline of the dollar in terms of foreign exchange, and the relatively small proportion of war costs financed from tax reve-nues.

World War I

Secretary McAdoo, equally anxious to hold down interest costs on the debt, issued the first Liberty Loan at 3.5 percent and fully exempt from income taxes. His point of view was set forth in 1918: "The higher the rate on Government bonds, the greater the cost to the American people of carrying on the war and the greater will be the depreciation in all other forms of investment securities. We cannot regard without concern declines in the general value of fixed investments."[12] McAdoo did raise the coupon rates on the second and third Liberty Loans, modifying and restricting the tax-exempt privileges, however. The third Liberty Loan Act (April 4, 1918) restricted interest on bonds to a maximum of 4.25 percent. This limitation still remains in the law. Unfavorable market conditions at the time of the fourth Liberty Loan (September 1918) caused the Treasury to revive substantial tax exemptions. The final war loan offered a choice between tax-exempt 3.75 percent and taxable 4.75 percent notes.

Despite the privileges attached to the Liberty bonds, they consistently sold below par in the open market, which led the Treasury, in the spring of 1918 (just before the third Liberty Loan), to establish a bond-purchase fund, administered by the War Finance Corporation, to support the prices of Liberty bonds. By June 30, 1920, when the bond-purchase fund was superseded by the 2.5 percent cumulative sinking fund, it had been used to purchase $1.7 billion of securities but had still failed to bring the price of any issue (except the fully tax-exempt first Liberty Loan) up to par. The fund was financed by the sale of certificates of indebtedness, a refunding operation in reverse—for the floating debt was increased, in order to support the prices of and to retire the long-term debt. Not until the beginning of 1920 did the Treasury begin to issue obligations carrying interest rates adjusted to market conditions.

World War II

To an even greater degree than his predecessors, Secretary Morgenthau was determined to keep interest rates low. Government obligations were issued according to a pattern of rates that had been fixed at the time of the first war-loan drive in December 1942.[13]

Treasury bills were issued weekly on a discount basis to yield ⅜ of 1 percent for a 91-day maturity. The other obligations included certificates of indebtedness yielding ⅞ of 1 percent for one-year maturities; Treasury notes yielding 1.25

percent with maturities ranging from 1.5 to 2.75 years; Treasury bonds yielding 1.5 percent for 5.5-year maturities, 1.75 percent for 6-year maturities, 2 percent for 10-year maturities, 2.25 percent for 15–17-year maturities (unavailable to commercial banks for seven years after issue), 2.5 percent for 26–27-year maturities (unavailable to commercial banks for ten years after issue).

The rate structure originated in the ascending interest curve that had developed during the depression. Rates of 3/8 and 7/8 of 1 percent were looked upon as sufficient reward for commercial banks, which, in purchasing the short-term debt, simply wrote up deposit balances on their books. A rate of 2 percent on ten-year bonds was looked upon as viable for savings banks, which would, it was believed, be the principal buyers, and a rate of 2.5 percent on twenty-six-year bonds was considered viable for insurance companies, which would provide the largest market for these obligations.

During the discussions preceding adoption of the curve, Federal Reserve officials argued unsuccessfully for higher short-term rates. A narrower overall spread, they maintained, would diminish the incentive to "play the pattern" of rates and would be less inflationary.* The Treasury responded that the pattern would not be inflationary because of rationing and price controls. The ·Treasury also proposed that the Reserve System maintain a large volume of excess reserves. This the Reserve System refused to do, on the ground that its purchases to maintain the rate pattern would automatically create the reserves needed for commercial bank purchases.

Scarcely any method of war finance with greater inflationary potential than that used in World War II could have been contrived. A steeply graduated curve is an inducement to the Treasury to float short-term obligations (the floating debt rose from $2 billion in 1941 to $59 billion in 1946). It makes speculation, in the form of "riding the interest curve," highly profitable. Individuals borrow heavily to speculate in government obligations whose prices are destined to rise as the term to maturity shortens.

A sharply graduated curve can be maintained only if the investors believe that it can *not* be maintained. Once investors conclude that the curve will not be altered they will buy longer-term obligations, which, despite their maturities, are in effect demand obligations. As banks and other investors "reach out," political pres-

---

* A rigidly pegged interest rate curve causes the prices of government obligations to rise as the term to maturity shortens. Otherwise the interest yield would not be on the curve. The rise in price generates capital gains for the speculator, often buying government securities on a very small margin. See Henry C. Murphy, *The National Debt in War and Transition* (New York: McGraw-Hill Book Company, Inc. 1950), chapter 14.

sures for maintenance of the curve and continued pegging operations by the Federal Reserve banks are engendered.

The wartime yield curve was maintained almost without change from 1942 until near the end of 1944. During 1945 and the first quarter of 1946 a marked decline in the yields on long- and intermediate-term bonds occurred as a result of growing confidence among investors that the Treasury and the Reserve banks would not deviate from their low-interest policy. Confident that long-term investments were as liquid as short obligations, investors shifted to intermediate- and long-term bonds. In the sixth, seventh, and eighth war-loan drives, investors showed increasing preference for the 2.25 percent bonds, whereas commercial banks, which were barred from purchasing them, bought outstanding bonds in the five-to-ten-year range. In order to do so, they shifted virtually all their holdings of Treasury Bills to the Reserve banks, sold certificates of indebtedness in the open market (the Reserve banks were forced to buy), and borrowed from the Reserve banks. As long as the short end of the curve was rigidly pegged, the Treasury and the Reserve banks were powerless to prevent a decline in long-term rates.

The Treasury defended its interest policy on the ground that it was in effect projecting, with a slight increase in short-term rates, the prewar interest curve. It asserted that low short-term rates were necessary to ensure the maintenance of low long-term rates. Long-term rates of 2.5 percent, the Treasury declared (and the Federal Reserve denied), could not be maintained if the Treasury bill rate were to increase above $\frac{3}{8}$ of 1 percent.

Through the war years the Treasury equated government credit with government bond yields, predicted economic stagnation in the postwar period, argued that savings are mechanically determined and unresponsive to the level of interest rates and firmly held that monetary policy was passé. "The fundamental factors underlying interest rates on government securities, which apply also to interest rates in other fields, give no indication of a change in the direction of a higher level of rates in the foreseeable future."[14]

The Korean War

During the Korean war the administration was adamant in its insistence that interest rates remain unchanged. Under pressure of an ultimatum from Federal Reserve officials, it was forced to give ground in 1951 (see Chapter 8). The accord which was then signed was finally implemented in 1953.

INVOLVEMENT OF THE COMMERCIAL BANKING SYSTEM

Maintenance of interest rates at artificially low levels, whether in war or peace, requires an expanding volume of commercial- and central-bank credit. The money supply rises, ownership of liquid assets by individuals and business firms mounts, and inflationary pressures, under conditions of relatively full employment, are intensified. The overriding reasons for financing a war from taxation or from sales of bonds to individuals and savings institutions are that these measures will restrain the growth of the money supply and other liquid assets, check inflationary forces, ease the transition to a postwar economy, preserve the competitive forces of the marketplace, and minimize the involvement of the commercial banking system in war and postwar finance. The degree of involvement of the commercial banking system in various wars is set forth in Table 7.6*

Table 7.6

Estimated Increase in Public Debt Financed by the Commercial Banking System[a] (Millions of Dollars)

	Civil War[b] 1860–1866	World War I 1916–1919	World War II 1940–1946	Korean War 1950–1953*
Increase in interest-bearing debt	$2,257	$24,265	$225,735	$8,737
Estimated amount financed, by commercial banking system	400	7,000	90,000	none
Ratio of estimated amount financed by commercial banking system to total increase in interest-bearing debt	18%	30%	40%	—

a. Data are for June 30 of each year.
b. Data for the Civil War do not include the greenbacks. If they were included (added to the increase in debt and to that financed by the commercial banking system) the ratio of estimated amount financed by the commercial banking system to the total increase in debt would rise to about 31 percent. The commercial banking system in World Wars I and II and the Korean war include the commercial banks and the Federal Reserve banks. The time span includes the periods of mobilization and demobilization.

Source: *The Statistical History of the United States from Colonial Times to the Present, op. cit.,* pp. 624, 631, 641–642, 720–721; *Federal Reserve Bulletin,* 1950, pp. 984, 1045, 1194, 1205 and 1953, pp. 957–958, 967, 984; and *Sixth Annual Report of the Federal Reserve Board* (Washington, D.C.: Government Printing Office, 1920), pp. 115–117.

* The Korean war data are not particularly significant as they were influenced by important shifts in debt ownership distribution. Between June 30, 1950, and June 30, 1953, total federal debt rose by $9 billion, the marketable debt fell by $8 billion, the nonmarketable debt fell by $4 billion, the newly issued convertible bonds rose by $12.3 billion, and special issues rose $9 billion. Federal debt held by the commercial banks fell by $7.7 billion and that held by the Federal Reserve banks rose by $6.4 billion. The Federal banks purchased government securities in order to finance the increase of money in circulation and in member-bank required reserves. The increase in the deposits (Table 7.9) of the commercial banks resulted from a sharp increase in loans; total investments remained relatively stable.

Contrary to expectations at the time of the passage of the National Currency Act (February 25, 1863) commercial banks played a relatively minor role in war finance during the Civil War. National banks were not established in large numbers until 1865, when state bank notes became subject to confiscatory taxation. By that time war-financing needs had begun to subside.

World War I

The expansion of commercial-bank credit in World War I took the form of purchases of the short-term debt, especially certificates of indebtedness, and of loans to customers to enable them to purchase Liberty bonds on the instalment plan (see Table 7.7.) Individuals were encouraged to borrow in order to buy war obligations.

Table 7.7
All Commercial Banks, World War I
(Millions of Dollars)

	Loans	U.S. Obligations	Other Securities	Deposits (Excluding Interbank)
June 20, 1917	$18,581	$1,300	$4,437	$22,486
June 30, 1919	22,814	4,864	4,657	29,306
Increase	4,233	3,564	220	6,820

Source: The Statistical History of the United States from Colonial Times to the Present, op. cit., pp. 631–632.

Many measures were adopted to facilitate credit expansion. They included reduction in reserve requirements for Federal Reserve notes and the deposit liabilities of member banks, encouragement to state banks to join the Reserve System, the impounding of gold in the Federal Reserve banks, and an embargo placed on gold exports. Superimposed on these measures were the credit policies of the Reserve System. In the attempt to counteract the effects of general credit expansion, the administration and the Reserve System endeavored (unsuccessfully on the whole) to control selected credit areas: stock exchange, investment credits, and business loans.

The expansion of Federal Reserve credit in World War I took the form largely of loans to member banks. Open-market purchases of bankers' bills and government obligations were relatively small, rising only $445 million from April 1917 to August 1919, whereas discounted bills rose $1,800 million. These consisted of advances to member banks secured for the most part by certificates of indebtedness. The principal factors causing member banks to borrow were the increases of money in circulation and in member-bank required reserves brought about by the expansion in bank deposits. The Reserve banks adjusted discount rates to the coupon rates on Liberty bonds, established preferential rates on loans to member banks against war paper, and rediscounted paper of nonmember banks when it was endorsed by member banks and secured by war paper.

Table 7.8

Discount Rates,
Member-Bank Collateral Notes
Maturing Within 15 Days,
Federal Reserve Bank of New York

January 1, 1917	3.0%
December 21, 1917	3.5
April 3, 1918	4.0
December, 1918	4.0

Source: Fourth Annual Report of the Federal Reserve Board Covering Operations for the Year 1917 (Washington D.C.: Government Printing Office, 1918), p. 37; and Fifth Annual Report of the Federal Reserve Board Covering Operations for the Year 1918 (Washington D.C.; Government Printing Office, 1919), p. 5.

In 1918 the Federal Reserve Board explained:

The rates of interest borne by the Treasury certificates of indebtedness and by the Liberty loan bonds have been determined by the Secretary of the Treasury within the limits fixed by Congress, and the Board has felt it to be its duty to adjust its discount rates in such manner as to assist the distribution of the various Treasury issues.[15]

The increase in the discount rate on December 21, 1917, followed the second Liberty Loan drive and was intended to bring the rate more nearly in line with market rates. The increase on April 3, 1918, followed increases in coupon rates on Liberty bonds and certificates of indebtedness. Throughout the period covered by Table 7.8 the preferential rates on member-bank collateral notes were substantially below open-market short-term rates. Even so, discount rates did rise in World War I, which they did not do in World War II, due to rigid pegging techniques.

The techniques used in World War I to inject central- and commercial-bank credit into the financial system of the United States had certain advantages. The Reserve banks could pressure commercial banks to repay their rediscounted loans —and did so—by raising the bank rate in 1920. Through 1920 and 1921, member banks reduced rediscounts by making use of the gold inflow and the cyclical retirement of the currency (see Chapter 9, p. 222). Commercial banks could, in turn, pressure their customers to repay loans. The whole process had the desirable results of squeezing some of the excess credit out of the banking system, of eliminating part of the war inflation, and of preventing wage increases from being frozen into the cost structure.

The rise in member-bank borrowings during World War I caused the interest curve to be negatively inclined, with short-term rates higher than long. This itself had the fortunate result of creating nonbank demand for the short-term debt and of inducing the Treasury, once revenues had exceeded expenditures, to use surplus funds to reduce the floating debt. Interest rates, not being rigidly pegged during the war, were freed in a reasonably short time of all controls in the postwar period.*

World War I was a crucial period in the development of central banking. Before 1914 central bankers had been able to fashion their policies in relative freedom from government influence. Their portfolios had consisted largely of trade bills. The budgets of the industrial nations had usually been balanced, and the latter therefore had little difficulty in selling obligations when necessary to savers and saving institutions. Following World War I, central banks to an increasing extent fell subject to the domination of Ministers of Finance.

World War II

The decision of the Treasury to finance World War II on the basis of a steeply inclined interest rate curve, low short-term rates and higher long-term rates, caused a gigantic expansion in commercial-bank and Federal Reserve bank credit. Several measures were taken to facilitate this expansion: The Reserve Banks agreed to maintain member-bank net free reserves in amounts necessary to maintain the yield curve (which turned out to be about $1 billion), to purchase all Treasury bills at not less than ⅜ of 1 percent, and to lend against government obligations at not less than par. In addition, the Reserve banks established a preferential discount rate of .5 percent on member-bank notes collateralled by Government securities maturing or callable within one year; lowered the reserve requirements of member banks in central-reserve cities; exempted war-loan accounts from member-bank reserve requirements; and lowered the reserve requirements against Federal

---

* Commercial-bank holdings of the public debt fell through 1920 and 1921, began to rise in 1922, and continued to rise slowly through the rest of the decade. The reduction in total debt affected nonbank holders, who, so to speak, received savings funds which they could invest or otherwise use.

Reserve notes and deposits. No action on gold redemption was required. Domestic redemption had ceased in 1933, and the entire domestic gold stock had been impounded by the Treasury in 1934.

From the end of 1939 to the end of 1945, Federal Reserve credit rose from $2.5 to $24 billion, mainly in the form of Treasury bills. The Reserve banks took the obligations that other purchasers did not want. The increase in Federal Reserve credit resulted, as it had in World War I, from the increase of money in circulation and the increase in the required reserves of member banks. Although the gold stock rose in World War I, it fell in World War II. Commercial-bank holdings of the public debt rose from $19 to $91 billion, which brought about the increase in bank deposits that forced the rise in required reserves.

The "success" of the individual loan drives was dependent upon sharp expansion in bank credit. The ratios of the expansion in Federal Reserve and commercial-bank credit in the eight drives during World War II ranged from 29 percent (in the third drive) to 50 percent (in the fifth drive). During the war-loan drives, the shift of deposits from private to government accounts gave member banks excess reserves, on the basis of which they purchased government obligations and extended loans against them. Loans against government obligations to others than dealers reached the staggering total of $1.8 billion in both the seventh and eighth loan drives, an indication of speculative interest in "riding the curve."

The government lifted every barrier to such transactions. All bank-supervisory agencies declared that they would not criticize banks for investing in the public debt, except for those securities that were ineligible for bank investment. Furthermore, loans extended by commercial banks to enable customers to purchase the public debt would not, if granted on a short-term or amortized basis, be subject to supervisory criticism. Nor would commercial banks be subject to criticism if they used their idle funds to make such investments and loans and if, in order to do so, they availed themselves of the privilege of borrowing from or selling Treasury bills to the Reserve banks.

Bank-supervisory officials frequently called the attention of commercial-bank officers to the needs to adjust their loan policies to war requirements; to meet the credit needs of war industries; to refuse credit for unnecessary accumulation of civilian inventories; and to place as many loans as possible on an amortized basis. These admonitions were really not necessary. In World War II the expansion of business and consumer credit depended upon the availability of goods; the real economy dominated the credit economy. Earning assets other than those related to the public debt showed no net increase during World War II, in contrast to the increases in World War I and the Korean War, when such assets reflected substantial rises.*

The financing techniques used in World War II greatly increased the difficulties of restoring competitive relations in the postwar money and capital markets. A sharply inclined interest curve, the rise in the floating debt, and hesitancy in the unpegging of the curve all intensified postwar inflation. The last factor resulted from belief that government credit is to be measured by bond prices, that once the curve was unpegged these prices would face a "bottomless pit," that low interest rates are a positive "good" in themselves, and that monetary policy should bow to fiscal polical as a control mechanism. It was argued that, if monetary policy were to be effective, interest rates would have to be raised to such heights that the economy would be plunged into deep depression.

The Korean War

The Korean War initially produced an upsurge of inflation that swept the Western world. Business investment in inventories and in construction and producers' durable goods soared. Consumers joined the rush and used credit to buy consumers' durables and real estate. The fiscal measures adopted (credit policy was still hampered by a pegged market) in coordination (which was crucial) with the productive powers of the economy helped to check the upward surge in prices and caused the wholesale price index to level off in 1951. Action by monetary authorities in selected credit areas reinforced these measures. Controls were imposed on consumer and mortgage credit, but they quickly encountered strong politicial opposition and were discarded for political expediency.*

Holdings of government obligations by commercial banks actually fell during much of the Korean War. This unprecedented wartime development resulted from two other unique developments: The Federal budget was balanced on a cash basis, and the flow of funds into government trust accounts absorbed the government securities occasionally sold by the commercial banks and other investors.

THE RESULT

The result of fiscal and monetary policies in World Wars I and II was to

---

* Under an executive order issued on August 9, 1941, the Board of Governors was for the first time directed to subject consumer credit to selective controls. Pursuant to this order, the Board issued Regulation W, effective on September 1, designed to reduce the demand for consumers' durable goods and to restrain overall increases in credit. The volume of consumer credit fell, but more as a result of the unavailability of durable goods than of the imposition of credit controls.

* Early in 1951 a general ceiling on wages and prices, as well as a voluntary credit-restraint program went into effect.

force sharp increases in the money supply. The increase during the period dominated by World War I (April 1917–December 1919) was about 42 percent, in that dominated by World War II (December 1941–December 1946) about 123 percent, and in that dominated by the Korean war about 12 percent. Annual increases averaged 17 percent, 25 percent, and 3 percent (see Table 7.9).

Table 7.9
Currency and Demand Deposits[a]
(Billions of Dollars)

World War I		World War II		Korean War	
1914	$11.6	1939	$36.0	1950	$115.2
1915	13.4	1940	41.9	1951	122.0
1916	15.6	1941	48.2	1952	126.5
1917 (April)	16.6	1942	62.6	1953	128.2
1917	18.3	1943	79.9		
1918	20.8	1944	90.7		
1919	23.5	1945	102.4		
		1946	107.6		

a. Figures are for the end of each year, unless otherwise noted.
Source: Milton Friedman and Anna Jacobson Schwartz, A Monetary History of the United States 1867–1960 (Princeton, N.J.: Princeton University Press, 1963), pp. 708–720.

The redundancy of the money supply in World Wars I and II was evidenced not only by inflationary pressures but also by increases in the ratio of the money supply to GNP.[16] Currency depreciation during the world wars was greatest in uncontrolled export prices; between 1941 and 1945 they rose from 110 to 190 (January–June 1939 = 100).[17]

In retrospect the increase in conventional money very likely would have been substantially less in World War I had individual income taxes been increased earlier and had they been placed at levels (particularly on lower incomes) that would have raised additional revenues.

The sale of government obligations would have depended less on an inflationary expansion of commercial-bank and Federal Reserve bank credit had they been issued at higher interest rates. The first Liberty Loan might have been sold to yield 5 percent, subsequent issues at closely similar rates and all should have been made fully taxable. Certificates of indebtedness should have been issued at rates that would have enabled them to find purchasers outside the banking system. The unwillingness to issue government obligations at or slightly above market rates forced the Reserve banks to adjust their discount rates to coupon rates on government securities. The mistake of imposing a 4.25 percent overall limitation on bond coupons has yet to be rectified.

Again in World War II the conventional money supply would have increased less had personal income-tax rates been raised and placed on a current basis earlier. Increases in income might well have been subjected to surtax rates and a Federal sales tax introduced. The level of tax rates, high as they seemed at the time in the United States, were lower than those in Canada and the United Kingdom.[18]

Inflationary pressures would probably have been less had proposals for the introduction of an "expenditures tax" to replace other taxes on personal income been adopted. Such a tax has the triple advantage (in wartime) of raising revenue, reducing consumer expenditures, and increasing savings available for bond purchases.

Government obligations might well have been offered at higher rates, with the longest-term obligations issued at perhaps 3.5 percent and others along a less steeply inclined curve, beginning at 2.5 percent for Treasury bills. To preclude a general conviction that the curve was immutable, occasional changes in interest rates on government securities could have been introduced.

This type of curve would have represented such a drastic change from the Depression-induced curve that in 1941 no one would have given its introduction serious consideration. What is forgotten in wartime, expecially in a "2 percent war," is that interest rates are destined to rise in the postwar period as a result of efforts to reintroduce a market economy, to combat inflation, to satisfy pent-up loan and investment demands, and to replace capital equipment destroyed by war.

In World War II finance ministers, perhaps influenced by the economics of John Maynard Keynes, assumed that the current monetary rate of interest represented the "real rate" of interest. They ignored the effect on real rates of the sharp increases in time preferences of individuals and business firms starved for houses, durable goods, and production equipment. The real rate had risen. When the monetary rate was prevented from rising, the inflationary gap widened, and the transition to a market economy proved difficult.

It is to be hoped that World Wars I and II were the last of the total wars. Another may bring the history of peoples and institutions to an end. The costs of "brush wars," exemplified by those in Korea and Vietnam, should be financed entirely from tax revenues. The Reserve System would then be left free to act as it deemed necessary to curb inflationary pressures resulting from increases in private demand. Under such conditions a balanced budget is the best guarantee of Federal Reserve independence.

Notes

1. Woodrow Wilson, *Congressional Record,* House, April 2, 1917 (Washington, D.C.: Government Printing Office, 1917), p. 120.

2. These data on national defense expenditures have been taken from *The Statistical History of the United States from Colonial Times to the Present* (Stamford, Connecticut: Fairfield Publishers, Inc., 1965); the Economic Reports of the Presidents; and *Federal Reserve Bulletin* (February 1972), p. A43.

3. *Annual Report of the Secretary of the Treasury on the State of the Finances for the Fiscal Year Ended June 30, 1946* (Washington, D.C.: Government Printing Office, 1947), p. 3.

4. B. H. Beckhart, *The Discount Policy of the Federal Reserve System* (New York: Holt, 1924), chapter 6.

5. See *The General Maximum Price Regulation,* Bulletin No. 879 (U.S. Department of Labor, Bureau of Labor Statistics, June 10, 1946).

6. "War and Postwar Wages, Prices, and Hours, 1914–1923 and 1939–1944," *Monthly Labor Review* (October 1945), p. 615.

7. Harvey C. Mansfield et al., *A Short History of the O.P.A.,* General Publication No. 15, May 29, 1947 (Office of Temporary Controls), pp. 155, 172–197.

8. Doris P. Rothwell, "Price Control since the General Maximum Price Regulation," *Monthly Labor Review* (October 1945), pp. 675–693. See also Colin D. Campbell, Ed., *Wage-Price Controls in World War II, United States and Germany* (Washington, D.C.: American Enterprise Institute, October 1971).

9. *The Statistical History of the United States from Colonial Times to the Present, op. cit.,* pp. 703, 716–717.

10. *Annual Report of the Secretary of the Treasury on the State of Finances for the Fiscal Year Ended June 30, 1944* (Washington, D.C.: Government Printing Office, 1945), p. 389.

11. For an excellent discussion of the management of the public debt see Tilford C. Gaines, *Techniques of Treasury Debt Management* (Glencoe, Ill.: Free Press of Glencoe, 1962).

12. *Annual Report of the Secretary of the Treasury on the State of the Finances for the Fiscal Year Ended June 30, 1917* (Washington, D.C.: Government Printing Office, 1918), p. 4.

13. An excellent discussion of interest-rate policy in World War II can be found in Elmus R. Wicker, "The World War II Policy of Fixing a Pattern of Rates," *The Journal of Finance,* Vol. XXIV, No. 3 (June 1969).

14. *Annual Report of the Secretary of the Treasury on the State of the Finances for the Fiscal Year Ended June 30, 1944* (Washington, D.C.: Government Printing Office, 1945), p. 7.

15. *Fifth Annual Report of the Federal Reserve Board* (Washington, D.C.: Government Printing Office, 1919), p. 5.

16. *Chart Book of Economic Statistics, 1967* (New York: Morgan Guaranty Trust Company, 1967), charts 15 and 23.

17. *Sixteenth Annual Report* (Basle, Switzerland: Bank for International Settlements, July 1946), p. 12.

18. R. A. Musgrave, "The Wartime Effort in the United States, the United Kingdom and Canada," *Proceedings of the Thirty-Sixth Annual Conference on Taxation under the Auspices of the National Tax Association* (Washington, D.C.: National Tax Association, 1944), pp. 301–302.

CHAPTER 8

Combating
Postwar
Inflation

THE SETTING

As World Wars I and II approached an end, predictions were frequently made that, as military expenditures fell and members of the armed forces returned to civilian life, the United States would face serious unemployment and sharp declines in prices and production. In both instances these pessimistic predictions were belied; in both instances the pent-up demand for goods by civilians and business firms had been grossly underestimated. The problem proved to be not one of combating recession but rather one of checking inflation.

World War I was followed immediately by a decline in prices and production and an increase in unemployment, but the downward movement came to an end in February and March 1919. Thereafter all indexes began to rise. The index of wholesale prices, which stood at 203 in November 1918 (1913 = 100) and fell to 193 in February 1919, rose with few interruptions to 247 in May 1920. Prices on the New York Stock Exchange rose steadily from February to November 1919. Street loans, the term then applied to brokers' loans, more than doubled. The dollar value of export trade increased enormously. Labor was in great demand.* Similarly, the approaching end of World War II caused a slight decline in business indexes; a moderate business cycle contraction began in February 1945 but

---

* The turning points in the business cycle were August 1918, March 1919, and January 1920.

ended in October. The expansion that followed continued, except for a temporary interruption in 1949, for nearly seven years.* The wholesale-price index, which stood at 57.9 in 1945 (1957–1959 = 100), soared to 96.7 in 1951, one of the most rapid increases in American history. The consumer-price index rose in the same period from 62.7 (1957–1959 = 100) to 90.5.

At no time after World War II was unemployment a particularly serious problem. Many who had entered the labor force during the war, including women and the elderly, voluntarily withdrew; the GI Bill of Rights induced many ex-service men to return to school. Veterans who did enter the labor force readily found employment in construction, wholesale and retail trade, finance, services, and government.

After reaching a peak in May 1920 the wholesale-price index fell rapidly, declining about 40 percent over the next eighteen months. A similar price decline did not occur after World War II. The index, save for occasional slight declines and periods of stability, rose continuously until in December 1969 it stood at 115.1, about 19 percent above the 1951 level and about 100 percent above the 1945 level. Since World War II the American economy has been subject to fairly continous inflationary pressures.

Federal Reserve policy, once it had regained its independence after World War I (November 1919), was influenced largely by the declines that occurred in the ratio of gold reserves to Federal Reserve notes and deposits. After World War II Federal Reserve policy was for several years saddled with the responsibility of holding interest rates close to wartime levels. The restrictive monetary policies of 1920–1921, coupled with a growing surplus in the Federal budget, induced credit contraction and prevented cost push from escalating prices. In the later period, ample credit permitted cost push to ratchet prices ever higher.

AFTER WORLD WAR I

Sources of Effective Demand

Made effective by liberal extensions of credit, foreign and domestic demand concentrated on an inadequate supply of goods and services. In 1919 the Allies purchased nearly $5 billion worth of commodities in the United States, mostly food products and finished manufactured goods. These purchases were financed through credit advances by the American government, flotation of foreign loans in the United States and by a sharp rise in open-book transactions. The United States

---

* The turning points in the business cycle were October 1945, November 1948, October 1949, and July 1953.

made direct credit advances of $2 billion to the Allies, spent $100 million on relief work in Europe, and purchased $526 million of Allied currencies to cover expenditures of the American army abroad. Foreign nations floated $436 million of securities in the United States. As exports grew, those interested in foreign trade fell victim to unbridled optimism. Exporters freely granted credits to European importers, as well as to importers in other nations, on open-book accounts. American banks extended liberal credit on the guarantees of European banks. The doctrine that credit standards usually applicable to domestic trade could somehow be disregarded in foreign trade gained wide acceptance.

By reason of heavy expenditures at home and abroad the deficit of the Federal government continued for months after the armistice. The peak of the Federal debt was not reached until August 31, 1919, at which time the short-term debt amounted to $9 billion and the bonded debt to $16 billion. Not until January 1920 was the Treasury able to reduce its floating debt to what it considered manageable proportions. Although the policies adopted had caused a "little inflation," Treasury officials were nevertheless convinced that they could help to readjust business to a peacetime basis and enable men discharged from the armed forces to find employment.

The rise in prices in the spring of 1919 buoyed business sentiment. Firms scrambled for inventories and duplicated orders as they engaged in speculative and protective buying. Commercial banks were caught in the upsurge of optimism and were ready to grant and renew loans freely. Trade credit was readily available. The quality of credit declined.

The book value of inventories rose sharply, reflecting rising prices and larger physical holdings on hand and in transit. Inventories were generally valued on a first-in, first-out (Fifo) basis and consequently conveyed a false impression of profits. A few companies set up inventory reserves, but, as later developments showed, they were grossly inadequate.

The increase in buying by consumers and business firms and the rise in the export trade induced an expansion of plants and equipment. In the case of the railroads this represented deferred replacement, but for other industries it involved mainly additional facilities. The funds needed for this expansion were obtained through the liquidation of government securities, sales of new securities, and bank borrowing.

Farmers, convinced that rising and high farm prices were a permanent phenomenon of an ever-expanding economy, eagerly borrowed to buy additional land and to increase crop yields. The total amount of farm mortgage debt increased from $4.3 billion in 1913 to $8.5 billion in 1920. Non-real estate agricultural loans extended by all operating banks increased in the same period from $1.5 to $3.5 billion.[1] The increase in farm-mortgage loans was particularly sharp in the west north central, east and west south central, and in the mountain states. It was in these areas of farm land speculation and large bank loans that bank failures were particularly severe in the 1920s.

Involvement of the Banking System

From the end of 1918 to mid-1920 loans to all categories of borrowers increased 37 percent and holdings of nongovernment securities 10 percent (see Table 8.1). The rapid increase in loans brought about the sharp rise in deposits. The increase in loans was accompanied by a decline in quality and the rise in deposits by an increase in velocity.

Table 8.1
Total Loans, Investments and Deposits
All Member Banks
(Billions of Dollars)

	December 31, 1918	June 30, 1920	Change Amount	Percent
Total loans	$14.2	$19.5	+5.3	+37
Total investments	6.4	6.0	− .4	− 6
Total loans and investments	$20.6	$25.6	+5.0	+24
Government securities	$ 3.5	$ 2.8	− .7	−20
Other securities	2.9	3.2	+ .3	+10
Total deposits	21.5	25.4	+3.9	+18

Source: *Banking and Monetary Statistics* (Washington, D.C.: Board of Governors of the Federal Reserve System, November 1943), pp. 72–73.

Through those eighteen months member-bank borrowing at Federal Reserve banks increased from $1.8 to $2.5 billion, reaching one of the highest points of all time. On June 30, 1920, member-bank borrowings from the Federal Reserve banks equaled about 10 percent of their total loans and investments. In 1969 figures this would mean borrowings of about $34 billion. The rise in borrowings resulted from a decline of $300 million in the gold stock,* an increase of $200 mil-

---

* Restrictions on gold exports had been removed on June 26, 1919, *Sixth Annual Report of the Federal Reserve Board Covering Operations for the Year 1919* (Washington, D.C.: Government Printing Office, 1920), p. 50.

lion in circulating money, and an increase of $267 million in required reserves (resulting from the rise in deposits).

Short-term interest rates increased sharply: the commercial-paper rate rose from 6 percent in December 1918 to 8.13 percent in July 1920. Standing above the discount rate, these rates induced member banks to use discount facilities freely. Long-term rates also rose but by smaller amounts. The interest curve became negatively inclined.

The decision by the Treasury to float Victory notes at relatively low interest rates forced the Reserve banks to enter into a "gentlemen's agreement" with the commercial banks to carry their subscriptions and their customers' subscriptions to the Victory Loan for six months at rates of interest borne by the obligations. In accordance with this agreement, discount rates remained unchanged until November 1919.† The effective discount rate, applicable to the bulk of borrowing, was that prevailing on war paper.

Table 8.2
Discount Rates, New York Federal Reserve Bank

In Effect	Commercial Paper 16–90 days	Collateral Loans Secured by Certificates of Indebtedness
1919		
January 1,	4.75%	4.00%
November 4	—	4.25
December 12	—	4.50
December 30	—	4.75
1920		
January 23	6.00	—
February 26	—	5.00
June 1	7.00	5.50

The flotation of the Victory notes was accompanied by a sharp rise in holdings of Federal obligations by member banks and in loans secured by these obligations. This increase in credit volume was supported, as already mentioned, by increases in Federal Reserve discounts. In the second half of 1919 war paper held by the commercial banks declined as their commercial and other loans increased.

---

† Elmus R. Wicker has pointed out that an important feature of the Fourth Liberty Loan "was the commitment made by almost all national banks to lend to their bond-purchasing customers at 4¼ percent for ninety days with renewals *at the same rate* for one year." Elmus R. Wicker, *Federal Reserve Monetary Policy, 1917–1933* (New York: Random House, 1966), p. 31.

Relation of Federal Reserve Policy to Inflation

Had the Reserve banks been able to raise their discount rates early in 1919, as a number of System officials desired, inflationary trends would probably have been less. Both the increase in private debt and the decline in quality could have been retarded.

Governor Benjamin Strong of the Federal Reserve Bank of New York, in testimony before the Joint Commission of Agricultural Inquiry, stated that it would have been desirable to have raised discount rates between January and March 1919, a period of price decline in many nations. He also cited the obstacles—the Victory Loan and large government expenditures.[2]

The low rates at which government obligations were issued during World War I inhibited increases in discount rates. A more realistic rate schedule would have eased the transition to normal functioning in the money and capital markets. A sharp rise in discount rates early in 1919, though it would have caused substantial declines in bond prices, would have benefited the economy as a whole by retarding inflation and reducing the severity of the 1920–1921 depression. Costs might have included extensive refunding of the Liberty Loans, the sale of Victory notes at market rates—and congressional recriminations. But they would no doubt have been fully justified in benefits to the economy.

Gustav Cassel, a distinguished Swedish economist of that period, declared that weak American discount policy had postponed the adoption of sound monetary policies in Europe as well. A deflationary policy in the United States, he remarked, would have caused European exchange rates to decline more than they actually did and would have forced earlier adoption of corrective action.[3]

The increase in discount rates in November 1919 marked the beginning of Federal Reserve independence:

> The disappearance of the Treasury from the long-term loan market and the rapid reduction of its requirements for short-term accommodation foreshadows the approach of the time when financial operations of the Government will cease to be the important factor in shaping Reserve Bank policies which they have been, and Federal Reserve Bank rates once more will be fixed solely "with a view of aiding commerce and business." [4]

Unable to increase their discount rates, the Reserve banks relied on various substitutes. They included public warnings, the use of moral suasion, and admonitions to banks to discriminate against speculative and non-essential loans and to ration credit. These measures were ineffective; banks define such terms as essential and non-essential credits in the light of their customers' needs and requirements and their importance as depositors. The Board itself admitted that "warnings were only a transitory expedient and were given only momentary attention by many banks." [5]

As another substitute for overall bank-rate increases, four Federal Reserve banks, under the authority of the Phelan Act, signed by the President on April 13, 1920, established progressive discount rates.[6] The basic purpose of the act, which was discussed in Chapter 4 (pp. 96–97), was to prevent excessive borrowings from the Reserve banks by a few member banks. Mounting political pressures forced abandonment of the progressive rates. Agricultural interests were convinced that the rates penalized rural banks and discriminated against those banks which were endeavoring to alleviate the developing agricultural distress.

The officials of the Reserve System, on the contrary, concluded that progressive rates did prevent a few banks from making excessive use of Federal Reserve facilities and thus improved the distribution of credit. In the post-World War II period various foreign nations and central bankers used such rates as an important anti-inflationary device.

Throughout 1919, certain Federal Reserve banks, whose reserves otherwise would have fallen below the legal minimum, were forced to borrow from other Reserve banks. The borrowing banks were Atlanta, Boston, New York, Philadelphia, Richmond, and Dallas; the lending banks were Cleveland, Chicago, Kansas City, Minneapolis, St. Louis, and San Francisco. Aside from Richmond and Dallas, the borrowing banks, at least those borrowing large amounts, were located in the industrial East. The need to borrow arose from the transfer of Treasury funds to other parts of the country and from the regional credit requirements of business and industrial borrowers.

Funds were obtained from the lending Reserve banks through the sale of acceptances and the rediscounting of eligible paper. The rates on interdistrict rediscounting were fixed by the Board for each transaction as it occurred. In general the Board set the rates higher than those prevailing at the Reserve bank receiving the accommodation.

Had the eastern Reserve banks not borrowed, their ratios of total reserves to combined deposit and Federal Reserve-note liabilities would have fallen below the legal minimum. The reserve ratio of the Boston bank, for example, would have fallen on December 26, 1919, to 24.3 percent; that of the New York bank to 36.2 percent; and that of the Philadelphia bank to 32.7 percent.

The principal restraint on postwar inflation was the 1918 Revenue Act, which became law on February 24, 1919. This act imposed a normal tax of 12 percent on 1918 incomes above $4,000. The combined normal and surtax rates reached as high as 77 percent. The act also imposed an income tax on corporations of 12 percent for 1918 income and 10 percent for subsequent years, as well as a combined excess-profits and war-profits tax.

Rising tax rates, together with a sharp reduction in expenditures, brought about a spectacular change in Federal finances. From a deficit of $13.4 billion in fiscal 1919, the budget moved to a surplus of $300 million in fiscal 1920 (there was no deficit again until fiscal 1931). This turnabout in Federal finances helped to restrain inflation, permitting a reduction in the floating debt and persuading the Treasury that its obligations could and should stand the test of the marketplace. The Federal Reserve had regained its independence.

AFTER WORLD WAR II

Our discussion of post-World War II inflation begins in 1945 and ends in 1951, the year of the accord between the Reserve System and the Treasury. Following World War I the Reserve System won its independence from the Treasury, about a year after the armistice. After World War II it took from six to eight years (see pp. 200-202). Consequently inflationary pressures were much more severe. Both periods gave proof that, in combating inflation in a free market economy, there is no substitute for monetary policy.

Much had to be learned and much endured before monetary policy was revived. The remainder of this chapter attempts to retrace the road back, which not only took many years but which was characterized by a succession of small steps. Looking back from the vantage point of 1970, when interest rates have reached levels not exceeded for 100 years, the slight increase in Federal Reserve discount rates from 1.5 to 1.75 percent in 1950 might seem fairly insignificant. Yet in the context of the period it was an extremely important step toward reassertion of Federal Reserve independence. The System was then engaged, as Allan Sproul stated, "in a public knockdown and dragout fight with the Treasury."[7] In order to understand the essence of this struggle, events are set forth in some detail.

Sources of Demand

The very raipd rise in consumer and wholesale prices (see pp. 175–176) after World War II resulted from an intense demand for goods and services by consumers, business, and state and local governments. Between 1945 and 1951 the consumer sector increased its demand for goods and services (at current prices) from $106 to $189 billion. Its purchases of new and existing homes rose from $7.2 to $24.5 billion.[8] Consumers were able to make these purchases by drawing on current income, by sharply increasing personal and mortgage debt and by equally sharply reducing their rate of savings.

In somewhat similar fashion the corporate sector, by use of cash income, sales of products and services, reductions in holdings of government securities, increases in bank and trade debt, and sales of corporate securities, was able not only to meet operating expenses but also to increase capital expenditures and to build up inventories.

Much the same developments occurred in the nonfarm noncorporate business sector, in the farm sector, and in the state and local government sector. In each instance cash inflow was supplemented by an increase in debt, and in the farm sector also by an actual reduction in financial assets.[9]

Total debt rose nearly 30 percent (see Table 8.3); only Federal debt declined, thanks to excess cash in the government's war-loan accounts and to a large budget surplus of $8.5 billion in fiscal 1948. War-loan accounts were reduced from a post-Victory Loan peak of $26 billion to a basic minimum of $3.3 billion.

Table 8.3
Net Public and Private Debt
(Billions of Dollars)

Year	Federal Government and Agency	State and Local Government	Private Corporate	Private Individual and Noncorporate	Total
1945	$252.7	$13.7	$ 85.3	$ 54.6	$406.3
1951	218.5	23.3	162.5	119.7	524.0

Source: Economic Report of the President. Transmitted to the Congress, January 1967 (Washington, D.C.: Government Printing Office, 1967), p. 278.

Involvement of the Banking System

Bank credit played a very important role in implementing demand. Loans by all insured commercial banks rose about 124 percent (see Table 8.4). Increases were particularly marked in business, real-estate, and consumer loans. A decline in holdings of government securities occurred, but obligations of state and local governments rose.

Table 8.4

Loans and Investment by All Insured Commercial Banks
(Billions of Dollars)

	December 31, 1945	December 31, 1951	Amount of Change	Percentage Change
Loans				
Business loans	$ 9.5	$25.7	+$16.2	+171%
Agricultural loans	1.3	3.3	+ 2.0	+154
Loans for purchasing or carrying securities	6.8	2.5	− 4.3	− 63
Real-estate loans	4.7	14.5	+ 9.8	+208
Consumer loans	1.4	7.7	+ 6.3	+450
Other loans	2.1	4.3	+ 2.2	+105
Total Loans	$25.8	$58.0	+$32.1	+124%
Investments				
U.S. government obligations				
Treasury bills	$ 2.5	$ 7.2	+$ 4.7	+188%
Certificates of indebtedness	19.1	7.5	− 11.6	− 61
Notes	16.0	11.3	− 4.7	− 29
Bonds	51.3	34.5	− 16.8	− 33
	$88.9	$60.5	−$28.4	− 32%
Obligations of state and local governments	3.9	9.0	+ 5.1	+130
Other securities	3.3	4.0	+ .7	+ 21
Total Investments	$96.1	$73.5	−$22.6	− 24%

Source: *Federal Reserve Bulletin* (April 1952), p. 416.

Business loans extended by commercial banks increased rapidly from mid-1945 to the end of 1947. They were stable in 1948, declined in 1949, and increased rapidly again after the outbreak of the Korean war. The sharp increase in business loans in 1946 and 1947 was required to finance increased inventories and receivables at rising prices and to finance expansion in plant and equipment. The rising loan volume aggravated inflationary pressures, causing prices to rise and stimulating further increases in loans. The exceptional volume of liquid assets accumulated by business firms during the war surprisingly did not act as a damper on external business financing, either because of uneven distribution or because of firms' determination to hold liquid assets until the future was more certain.[10]

In 1948 business loans grew relatively little. Businesses financed larger proportions of their capital-expansion programs from retained earnings and securities sales. Programs to encourage restraint in lending, under the leadership of The American Bankers Association and bank-supervisory agencies, may also have helped to limit loan expansion.[11]

The sharp contraction in business loans in 1949, when the first phase of post-war inflation ended, resulted from inventory liquidation, a reduction in other working-capital requirements, and postponement of further capital expenditures. Business paid off large amounts of bank credit with the proceeds of security flotations, including public and private placements.[12]

Business loans began to rise sharply in mid-1950, and continued to rise until the end of 1952, mainly as a result of the effects of the Korean war upon inventories. Defense and defense-related industries were heavy borrowers.

The rise in consumer credit reflected the growing availability of consumers' durable goods, substantial increases in repair and modernization loans, increases in the cost of living (which forced consumers to borrow), and active promotional work by lending institutions. Real-estate credit increased as loans were granted at rising prices to purchase existing houses as well as to build new houses, to refinance morgage debt, and for other purposes. About 40 percent of the loans were extended on new properties, another 40 percent to finance home purchases and the balance for other purposes. About 35 percent of all real-estate loans were underwritten by the federal government. In the case of both consumer and real-estate credit, the amount borrowed reflected not only the underlying economic factors but also a general easing of lending terms (except as tightened on occasion by selective credit regulations).

From the end of 1945 to the end of 1951 loans to farmers increased from about $1.3 billion to more than $3.3 billion, the result of rising prices and machinery purchases. Loans on stocks and bonds fell from $6.8 billion to $2.5 billion (see Table 8.4), due to the termination of wartime speculation in government securities and to changes in margin requirements. Because of their tax-exempt status, obligations of state and political sub-divisions were acquired in large volume.

The Money Supply • The sharp increase in the loans of commercial banks and in purchases of state and local obligations were made possible, to a considerable extent, by the liquidation of a substantial volume of Federal obligations. The balance of the increase, about one-fourth of the total, reflected credit expansion. During the war the active money supply (demand accounts adjusted and currency outside banks) increased $66 billion, in the postwar period $22 billion. In contrast to the sharp war-time increases in both currency and demand deposits, the postwar rise was concentrated in demand deposits (see Table 8.5). The increase in deposit totals was accompanied by a sharp rise in deposit turnover.

Viewed against its relationship, in periods of active business, to GNP the money supply at the end of the war was redundant. The volume of deposits exist-

Table 8.5

The Money Supply
(Billions of Dollars)

Year [a]	Deposit Component	Currency Component	Total
1939	$30	$ 6	$ 36
1945	76	26	102
1951	98	26	124

a. End of year figures.

Source: *Economic Report of the President*. Transmitted to the Congress, January 24, 1956 (Washington, D.C.: Government Printing Office, 1956), p. 215.

ing at that time was sufficiently large to finance a substantial rise in business activity simply by increased use.

In order to moderate price increases after the war, monetary policy should have been directed toward checking increases in total bank credit (possibly even toward bringing about a decline) and toward dissuading financial intermediaries from increasing their total loans and investments by reducing their holdings of government obligations. These objectives could not have been accomplished unless fiscal, debt-management, and monetary policies were coordinated in vigorous action —and united effort was impossible as long as the administration tenaciously refused to allow interest rates to respond to market forces.

Cost Push • When intense demand is backed by ample credit, labor costs rise sharply. Average gross weekly earnings in manufacturing increased from $44.20 in 1945 to $63.34 in 1951. The increase in wages, which would have been even larger had fringe benefits been included, was reflected in a sharp rise in unit labor costs. These developments were quite different from those in 1920–1930, when hourly wages remained steady and unit labor costs fell.[13]

Granted that there can be no sustained increase in prices in the absence of a rise in monetary volume or velocity; nevertheless in an inflationary environment, a rise in unit labor costs (often forced by the monopolistic power of trade unions) can itself cause an increase in prices and raise borrowing needs, which if granted, may cause additional increases in money volume or velocity. Furthermore, wage increases, often granted in anticipation of continuing inflation, are practically irreversible when unemployment is politically unacceptable.

Demand pull and cost push are closely intertwined causes of inflation. Demand pull is basic, made effective by a plentiful supply of money and credit, with cost push playing a subsidiary but by no means unimportant role. Only by moderating the pressure of monetary demand can the threat of an inflationary wage push be removed.

Tax Policy

The administration was well aware of the need to combat postwar inflation and was convinced that it could do so most successfully by relying on tax policy. The use of the interest rate, it feared, might undermine the "credit" of the government and increase the difficulties of debt management. The administration's tax program was much more conservative in the early postwar period than was that of Congress. The administration wished to continue tax rates; Congress to reduce them. But after the outbreak of the Korean war both agreed that taxes should be sharply increased.

Secretary of the Treasury Fred R. Vinson, in appearances before congressional committees in October 1945, recommended limited tax reductions in order to ease the transition from wartime conditions to a peacetime economy. Going beyond his recommendation, the Revenue Act of 1945 reduced tax liabilities for calendar years 1946 and 1947 by nearly $6 billion annually.[14] It did this by repealing the excess-profits tax, reducing the corporate surtax rates, reducing individual income-tax rates, granting certain benefits to members of the armed forces, and postponing increased taxes for old-age and survivors' insurance.[15]

A bill passed by Congress in 1947 would have reduced individual income-tax liabilities an additional $3–5 billion. This legislation was vigorously opposed by Secretary of the Treasury John W. Snyder, who recommended that surplus revenues not be decreased but be used to reduce the public debt. The bill was therefore vetoed by President Harry S. Truman, who noted that it provided for the wrong type of tax reduction at the wrong time.[16]

Not to be thwarted, in March 1948 Congress passed a bill effecting substantial increases in per capita exemptions and reductions in individual income-tax rates and providing for income splitting by married couples. President Truman vetoed this bill on the ground that to reduce government income by $5 billion exhibited "reckless disregard for the soundness of our economy and the finances of our Government." [17] The bill was passed over the President's veto on April 2, 1948.

Continued inflationary pressures induced President Truman in his budget message of January 3, 1949, to recommend new tax legislation to raise additional revenues of $4 billion:

> In a period of high prosperity, it is not sound public policy for
> the Government to operate at a deficit. A Government surplus at
> this time is vitally important to provide a margin for contingen-
> cies, to permit reduction of the public debt, to provide an ade-
> quate base for future financing of our present commitments, and
> to reduce inflationary pressures.[18]

Whether because of inertia or because of active opposition, Congress did not
adopt these recommendations but yielded to heavy public pressure opposing tax increases.

On July 11, 1950, in the midst of discussions of an important tax revision
bill that had been passed by the House of Representatives, the Senate Committee
on Finance suspended its inquiry upon the recommendation of the Secretary of the
Treasury. The President was now ready to propose tax increases rather than tax revisions because of the outbreak of the Korean war. The resulting legislation is discussed in Chapter 7.

From a deficit of $42.1 billion in the national-income accounts in calendar
year 1945 the Federal government moved into a surplus of $3.5 billion in 1946.
This dramatic turnabout had resulted from a very sharp decline in expenditures
and a small decline in receipts. From the beginning of 1946 to the end of 1951
the Federal government enjoyed a surplus of $38.2 billion on national-income ac-
counts. The surplus might well have been much larger had Congress not overrid-
den the President's tax veto in 1948, but it was nevertheless an extremely important anti-inflationary weapon. Its effectiveness was enhanced by the increasing
importance of the personal income, employment, and excise taxes and the decreasing importance of corporation taxes in total tax receipts. Large as the Federal
surplus on national-income accounts was, however, it was not large enough to
counteract the inflationary consequences of private debt increase, stimulated by the
easy-money policy of the Reserve System.

Debt Management and Inflation

The size, maturity, and ownership distribution of the Federal debt (see Table
8.6) are potent weapons for influencing the credit policies of commercial banks
and financial intermediaries and for combating either inflationary or deflationary
developments. Equating yields on government obligations with the credit standing
of the government itself, the Treasury insisted that the yields on government
bonds remain substantially unchanged. In the early postwar years this point of
view was supported by the Reserve System. Not until 1951 did the System insist

Table 8.6

Ownership of Federal Securities, by Classes of Investor
(Billions of Dollars)

	February 28, 1946	June 30, 1947	June 30, 1948	December 31, 1951	Change, 1946–1951
Nonbank investors					
Individuals	$ 63.9	$ 66.2	$ 65.5	$ 64.6	+$ .7
Others					
Insurance companies	24.4	24.6	22.8	16.3	− 8.1
Mutual-savings banks	11.1	12.1	12.0	9.8	− 1.3
Corporations	19.9	13.9	13.5	20.8	+ .9
State and local governments	6.7	7.1	7.8	9.5	+ 2.8
Miscellaneous investors	9.1	9.8	9.1	11.0	+ 1.9
US government accounts	28.0	32.8	35.8	42.3	+ 14.3
Total	$163.1	$166.5	$166.5	$174.3	+$11.2
Banks					
Commercial banks	$ 93.8	$ 70.0	$ 64.6	$ 61.4	−$32.4
Federal Reserve banks	22.9	21.9	21.4	23.8	+ .9
Total	$116.7	$ 91.9	$ 86.0	$ 85.2	−$31.5
Total interest-bearing debt	$279.8	$258.4	$252.5	$259.5	−$20.3

Source: *Treasury Bulletin* (April 1952), p. 33.

that it be freed from responsibility for keeping bond prices at or above par, a responsibility that made it impotent to check inflationary developments.

Had it not been for this policy the maturity of the debt could probably have been extended, the floating debt substantially reduced, the liquidity of commercial banks and financial intermediaries sharply curtailed, and the decline in the average maturity of the debt checked. (Even the 4.25 percent coupon limitation on bonds would probably have proved no barrier to an extension of the debt in this period, considering the initial low level of long-term rates.) The Treasury, however, was not willing to use debt management as an active positive tool in arresting the rapid erosion of dollar purchasing power.

Public debt-management policies from 1946 to 1951 may be divided into three phases. The first comprised the sixteen months from February 28, 1946 (when total Federal debt reached its postwar peak), to June 30, 1947. The sharp reduction in total debt resulted from use of the excess cash in the government war-loan accounts. This was drawn upon to retire short-term debt largely held by commercial banks. Their holdings of bonds actually rose. This reduction in government-debt holdings by commercial banks exceeded the decline in the total

Federal debt, which was made possible by an increase in the debt held by the investment accounts of the government.

The second phase covered the twelve months from June 30, 1947, to June 30, 1948. The funds used for debt retirement resulted from a budgetary surplus of about $8.5 billion, which was used first to retire debt held by the Reserve banks. As this action would have caused a sharp increase in member-bank borrowing unless offset, the Reserve banks purchased securities in amounts equal to those retired. These securities, principally long-term bonds, were acquired from commercial banks, insurance companies, and other nonbank investors. The open-market operations of the Reserve banks thus held net free reserves of commercial banks to a substantial figure and enabled the commercial banks—and indirectly financial intermediaries—to meet a large demand for loans.

The third phase covered the thirty months from June 30, 1948, to December 31, 1951, a period marked by the slight recession of 1949 and the beginning of the Korean war. The public debt, instead of declining as it had in previous periods, rose $7.0 billion. Table 8.6 shows that nonbank holdings of the debt rose $7.8 billion. The rise was sufficiently large not only to finance the deficit but also to absorb an aggregate reduction in debt by the commercial and Federal Reserve banks of about $1 billion. Commercial banks reduced their debt holdings $3.2 billion, and the Reserve banks increased theirs $2.4 billion. Inverse fluctuations in holdings of government obligations by the commercial banks and the Federal Reserve banks reflected the changes which were ordered in member-bank reserve requirements. An increase in these requirements caused the Reserve System to purchase government securities in order to maintain the existing interest rate structure. Government obligations passed from ownership by member banks to ownership by Reserve banks. An increase in reserve requirements in this period therefore had the effect of reducing interest-bearing assets (government obligations) on the books of member banks and of increasing non-interest-bearing assets (deposits due from the Reserve banks). In this way purchases of government obligations by the Reserve banks kept net free reserves at a figure that supported the interest structure and permitted member banks to increase their loan portfolios substantially. The initiative for open-market operations in reality passed from the Reserve System to member banks.

As it was, changes in the total debt and in the ownership distribution of the debt did exert rather slight anti-inflationary pressure. The huge cash holdings at the end of the war, along with the large budget surplus of 1948 slightly reduced the liquidity of commercial banks. The flow of savings into government trust accounts exceeded the sale of obligations by insurance companies and mutual savings banks.

Much more could have been accomplished had the Treasury been willing to institute vigorous policies aimed at further reduction of the floating debt and at the extension of debt maturities. Obviously such policies would have entailed substantial price declines in outstanding marketable issues. No government, however, is legally or morally obligated to peg the prices of coupon obligations. The small investor was protected against price declines by his ownership of redemption obligations, but he had no protection against the rapid erosion of his purchasing power. So rapid was this erosion that a redemption obligation purchased in 1941 had by 1951 brought no interest return but had actually lost about 25 percent of the value of its principal. Better an increase in interest costs on the debt than a decline in the purchasing power of money!

Squirming in the Straitjacket

In March of 1951, the Federal Reserve System acting in accord with the Treasury, made a decisive break away from the pattern of support for Government security prices that had limited the effectiveness of policies of credit restraint during the postwar period. This was the culmination of a series of steps beginning in 1946, which had brought about a gradual unfreezing of the wartime pattern of supported prices and interest rates on Government securities. . . . So long as rigid support for Government securities had continued, the initiative for reserve creation rested almost wholly with holders of Government securities who chose to sell. In the face of intensifying demands for credit in the private sector of the economy, this meant that sellers of Government securities to the Federal Reserve could obtain funds practically without limit for use in satisfying other borrowing demands. The resulting monetization of the Goverment debt also provided new bank reserves, which served as a base for a further possible multiple-credit expansion.[19]

The transition to freer markets, explained the Reserve bank, had to be made cautiously. Investors in government securities had become conditioned to markets that held prices at or above par, and a sharp decline might prove a shock to the market.

The year 1946 brought the elimination (between April 25 and May 10) of the preferential rate of .5 percent per annum on advances to member banks secured by U.S. obligations running one year or less. The discount rate became 1 percent per annum. Abandonment of the preferential rate was quickly followed by increases in the buying rates on acceptances (July–August 1946). Other changes included an increase in securities-loan margin requirements and a revision of Regulation W (on consumer credit), for the purpose of simplifying procedures, making them uniform and administratively more workable, and preventing abuses in the use of consumer credit.

In making these various changes the Board stated clearly that it did not "favor a higher level of interest rates on U.S. securities than the Government is now paying." [20] Actually, however, these steps, though ineffective in checking inflation at the time, were the first in a long series that eventually freed the money and capital markets from government control.

The most important action taken in 1947 was the discontinuation of the posted rate ($\frac{3}{8}$ of 1 percent) on all Treasury bills issued on or after the 10th of July. The Reserve System explained that this step, taken after consultation with the Secretary of the Treasury, would end a wartime procedure that was no longer required. This agreement by the Treasury had come only after the Reserve System agreed in its turn to hand over 90 percent of its net earnings to the Treasury (see pp. 113–114). The Treasury-bill rate then began to find its level in the market, and by the end of the year it had risen to nearly 1 percent.

Even though short-term interest rates could not be completely free while long-term rates were pegged, this action, marking the first break in the wartime pattern of rates which had existed since 1942, was extremely significant. In introducing a degree of flexibility into the short-term market, it engendered some uncertainty over the future of the whole rate structure. Consistent with this step, the maturities of newly offered Treasury certificates were shortened in August and September, and higher rates were placed on new issues.

Support of the Bond Market • Following the end of the Victory Loan campaign, the prices of long-term bank-restricted government bonds had begun to rise sharply. Demand was stimulated by the knowledge that no new large offerings of government bonds were imminent and that new bond issues by other borrowers could not begin to fill the gap. By April 1946 the bull market in bonds had run its course. This resulted in part by sales of marketable government bonds from the Treasury's investment accounts and by a reduction in Treasury bonds held by the Reserve System. Market yields began to rise, but nevertheless government bond prices still remained well above par.

In the last quarter of 1947 money-market uncertainties, brought about by the rise in short-term rates coupled with growing demand for funds, caused corporate and municipal bond yields to rise. Commercial banks and savings institutions began to sell bonds to meet loan demands. In the absence of other buyers the Reserve

System and the Treasury (using its trust funds) found it necessary to purchase large amounts of government bonds. In many instances the sellers then purchased Treasury bills. The Reserve System's holdings of short-term government paper fell as its holdings of long-term obligations rose. The market had begun to "play the pattern of rates" in reverse.

In November and December 1947 the Federal Reserve and the Treasury, in order to maintain the fixed rate structure, were compelled to support the market prices of government bonds at a level considerably above par. The Federal Reserve became a "reluctant buyer," purchasing only those securities that could not find a market elsewhere even after earnest efforts. A large backlog of unsold government securities accumulated. In order to overcome this reluctance, at least one dealer sold government bonds on the New York Stock Exchange rather than on the over-the-counter market, thus forcing the Reserve banks to buy them. Otherwise the sale price would have fallen below the pegged level, and the new price would have been a matter of public record.

On December 24, 1947, the Reserve System reduced its buying price on Victory bonds to 100.25 and made comparable reductions in its buying prices for other obligations. The issues that had sold at substantial premiums reflected the sharpest declines. No issue was permitted to fall below par, however. Yields were restored to their 1944 levels, those that had existed before heavy purchases of long-term bonds by commercial banks.

The dropping of the pegs caused a deluge of sales, which compelled the Reserve System to purchase $8.1 billion of bonds through 1948, in order to maintain the new pegs. In the same period it sold $7.3 billion of short-term securities, as the market continued to play the curve in reverse. The net release of total Federal Reserve credit was held to $900 million.

The measures taken by the Reserve System in the short- and long-term money markets in 1947 were the first cautious steps towards an independent credit policy. The abandonment of rigid pegs in the short-term market was particularly significant. Investors began to question the immutability of the curve. When the prices of long-term bonds were finally permitted to decline, investors became convinced that the curve was indeed subject to change.

In the early postwar years the Reserve System reiterated that it lacked sufficient power to combat inflationary pressures, although, of course, it possessed ample weapons to combat deflation. Federal Reserve support for the government-securities markets precluded effective use of open-market operations.

Some of the measures that the System sought as substitutes for effective open-market operations were; first, the power to vary within wider limits the level of primary reserves; second, the authority to relate reserve requirements to types of deposits; third, the establishment of a secondary-reserve requirement, which could be adjusted to changing conditions; and, fourth, legislation permitting the Reserve Board to exercise permanent control over consumer credit. As these proposals were studied, it became apparent that there was no substitute for freely functioning money and capital markets that could, through interest-rate changes, equalize the supply and demand of funds uninfluenced by support policies of the central bank.

Even though the Reserve System was not given the powers it sought, inflationary pressures abated somewhat in 1948 and considerably in 1949. Consumer prices rose at a slower rate in 1948 and actually fell in 1949. Wholesale prices reached a peak in August 1948 and then began a decline that continued until April 1950, when private and government demand resulting from the Korean war provoked a rapid increase.

In the first nine months of 1948, when inflationary pressures were still operating, the Federal Reserve System relied upon modest increases in rates on Treasury bills and certificates, modest increases in discount rates, a slight rise in the minimum buying rates on bankers' acceptances, and an increase in member-bank reserve requirements. It continued to support government bond prices above par.

The rise in short-term rates, along with the rise from 1 to 1.25 percent in the discount rate between January 12 and 19 and to 1.5 percent between August 13 and 23, 1948, probably exerted a slight though not measurable restraint on consumer and business intentions.

Reserve requirements were raised to the highest levels that have ever prevailed in the Federal Reserve System. Through 1948, the increase in required reserves amounted to $2.3 billion (see Table 3.4), financed principally by a $700 million increase in the Reserve System's open-market portfolio, by a rise of $1.5 billion in the gold stock, and by an increase in member-bank borrowings of $140 million. In order to meet the new requirements, while continuing to extend loans and to acquire short-term government securities, commercial banks reduced their holdings of government bonds. The portfolios of the Reserve banks mirrored these developments; bond holdings increased and short-term government securities decreased. Member-bank borrowings remained at fairly low levels and excess reserves at high levels. The pegged market, requiring the purchase of securities by the Reserve banks, negated the restrictive effects of the increases in reserve requirements.

Upon the urgent recommendation of the Board of Governors, the Council of

Economic Advisers and President Truman, the Congress by joint resolution authorized the Board, on August 16, 1948, to reinstate consumer-credit controls until June 30, 1949. The Board's earlier powers of control had been terminated on November 1, 1947.

Action in Recession of 1949 • "Throughout the year 1949, the general and selective instruments available to the Federal Reserve authorities were coordinated in a flexible program for adjusting the availability and cost of credit to the changing needs of the economy." [21] The Board of Governors shifted the emphasis of its credit policy from restraint to ease, including sharp reductions in member-bank reserve requirements, which from May 1 to September 1 released $3.8 billion (see Table 3.4). Member banks quickly invested the released funds in government obligations. To prevent sharp price increases and disorder, the Reserve System sold Treasury bills and certificates on the market. The Treasury also cooperated by increasing its weekly offerings of bills, as a means of financing the deficit. Through 1949 commercial banks increased their holdings of government obligations $4.4 billion, and the Reserve banks reduced their holdings an equal amount.

The moderation of consumer buying pressures caused the Board to relax instalment-credit terms effective March 7 and again on April 27. The Board's temporary authority which ended on June 30, 1949, was followed by a further easing of market terms and a sharp increase in total instalment credit, resulting not only from a continued rapid rise in automobile sales but also from smaller down payments and longer maturities. By the end of the year total instalment credit had reached the record-breaking total of $11 billion. Beginning in March 1949 the Board eased the regulations governing the use of credit in the securities market. Margin requirements were reduced from 75 to 50 percent effective March 30. Customers' debt balances then increased, and public participation in the stock market rose.

The discount rate had not been lowered in 1949, despite requests by the Federal Reserve Bank of New York on three separate occasions between September 15 and October 6 that it be permitted to do so. Decision was deferred by the Board until October 10, when the request was finally rejected. Britain's devaluation of the pound on September 21, as well as an upturn in general economic activity, had dissuaded the Board from giving its approval. The recession was over; and, even if it had not been, the discount rate already stood at a low level.

The recession of 1949, which had begun in November 1948, had run its course by October 1949. The economic environment then changed dramatically, and inflationary pressures once again challenged credit and monetary policy. The Reserve System had acted swiftly to counter the business decline, shifting the emphasis of credit policy from restraint to ease. From the beginning to the end of 1949, the Treasury-bill rate had declined from 1.160 to 1.097; the yield on seven-to nine-year government-taxable bonds from 1.88 to 1.68; and that on government-taxable bonds with maturities of fifteen years or more from 2.42 to 2.19. The Reserve System thus undertook to maintain "orderly conditions" in the government-securities markets and to avoid unnecessarily sharp temporary declines in interest rates. Beginning in November 1949 the Federal Open Market Committee authorized the purchase and sale of bills and certificates at somewhat lower prices in order to increase yields. The System had begun to initiate a policy of mild restraint.

FREED BY THE KOREAN WAR

The 1951 *Annual Report* of the Federal Reserve Bank of New York pointed out that the Korean War had begun (June 1950) when the economy had already fully recovered from the minor recession of 1949 and was operating close to capacity.[22] Remembering the shortages of goods during World War II, individuals, businesses and even the government began a competitive scramble for available supplies—concentrated at the beginning of the war (June 25, 1950) and again at the time of Chinese intervention (November 26, 1950). These upsurges in demand provoked immediate responses in prices. All price indexes rose sharply during the second half of 1950, to level off or even to decline in 1951.

The Treasury Department wished to finance the Korean war at stable, low interest rates. The Federal Reserve System, in view of the inflationary pressures in 1950 and uncertainties about the duration and scope of the war, wished to avoid freezing the interest curve. This disagreement was the basis of conflict, which finally ended in a victory for the Reserve System.

The administration believed that inflationary pressures could be checked by employing selective credit controls, by increasing member-bank reserve requirements and by financing war costs from current tax revenues. These measures, it believed, would have to be supplemented by wage and price controls and the use of priorities and allocations in order to promote the most effective use of scarce materials. Reliance on such measures would presumably avoid an increase in interest rates.

Consumer-credit controls, imposed by Regulation W under the Defense Production Act, soon encountered strong political opposition. They were in force from September 8, 1950, to May 7, 1952, but were then suspended and have never been renewed. The controls imposed by the Board of Governors had the effect of increasing down payments and shortening instalment-loan maturities. The Board was credited with checking the advance in instalment credit during the final months of 1950 and with causing a decline in the first half of 1951. Once the controls were removed the total volume of instalment credit rose sharply. It was the very effectiveness of those controls that had caused their suspension.

Regulation X, which represented the first attempt anywhere to restrain inflationary pressures through a comprehensive control of mortgage-lending terms, was issued on October 12, 1950, also under the Defense Production Act. The Board of Governors was given authority to prescribe maximum amounts which could be borrowed, maximum maturities, and minimum amortization schedules for conventional mortgages. These restrictions were dovetailed with those imposed on Federal Housing Administration and Veterans Administration mortgages.

Subject to persistent congressional attack and modification, Regulation X was finally suspended on September 16, 1952, at the very time when, according to many students, it was proving most effective. The Federal Reserve System favored Regulation X by reason of its inability, in view of the pegged bond market, to exercise general credit control and because of the increase in real-estate mortgages held by the commercial banks and the effect of this increase on the money supply.

As still another effort to check inflation and at the same time avoid increases in interest rates, the administration instituted a voluntary credit-restraint program, under Section 708 of the Defense Production Act. The purpose of the program was to encourage financial institutions to enter into voluntary agreements to channel loans into essential defense purposes and to curtail nonessential credit.

A vast organization, consisting of a national committee and forty-three regional committees, was established; it issued innumerable bulletins for the guidance of lending officers. The program came to a sudden end when President Truman, in order to permit states to issue soldiers' bonus bonds (clearly a nonessential use of credit) exempted all state and local issues from its control in March 1952. The administrators, who had devoted countless hours of dedicated work, returned to their respective business in great resentment and frustration. Although it is quite impossible to evaluate precisely the effectiveness of the program, its impact on the economy was probably minor. To be effective, programs of this character must be reinforced by vigorous monetary and fiscal policies—and if such rigorous policies exist the voluntary programs are not required.

The rapid increase in stock prices through 1950, accompanied by a sharp rise in customers' debit balances, caused the Board of Governors to increase margin requirements from 50 to 75 percent of market value, under Regulations T and U, effective on January 17, 1951. This action was given credit for checking the advance in stock-market credit. With its mission accomplished, margin requirements were reduced to their former levels effective February 20, 1953.

Except for stock-market credit, selective credit controls encountered devastating opposition from various interests. Controls over stock-market credit seemed immune, probably because the individuals and institutions associated with Wall Street had less political weight and because countering securities speculation seemed desirable.

Selective credit controls, even though they prove effective in certain homogeneous areas of credit, cannot be applied, either voluntarily or otherwise, to the heterogeneous business loans of commercial banks. In this sphere general credit controls are indispensable. It was with this thought in mind that the Reserve System, reinforced as it was by the knowledge that the effects of increases in member-bank reserve requirements are completely negated by a pegged interest curve, decided to challenge the Treasury. The effect of the increase in member-bank reserve requirements early in 1951, the principal factor in bringing about a rise in required reserves of $2 billion during the first quarter, had been offset by a nearly equivalent increase in the open-market portfolio of the Reserve System.

As an initial effort to escape the interest straitjacket, the Board approved on August 18, 1950 an increase from 1.5 to 1.75 percent (effective August 21) in the rate on discounts and advances at the Federal Reserve Bank of New York. Within a few days all the Reserve banks had followed suit.

The action was taken, the Board explained, because of "excessive" expansion in loans and holdings of corporate and municipal securities by member banks. The psychological impact of this step was weakened by an accompanying statement that the Board and the Federal Open Market Committee would use all means at their command "to restrain further expansion of bank credit consistent with the policy of maintaining orderly conditions in the Government securities market." [23]

The Reserve System itself has never defined "orderly conditions" in the government-securities market. Various suggestions have included absence of erratic price fluctuations, establishment of general support points, and temporary stabilization of the prices of new issues.

Secretary Snyder once defined a stable long-term government bond market as one in which prices and yields fluctuate within a moderate range over a considerable period without exhibiting any pronounced upward or downward trend. He added that he did not mean a pegged market but did have in mind the type of market that had existed from the time of the Japanese surrender to the beginning of the Korean war. How Secretary Snyder could have viewed this market as one which was not pegged is an unexplained mystery.[24]

Conflict with the Treasury

The increase in the discount rate was instituted without consultation with the Treasury. Indeed the conflict between the two bodies had reached a point at which there was no longer consultation at either staff or executive levels. After the decision had been reached, the Board informed the Treasury of its action on Friday afternoon, August 18. The Treasury, viewing the increase as a *fait accompli*, made no public comment.[25] But it immediately announced the terms of its September–October 1950 refunding. For the $13.6 billion of maturing government obligations, it offered to exchange thirteen-month notes, at 1.25 percent interest, which was slightly under the market rates prevailing before the Reserve System's decision. The interest rate and maturity of these obligations were the same as in the May–June 1950 refunding.

The inconsistency between the actions of the Federal Reserve System and the Treasury Department was apparent to all, and it was clear that the former would have to support the refunding operation to prevent massive attrition.

The Reserve System could not reverse its action. At the time of the Treasury's announcement it held $2.4 billion of the maturing issues. To prevent an overwhelming rejection of the Treasury offering, it purchased an additional $8 billion worth, raising its total holdings to $10.4 billion. It exchanged the entire amount for the new issue, which left $3.2 billion of the maturing issues with other holders ($800 million were exchanged, and $2.4 billion were redeemed for cash). The amount exchanged by the Federal Reserve System amounted to about 77 percent of the maturing issues and that exchanged by other holders to 6 percent.[26]

As the Reserve System purchased the maturing issues, it sold Treasury bills, certificates of indebtedness, and Treasury notes at yields in line with the action taken with respect to the discount rate. Consequently the net increase in holdings of government securities was held to $1.2 billion, and the effect upon member-bank reserves was softened somewhat by a decline in the gold stock and an increase in circulating money.

The Treasury returned to the market in November 1950 to refund $8 billion of securities maturing in December and January. On the advice of Federal Reserve authorities, a five-year 1.75 percent note was offered in exchange. The Reserve System was compelled to purchase $2.7 billion of rights, only partly offset by sales of $1.3 billion of Treasury notes due in 1951. These purchases released Federal Reserve funds to the market—directly contrary to the System's policy objectives.

The conflict had to be resolved. The future of the Reserve System was at stake. Was it to be simply a subdepartment of the Treasury, subject to rigorous control? Or was it to be in fact, as it was in law, an independent agency within, but not of the government. Should the government adjust its debt-management policies to credit action by the Reserve System?

The Accord • No Treasury securities were scheduled to mature in the first five months of 1951, and it was during this "open" period that the Reserve System forced the Treasury to enter into an accord. Throughout January and February, speeches, interviews, charges, and countercharges followed in quick succession until finally accommodation was reached. During the discussions Secretary Snyder fell ill, and it was suggested that the discussions be postponed until his recovery. But members of the Federal Open Market Committee made it clear that, though they were distressed by the Secretary's illness, the question of future Federal Reserve and Treasury relations could not be postponed. As President Sproul stated:

> The pressures were too great. We were being forced to put large amounts of reserve funds into the market each day in support of the longest-term Government bonds at premium prices, a policy which we considered to be profoundly wrong. Inflationary pressures were again strong. We said, therefore, that unless there was someone at the Treasury who could work out a prompt and definite agreement with us as to a mutually satisfactory course of action, we would have to take unilateral action.[27]

An ultimatum had been issued. The Board of Governors had considerable support in Congress and was thus freed of its wartime subservience to the Treasury.

On March 4, 1951 Secretary Snyder and the Chairman of the Board of Governors, Thomas B. McCabe, announced that they had reached full accord on debt-management and monetary policies for financing government requirements and minimizing public-debt monetization.

There were several terms. First, in view of the large volume of 2.5 percent long-term bonds in the market, the Treasury would offer to exchange a nonmarketable 2.75 percent twenty-year bond redeemable at the holder's option before maturity only by conversion into a five-year marketable Treasury note. The purpose of this provision was to discourage the liquidation of Treasury bonds maturing in

1967–1972, as well as their monetization through the support operations of the Federal Reserve System.

Second, the Federal Reserve System agreed to purchase limited amounts of long-term government obligations should private holders begin to sell them once the terms of the accord had been announced. If sales proved to be excessive, open-market purchases would be made on a scaledown of prices.

Third, the Federal Reserve System agreed to maintain its discount rate at 1.75 percent for the remainder of the year and to conduct its open-market operations in a manner that would assure satisfactory refunding of maturing Treasury issues. It was agreed that the Federal Reserve System would immediately reduce or discontinue purchases of short-term securities and would permit the short-term market to adjust to a position at which banks would depend upon borrowing from the Reserve banks to adjust their own reserves. This policy assumed a level of short-term interest rates that would fluctuate, in response to market forces, around the Federal Reserve discount rate.

Finally, it was agreed that more frequent conferences between Treasury and Federal officials and staff would be held so that closer collaboration on government financing might be achieved.

On April 2, 1951, William McChesney Martin, Jr. succeeded Mr. McCabe as Chairman of the Board of Governors of the Federal Reserve System, a post which he was to hold until January 31, 1970. In taking his oath of office Chairman Martin stated that he believed in a "strong, vigorous, independent, and responsible Federal Reserve System."[28]

The exchange operations removed $13.6 billion (of a total of $19.7 billion) of the bank-restricted bonds maturing in 1967–1972 from the market. Until the exchange had been effected the Reserve System continued its support operations, but at declining prices. Once the exchange was completed, moderate purchases sufficed to prevent disorderly conditions in the market. After June 1951 the Reserve System purchased practically no long-term bonds. Prices broke par in April and fluctuated around 97 during the latter half of the year. The breaking of par may not seem particularly significant now, but then it was a momentous development. Not since the Great Depression had any long-term government bond broken or been allowed to fall below par.

Beginning in March the Reserve System withdrew its support from the market for short-term government securities. Short-term rates were thereafter determined by market forces except for support at times of Treasury refunding or seasonal strain. Member banks began to make greater use of the discount window.

Federal Reserve Independence

Despite the accord, the Reserve System was not entirely free. It had agreed not to raise its discount rate through 1951. Actually, the rate was not increased until January 16, 1953, when it was raised to 2 percent at most of the Reserve banks.* The System also had agreed to maintain "orderly conditions" in the government securities market. Not until March 5, 1953, did the Federal Open Market Committee change this policy to one of "correcting a disorderly situation in the Government security market." This change in wording, in a directive issued on March 5, 1953, was extremely important. It meant that the Federal Reserve would intervene in the market not to foster "orderly conditions," however these might be defined, but simply to prevent "disorderly conditions," the type of situation, for example, which existed at the outbreak of World War II. The directive included several instructions. It stated that, first, under current conditions operations in the System account should be confined to the "short end" of the curve (not including correction of disorderly markets). This provision was the basis of the "Treasury bills only" policy. Second, the policy of the Federal Open Market Committee is not to support any pattern of prices and yields in the government securities market and intervention is solely to effectuate the objectives of monetary and credit policy. Third, the Committee will refrain, during periods of Treasury financing, from the practice that has been followed on previous occasions of purchasing any maturing issues for which an exchange is being offered, when-issued securities, and outstanding securities of maturities comparable to those offered for exchange.[29]

Two years after the accord, the Federal Reserve System was thus free of Treasury domination. In its quest for independence the accord had been the indispensable step.†

A FINAL NOTE

The inability of the Reserve banks to exercise general credit control contributed to the inflation that beset the American economy after World Wars I and II. Reliance upon general credit controls is evinced by an increase in net borrowed reserves, which must at times be very sharp to be effective, and by an increase in all interest rates, including the discount rate. Once such a policy is instituted, increases in member-bank reserve requirements prove effective and the effectiveness

---

* Late in 1951 and throughout 1952 Reserve policy was to force member banks into debt and force increases in open-market rates, even though the discount rate was not raised.

† This independence was again curtailed with the adoption of Operation Twist (see Chapter 15 and the discussion of even keel, p. 123).

of selective credit controls, were they to be employed, is increased. Tardiness in permitting Reserve banks to institute general credit controls after World War II is illustrated by the infrequent and small increases in discount rates in that period (see Table 8.7).

Table 8.7
Changes in Discount Rates, New York Federal Reserve Bank

April 6, 1946	.50% to 1.00%
January 12, 1948	1.00% to 1.25%
August 13, 1948	1.25% to 1.50%
August 21, 1950	1.50% to 1.75%
January 16, 1953	1.75% to 2.00%

Source: *Federal Reserve Bulletin.*

The problems besetting the Federal Reserve System from the end of World War II to the accord with the Treasury in 1951 were a legacy of the monetary policies adopted in the war. Gradually the conviction grew in the United States and abroad that—if the price mechanism were to regain its historic role, if savings were to be stimulated, if the interest rate were to channel credit and savings into the most productive uses, if cost analysis were once again to control business decisions, and if production were to be directed toward consumer preferences—free-market economies would have to be restored. Restoration required liquidation of price and foreign-exchange controls, the end of inflation, stabilization of currencies, freeing of interest rates, balancing of government budgets, elimination of "indexation" (tying wages, interest rates, and the like to price changes), termination of subsidies, and elimination of deficits in nationalized industries. Where market economies were restored early, as in Belgium, West Germany, and Italy, recovery was greatly accelerated. Where restoration was delayed, as in the Netherlands, Scandinavia, and the United Kingdom, recovery was slower, and economic stagnation resulted.

The Subcommittee on General Credit Control and Debt Management of the Joint Committee on the Economic Report, after studying this period with care, arrived at the following recommendations, which provide a fitting conclusion to this chapter:

We recommend that an appropriate, flexible and vigorous monetary policy, employed in coordination with fiscal and other policies, should be one of the principal methods used to achieve the purposes of the Employment Act [of 1946]. Timely flexibility toward easy credit at some times and credit restriction at other times is an essential characteristic of a monetary policy that will promote economic stability rather than instability. The vigorous use of a restrictive monetary policy as an anti-inflation measure has been inhibited since the war by considerations relating to holding down the yields and supporting the prices of United States Government securities. As a long-run matter, we favor interest rates as low as they can be without inducing inflation, for low interest rates stimulate capital investment. But we believe that the advantages of avoiding inflation are so great and that a restrictive monetary policy can contribute so much to this end that the freedom of the Federal Reserve to restrict credit and raise interest rates for general stabilization purposes should be restored even if the cost should prove to be a significant increase in service charges on the Federal debt and a greater inconvenience to the Treasury in its sale of securities for new financing and refunding purposes.[30]

Notes

1. *The Statistical History of the United States from Colonial Times to the Present* (Stamford, Conn.: Fairfield Publishers, Inc., 1965), pp. 286–287.

2. *Agricultural Inquiry,* Hearing before the Joint Commission on Agricultural Inquiry, 66th Cong., 1st sess. under Senate Concurrent Resolution 4. Par. 13 (Washington, D.C.: Government Printing Office, 1921), pp. 763–764.

3. Gustav Cassel, *Money and Foreign Exchange after 1914* (New York: The MacMillan Company, 1923), p. 199.

4. *Federal Reserve Bulletin* (October 1919), p. 910. Because of the improvement in its position, the Treasury withdrew its opposition to an increase in discount rates.

5. *Seventh Annual Report of the Federal Reserve Board Covering Operations for the Year 1920* (Washington, D.C.: Government Printing Office, 1921), p. 12.

6. B. H. Beckhart, *The Discount Policy of the Federal Reserve System* (New York: Holt, 1924), pp. 304–310.

7. Allan Sproul, *Address to the Mid-Winter Meeting of the New York State Bankers' Association,* January 25, 1954 (mimeographed), p. 5.

8. *Flow of Funds in the United States 1939–1953* (Washington, D.C.: Board of Governors of the Federal Reserve System, December 1955), p. 73.

9. *Ibid.,* pp. 104, 115 and 160.

10. *Thirty-Third Annual Report of the Board of Governors of the Federal Reserve System Covering Operations for the Year 1946* (Washington, D.C.: June 17, 1947), p. 18.

11. *Thirty-Fifth Annual Report of the Board of Governors of the Federal Reserve System Covering Operations for the Year 1948* (Washington, D.C.: June 30, 1949), pp. 16–17.

12. *Thirty-Sixth Annual Report of the Board of Governors of the Federal Reserve System Covering Operations for the Year 1949* (Washington, D.C.: June 30, 1950), p. 16.

13. *Chart Book of Economic Statistics 1968* (New York: Morgan Guaranty Trust Company, 1968), chart 13.

14. *Annual Report of the Secretary of the Treasury on the State of the Finances for Fiscal Year Ended June 30, 1945* (Washington, D.C.: Government Printing Office, 1946), p. 2.

15. *Annual Report of the Secretary of the Treasury on the State of the Finances for Fiscal Year Ended June 30, 1946* (Washington, D.C.: Government Printing Office, 1947), pp. 92–93.

16. *Annual Report of the Secretary of the Treasury on the State of the Finances for Fiscal Year Ended June 30, 1947* (Washington, D.C.: Government Printing Office, 1948), pp. 217–246.

17. *Annual Report of the Secretary of the Treasury on the State of the Finances for Fiscal Year Ended June 30, 1948* (Washington, D.C.: Government Printing Office, 1949), p. 326.

18. *Annual Report of the Secretary of the Treasury on the State of the Finances for Fiscal Year Ended June 30, 1949* (Washington, D.C.: Government Printing Office, 1950), p. 21.

19. *Thirty-Seventh Annual Report of the Federal Reserve Bank of New York, 1951* (March 14, 1952), p. 22.

20. *Thirty-Third Annual Report of the Board of Governors of the Federal Reserve System Covering Operations for the Year 1946* (Washington, D.C.: June 17, 1947), p. 93. For a discussion of this period by one who was intimately associated with its developments, see Allan Sproul, "The Accord," *Monthly Review* (Federal Reserve Bank of New York, November 1964), pp. 227–236.

21. *Thirty-Sixth Annual Report of the Board of Governors of the Federal Reserve System Covering Operations for the Year 1949* (Washington, D.C.: June 10, 1950), p. 3.

22. *Thirty-Seventh Annual Report of the Federal Reserve Bank of New York, 1951* (March 14, 1952), p. 5.

23. *Monthly Review of Credit and Business Conditions*, Vol. 32, No. 9 (Federal Reserve Bank of New York, September 1950), p. 97.

24. *Monetary Policy and the Management of the Public Debt*, Part 1, Joint Committee on the Economic Report, 82nd Cong., 2nd sess., 1952 (Washington, D.C.: Government Printing Office, 1952), pp. 92 ff.

25. *Monetary Policy and the Management of the Public Debt*. Hearings before the Subcommittee on General Credit Control and Debt Management of the Joint Committee on the Economic Report, Congress of the United States, 82nd Cong., 2nd sess., pursuant to Section 5 (A) of Public Law 304 (Washington, D.C.: Government Printing Office, 1952), pp. 519 ff.

26. *General Credit Control, Debt Management and Economic Mobilization*, Joint Committee on the Economic Report 82nd Cong., 1st sess. (Washington, D.C.: Government Printing Office, 1951), p. 5.

27. *Monetary Policy and the Management of the Public Debt, op. cit.*, p. 522.

28. *Federal Reserve Bulletin* (April 1951), p. 377.

29. *Fortieth Annual Report of the Board of Governors of the Federal Reserve System Covering Operations for the Year 1953* (March 1, 1954), p. 88.

30. *Monetary Policy and the Management of the Public Debt,* Report of the Subcommittee on General Credit Control and Debt Management of the Joint Committee on the Economic Report, 82nd Cong., 2nd sess. (Washington, D.C.: Government Printing Office, 1952), p. 36.

CHAPTER 9

Working Toward Economic Stability

THE TWO POSTWAR DECADES

In the 1920s Federal Reserve policy was directed toward stabilization of European currencies and reduction of cyclical fluctuations in domestic business activities. In the 1950s it was directed principally toward cyclical stability. Currency stabilization and closely related problems of world economic reconstruction were then the province of the Bretton Woods institutions, assisted by huge loans and grants-in-aid from the U.S. Treasury (see Chapters 11 and 16 for further details).

In the 1920s Reserve policy was formulated largely by the Federal Reserve Bank of New York under the leadership of Governor Benjamin Strong; in the 1950s it was directed mainly by the Board of Governors, whose chairman was William McChesney Martin. Economic stability is, of course, never far from Federal Reserve consideration. In the two postwar decades, however, Reserve officials were able to give priority to stability in business conditions, undeterred by the pressing needs of war finance, strong inflationary pressures, serious depression, or huge deficits in the balance of payments.

Furthermore, the political environment of the two decades favored independent Federal Reserve action. In the 1920s the Federal budget was in surplus, and the Federal debt was being rapidly reduced. Although the Federal Government and agency debt was rising in the 1950s, the increase in net debt, once the administration of Dwight D. Eisenhower had taken office, did not exceed 8 percent. The attitudes of the Eisenhower administration toward monetary and economic policies promoted Federal Reserve independence, as had those of the administrations of Warren G. Harding, Calvin Coolidge, and Herbert Hoover.

The two decades were highly prosperous. Industrial production began to rise in 1921 and continued to rise, except for a major interruption in 1924 and a minor one in 1927, to a peak in 1929 that was twice as high as that of 1921. The 1929 peak was not surpassed again, except for brief periods in 1936 and 1939, until the United States felt the impact of Allied war demand in 1940.

Also, in the 1950s the index of industrial production (1957–1959 = 100) rose rapidly, increasing from 81.3 in 1951 to 109.7 in 1961. Real GNP (1958 prices) increased from $383 billion in 1951 to $497 billion in 1961. Declines occurred during only two years, 1954 and 1958. Personal-consumption and state- and local-government expenditures rose without interruption. Following a sharp increase in the early part of the decade and a decline in 1954, Federal expenditures leveled off and remained fairly stable. Only such items as expenditures on business inventories, construction, and producers' durable equipment reflected important cyclical swings.

In these two postwar decades, cyclical expansions were long and contractions short. In addition, during the contractions the rise in unemployment, the decline in industrial production, and the drop in GNP were relatively modest (see Table 9.1).

Table 9.1
Cyclical Expansions and Contractions

Expansions		Contractions	
Period	Duration (months)	Period	Duration (months)
July 1921—May 1923	22	May 1923—July 1924	14
July 1924—October 1926	27	October 1926—November 1927	13
November 1927—August 1929	21		
October 1949—July 1953	45	July 1953—August 1954	13
August 1954—July 1957	35	July 1957—April 1958	9
April 1958—May 1960	25	May 1960—February 1961	9
Average	29.1		11.6
Peacetime average cycles (1854–1961)	26		20

Source: Business Cycle Developments (U.S. Department of Commerce, Bureau of the Census, October 1968), p. 65.

The expansions in the 1950s were much longer than in the 1920s; the contractions a trifle shorter. Only to those who were convinced that booms could be perpetuated did the contractions in the 1950s seem inexcusable; they overlooked the vital point that price stability can be achieved only when the price rise of a boom is offset by a decline in recession. This occurred in the 1920s but not in the 1950s. The result was that consumer prices were stable in the 1920s but rose in the 1950s. Gains in productivity tended to be passed on to consumers in the 1920s but not in the 1950s.

To those living in the exuberant atmosphere of the 1920s, depression and stagnation were unthinkable. It was a "new era" in which recurrence of depression comparable to that of 1921 seemed impossible. The business community "guaranteed" lasting prosperity by paying wages high enough to enable workers to consume the ever-mounting production of the nation's multiplying factories. What workers lacked in immediate purchasing power could be made up by increases in consumer credit, itself largely an innovation of that decade.

There were those who doubted that an economic utopia had been achieved. In 1929 Wesley Clair Mitchell expressed doubts that the cycle had been permanently ironed out. That the United States had not suffered a severe depression since 1921 was no guarantee, he cautioned, that it would be "equally prudent, skillful and fortunate in the years to come." Past experience suggested that the pace would slacken and that years might pass before another such steady advance occurred. His appraisal proved all too true.[1]

In the 1950s the possibility of a depression or even of a severe recession was seldom taken seriously. The "new economics," it was asserted, had the knowledge and the tools to ensure continuing high levels of prosperity. To be sure, as the decade drew to a close optimism was somewhat dampened by price pressures and growing deficits in the balance of payments. But the optimists declared that even these problems could be erased by stimulating rapid economic growth. Accelerated growth could be relied upon, so they declared, not only to eliminate the deficit in the balance of payments but also to reduce unemployment and even to dampen inflationary pressures.

In its first annual economic report (1953) the Eisenhower administration cast doubts upon the premises of these optimists. It is not easy, the report pointed out, to achieve economic stability. Control of the cycle is an art rather than a science. Correct action must be taken at the right moment. But what is the correct action? What is the right moment? How can we foretell the effects of particular actions on psychological attitudes? How can we foretell the economic consequences?

In pursuit of this art, the administration declared, we must avoid a doctrinaire position, endeavor to harmonize fiscal and monetary policy, and we must act promptly and vigorously. Even with the best intentions and the most careful analyses of existing conditions, actions may not produce the anticipated results. Monetary managers were likened to tightrope walkers balancing precariously between inflation and deflation.

RESPONSIBILITY

In the 1920s the Federal Reserve System had full responsibility for economic stabilization. The active use of fiscal and debt-management policy to influence economic conditions was alien to contemporary thought. Public opinion held that the Federal budget should be kept continuously in balance. In fact, it was continuously in surplus. Fiscal policy, in the absence of unemployment insurance and old-age pensions, could not play even a passive role. There were no built-in stabilizers. The Federal Reserve, young and inexperienced, not only had full responsibility for taking appropriate action but also had the task of analyzing and evaluating current trends. There was no Council of Economic Advisors with which it could share this task.

In the 1950s it was commonly believed that Federal Reserve policies should be reinforced by appropriate Federal tax, expenditure, and debt-management policies. Appropriate action in those areas was to be supplemented by that of the built-in stabilizers, consisting of the revenue and expenditure effects of unemployment insurance and of old-age pensions and the countercyclical effects of fluctuations in Federal personal and corporate income taxes.

The Federal budget should be brought into balance, so it was believed, only over the course of a business cycle. Model builders pointed out that declining tax revenues in a recession, resulting mainly from the action of the built-in stabilizers, would generate a Federal deficit, which, if financed by short-term obligations sold at declining interest rates to commercial banks, would increase the money supply, as well as the liquidity of the commercial banks. Commercial banks would themselves be able to buy short-term government obligations on the basis of excess reserves resulting from deliberate enlargement of the open-market portfolios of Reserve banks. They would also be able to meet loan demands at declining interest rates. The increased money supply would flow into consumer hands through increases in unemployment insurances and old-age pensions. If the deficit arising from the built-in stabilizers were insufficient to stimulate the economy, tax rates could be reduced or expenditures increased.

In a boom the opposite sequence would occur. Surplus government revenues would be used to retire the short-term debt held by commercial banks. The banks' liquidity would thus be reduced and their ability to meet loan demands curtailed. During a boom this action would be accompanied by a decline in unemployment-insurance payments and in applications for old-age pensions. Also in a boom the Reserve System would, through a positive open-market policy, force member banks into debt, causing an increase in interest rates and reducing the availability of commercial bank credit. To reinforce this action by the Reserve System the government would at the same time issue long-term bonds at rising interest rates, in order to soak up the volume of funds available for investment.

A floor would thus be placed under recession and a ceiling on the boom. Such was the theoretical basis of countercyclical action—part automatic, part contrived, and easier to express in theoretical terms than to translate into practice. Actually the model never was completely translated into practice in the 1950s. Debt management contributed to, rather than countered cyclical tendencies. Only once were tax rates reduced as an economic stimulus (see pp. 233–234). The increase in the Federal debt in a recession was not offset by decreases in boom periods. Again, as in the 1920s, monetary policy, this time abetted by the built-in stabilizers, had main responsibility for tempering the cycle.

SIMILARITIES AND DISSIMILARITIES

There were many similarities in economic and financial developments during the two postwar decades of the twentieth century: the need to reconstruct currencies, to reestablish international currency and trade relations, to repair war damages, and to reactivate international capital markets. In the 1920s these problems were handled by both central and private bankers, in the 1950s mainly by governments and international lending institutions. Again in the 1970s the United States faces similar problems.

A chronology of the stabilization of selected currencies highlights certain parallels (see Table 9.2). A crucial decision in the twenties was the action taken in 1925 to stabilize the British pound at its prewar level, $4.867. In view of the inflation that had occurred, the loss of certain export markets, and the under valuation of the French franc, this action, which overvalued the pound, subjected British currency to constant pressure. The Bank of England was repeatedly forced to appeal to the Federal Reserve System and other central banks for help.

British public opinion after World War II did not urge that the wartime value of the pound ($4.03) be continued. In 1949 it was devaluated to $2.80 and in 1967 to $2.40. Despite these devaluations, Great Britain has required intermit-

Table 9.2
Stabilization of Selected Currencies[a]

Currency	After 1918	After 1945
German mark	1924	1953
British pound	1925	1949
French franc	1926	1960
Italian lira	1927	1960

a. The years after World War II are those in which parity was established with the help and approval of the International Monetary Fund. Actually the mark and the lira had achieved de facto stabilization earlier. After World War I the French franc was stabilized de facto in 1926 and de jure in 1928. In neither period could stabilization be considered permanent.

Source: *Federal Reserve Bulletin* (August 1928), p. 562; and *Thirtieth Annual Report* Bank for International Settlements (Basle: June 13, 1960), p. 164.

tent financial aid, just as she had in the interwar period. The British economy has been plagued by constant inflationary pressures and has failed to display the dynamic qualities of such other economies as those of the Common Market nations and Japan.

Among the difficult problems following World War I were those which concerned German reparations and inter-Allied debts. The payment of reparations would be expected to produce a sharp increase in German exports, and payments of inter-Allied debts would be expected to produce similarly sharp increases in the exports of France, Italy, and Great Britain. But attempts to increase exports were hindered by growing trade restrictions, notably the sharp rise in American tariff rates. For several years the problem was held in abeyance by large private loans extended to German borrowers by American investors, which enabled the German government to pay its reparations to the Allied powers and they, in turn to meet payments on war debts. When the flow of funds from the United States ceased after the stock-market collapse in 1929, the whole fabric of international finance was torn asunder.

The 1950s were not beleaguered by problems of war debts or reparations. Profiting by the mistakes of the 1920s, the United States canceled the greater part of the aid it extended during the war, and the reparations that were required were paid in kind. Efforts were made to reduce trade barriers, to eliminate exchange controls, and to organize trading partnerships. The establishment of the European Common Market and the European Free Trade Association afford examples of this trend.

THE QUALITY OF CREDIT

Professors Edwin F. Gay and Leo Wolman, in a report which they prepared for the Hoover Committee on *Recent Social Trends in the United States,* stated:

> In some way, the excessive multiplication of credit may, and does, convert prosperity into depression. The failure to exercise effective control over the issue and use of credit may, and does, result in the diversion of large amounts of credit into speculative enterprises which are bound to breed ultimate collapse. . . . Unthinking competition among numerous banks, in the quest for business and profits, may adulterate the investment portfolios of many banking institutions and weaken the safeguards of the depositor. And ignorant, inefficient and lax public supervision over the financial institutions of a country may nullify reasonable standards of regulation imposed upon banking management by the law.[2]

Developments through the 1920s gave ample evidence that long-run stabilization of prices and business conditions cannot be achieved unless the quality of credit remains high. Lenders must appraise realistically a borrower's income-producing ability and his underlying collateral. They must not rely on such unrelated factors as continued inflation or rapid increases in economic growth or in population to bail out unsatisfactory credits. If a decline in the quality of credit results in rising loan delinquencies, it may trigger a decline in economic activity. Even if a decline in quality does not trigger a recession, it will accelerate a downturn once it begins.[3]

The longer a boom persists, the greater the danger that the quality of loans will fall. Lending officers who have not encountered a serious recession come to the fore. They are often confident that prosperous conditions can and will be maintained, that the "new era" will suffer no setback and the "new economics" can cope with any untoward development.

Financial institutions succumb, consciously or not, to the temptation to lower credit standards. Banks and other institutions venture into new lending fields, often without adequate knowledge of risks; loans are extended to marginal borrowers; maturities are lengthened; down payments are reduced; balloon notes become more common; repayments are predicated upon favorable concatenation of circumstances that may not occur; loans are extended against speculative ventures.

Not only does the quality of credit extended by banks and other financial institutions decline, but trade credit is also vulnerable. Standards are lowered to increase sales. Cash discounts tend to be eliminated. Terms are lengthened, slow-paying accounts increase, and collections become slipshod. The longer the accounts are past due, the sharper is the depreciation in their ultimate value. Once a reaction sets in, trade credit declines precipitously, often, as the Radcliffe Report pointed out, with catastrophic results.[4]

The Federal Reserve Board was not unmindful of this problem in the 1920s. After making the point in its 1923 report that a central bank's reserve ratio is no longer a dependable guide in a world in which the gold standard has been suspended and in which the flow of gold is governed by factors other than the normal forces operating on the balance of payments, the Board examined other possible criteria. One of the most important, it declared, is the use to which increases in credit are devoted. If credit is used productively, mainly to finance short-term operations in agriculture, industry, and trade, maladjustments will probably not arise between the volume of production and consumption which, in turn, are followed by price and other economic disturbances. Protection against a misuse of credit, it concluded, requires close acquaintance with changes in the quality and character of commercial-bank portfolios.[5]

The Board's analysis proved particularly pertinent to developments in the 1920s. In the second half of the decade the quality of credit for urban mortgage loans and domestic and foreign bond issues declined sharply. Increases in bank credit resulting from Federal Reserve activities to support the British pound found their way into stock-exchange loans. The rapid expansion of these loans brought about maladjustments in domestic and foreign money and capital markets and eventually forced the Reserve System to contract credit, with a resulting depressive effect upon world commerce and trade. The 1950s were also not immune to such developments. Required down payments were lowered, and maturities were extended for consumer credit and urban mortgage loans. Credit quality had declined.

USES OF BANK FUNDS, 1921–1929

The commercial banking system underwent a radical transformation from 1921 to 1929. The category of "all other loans" (i.e. other than collateral and real estate), then the only measure of business loans, was only slightly higher in

1928 ($14.4 billion) than in the depression year 1921 ($14.0 billion). The sharp increase in the "all other loans" in 1929 ($2 billion) resulted from loans extended to customers to finance stock-market speculation at a time when the Federal Reserve System was attempting through moral suasion to reduce the volume of collateral loans. In other words, these loans were, in part, a disguised form of collateral loan. The more speculative and less liquid types of loan, against real estate and other collateral, greatly exceeded the 1921 totals.[6]

That the increase in business loans was so small is paradoxical in view of the rapid rise in business activity. Industries most heavily dependent upon bank credit—for example, manufacturing and agriculture—declined in relative economic importance, whereas industries that were less dependent (service trades, transportation, and utilities) gained. Changes in the asset structures of manufacturing and trade concerns weakened the demand for short-term funds and strengthened the demand for long-term financing. Fixed assets grew in relative importance, cash increased in proportion to total assets, and receivables and inventories became relatively less important among business assets.[7]

The sharp decline in the Federal debt provided savings for financing borrowing requirements, thus rendering business enterprises less dependent upon bank credit. Business firms still smarting from the commercial banks' refusal to extend and renew loans in the depression of 1921 preferred to borrow through issues of debentures and bonds in the capital markets.

Collateral loans increased spectacularly, rising about 40 percent between 1924 and 1929. These loans were extended principally against stock-exchange collateral and were granted for many purposes: to finance business credit needs (such loans are now classified as commercial and industrial loans); to finance personal credit needs (now classified as personal loans); to finance the purchase and carrying of new security issues by investment bankers, pending sale to individual investors; to finance the security inventories that brokers held either in short-term trading accounts or in longer-term investment accounts; to finance the delivery or clearance of securities traded; and to finance the purchase of securities by customers of brokerage houses. This last purpose was the predominate reason for the sharp increase occurring during the second half of the decade.

At the time of the stock-market crash (October 1929) the collateral loans of all commercial banks were estimated at $14 billion, an amount equal to 40 percent of all loans. To be added to this total were the security loans extended by corporations, investment trusts, and individuals (amounting to $3.9 billion) and those extended by private banks, brokers, and foreign banking agencies (totaling $1.5 billion). All security loans extended by all lenders probably reached a grand total of $19.4 billion.[8]

Only the New York City banks, which at the time of the stock-market crash held $1.1 billion of brokers' loans, felt responsible for the market. Other lenders were mainly "fair weather" lenders, who could be expected to run for cover at the first hint of real difficulty. As the storm clouds gathered, they withdrew their funds rapidly, forcing the New York City banks to take over their loans in order to prevent the closing of the stock exchange.

The increase in total commercial bank loans from 1922 to 1929 amounted to 44 percent, the increase in investments to 46 percent. Loans, which had amounted to 83 percent of deposits in 1921, fell to 73 percent in 1929, and investments, which had amounted to 26 percent in 1921 rose to 28 percent in 1929. These trends were the opposite of those of the 1950s, when the loan-deposit ratio rose, and the investment-deposit ratio fell.

The decline in bond yields was very sharp in 1921 and 1922, and it was in those years that commercial banks added substantially to their holdings of government obligations. This action resulted from the need to build up earning assets reduced by the decline in loans and from the need for government obligations to serve as collateral for government deposits and as security for loans obtained from the Reserve banks.

For the rest of the decade, commercial bank holdings of government obligations remained stable, a remarkable development in itself, in view of the rapid retirement of the Federal debt. Debt reduction, primarily affecting holdings by noncommercial banks, raised the proportion of the Federal debt held by commercial banks from 13 percent in 1920 to 32 percent in 1929, but there were wide differences among individual banks. The central reserve-city and reserve-city banks increased their holdings of government obligations, while the country banks—which really needed such obligations as secondary reserves—reduced their holdings.

Holdings of state and municipal obligations doubled, and holdings of "other securities" increased about 70 percent. As the decade wore on many obligations were purchased primarily for income. Commercial banks engaged in intense competition for deposits. Underwriting syndicates, including the security affiliates, compromised standards for price. Income became more important than quality.

Demand deposits adjusted and time deposits of commercial banks rose sharply (see Table 9.3). The rapid increase in time deposits, exceeding that at mutual-savings banks, resulted not only from avid competition by commercial banks for funds for use in collateral and real-estate loans and for investments but also from inducements offered to customers to shift their deposits from the demand to the time category, thus releasing reserves for further credit expansion.

Table 9.3

Deposits in all Commercial Banks
(Billions of Dollars)

	Demand Deposits Adjusted	Time Deposits
June 30, 1921	17.1	10.9
June 29, 1929	22.5	19.6

Source: *Banking and Monetary Statistics* (Washington, D.C.: Board of Governors of the Federal Reserve System, November 1943), p. 34.

FEDERAL RESERVE POLICY, 1922–1929

For the Reserve System the 1920s were a time to experiment, a time to develop procedures and policies. It did so in open-market operations, in the purchase of domestic and foreign bills of exchange, in the development of resale agreements, and in close working arrangements with foreign central banks. It promoted economic research and examined the multitudinous guides to credit policy.

During the 1920s open-market operations developed into a primary instrument of Federal Reserve policy. Before 1922 they had been small in scale and importance and were carried on largely by individual Federal Reserve banks in order to provide necessary earnings and to promote the use of trade acceptances and dollar bills of exchange. Closely related to the rise in the importance of open-market operations was a tendency toward the centralization and formalization of decision-making (Chapter 2).

The growing emphasis on open-market operations relegated the discount rate to a position of secondary importance. Changes were made in order to adjust discount rates to changes in open-market rates that had, in effect, been brought about by open-market operations. The principal changes in open-market operations from 1922 through 1929, along with correlative alterations in discount rates, are set forth in Table 9.4.

Policy 1922–1923

During the war and, the immediate post-war years, member-bank borrowings increased rapidly, reaching a peak of $2.8 billion in October 1920 (Chapter 7,

Table 9.4
Open-Market Operations, 1922–1929

Period	Operation	New York Federal Reserve Bank Discount Rate	
		In effect	
January 1922–May 1922	Purchase, $365 million	January 1, 1922	4.5%
		June 22, 1922	4.0
June 1922–July 1923	Sale, $494 million	February 23, 1923	4.5
December 1923–September 1924	Purchase, $469 million	May 1, 1924	4.0
		June 12, 1924	3.5
		August 8, 1924	3.0
November 1924–March 1925	Sale, $212 million	February 27, 1925	3.5
April 1926	Purchase, $63 million	January 8, 1926	4.0
		April 23, 1926	3.5
August 1926–September 1926	Sale, $37 million	August 13, 1926	4.0
May 1927–November 1927	Purchase, $288 million	August 5, 1927	3.5
January 1928–August 1928	Sale, $497 million [a]	February 3, 1928	4.0
		May 18, 1928	4.5
		July 13, 1928	5.0
August 1928–December 1928	Purchase, $358 million		
January 1929–July 1929	Sale, $480 million		
July 1929–October 1929	Purchase, $269 million	August 9, 1929	6.0

a. In 1928 and 1929 open-market operations included dealings in both U.S. securities and bankers' accep-tances. Data were obtained from various issues of the *Federal Reserve Bulletin* and from *Banking and Monetary Statistics* (Washington, D.C.: Board of Governors of the Federal Reserve System, November, 1943), pp. 369–371.

Source: The timing of policy operations except those for 1928 and 1929 are taken from *Operations of the National and Federal Reserve Banking Systems*. Subcommittee on Banking and Currency. U.S. Senate. 71st Cong. 3d Sess. 1931 (Washington, D.C.: Government Printing Office), p. 803. The data given are monthly averages of daily data, except for April 1926 which are end of the month data.

p. 166). A rapid decline then set in, which reduced the total to $1 billion by January 1922; this resulted from an increase in the gold stock ($800 million) and a decline of money in circulation ($1.1 billion).[9] Member banks in New York City and Chicago were able to reduce their borrowings substantially, in the reserve cities to a lesser extent, and in country towns very little. The inflow of gold re-flected in the main the liquidation of borrowings by foreign countries, and the re-ceipt of currency reflected the liquidation of loans by domestic borrowers.[10] Loan liquidation proceeded at a much faster pace in metropolitan centers than in country areas.[11]

The decrease in member-bank borrowings in 1921 was accompanied by suc-cessive reductions in discount rates [12] (see Chapter 10). The decline in the volume of member-bank borrowings and the rates charged on those borrowings quickly eroded the net earnings of the Reserve banks. Net earnings in 1922 were only 41 percent of those in 1921 and were smaller than those in any year since 1917. Cost could not be reduced proportionately.[13]

The sharp reduction in net earnings induced those Reserve banks which particularly were affected to add to their holdings of government obligations (Table 9.4, p. 219). They did so individually and on their own initiative, without reference to current business conditions—which had shown marked improvement since the 1921 depression—but with sole emphasis on their own income accounts.[14]

Actually, purchases of government obligations caused the net earnings of the Reserve banks to decline still more. Member banks used the funds released to make further reductions in their borrowings. Although Federal Reserve officials were aware in a general way of the inverse relationship between member-bank borrowings and open-market operations, this inverse relationship never had been so vividly portrayed as in 1922–1923.[15] Never in the future would doubt again exist of the validity of this relationship.

Following the purchase of these securities, the Reserve System decided that in the future, securities should not be purchased for the sole purpose of covering dividends and expenses. Rather than to purchase securities for this purpose, which might lower interest rates at an inappropriate time, dividends and expenses would be paid from accumulated surplus.*

Beginning in June 1922, the System reduced its holdings of U.S. obligations slowly at first and then more rapidly, until they fell to $95 million early in July 1923. Holdings of acceptances increased slightly so that the decline in the open-market portfolio was less than that reflected simply in the ownership of United States securities (Table 9.4, p. 219).

Various reasons have been cited for this reduction in open-market holdings, accompanied as it was by an increase in the discount rate at the Federal Reserve Bank of New York in February 1923. In a letter to Governor Montagu Norman of the Bank of England, Governor Benjamin Strong of the Federal Reserve Bank of New York pointed to the rise of market interest rates above the discount rate, to the fact that industrial production was nearing capacity, and to the emergence of substantial labor shortages, and then voiced conviction that further increases in bank credit would simply serve to increase prices.[16] Still another reason cited by Governor Strong was the need to offset the effect of gold imports on member bank reserves.[17] The Reserve banks had already begun to circulate gold certificates

---

* For a further discussion of this period and of the steps leading to the harmonization of open-market operations, see Chapter 2.

and coins in order to prevent their own reserve ratios from rising. Some of the reasons cited may have been rationalizations after the event; the compelling reason for this action seems to have been the desire of the U.S. Treasury, at a time of large surplus revenues, to obtain U.S. obligations for redemption without being compelled to purchase them at rising prices in the open market.[18]

This reduction in open-market holdings not only fulfilled its primary purpose of providing the Treasury with U.S. obligations, but by causing market interest rates to rise, it retarded somewhat the growth of commercial bank credit and helped to check the upward thrust of commodity prices. The basic purpose, like the expansion in the open-market portfolio of 1922, was not that of influencing economic developments. Both of these operations did have important economic effects, but the primary purpose on the first occasion was to increase earnings of the Reserve banks and, on the second, to assist the Treasury with the redemption of the debt.

The purchase and sale of U.S. obligations in 1922 and 1923 were not conducted as a system operation. Each Federal Reserve bank conducted its operations individually and on its own initiative, although an effort was made through the establishment of "The Committee of Governors on Centralized Execution of Purchases and Sales of Government Securities by Federal Reserve Banks" [19] to prevent purchases and sales from disrupting the government securities market (see Chapter 2).

Policy 1924

The large open-market purchases between December 1923 and September 1924 (Table 9.4) were the first to be handled in a joint investment account and the first to be directed solely towards influencing economic conditions. This action resulted from decisions taken at a meeting of the Open-Market Investment Committee (December 3, 1923), which were approved by the Federal Reserve Board and concurred in by all twelve Federal Reserve Banks [20] (see Chapter 2).

The National Bureau chronology fixes the beginning of the recession in May 1923 (Table 9.1). Action by the Reserve System was a bit tardy, and when it occurred it is not clear whether it was taken to counter the decline or to rebuild the security holdings of the Reserve Banks. The acceleration of the decline in employment, production, and retail sales in the first six months of 1924 caused the Reserve System to place increased emphasis on the state of the economy. By July 1924 indexes of business activity were lower than at any time since the 1920-

1921 depression. There could be no question but that the nation was suffering from serious decline. Paralleling the decline in business activity and extending into the period of recovery the Reserve Banks increased their open-market portfolio from $127 million on January 2, to $619 million on September 17, 1924. Abetted by a sharp increase in the gold stock and by a seasonal decline of money in circulation (itself offsetting the decline in bill holdings), this action enabled member banks to reduce their borrowings at the Reserve banks and to increase their reserve balances. Money market interest rates fell to the lowest levels since 1916. The Reserve System responded by approving three reductions in the discount rate at the Federal Reserve Bank of New York.

The principal objectives of Federal Reserve policy, as stated by officials of the System, were: to bring about recovery in business conditions and business confidence, to enable member banks to reduce their indebtedness at the Reserve banks, to relieve continuing pressure for loan liquidation in agricultural areas, to give the Reserve banks assets that might be sold later to check possible incipient inflation, to establish interest rates in the New York money and capital markets lower than those prevailing abroad in order to promote the flow of funds to foreign markets, and to further the resumption of gold payments by the United Kingdom. This last goal was by far the most important.[21]

The results of the policy, according to a memorandum prepared by Governor Strong, were: the pressure for loan liquidation was relaxed, a receptive capital market was created for the flotation of foreign and domestic issues, sterling rose in the foreign exchange markets, and stimulus was given to business recovery.

Open-market operations also induced a rapid increase in member-bank credit during the second half of 1924, which took the form largely of a rise in security loans and investments. Commercial loans reflected only a moderate increase.

The fact that the cheap money policy had had this effect on member-bank loans and investments caused certain Federal Reserve banks, as they later evaluated the policies, to state that the operations were excessively large. Funds not required for business needs swelled bankers' balances and security loans and investments on the books of member banks.[22]

It was possible, too, that the policies, instituted partly to assist monetary reconstruction in Europe, had rendered actual disservice. Open-market operations raised sterling-exchange rates to levels that could not be maintained on purely economic, as distinct from financial, grounds. To force interest rates in the American money market to artificially low levels, engendering inflationary developments and compelling a policy reversal, which in turn forced interest rates to artificially high levels, did not help European monetary recovery.

Sales in 1924–1925

The decline in open-market holdings from November 1924 to March 1925 along with the increase in the bank rate from 3 to 3.5 percent at the Federal Reserve Bank of New York, was designed to check an expansion in security loans that itself had resulted from the earlier easy-money policy. Interest rates rose, and increase in brokers' loans was halted.

A Year to Emulate, 1926

In the catastrophic 1930s, 1926 came to be regarded as a year to emulate, possessing as it did a variety of desirable features. The physical output of industry exceeded that of any previous year. There was practically no unemployment, and total wage payments were well maintained. Construction had continued in large volume, and crop yields had been generally large. The movement of goods through retail and wholesale trade had been orderly and sustained by continuous consumer demand. There had been no evidence of inventory accumulation. And, despite exceptionally active business, commodity prices had declined in December to a point 6 percent lower than that of a year before, stimulating buying and permitting consumers to share in increased productivity.

The credit policy of the Reserve banks had been to continue discount rates unchanged save for an adjustment at the New York bank and to maintain the System's open-market portfolio with relatively small changes. It had been an exceptional year, of steady growth with declining prices—so exceptional that it has not recurred.

Purchases in 1927

The decision to increase open-market holdings of U.S. securities from $254 to $705 million between May 11 and November 16, 1927, was one of the most crucial in the history of Federal Reserve policy. When added to an increase of about $100 million in acceptance holdings, the rise in the open-market portfolio was sufficient not only to offset a reduction in the gold stock and an increase of money in circulation but also to cause a sizable increase in member-bank reserve balances.

The effect was to bring about a reduction in both short- and long-term interest rates and a sharp increase in the security loans and investments of member banks. New York City banks increased their security loans, other banks their investments. Business loans extended by commercial banks rose but by a very small amount.

The decline in open-market rates was accompanied by a reduction in the discount rates at all Federal Reserve banks, beginning with Kansas City on July 29 and ending with Minneapolis on September 13 (see Chapter 2). Because these reductions came at a time when the speculative impulse needed only a generating spark, it was inevitable that the resulting expansion of credit would swell total security loans to brokers and would provide the basis for a stock-market advance. The growing importance of time deposits expanded credit at a large multiple of the rise in excess reserves.

The main reason for the adoption of this policy was the weakness in sterling exchange and an appeal from the Bank of England for assistance. The decline in business activity had been slight, resulting principally from the decision of the Ford Motor Company to substitute its Model A for the Model T. The action did strengthen sterling exchange and induced France to draw gold from the United States to reestablish its gold standard. The short-run benefits, however, seemed to have been completely outweighed by long-run disadvantages. The resulting sharp increase in security loans forced a reversal early in 1928, and by August, pound sterling had fallen to a point lower than that reached before the System adopted the policy.

Policy 1928–1929

Open-market holdings were reduced in the first halves and increased in the second halves of 1928 and 1929 (Table 9.4). The reversal each autumn of the policy initiated each spring grew out of a schizophrenic credit policy. The Reserve System sought to terminate speculative orgies on the stock exchange without hurting business, which at that time was impossible. The Federal Reserve System could not then, as it can now, fall back upon selective control of security loans. It was compelled to rely on the restraining influence of interest rates, i.e., on general credit controls, which are not without their influence on general business activity..

The rapid increase in Stock prices and security loans resulting from the easy-money policy of 1927 convinced Reserve officials that a restrictive policy should be instituted.[23] They justified their position on the grounds, first, that an increase in stock-market credit by raising stock prices tends to encourage the flotation of stocks and the use of funds resulting from it; second, that such an increase will, if financed by increases in bank credit, expand the money supply and, if financed by noncommercial bank funds, increase the velocity of bank deposits; third, that rising stock prices result in capital gains, which, whether realized or not, encourage participants to increase consumption; and, fourth, that optimism based on rising stock prices encourages people to activate their idle balances. A sharp decline in stock-market credit and stock prices has reverse effects.

Contemporary observers argued that the soundness or unsoundness of brokers' loans could not be judged by the security or protection of individual loans. The problem had much wider implications, involving the cyclical effects of increases in security loans, the liquidity of bank portfolios, and the contingent effects on the banking system of loans for "the account of others," i.e. loans by others than commercial banks.

The $497 million reduction in Federal Reserve holdings of U.S. obligations and acceptances (see Table 9.4) between January and August 1928, coupled with a decline of about $200 million in the gold stock, forced an increase of nearly $600 million in member-bank borrowing. The reduction in the portfolio of securities and bills was accompanied by three increases in discount rates. Short-term money rates advanced substantially, and the interest curve became negatively inclined.

This restrictive policy had the desired result of slowing down the increase in security loans. Between January and August 1928 security loans of the reporting member banks fell by .6 percent. Total brokers' loans increased nearly 12 percent, but as a result of a sharp increase in loans for the "account of others." Bank loans to brokers fell. The policy was working. Had it been continued through the autumn of 1928, the stock-market break would probably have occurred a year earlier than it did—but the Great Depression might have been less severe.

Convinced that it could penalize speculation without hurting business, the Federal Reserve System rapidly increased its holdings of acceptances in the autumn of 1928, in order to relieve seasonal credit pressures. This increase permitted member banks to reduce their borrowing at the Reserve banks and to increase their reserve balances. Reporting member-bank credit expanded again—in the form of security loans. All classes of lenders—New York City banks, out-of-town banks, and the "others" participated in this rise. The purchase of acceptances aggravated the very situation that the Reserve System was trying to correct.

In the spring of 1929 a sharp decline in Federal Reserve holdings of acceptances and securities (see Table 9.4) occurred. The decline in the open-market portfolio of the Reserve banks was enough to offset an increase in the gold stock and, in addition, to force an increase in member-bank borrowing. Credit expansion at reporting member banks was held to .7 percent. Total brokers' loans rose, but the rise was again accounted for by increases in loans for the "account of others." Bank loans to brokers fell.

"For a number of weeks from February to May," according to the Federal Reserve Bank of New York, "the directors of the Federal Reserve Bank of New York voted an increase in the discount rate from 5 to 6 percent. This increase was not approved by the Federal Reserve Board." [24] Similar recommendations by the directors of the Federal Reserve banks of Boston, Chicago, Philadelphia, and Kansas City also met with refusal.

In its Annual Report for 1929 the Federal Reserve Board asserted that an increase in discount rates was not the most appropriate method of dealing with a situation that called for the use of "direct pressure." "Direct pressure" consisted in issuing admonitions to member banks, pointing out that the growth in security loans was contrary to the spirit of the Federal Reserve Act. It also consisted in the bringing of pressure upon member banks to reduce their borrowing at the Reserve banks by calling in at least part of their brokers' loans. "Direct action," or moral suasion was not successful. It caused member banks to hide their security loans in the "all other loans" category. It drove business from the cooperating to the noncooperating banks. The reduction of member-bank borrowing in districts where Reserve banks had vigorously pursued this policy simply led to increases in other districts.

The Straddle Policy • Following a two-day special conference with the governors of the Federal Reserve banks, the Federal Reserve Board authorized the New York Reserve Bank to raise its discount rate to 6 percent effective August 9, 1929. This increase of one percent, preceded by no warning from the Board, coming at a time of year when rate advances had been the exception, and not foreshadowed by a rate rise at the Bank of England, was designed as a gesture against the continued use of credit for speculative purposes, which had raised the total of brokers' loans by $265 million in one month.

On the same date the acceptance buying was lowered from $5\frac{1}{4}$ to $5\frac{1}{8}$ percent at the Federal Reserve Bank of New York. This action was an attempt to compromise the conflicting goals of Federal Reserve officials, who wanted to deflate the stock market and still make credit available for fall financing. For the first time in the history of the System a discount-rate increase was accompanied by a reduction in the buying rate on bills.

The inconsistency of this action was dubbed a "straddle" and was correctly interpreted by the speculative fraternity as a bullish factor. The lowering of the bill rate presaged a rapid increase in the bill holdings of the System and a shift in the composition of Federal Reserve credit from "bills discounted" to "bills purchased." With the shifting of the burden from the rediscount to the open-market shoulder, market interest rates eased. The effectiveness of the 6 percent discount rate was thus nullified.[25]

The Panic • Between August 14 and October 23, the date of the stock-exchange panic, the Federal Reserve banks increased their bill portfolio by $261 million. Member-bank indebtedness fell $232 million. Security loans by reporting member banks outside New York City increased sharply. The purchase of bills in the money market enabled New York City reporting member banks to reduce their borrowing substantially, so that they were in a favorable position to meet the crisis when it occurred—a chance by-product of a policy that postponed the collapse and undoubtedly increased its severity.

The basic cause of the panic was the rise in stock prices caused by individual and gigantic pool operations, purchases by investment trusts, and rapid expansion of borrowing to a point warranted only by the most euphoric judgments of prospective economic conditions and corporate earnings. It was, in Thorstein Veblen's language, "the capitalized values of imbecility." [26] The immediate causes were reports of smaller corporate earnings, the flooding of the market with new security issues, the rise in the London bank rate to 6.5 percent, the Hatry failure in London, the cessation of European participation in the American market, and a decline in business activity that had become clearly evident by October. All these factors shook the confidence of American speculators and resulted in a break of unprecedented severity.

The panic brought about a very sharp change in the composition of brokers' loans. Within a week the "others" had withdrawn $1.4 billion and the out-of-town banks, $700 million. The New York City banks, as the occasion demanded, replaced those withdrawals automatically, crediting the deposit accounts of the withdrawing lenders and taking over the loans themselves. The replacement by New York City banks of the loans withdrawn by other lenders prevented interest rates from rising to even higher levels and indeed prevented the closing of the stock exchange. The renewal rate was pegged at 6 percent, the lowest rate known during any major panic.

Table 9.5

Fluctuations in Brokers' Loans,
October–November 1929
(Millions of Dollars)

	October 23	October 30	November 6	November 13
Out-of-town banks	$1,733	$1,005	$ 963	$ 812
"Others"	3,823	2,464	2,399	2,204
Own accounts	1,077	2,069	1,520	1,156
Total	$6,633	$5,538	$4,882	$4,172

Source: *Banking and Monetary Statistics* (Washington, D.C.: Board of Governors of the Federal Reserve System, 1943), p. 498.

As the New York banks took over the loans to brokers that had been called by out-of-town banks and "others" (the invisible banking system thus merging with the visible) it became necessary to increase their reserve balances with the New York Federal Bank. Between October 23 and 30 the net demand deposits of the member banks in New York rose $1.6 billion, reflecting an increase in total loans and investments of $1.4 billion, nearly all of which resulted from the increase in loans against securities (see Table 9.5). The reserves were partly supplied by borrowing from the Reserve Bank and partly by heavy open-market purchases—which began on the first day of the panic.

Looking back over the span of years, people question how the collapse of the stock market could have ushered in the Great Depression. Vast numbers of individuals had purchased stocks on thin margins. Once the decline set in, their equity evaporated. The loss of paper profits turned their optimism sour. Consumers reduced their expenditures and held back from investment in homes and long-term projects. Corporate executives were similarly discouraged. The decline in consumer and business purchases forced the scales, already tipping toward recession, to depression lows.

An Evaluation

The 1920s were marked by sagging ethical standards in many fields of finance, by an epidemic of bank failures in rural areas, by a tendency toward longer-term and more speculative commercial-bank assets, and finally by an orgy of speculation that engulfed the nation. The Reserve System endeavored to achieve several policy goals simultaneously: strengthening and stabilizing European currencies, curbing the use of credit in domestic securities speculation, and stimulating business activity during the declines of 1924 and 1927. Not only did these goals

prove mutually inconsistent, but also the System, unable to set margin requirements on security loans, lacked the necessary tools to bring about even a partial
synthesis.

Apart from this weakness, the easy-money policies of 1924 and 1927,
adopted primarily to assist British sterling, were partly responsible for a decline in
the quality of credit, especially in foreign and domestic bonds and in security loans.
The decline eventually undermined the efforts of the Reserve System to moderate
the business cycle and to stabilize European currencies.

CREDIT TRENDS IN THE 1950s

At the end of 1950 total net public and private debt amounted to $486 bil-
lion and at the end of 1960 to $874 billion. Excluding Federal debt, which re-
flected only a relatively small increase, net public and private debt increased from
95 to 124 percent of GNP. This increase resulted not only from a sharp rise in
consumer demand for durable goods and housing; in business demand for working
capital and for plant and equipment; and in state and local demand for roads and
schools, but also from marked relaxation in lending terms, which particularly affected the consumer and urban mortgage markets.

The increase in bank-held debt amounted to $70 billion, a sum equal to
about 18 percent of the increase in total debt. Business loans rose steadily, except
for short interruptions that resulted mainly from inventory liquidations. An increasing proportion took the form of term loans, which, in being tailored to borrowers' needs and in being amortized, were regarded as a superior substitute to the
debentures of the 1920s.

Directly or indirectly commercial banks financed a large part, perhaps as
much as 50 percent, of the increase in consumer credit. Loans to individuals on
the statements of commercial banks reflected the amount of direct financing and
arose from the competitive desire to maintain and increase their share of a profitable market. Bank loans to sales-finance companies reflected the amount of indirect
financing.

This period witnessed a sharp increase in maturities on instalment loans and
a sharp decline in down payments. The one development is closely related to the
other. Often the easier credit terms were granted to "risk" borrowers: young people and wage and salary earners in lower-income groups.

Total mortgage debt increased from $73 to $207 billion. That held by commercial banks rose from $13 to $28 billion falling from 19 to 14 percent of the

total. At the end of the decade about 45 percent of the residential mortgage loans held by commercial banks were insured by the Federal Housing Administration or guaranteed by the Veterans Administration.

Financing terms eased over the decade. The loan-to-value ratio rose, down payments fell, and average maturities on new loans lengthened. The rate at which mortgage debt was repaid through amortization declined. Lending on second mortgages also became more important. In distinct contrast to the 1920s, however, loans were amortized.

More than 20 percent of the total increase ($40 billion), in state- and local-government securities was acquired by commercial banks, which bought them to obtain the tax-exempt returns necessary to pay rising interest rates on savings and time accounts. The longer the maturity of the obligation, the higher, usually, was the yield, which tempted banks to "reach out" on the interest rate curve. They thus sacrificed liquidity for yield and became increasingly vulnerable to interest-rate changes.

Holdings of Federal obligations by commercial banks reflected practically no net change, although there were important intermediate cyclical changes. Holdings increased sharply during periods of credit ease and fell with equal rapidity in subsequent periods of restraint.

The monetization of debt carried deposit totals far above those of the war period. Deposit turnover increased rapidly. As in the 1920s, time deposits rose more rapidly than demand. The competitive position of banks in relation to financial intermediaries was aided by relaxations in the terms of Regulation Q.

Contrary to developments in the 1920s, however, the loan-deposit ratio rose sharply. Similar to the situation then, bank assets tended to lengthen and the quality of assets to fall. The capital accounts of commercial banks relative to total assets rose; relative to risk assets they fell. The ratio of cash and government securities to total assets declined.

There was no dearth of purchasing power. Throughout the decade consumer prices rose 22 percent. The implicit price deflators of GNP also rose sharply in the case of the services purchased by consumers, producers' durable equipment, and residential structures. The building boom of the 1950s was accompanied by rising costs, whereas the building boom of the 1920s was characterized by falling costs. This redundancy of purchasing power created an environment in which cost push operated to spiral prices upward. Until towards the end of the decade, unit labor costs steadily increased, whereas in the 1920s they had fallen.

The inflationary trends over the whole decade called for restraining action by the Federal Reserve banks and the Federal government. An effort should have been made to reduce and to lengthen the Federal debt, yet marketable Federal debt increased from $155 to $184 billion, and average maturity fell from eight years and two months to four years and four months.

FEDERAL RESERVE POLICY IN THE 1950s

When the Eisenhower administration took office in January 1953, it predicated its initial policies upon a continuation of inflationary trends. Many raw materials were in short supply, manufacturers were maintaining protective inventories, strategic materials were still subject to government control, business demand for credit was large and failed to reflect the usual seasonal decline, and consumer credit was continuing to increase.

The administration's decision to remove price controls convinced many people that restrictive credit policies should be relied upon to check possible inflation. The Federal Reserve System raised the discount rate from 1.75 to 2 percent between January 16 and 23, 1953, the first increase since August 1950; it afforded tangible evidence that the System had finally achieved the independence presaged by the accord of 1951.

Open-market holdings remained stable in the first four months of 1953; in face of a strong credit demand, banks found it necessary to rediscount. The New York City banks, in particular, were subject to constant pressure and were forced to make necessary adjustments in their portfolios. The discount mechanism was again activated. Margin requirements on security loans were lowered from 75 to 50 percent, effective February 20, 1953. This action may seem inconsistent with other monetary policies, but common-stock prices had fallen, and customers' debit balances had remained at relatively low levels.

The Treasury harmonized its policies with those of the Reserve System and sought to obtain the funds it required from investors other than banks. It issued (for payment on May 1, 1953) a 30-year, 3.25 percent bond, in the amount of $1 billion. The President recommended that the excess-profits tax, due to expire on June 30, 1953, be extended for another six months. Maximum interest rates on FHA and VA mortgages were raised to 4.5 percent.

These restrictive policies had more potent effects than had been anticipated. A record level of security issues, rapid expansion in consumer and mortgage credit, a continued demand for short-term credit, expectations that the Treasury would be a heavy borrower for the rest of the year, and heavy sales of government securities by commercial banks (particularly in large cities) caused investors to fear that interest rates would continue to rise. The government securities market became demoralized. The new 3.25 percent bonds fell below par. Money-market interest rates advanced sharply. Early in June there were practically no bids for Treasury securities.

A Change in Policy

By mid-May it had become apparent that inflationary pressures had receded. The System began to purchase Treasury bills, increasing its holdings from $515 million on May 6 to $740 million by the end of the month. The market was slow to register the change in Federal Reserve policy. To convince investors that a change had indeed occurred, the Board of Governors announced on June 24 a reduction in member-bank reserve requirements effective early in July that released $1.2 billion of reserves (see Chapter 3, Table 3.4). This action, coupled with the purchase of $1 billion in Treasury bills (May 6–July 29), persuaded even the most recalcitrant skeptics. Member-bank borrowing fell sharply, and excess reserves rose. Net borrowed reserves, which in February had approached $700 million, became net free reserves of nearly $400 million in July. The change.in the money market was dramatic. The pressures on the New York City and Chicago banks, which had been particularly acute, were eased. Money-market rates declined sharply.[27]

Contractions and Expansions

Following these initial developments, the economy experienced three periods of contraction and two of expansion (see Table 9.1). Credit was, of course, eased in periods of business contraction and was made less available when demand pressed against productive capacity.

An attempt has been made in Table 9.6 to select the months in which Federal Reserve policy changed. The months selected must be regarded simply as approximations. Policy does not abruptly change on a particular date or even in a particular month. The transition from one type of policy to another usually occurs in slow steps over several weeks.

Nor should the dates of changes in Federal Reserve policy be expected to coincide with the business cycle turning points of the National Bureau of Economic

Research (see Table 9.1). These were selected after the event, when all information was at hand. The Reserve System had to appraise the passing scene; it was not afforded the advantage of hindsight. Even so there is a close correspondence. The Reserve System changed the direction of its policy with remarkable acumen.

Table 9.6
Federal Reserve Policy Action, 1952–1961
(Millions of Dollars)

Period	Changes in Amounts of U.S. Securities Bought Outright (Average Daily Data)	New York Federal Reserve Discount Rate	
Restriction, December 1952–May 1953	+$ 5	January 1, 1953	1.75%
		January 16, 1953	2.00
Ease, May 1953–December 1954	+ 1,007	February 5, 1954	1.75
		April 16, 1954	1.50
Restriction, December 1954–November 1957	− 1,612	April 15, 1955	1.75
		August 5, 1955	2.00
		September 9, 1955	2.25
		November 18, 1955	2.50
		April 13, 1956	2.75
		August 24, 1956	3.00
		August 23, 1957	3.50
Ease, November 1957–July 1958	+ 1,942	November 15, 1957	3.00
		January 24, 1958	2.75
		March 7, 1958	2.25
		April 18, 1958	1.75
Restriction, July 1958–May 1960	+ 479	September 12, 1958	2.00
		November 7, 1958	2.50
		March 6, 1959	3.00
		May 29, 1959	3.50
		September 11, 1959	4.00
Ease, May 1960–February 1961	− 67	June 10, 1960	3.50
		August 12, 1960	3.00

Source: *Federal Reserve Bulletin.*

Credit Ease—May 1953 to December 1954

Through the recession and continuing until December 1954, the Reserve System followed a policy of "active ease." It reduced discount rates twice: from 2 to 1.75 percent in February and from 1.75 to 1.50 percent in April 1954. The Board of Governors also reduced member-bank reserve requirements twice. The first reduction released, as stated above, $1.2 billion of reserves, and the second, in effect from June 16 to August 1, 1954, released $1.6 billion. Open-market operations were directed toward maintaining substantial amounts of net free reserves.

Expansive monetary policy was reinforced by fiscal and debt-management policies. A 10 percent reduction in individual income-tax rates became effective January 1, 1954, and an excise-tax reduction on April 1. The tax reductions on a full-year basis amounted to $7.4 billion, offset in part by an increase of $1.3 billion in social-security contributions, making a net reduction of $6.1 billion. The tax reduction of 1954 was the only instance in the decade of the active use of fiscal policy to stimulate recovery. To cover the resulting deficit, the Treasury sold short- and intermediate-term obligations, which, it was believed, would not compete for investment funds and would find a ready market among commercial banks.

The decline in GNP resulted from a fairly sharp decrease in government purchases of goods and services, inventory liquidation, and a decline in expenditures on producers' durable equipment. Personal-consumption and construction expenditures continued to rise.

The overall decline in economic activity was slight. Consumers maintained their expenditures and reduced their rate of saving; businessmen increased the flow of dividends to stockholders; the easing of mortgage terms stimulated construction; states and municipalities expanded programs of school and road construction; decreases in Federal taxes and increases in unemployment-insurance and social-security payments helped to bolster personal incomes; corporate tax liability fell. The shift to a policy of active ease by the Federal Reserve System had provided a propitious climate for the recovery that took place.

As open-market operations accelerated, some members of the Federal Open Market Committee became convinced that the action taken on March 4–5, 1953, confining operations to the short-end of the curve, should be rescinded in order to give to the manager of the account greater discretion and freedom of action. This school of thought was led by President Allan Sproul of the New York Federal Reserve Bank but was opposed by Chairman William McChesney Martin of the Federal Reserve Board. After considerable discussion, the Open Market Committee continued, with few exceptions, to confine its operations to short-term securities until the balance of payments crisis of 1961.

The arguments of the two schools of thought are set forth in Chapter 18. Chairman Martin feared that purchases of other than short-term Treasury obligations would again enmesh the Reserve System in the unwelcome task of pegging yields. As it was, Federal Reserve open-market operations in the 1950s were conducted almost wholly in short-term securities, preferably Treasury bills, and avoided issues involved in or related to Treasury financing. In consequence, as a joint Treasury-Federal Reserve study pointed out:

> This period saw the development of a broad, active, and self-reliant U.S. Government securities market that would readily accommodate Treasury debt management operations without official support, and could accommodate Federal Reserve buy-and-sell transactions in the volume consistent with a flexible monetary policy.[28]

Credit Tightening—December 1954 to November 1957

For nearly three years the index of industrial activity stood above the long-term trend. Real GNP rose rapidly in the second half of 1954 and through 1955, thereafter remaining on a plateau until a decline in the fourth quarter of 1957. The consumer was the initiating factor in recovery. His expectations became buoyant, and his purchases increased. Automobile production and home building increased spectacularly. The decline in business inventories ceased. Plant expansion and investment joined the upward procession. Federal purchases of goods and services leveled off, but state and local purchases continued to rise.

Business and financial developments in this period were followed with meticulous care at the frequent meetings of the Federal Open Market Committee. By May 10, 1955, the committee reported that recovery was an accomplished fact (some nine months after it had begun), and by December 17, 1957, it agreed that the economy was again in recession.

When indexes are rising rapidly, as they did through 1955, interpretation of the passing scene is simplified. When they begin to move sideways, as they did in 1956 and 1957, analysis becomes much more difficult. It was further complicated in those years by the President's illness and the Suez crisis. Those in charge of the open-market account translated policy directives into action; net free reserves were converted to net borrowed reserves by the end of March 1955. Policy was becoming progressively firmer. Fluctuations thereafter reflected the changing economic appraisals of the Federal Open Market Committee.

Many considerations governed Federal Reserve policy. In the field of credit they included the extent to which bank credit was employed to finance plant and equipment expenditures and the extent to which lending terms were liberalized in real-estate and consumer instalment loans. In production they included changes in inventories, employment, labor productivity, capacity utilization and cost-push pressures. Especially careful consideration was given to price indexes: sensitive commodity, wholesale, and consumer prices. The tools of policy were used continuously to promote recovery yet to prevent inflation as much as possible.*

Through the 1950s the Reserve System was faced with an embarrassment of riches in the abundance of statistical material on which to base its decisions. These included not only the data mentioned in the above paragraph, but in addition, a whole series of additional data which were set forth each month in a publication of the U.S. Department of Commerce, *Business Conditions Digest*. These data include leading, coincident, and lagging cyclical indicators. Leading indicators are those which usually reach peaks or troughs before the corresponding turns in aggregate economic activity and are carefully watched for clues to future developments. Of equal interest, although subject to careful interpretation, are data on anticipated expenditures by businessmen or consumers.[29] Abundance of data will not in themselves assure well-conceived policy, unless central bank officials possess the competence to translate the data into effective action and are undeterred by political pressures.

Changes in the discount rate responded to changes in open-market rates brought about by fluctuations in net free and net borrowed reserves. Increases in discount rates (four in 1955, two in 1956, one in 1957) raised the level from 1.5 to 3.5 percent. Discount policy was reinforced by discount-window policy: control exercised over borrowing by member banks.

Increases in discount rates were made in modest steps. This resulted from a natural hesitancy to use a mechanism which for so many years had been a museum piece and from the conviction that small increases would have a significant effect in curtailing credit. It was argued that small increases, by causing capital losses on government obligations (which loomed large in commercial-bank portfolios), would have a "locked-in" effect, i.e., commercial banks would hesitate to sell government obligations to make loans. As Ascher Achinstein has pointed out, this theory is comforting for those who wish to avoid unpopular high rates,[30] but it received little empirical support in 1955. Commercial banks, convinced that small increases in discount rates heralded still higher rates, engaged in anticipatory selling. Even before the rise in the discount rate in April they had reduced their government portfolios by $5 billion.

---

* In the 1950s, Federal Reserve officials were very concerned about the liberalization of credit terms in the mortgage and consumer credit markets. There was extensive use of mortgages requiring no down payments and a marked lengthening of terms. Savings-and-loan associations increased their borrowing from Federal Home Loan Banks. Mortgage lenders arranged for temporary financing by "warehousing" large amounts of mortgages with commercial banks. Consumer-credit terms were similarly liberal, particularly in 1955. Still another development that caused concern was the use of bank credit to finance capital projects. On August 7, 1956, the Open Market Committee declared -that the System should do what it could to "discourage" the financing of plant and equipment expenditures out of bank credit when such demands should be satisfied in the long-term capital market.

Fiscal policy reinforced monetary policy negatively by maintaining a tight rein on expenditures and avoiding tax cuts. This negative policy did produce a small cash surplus in the calendar years 1956 and 1957, but it resulted in a slight deficit in 1955. Debt-management policy was pro- rather than counter-cyclical. The average maturity of the Federal marketable debt fell sharply. Contrary to the model presented on p. 212, short- rather than long-term obligations were sold.

Credit Ease—November 1957 to July 1958

The recession of 1957–1958 was short-lived and mild. The principal cause was inventory disinvestment. Corporate expenditure on capital equipment fell slightly. Corporate liquidity had declined, and financing terms had become unfavorable. Consumers reduced their purchases of durable goods, but their other expenditures increased. Construction expenditures held up well, and total government purchases of goods and services rose. Various factors accounted for the mildness of the decline: defense orders were stepped up, larger government-support payments expanded farm incomes, corporations maintained dividend payments, and the built-in stabilizers began to work.

The Federal Reserve System followed customary procedures in combating the recession. Discount rates were reduced in November 1957, in the first of four successive waves. Following a substantial decline in stock-market credit, margin requirements were reduced from 70 to 50 percent, effective January 16, 1958. In mid-February the Board announced a first round of reductions in member-bank reserve requirements (see Chapter 3, Table 3.4). Further reductions were announced in mid-March and mid-April. About $1.5 billion of reserve balances were released to member banks. The reduction in reserve requirements, coupled with vigorous open-market operations, not only offset the effect of gold exports—the beginning of a long drain—but also pushed net free reserves to $500 million. Credit demands eased, commercial banks added to their investment portfolios, and interest rates tumbled.

Administration action included various measures to spur building activity, a temporary lengthening of the eligibility period for unemployment benefits, a speed-up of defense procurement, acceleration of grants-in-aid and tax refunds to State and local bodies,[31] and larger allocations for the Federal highway program.

In the second half of 1957 government receipts exceeded disbursements by $1.6 billion. In the first half of 1958 the situation changed completely. Government disbursements exceeded receipts by $8.2 billion (at seasonally adjusted annual rates). This "turn-around" of $9.8 billion—most of which reflected a decline in receipts—had a greater expansive impact on the economy than fiscal operations had had in either of the other two postwar contractions.[32]

As in the 1953–1954 recession, the Federal government took advantage of the decline in interest rates to issue longer-term securities. Between September 1957 and June 1958 the Treasury put out seven issues of bonds, totaling $16 billion, either for cash or in exchange for maturing securities. The bonds ranged in maturity from six to thirty-two years. Debt operations during the period of high interest rates in fiscal 1957 had been concentrated at the "short end" of the curve. This policy, which directly contradicted that embodied in the model presented on pp. 211–212, was reversed once interest rates began to decline.

During the latter half of June 1958 severe pressures developed in the Treasury bond market. A large volume of government securities had been purchased, some outright and some on unduly thin margins, by temporary holders in the expectation of further easing of interest rates. The growing recognition that business activity was rising and that the Reserve banks might tighten credit policy caused a sharp reversal of expectations. Prices began to decline and margin calls forced speculators, as well as institutional investors, to sell. The Treasury endeavored to halt the decline by purchasing $600 million of a newly issued seven-year bond.

A new round of selling was precipitated by an announcement that American troops had landed in Lebanon. The situation had so deteriorated that by mid-afternoon of July 18, 1958, there were no bids for government obligations. Despite a large volume of net excess reserves the market had become disorderly. The Federal Open Market Committee authorized the manager of the open market account to purchase government obligations without limitation on maturity or amount. A small volume of government securities other than Treasury bills was purchased, and the disorder passed. The authorization was terminated on July 24.

Remedial steps were taken in the effort to curtail future speculations in government securities. The Comptroller of the Currency issued instructions to national-bank examiners throughout the country, prescribing minimum margin requirements. The New York State Banking Department took parallel action, and the New York Stock Exchange proceeded against one of its member firms that had failed to meet the Exchange's margin requirements.

Credit Restriction—July 1958 to May 1960

On July 29, 1958, the Federal Open Market Committee reported that April had marked the trough of the recession, that there was growing evidence of business improvement, and that the Reserve System should recapture the reserves that had been placed in the market in June to correct disorder. Open-market holdings were reduced, but exports of gold and the seasonal expansion in the currency were not offset. Member-bank borrowing began to rise. By the end of the year net free reserves had been converted into net borrowed reserves. Discount rates were increased and margin requirements were raised.

Table 9.6 shows that open-market holdings increased during the period of restraint. The increase was small relative to gold exports and currency increases, which forced a decline in excess reserves and an increase in member-bank borrowing. Pressure on interest rates was heavy and would have been heavier had not a small amount of vault cash been allowed to count as part of required reserves. All interest rates—but particularly short-term rates—rose sharply, with the result that occasionally the interest curve was negatively inclined for the first time since the late 1920s.

The reasons for moving toward restraint in the early stages of revival were a rapid increase in total debt and a decline in its quality, a sharp rise in the loan portfolios of commercial banks, continued advances in consumer prices, and a heavily adverse balance of payments. These factors called for a restrictive policy, despite the higher level of unemployment, which was tending to become more structural than cyclical and which in consequence was not wholly responsive to monetary policy.

Credit Ease—May 1960 to February 1961

Even before the summer of 1960 the strength of final demand began to ebb. Inventories fell, personal consumption dropped, and financial savings increased. Outlays on residential construction were reduced, and unemployment was rising. The recession proved to be the mildest that the country had experienced since World War II. Even so, unemployment continued to be a serious problem. By early 1961 it had risen to 7 percent, and more than half the labor markets were classified as having "a substantial labor surplus." There was a significant rise in long-term unemployment and the unemployment of heads of families.

During each of the postwar booms unemployment, though reduced, rose above the maximum reached in the preceding cycle. This led to continued discussion between those who believed that unemployment could be rectified only by increasing monetary demand and those who believed that correction required certain structural changes—like job training, education, and elimination of racial discrimination. As time went on more emphasis was given to the need for structural change.

Once the decline started, the Federal Reserve System moved rapidly toward easier money, principally by allowing member banks to include all their vault cash in required reserves and by reducing the reserve requirements of the central reserve-city banks. The open-market portfolio actually fell slightly. The reduction in reserve requirements not only offset a substantial gold loss but also brought about a sharp increase in net free reserves. Discount rates were reduced to 3 percent and margin requirements to 70 percent. Money rates, particularly short-term rates, fell sharply. But even at their low points all interest rates stood above their previous recession lows. In the postwar period cyclical swings fluctuated about a strong upward secular trend.

The upward trend in interest rates through the 1950s was evidence that the supply of savings had lagged behind demand. This situation could have been partly rectified had the Federal debt been reduced, the reductions in prosperity exceeding the increases in recession. Reductions would have provided savings to meet part of the demand for lendable funds, inflationary pressures would have been less acute, and the burden on the banking system and the capital markets would have been smaller. Cyclical fluctuations in interest rates would also have been less pronounced.

The experience in the 1950s does, however, underscore the impressive cyclical resilience of the postwar economy. Declines in business activity were short-lived. Depressions were avoided. The Reserve System was pragmatic and flexible in its approach. It avoided a doctrinaire position and did not fall victim to any single-cause explanation of the business cycle.

In both the timing of its policies and the degrees of monetary relaxation or restraint that it employed, the Reserve System, assisted by built-in stabilizers, made an important contribution to economic stability. It may have moved too far toward ease in 1954 and may have been tardy in imposing restraint in 1955. But at that time the efficacy of the built-in stabilizers in preventing serious depression had not been fully tested. The Reserve System feared depression in 1954 and did not wish to bring the expansion of 1955—the first one not influenced directly by the aftermath of World War II or the Korean war—to an untimely end. Over the whole period the System would have been justified in following a more restrictive credit policy, in view of the use made of bank credit, cost-push pressures, and growing reluctance by foreigners to hold dollars; these factors were by-products of the continuing American deficit in the international balance of payments (see Chapter 12).

CONCLUDING OBSERVATIONS

Both the 1920s and 1950s were characterized by minor cycles and rapid increases in production. In both decades depression was avoided. In the 1920s Federal Reserve action was abetted by fiscal and debt-management policies; in the 1950s fiscal policy, save for the built-in stabilizers, played a minor role, and the Federal debt was managed in such fashion that it contributed to, rather than countered cyclical tendencies.

In the 1920s, the Reserve System relied on changes in the discount rates, open-market operations, and direct pressure. In the 1950s, in addition to these tools, it relied on changes in member-bank reserve requirements and margin requirements on security loans. Substantial reductions in reserve requirements were ordered during recessions but not during periods of economic expansion. Reserve requirements were reduced and cash included in reserves to increase the competitive power of member banks, whose officers believed that requirements were unreasonably high in comparison with those of nonmember banks; to stimulate business activity, and to ensure an "adequate" increase in the money supply.

Surface phenomena, which seemed to indicate satisfactory underlying economic situations, masked disquieting credit developments. These consisted mainly of changes in the use of bank credit and in lending standards. In the 1920s they included a sharp rise in stock-exchange loans and a decline in the quality of credit in foreign and domestic bonds and mortgage loans. In the 1950s they were evidenced by a decline in the quality of consumer and mortgage credit, and the use of credit in financing capital projects. Control over margin requirements kept security loans from becoming in the 1950s the problem that they had been in the 1920s. The decline in the quality of credit in the 1920s had intensified the Great Depression, in fact had probably made it "great;" and the decline of quality in the 1950s intensified cost-push pressures and thus contributed to balance-of-payments deficits in the 1960s.

If these two decades offer any lesson it is that central banks must be continuously alert to changes in net public and private debt, not only in quantity but also in use, amount monetized, type monetized, and improvements or deterioration in quality. Quite apart from quantity of debt, changes in its structure and quality directly affect cyclical fluctuations, inflationary pressures, and the ability of a central bank to stabilize the economy.

The character and structure of the debt may themselves help to condition central-bank policy. A large volume of debt that depends for repayment upon future income (consumer debt) may dissuade monetary authorities from taking anti-inflationary measures even when they are justified. A deterioration in quality may induce a government or central bank to follow inflationary policies in order to "validate" debt. Debt is "validated"; however, the thrifty are victimized.

Notes

1. Wesley C. Mitchell, "A Review," *Recent Economic Changes in the United States,* II (New York: McGraw-Hill, 1929), pp. 890–891, 909–910.

2. Edwin F. Gay and Leo Wolman, "Trends in Economic Organization," *Recent Social Trends in the United States,* One Volume Edition (New York: McGraw-Hill, 1934), pp. 252–253.

3. Address by C. Canby Balderston, formerly Vice Chairman of the Board of Governors of the Federal Reserve System, before The American Bankers Association Monetary Conference, Princeton, N.J., March 19, 1965.

4. *Committee on the Working of the Monetary System.* Report (London: Her Majesty's Stationary Office, August 1959), pp. 102–106.

5. *Tenth Annual Report of the Federal Reserve Board Covering Operations for the Year 1923* (Washington, D.C.: Government Printing Office, 1924), pp. 29–39.

6. *All Bank Statistics, United States, 1896–1955* (Board of Governors of the Federal Reserve System, April 1959), p. 34.

7. See Neil H. Jacoby and Raymond J. Saulnier, *Business Finance and Banking* (New York: National Bureau of Economic Research, 1947), chapter 3.

8. B. H. Beckhart, *The New York Money Market,* Vol. III (New York: Columbia University Press, 1932), pp. 77–78.

9. *Banking and Monetary Statistics* (Washington, D.C.: Board of Governors of the Federal Reserve System, November 1943), p. 369.

10. *Federal Reserve Bulletin* (April 1923), p. 410.

11. *Ninth Annual Report of the Federal Reserve Board Covering Operations for the Year 1922* (Washington, D.C.: Government Printing Office, 1923), p. 8.

12. *Eighth Annual Report of the Federal Reserve Board Covering Operations for the Year 1921* (Washington, D.C.: Government Printing Office, 1922), p. 33.

13. *Ninth Annual Report of the Federal Reserve Board Covering Operations for the Year 1922* (Washington, D.C.: Government Printing Office, 1923), pp. 18–25.

14. *Operation of the National and Federal Reserve Banking Systems.* Hearings before a Subcommittee of the Committee on Banking and Currency. U.S. Senate, 71st Cong., 3rd sess. Pursuant to S. Res. 71. Appendix, Part 6. Federal Reserve Questionnaires (Washington, D.C.: Government Printing Office, 1931), pp. 799, 803–804, 811.

15. *Tenth Annual Report of the Federal Reserve Board Covering Operations for the Year 1923* (Washington, D.C.: Government Printing Office, 1923), p. 14.

16. Lester V. Chandler, *Benjamin Strong, Central Banker* (Washington, D.C.: The Brookings Institution, 1958), p. 221.

17. Elmus R. Wicker, *Federal Reserve Monetary Policy 1917–1933* (New York: Random House, 1966), p. 71.

18. *Operation of the National and Federal Reserve Banking Systems, op. cit.,* pp. 799–812.

19. Chandler, *op. cit.,* p. 215.

20. *Operation of the National and Federal Reserve Banking Systems, op. cit.,* p. 800.

21. *Operation of the National and Federal Reserve Banking Systems, op. cit.,* p. 805.

22. Chandler, *op. cit.,* pp. 244–246.

23. For a detailed discussion of this period see Benjamin Haggott Beckhart, James G. Smith and William Adams Brown, Jr., *The New York Money Market,* Vol. IV (New York: Columbia University Press, 1932), part one.

24. *Fifteenth Annual Report Federal Reserve Bank of New York for the Year Ended December 31, 1929* (New York: Federal Reserve Bank of New York, February 25, 1930), p. 6.

25. For a detailed scholarly discussion of this period, see Stephen V. O. Clarke, *Central Bank Cooperation 1924–1931* (New York: Federal Reserve Bank, 1967).

26. Thorstein Veblen, *The Theory of Business Enterprise* (New York: Charles Scribner's Sons, 1935), p. 106.

27. A discussion of this period is to be found in *United States Monetary Policy: Recent Thinking and Experience.* Hearings before the Subcommittee on Economic Stabilization of the Joint Committee on the Economic Report, Congress of the United States 83rd Cong., 2nd sess., Pursuant to Sec. 5(a) of Public Law 304, December 6 and 7, 1954 (Washington, D.C.: Government Printing Office, 1954).

28. *Report of the Joint Treasury-Federal Reserve Study of the U.S. Government Securities Market* (Washington, D.C.: The Federal Reserve System, April 1969), p. 7.

29. For a description and discussion of these various series see *Business Conditions Digest,* (U.S. Department of Commerce, Bureau of the Census, September 1971).

30. Ascher Achinstein, *Federal Reserve Policy and Economic Stability 1951–1957.* Senate Report 2500, 85th Cong., 2nd sess. (Washington, D.C.: Government Printing Office, 1958), pp. XI and 6–7.

31. *Economic Report of the President.* Transmitted to the Congress January 20, 1959 (Washington, D.C.: Government Printing Office, 1959), p. 41.

32. *Ibid.,* pp. 44 and 200.

Struggling with Depression

CHAPTER 10

THE THREE DEPRESSIONS

In the late 1920s the Federal Reserve Bank of New York instructed and entertained classes in money and banking with motion pictures of bank runs during the panic of 1907. Long lines of depositors, herded into queues by mounted policemen, were seen anxiously waiting for bank doors to open so that they might quickly convert their deposits into cash. The implication was that bank runs were a relic of an unenlightened past and could not possibly recur in this more sophisticated age. Within a few years this motion picture was relegated to an inactive file. Bank runs were again dominating the financial news, and bank failures were occurring on a scale never before witnessed in American history.

Not that the Reserve System was responsible for the collapse of the banking system. But its operations have not prevented several serious depressions. Three have occurred since its establishment; one was among the most oppressive ever to blast the American economy.

Depressions	Duration
January 1920–July 1921	18 months
August 1929–March 1933	43 months
May 1937–June 1938	13 months

These depressions varied greatly not only in length but also in severity. The Federal Reserve Board Index of Industrial Production declined 32 percent in the first, 53 percent in the second and 33 percent in the third. Judged by duration and severity the second depression easily merited the adjective "great."

At least five other declines in business activity have taken place, but they were relatively mild; the Index of Industrial Production declined between 5 and 18 percent. The mildness of these declines justifies calling them "recessions," whereas declines of 25 percent or more, to draw an arbitrary line, may be termed a "depression."

THE FIRST DEPRESSION—JANUARY 1920 TO JULY 1921

The Nature of the Depression

There were many reasons for the decline in business activity. The cessation of war expenditures and foreign aid caused exports to collapse. From 1920 to 1921 exports fell from $8.7 to $4.6 billion and imports from $5.8 to $3.3 billion. Federal expenditures declined from $18.5 billion to $6.4 billion and a Federal deficit of $13 billion was converted into a surplus of $300 million.[1] These developments, by cutting into domestic buying power, brought about a drastic liquidation in top-heavy inventories. Prices tumbled, particularly for foodstuffs and raw materials, drying up buying power in farm areas and raw-material producing nations. A sharp drop in plant and equipment expenditures followed; by further reducing consumer income, it aggravated the decline.

The depression was particularly severe in centers of durable goods production. The physical output of steel fell more than 50 percent, the dollar value of industrial machinery 44 percent, that of construction materials about 40 percent, that of passenger cars about 40 percent.[2] The duration of this depression, severe as it was, was somewhat shorter than average peacetime contractions. The sharp price decline, abbetted by downward flexibility in wages, finally evoked demand from consumers and business firms. Automobile production and construction activity sparked the rise.

This depression was no more severe, as measured by the decline in the production index, than that of 1937-1938, possibly because of the staying power of the commercial-banking system. Although losses on loans and securities were heavy, bank suspensions, either in number or deposit liabilities, were not sufficient to undermine confidence in all credit institutions.

The Price Decline • Wholesale prices had reached a peak in England and Japan in March 1920; in France and Italy in April; in the United States, India, and Canada in May; in Sweden in June; in the Netherlands in July; and in

Australia in August. Within the short space of five months prices began to decline rapidly in the greater part of the world. In the United States wholesale prices tumbled from a peak of 247 (1913 = 100) in May 1920 to 138 in January 1922. Only in those nations in which large public deficits were met by the constant issuing of fiat money did prices continue to increase. The first warning of the general decline in prices was the collapse of the silk market in Japan, where from January to May 1920 the index of raw-silk prices fell by more than 50 percent.

The decline in wholesale prices was particularly severe for farm products, foods, metal and metal products, chemicals, and drugs. Less severe were the declines in fuel and lighting, clothing, house furnishings, and building materials. The unevenness of the price decline worsened the economic position of various economic groups, particularly producers of foodstuffs and raw materials. It thus weighed heavily upon the raw-material producing nations, which customarily negotiate large foreign loans while export prices are high and often find that they must repay when markets are depressed. Foodstuffs are particularly subject to the vicissitudes of the market. A relatively slight surplus results in a disproportionately steep price decline. A slight shortage brings about a steep rise.

Credit developments themselves played an important role in the collapse of prices. Loan volume had increased sharply, and quality had deteriorated during the upswing of the 1919 credit and business cycle. From the middle of 1918 to the middle of 1920 total loans of all commercial banks had risen from $21 billion to $29 billion. By June 1922 they had fallen to $25 billion (see Table 10.1). As prices fell, loans were frozen. Banks that forced loan collections—and many did—found themselves dealing in automobiles, silk, and sugar and began to sell these goods at depressed prices.

An example of the decline in loan quality can be found in the acceptance market. Many abuses developed: the renewal of acceptances, the practice of banks discounting their own acceptances, the use of acceptances to finance speculative and long-term investments, failure to relate acceptances to specific transactions, use of acceptances to grant loans to borrowers beyond the limits prescribed by Section 5200 of the U.S. Revised Statutes, and use of acceptances to secure overdrafts. Deterioration in the quality of acceptances was recognized long before the 1920-1921 depression. It was not the result of the depression but occurred earlier and aggravated its severity.

Terms of trade turned against farm areas as they did against raw-materials-producing nations. With the decline in agricultural prices, the funds flowing into farm areas fell, but the volume flowing out remained high as long as farmers and farm communities continued to purchase non-farm products and to repay debts. The reserves of local banks declined, forcing them in turn to accelerate liquidation of loans and investments.

The Money Supply • During the depression (January 1920–July 1921) the money supply (currency held by the public and demand deposits adjusted) fell $2.4 billion, or slightly more than 10 percent. Along with the decrease in deposit totals, deposit turnover fell. The decline in deposits resulted from a reduction in commercial bank loans of somewhat similar magnitude. Investments showed little change.

The decline in loans, which brought about the decrease in the money supply, was not uniformly proportional throughout the country. Liquidation was much sharper in the agricultural then in industrial communities and in fact continued unabated in farm areas throughout the 1920s. In Iowa, for example, the loans of all banks, which had risen from $500 million in 1913 to $991 million in 1920, fell to a low of $141 million in 1933. The same trend occurred in North Dakota; loans of all banks rising from $75 million in 1913 to $202 million in 1920 and falling to $25 million by 1935.

In an industrial state such as Pennsylvania, the loans of all commercial banks rose from $1.2 billion in 1913 to $2.2 billion in 1920, receding to $2 billion in 1922. They then began to rise again reaching a peak of $3.5 billion in 1929, far above the high point of 1920. Fluctuations in New York State were similar to those in Pennsylvania. The loans of all commercial banks rose from $2.5 billion in 1913 to $6 billion in 1920, receded to $5.0 billion in 1922, and increased again to $9.5 billion in 1930. The effect of the depression upon bank loans in industrial areas was thus sharp but not prolonged; in the rural areas it was both sharp and prolonged.[3]

From mid 1919 to mid 1920, when loans were increasing rapidly, the investment portfolio decreased. During the next year, when loans were falling rapidly, it remained stable; thereafter it rose, with the rise in 1922 offsetting the decline in loans.

Federal Reserve Policies • In the depression of 1920–1921 there was no serious discussion of the desirability of government intervention. In his annual report for fiscal 1921, Secretary of the Treasury Andrew W. Mellon stated: "The nation cannot continue to spend at this shocking rate [Expenditures for fiscal 1921 were $5 billion, in contrast to $6 billion in 1920 and $14 billion in 1919]. . . . This is no time for extravagance or for entering upon new fields of expenditures

Table 10.1
All Commercial Banks
(Billions of Dollars)

Year (a)	Total Loans	Total Investments	Government Securities	Other Securities
1918	$21	$7.5	$3.0	$4.5
1919	23	9.5	4.9	4.6
1920	29	8.4	3.6	4.8
1921	26	8.4	3.3	5.1
1922	25	9.4	3.8	5.5
1923	27	10.3	4.6	5.7

(a) All data are for June 30 or the nearest date for which they were available.

Source: *The Statistical History of The United States from Colonial Times to the Present* (Stamford, Conn., Fairfield Publishers, Inc., 1965) p. 631.

. . . . Expenditures should not even be permitted to continue at the present rate." [4] Secretary Mellon, to be sure, did recommend a further reduction in taxes beyond that provided in the Revenue Act of 1921. He reasoned that tax rates existing then had impaired incentive, had caused a decline in savings, had interfered with the freedom of business transactions, and had diverted capital from productive uses. He estimated that the Revenue Act of 1921 would reduce the aggregate tax burden by $835 million.

Mellon's arguments for a reduction in tax rates were not couched in terms of budgeting for a Federal deficit or of stimulating consumer income. He would have opposed such proposals vigorously, convinced as he was that the public debt should be reduced. He took pride in the fact that government debt, consisting principally of the floating debt, had been reduced $300 million in fiscal 1921. He believed that further reductions should and would occur if the government exercised the strictest economy. The Secretary believed that tax reduction would, by releasing the energies of the private sector, provide an important stimulus. This was as far as he would go.

The attitude of the Federal Reserve System was similar to that of the United States Treasury. It did not entertain the possibility of embarking on countercyclical action. Had it done so, it would, of course, have relied upon large open-market operations.

One finds practically no discussion of open-market operations in the annual reports of the Federal Reserve Board or in the resolutions of the Federal Advisory Council. What discussions took place centered on the advisability of purchasing bankers' acceptances in order to build up a discount market. The Council itself was principally interested in discount rate policy and in the criteria of that policy. Not that the effects of open-market operations were unknown, it was simply that discount policy seemed the appropriate credit policy at the time. The Council agreed that the principal guide to discount policy was the reserve ratio of the Federal Reserve banks.

On November 5, 1920, when deposit and note liabilities of the Reserve banks reached a peak, the ratio of reserves held against the aggregate of these liabilities amounted to 43 percent. The increase in gold reserves and the decline in liabilities raised it to 70 percent by the end of 1921. Through 1922 the ratio fluctuated between 73 and 79 percent. Apparently the Reserve Board regarded this ratio as satisfactory, if not a bit high, for action was taken to stabilize the ratio by putting gold certificates and coins in circulation. This action was opposed by the Federal Reserve Council, which insisted that the nation's gold be mobilized with the Reserve banks.

In emphasizing the reserve ratio, as the System did through 1921, it was simply following the traditional policy of the Bank of England. Not until 1923 did the Board question its value as a guide to credit policy (see Chapter 9).[5]

During the depression of 1920–1921 and into the period of recovery, substantial declines took place in member-bank borrowing. This resulted not from open-market operations but rather from a heavy gold inflow and a cyclical retirement of the currency. Bills discounted, which had been rising steadily since August 1917, reached a peak of $2.8 billion in October 1920. From that point, the highest in the history of the System, the total fell to $396 million in August 1922. The reasons for this decline are clear from Table 10.2.

The difference between the two sums, $2.4 billion, is of course, equal to the decline in bills discounted. Purchases of government securities by the Federal Reserve banks played no role in causing member-bank borrowing to decline. The small increase was more than offset by the decline in bills bought and in other Federal Reserve bank credit.

The Port of New York was the chief recipient of the gold sent by foreign nations to liquidate indebtedness and to purchase goods. Had foreign nations been able to pay debts or to buy goods by selling their own products freely in the United States, the gold inflow would have been smaller, and member-bank indebtedness would have remained at a higher level (unless the Reserve System had engaged in extensive open-market operations). High American tariffs inhibited the inflow of foreign goods.

Table 10.2
Changes in Member-Bank Reserves and Related Factors
October 1920–August 1922
(Millions of Dollars)

Factors Causing Decline in Bills Discounted		Offsetting Factors	
Federal Reserve Credit:		**Federal Reserve Credit:**	
U.S. Securities	(+)$ 192	Bills bought	(−)$144
Gold stock	(+) 985	All other	(−) 84
Treasury currency	(+) 165	Treasury cash holdings	(+) 10
Money in circulation	(−) 1,225	Treasury deposits at	
Nonmember Bank Deposits	(−) 2	Federal Reserve banks	(+) 10
Other Federal Reserve accounts	(−) 47		
Member-bank Reserve balances	(−) 16		
Total	$2,632	Total	$248

Source: *Banking and Monetary Statistics* (Washington, D.C.: Board of Governors of the Federal Reserve System, November 1943), p. 369.

Gold imports came in large amounts from France, Sweden, the Netherlands, the United Kingdom, Canada, British India, China, and Australia. As gold entered the Port of New York, the reserves and deposit liabilities of the New York commercial banks increased. They were enabled to reduce their indebtedness to the Reserve bank, to increase their investment holdings, and were in a position to extend loans.

John Maynard Keynes accused the Federal Reserve System of "sterilizing" gold in those years and thus prolonging and deepening the depression. There was, however, no conscious sterilization as there was later when the Treasury took positive action in the 1930s. Possibly what he had in mind was that the Reserve banks should, as soon as the depression got under way, have engaged extensively in open-market operations. By reducing member-bank borrowing such operations would have caused a decline in interest rates and would possibly have induced American loans and funds to flow abroad. European nations would have been under less compulsion to send gold to the United States, and deflationary pressures might then have been less severe.

Discount Rate Policy • Changes in discount rates at the Federal Reserve Bank of New York through the period of contraction are shown in Table 10.3. They were high throughout the depression and were not reduced until recovery was already under way. Rates on war paper remained consistently below rates on commercial paper until July 21, 1921, at which time they were equalized.

Table 10.3
Discount Rates at the Federal Reserve Bank of New York, 1920–1921

Effective Date	Commercial Paper (60–90 days)	Notes Secured by Treasury Notes and Certificates of Indebtedness (90 days)
January 1, 1920	4.75%	4.75%
January 23, 1920	6.00	—
February 26, 1920	—	5.00
June 1, 1920	7.00	5.50
February 5, 1921	—	6.00
May 5, 1921	6.50	—
June 16, 1921	6.00	—
July 21, 1921	5.50	5.50
September 22, 1921	5.00	5.00
November 3, 1921	4.50	4.50

Source: Seventh Annual Report of the Federal Reserve Board Covering Operations for the year 1920 (Washington, D.C.: Government Printing Office, 1921), pp. 60–61; and Eighth Annual Report of the Federal Reserve Board Covering Operations for the year 1921 (Washington, D.C.: Government Printing Office, 1922), p. 37.

The adoption and maintenance of high discount rates during the contraction was subject to much criticism at the time. Discount policy, however, resulted from the conviction that reserve ratios were low and that high discount rates were required to drive war paper from commercial-bank portfolios and to restore the banks to normal functioning. The Bank of England followed much the same policy. Both central banks delayed reducing bank rates until market rates fell; they fell in the United States as the gold stock increased and money in circulation declined.*

Interdistrict Discounting • It will be recalled that in the fall of 1919 and in the spring of 1920 the eastern Reserve banks had been forced to seek accommodation from other Reserve banks (see Chapter 8, for details). Funds were required to finance industrial needs and to aid the government in its fiscal operations. The picture then changed, and through the greater part of 1920 and 1921 the Federal Reserve banks of Boston, Philadelphia, Cleveland, and San Francisco extended credit to other Federal Reserve banks, especially to those in agricultural areas which were forced to borrow to meet seasonal requirements and to finance the net outward flow of funds.

Interdistrict rediscounting was under the supervision of the Federal Reserve Board. All requests were approved, and none were refused. The reserves of the

---

* In March 1921 Secretary of the Treasury Mellon asked for a reduction in discount rates, for President Warren G. Harding was anxious to help the farmers. Comptroller of the Currency John Skelton Williams had proposed that discount rates be reduced as early as December 1920. Elmus R. Wicker, *Federal Reserve Monetary Policy, 1917–1933* (New York: Random House, 1966), chap. 3.

Federal Reserve banks were shifted about in such a manner as to keep the reserves of all twelve banks above the legal minimum (40 percent against notes and 35 percent against deposits).[6] Otherwise the percentage of reserves at the New York Reserve Bank at one time would have fallen to 34.2 percent, that at Richmond to 25.6 percent, that at Atlanta to 17 percent, that at Minneapolis to 18 percent, that at Kansas City to 15.9 percent, and that at Dallas to 9.2 percent. If one assumes that these figures would have represented the reserve ratios against Federal Reserve notes, the Board of Governors would have been compelled to impose a tax of 16 percent on the uncovered portion of notes issued by the Federal Reserve Bank of Dallas. This tax would have been added to the then current discount rate, 6 percent, increasing it to 22 percent!

The Federal Reserve Advisory Council took the position that no limit should be placed on interdistrict discounting, that the Reserve System was a single central bank and should be so regarded. No interdistrict rediscounting has taken place since December 9, 1921, when the Dallas bank borrowed $1 million from Boston; all interdistrict rediscounts were retired by December 15, 1921. Since that time the reserves of the Federal Reserve banks have been moved about by shifts in the open-market portfolio which take place in a strictly mechanical fashion in order to equalize the reserve percentages of the Reserve banks as long as the requirements were in effect.

Political Repercussions • The decline in prices, resulting in the usual hardship for debtor classes, engendered acute political antipathy toward the Reserve System. However, criticism was not directed at fiscal policy which had not entered public consciousness as a countercyclical instrument. Emphasis on fiscal policy came more than a decade later. The Federal Reserve Board was accused of having decided to embark upon a drastic policy of deflation at a secret meeting held on May 18, 1920; of denying funds to the farmer so that they could be used on Wall Street; and of discriminating against small banks by demanding excess collateral against the loans granted them. System officials were accused of profiting from large salaries, of causing losses of several billion dollars to holders of Liberty bonds, and of fostering Wall Street speculation.

These charges and many others like them led to an investigation of the System by the Joint Commission of Agricultural Inquiry. Provision for the Commission was incorporated in a resolution which passed the Senate on May 31 and the House on June 7, 1921. The Commission took extensive testimony, filling three volumes of 2,400 pages. Its findings completely exonerated the Reserve System from its critics' charges.

The criticism and investigation did lead to passage of the Dirt Farmer Amendment, enlarging the Board from seven to eight members with the understanding that a "dirt farmer" would be appointed (see Chapter 2, for details), and to passage of two amendments permitting the discounting of longer-term agricultural and livestock paper. Finally, the Agricultural Credits Act was passed on March 4, 1923, which inter alia established the Federal Intemediate Credit banks and the National Agricultural Credit corporations.

An Evaluation

Convinced that liquidation was necessary to rid the economy of excesses and to establish a firm basis for recovery, the Federal Reserve System followed a restrictive policy in the first of the three depressions. Discount rates were not reduced and open-market purchases were not undertaken. The inflow of gold and the decline of money in circulation caused member-bank borrowing to decline and increased the reserve ratio, which the Reserve Board believed should be the principal guide to policy in that troubled period. Once discount rates began to be reduced in May 1921, further reductions followed one another in quick succession.

The failure of the Reserve System to respond to the decline in business activity (even though its response might not have been entirely successful) stands in sharp contrast to its quick response on other occasions, including 1929. Intervention by the Reserve banks would probably have moderated the liquidation of bank credit, enabled commercial banks to increase their investment portfolios more rapidly, promoted fuller functioning of the capital markets, and eased the strain on European currencies. It might even have stimulated an earlier recovery. Had this action been accompanied on the part of the Federal Government by a retention of and a further lowering of the rates established in the Underwood Tarriff Act of 1913, a powerful stimulus would have been given to economic progress throughout the world.

THE SECOND DEPRESSION— AUGUST 1929 TO MARCH 1933

Nature and Severity

According to the chronology of the National Bureau of Economic Research,[7] the Great Depression begun in August 1929 and continued until March 1933. This contraction, lasting forty-three months, has been exceeded only by the one of sixty-five months from October 1873 to March 1879.

GNP in constant dollars (at 1958 prices) declined during the four-year period from $203.6 billion to $141.5 billion. In current dollars it fell from $103.1 billion to $56 billion. If we project the growth in GNP during the 1920s through 1933, the loss in GNP reaches the astounding total in 1929 dollars of nearly $185 billion.

Unemployment rose from 1.55 million in 1929 to 12.83 million in 1933, from 3.2 to 24.9 percent of the labor force. Full employment gave way to a situation in which one out of every four in the labor force was unemployed. Those who were employed suffered a substantial decline in wages. Average weekly earnings in all manufacturing fell from $25.03 in 1929 to $16.73 in 1933. Even when adjusted for the decline in consumer prices the drop in wages of those employed was substantial.

The depression was worldwide, affecting industrial and agricultural nations, communist and capitalist powers. It resulted in political upheaval, revolution, and military aggression. It was an important factor in engulfing nations in World War II. For many years it continued to influence government policy even though current economics situations had completely changed.

Through 1930 the decline in business activity, though severe, was regarded as a conventional depression, rather like that of 1920-1921. Early in 1931 a slight improvement occurred, and many people concluded that the worst was over. Industrial production, which had fallen from 126 in May 1929 (1923–1925 = 100) to 76 in December 1930, started to rise, reaching 90 in April 1931.[8] Belying optimistic expectations it began to decline once again, tumbling to 60 in March 1933. The principal reasons for the renewed decline, marking descent into the Great Depression, were domestic and international liquidity crises and the resulting collapse of credit systems.

Liquidity crises result from the shifting of funds from assets of less acceptability to assets of greater acceptability: from savings to demand deposits, from deposits to currency, from currency to gold, from one commercial bank to another, and from one country to another. It is relatively easy to shift demand deposits, the result of credit creation, to other banks, financial intermediaries and financial institutions in other nations. It is the reverse process that may, if the amounts are large, creditors insistent, and liquid assets small, cause the breakdown of banking systems and undermine currencies. Liquidity shifts of ominous proportions result from lack of confidence in individual banks, banking systems, or currencies. They are aggravated when financial institutions fail to cover short-term liabilities with short-term assets, when short-term funds are used to finance long-term credit needs, when lending standards have deteriorated, and when savings and time deposits are treated as demand deposits subject to sudden withdrawal. Liquidity crises are also aggravated if a nation has a unit rather than a branch banking system and if the gold exchange standard, with its concentration of short-term liabilities in a few key-currency nations, is of importance.

Banking Problems

The banking system entered the Great Depression in a weakened condition. The 1920s had witnessed a deterioration in asset quality resulting not only from changed lending standards (see Chapter 9, for details) but also from growing laxity in chartering and supervision of banks. This laxity had resulted from a competitive struggle between the state and national systems to increase the number of banks in their respective domains.

In state banking systems political considerations frequently dictated the appointment of bank superintendents and examiners. Records were imperfectly kept, and reports were incomplete and inadequate. Bank examiners frequently counted upon entering the employ of banks they examined. The quality of bank management declined. Bank officers received salaries and bonuses especially in those instances in which the officers controlled the banks, far out of line with services rendered.

Coupled with these developments, which were reflected in a decline in asset quality, were others associated specifically with the Great Depression: rapid decline in security values, in prices of urban and farm real estate, and in commodity prices.

Waning confidence in the banking system was evinced in the rapid withdrawal of currency by depositors (tellers' runs) and in the shifting of deposits to other institutions (clearinghouse runs). Tellers' runs were reflected in changes in the volume of hoarded currency, taking the form of large denomination bills.[9] Each successive wave of bank failures provoked currency drains, which resulted in further bank failures. A crucial failure was that in December 1930 of the state chartered Bank of United States in New York City, with its 400,000 depositors at fifty-nine branches; this failure caused heavy withdrawals in New York and elsewhere. The contagion of fear knew no geographical limits.

In September 1931, after the suspension of the gold standard in England, currency hoarding was greatly accelerated (Chapter 11, p. 304). This new upsurge was accompanied by a sharp rise in bank failures. A further wave of failures late in 1932 and early in 1933 led to another major hoarding movement. These

failures resulted in part from a law enacted in July 1932, requiring the Reconstruction Finance Corporation (RFC) to submit each month to the President, the
Senate, and the House of Representatives a statement listing the banks to which
loans and advances had been extended, as well as the amount and interest rate of
each loan. In August 1932, the Speaker of the House of Representatives instructed
the RFC to make the names public. The inclusion of a bank on this list was interpreted as a sign of weakness and subjected it to a run.

Clearinghouse runs centered on individual banks and on banks in particular
regions. Deposits were shifted from state to national banks, from nonmember to
member banks, from banks in smaller towns to those in larger communities, from
banks in the West to banks in the East, from outlying regions to money-market
centers. Deposits were shifted from commercial banks to postal-savings banks and
to mutual-savings banks, whose deposit liabilities grew as the deposit liabilities of
other banks fell. There was an unceasing quest for safety.

If, in the middle of 1931 before European banking difficulties became so
serious, the Federal government had been able and willing to guarantee the liabilities of all banks, pending banking reform and reorganization, the depression might
have ended. At least it probably would not have plunged to such depths. In February 1933, renewed banking difficulties led to the temporary closing of all banks
by official action, first in a few states and finally, by presidential proclamation,
throughout the country.

The developments through these years highlight the need to concentrate in
discussions of monetary policy on problems of individual banks as well as on
those of the banking system as a whole. The individual bank bears the brunt of
tellers' and clearinghouse runs. To replenish the reserves depleted by the one run
or the other, the individual bank must liquidate assets or borrow from other institutions. Security values are then depressed, credit becomes less available, and other
institutions, exemplifying the domino theory, become quickly involved.

Throughout the Great Depression, the American gold stock experienced a
modest increase. From $3,997 million at the end of 1929 it rose to $4,036 million
at the end of 1933 (at $20.67 a fine ounce) just before devaluation. Heavy gold
exports to France, Belgium, the Netherlands and Switzerland during the depression years were offset by equally heavy imports from Argentina, Canada, Chile,
Japan, Mexico, and the United Kingdom. There were important interim fluctuations. The gold stock reached a peak of $4,708 million at the end of August 1931,
to fall more than $700 million during the next two months. This drop represented
the only important short-term drain, aside from a decline of $200 million in the

first two months of 1933—which occurred when the American people began to lose confidence in the government's ability to maintain the gold standard. Loss of confidence had shifted from the banking system to the monetary standard.[10]

The number of commercial banks in operation in the United States declined from 24,026 on December 31, 1929, to 13, 949 on June 30, 1933, a decrease of 10,077, or about 42 percent.[11] The decline resulted from mergers, amalgamations, and suspensions—but mostly from suspensions. This abominable record is to be contrasted with those of Great Britain and Canada, where not a single important bank failed.

Bank suspensions left innumerable towns and many counties totally bereft of banking facilities. It was estimated that in the United States in 1936 there were 2,000 bankless towns with populations of 1,000 or more each. Many remedies were proposed or adopted: establishment of cooperative credit associations and cash depositories, liberalization of laws on the establishment of branch banks, and the establishment at post offices of giro accounts based on European models.

From December 31, 1929, to June 30, 1933, deposit liabilities fell from $51 billion to $32 billion. Of this decline of $19 billion, about $7 billion was accounted for by the deposits of the suspended banks, causing losses to depositors of $1.4 billion.[12] The effect of bank suspensions on the total community cannot be judged simply by dollar losses to depositors. Bank failures generated a universal scramble for liquidity, which caused the banking system to collapse and the economic system to plunge still lower.

The rapid decline in loans, at once a product and a cause of the Great Depression, is set forth in Table 10.4. Purchasing power was destroyed. Individuals

Table 10.4

Assets and Liabilities of all American Commercial Banks—1929 to 1934 (Billions of Dollars)

Year	Total Loans	Total Investments	Cash Assets	Total Deposits
1929	$36.1	$13.7	$ 9.0	$49.4
1930	35.0	14.4	10.9	51.3
1931	29.3	15.7	10.0	47.3
1932	22.0	14.3	7.0	35.7
1933	16.5	14.1	7.4	32.1
1934	15.7	17.1	9.6	36.8

Source: *All Bank Statistics, United States 1896-1955* (Washington, D.C.: Board of Governors of the Federal Reserve System, 1959), pp. 34–36.

and firms were forced into bankruptcy. Often credit was unavailable at any price. The credit system ceased to function.

All data in the above table are for June 30 or the closest date for which they are available. Although total investments remained fairly stable, their composition changed. Holdings of U.S. obligations and the obligations of state and their political subdivisions rose. Holdings of other securities fell.

Federal Reserve Policy

Throughout the Great Depression the Federal Reserve System was confronted with a series of rapid and momentous developments. Each day brought its pressing crises and the need for immediate decisions. Time did not permit prolonged consideration and discussion. The statistical bases for the formulation of policy were frequently lacking. There were, for example, no reliable data on unemployment and no statistics on GNP. There were, to be sure, data on industrial production, contracts awarded, factory employment, factory payrolls, freight carloadings, and commodity prices. In fact, many of these data were gathered by the research departments of the Reserve System. It was on the basis of existing data and of the interpretations of these data, influenced by current attitudes, that decisions were made.

The Federal Reserve was not assisted in its efforts to stay the depression either by deposit insurance or by fiscal policy. To be sure, the RFC established on January 22, 1932, had been empowered to lend to any bank, savings bank, or trust company. It came late in the Great Depression, and was hampered in its lending activities by rigid, stringent rules. Its effectiveness was further impaired by the requirement that the names of borrowing banks be published.

A sharp decline in business activity today would induce the administration to call for a reduction in Federal tax rates, an increase in expenditures, or both. Even had the administration been willing during the Great Depression to embark upon an active fiscal policy, the scope of possible operations would have been limited. Federal tax receipts in fiscal 1930 amounted to only $4 billion, GNP about $100 billion. Tax receipts did not then decline simultaneously with income; payments for one year were based on income for the preceding year. Only since 1944 has the Federal personal income tax, through payroll deductions, been related directly to current income. Federal expenditures were small and could not be increased rapidly except through such devices as the Civilian Conservation Corps and the

Works Progress Administration, which were initiated by the Roosevelt administration.

Individual and corporate income-tax rates were, to be sure, reduced by Congress in December 1929. These reductions applied to income taxes for the calendar year 1929, mostly payable in 1930, and were adopted to relieve individuals and corporations from part of their tax liabilities at a time when a large surplus of receipts was anticipated. The action was not viewed as a measure to counter the effects of the Great Depression, which was not yet even a gleam in the eyes of the bears.

During the depression itself Secretary of the Treasury Mellon recommended "a vigorous and continued effort to reduce expenditures" [13] and increased taxation with a view to balancing current receipts and expenditures, exclusive of the sinking fund and other statutory debt retirements. The Treasury's revenue program was based mainly upon a return in principle to the general plan of taxation that had existed under the Revenue Act of 1924.

In accordance with these recommendations, the Revenue Act of 1932 provided for increases in corporate and individual income-tax rates (applicable to 1932 incomes, payable in 1933), for increases in existing excise taxes, for the imposition of new excise taxes, and for higher postal rates.

Notwithstanding the increase in tax rates, the deficit experienced in fiscal 1933 ($2.6 billion) was practically equal to that of fiscal 1932 ($2.7 billion). The federal deficit during the Great Depression (fiscal years 1930 through 1933) totalled $5 billion, equalling about 30 percent of expenditures. The deficit resulted more from a decline in receipts than an increase in expenditures. The decline in receipts itself resulted from a sharp decline in individual income and heavy corporate losses. Had tax rates been reduced instead of increased, the depression might have been stayed and tax receipts been larger.

Not only the administration but also Americans in general supported higher tax rates as a means of balancing the budget. It would have seemed inconceivable that the budget might be brought into balance by lowering tax rates. Only an increase in tax rates, so it was thought, would balance the budget and eliminate the deficit. As time went on the attitude of the Hoover administration towards deficits changed somewhat. Secretary Mellon became less adamant and the attitude of President Franklin D. Roosevelt toward deficits was in distinct contrast to that of candidate Roosevelt.

In the absence of expansionist policies on the part of the government, the Federal Reserve System itself had main responsibility for checking the decline in economic activity and of promoting recovery. The principal decisions of the System, as they were reflected in open-market operations and changes in the discount rate, are shown in Table 10.5. Purchases of bankers' bills are not included in open-market operations but are discussed separately.

Table 10.5
Federal Reserve Policy Decisions, 1929–1933

Period	Changes in Holdings of U.S. Securities	Discount Rate New York Federal Reserve Bank	
1. October 23–December 31, 1929	Purchase of $ 375 million	In effect August 9, 1929 November 1, 1929 November 15, 1929	6.0% 5.0 4.5
2. December 31, 1929–September 16, 1931	Purchase of $ 231 million	February 7, 1930 March 14, 1930 May 2, 1930 June 20, 1930 December 24, 1930 May 9, 1931	4.0 3.5 3.0 2.5 2.0 1.5
3. September 16, 1931–October 28, 1931	Sale of $ 15 million	October 9, 1931 October 16, 1931	2.5 3.5
4. October 28, 1931–February 24, 1932	Purchase of $ 14 million	No change	
5. February 24, 1932–December 28, 1932	Purchase of $1,110 million	February 26, 1932 June 24, 1932	3.0 2.5
6. December 28, 1932–March 8, 1933	Purchase of $ 30 million	March 3, 1933	3.5
7. March 8, 1933–December 27, 1933	Purchase of $ 551 million	April 7, 1933 May 26, 1933 October 20, 1933	3.0 2.5 2.0

Source: *Nineteenth Annual Report of the Federal Reserve Board Covering Operations for the year 1932* (Washington, D.C.: Government Printing Office, 1933), pp. 103–194; *Twentieth Annual Report of the Federal Reserve Board Covering Operations for the Year 1933* (Washington D.C.: Government Printing Office, 1934), p. 146; and *Banking and Monetary Statistics* (Washington, D.C.: Board of Governors of the Federal Reserve System, November 1943), pp. 383–387.

The four years are divided into small segments in order to reveal changes in policies as these were affected by rapidly changing economic developments. Over the whole period open-market operations raised Federal Reserve holdings of U.S. securities from $136 million on October 23, 1929, to $2,432 million on December 27, 1933. (They remained close to this total for the next eight years.) The discount rate at the Federal Reserve Bank of New York fell from 6 to 2 percent.

Period 1: Federal Reserve Policy After the Crash

The 1929 break in stock prices, coupled with rumors that the stock exchange would close, caused, as was noted in Chapter 9, a sudden heavy withdrawal of funds by "others" and by out-of-town banks. These huge withdrawals would probably have closed the stock exchange but for the willingness of New York City banks to replace with their own funds the loans that had been called. In doing so they were assured by the Federal Reserve Bank of New York that reserve credit would be made available in sufficient amounts to maintain necessary reserves.

The Federal Reserve Bank of New York, from October 23 to October 30, 1929, added $141 million of U. S. securities, purchased either outright or under repurchase agreements, to its portfolio. The eleven other Reserve banks added only $11 million of such securities to their portfolios. In the same week loans to member banks in the New York district rose $139 million. Open-market operations and discounts provided the funds that New York City banks needed to meet increased reserve requirements and the flow of funds to interior banks.

Purchases of securities by the Federal Reserve Bank of New York were made on its own initiative. The Federal Reserve Board acknowledged the legal right of the New York bank to purchase securities but believed that its own authority had been challenged by lack of consultation. In an effort to recoup its prestige the Board told Governor George L. Harrison that it would approve his request for a reduction in the New York discount rate from 6 to 5 percent only if the New York bank made no further purchases except with the approval of the Board. The New York discount rate was reduced effective November 1.

After considerable discussion the Federal Reserve Board finally approved a recommendation by the Open Market Investment Committee authorizing Reserve banks to purchase government securities in amounts not to exceed an additional $200 million for the accounts of those banks that might wish to participate in the purchases. The committee used this authorization to acquire $165 million in government securities by the end of the year.

Irritated by the independence of the New York Federal Reserve Bank and incensed by what it termed "insubordination," the Reserve Board in March 1930 established the Open Market Policy Conference, consisting of representatives of each of the twelve Reserve banks (see Chapter 2, for details). The purpose was to limit the authority and to dilute the influence of the Federal Reserve Bank of New York.

The purchase of securities and bills by the Reserve banks in the final quarter of 1929 offset the effects of a decline in the gold stock and a seasonal increase of money in circulation and enabled member banks to reduce their borrowings. Open-market interest rates fell sharply. There was no evidence yet of a credit collapse,* although it was clear that business activity was declining. The decline in business activity, the Federal Reserve Bank of New York reported in its 1929 report, was an important consideration in the steps taken toward easier money conditions.

Period 2: The Lowering of the Bank Rate

The next period, about twenty-one months of rapidly declining activity (see Table 10.5), was characterized mainly by a sharp reduction in discount rates. That at the Federal Reserve Bank of New York fell from 4.5 percent at the end of 1929 to 1.5 percent in the spring of 1931. Official buying rates on acceptances were reduced to 1 percent.

The discount rates at the other Federal Reserve banks on May 9, 1931, when the New York rate was reduced to 1.5 percent, were at much higher levels, except for that in Boston, which was 2 percent; at six Reserve banks it was 3 percent and at four 3.5 percent. The low rate at the New York bank reflected its desire to inaugurate vigorous policies of monetary ease; its managers were acutely aware of the liquidity pressures on the banking system and of the need to create a favorable environment for business recovery.[14]

The System's holdings of U.S. securities increased only $231 million during those twenty-one months, an increase which was largely offset by the decline in bills bought. One reason for this astonishing low increase was the conviction of various Reserve bank officials that vigorous action was not necessary while the gold stock was rising rapidly. This rise enabled member banks to reduce their indebtedness and caused excess reserves to rise to $100 million by the middle of 1931 (see Table 10.6).

That Federal Reserve policy was not heavily expansionary in this period is difficult to understand. Industrial production was declining rapidly, and wholesale prices, particularly those of farm products, were falling sharply. Unemployment was rising, banks were failing, money was being hoarded, and bank credit was declining at about 4 percent per annum. The situation called for greatly expanded

---

* The reduction in stock exchange loans which affected primarily "others" and the out-of-town banks had not as yet affected the total loans and investments of member banks which were slightly higher on December 31 than they had been on October 2, 1929. Total deposits increased as demand deposits rose and time deposits fell.

Table 10.6

Factors Affecting Member-Bank Borrowings
December 31, 1929–September 16, 1931
(Millions of Dollars)

Causing Decreases			Causing Increases		
Federal Reserve credit			Federal Reserve credit		
U.S. Securities	(+)$	231	Bills bought	(−)$	174
Other	(+)	8			
Other Federal Reserve accounts	(−)	28	Non-member bank deposits	(+)	194
Treasury deposits with Federal			Member bank reserve		
Reserve banks	(−)	25	balances	(+)	63
Treasury currency	(+)	1	Money in circulation	(+)	223
Gold stock	(+)	732	Treasury cash	(+)	3
Totals		$1,025			$ 657
		Bills discounted	−369		

Source: *Banking and Monetary Statistics, op. cit.*, pp. 384–386

open-market operations, which might have lessened the pressure for liquidation at home and abroad.

The explanation lies in attitudes prevailing in the 1930s. For example, the Federal Reserve Advisory Council could recommend on February 17, 1931, that "the situation will best be served if the natural flow of credit is unhampered by open-market operations or changes in the rediscount rates." [15] It would scarcely recommend inaction in similar circumstances today. But at that time many were convinced that a depression was required to purge the economic system of the excesses of the boom.

The inflow of gold and the shifting of funds from the interior of the country to New York City enabled New York banks to repay loans from the Reserve bank and to accumulate excess reserves. By mid-1931 net excess reserves were a phenomenon of the central reserve-city banks. Borrowing and excess reserves were about equal at reserve-city banks. Borrowing exceeded excess reserves at the country banks.

Declining interest rates were largely a money-market development, and even there they bore small relation to the availability of credit. As the Federal Reserve Bank of New York stated in 1931:

> In the modern business world the great bulk of transactions between governments, corporations and individuals is based on documents representing promises to pay given amounts of money on demand or after stated intervals . . . if the banks . . . lose confidence in the stability of their depositors, they give primary

attention to liquidity rather than to the credit needs of the business community . . . the normal functioning of the credit mechanism becomes impossible. . . .[16]

Period 3: Federal Reserve Policy During the Gold Drain

The international liquidity crisis which affected Austria, Germany and the United Kingdom in quick succession (see Chapter 11, *passim*) fell next with severe impact on the United States. Dollar exchange soon dropped below the gold export point vis-a-vis the currencies of Belgium, France, the Netherlands, and Switzerland. In slightly more than a *month,* $724 million in gold was either exported or earmarked for foreign accounts. About three-fifths of this gold was taken by France and most of the remainder by Belgium, Switzerland, and the Netherlands. In November the gold inflow was resumed, and the gold stock rose as a result of shipments from Canada, Latin America, and the Far East.

Table 10.7

Liquidity Crisis, 1931
(Millions of Dollars)

	Week Ended September 19	Week Ended October 31	Change
Gold Stock	$ 5,013	$4,289	−$ 724
Money in circulation	5,108	5,513	+ 405
Federal Reserve Credit			
Bills discounted	$ 269	$ 713	+ $444
Bills bought	212	726	+ 514
U.S. securities	741	727	− 14
Other	43	46	+ 3
Total Reserve Credit	$1,265	$2,212	+ $947

Source: *Federal Reserve Bulletin* (October 1931), p. 560; and (November 1931), p. 609.

The foreign and domestic drain, amounting to $1,129 billion (gold stock decrease and currency increase), was financed by a sharp increase in bills discounted and in bills bought. U.S. securities actually fell.

The Federal Reserve Bank of New York felt the major impact of the liquidity drain, not only from the decline in the gold stock and from the increase of money in circulation, but also from the loss of bankers' balances to the interior. New York City was, in fact, the focal point of the drain.

During this period the New York Federal Reserve Bank increased its discount rate twice, from 1.5 to 3.5 percent (see Table 10.5). Both advances were accompanied by increases in the bank's buying rate for acceptances, but this action was not taken until after member banks had sold to the Reserve bank a large volume of bills that they had acquired when lower rates were in effect. On each of two days, September 24 and October 9, 1931, the New York Federal Reserve Bank bought for its own account and for other Federal Reserve banks more than $100 million in bills.

As a consequence of this rapid increase in bills discounted and bills bought, total Federal Reserve credit increased to the highest level since 1921. The rise of $444 million in bills discounted meant that the internal and external drains were allowed to have their effects on the money market. Short-term money-market rates doubled, and member banks came under pressure for further liquidation.

Modern works on Federal Reserve policy have severely criticized this policy. To their authors it has seemed inconceivable that the Reserve System would follow a deflationary policy in the midst of the Great Depression. The American gold standard was in no danger, the international balance of payments showed a surplus of $500 million in 1931, and short-term liabilities to foreigners were small. Critics have maintained that the gold and currency drain should have been offset by open-market operations. A period of deep depression, they have reminded us, is not the time to abide by classical gold-standard rules.

But in 1931 the Reserve System feared that, if interest rates were not raised, the gold drain would accelerate. A flight of domestic capital might occur as investors sought refuge for their funds in France, whose currency was then highly regarded. This policy received virtually unanimous support among Federal Reserve officials and was widely acclaimed in the financial press. Prevailing attitudes in the 1930s led the Reserve System to take deflationary action, despite the depression and the underlying strength of the dollar. Opposite attitudes in the 1960s caused the Reserve System to offset gold exports despite a high level of business activity and the weak position of the dollar.

Period 4: Federal Reserve Policy and Free Gold

It should be noted in Table 10.5 that, even after the resumption of the gold inflow (October 28, 1931–February 24, 1932) discount rates were not reduced, and U.S. securities were purchased in small amount.

Industrial production was declining, employment dropping, commodity prices collapsing, member-bank loans and deposits falling sharply. Bank failures continued at a high level, and currency was increasingly hoarded.

Why under these circumstances did the Federal Reserve System not turn to an expansionary policy? The answer lies in the effects of open-market purchases of government securities upon the volume of "free gold." It will be remembered that at that time Federal Reserve notes were specifically backed by gold, gold certificates, and eligible paper, including loans to member banks secured by government obligations. Government obligations owned by the Reserve banks themselves could not serve as collateral.

 ⁻ Under the rules then prevailing, purchases of government obligations by the Reserve banks, by causing declines in member-bank borrowing, reduced the amount of "free gold." Gold had to be substituted for bills discounted as they were reduced through repayment.* The amount of gold held by the Reserve banks that was not required as reserves against their deposits or as collateral against Federal Reserve notes declined. Declines in the amount of "free gold," if continued, would sooner or later be reflected in deficient reserves against deposits or would act as an obstacle to the issue of Federal Reserve notes (see Chapter 5 for further discussion).

On February 24, 1932, the Reserve banks held slightly more than $400 million in free gold; less than in the preceding year because of the gold exports, the increase of money in circulation and a small rise in holdings of U.S. securities. The amount would have fallen more had it not been for a substantial increase in member-bank borrowing. Although this increase "freed" more gold, it also kept money-market interest rates high and subjected commercial banks to further pressure. An expansionary policy could not be pursued without resolving this dilemma.

To enable the Reserve System to engage in extensive open-market operations, the Glass-Steagall Act was passed on February 27, 1932 (see Chapter 5, p. 111). It permitted the Reserve banks to use government securities that they themselves owned as collateral for Federal Reserve notes. Although originally conceived as a temporary measure, this enactment has become a permanent part of the Federal Reserve Act.

The Glass-Steagall Act in effect made the Federal Reserve note a general asset currency, comparable to Federal Reserve deposit liabilities. It also liberalized the sections of the Federal Reserve Act regulating rediscounting by member banks so that groups of banks or individual banks lacking eligible paper might nevertheless have access to rediscount facilities. The act thus permitted smaller member banks

---

* Open-market purchases of bankers' acceptances did not have the same effect, for they could be used as collateral against Federal Reserve notes. The amount available for purchase was not large, however. In January, 1932, the Reserve System held for its own account or the accounts of foreign correspondents about half of all outstanding bankers' acceptances.

in exceptionally exigent circumstances to borrow on their own promissory notes secured to the satisfaction of the lending Reserve bank at a rate not less than 1 percent per annum higher than the highest discount rate of that Reserve bank. Those promissory notes were not, however, to be used as collateral for Federal Reserve notes (see Chapter 5). This privilege was later extended to all member banks, and the penalty rate was reduced from 1 to .5 of 1 percent above the highest discount rate.

Period 5: The Great Purchases of the Federal Reserve

Elimination of the concept of free gold, which was, after all, simply a technical consideration, made it possible for the Reserve System to engage in huge open-market operations. It proceeded slowly at first, then rapidly, until the Reserve System was adding $100 million in government obligations to its portfolio each week. In five months the portfolio more than doubled, from $741 million on February 24 to $1,851 million on August 10, 1932. By today's standards, the amounts involved seem small, but then they seemed huge; in percentages they seem enormous even today (see Table 10.8).

Table 10.8
Factors Affecting Member-Bank Reserve Balances
February 24–December 28, 1932
(Millions of Dollars)

Increasing Reserves		Decreasing Reserves	
Federal Reserve credit		Federal Reserve credit	
U.S. government securities	(+)$1,110	Bills discounted	(−)$568
Gold stock	(+) 155	Bills bought	(−) 100
Treasury currency	(+) 149	All other	(−) 8
Treasury deposits	(−) 7	Money in circulation	(+) 94
Non-member bank deposits	(−) 7	Treasury cash	(+) 39
		Other Federal Reserve accounts	(+) 14
Total	$1,428	Total	$823
	Increase in member-bank reserve balances	$604	
	Increase in excess reserves	$527	

Source: *Banking and Monetary Statistics* (Washington, D.C.: Board of Governors of the Federal Reserve System, 1945), pp. 386–387.

Purchases of government securities plus the increase in the gold stock and in Treasury currency not only offset the effect on member-bank reserves of such factors as the decrease in bills discounted and bills bought, the decline in the gold stock, and the increase in money in circulation, but also actually increased member-bank total and excess reserves (see Table 10.8). Purchases of government securities immediately increased the reserve balances of New York banks. Later these funds were distributed, largely through Treasury disbursements (including advances by the RFC), to interior banks and other institutions. Funds distributed in this fashion often found their way back to New York City or Chicago in the form of bankers' balances.

The concentration of excess reserves in the money market brought about a substantial reduction in money-market rates. By the end of 1932 the call-loan rate had fallen to 1 percent, prime bankers' acceptances to ⅜ of 1 percent, the average yield on U.S. Treasury notes and certificates to .04 percent, and rates on prime commercial paper to 1.38 percent. Long-term rates fell substantially but, as in all such periods, not as much as did short-term rates. The interest curve became sharply ascending, a condition that lasted many years and came to be considered "normal." Through 1932 rates charged borrowing customers in New York City declined from 4.51 to 3.78 percent, in seven other northern and eastern cities relatively less, and in eleven southern and western cities still less. Credit was becoming more available in New York but not markedly so elsewhere. Doubtless credit would have become more available had open-market operations been of even larger magnitude. Despite the sharp fall in open-market rates the Federal Reserve Bank of New York did not see fit to reduce its discount rate to the low level of 1.5 percent reached on May 9, 1931 (see Table 10.5).

Although business activity was at an abysmally low level at the end of 1932, there were encouraging signs of renewed activity. In the second half increases occurred in aggregate industrial output, in freight carried by the railroads, in factory employment, and in factory payrolls. An increase in industrial output was limited largely to textiles, leather products, and food processing. In the autumn there were seasonal increases in coal output and automobile production. Depressed business conditions at the end of the year reflected mainly the low level of activity in heavy industry.

Consumers and businessmen were in positions to finance a substantial revival in business. The public held stocks of hoarded currency that would be spent once confidence had been restored. Similarly, the low levels to which deposit velocity had fallen meant that a substantial increase in activity could be financed by an increase in deposit activity alone, without a rise in deposit volume. Bank suspensions were about one-third less in 1932 than in 1931 and were fewer in the latter half of the year than in the first half.

The nation could have enjoyed a substantial revival had the RFC not been compelled to publish the names of borrowing banks, causing them to fall subject to public distrust and currency and deposit runs. Bank suspensions increased substantially in December 1932 and January and February 1933. The result was a sharp rise in demand for currency and gold. The American people had at last begun to lose confidence in their monetary standard.

Period 6: Federal Reserve Policy and the Bank Holiday

With a little more courage and a little more statesmanship, the banking collapse could have been avoided. Had the RFC been given authority to extend loans to distressed banks more freely and had political considerations not dictated the public listing of borrowing banks, the commercial banking system might have continued to function and the upturn in business activity that had begun in mid-1932 might not have been checked. The advocates of dollar devaluation would surely have been less persuasive. The administration might have been more willing to enter into cooperative relations with other nations at the London economic conference (see Chapter 11 below). Exchange controls and other trade barriers might not have been tightened. The world might have been less fragmented. But instead the United States plunged into unprecedented and unnecessary financial chaos, which engulfed the world.

As 1932 came to a close there was a spirit of uneasiness in the country. The newly elected administration had not yet revealed its economic policies. Unemployment was still extremely serious and local relief funds were insufficient. Share-the-work-plans, reflation, free silver, technocracy, and barter arrangements were topics of common discussion. Bank suspensions began to rise.

When Governor Oscar K. Allen of Louisiana proclaimed a bank holiday on February 4, 1933, and Governor William A. Comstock of Michigan proclaimed an eight-day holiday beginning February 14, the country became convinced that the banking system was near collapse. By Inauguration Day, on March 4, practically all banks had restricted deposit withdrawals or had been closed. On March 6, the suspension of banking activities was made complete by the declaration of a national holiday by President Roosevelt. The proclamation prohibited all payments of gold and other currency that might facilitate hoarding, the paying out of deposits, extension of loans and discounts, transactions in foreign exchange, and all other banking operations not specifically authorized by Secretary of the Treasury William H. Woodin.

On March 10 the President conferred upon the Secretary of the Treasury power to license member banks of the Federal Reserve System found to be in satisfactory condition. A similar power was conferred upon state banking authorities respecting nonmember banks. On March 13 the Reserve banks were reopened, and for the next several days most commercial banks were permitted to conduct business.

Three days after the banking holiday 5,077 member banks were allowed to engage in unrestricted operations and by March 22, 6,800 nonmember banks; a total of 11,877. The number increased rapidly until at the end of 1933 the number of banks in unrestricted operation had grown to 14,211. Those not in operation were in liquidation or had been merged with other institutions.[17]

Federal Reserve statements reflected the dramatic developments shaking the financial world. Bank suspensions and the spread of banking holidays in January and February had generated renewed hoarding of currency. Gold was being withdrawn from the Reserve banks both for export and for domestic hoarding. Deposits were being shifted rapidly about the country from presumably weaker to presumably stronger institutions. From January 4 to March 8, 1933, money in circulation rose by $1,868 million, and the gold stock fell $281 million; member-banks reserve balances fell $738 million, bills discounted rose $1,163 million, bills bought rose $384 million, and holdings of U.S. government obligations rose only $30 million.[18]

The Federal Reserve System seemed paralyzed. The panic called for massive open-market purchases of government securities from all holders: individuals, banks, and corporations. Only a small amount was bought. Member banks were forced heavily into debt, and money-market interest rates rose. Member banks were compelled to sell investments, and loan liquidation continued.

On March 3 the discount rate was raised at the New York Federal Reserve Bank from 2.5 to 3.5 percent. Buying rates on acceptances had been increased from .5 percent to 3.5 percent on ninety-day bills. A panic does not justify an increase either in the discount rate or in acceptance-buying rates. It calls instead for huge open-market operations to maintain the existing level of interest rates and to prevent credit liquidation. The conditions that produce a panic quickly subside.

The New York City banks felt the full force of the panic. Out-of-town banks and corporations and local depositors withdrew huge amounts (see Table 10.9).

Once confidence was restored, the panic quickly passed. By June, $1,900 million in currency had flowed back into the banks. The Reserve banks began to buy

Table 10.9

Net Losses by New York Banks
February 14–March 3, 1933
(Millions of Dollars)

Transfers to inland banks and corporations	$ 403
Currency payments	545
Gold losses	279
Total	$1,227

Source: *Nineteenth Annual Report Federal Reserve Bank of New York for the Year Ended December 31, 1933* (March 22, 1934), p. 6.

government obligations and by the end of 1933 had added $551 million to their portfolios (see Table 10.5). The discount rate was reduced to 2 percent and acceptance buying rates to .5 percent. Market interest rates declined and credit liquidation ceased. The Great Depression was over. The resumption of previous economic-growth rates still lay, however, in the distant future.

NEW DEAL BANKING LEGISLATION

Having come into office without a well-conceived or integrated economic program, the Roosevelt administration improvised, first in one direction and then in another, a whole series of measures designed to restore prosperity and to reconstruct the economic life of the nation. Monetary measures included dollar devaluation (see Chapter 11) and many efforts to raise the price of silver.* Banking legislation included such measures as the Emergency Banking Act of 1933, the Banking Act of 1933, and the Banking Act of 1935.

The Emergency Banking Act of 1933, signed into law six days after President Roosevelt assumed office, confirmed his previous actions relating to gold, silver, and the foreign exchanges; provided for the appointment of conservators to take charge of insolvent national banks and banking associations in the District of Columbia; provided for the issue of preferred stock by national banks in order to strengthen their capital position; and authorized the RFC to purchase the preferred stock of national banks and trust companies and to make loans against such stock.† It provided for the issue of Federal Reserve bank notes against direct obligations of the United States and against eligible paper during an emergency, and authorized the Federal Reserve banks to lend directly to individuals, partnerships, and corporations.

---

* For lack of space, we shall not discuss these efforts; all silver-purchase legislation has now been repealed and the price of silver stands above its previous "monetary value."
† Authority to purchase capital notes and debentures was added on March 24, 1933, in an amendment.

This measure was, as its title implies, an emergency measure. The important provisions related to the appointment of conservators and to the purchase of preferred stock and capital notes by the RFC.

In the rehabilitation and strengthening of the banking system the RFC played a stellar role, lending against the assets of both open banks and of banks in liquidation (thus unfreezing deposits), and purchasing their capital notes and preferred stock (thus providing the essential capital for successful functioning of the banking system, which could not at that time be procured locally).

In his final report on the activities of the RFC, Secretary of the Treasury Robert B. Anderson declared that in the course of its life (1932–1957) the agency had authorized a total of 15,409 loans to more than 7,300 banks and trust companies. Authorizations had amounted to $2.5 billion and disbursements to $2.0 billion. Loans had been extended to banks in forty-eight states, the District of Columbia, Alaska, Hawaii, and Puerto Rico. Actual disbursements had been particularly large in states like California, Illinois, Michigan, Ohio, and Pennsylvania.[19]

Equally important was the rehabilitation of the capital structures of commercial banks, which was prerequisite not only to their efficient functioning but also to membership in the Federal Deposit Insurance Corporation. In its 1934 report the FDIC asserted that a net sound capital of 10 percent of deposits was considered a minimum for safety and reported that more than one-third of all commercial banks that had not been members of the Federal Reserve System when they applied for membership in the FDIC had a net sound capital of less than this amount. One-tenth of these banks had no net sound capital.[20]

Throughout its existance the RFC authorized loans on and subscriptions to preferred stock and purchases of capital notes or debentures totaling $1.3 billion for 6,868 banks and trust companies. The amount actually disbursed was $1.2 billion. Purchases of preferred stock and capital notes were particularly heavy in the final quarter of 1933 and throughout 1934 and 1935. The amount of such investments had been substantially reduced by 1947. The readiness of the RFC to strengthen the capital structure of commercial banks enabled many of them to obtain additional funds locally through stock subscriptions, directors' guarantees, and purchase by local interests of temporarily depressed assets.

The loans which the RFC granted to commercial banks plus its work in rehabilitating their capital structures helped the banking system to function once again. It did not, however, function as fully as might have been expected. Many lending officers were still shell shocked by the events of the Great Depression. They were frequently loath to extend credit except to first-class risks and were equally loath to purchase any but short-term obligations. To help overcome this attitude the Federal Government introduced various programs of loan insurance and guarantees.

Banking Act of 1933

The Banking Act of 1933 contained numerous provisions designed to strengthen the banking system. It created the FDIC, severed the ownership relationship between commercial banks and security affiliates, required institutions to choose between operating as a commercial or as an investment bank, and prohibited member banks from acting as the medium or agent for nonbanking corporations in lending on the security of stocks. It limited dealings in investment securities by member banks and brought bank holding companies except, as was later discovered, the one-bank holding companies, under the supervision of the Federal Reserve Board. It introduced various limitations on loans by member banks, authorized shareholders in national banks to cumulate their shares in the election of individual directors, and ended the double liability on the shares of national banks.

This law authorized the Federal Reserve Board to remove an officer or director of a member-bank that continued to violate banking laws or to engage in unsafe or unsound practices, brought all foreign transactions of the Reserve System under the direct control of the Federal Reserve Board, forbade Reserve banks from engaging in open-market operations except in accordance with Reserve Board regulations, lengthened the terms of office for Board members to twelve years, provided for Reserve membership by mutual-savings banks, and required the Federal Reserve Board to keep informed of the "general character and amount of the loans and investments of its member banks."

These provisions were designed to strengthen the power of the Federal Reserve Board and to prevent any Federal Reserve bank from challenging that authority. A coordinated central banking system was evolving into one under centralized control.

The act also prohibited payment of interest on demand deposits and gave the Federal Reserve Board power to regulate interest paid on time deposits. Prohibiting interest on demand deposits would, it was hoped, reduce the concentration of bankers' balances and other demand deposits in New York City and lead to a wider dissemination of excess reserves. Regulating interest paid on time deposits would, it was hoped, prevent banks from employing their funds, as many had done before the Great Depression, in ways that sacrificed safety to income.

Banking Act of 1935

As the Board of Governors pointed out in 1935, the Banking Act of 1935 incorporated "into law much of the experience acquired by the System during the more than two decades of its operations." [21] It reflected a broader conception of the System's functions in the nation's economic life than had existed when the System was first established, and it defined more clearly and fixed more firmly the responsibilities of the Board and of the Reserve banks.

The act, which was adopted after extensive congressional hearings, contained three titles. The first provided for a permanent plan of deposit insurance, the second amended the Federal Reserve Act in important particulars, and the third introduced a number of technical amendments to the banking laws.

Title II, the most important from our point of view, reconstituted the Federal Reserve Board as the Board of Governors of the Federal Reserve System. The ex-officio membership was eliminated; all seven appointed members were thenceforth called "governors" (see Chapter 2, pp. 33–34). The Federal Open Market Committee was established, the lending powers of the Federal Reserve banks were broadened, and the power of the Board of Governors to change member-bank reserve requirements was altered and clarified (Chapter 3 above). The act thus placed greater responsibility for the direction of national credit policies upon the Board of Governors while preserving the autonomy of the regional banks in their relations with member banks.

The vast amount of banking and monetary legislation enacted from 1933–1935 had several basic objectives: delegation to the Treasury of complete control over the monetary standard, centralization of Federal Reserve credit policies in the Board of Governors and the Federal Open Market Committee, and elimination of various abuses in commercial-banking practices (for example, those associated with the operation of security affiliates and holding companies and with various lending and investing operations).

The legislation did not establish specific criteria for monetary or credit policy. The criteria included in the legislation were couched in general terms and included such objectives as the prevention of "injurious credit expansion or contraction," the prevention of "the excessive use of credit for the purchase or carrying of securities," and the accommodation of commerce and business. Couched in such general loose terms, the Reserve officials could initiate policies which represented their own aims or which were mandated by the United States government.

THE THIRD DEPRESSION—MAY 1937–JUNE 1938

The economic rehabilitation of the banking system paralleled its legal reconstruction. Total earning assets of the commercial banks rose quickly, responding to the rapid increase in excess reserves and reflecting large Federal deficits (see Table 10.10).

Table 10.10
Assets and Liabilities of all Commercial Banks
(Billions of Dollars)

Date	Total Loans	Total Investments	Total Deposits [a]	Member Banks Total Excess Reserves [b]
June 29, 1929	$35.7	$13.7	$45.1	$ .042
June 30, 1933	16.3	14.0	28.5	.363
June 30, 1936	15.6	23.0	41.0	2.593
June 30, 1937	17.4	22.0	42.8	.876
June 30, 1938	16.1	21.1	41.8	2.762
June 30, 1939	16.4	22.9	45.6	4.246
June 30, 1940	17.4	23.7	50.0	6.696
June 29, 1941	20.4	27.3	56.5	5.351

a. Excluding interbank deposits.
b. Monthly averages of daily figures.

Source: *Banking and Monetary Statistics* (Washington, D.C.: Board of Governors, 1943), pp. 19, 396.

The increase in earning assets took the form principally of a sharp rise in holdings of government obligations; loans lagged far behind. By 1941 total investments were twice those of 1929, whereas loans were only 57 percent as large. Deposits, reflecting the monetization of government securities and imports of gold, soared and as early as 1939 equalled those of 1929. Deposit turnover, which had begun to decline in 1929, continued to do so until 1945. Loans, expressed as a percentage of deposits, declined through those years; the ratio of capital accounts to risk assets remained steady. The commercial banking system was financially liquid, in fact too liquid.

Economic recovery had been fairly vigorous. By 1937 GNP in constant prices equaled the 1929 level. The implicit price deflator was stable. Money wages had increased more rapidly than had consumer prices. Unit labor costs were declining.

Unemployment, though still large, was declining. The stage seemed set for a vigorous rise in economic activity, when, to the amazement and chagrin of those plotting the nation's economic course, the economy plunged into another depression just four years after the inauguration of the New Deal. The contraction, which began in May 1937 and continued until June 1938, was very sharp. The Federal Reserve Index of Industrial Production (1923–1925 = 100) fell from 118 to 77 (the 1929 average had been 119).

GNP fell about 7 percent in current dollars. The decline in this period which resulted from inventory disinvestment, a drop in the demand for consumer and producer durables, and a drop in nonresidential construction, was ascribed to four major factors.

First, member-bank reserve requirements had been increased. Excess reserves of member-banks amounting to $3 billion in mid-1936 were large enough to provide the basis for a 100 percent increase in the existing volume of deposits, which were already as large as they had been at any previous time. To reduce the potential inflationary threat of these excess reserves (wholesale prices of industrial materials were rising sharply) the Board of Governors increased member-bank reserve requirements by 50 percent effective August 15, 1936. (The large volume of excess reserves had already caused the New York City banks to lengthen the maturities in their investment portfolios in order to reach out for yields. This tendency had to be checked, according to the Federal Reserve Bank of New York.)

Almost immediately after the ordered increase in reserve requirements, which reduced excess reserves to $1.9 billion, the expansion of excess reserves was resumed. The inflow of gold had so accelerated that by the end of the year excess reserves had increased to $2.2 billion. Consequently the Board of Governors announced further increases in member-bank reserve requirements effective March 1 and May 1, 1937, which, with the earlier increase, raised member-bank reserve requirements to their legal maximum. With this action the Board eliminated $1.5 billion of excess reserves, which it deemed superfluous to the current and future needs of commerce, industry, and agriculture. The total was reduced to $900 million for all member banks and to $150 million for New York City member banks alone. The Reserve System was then in a position to effect future changes in member-bank reserve requirements through open-market operations, which were considered a more flexible instrument.

When the increases were initiated, excess reserves were widely distributed among member banks. Balances with correspondent banks were twice as large as they had generally been in the past. All but a few banks were able to meet the new requirements, either by using their excess reserve balances or by drawing on half their bankers' balances. In other words the effects of the action were expected to be anti-inflationary rather than deflationary.

Second, accompanying the action by the Board of Governors in raising member-bank reserve requirements, the U.S. Treasury, on December 31, 1936, began to sterilize increases in the gold stock resulting from imports or domestic gold production. The one action had the effect of reducing excess reserves and potential credit expansion and the other prevented increases in the gold stock from increasing total reserves and actually brought about an increase in the required reserves. In this way action by the Treasury in reducing potential credit expansion supplemented that by the Reserve System.

The Treasury customarily paid for gold imports or for gold domestically produced with checks drawn on its accounts with the Federal Reserve banks. It customarily replenished these accounts by giving the Reserve banks a gold-certificate credit. Under the gold-sterilization policy, the Treasury replenished its account at the Reserve banks by shifting deposits from commercial banks, which it replenished, in turn, by selling obligations to commercial banks or to the market. Obligations sold to commercial banks raised their deposits and thus their required reserves rose. The net effect then of a gold sterilization policy might be that of bringing about an increase in required reserves. Gold imports would then have the paradoxical effect of tightening the money market.

In any event, gold sterilization prevents additional gold resulting either from imports or domestic production from increasing member-bank reserves and prevents declines in the gold stock through exports from reducing member-bank reserves. Between December 24, 1936, and September 11, 1937, the Treasury's policy raised the inactive gold stock by about $1.4 billion. Then $300 million was released; the balance, $1,183 million, was released on April 14, 1938. Both actions were attempts to halt the depression.

Still a third reason cited for the new depression was a sharp change in the government's fiscal position. Between fiscal 1937 and fiscal 1938 total Federal expenditures fell by $1 billion, or by about 13 percent. Total revenues increased $600 million, or by about 12 percent. The net deficit consequently fell by $1.6 billion, or by about 60 percent. The decline in expenditures resulted from decreases in funds spent on relief, work relief, and public works. The administration was convinced that recovery was assured. The rise in revenues was accounted for by increased income taxes and receipts from new social-security levies.

The fourth was the enactment of the undistributed-profits tax. In a message to the Congress on March 3, 1936, in which he decried the "large growth" of corporate profits during the 1920s, President Roosevelt proposed that, instead of the corporate income tax, the excess-profits tax, and the capital-stock tax, a tax be levied on corporate profits not distributed as dividends. The tax was to be graduated in .relation to the percentage of adjusted net income retained. The larger the percentage of undistributed profits, the higher the tax. The legislation finally enacted on June 22, 1936, departed from these broad principles and formed part of the hybrid corporate tax structure. The reasons cited in its favor were that it would increase Federal revenues while reducing inequalities in taxation; would guarantee fairer distribution of the tax load; would reduce the proportion of national income saved; and would increase consumption. In accordance with Keynesian doctrines it was believed likely to stimulate economic growth. Some proponents declared that it would curb the reputed overexpansion of corporate facilities, which were frequently cited as a cause of the 1929–1933 depression. Others affirmed that an undistributed-profits tax would bring corporate investment under necessary control. The stockholder would be able to decide whether to invest his dividends in the corporation disbursing them or in some other enterprise. Those who opposed the tax pointed out that it would deprive business of investment funds, that it would hamper the growth of small and new business, that it would accentuate cyclical fluctuations, and that it put a "penalty on prudence and a bounty on improvidence." The debate was acrimonious. Businessmen just recovering from the traumatic experience of the Great Depression again fell prey to anxieties.[22] Expenditures on plant and equipment fell sharply.

   An Appraisal • Although in fiscal years 1936–1938 the undistributed-profits tax produced no more than $400 million in revenue, its psychological impact was severe. Regarding it more as a reform than as a revenue measure, administration spokesmen launched sharp attacks on the business community. Fear and uncertainy increased, business confidence waned, and expenditures on producers' durable equipment fell one-third. This decline caused a decline in consumer expenditures, which were further reduced by rising social security taxes.

   Despite the fact that the Reserve System had raised member-bank reserve requirements shortly before the depression, this action, together with that of the Treasury's in sterilizing gold, probably played a minor role in the decline. Net free reserves never fell below $500 million. Short- and long-term interest rates rose modestly. The principal causes of the third depression seem to have been the changed fiscal position of the government and, above all, the psychological impact of the undistributed-profits tax. (Some students have also emphasized the rise in construction costs and its effects on new building.)

The banks of New York City, which bore the brunt of the increase in reserve requirements, began to sell government obligations in March and April 1937, in order to meet the new requirements and the withdrawal of bankers' balances occasioned by them. They concentrated their sales on long-term bonds on which they could realize profit, rather than on short-term bills or notes, which they already held in substantial volume. As a result, yields on long-term government bonds rose from a little over 2.25 percent in February to 2.75 percent in early April.

In order to stabilize the market, that is, to prevent further price declines and to restore prices to their previous levels, the Federal Open Market Committee, in March 1937, increased the System's holdings of bonds by $104 million and reduced holdings of bills and notes by the same amount. The total portfolio remained the same. Between April 4 and April 28 the System again purchased $96 million of Treasury bonds, increasing its total portfolio by this amount. Bond prices stopped declining and, under the pressure of rapidly increasing excess reserves, resumed their long-term rise.

The third depression, it must be emphasized, had a long-lasting effect on the attitude of the government towards monetary policy. That it followed an increase in reserve requirements and a slight increase in interest rates was one of the factors causing the government over the next fourteen years to oppose credit policies that might induce even moderate rises in interest rates.

Federal Reserve Policy • Once the downturn occurred, action was taken quickly by the Federal Reserve System. Through August and September 1937 discount rates were reduced from 2 to 1.5 percent at ten Reserve banks and from 1.5 to 1 percent at the New York Federal Reserve Bank (it was already at 1.5 percent at the Cleveland Federal Reserve Bank). Effective November 1, 1937, the maximum loan value of securities was increased from 45 to 60 percent, and effective April 16, 1938, a reduction in member-bank reserve requirements was ordered (see Chapter 3).

The reduction in the discount rate was voted to induce member banks to borrow from their local Reserve banks, rather than to borrow outside their Reserve districts, or to liquidate securities. The increase in the maximum loan value of securities followed a sharp decline in security prices, a decline in security loans, and a decrease in security offerings. The reduction in reserve requirements, occurring when excess reserves were $1.7 billion, had, in effect, been ordered by President Roosevelt as part of a general recovery program. This action, which increased excess reserves by about $750 million, was not only not necessary but, in adding to the already huge volume of excess reserves, forced interest rates close to the vanishing point. Coupled with desterilization of gold and continued gold imports it raised excess reserves to $7 billion by mid-1940.

Monetary action was supplemented by various fiscal measures. The undistributed-profits tax was repealed. Federal expeditures on work relief increased, tax receipts fell, and the deficit in the national-income accounts rose from $400 million in 1937 to $2.1 billion in 1938. What caused production eventually to rise and unemployment to decline was, of course, preparation for war.

CONCLUDING OBSERVATIONS

Monetary and fiscal policies differed greatly in the three depressions. In the first (1920–1921) both policies were deflationary. In the second (1929–1933) tax policy was deflationary, government expenditures mildly antideflationary, and monetary policy, though vacillating, on the whole antideflationary. In the third (1937–1938) monetary and fiscal policy were violently expansionist. In the course of only twenty years policy had been completely reversed and attitudes greatly changed.

Despite the deflationary monetary and fiscal policies in the first depression, it lasted a relatively short time. Had expansionist policies been adopted its duration and severity might have been even less. The ability of the banking system to withstand the 1921 depression was an important sustaining force. Bank failures, though numerous, were concentrated among small banks in farm areas; the banking system itself did not collapse.

It was the collapse of the whole banking system that caused the depression of 1929–1933 to plunge to lower depths. The collapse was largely the result of declines in the quality of credit, standards of bank supervision, and ethical standards in the banking community. As the banking system weakened, the depression deepened, causing bank failures to increase, which in turn produced devastating liquidity crises.

Today deposit insurance engenders confidence in the banking system that should help to prevent bank failure epidemics. It does not and cannot, of course, prevent money-market disturbances arising from "disintermediation," that is, resulting from shifting funds from savings and savings institutions to demand deposits and currency. Nor does it insure against the emergence of foreign liquidity crises, the movement of funds from one nation to another because of dwindling confidence in the currency of a particular nation or group of nations. Liquidity crises, a dominant characteristic of the Great Depression, are by no means relegated to the inactive file of bank history.

Credit and monetary developments played a minor role in the 1937 depression. Interest rates continued low, but the confidence of the business community was shaken by the policies of the administration, which often seemed erratic and irrational. Bankers were caught in the same psychological downdraft. Lending policies were still influenced by the nightmarish memories of the Great Depression.

The danger now is not that the United States faces depressions comparable to those that we have been studying, since built-in stabilizers will help sustain income, while fiscal and monetary policies will be expansionist. Rather, the danger is continued inflation and progressive erosion of the value of money.

Notes

1. *Historical Statistics of the United States 1789–1945* (Washington, D.C.: U.S. Bureau of the Census, 1949), pp. 244, 296–299. Data on federal expenditures and the deficit are for fiscal years.

2. *Historical Statistics of The United States 1789–1945, op. cit.,* pp. 180–182, 186.

3. *All-Bank Statistics, United States 1896–1955* (Board of Governors of the Federal Reserve System, April 1959), pp. 364, 734, 774, and 868.

4. *Annual Report of the Secretary of the Treasury on the State of the Finances for the Fiscal Year Ended June 30, 1921* (Washington, D.C.: Government Printing Office, 1922), p. 31.

5. *The Federal Reserve Re-examined.* A study made by the New York Clearing House Association (New York: The New York Clearing House Association, 1953), pp. 10–12.

6. For description of certain subterfuges see B. H. Beckhart, *The Discount Policy of the Federal Reserve System* (New York: Holt, 1924), pp. 331–334, 432–436.

7. *Business Cycle Developments* U.S. Department of Commerce (Bureau of the Census, October 1968), p. 65.

8. *Twenty-second Annual Report of the Board of Governors of the Federal Reserve System Covering Operation for the Year 1935* (Washington, D.C.: Government Printing Office, 1936), pp. 186–188.

9. See the chart in *Twentieth Annual Report of the Federal Reserve Board Covering Operations for the Year 1933* (Washington, D.C.: Government Printing Office, 1934), p. 5.

10. *Banking and Monetary Statistics* (Washington, D.C.: Board of Governors, November 1943), pp. 375–376.

11. *Ibid.,* p. 19.

12. *Ibid.,* pp. 19 and 283.

13. *Annual Report of the Secretary of the Treasury on the State of the Finances for the Fiscal Year Ended June 30, 1931* (Washington, D.C.: Government Printing Office, 1932), p. 32.

14. Attitudes of Federal Reserve officials throughout this period are detailed in Elmus R. Wicker, *Federal Reserve Monetary Policy 1917–1933* (New York: Random House, 1966), chaps. 11, 12.

15. *Eighteenth Annual Report of the Federal Reserve Board Covering Operations for the Year 1931* (Washington, D.C.: Government Printing Office, 1932), p. 220.

16. *Seventeenth Annual Report Federal Reserve Bank of New York for the Year Ended December 31, 1931* (New York: April 6, 1932), pp. 5–6.

17. *Annual Report of the Secretary of the Treasury on the State of the Finances for Fiscal Year Ending June 30, 1933* (Washington, D.C.: Government Printing Office, 1933), p. 24; and *Twentieth Annual Report of the Federal Reserve Board Covering Operations for the Year 1933* (Washington, D.C.: Government Printing Office, 1934), p. 22.

18. *Banking and Monetary Statistics op. cit.*, p. 387.

19. *Secretary of the Treasury's Final Report on the Reconstruction Finance Corporation* (Washington, D.C.: Government Printing Office, 1959), pp. 53, 57.

20. *Annual Report of the Federal Deposit Insurance Corporation for the Year Ending December 31, 1934* (August 15, 1935), pp. 51 and 54.

21. *Twenty-Second Annual Report of the Federal Reserve Board Covering Operations for the Year 1935* (Washington, D.C.: Government Printing Office 1936), p. 5.

22. For a discussion of this proposal see Roy G. Blakey and Gladys C. Blakey, "The Revenue Act of 1936," *The American Economic Review*, Vol. XXVI, No. 3 (September 1936), pp. 466–482.

Adjusting to the Changing Gold Standard

CHAPTER 11

PRELUDE

Ninety-three Years without Devaluation

From 1821 to 1914 Great Britain was uninterruptedly on the gold-coin standard. The Bank of England was under legal obligation to buy bar gold offered at £ 3.17s.9d. a standard ounce and to redeem its notes with sovereigns, equivalent to a selling price of £3.17s.10½d. With the weight of pure gold in the British sovereign equalling 113.001 grains troy, and the American dollar equalling 23.22 grains troy, the ratio of the one to the other (that is, the mint par of exchange in 1914), was $4.8665 +. Costs of shipping the gold, loss of interest while the gold was in transit and freight and insurance charges determined the range of exchange rate fluctuations on either side of this figure. Ordinarily, the range was between about $4.84 and $4.88. At the lower figure gold entered the United States and at the higher it left.

The gold points (as the lower and upper range of fluctuations were termed), were influenced not only by the factors which we have mentioned but also by specific actions on the part of central banks. Thus, the Bank of England might redeem its notes in relatively light weight sovereigns, which were still within the limits of tolerance permitted by the coinage acts. The Bank, too, might grant interest free advances against gold imports. Each action would affect the gold export and import points.

Other expedients were used by other central banks. Thus, the Bank of France prior to 1914 had the right to redeem its notes in French gold coins or in 5 franc sliver pieces, either of which possessed the full legal tender power. Should a bullion arbitrageur seek to redeem his bank notes in gold, he might be met with a counter-offer to redeem the notes in silver coins. Should he insist, the Bank of France might offer to sell him gold bars or foreign gold coins at a premium. This would cause the French franc to depreciate in terms of other currencies. Other central banks (the Reichsbank for example) might confine the redemption of its notes solely at the head office, or might use moral suasion (Germany, Austria-Hungary and Russia) to dissuade exporters from demanding gold. The Bank of England did not resort to such extreme expedients. The world had confidence that its obligations would be honored.

The gold content of the American dollar, save for relatively slight changes in 1834 and 1837, remained unchanged from 1792 to 1934. The record, however, was not as unblemished as this statement might imply. Prior to the Civil War the United States was on the bimetallic standard, or rather on an alternating standard, as the ratio initially established, 15 to 1, favored silver until changed in 1837 to 16 to 1, which favored gold. For eighteen long years from 1861 to 1879 gold payments were suspended. Even when resumption took place (January 1, 1879) the country was torn by acrimonious discussions of the desirability of restoring bimetallism. The question was settled, at least for the time being, by the Gold Standard Act of March 14, 1900, which established the dollar consisting of 25.8 grains of gold 9/10 fine as the standard unit of value. Thirty-four years later the dollar was sharply devalued (January 30, 1934) and in another thirty-eight years (April 3, 1972) it was devalued again.

That the United States in 1900 adopted the gold standard was not surprising in view of the leadership of Britain. Germany had done so in 1871, the Scandinavian nations in 1873, and the Latin Monetary Union in 1874. The British pound was the key currency of the world. As David Lloyd George once remarked, "the British bill of exchange had the authentic ring of gold."

That the foreign-exchange value of pound sterling could remain stable for almost a century seems incredible to modern man living in an age of violent changes in the domestic and foreign value of all monies of the world. The Victorian period provided a stable world environment. It was not disturbed by world conflict (Pax Britannica), not convulsed by revolutionary changes in prices, or not subject to continuous wage pressures. It emphasized the value of personal and public thrift. In recent decades the British bill of exchange has lost its authentic ring. There have been successive devaluations of the pound: in 1931, in 1949, and in 1967.

A Sterling Standard

The focal point of the international gold standard of the Victorian period was London. There the world's short- and long-term money and capital markets were centered. Sterling letters of credit financed world trade; capital exports financed economic development in all nations. Great Britain was a creditor nation on both short- and long-term accounts. Short-term acceptance credits exceeded short-term deposit liabilities, with the result that the British financial system stood impregnable against possible liquidity crises.[1]

Buttressing the position of the British pound as the key currency of the world was the absence of exchange and trade barriers. Funds flowed in and out freely. There were no foreign-exchange controls. Their imposition would have seemed an act of madness to British bankers. Goods also flowed freely in and out of England. Protectionist devices in the form of import duties, quota restrictions, export subsidies, and the like were nonexistent. Foreign borrowers could always repay debts by shipping goods. British banking houses endeavored (not always successfully) to limit foreign debts to the ability of borrowers to repay and endeavored to insure that the funds were used in such fashion (for example, in the development of agricultural and mineral resources) that they would contribute to export earnings.

A further underpinning to world confidence was orthodox fiscal policy. The British budget was usually in balance. The British national debt had, in terms of pound sterling, fallen by 22 percent from the battle of Waterloo to the battle of the Marne, and in terms of annual national income it had fallen from 200 to about 30 percent.

The intricate web of international financial relations rested on gold reserves in the banking department of the Bank of England (including notes of the Issue

Department) amounting to only £ 50 million at the end of 1913. Aside from certain critical periods this amount proved adequate. If reserves fell, the Bank of England raised its discount rate. In various ways this action checked the outflow of funds and induced an inflow. Higher interest rates in England attracted fluid capital, checked the granting of foreign loans, and, through its effects on security prices, attracted investment funds. If continued for long, credit contraction in England would depress commodity prices and increase exports. But it was mainly through its effect on the inflow and outflow of short- and long-term funds that changes in the Bank rate influenced sterling exchange and caused the gold reserves of the Bank of England to rise or fall. It was a common saying that a 7 percent rate would draw gold from the ground.[2]

Changes in the British discount rate showed a close inverse correlation to fluctuations in the gold reserves of the Bank of England. The Bank, thus, abided by the rules of gold standard and was willing that Britain be subjected to the discipline of the balance of payments.

The Leadership of London

An increase in the British Bank rate influenced business decisions all over the world. Businessmen in New York, Shanghai, Bombay, and Buenos Aires drew in their horns, convinced that the directors of the Bank of England, the acknowledged experts in many financial fields, would not have taken such action unless something were amiss. The resulting reduction of inventories and postponement of plans for capital expansion dampened inflationary pressures and caused cyclical downturns in prices, which were abetted by downward flexibility in wages.

Occasionally, the Bank of England relied not simply on Bank rate pressures but also made use of moral suasion. For example, in 1906 the Bank, worried about speculative developments in the United States, advised British bankers to lighten their American commitments. They did so in time to avoid involvement in the American panic of 1907. The leadership of London was an important reason for parallelisms in the business cycles of industrial nations before 1914.

Economic integration in the Victorian period resulted not only from British leadership but also from currency convertibility, freedom for money and capital transactions, and freedom for personal travel and trade.* Certain basic concepts were shared in common, such as the support given to free market forces, conviction

---

* Czarist Russia was the only important nation then requiring passports for entrance into the country. Outside Russia and the United States, tariff rates were relatively low, and the United Kingdom had none.

that an international division of labor was advantageous to all nations, and opposition to government intervention and controls.*

Disintegration

The international gold standard, which was really a sterling standard with London as its focal point, ended with the guns of August 1914. The ensuing half-century has witnessed many attempts to rebuild a comparable international monetary system, but none has proved successful. All have failed mainly because the political and economic environments have not been conducive to success.

There are now two international monetary centers, London and New York, instead of one. Neither is completely sovereign. Both have been challenged by the rise of money and capital markets on the Continent and the emergence of the Eurodollar market. Each is a heavy debtor on short-term account. Each, like Victorian Britain, is a creditor on long-term account, with the important difference that modern Great Britain and the United States have applied trade and exchange restrictions of varying intensity, making it difficult at times for debtors to service their debts. Each nation often grants loans only if the proceeds are to be used domestically; "tied" loans were the exception in the Victorian period. Borrowers then could spend loan funds in the cheapest markets.[3]

Over the past half-century nations have fallen victim to the seductive lure of protectionism and foreign-exchange controls and to the enticingly superficial appeal of autarchy; they have been plagued by inflation and devaluations, buffeted about by tidal flows of "hot money" (money in unceasing quest for havens of refuge), and trapped into using short-term funds to finance long-term credit needs. Confidence in currencies wanes, and gold is hoarded. Inflationary pressures caused by the monetization of both public and private debt continue unabated.

The portfolios of central banks now consist mainly of government obligations, whereas before 1914 the requirement that central banks redeem their notes in gold coin induced them to restrict their earning assets mainly to short-term commercial bills. This change in the portfolios of central banks resulted not only from the financial requirements of World Wars I and II but also reflects present insistence on "full" employment, even at the risk of currency depreciation. Often unwilling to check inflation by deflationary measures, nations resort to more controls, which in the long run not only substitute direction for the competitive forces

---

* There were exceptions, but in comparison to present economic systems—some completely controlled, others partially controlled, a few relatively free—a distinct overall difference emerges.

of the market place but also provoke further inflation and eventually lead to currency devaluation and to increases in the price of gold.

GOLD AND CENTRAL BANKING

It has been estimated that in November 1914, as the Reserve banks prepared to open for business, the United States had a gold stock of $1,835 million (at $20.67 an ounce). Of this amount $666 million was in the form of gold coins held by commercial banks and the public, $913 million in circulating gold certificates held by commercial banks and the public and secured 100 percent by gold in the Treasury, and $256 million in uncommitted gold held by the Treasury.[4]

The Federal Reserve Act required that the capital subscriptions of member banks be paid in gold or gold certificates, and the Federal Reserve Board recommended that member banks pay in their reserve deposits as far as possible in this form. By the end of 1914 the Reserve banks held $229 million in gold and gold certificates, equal to about 12 percent of the nation's monetary gold stock (one of the uses to which the Reserve banks put their gold holdings was the establishment of the gold settlement fund—Chapter 3).

On December 31, 1970, the monetary gold stock of the United States stood at $11.1 billion (at $35 an ounce), which, except for the gold in the Exchange Stabilization Fund, was held by the Treasury. The Federal Reserve banks held claims of $10.5 billion against the gold stock, in the form of gold-certificate credits, and from January 1934 to August 1971 were free to redeem these credits to meet demands for gold from foreign central banks and monetary authorities.

Despite the increase in the gold stock between 1914 and 1970, from about $2 to $11.1 billion, the ratio of gold and gold-certificate reserves of the Federal Reserve banks to their combined note and deposit liabilities fell from about 88 to 13 percent. This sharp decline resulted from increased liabilities (notes plus deposits) of the Federal Reserve banks, which greatly outstripped the increases in reserves. Consequently the required gold-certificate reserves against both Federal Reserve notes and deposits were eventually eliminated.

These data are only for the beginning and the end of the period. In between there were tremendous fluctuations in the gold stock, revolutionary changes in the gold standard, and convulsions in the price of gold.*

---

* Only by an act of Congress can the United States alter the statutory gold content of the dollar or change the par value of the U.S. dollar. The United States has no legal commitment to buy or sell gold; the practice dating from 1934 could be changed without notice, and was, in fact, changed in August 1971, when the U.S. suspended convertibility.

Gold and Credit

As long as nations include gold, gold certificates, or their equivalent in central-bank reserves and buy and sell gold at relatively fixed prices, imports, exports, production, and sales will be directly related to the credit system. Increases in the gold stock, unless offset, permit expansion in central- and commercial-bank credit, and decreases induce contractions.

The gold stock of the world is related, more or less directly, to the volume of central- and commercial-bank credit. The relationship may not be a fixed one. The effects of increases and decreases in gold stocks on bank reserves may be offset, and credit tends to expand in increasing multiple relationship to a given increase in gold.

To the extent that central banks hold their reserves not only in gold but also in foreign exchange, as many do, increases and decreases in holdings of foreign exchange have the same effects on the credit system as changes in the gold stock. Similarly, now that central banks have begun to hold their reserves in Special Drawing Rights (see Chapter 16) increases and decreases in such rights will have the same effects on the credit system as do changes in holdings of gold and foreign exchange.

The Functions of Gold

In the modern world gold serves many functions. These are deeply rooted in the historic past and find confirmation in the psychological attitudes and practices of modern man. Having large value in small bulk, possessing durability and homogeneity, gold has for centuries been used in trade and commerce to purchase goods and services and especially in modern times to settle international balances. It is not subject to tariff duties or import quotas as it crosses frontiers. As President Charles de Gaulle once said, "gold does not change in nature . . . [it] can be made either into bars, ingots or coins . . . [it] has no nationality . . . the immutable and fiduciary value par excellence . . . today no currency has any value except by direct or indirect relations to gold." [5]

Gold is the one indisputable liquid asset. It is beyond the control of any one nation or group of nations. Its advantages are such that nations do not seem ready, certainly not at the present time, to give it up as a liquid asset and to substitute money controlled by an international body, involving as this would a heavy impairment of sovereignty.[6]

Gold serves as the common denominator for the currencies of nations belonging to the International Monetary Fund. For example, until 1972 the American dollar was defined as equivalent to .88671 grams of gold, the French franc to .160 grams, and the British pound to 2.13281 grams. These weights determined the par value of currencies in terms of one another. Relating the weight of the gold dollar with that of the British pound yielded a par value of $2.40 to each pound. By the rules of the International Monetary Fund, currencies were permitted to fluctuate above and below par by as much as 1 percent.* The range of fluctuation has subsequently widened to 2.25 percent (see Chapter 17).

When a nation decides to devalue its currency, as many have, it simply reduces the gold weight of the currency unit. When Britain devalued in 1967, it reduced the weight of its currency unit from 2.48828 to 2.13281 grams. The willingness of the United States, until August 1971, to buy and sell gold (sales were at times made grudgingly) at $35 an ounce minus and plus .25 percent was the keystone of the postwar international gold standard.

Gold, as opposed to the gold standard, satisfies a widespread and insistent demand for an asset that is immune to currency and political disorders. The events of the past fifty years have induced individuals in all nations to hoard gold, whether such action is permitted legally or not. So great was the confidence in leading currencies before 1914 that relatively little gold was hoarded, except in British India. The propensity of the Indians to hoard gold was then looked upon as a quaint custom of a far-away people. That quaint custom has now spread over the entire world, keeping large amounts of gold from the vaults of central banks, where it would add to what is called "international liquidity." Confidence in currencies induced investors in the pre-1914 period to purchase long-term bonds. The volume of "hot money," placed in short-term obligations and shuffled among nations, was very small. Lack of confidence in the purchasing power of currencies accounts for the current unwillingness of individual investors to shift from short-to-long-term debt obligations.

Gold Supply and Demand

The relation of gold to central- and commercial-bank credit and its role in the settlement of international claims account for the importance given to increases in the supply of gold from mining, dishoarding, and Russian sales and to in-

---

* Many nations have adopted narrower ranges. The signatories of the European Monetary Agreement limited fluctuations to approximately .75 percent on either side of parity. The British pound fluctuated approximately .83 percent on either side of parity.

creases in demand on the part of industry and individuals. The difference between supply and demand, if any, goes to increase the reserves of central banks.

Gold production in the noncommunist world amounts to about $1.4 billion annually. Russian production is not known, but Western experts estimate it at $350 to $600 million a year. Estimates of Russian gold stocks vary from $4 billion to as high as $10 billion. The Soviet government, anticipating an increase in the world price of gold, has in recent years restricted its sales to meet urgent import needs.

Gold production outside the USSR increased rapidly from 1945 to 1965, reflecting mainly a rise in South African production, owing to new mines, improved techniques, and the mining of uranium as a by-product. Elsewhere gold production declined. After reaching 31 million fine ounces in 1965, South African production has itself tended to become stable. The official price in American dollars has not risen. Mining costs have increased, reflecting general inflation, and gold mining has, in consequence, tended to become less profitable.

Various nations have adopted devices to ease the position of the gold-mining industry: tax relief, subsidies for marginal production, and permission to sell varying amounts of new gold production on black markets. The devaluation of the British pound in September 1949 afforded some relief for gold producers in the sterling area as did that of November 1967. The devaluation of the American dollar in 1972 afforded still further relief.

Demand for gold arises from increases in official gold stocks, industrial use, and private hoarding.[7] Industrial needs for gold include demand from the jewelry, dental, electrical, electronic, and aerospace industries. Additions to private holdings reflect deep-rooted confidence in gold as a standard of value and distrust of paper currencies—as well as a human desire to escape the payment of taxes. Miroslav A. Kriz has estimated that in 1967 $3 billion were siphoned into private holdings. Private demand not only absorbed all the newly mined gold but also reduced official stocks by about $1.6 billion.[8] The alleged gold shortage resulted from this explosion of private demand and lack of sales on the part of the Soviet Union.

As Kriz has pointed out, gold production, despite fears expressed in the 1920s and early 1930s, has over time contributed heavily and steadily to international reserves. Of all the gold ever mined, about $80 billion, more than three-fourths, has been mined in this century and about one-third in the past twenty years.

International Arrangements

There is extensive private trading in gold bars and coins, amounting perhaps to several billion dollars a year. Quoted prices reflect public reactions to political and monetary developments. London is the most important bar market (the London gold market reopened March 22, 1954) and Paris and Zurich the most important coin markets. Other markets can be found in Beirut, Kuwait, Dakar, Mexico City, and Toronto, In recent years the price of gold in London has risen above the U.S. Treasury selling price, evidencing private demand.[9]

To prevent the price of gold from rising to panic levels, as it did temporarily in 1960, and to exercise a moderating influence on the market, a gold pool was established in October 1961, by the central banks of the United Kingdom, Belgium, France, Italy, the Netherlands, Switzerland, West Germany, and the United States.* The Bank of England undertook to act as agent for the group, with authority to draw on the gold reserves of these central banks and to sell the gold thus obtained and with authority also to buy gold when the price fell below the United States selling price.

The gold pool thus consisted of a selling consortium which could be invoked when necessary to stabilize the gold market. It consisted, too, of a buying syndicate, coordinating gold purchases in London by a group of central banks. The basic objective, as the Bank of England pointed out, was to avoid unnecessary and disturbing fluctuations in the price of gold that might undermine confidence in the stability of world currencies.

Waning confidence in the dollar prompted an acute private demand for gold amounting to about $2 billion in the spring of 1968, which was met largely by drawing upon American official stocks. So massive was the drain that on March 16 and 17, governors of the central banks of Belgium, West Germany, Italy, the Netherlands, Switzerland, the United Kingdom, and the United States decided to refrain thereafter from supplying gold to the London or any other private gold market. Moreover, these central banks agreed that they would no longer buy gold from the market and that they would not sell gold to monetary authorities to replace gold sold in the private markets.[10] A two-price "system" for gold was thus established: the central bank price which governed transactions among central banks and which was $35 per fine ounce, and the open-market price. As Pierre-Paul Schweitzer, Managing Director of the IMF, pointed out, this decision in-

---

* France withdrew in June 1967; the Federal Reserve Bank of New York has acted as agent for the U.S. Treasury in all gold-pool transactions.

volved "no departure from the obligation of these countries to maintain the par value of their currencies established with The International Monetary Fund." [11] In line with this decision the London gold market was closed March 15–April 1, then reopened under various restrictions. (The seven nations that had signed the agreement agreed to support the pattern of exchange rates then existing. They thus agreed to continue to buy dollars in the foreign-exchange markets, which they had discontinued doing for a few days in the case of travelers' checks.) Since the establishment of the two-price system, the open-market price of gold has fluctuated within a wide range, mirroring international political and financial crises and shifting confidence in key currencies.

In view of the commitment by central banks in Western Europe and the United States to restrict purchases and sales of gold to one another, a temporary decline in the open-market price through the second half of 1969 stimulated lengthy discussion of the legal obligation of the IMF itself to purchase gold at the mint price. This obligation seemed perfectly clear. Article V, Section 6, of the IMF Articles of Agreement reads, "Any member desiring to obtain, directly or indirectly, the currency of another member for gold shall, provided that it can do so with equal advantage, acquire it by the sale of gold to the Fund." This section did not differentiate between newly mined gold and gold that formed part of central-bank reserves or private stocks.

The basic controversy involved the right of South Africa to sell gold to the IMF. The United States first opposed IMF decisions to purchase gold from South Africa but later acquiesced, following an exchange of letters between the Minister of Finance of South Africa and the Managing Director of the Fund. Although the import of this correspondence even now is not entirely clear, apparently South Africa has the right to sell gold to the Fund in any amount in exchange for other currencies. The currencies to be purchased are to be determined in consultation with the Managing Director.[12] The BIS in its *Fortieth Annual Report* stated that the arrangements had effectively put a floor of $35 per fine ounce (less the Fund's charge of .25 percent) to the price received by South Africa for its gold. The arrangements did not, however, put a ceiling on the price to be received in the open-market.[13] The IMF may itself use the gold it acquires from South Africa to purchase the currency of any member nation. In 1970 it acquired the equivalent of $640 million. In consequence of these arrangements and the suspension of convertibility by the United States, the IMF may in time replace the United States as the keystone of the present international gold standard.

GOLD MOVEMENTS
AND THE FEDERAL RESERVE SYSTEM

Since the establishment of the Federal Reserve System four massive gold movements have occurred—three inward and one outward. They have been associated less with surpluses and deficits in the trade balance than with massive movements of short- and long-term funds (see Table 11.1).

Table 11.1
Gold Movements
(Millions of Dollars)

Period [a]	Gold-Stock Changes	
1914–1917 [b]	$1,526 to $2,868	+$1,342
1920–1924 [b]	2,639 to 4,212	+ 1,673
1934–1941 [c]	8,238 to 22,737	+14,499
1957–1971 [c]	22,857 to 10,206	−12,651

[a] Data are end-of-year figures.
[b] At $20.67 an ounce in this period.
[c] At $35 an ounce in this period.

Source: *Banking and Monetary Statistics* (Washington, D.C. Board of Governors of the Federal Reserve System, November 1943), pp. 536–538; and *Economic Report of the President*, transmitted to the Congress January 1972 (Washington, D.C.: U.S. Government Printing Office, 1972), p. 302.

The Gold Inflow

The very rapid inflow of gold between 1914 and 1917 which was discussed in Chapter 6, provided the basis for the war-induced expansion in commercial-bank loans and investments. The Reserve System which had practically no security portfolio and lacked power to raise member-bank reserve requirements, was unable to take offsetting action. It was never suggested that the Treasury itself sterilize gold imports.

Following a period of loss to those nations with which the United States in World War I had an adverse blance of payments, the gold inflow was resumed. Until the end of August 1922 its effect on member-bank reserves was offset by the decline in member-bank borrowing. High discount rates induced member banks to use the gold inflow to repay their borrowings at the Reserve banks. In the second half of this period, the increase in the gold stock about equaled the increase of money in circulation. Again the effect on member-bank reserves was offset. Over the whole period 1920–1924, the increase in the gold stock did not by itself provide the basis for credit expansion.

The next gold inflow, the largest that the world has ever experienced, occurred after the devaluation of the dollar in 1934. (The outflow during the liquidity crisis of 1931, discussed in Chapter 10, was immediately followed by an equivalent inflow and consequently has been omitted from this discussion.) The golden avalanche resulted from a heavy export balance, a huge influx of foreign capital, and heavy withdrawals of American capital from Europe. These factors, which reflected the undervaluation of the dollar in the foreign exchange markets, and the fear of possible currency difficulties and war in Europe, varied in relative importance over the years. The balance of goods and services was particularly important in 1934 and again towards the end of the decade, when the military requirements of the belligerent nations impinged on the American economy. The inflow of foreign funds was heavy in 1935 and 1936 and again in 1939 and 1940.

Gold imports came principally from the United Kingdom (which often served as an entrepôt, particularly for South African gold), Australia, British India, Belgium, Canada, France, Hong Kong, Japan, Mexico, the Netherlands, the Philippines, Sweden, and Switzerland. The United States absorbed gold far in excess of current production (which itself was rising under the impetus of higher gold prices) and drew heavily upon the gold reserves of other nations and upon gold hoards in Western Europe and the Far East.

The bulk of gold imports arrived at the Port of New York and therefore initially affected the assets and liabilities of the Federal Reserve Bank of New York and the reserves of its member banks in New York City.

Increased reserves in New York City banks were then disseminated over the country, principally through Treasury transactions. The Treasury borrowed more in the New York area from commercial banks, individuals, and financial institutions than it spent, and transferred the excess to various parts of the nation to meet relief and other government expenditures. The decline in Treasury deposits with New York commercial banks was matched by an increase in these deposits elsewhere. As they were drawn upon, they were transferred to the ownership of business firms and individuals. A small part found its way back to New York as deposit balances of banks and business firms.

Problems

By the end of 1940 the United States held slightly more than 75 percent of the world's reported gold reserves. The rapid concentration of the gold stock in the United States gave rise to at least two crucial questions: First, what would be the effect of this concentration upon the American credit system and price structure? Second, what would be its effects upon gold use by other nations and upon the international gold standard?

The war and postwar inflation answered the first question (see Chapter 8). In trying to answer the second question, the President of the Reichsbank in Nazi Germany, Walther Funk, said on July 26, 1940, that "in any case gold will in the future play no role as a basis of European currencies, for a currency is not dependent upon its cover but on the value which is given it by the state, i.e., by the economic order as regulated by the state." [14] Germany would never, he continued, pursue a monetary policy that would make it in any way dependent upon gold, for it is impossible to tie a nation to a medium the value of which it cannot determine for itself. The governor of the Bank of Italy obediently echoed these ideas. The Nazis were intent on eliminating gold as a basis of monetary systems, and in their more exuberant moments, eliminating the interest rate as well.

On both counts the Nazis were proved wrong. Gold formed the basis of the Bretton Woods Agreements (see p. 315) and gold flows played an important role in postwar German monetary policy. The role of the interest rate and of interest rate changes in economic development became increasingly recognized in the postwar world, communist as well as capitalist.

The increase in "high-powered money" (that is, member-bank reserves) from the end of 1933 to the end of 1941 amounted to $9,723 million (see Table 11.2). The principal factor was a sharp rise of $18,701 million in the gold stock and the much smaller increase of $944 million in Treasury currency. The increase in Treasury currency resulted from the increase in silver coins and certificates, slightly offset by a reduction in national bank notes and Federal Reserve bank notes. Silver certificates met the full demand for paper money of $1 denomination and was increasingly substituted for Federal Reserve notes in meeting the demand for paper money of $5 denomination.

As pointed out earlier, the increase in member-bank reserves was so rapid that fear grew of possible inflation. This fear caused the Federal Reserve System to raise member-bank reserve requirements and the Treasury to sterilize gold imports for a time (Chapter 10, above). In retrospect it would seem better had the Treasury adopted its sterilization policy in 1934 and continued it until the end of 1941, when the gold inflow ceased. The cost to the Treasury would have been the interest charges on an increased public debt of about $15 billion. Had this policy been instituted, the Reserve banks, by changes in member-bank reserve requirements and open-market operations, would have been able to keep excess member-

Table 11.2

Increase in Member-Bank Reserves
December 31, 1933–December 31, 1941
(Millions of Dollars)

Factors of Increase		Factors of Decrease	
Gold Stock [a]	+$18,701	Reserve-bank credit	−$ 327
Treasury currency outstanding	+ 944	Money in circulation	+$5,641
Other Federal Reserve accounts	− 69	Treasury cash holdings	+ 1,931
		Treasury deposits at	
Total	$19,714	Federal Reserve banks	+ 864
		Nonmember-bank deposits	+ 1,228
		Total	$9,991

Increase in total member-bank reserves	$9,723
Increase in required reserves [b]	6,638
Excess member-bank reserves (Dec. 31, 1941)	$3,085

[a] Including the profits from gold devaluation.
[b] Resulting from increases in member-bank deposits and reserve requirements.

Source: *Banking and Monetary Statistics* (Washington, D.C.: Board of Governors of the Federal Reserve System, 1943), pp. 376–377.

bank reserves at levels appropriate for the stimulation of business activity, but below the level which would have provoked dangerous credit expansion.

The sterilization of gold imports would have given recognition to the abnormal character of the inflow and to the possibility of a later outflow as the world gold supply became redistributed. Abnormal inflows resulting from gigantic movements of "hot money" should not by themselves be allowed to cause sharp reductions in interest rates that force banks to purchase long-term government obligations by reason of a sharply inclined interest curve. As holdings of these obligations increased, the reversal of policy became more difficult and its effects on the capital markets more drastic.

The Gold Outflow

The post-World War II period was marked by a dramatic redistribution of the world's monetary gold stock. After a relatively small increase in the early postwar years, as shown in Table 11.3, the American stock fell precipitately and would have fallen more had it not been for the willingness of European nations to hold dollars.

A postwar redistribution of the world's gold stock was to be expected, but Europe's huge gain was larger than was justified simply by its economic resurgence. It also reflected a disturbing loss in American competitive power and an

Table 11.3
Estimated Monetary Gold Reserves
of
Central Banks and Governments
(Millions of Dollars)

Date [a]	United States	Industrial Europe [b] and United Kingdom	Other Nations, IMF, and BIS	Total
1945	$20,083	$ 6,514	$10,403	$37,000
1950	22,820	6,219	10,361	39,400
1970	10,732	18,500	12,053	41,285

[a] End of December.
[b] Industrial Europe includes Austria, Belgium, Denmark, France, Germany, Italy, the Netherlands, Norway, Sweden, and Switzerland.

Source: Bank for International Settlements, *Twenty-First Annual Report* April 1, 1950–March 31, 1951 (Basle: June 11, 1951), pp. 161, 163; and *Federal Reserve Bulletin*, (July 1971), pp. A92–A93.

equally disturbing inability or unwillingness to cope with the continuous deficit in the United States' balance of payments. The entire gold loss was offset by Federal Reserve open-market operations.

As a result of the four gold movements, shown in Table 11.1, the gold stock of the United States rose from about $2.5 billion at the end of 1914 to $10.7 billion at the end of 1970 (at $35 an ounce). Meanwhile the deposit and note liabilities of the Federal Reserve banks rose from $312 million to $87 billion and the deposit liabilities of all commercial banks from $21 billion to $481 billion. The gold stock, measured as a percentage of these deposit liabilities, fell from about 12 percent to 2.2 percent.

Despite frequently expressed fears of deflation arising from an alleged lack of gold through these years, there was abundant purchasing power in the period as a whole. In fact, purchasing power was heavily redundant, and wholesale prices (1947–1949 = 100), despite important intermediate variations, rose from 45 in 1914 to 140 in 1970.

ATTEMPTS TO REESTABLISH THE INTERNATIONAL GOLD STANDARD IN THE 1920s

War and postwar inflation, by reducing the purchasing power of currencies or rendering them completely worthless, made currency reform an early order of business in the 1920s. Stable currencies were prerequisite to political stability, the accumulation and productive investment of savings, industrial peace, internal economic growth, import and export trade, and foreign investment.

The basic requirements for the stabilization of currencies were set forth in the Report of the Financial Commission of the Genoa Conference of 1922, which itself was convened to consider such problems as international indebtedness, currency reform, and tariff relationships. The basic requirements were balancing national budgets, freeing central banks from political controls, prudent administration of financial institutions, and abolition of exchange controls. Once these requirements had been satisfied, the gold value of a currency could be fixed. The report called attention to the fact that currency reforms would be facilitated by continuous cooperation among central banks of issue.[15]

The balancing of government budgets had the highest priority, for it would revive confidence in currencies. A decline in velocity would result even though the volume remained the same. Goods would reappear on the markets, and prices would begin to fall. The value of a currency, often still irredeemable in foreign exchange, would begin to rise. Indeed it could rise so rapidly, because of repatriation of monies formerly sent abroad, that action might have to be taken to keep its value down. Once a currency had "found its level" in the foreign-exchange markets, a decision to stabilize it in terms of gold could be taken.

In the 1920s currency reform involved a return to some type of gold standard, in order to permit the stabilization of exchange rates in terms of one another. The standards established included gold coin (the United States, France, and Switzerland), gold bullion, (the United Kingdom), and gold exchange (Germany). Most nations established either the gold bullion or gold exchange standard. The gold exchange standard differed from the other two in that central bank liabilities were not redeemed in gold coin or bullion at home but rather in drafts drawn on a country which itself redeemed its liabilities in gold coin or bullion.

The gold-exchange standard in the 1920s, as in the 1960s, came under French attack. Criticism centered on the fact that the gold exchange standard enables a nation to acquire reserves by borrowing in a gold-standard country, thus permitting a multiple expansion of credit on a given gold base. (This criticism would lose much of its force if exchange reserves were held exclusively with central banks.) It does not require that a debtor nation take corrective action against a deficit in its balance of payments as long as it can continue to obtain foreign loans. Nor is a key-currency nation required to take corrective action against a deficit in its balance of payments as long as other nations are willing to hold its currency (see Chapter 17).

The gold-exchange standard subjects deposit holding centers to the vulnerability of sudden runs. Deposits in the 1920s resulted partly from borrowing, like the German deposits in New York, and partly from a flight of capital, like the French deposits in London. Whether borrowed or owned, they put the key-currency centers in a hazardous position.[16]

Before 1914 the gold-exchange standard was confined to a few areas like the Austro-Hungarian Empire, India, the Philippines, Mexico, and the Straits Settlement. The short-term foreign currency assets of these governments were built up either by foreign-trade balances with Great Britain or the United States or by loans from these nations. The bulk of the exchange assets was held in Britain. The amount, however, was not large. Great Britain's deposit liabilities to foreign creditors were smaller than were the acceptances that British banks had negotiated on their account.

The Federal Reserve System played a significant role, directly and indirectly, in helping certain nations to fix relationships between their currencies and gold between 1923 and 1928.[17] It participated actively in international conferences, eased interest rates in 1924 to facilitate the flotation of foreign loans, eased them again in 1927 to strengthen sterling exchange, and entered into arrangements to purchase foreign bills of exchange.

Easing interest rates in 1924 facilitated flotation of the Dawes loan, which was a prerequisite for the stabilization of the mark. The total amounted to $200 million and the American portion to $100 million. As a further measure of assistance, the Federal Reserve Board ruled that the Reserve banks could purchase German trade bills payable in dollars and in the United States when endorsed by the German Gold Rediscount Bank and an American banking institution.

But it was in connection with the stabilization of sterling and its restoration to prewar parity that the Reserve System played its most important role. To help Great Britain return to gold the Federal Reserve Bank of New York, in 1925, in cooperation with other Federal Reserve banks, advanced a two-year credit of $200 million to the Bank of England, and J. P. Morgan & Company advanced a credit of $100 million to the British government. To help Great Britain remain on gold the Reserve System eased interest rates in 1927. Although the credit that the Reserve System had granted to Britain in 1925 was not used, nevertheless its existence undoubtedly enhanced the assurance with which Britain returned to the gold standard.[18]

Other credit arrangements entered into by the Reserve System for the purpose of currency stabilization included loans extended to the Bank of Poland, the National Bank of Belgium, and the Bank of Italy. The Bank of France, possessing large foreign balances, did not find it necessary to obtain foreign credits. The repatriation of funds held abroad by French nationals in the period 1926–1928, when France was moving toward stabilization, added substantially to its reserves. The adoption of an exchange rate that was low in relation to the purchasing power of the currency induced a heavy inflow of funds.

Between 1923 and 1928 thirty nations returned to gold; Austria was first and France last. It was a period in which cental banks and bankers were beginning to cooperate on a continuous basis in the attempt to solve world monetary problems. Failure to solve these problems was not so much the fault of central banks as it was that of governments which did not provide the type of world environment (freedom from currency and trade controls) in which international monetary standards could have functioned.

THE INTERNATIONAL LIQUIDITY CRISIS

A little more than three years after France had stabilized its currency, marking the end of what seemed the successful reestablishment of the international gold standard, the British government announced, on September 20, 1931, that it had relieved the Bank of England of its obligation to sell gold at the statutory price. Britain, which resumed gold payments in 1925, was forced to suspend after a short six years. Britain's action resulted form a liquidity crisis which started in Vienna in May 1931 and shortly engulfed the whole world. The publication of the balance sheet of the Creditanstalt, revealing losses equal to its entire capital, led to heavy withdrawals by domestic and foreign depositors and to a flight of capital.

The crisis spread to Germany, which in a few weeks lost gold and foreign exchange totaling nearly $2 billion. All banks were closed on July 13, and foreign-exchange restrictions were imposed on July 15, 1931. Confronted not only by a foreign run but also by a domestic drain of huge proportions, the Reichsbank suffered an acute increase in note liabilities, a sharp shrinkage in gold and foreign-exchange reserves, and a resulting sharp increase in discounted bills. It stood ready to grant domestic credits freely, however, at interest rates that reached temporary peaks of 15 percent for the discount rate and 20 percent for the Lombard rate, the rate charged on security loans. To help meet the foreign drain, the Reichsbank arranged for $100 million in foreign credits, $25 million of which were advanced by the Federal Reserve banks. These credits were initially granted for a period of three weeks but were successively renewed until their expiration in

March 1933. Had the IMF or swap agreements existed then, direct or indirect assistance might have been extended to Germany sufficient to enable it to weather the crisis and to avoid imposition of restrictive measures.

The liquidity crisis next engulfed England. So heavy was the attack on sterling that the Bank of England was forced to arrange credits of $125 million with the Federal Reserve banks and credits of a similar amount with the Bank of France. The British government itself arranged additional credits of $400 million, half in New York and half in Paris. Borrowing of this magnitude ($650 million) did not suffice to save the pound. The collapse of a key currency, as Stephen V. O. Clarke has pointed out, contributed substantially to the disruption of the international economy.[19]

In addition to the large credits extended to Germany and Great Britain, the Reserve banks extended smaller credits to the national banks of Austria and Hungary. The Bank for International Settlements joined in granting these credits, as in those to Germany.

An important cause of the crisis, which caused a worldwide suspension of gold payments, imposition of exchange controls, and further increases in trade barriers, according to the 1931 report by the Reichsbank, was the complicated mass of political debts. They included war debts and reparations (brought to an end by the Hoover moratorium of 1931) which, in view of the trade barriers of the 1920s, could only with great difficulty be paid in goods. Payment of reparations was effected through using the dollar exchange borrowed by German firms and municipalities without difficulty from receptively eager American banks and industries. Their borrowings, which far exceeded their capacity and the capacity of the German economy to repay, could be continued and refinanced only in an optimistically prosperous America. Once the bubble burst, liquidity crises, debt defaults, and pervasive bankruptcies were inevitable.

Other factors listed by the League of Nations that were responsible for the liquidity crisis and which were quite as basic, included the use of banks in central Europe of short-term domestic and foreign funds to finance the capital needs of industry, the decline in the liquidity of banks in the form of self-liquidating paper and short-term shiftable assets, and the tendency of commercial banks on the European continent and elsewhere to allow deposit liabilities to increase without a concomitant rise in capital funds. Also, overhanging world banking systems and money markets was a huge volume of international short-term indebtedness which resulted not only from the practice of Central European banks of borrowing short and lending long but also from the growing use of the gold exchange standard.

In the more stable years preceding World War I international short-term liabilities were small in amount. The huge total reached at the end of 1930 resulted from an accumulation going back to 1925 and was represented by:

1. funds employed in financing foreign trade
2. central-bank and other monetary and banking reserves
3. funds held to meet interest, dividend, and amortization payments on long-term loans and other liabilities
4. "hot money" seeking refuge from currency and political difficulties
5. short-term borrowings often employed, as in the case of Austria and Germany, in long-term investment.

All of these various funds save for those classified under 1 and 3 constituted a source of danger. Funds appearing under 2 and 4, representing owned reserves, were a threat to the nation holding them and funds appearing under 5 were a threat to the borrowing nation. Funds accumulated under 1, 2, and 3 would be held mainly in London and New York.

The situation was impermanent. As long as business activity remained high, prices steady, and new loans easy to obtain, service on the accumulated debt could be maintained and maturing credits refinanced. But the decline in security values, commodity prices, international lending, and world trade led to banking difficulties that brought on a world crisis in confidence.

In reviewing these developments several years after the event, the BIS suggested that central banks should keep close watch on their nationals' foreign borrowing, should possess monetary reserves sufficiently large to meet runs, should permit those gold exports which reflect a lack of equilibium in international payments to exert their full effect on the domestic credit structures, and should endeavor to prevent use of short-term credits for purposes properly requiring long-term financing. "The position in 1930," the BIS concluded, "was due largely to the overgrown foreign exchange standard which is unlikely in the future to assume the same proportions." [20] Unfortunately, this prophecy proved incorrect.

AMERICAN COUP DE GRACE AT THE LONDON CONFERENCE

Roosevelt and the Conference

In an attempt to salvage what could be saved, to build anew and to resurrect economic and political internationalism, President Herbert Hoover in May 1932, took the initial steps toward convening a world economic and monetary conference, the purpose of which was to evolve cooperative action on international economic problems and to formulate foreign exchange stabilization agreements.

High hopes were aroused on every continent, reported the BIS in its *Fourth Annual Report,* by the convocation of the World Conference in London in June 1933. These hopes "were dashed to the ground when this vast assembly met and promptly discovered that it was either in disaccord on fundamentals (especially as regards early currency stabilization) or, if in agreement on some fundamentals (for example on the economic side) in disharmony as to the ways and means of reaching the agreed objectives." [21]

In a "fireside chat" on May 7, 1933, President Franklin D. Roosevelt declared most emphatically that the "great international conference that lies before us must succeed. The future of the world demands it and we have each pledged ourselves to the best joint efforts to that end." [22]

Despite those ringing words, Roosevelt brought the conference to an abrupt end by asserting in a special message to the delegates on July 3, 1933, that he would regard it "as a catastrophe amounting to a world tragedy" if the conference were to concern itself with foreign exchange stabilization. The United States, he continued,

> seeks the kind of a dollar which a generation hence will have the same purchasing and debt-paying power as the dollar value we hope to attain in the near future . . . old fetishes of so-called international bankers are being replaced by efforts to plan national currencies with the objective of giving to those currencies a continuing purchasing power which does not greatly vary in terms of the commodities and the need of modern civilization.[23]

To emphasize his point, he added, "The sound internal economic system of a nation is a greater factor in its well-being than the price of its currency in changing terms of the currencies of other nations."

The conference came to an abrupt halt. Had it succeeded in realizing the high hopes of its initiators, much of the Western world (outside the Japanese, German, and Russian spheres of influence) might have become more closely knit economically and financially.

That President Roosevelt reversed his initial endorsement of the aims of the conference and adopted a totally different point of view resulted from his conversion to the Warren-Pearson price theories. "The worldwide attempt," asserted these authors, "to maintain a fixed price for gold resulted in a collapse of commodity prices." If price chaos were to be avoided in the future, the scientific principles that govern prices had to be discovered, made common knowledge, and applied. Credit management cannot by itself bring about a lasting increase in prices; all that it does is "to throw commodity prices out of line with gold by a limited amount." [24]

To achieve price stability, nations would have to adopt a compensated dollar whose weight in gold would vary directly with commodity prices. As commodity prices rose, the weight of the gold dollar would rise. The dollar value of the reserves of central banks would fall. The dollar value of the output of gold mines would also decline, resulting in lower profits and in a decrease in physical output. If, on the other hand, commodity prices fell, the weight of the gold dollar would fall, resulting in an opposite sequence of events to those which we have described.

In periods of inflation the weight of the gold dollar would rise, and the dollar price of gold would fall. In periods of deflation the reverse would occur. The cure for deflation would thus be an increase in the dollar price of gold. The price level, Warren and Pearson maintained, is directly related to the value of gold, and changes in the price level result solely from changes in the value of gold. To raise the price level in the United States, which was the administration's basic objective in 1933, the price of gold had to be increased from $20.67 an ounce to some higher figure. The weight of the gold dollar had to be reduced.

The administration apparently concluded that the reestablishment of the wholesale-price level of 1926 was necessary to insure farm and industrial prosperity and to bring about equitable relations between debtor and creditors. But to reestablish that level the wholesale index would have to increase about 50 percent. To reestablish the 1926 wholesale food-price level the relevant index would have to increase about 67 percent. Actually, when devaluation occurred, the price of gold was raised slightly above 69 percent, from $20.67 to $35 an ounce. Presumably this decision was designed to give a sharp impetus to an increase in food prices.

The failure of the London Conference led, as the BIS pointed out, to a series of retrograde developments—more moratoria on public and private debts; more transfer impediments; more artificial clearings; more gold hoarding than during any year on record; more conversion of foreign balances and their repatriation into the home currency, or in gold, by private and central banks; almost complete cessation of long-term lending abroad; and further limitation or reduction in the volume of short-term credits.

International economic relations were shattered. Only as nations began to realize the catastrophic results of their policies did they begin the long and arduous trudge back to a saner world. They first had to succumb, so it seemed, to the virus of nationalism before they were willing to take remedial measures.

Currency Blocs

One of the first reactions to the conference's failure was formation of the "gold bloc" by those nations (France, the Netherlands, Italy, Belgium, Switzerland, and Poland) determined to preserve the status quo in their monetary systems. On July 3 their representatives confirmed their intention "to maintain the free functioning of the gold standard in their respective countries at the existing gold parities and within the framework of existing monetary laws." [25] The failure of the conference also led to the establishment of the sterling area, a group of nations centering around the pound sterling, which, in a currency declaration, stated that they recognized the importance of stable exchange rates between the countries of the Empire, in the interests of trade. These nations were shortly joined by Sweden, Denmark, and Argentina. In addition, several countries consisting of Canada, Cuba, Mexico, other Latin American nations, and the Philippines constituted an informal group, termed the dollar bloc. Their currencies centered about the American dollar.

The breakup of the conference thus resulted in the formation of three important monetary blocs, consisting of the gold, sterling, and dollar-bloc nations. In addition, there were mark, ruble, and yen blocs; the mark bloc grew in importance as Germany spread its influence among the Danubian nations through exchange controls and military conquests.

American Gold Policy

Following the breakup of the London Conference, President Roosevelt took steps to raise the price of gold. On August 28 he issued an executive order which revoked previous orders and which contained comprehensive provisions respecting the acquisition, hoarding, exportation, and earmarking of gold coin, bullion, and currency and respecting operations in foreign exchanges. All holders, with certain exceptions, were required to turn over their stocks of gold coin, bullion, and gold certificates to the Federal Reserve banks. In an executive order of August 29, the President authorized Secretary of the Treasury William H. Woodin to purchase all newly mined domestic gold at prices that would equal the highest price obtainable for the depreciating dollar each day on any of the world's free-gold markets. On

October 25 the RFC was assigned the power to buy and sell gold; to acquire, hold, and earmark gold for foreign accounts; and to export and otherwise dispose of its gold holdings.[26] The RFC purchased gold at continuously increasing prices, reducing by main force the price of the dollar in the foreign-exchange markets. At that time the dollar was basically very strong; it would not have declined had it not been for determined efforts by the U.S. government.

When the President authorized the RFC to purchase gold at increasing prices, he stated that this action was "a policy and not an expedient," that it was a move toward a managed currency, that it was designed to restore commodity price levels, and that once these were restored ". . . we shall seek to establish and maintain a dollar which will not change its purchasing and debt-paying power during the succeeding generation." [27]

These many developments culminated in the Gold Reserve Act of January 30, 1934, which until August 15, 1971 continued as the basic monetary statute of the nation. Under the provisions of the act the President fixed the weight of the dollar at $15\frac{5}{21}$ grains, $\frac{9}{10}$ fine. This weight was 59.06 percent of the former weight of $25\frac{8}{10}$ grains, $\frac{9}{10}$ fine, and was the equivalent of $35 per fine troy ounce.

Secretary of the Treasury, Henry Morgenthau Jr., (who was appointed on January 1, 1934, following Secretary Woodin's resignation on December 13, 1933) announced that he would buy through the Federal Reserve Bank of New York any or all gold offered at $35 an ounce, less the usual mint charges and .25 percent for handling charges. He also announced that, whenever exchange rates with gold-standard currencies should reach the gold-export point, he would sell gold to central banks at $35 per ounce plus a handling charge of .25 percent. Exports were to be made only to foreign central banks, buying and selling gold at fixed prices.[28]

The initial effect of the Gold Reserve Act upon the Federal Reserve statement was simply to substitute gold certificates for gold; one asset was swapped for another. There was no change in total assets and no change in any liability, including member-bank reserves. In their actual use of the gold "profits" of 2.8 billion, Congress and the Treasury showed commendable prudence. Only a fraction was used in a manner that increased member-bank reserves. The largest portion, $1.8 billion, was sequestered in the inactive Stabilization Fund. The next largest portion, $645 million, was used to retire the national bank notes and employed in a fashion that, when all operations had taken place, had no effect on member-bank reserves.

Much more important than the "accounting effects" of the Gold Reserve Act was the assumption by the Treasury of control over monetary and credit policy. The Federal Reserve System was relegated to a secondary position and did not achieve relative independence until the accord of 1951 (see Chapter 8).

Devaluation resulted not from weakness of the dollar but rather from unqualified acceptance of the Warren-Pearson price theory. This theory was wholly mechanistic, correlating commodity and gold prices while ignoring the volume, use and quality of credit, and the volume and use of currency. Indeed the authors declared that changes in the volume and use of credit could produce only temporary aberrations. The basic, and in fact the sole, determinant of commodity prices was considered to be the price of gold.

Actually, devaluation had no economic justification. The balance of payments was in surplus. American costs had adjusted themselves to the decline in prices. Debt was being refinanced. The basis was laid for a sharp cyclical upturn in business activity, which would be followed sooner or later by a cyclical rise in farm and raw material prices.

The Tripartite Agreement

The decision to devalue the dollar set back world recovery by forcing the gold-bloc countries to ship huge amounts of gold to the United States and compelling them eventually to devalue their own currencies. Following a loss of $2.1 billion in gold during the preceding eighteen months the French government suspended gold payments on September 26, 1936. Its action was followed shortly by the devaluation of the currencies of Italy, the Netherlands, Switzerland, and a host of other countries. German currency remained immobile behind the iron wall of Nazi controls.

The day before the devaluation of the French franc, the American, British, and French governments declared their intention to foster conditions that would contribute to the restoration of order in international economic relations, to avoid competitive currency depreciation, to arrange consultations in order to avoid any disturbance that might result from the devaluation of the franc, and to relax barriers to trade and exchange. Later Belgium, the Netherlands, and Switzerland announced their intention of cooperating in this declaration. The Warren-Pearson theory was thus laid to rest, and the goals of the London Conference were vindicated.

The countries signatory to the agreement decided, subject to twenty-four hours' notice, to sell gold to each other's exchange funds. The new system, reported the BIS in its *Seventh Annual Report,* could be described as a daily gold settlement system.[29] Although France was not able, in view of the threat of World War II, to maintain initial exchange rates, this agreement was extremely important in providing a basis for collaboration and recognition, even on the part of the United States, of the essential role of stable exchange rates in promoting world recovery.

As a President of the BIS, Dr. J. W. Beyen, pointed out, stable exchange rates lead nations to observe certain principles in their cost and price structures and credit policies.[30] These rules are in the direct interest of the people concerned, since their purpose is the maintenance of sound currencies at home and the establishment of monetary and credit relations with other nations that will help rather than impede the international exchange of goods.

ANOTHER ATTEMPT TO REESTABLISH AN INTERNATIONAL MONETARY STANDARD

Currency Stabilization

As World War II approached its end, the nations of the world realized that one of their most important peacetime tasks, once hostilities ended, would be to sweep away the debris of inflated and worthless currencies and to reestablish the badly shattered international monetary standard. Economic controls would have to be abandoned, subsidies eliminated, government budgets balanced, interest rates unpegged, banking systems reestablished, blocked balances unfrozen, exchange rates stabilized, and massive dollar assistance provided.

The task proved more difficult than it had been after World War I, not only because the material destruction was greater, the disorganization of economic life more severe, and loss of foreign investment larger, but also because the economic attitudes that had developed during the depression continued to govern—even though conditions had changed radically. These attitudes often delayed the adoption of measures that would have speeded recovery—particularly was this the case in the United Kingdom and Scandinavia, where action to release the dynamic forces of free competitive markets was long postponed.

The Western nations, once they had stabilized their currencies, adopted the gold-exchange standard based on the American dollar.* Most nations held some

---

* The nations of the sterling area relied on the British pound, which itself relied from time to time on massive American assistance (for the dates when the main currencies were stabilized after World Wars I and II, see Chapter 9).

gold, and many held rather large amounts, but all bought and sold dollars in order to keep the foreign-exchange value of their currencies within limits prescribed by the IMF. The willingness of the U.S. Treasury to buy and sell gold, within narrow limits, was the basis of the new international monetary system. The preservation of this system was deemed so vital to international economic stability that nations were willing, though reluctantly as time went on, to allow their dollar holdings to grow rather than to embarrass the United States by asking for gold redemption.

At the end of World War II (and at the end of World War I) nations found themselves with more money (currency plus bank deposits) than was compatible with existing price and income levels. Physical controls imposed during the war had prevented the increased money supply from being entirely absorbed in open inflation. Three solutions to this problem were adopted.

The first was open inflation, allowing prices to adjust themselves to the money supply, followed, for example, in Italy. The second was to destroy a substantial portion of the existing money supply, as West Germany did, converting old money into new at an average ratio of about 10.5 to 1. The third was to try to increase production to a level commensurate with the money supply, relying on the use of controls to hold down prices until this level was reached; this policy was followed in the United Kingdom.

The policies followed in Italy and Germany permitted economic controls to be lifted; those followed in the United Kingdom required that controls be continued.* The continuation of controls led to what is termed "suppressed inflation." Individuals could not use their earnings to purchase the goods they desired at any price, and their productivity declined; business firms, subject to many controls, found their initiative sapped and did not adapt new processes or produce goods that consumers desired. In order to increase productivity among coal miners and thus to increase coal production, for example, the British government (despite the outcry for "fair shares") sent scarce consumer goods to mining villages.[31]

Eventually most controls were abandoned in the United Kingdom and elsewhere, occasionally to be reinstated, but the nations which reflected the quickest recovery at the end of the war and the greatest continuous economic growth were those which first reinstituted and continuously maintained free market economies.

Contrary to the situation after World War I when American private capital markets, assisted by the Federal Reserve System, financed economic reconstruction

---

* American advisers in Germany wanted controls continued, but the German government wisely decided otherwise.

and currency stabilization, the much larger aid required by European and other nations after World War II was provided by loans and grants extended by the U.S. government. As indicated in Table 11.4, American assistance to all nations during the period of monetary reconstruction amounted to about $33 billion (total exports of $37,255 million minus liquidation of gold and dollar assets of $3,633 million).

Table 11.4

Financing Surplus American Exports, January 1, 1946–December 31, 1950 (Millions of Dollars)

Surplus of exports of goods and services	$34,444
Means of financing the surplus:	
Liquidation of gold and dollar assets of foreign nations	$ 3,633
Dollar disbursements by the International Monetary Fund	739
Dollar disbursements by the International Bank for Reconstruction and Development	548
United States Government:	
Grants	17,293
Long- and short-term loans	8,372
United States private sources:	
Remittances	2,847
Long- and short-term capital	3,823
Total	$37,255
Errors and omissions	−$ 2,811

Private capital exports, in this period played a relatively minor role and were used mainly to develop the oil resources of the Near East and Latin America. The liquidation of gold and dollar assets by foreign nations ended by 1949, when their economies had been reconstructed. Thereafter these nations accumulated dollars in increasing amounts. Had provision been made for repayment of the grants, the American balance of payments problem in the 1960s would have been eased. In the late 1940s, however, economists were convinced that the dollar gap would continue indefinitely.

Institutional Support

Although officials of the Federal Reserve System participated in various international conferences, they did not play an initiating or guiding role in currency stabilization in the 1950s, as they had in the 1920s. This role was assumed by the Treasury, the BIS, and the IMF.

The foreign activities of the Federal Reserve System included serving as a depository for foreign central banks and the Bretton Woods institutions, operating the American Exchange Stabilization Fund, serving as fiscal agent for the Export-Import Bank and occasionally extending short-term loans to foreign central banks against gold collateral. These loans, granted at the regular discount rates, reached a peak of nearly $260 million in August 1948. In the 1960s, when the dollar and pound were under attack, the Reserve System did begin to play an increasingly active role, particularly through swap arrangements, in solving the acute problems of defending key currencies (see Chapter 16).

Assisting in restoration of an international monetary standard after World War II were two international institutions of great importance: the BIS, founded in 1930, and the IMF, established in 1945.

The BIS emerged from the Hague Agreements on Reparations and was established to formalize central-bank cooperation, which had evolved informally in the 1920s. Its members now include not only the central banks of all European countries (with the exception of the USSR), but also the central banks of Canada and Japan. The membership is a homogeneous one, in that the members are all located in industrially developed nations. The directors, consisting of representatives of central banks, share a common interest in protecting the stability of currencies and bring their rich banking experience to bear on specific problems.*

In the early postwar years the BIS played a very important role in the reestablishment of a system of multilateral payments among European nations. The initiating impulse was the conclusion, immediately after the war, of about thirty bilateral payment and monetary agreements providing for reciprocal overdraft facilities totaling about $650 million, which gradually evolved into a rudimentary type of multilateral clearance system and in turn spawned a full-fledged multilateral clearing arrangement, the European Payments Union (EPU). As the BIS pointed out, the EPU offered no substitute for full convertibility but was an important cooperative step toward that goal. By the end of 1958 all the major Western European countries had jointly established the nonresident convertibility of their currencies. The monetary cooperation initiated by the EPU has continued within the framework of the European Monetary Agreement.[32]

---

* The BIS was constituted as a limited liability company, with each share of stock carrying one voting right. Voting rights, however, are not acquired with the ownership of the shares but are reserved under the statutes for the central banks of the countries where the shares were originally issued. If the central bank of any of these countries does not desire voting rights, which is the case with the Federal Reserve Banks, the Board of Directors of the BIS may appoint another financial institution of the same country to exercise them in its place. The Board of Directors of the BIS has appointed the First National City Bank of New York to exercise the American voting rights. (Letters from Antonio d'Aroma, Secretary General of the BIS, October 2, 1969, and Gabriel Ferras, General Manager of the BIS, November 25, 1970.)

The IMF, whose Articles of Agreement were drafted at the Bretton Woods Conference of 1944, was established to promote international monetary cooperation and consultation, to end competitive currency depreciation, to help eliminate exchange controls, to stabilize exchange rates, to facilitate orderly changes in exchange rates, and to remedy the reputed defects of the international gold standard.*

The IMF is a worldwide organization with 117 members (on April 30, 1971; on December 27, 1945, there were but 22 members). The membership is heterogeneous, consisting of nations at various stages of economic development and with diverse attitudes on monetary issues. As indicated in Chapter 16, each member nation is assigned a quota which sets its contribution to the resources of the IMF, which determines access to the credit facilities of the IMF and which fixes, with approximate limits, its voting rights.

The IMF agreement provided that the initial par values of members' currencies were to be established in consultation with the IMF and were to be changed only after further consultation with the IMF. By December 18, 1946, the IMF had accepted the initial par values of the currencies of thirty-three members. A host of changes occurred in 1949, when thirteen members, accounting for 65 percent of world trade, devalued their currencies. This mass move was initiated by action on the part of the United Kingdom.

In the so-called "transitional period" (1945–1950), during which industrial nations were rebuilding their economies, the IMF lent the equivalent of $785 million (the bulk of which were in dollars) for currency stabilizations. The largest loans were to France, India, the Netherlands, and the United Kingdom. The IMF would have lent more, even at the risk of freezing its assets (that is, lending dollars against currencies of limited acceptability) had it not been for the inauguration of the European Recovery Program (the Marshall Plan) in April 1948. During the existence of this program the IMF marked time. The industrial nations required long-term development money, which was not a proper responsibility of the IMF. Therefore, the IMF concentrated its efforts on prodding member nations to eliminate exchange controls on current accounts, in order to establish orderly cross rates, and to abandon multiple currency practices. The Anglo-American Financial Agreement, under the terms of which the United States and Canada lent

---

* According to an article in the Bank of England *Quarterly Bulletin,* March 1969, pp. 37–51, "The International Monetary Fund: use and supply of resources," the process of legal interpretation has enabled the Fund to adjust itself, at least partially, to the changing world situation which could not be foreseen at Bretton Woods. The founding fathers of the IMF envisaged a world in which the main danger would be from deflation; could not foresee the possibility of a prolonged U.S. balance-of-payments deficit; the unification of world financial markets through use of Euro-dollars and massive movements of short- and long-term capital funds; or the magnitude of economic problems of the developing world.

the United Kingdom $5 billion, provided for convertibility of sterling on current transactions after July 15, 1947. This agreement was correctly regarded as an extremely important step toward general convertibility. Unfortunately it proved abortive and was ended on August 21, 1947.

The New International Monetary Standard

In 1965 the IMF declared that the existing international monetary system

> comprises a spectrum of customary institutional and legal arrangements which govern the conduct of international economic transactions, the methods of financing deficits and surpluses in international payments, and the manner in which countries are expected to respond to such surpluses and deficits.[33]

The present system, continued the Report, comprises the Articles of Agreement of the IMF, which were drafted and adopted to foster the interconvertibility of currencies. It includes, too, the "par value system," under which each country is obligated to maintain a fixed value for its currency relative to gold and other currencies. It includes, too, those provisions of both the Articles of Agreement of the IMF and of the General Agreement on tariffs and Trade which subject exchange and trade and controls to international regulation and surveillance. Finally, the international monetary system includes all arrangements respecting external reserves.

The system, the Report explained, combines two features complementary in character: the financing of imbalances and the elimination of imbalances. Obviously the task of managing the international monetary system is lightened if major payments disturbances do not arise in the first instance.

In some respects the international monetary standard of the 1950s seemed to have better prospects for success than had that of the 1920s. In the 1950s nations were not beleaguered with reparations and war debts. The United States had canceled repayment of the greater part of the loans that it had extended during the war, and reparations, to the extent that they were paid, were usually paid in kind. Postwar assistance took the form largely of grants-in-aid.

Furthermore, the United States recognized its obligations as a creditor nation. Beginning in 1947 tariff rates were lowered on six separate occasions, including those of the Kennedy Round. The ratio of duties to dutiable imports fell from 37 percent in 1941 to 12 percent in 1967. The Kennedy Round agreements, when they take effect, will probably reduce this ratio to about 5 percent.[34] (The results of the Kennedy Round in terms of eliminating nontariff barriers like quotas, were modest. When acute balance-of-payments difficulties arose in the 1960s the United States invoked various protectionist devices; see Chapter 12).[35] The lowering of tariff barriers following World War II, accompanied by the establishment of trading partnerships like the Common Market and the European Free Trade Association, augured well for the maintenance of an international monetary system.

There were, however, important countervailing influences, including the persistent difficulties of the British economy and its failure to forge ahead; the lavish granting of loans to developing nations far beyond their capacity to repay; the failure of nations to reduce trade restrictions on the nontropical agricultural products and on the labor-intensive industries of developing countries; and finally the long-continued deficit in the United States' balance of payments, which threatened to replace its liberal trade with restrictive policies and thus to undermine the international monetary system (see Chapter 16).

CONCLUDING OBSERVATIONS

Gold has in the past played—and doubtless will continue to play in the future—a significant role in international monetary relationships. The par values of currencies are fixed by the relative gold weights of currency units. The purchase and sale of gold by central banks at relatively fixed prices in terms of currency units affect central-bank and commercial-bank reserves and credit expansions and contractions. Continued loss or gain of gold reflects a fundamental disequilibrium in international economic relationships (for a discussion of "paper gold," see Chapter 16).

The gold standard of the Victorian period was really a sterling standard. It rested upon the firm foundation of Great Britain's position as short- and long-term creditor in the money and capital markets, upon the economically liquid condition of the British banks, upon functional specialization of financial institutions, upon a fiscal policy that sharply reduced British government indebtedness in terms of national income, and upon the absence of British trade and exchange barriers.

Foreign trade was financed by self-liquidating bills of exchange. Capital was exported to develop the capital equipment and resources of a borrowing nation in a manner that would contribute to its export capacity and thus to its ability to repay international indebtedness.

Since the end of World War I the gold standard has developed into a gold-exchange standard, which, unless skillfully managed, carries the seeds of its own destruction; a key-currency nation can put off remedial action against internal inflation and external balance-of-payments deficits as long as other countries are willing to hold its currency. Balance-of-payments deficits help to provide the basis for credit expansion and price increases in other nations and generate a huge volume of "hot money" rushing madly from market to market in search of security.

As credit expands, public and private deficit financing is incited. Commercial banks enter new lending fields, borrow short to lend long, credit standards fall, and the quality of credit suffers. Eventually the day of reckoning arrives, and central bankers rush to hurried conferences in an effort to patch up a shattered world monetary system.

What is likely to be forgotten, now that the reasons for the successful functioning of the gold standard in the Victorian period are shrouded in history, is that no international monetary standard, gold or otherwise, can long endure unless it is supported by appropriate trade and credit policies in the key-currency nations. Appropriate trade policies are liberal trade policies, and appropriate credit policies are those that encourage qualitative lending standards and stabilize, in terms of the consumer-price index, the domestic purchasing power of currencies.*

In the 1920s trade policies were highly protectionist, and qualitative lending standards tended to deteriorate. The consumer-price index was stable, but this stability reflected what came to be called "negative inflation." Had the index reflected increases in productivity, it would have fallen. That it did not was the result of the bolstering effect of credit expansion and a decline in qualitative standards.

In the 1960s American trade policies were liberal, but qualitative credit standards fell, and the consumer-price index rose continuously. As time passed, the problem, according to Chairman Samuel Schweizer of the Swiss Bank Corporation, was not to make dollars as "good as gold" but rather to prevent gold from becoming as bad as dollars. Other aspects of this problem are discussed in Chapter 15.[36]

---

* The index should be adjusted for changes in productivity. If productivity is in general rising, an index of consumer prices, if it were to be considered noninflationary, would be expected to decline.

Notes

1. See Peter H. Lindert, *Key Currencies and Gold 1900–1913* ("Princeton Studies in International Finance No. 24, International Finance Section, Department of Economics." [Princeton: Princeton University Press, 1969]). For a discussion of the history of the gold standard in the United States, see Margaret G. Myers, *A Financial History of the United States* (New York: Columbia University Press, 1970).

2. For a discussion of central-banking policy in this period see Arthur I. Bloomfield, *Monetary Policy Under the International Gold Standard 1880–1914* (New York: Federal Reserve Bank, 1959). Also see Ralph A. Young, "Making Peace with Gold," *The Morgan Guaranty Survey* (June 1968), pp. 3–14; and A. G. Ford, "The Truth about Gold," *Lloyds Bank Review* (July 1965), No. 77, pp. 1–19.

3. For a discussion of impediments to trade other than tariffs see Norman S. Fieleke, "The Buy-American Policy of the U.S. Government: Its Balance-of-Payments and Welfare Effects," *New England Economic Review* (Federal Reserve Bank of Boston, July–August 1969), pp. 2–16.

4. "A Note on Gold in 1914," *Monthly Review* (New York: Federal Reserve Bank, April 1964), p. 79.

5. Charles de Gaulle, 11th Press Conference, Paris, February 4, 1965, p. 6.

6. See Miroslav A. Kriz, "The Future of Gold-Discussion," *Papers and Proceedings of the Eighty-First Annual Meeting* of the American Economic Association, Chicago, December 30, 1968; and *The American Economic Review*, Vol. LIX, May 1969, No. 2, pp. 353–356.

7. "Annual Gold Review," *Monthly Economic Letter* (First National City Bank of New York, January 1968), pp. 8–11.

8. "New Perspectives on Gold," *Monthly Economic Letter* (First National City Bank of New York, April 1968), pp. 39–42.

9. International Monetary Fund, *1967 Annual Report* (Washington, D.C.), p. 122.

10. *International Financial News Survey* (International Monetary Fund, Vol. XX, No. 11, March 22, 1968).

11. *The New York Times,* September 28, 1968, pp. 45–46.

12. Article VII, Section 2 (ii); see *International Financial News Survey* (International Monetary Fund, Vol. XXII, No. 2, January 16, 1970).

13. Bank for International Settlements, *Fortieth Annual Report,* April 1, 1969–March 31, 1970 (Basle: June 8, 1970), p. 112.

14. Bank for International Settlements, *Eleventh Annual Report,* April 1, 1940–March 31, 1941 (Basle: June 9, 1941), p. 96.

15. *Federal Reserve Bulletin* (June 1922), pp. 678-680.

16. An excellent discussion of the gold-exchange standard is included in the testimony by Friedrich Lutz in *The United States Balance of Payments,* Hearings before the Joint Economic Committee, 1st sess. of the 88th Cong. of the United States, Part 3, The International Monetary System: Functioning and Possible Reform, November 12, 1963 (Washington, D.C.: Government Printing Office, 1963), pp. 338–349.

17. See Stephen V. O. Clarke, *Central Bank Cooperation, 1924–1931* (New York: Federal Reserve Bank, 1967).

18. *Thirteenth Annual Report,* Federal Reserve Bank of New York, for the year ended December 31, 1927 (February 2, 1928), p. 17.

19. For a detailed account of this period, see Clarke, *op. cit.*

20. Bank for International Settlements, *Sixth Annual Report,* April 1, 1935–March 31, 1936 (Basle: May 11, 1936), p. 44.

21. Bank for International Settlements, *Fourth Annual Report,* Arpil 1, 1933–March 31, 1934 (Basle: May 14, 1934), p. 5.

22. *The New York Times,* May 8, 1933, p. 2.

23. *The New York Times,* July 4, 1933, p. 1.

24. George F. Warren and Frank A. Pearson, *Prices* (New York: Wiley, 1933), pp. 303, 362, 369.

25. Bank for International Settlements, *Fourth Annual Report, op. cit.,* p. 13.

26. The Executive Orders are to be found in the *Federal Reserve Bulletin* (September 1933), pp. 534–538.

27. *The New York Times,* October 23, 1933, p. 3.

28. *Federal Reserve Bulletin* (February 1934), pp. 61–70.

29. Bank for International Settlements, *Seventh Annual Report,* April 1, 1936–March 31, 1937 (Basle: May 31, 1937), p. 23.

30. Bank for International Settlements, *Eighth Annual Report,* April 1, 1937–March 31, 1938 (Basle: May 9, 1938), p. 115.

31. In this section we have drawn heavily on an unpublished manuscript by Vera Lutz, "The Record of Inflation: European Experience since 1939" (The American Assembly, Columbia University, 1952).

32. Bank for International Settlements, *Fifteenth Annual Report,* April 1, 1944–March 31, 1945 (Basle: Autumn 1945), p. 100; *Sixteenth Annual Report,* April 1, 1945–March 31, 1946 (Basle: July 1946), p. 54; *Nineteenth Annual Report,* April 1, 1948–March 31, 1949 (Basle: June 13, 1949), pp. 200–213; *Twenty-first Annual Report,* April 1, 1950–March 31, 1951 (Basle: June 11, 1951), p. 238.

33. International Monetary Fund, *1965 Annual Report* (Washington, D.C.: August 30, 1965), p. 9.

34. *Monthly Economic Letter* (First National City Bank of New York, September 1967), pp. 100–104; and *Economic Review* (Federal Reserve Bank of Cleveland, September 1967).

35. For a discussion of the implications of the Kennedy Round, see *Economic Report of the President* (Washington, D.C.: Government Printing Office, 1968), pp. 187–194.

36. Quoted in *Press Review,* Bank for International Settlements (Basle: March 10, 1966), p. 1.

Che
Jntractable
Problem of
CHAPTER 12 # the 1960s*

AN UNUSUAL DEVELOPMENT

The persistent deficit in the balance of payments emerged as the really intractable economic problem of the United States in the 1960s. Innumerable were the optimistic forecasts of its early solution. All proved unfounded. The dollar weakened, and, as it weakened, it was generously supported by various foreign nations, particularly by West Germany and Japan. Nations prostrate at the end of the World War II succored the economic colossus of the West. The support, which represented close monetary cooperation, arose from a desire to prevent the newly created gold-exchange standard from collapsing and to dissuade the United States from withdrawing military support from Western Europe and Asia. The action was founded on economic and political motivation.

That the United States would suffer long-continued payments deficits and that dollar scarcity would turn into dollar glut were unforeseen developments of such revolutionary import that they cast into discard economic forecasts of the early

* The author is indebted not only to the members of the review committee but also to Ivar Rooth, at one time Governor of the Sveriges Riksbank and Managing Director of the International Monetary Fund for assistance with this chapter.

post-war period. Leading economists, particularly those in Great Britain, had affirmed with dogmatic certitude that, by reason of the high productivity of the American economy, the world's principal economic problem would be an indefinite continuation of dollar scarcity. It was to protect the world against this contingency that the scarce-currency clause was introduced into the Articles of Agreement of the International Monetary Fund. (Article VII permits the IMF, if it deems such action appropriate, to declare a currency "scarce." The issue of a formal declaration authorizes member nations to impose limitations on freedom of exchange operations in the scarce currency.) Suggestions that dollar scarcity might turn into a dollar glut would have been looked upon as droll forecasts by the uninformed.

Some of the reasons for this dramatic change, some of its adverse consequences, and the principal policies adopted by the U. S. administration and the Federal Reserve System form the basic discussion of this and succeeding chapters.

In the early 1950s, the deficit in the American balance of payments with few exceptions, had been relatively modest, had caused no decline in the monetary gold stock, and had provided many nations with needed dollar reserves. The European economies were being rebuilt and relied on American assistance. Once they had been reconstructed, a prerequisite for economic growth and well-being, their competitive power was enhanced. For this and other reasons, dollar scarcity turned into dollar glut. The idealistic one-world concept of the 1950s yielded to the hard reality of worldwide competition.

Magnitude of the Deficit

Broadly speaking, the balance of payments, whether in surplus or deficit, is the net result of all transactions which enter into international commerce. Varied are the definitions which are employed and many are the statistical quicksands.

The basic problem is to separate the items which cause the surplus or deficit from those which "settle" or "finance" the surplus or deficit. In other words, what items should be placed "above the line" and which "below."

There is no dispute that changes in the gold stock are a settlement item and belong below the line. This is true even though the gold outflow, as in 1967, moved into private hoards rather than into the vaults of central banks. Similarly, increases or decreases in short-term liabilities (under one year) to foreign governments and to foreign central banks, in holdings of convertible currencies and SDR's (refer to Chapter 16) and in borrowings at the IMF are all settlement items. Included, too, are certain nonliquid liabilities such as the non-marketable, non-convertible, medium-term United States securities sold to foreign official holders.*

To these data, which measure the deficit on an official reserve transactions basis, should be added changes in liquid liabilities to foreign commerical banks, to business firms, to individuals and to various international organizations (excluding the IMF) to obtain a complete picture of the manner in which the deficit, on a total liquidity basis, is financed. These liabilities must be included inasmuch as nonofficial liabilities may quickly become official liabilities, should foreign creditors shift them to a central bank.

However measured, the United States has for many years suffered serious deficits in its balance of payments. The loss of gold, the continued pressure on the dollar, and the growing unwillingness of foreigners to hold the ever-growing volume of dollars are evidence that the balance of payments has been in fundamental disequilibrium.

The points we have been making can best be illustrated by reference to the deficit in the balance of payments in 1967 and the manner in which it was financed (see Tables 12.1 and 12.2). The liquidity deficit of $3.5 billion was 2.6 times that of 1966 and only exceeded in the postwar period by the roughly comparable deficits of 1959 and 1960 and by the stupendous deficits of 1969, 1970 and 1971. The massive 1971 deficit, following a succession of large deficits, forced the suspension of convertibility by the United States (see Chapter 17). The 1967 deficit was caused mainly by the failure of merchandise exports to match increases in imports and by sharp increases in military expenditures abroad (mainly in Vietnam). In 1968 the balance of payments recorded a surplus on the liquidity basis of $168 million. This gigantic turnaround from 1967 resulted from a very sharp temporary spurt in purchases of American securities by foreign investors.

Even a larger switch occurred in 1969 [1] when the 1968 surplus of $168 million turned into a deficit of $7,012 million (see Table 12.3). This dramatic change was accounted for by a multitude of financial transactions, including roundabout flows through the Euro-dollar market (see Chapter 15). A deficit in the balance of payments is best measured by the liquidity balance, which is a broad indicator of all potential pressures on the dollar. The official reserve transactions balance simply takes account in the main of changes in liabilities to foreign governments and

---

* These are the so-called Roosa bonds. At the end of October 1971, foreign official institutions (primarily German, Canadian and Swiss) owned $9.2 billion of United States Treasury bonds and notes of which $7.5 billion were payable in dollars and $1.7 billion in foreign currencies. The amount payable in foreign currencies (1.7 billion) should be deducted from the gold stock as of that date ($10.2 billion) to arrive at a figure, $8.5 billion, more representative of the actual gold holdings of the United States.

Table 12.1
U. S. Balance of Payments, 1967
(Billions of Dollars)

	Demand for Dollars or Supply of Foreign Currencies	Supply of Dollars or Demand for Foreign Currencies
Exports of goods and services	$46.2	
Imports of goods and services		$41.0
Remittances and pensions		1.2
U.S. government grants and loans (net)		4.2
U.S. private capital outflow (net)		5.7
Foreign capital inflow (net)	3.4	
Errors and unrecorded transactions		1.0
Total	$49.6	$53.1
Deficit (liquidity basis)	3.5	

Source: *Federal Reserve Bulletin* (September 1969), p. A72. Also see John Hein, "Understanding the Balance of Payments" *The Conference Board*, New York. 1970.

Table 12.2
Financing the 1967 Deficit on a Liquidity Basis
(Millions of Dollars)

Change in official reserves	
Decline in gold stock	−$1,170
Offset in large measure by an increase in convertible currencies[a]	+ 1,024
Offset in small part by a reduction in U.S. borrowings at the IMF	+ 94
Total reduction in official reserves [b]	−$ 52
Change in liquid liabilities to all foreign accounts	+$3,492
Dollars required to settle balance on a liquidity basis	+$3,544

    a. The increase in holdings of convertible currencies had little basic significance for they consisted mainly of the then relatively weak British currency, acquired by the Reserve System under a "swap arrangement" to support the pound.

    b. To the decline in official reserves of $52 million must be added the increase in liquid liabilities to all foreign accounts to obtain the dollars required to settle the balance on a liquidity basis.

Source: *Federal Reserve Bulletin* (September 1969), p. A72.

central banks. An indication of changes in the competitive economic strength of the U. S. is furnished by data on exports and imports of nonmilitary merchandise. The trade balance has suffered, for reasons to be explained later, a grievous decline in recent years.

How Deficits are Camouflaged

Special measures have been taken from time to time to reduce the liquidity deficit, in order to make a bad situation appear better. Foreign monetary authorities have, at the urging of American officials, shifted dollar assets of less to those of more than one-year maturity. The liquidity deficit of 1966 was offset to the extent of $788 million by such action of foreign monetary authorities and to the extent of $319 million by similar actions of international and regional organizations. Foreign purchases of long-term U. S. securities, representing a portion of American defense expenditures abroad, have also been encouraged by the United States as a means of reducing the liquidity deficit. Debt prepayments, too, have played an important role.[2] To encourage central banks to hold U.S. securities, tax exemptions previously granted to certain central banks were extended to all in 1961.[3]

In relation to GNP, the balance-of-payments deficit for 1967 was small, amounting to only .46 percent, but this relationship has little or no significance. It is the absolute difference between the demand for and supply of dollars that is important. It was this difference which caused the short-term indebtedness of the United States to soar, which inundated the world with redundant dollars, forcing their price down (in terms of other currencies) and compelled the United States to defend its declining reserves—and finally to suspend convertibility.

Table 12.3
Balance-of-Payments Deficits, 1958–1971
(Millions of Dollars)

Year	Liquidity Basis	Official Reserve-Transactions Basis
1958	−$3,365	n.a.
1959	− 3,870	n.a.
1960	− 3,901	−$3,403
1961	− 2,371	− 1,347
1962	− 2,204	− 2,702
1963	− 2,670	− 2,011
1964	− 2,800	− 1,564
1965	− 1,335	− 1,289
1966	− 1,357	+ 266
1967	− 3,544	− 3,418
1968	+ 168	+ 1,638
1969	− 7,012	+ 2,700
1970	− 3,848	− 9,819
1971 ᵖ	−22,175	−29,629

Source: *Economic Report of the President.* Transmitted to the Congress February 1971 (Washington, D.C.: Government Printing Office, 1971), p. 299; *Survey of Current Business,* March 1971, p. 33; *Federal Reserve Bulletin* (November 1971), p. A74; and *Economic Indicators,* Council of Economic Advisors, February 1972, p. 25.

Over the whole period (end of 1957 to end of 1970) the total deficit (liquidity basis) which amounted to $37.2 billion was financed in the following manner (see Table 12.4):

Table 12.4
Financing the Balance-of-Payments' Deficit
(Billions of Dollars)

Net reduction in gold stock, in holdings of convertible currencies and in the reserve position in IMF	$ 9.7
Net increase in short-term liabilities	27.5
	$37.2

Source: Economic Report of the President. Transmitted to the Congress, February 1971, op. cit., p. 304 and the Federal Reserve Bulletin, (July 1970), pp. A75 and A76. The decline in the American gold Stock led to massive redistribution of gold holdings, increasing those of Belgium, France, West Germany, the Netherlands, Italy, and Switzerland—striking evidence of the economic recuperation of Continental Europe and of the relative decline in the economic position of the United States.

EXPORTING INFLATION

The deficit in the American balance of payments was settled mainly by an increase in short-term, or, more correctly, liquid, liabilities owed to foreigners (see Table 12.4). From the point of view of foreigners these are liquid assets. The terms "liquid liabilities" and "liquid assets" are thus used interchangeably. To illustrate the use of such liabilities and the reason for their increase, let us assume that the American government in the course of a year spends $500 million in Germany on the maintenance of American troops. The U.S. government obtaining dollars from domestic taxation or borrowings, transfers these to the Deutsche Bundesbank (the German central bank) in return for German currency. The Deutsche Bundesbank now has dollars formerly possessed by the American government.

The Deutsche Bundesbank might decide voluntarily to keep the dollars as part of its reserves, because of their importance as an international currency. Or it might sell the dollars to German commercial banks and firms requiring dollars in their trading and financial operations, including those in the Eurodollar market.

If there were a demand for American goods or securities it would sell dollars in the foreign-exchange market. The United States' short-term liability would be extinguished by exports of goods and securities. If there were no demand for dollars, the Deutsche Bundesbank could ask the U. S. Treasury to redeem the dollars in gold or could retain the dollars. It would probably do the latter, for the American government has brought pressure upon foreign governments not to draw upon the American gold stock, an action which actually voids the gold-exchange standard and substitutes a political exchange standard in its place.

Dollar Holdings

The retention of dollar holdings may be voluntary or involuntary. Until 1958 dollar balances were voluntarily retained. Not subject to exchange controls and redeemable in gold, dollars were eagerly sought. Since then, as the dollar has come under increased suspicion, some nations, like Belgium, France, the Netherlands, Spain, and Switzerland, have converted substantial parts of their dollar holdings into gold. Nations that did not convert directly did so indirectly by buying gold in the London market; as long as the gold market functioned freely, the United States was forced to send gold to London to prevent the price from rising above an acceptable maximum.

Liquid Liabilities and Assets

Of the total volume ($59.9 billion) of liquid liabilities owed to foreigners, as reported by banks and brokers in the United States at the end of August, 1971, $40.7 billion were owed to foreign central banks and governments and their agencies, to the BIS, and to the European Fund.[4] Of the balance, $17.2 billion were owed to nonofficial holders, $1.5 billion to various international and regional organizations, and about $544 million were owed to the International Monetary Fund. Amounts were also owed to many nations, but the largest creditors were the United Kingdom, Japan, Germany, Italy, Switzerland, France, Canada, Venezuela, and Mexico.

Total liquid liabilities to foreigners began to exceed the gold stock in 1960, and toward the end of 1971 they did so by nearly $50 billion. Liquid liabilities to foreign central banks and governments exceeded the gold stock by $30 billion.

At the end of August 1971, liquid claims on foreigners reported by American banks amounted to $12.4 billion. The claims, except in the case of Japan and certain Latin American countries, are due, however, from countries different in the main from those to which liabilities are owed. In other words, American short-term creditors are not at the same time its short-term debtors.

A continual transfer of liquid assets takes place between official and nonofficial holders. Transfers may arise from increased deposits in the Eurodollar market by official institutions, from swap transactions between the United States and foreign monetary authorities, from the flight of funds from official reserves in one money market to commercial banks in another, and from the desire of monetary authorities to influence domestic credit conditions.[5] Shifts in ownership, often with concomitant geographical shifts, serve to complicate the statistics on the precise geographical origin of the funds.

Foreign liquid dollar assets fulfill many functions. They serve as liquid reserves for foreign central and commercial banks, finance international transactions, nourish the Eurodollar market, and help to protect many Latin American individuals and corporations against domestic inflation and currency disorders. The current total resulting from the continuous deficit in our balance of payments is much larger than would be required to render these services efficiently. Consequently they have generated inflationary pressures abroad.

Inflationary Implications

The increase in dollar holdings at European central and commercial banks, unless offset, permits a multiple expansion of domestic credits. Offsetting measures have included increases in reserve requirements, open-market sales of securities, charging foreigners for the permission to open and maintain demand deposits, and placing ceilings on the expansion of bank credit.

The rise in liquid dollar assets held by European banks is, according to many students, evidence of the export of inflation. They point out that the deficit in the American balance of payments is as large as it is because of domestic inflationary pressures. Had these pressures been kept under control both the deficit and liquid liabilities would have been smaller. The role of the dollar as an international currency has induced other nations to continue financing the deficits in the United States' balance of payments, an action which intensified inflationary pressures both here and abroad.

The rise in liquid dollar assets not only provoked the export of inflation but also facilitated the economic penetration of Europe by American industry. These ever-growing assets formed the basis of the Eurobond market, which, once controls were imposed on American capital exports, enabled American firms to borrow abroad in order to build capital equipment and to invest in European industry (see Chapter 13).

FAILURE TO APPLY THE DISCIPLINE OF THE BALANCE OF PAYMENTS

Despite the heavy imbalance, the United States economy was not subjected to what is called "the discipline of the balance of payments" (the reasons for unwillingness to apply discipline are discussed in Chapters 13 and 14). It means the adoption of restrictive credit and fiscal policies in response to a deficit, particularly if long continued. The purpose of such policies is to reduce domestic demand; to check increases in unit labor costs and in prices; to force a shakeout in surplus labor, to encourage the movement of labor to expanding firms; to subject management to the discipline of cost pressures; and to encourage increases in productivity. Firms begin to liquidate inventories, prices decline, and the U.S. becomes a good market in which to buy goods. Rising unemployment reduces imports and travel abroad. American manufacturers begin to seek foreign markets and to price and style goods for those markets.

A rise in interest rates and a reduction in the availabilty of credit would not by itself, however, force a reduction in foreign aid or military expenditures by the American government. These expenditures, which are not interest sensitive would have to be curtailed by the government on its own initiative. If it were unwilling to do so, as was the American government in the 1960s, it would probably subject the economy to direct economic controls, as it did in 1971, and in doing so, would undermine the free market economy. It has been pointed out that the United States had rendered a real service to Europe in the days of the Marshall Plan by requiring that Europeans accept the necessary monetary and fiscal discipline to ensure that the aid extended served to correct and not to perpetuate the deficits in their balance of payments.[6]

A basic rule of the international monetary standard, whether it be gold, paper gold, or credit, is that nations with long-standing balance-of-payments deficits must submit to the discipline of the balance of payments. Deficit nations have the responsibility of making necessary adjustments and must be willing to take deflationary action, and are frequently required to do so in order to obtain credits from the IMF. "Surplus" nations, on the other hand, cannot be expected to inflate nor to continuously revalue their own currencies in order to strengthen those of deficit nations.

Gold Exports Offset

American monetary authorities (for reasons discussed later) did not permit gold exports to exercise credit restraint. Their effect, as well as the effect of currency increases on member-bank reserves in the 1960s was more than offset, as shown in Table 12.5, by Federal Reserve purchases of securities. Had the discipline of the balance of payments been imposed, the volume of "discounts and advances" would have risen sharply. In reality, the opposite occurred.

Table 12.5

Factors Affecting Member-Bank Reserves from December 1957 to December 1971 (Average daily data, Millions of Dollars)

Decreasing Reserves		Increasing Reserves	
Discounts and advances	(—)$ 608	U.S. Government securities	(+)$45,176
Gold	(—) 12,637	Float	(+) 2,452
Currency in circulation	(+) 29,128	Other Federal Reserve assets	(+) 1,030
Treasury deposits	(+) 1,541	Treasury currency	(+) 2,467
Other deposits	(+) 542	S.D.R.'s	(+) 400
Other Federal Reserve accounts	(+) 1,224	Treasury cash	(—) 315
		Foreign deposits	(—) 55
Total	$45,680		$51,895

Source: *Federal Reserve Bulletin*, (February 1958), p. 148, and *Federal Reserve Bulletin*, (January 1972), p. A4.

The factors leading to an increase in member-bank reserves totaled $51,895 million and those to a decrease, $45,680 million, making a net increase of $6,215 million. By reason of the inclusion of currency and coin, member-bank total reserves actually rose by $11,896 million. Inasmuch as deposit expansion took the form largely of time deposits, an increase in reserves of this magnitude provided the basis for a sharp multiple expansion in credit.

There may have been justification in this period for the use of open-market operations to offset the effect on member-bank reserves of increases in the currency. These increases involved simply an exchange of currency for deposits, an exchange of one domestic liability for another. Offsetting the effect of all gold exports was quite a different matter and could not be similarly defended. As the IMF pointed out in its 1969 Annual Report:

> The most disappointing aspect of international payments in the past several years has been the continuing lack of effective adjustment by the United States and the United Kingdom. In both countries the root difficulty has been the weakness of the current account position resulting mainly from insufficient control over the expansion of demand.[7]

Failure to apply the discipline of the balance of payments resulted in inflationary trends at home and abroad. Benign neglect eventually threw the world into monetary chaos.

OVERCOMMITTED ABROAD, UNDERCOMMITTED AT HOME

Overcommitted abroad and undercommitted at home describes in succinct fashion, in the words of ex-President Sproul of the Federal Reserve Bank of New York, the American dilemma in the 1960s—the imbalance in the balance of payments and turbulence in the streets. From the beginning of 1960 to the end of 1969, foreign loans and grants by the U.S. government (less scheduled and unscheduled repayments) totaled $35 billion. Military expenditures abroad totaled an equal amount, $35 billion, partly offset by military sales of $9 billion. Total net government assistance thus amounted to $61 billion. Loans, grants, and military expenditures rose sharply as the Vietnam war intensified. Despite various measures by the federal government intended to reduce the dollar drain from foreign loans and war expenditures, it continued large, and in fiscal 1969 was estimated at more than $2 billion. Among actions to reduce the foreign-exchange costs of foreign aid was the tying of such aid; that is, a requirement that the dollar proceeds of grants and loans be spent in the United States. Not only did this policy increase the cost of foreign aid to the United States government to the extent that American prices were higher than those in foreign nations, but it also gave American concerns complete protection against what might have proved the invigorating effects of foreign competition.

Should military assistance and economic aid be continued in future years, the cost to American taxpayers and the burden on the balance of payments can each be reduced by:

1. lowering or eliminating import restrictions (tariff and non-tariff) on the products of other nations.[8] This action would permit nations to pay with their own products for at least part of the assistance and aid received.

2. routing economic aid through the International Bank for Reconstruction and Development (the World Bank). Not only would this action absolve the United States from charges of political favoritism and manipulation but it would enable the nations receiving the aid to spend the currency proceeds in the cheapest markets. Loans granted by the World Bank cannot be "tied."

Removal of economic shackles on world trade is a matter of first priority. Aid would give way to trade.

Still another factor in the adverse balance of payments was the outflow of private capital, including direct investment, portfolio purchases, and long-and short-term loans. The outflow of direct investment had shown a strong upward trend after the mid-1950s with a pronounced bulge in 1956–1957, corresponding to a worldwide investment boom, and another bulge in 1965–66, when automotive investments abroad were particularly large.[9]

From the beginning of 1960 to the end of 1969 direct investments rose more than $39 billion and other long-term investments (including portfolio investments) rose to $12 billion.[10] The outflow of short-term funds totaled nearly $10 billion, which brought the total outflow to $61 billion. With an inflow of foreign funds, amounting to $25 billion, the net outflow came to about $36 billion.

Private foreign investments have yielded a handsome return to the American economy. Income more than doubled between 1960 and 1969, rising from $3 to $8 billion a year and totaling $52 billion for those eight years. The total income on American government investments abroad was rather small, only about $5.6 billion. Despite the fact that private foreign investments yielded important returns to the American economy, it was these which fell subject to increasing foreign-exchange controls imposed by the administration.

Partly offsetting the income received on foreign investments by Americans were payments of interest and dividends on investments owned by foreign citizens. These rose rapidly through the years, totaling about $15 billion over the whole period. If one takes account of payments made on foreign-owned domestic investments, the net income on American government and private investments abroad was about $43 billion.*

The net adverse balance on travel more than doubled in the 1960s, from $700 million in 1960 to $1.8 billion in 1969 and over the period totaled about $13 billion. Efforts made by the American government to encourage foreign tourism may have reduced the growing imbalance but did not alter the trend. These measures were supplemented by the protectionist device of reducing duty-free imports of goods by tourists from $500 wholesale value to $100 retail value.

The Organization for Economic Cooperation and Development in Paris, concluded on March 30, 1967 that, although tourism was the largest single item in world trade, there was unlimited scope for further expansion and in view of the competitive character of the industry, a nation could not hope to benefit from

---

* Income on private foreign investment ($52 billion) plus income on American government loans ($6 billion) minus income on dollar investments owned by foreigners ($15 billion).

it in the absence of an overall national policy. The international tourist was looked upon as the true economic man, seeking the cheapest markets.[11]

Still another development, perhaps the most disquieting of all, was the decline in the favorable trade balance from $6.7 billion in 1964 to $700 million in 1969. The favorable trade balance had long been regarded as the one item that would solve the balance-of-payments problem by offsetting all deficits.

Although world exports in those years expanded considerably faster than did the volume of world output, the United States failed to maintain its share of export markets.[12] This failure generated fears that the competitive role of the United States had declined. Studies by the Federal Reserve Bank of Boston showed that, on the basis of quality and price, the competitiveness of American industry in foreign markets had indeed suffered a sharp decline in the late 1950s and early 1960s.[13] According to the IMF, export prices of American manufacturers rose much more rapidly through 1967 and 1968 than did those of manufacturers from competing industrial nations.[14] Another study by the Boston bank compared practices of small American manufacturers with those of their more successful Scandinavian counterparts, and showed that the success of the latter is attributable to willingness to adapt products to export markets; to quote prices including cost, freight, and insurance; and to frequent visits by officials to export markets. Small American exporters seldom or never visited their export markets, showed little patience with intricate export documentation, and found the granting of credit a time consuming, vexing problem. Inflexibility in complying with the demands of foreign markets, both in product and price quotations, as well as absence of an aggressive management attitude, were important factors in American failure to compete effectively in export markets.[15]

Rising personal income at full-employment levels stimulated the growth of imports. Imports of consumer products, food and nonfood, durable and nondurable, speeded up.[16] A marked acceleration occurred in imports of capital equipment and automobiles. If American industry has become less competitive, then according to the *Federal Reserve Bulletin,* some part of the rapid rise in merchandise imports since 1965 must reflect not a temporary aberration but a new trend that can be changed only slowly and with difficulty.[17] The Bulletin concluded that a return to overall equilibrium in the balance of payments could hardly be envisaged without a substantial recovery and further improvement in the trade surplus.[18]

THE UNITED STATES AS WORLD BANKER

The rapid growth in the liquid liabilities of the United States not offset by liquid claims or monetary reserves has resulted in the United States' becoming a highly illiquid "commercial bank." If a "balance sheet" were constructed (see Table 12.6), current private liabilities would appear twice as large as current private assets—and would exceed total monetary reserves by a wide margin.

Table 12.6
Balance Sheet of U.S.
as a Commercial Bank, December 31, 1969
(Billions of Dollars)

Current Assets			Current Liabilities	
Private short-term assets and claims	$ 2.6		To foreign commercial banks	$23.6
U.S. monetary reserve assets	17.0		To other private creditors	5.2
(gold	$11.9)		To foreign official agencies	13.0
(convertible currencies	2.8)			
(IMF position	2.3)			
Total	$19.6			$41.8

Source: David T. Devlin. "The International Investment Position of the United States: Developments in 1970." *Survey of Current Business*, Vol. 51, No. 10, October 1971, p. 21.

As an "investment bank" the United States is in incomparably better shape than it is as a commercial bank. American private investments abroad are more than twice as large as foreign private investments in the United States. Even if the long-term foreign assets of the U.S. government are eliminated, as being of somewhat dubious value, the investment balance sheet promises continued strength to the American economy (see Table 12.7).

Table 12.7
Balance Sheet of U.S.
as an Investment Bank, December 31, 1969
(Billions of Dollars)

Long-Term Nonliquid Assets			Long-Term Nonliquid Liabilities	
U.S. government	$ 30.7		U.S. government	$ 2.4
Private	96.3		Private	39.5
(Direct investments	$71.0)		(Direct investments in U.S.	$11.8)
(Foreign bonds	11.7)		(Corporate bonds	4.8)
(Foreign stocks	7.0)		(Corporate stocks	18.1)
(Other claims	6.6)		(Other liabilities	4.8)
Private short-term non-liquid	11.4		Private short-term non-liquid	2.9
Total	$138.4			$44.8

Source: See Table 12.6.

The United States will remain a strong investment bank and will gain liquidity as a commercial bank once the deficit in the balance of payments is eliminated and a surplus emerges. The resulting reduction in short-term liabilities, aided no doubt by simultaneous funding operations, will, in the long run, help to reestablish the dollar as a key currency.

CONCLUDING OBSERVATIONS

The besetting international economic problem of the 1960s was not a shortage but a surfeit of liquidity. Evidenced by the soaring volume of liquid dollar liabilities, it originated in the prolonged American balance-of-payments deficit, which itself resulted mainly from the great discrepancy between the social and political aims of government and the requirements of monetary stability.[19]

President Alfred Hayes of the Federal Reserve Bank of New York noted in a speech in Basel on June 10, 1968, that the American dollar had acquired its role as a trading currency through the stern judgment of market forces and had become the major reserve currency through the free choice of monetary authorities. The dollar had acquired this status not through divine right but through the freely expressed judgment of foreign merchants, traders, banks, and governments; it can retain its status only as long as it commands world confidence.[20]

The dollar would command confidence at home and abroad if monetary and fiscal policies were directed not towards the moderation but the termination of inflation, not towards the moderation but the termination of the balance-of-payments deficits.

Notes

1. Evelyn M. Parrish, "The U.S. Balance of Payments: Fourth Quarter and Year 1969." *Survey of Current Business,* Vol. 50, Number 3, (March 1970), pp. 25–48.

2. "Balance of Payments Review," *Monthly Review* (Federal Reserve Bank of Richmond, September 1967), pp. 8–10.

3. *Annual Report* (Federal Reserve Bank of New York, 1961), p. 34.

4. *Federal Reserve Bulletin* (March 1972), p. A78; Leon Korobow, "Foreign Liquid Assets in the United States." *Monthly Review* (Federal Reserve Bank of New York, June 1968), pp. 117–125. The European Fund was established by the European Monetary Agreement, which itself came into force on December 27, 1958, to grant short- and medium-term balance of-payments assistance to the member nations. As of March 1970, its only loans were one to Greece of $15 million and another to Turkey of $100 million. Bank for International Settlements, *Fortieth Annual Report* 1st April 1959–31st March 1970 (Basle: June 8, 1970), p. 165.

5. Peter Fousek, *The Balance of Payments Statistics* (Washington, D.C.: Government Printing Office, 1965).

6. M. Roger Auboin, in an article in *Agence Économique et Financière* (Zurich edition) May 15–16, 1967.

7. International Monetary Fund, *1969 Annual Report* (Washington, D.C.: August 13, 1969), p. 11.

8. Cf., *Non–tariff Distortions of Trade.* A statement on National Policy by the Research and Policy Committee of the Committee for Economic Development (Committee for Economic Development, New York), September 1969. See also *United States International Economic Policy in an Independent World.* Report to the President submitted by the Commission on International Trade and Investment Policy, (Washington, D.C.: July 1971).

9. *Federal Reserve Bulletin* (April 1968), p. 353.

10. *The Morgan Guaranty Survey* (March 1969).

11. Quoted in the *Press Review,* No. 64, Bank for International Settlements (Basle: April 3, 1967).

12. *Monthly Economic Letter* (First National City Bank of New York, April 1966), p. 45. See also *U.S. Foreign Trade–A Five Year Outlook with Recommendations for Action* (Washington, D.C.: Department of Commerce, 1969).

13. "Is the United States Pricing Itself Out of World Markets?" *New England Business Review* (Federal Reserve Bank of Boston, July 1965), pp. 2–7.

14. International Monetary Fund, *1969 Annual Report* (Washington, D.C.: August 13, 1969), p. 5.

15. -"U.S. and Scandinavian Export Practices Compared." *New England Business Review* (Federal Reserve Bank of Boston, September 1965), pp. 10–13. See also "Machinery Exports to World Markets by Major Exporting Countries, 1955–1965" *Capital Goods Review* (Machinery and Allied Products Institute), No. 66, July 1966.

16. *Federal Reserve Bulletin* (April 1968).

17. *Ibid.,* p. 352.

18. Further discussion of the international price competitiveness of American industry can be found in a report by Irving B. Kravis and Robert E. Lipsey, "New Measures of International Price Competitiveness, 1953–1964." *Forty-Eighth Annual Report* (New York: National Bureau of Economic Research, June, 1968), p. 21–28. See also "The Pattern of United States International Trade" *Economic Review* (Federal Reserve Bank of Cleveland, August 1970), pp. 3–17.

19. See Karl Blessing, "International Monetary Problems," *Progress* (Unilever Quarterly), February 1966.

20. Quoted in *Press Review,* No. 112, Bank for International Settlements (Basle: June 12, 1968).

Domestic Credit Trends in the 1960s

CHAPTER 13

THE NEW ECONOMICS

Reinforced by the automatic stabilizers, monetary policy in the 1950s had been able to forestall depression and restrict cyclical declines to moderate recessions. The record was impressive. GNP in real terms increased by about 40 percent and industrial production by 45 percent. Employment rose from 59 million to 66 million. Partially offsetting these impressive gains was a rise of about 24 percent in the consumer price index, half of which occurred during the Korean war.

In President Dwight Eisenhower's final Economic Report, the Council of Economic Advisers listed the conditions essential for an even more dynamic American economy: elimination of deterrents to increased labor and management productivity; an economic environment (resulting largely from a revision of the tax structure) favorable to individual initiative and effort; reduction in unemployment through vocational training and the elimination of racial discrimination; and adoption of the goals of "reasonable price stability in the Employment Act of 1946." [1]

The economic record of the 1950s, according to President John F. Kennedy's first Economic Report, was not good enough. In two months out of three the unemployment rate had been 4 percent or more.[2] Momentum had to be increased not by adopting the measures of the Eisenhower administration, which, it was asserted, had not progressed beyond trying to moderate the cycle, but through policies designed to accelerate economic trends. Top priority had to be given to rapid economic growth and full employment. Government policy was to keep unemployment far below the levels of the 1950s and to make full prosperity the normal state of the American economy.

Basic Premises

The economic philosophy of the Kennedy administration, which greatly influenced its fiscal and monetary policies, and which carried over into the Johnson administration, was based on the following convictions:

First, the United States had to make optimum use of its tremendous productive capacity, which it could do only if unemployment were reduced to 4 percent of the labor force. This rate was to be regarded simply as a temporary target to be lowered further as the labor force acquired skills and mobility and as industries moved to depressed areas.

Second, that unemployment exceeding 4 percent of the labor force resulted from deficient demand, rather than from structural maladjustments in the labor supply. The instruments of fiscal policy (purchases of goods and services, transfer payments, subsidies, grants-in-aid, and taxes) were the government's most powerful tools, the Council of Economic Advisors pointed out, for expanding or restraining overall demand. Fiscal policy had to be used to eliminate the "fiscal drag" (see Chapter 14).

Third, unemployment could be reduced to 4 percent of the labor force without causing inflation. This point of view assumed that the labor force was mobile, that workers of different skills would increase to meet employment demand, that productivity would continue to rise, that productive capacity was available, and that no production bottlenecks of the type so prominent in 1937 would develop. It assumed, too, that official data on unemployment were a good measure of the use of the labor force and consequently a good guide to monetary and fiscal policy. Recent studies, which emphasize the structural character of unemployment, cast doubt on this premise and urge the collection of data on job vacancies, so that the demand for particular types of labor can be matched with supply. According to this point of view, the two series together, job vacancies and the specific skills of the unemployed, give a more balanced picture of labor demand and supply than do crude unemployment data alone.[3] Actually the record shows that, as unemployment approached and fell below 4 percent of the labor force, wholesale prices began to rise rapidly, and the increase in consumer prices accelerated. Commodity prices evinced more stability when unemployment fluctuated around 5 percent of the labor force. Cost push proved a weaker inflationary force.

Fourth, if inflation developed, it could be held in check by wage and price guidelines. Fifth, the Federal budget should be balanced only at a 4 percent unemployment level. And, finally, monetary policy was to support the objectives of fiscal policy within the limits of preventing heavy deficits in the balance of payments. The Council, on the whole, did not favor use of general credit controls to correct the deficit, maintaining that increases, particularly in the long-term interest rate impaired growth by curbing construction, checking plant and equipment expenditures, redistributing income in favor of the wealthy, and making the fiscal problems of government more difficult.

Such, then, were some of the basic premises of the New Economics. It held that unemployment was mainly the result of deficient demand, which could be rectified by a reduction in tax rates, an expansive monetary policy, a standby program of public works, and strengthened unemployment insurance. The adoption of these measures would spur economic growth and growth itself would bring the Federal budget closer to balancing and would even help resolve the imbalance in foreign payments. Rapid growth, it was held, would spur productivity, increase the competitive position of the United States, and induce Americans to invest their funds domestically. (A careful study of this question by Jack C. Rothwell, then with the Federal Reserve Bank of Philadelphia, failed to reveal "any clear-cut tendency for an acceleration in the rate of growth to bring about an improvement in our balance of payments.") [4] The premises of the New Economics explain the long delay in applying the discipline of the balance of payments. Through most of the decade fiscal and monetary policy was directed toward reducing unemployment as measured by official data.

The increased demand resulting from a reduction in tax rates would, the Council admitted, increase imports. But, it maintained, the increase would come from raw-materials nations, which would spend the bulk of their earned dollars in the United States. It was estimated, for example, that for each dollar that the American people spent in Latin America, Latin Americans would spend 50 cents here. It was contended that imports would not come from those nations which might demand gold for dollars. Actually, once tax rates were reduced, the increase was mainly in imports from Japan, France, West Germany, Italy, the United Kingdom, and Canada: imports from Latin American countries showed a very slight increase.

Optimism Unlimited

The 1966 Economic Report concluded in an optimistic vein that the American economy had taken a giant step toward achieving the Employment Act's goal of "maximum employment, production and purchasing power."[5] It was the fifth year of uninterrupted economic expansion and the second year of declining unemployment. Living standards, the report continued, had risen at an unprecedented rate, and employment had forged ahead dramatically. The Council of Economic Advisers concluded that a vigorous economy could carry the new burdens of national defense at no sacrifice of consumer standards or enlarged capital stock. A vigorous economy would, furthermore, lend strength to the dollar as a basic reserve currency.

Economic data seemed to vindicate the optimism of the administration. From 1960 to 1969, GNP in 1958 prices, rose from $488 billion to $727 billion, about 45 percent. Per capita disposable personal income, again in 1958 prices, rose from $1,883 to $2,517 and per capita personal expenditures from $1,749 to $2,301. Civilian employment increased from 66 million to 78 million, and the unemployment rate fell as low as 2.9 percent of the labor force.

PRICE PRESSURES AND DEBT INCREASES

Despite these indications of economic wellbeing, the decade was not without cause for various misgivings. In an address before the Alumni of Columbia University on June 1, 1965, Chairman William McChesney Martin of the Board of Governors of the Federal Reserve System called attention to the disquieting similarities between developments in the 1960s and those in the 1920s. He pointed out that each period had experienced a number of years of uninterrupted prosperity, a marked increase in debt and in the effective money supply, a sharp rise in international indebtedness, and a deterioration in the payments position of the United Kingdom. Both eras had engendered optimistic predictions that the United States would enjoy an indefinite period of prosperity.

The Johnson administration finally began to share these concerns. In his Economic Report for 1968, President Johnson warned that, unless the nation acted firmly and wisely to control its balance-of-payments deficit, it would risk a break-down in its financial system, a possible reversion toward economic isolationism, and a spiraling slowdown in world economic expansion. To bring the balance of payments under control, fiscal affairs would have to be ordered and the wage-price spiral controlled.[6]

There were many reasons for the growing pessimism : developing price pressures, a sharp increase in Federal deficits resulting mainly from the Vietnam war, a rapid increase in the quantity and a deterioration in the quality of debt, a decline in the liquidity of commercial banks and, in consequence, a growing reliance by commercial banks on borrowed funds obtained from the Federal funds market, issues of negotiable certificates of deposit and commercial paper, and from the Eurodollar market.

Price Pressures

By the end of 1969 the consumer-price index, which had risen without interruption through the 1960s, stood 27 percent above the 1960 level, and the wholesale-price level, which had started to rise in 1965, stood 15 percent above. The implicit price deflator for total GNP rose from 103 to 128 between 1960 and 1969. Although these increases were small in comparison with those in some other countries, they were not consistent with the status of a reserve-currency nation suffering a continuous deficit in its balance of payments.

The rise in prices reflected not only the tugging force of demand-pull, itself a result of increases in money volume* and turnover, but also the pressures of cost push. The money supply began to accelerate in 1961 and over the whole period (December 1959–December 1969) rose about 43 percent. Money turnover reached its highest level in at least a half-century.[7] The pressures of cost push emerged when unemployment fell to 5 percent or less of the labor force and were evidenced (beginning in 1966) by rapid increases in unit labor costs. In a study of inflationary pressures in Great Britain, Pearce and Taylor found that price stability would not be secured with margins of spare capacity in manufacturing much below 10 percent. Such margins are compatible with a British unemployment rate of 2.50 to 3 percent.[8]

During a period of high level activity, demand pull acts on the balance of payments by drawing in imports and by depressing exports. Cost push tends to reduce exports and may, even in a period of unemployment, cause a balance-of-pay-

---

* The money supply (currency outside banks and demand deposits) was probably underestimated. Cf. *The Wall Street Journal*, November 30, 1970, p. 12.

ments deficit. The two forces do not function in isolation but interact to aggravate the deficit.[9]

Debt Increases

The rise in the money supply itself resulted from sharp increases in the loans and investments of commercial banks, which more than doubled from the end of 1959 to the end of 1969. For most of those years Federal Reserve action provided, without cost to member banks, the reserves necessary to support the expansion in their deposit liabilities resulting from increases in their loans and investments. Since a rising proportion of the total deposit volume consisted of time accounts, the increase in required reserves was less than would have been the case had demand deposits increased more rapidly.

Net public and private debt (from the end of 1959 to the end of 1969) increased $867 billion, about 104 percent, compared with an increase of GNP in current dollars of about 80 percent and in deflated dollars of about 53 percent. Per capita debt rose from about $4,700 to more than $8,300; as a percentage of total personal income, net public and private debt increased from about 217 to 227 percent. This increase, along with the climb of interest rates in the latter part of the decade to the highest level in more than a century, caused a larger share of current income to be absorbed by debt charges. The financial assets of individuals rose, but those who held such assets were not necessarily those who had incurred debt.

The ratios of various types of debt to GNP varied greatly. Federal debt fell sharply, consumer debt and state and local debt increased rapidly, corporate and mortgage debt rose more slowly. Data of aggregate debt convey little information on the inflationary thrust of debt increases and the ability of debtors to discharge their obligations. These factors can be determined only by studying the methods employed in financing the debt and changes in its quality.

Although Federal debt fell in relation to GNP, it rose rapidly in absolute amount. This resulted from a very sharp increase in military and non-military expenditures, not matched by a rise in tax receipts. Between fiscal 1960 and 1969 the expenditure account of the Federal budget showed a deficit of about $34 billion, to which would be added net lending of about $23 billion. The expenditure account showed a slight surplus in fiscal 1960 and again in 1969; in between it reflected annual deficits peaking at $19.1 billion in fiscal 1968.[10] The increase in the total interest-bearing public debt from December 31, 1959, to December 31, 1969, came to $77 billion and was financed largely in two ways: by government investment accounts totaling $38 billion—representing a type of forced savings, this rise was non-inflationary; and by the Federal Reserve banks, totaling $30 billion. The Reserve System purchased securities to offset the effect on member-bank reserves of increases in circulating money and declines in the gold stock. As we have mentioned, the purchase of securities to offset the total amount of gold exports meant that the economy was not subject to the discipline of the balance of payments.

Purchases by the U.S. investment accounts and by the Reserve banks financed about 88 percent of the increase in Federal debt. The balance ($9 billion) was financed by individuals ($11 billion), state and local government ($7 billion), and miscellaneous, mainly foreign, investors ($11 billion). These increases, totaling $29 billion, were offset in large part by decreases in securities held by commercial banks ($4 billion), by mutual-savings banks and insurance companies ($9 billion), and by other corporations ($8 billion).

The average maturity of the marketable interest-bearing debt, as it moved from investment to liquidity holders, declined from four years and seven months in December 1959 to three years and eight months in December 1969. There was a very sharp increase ($31 billion) in marketable securities maturing within one year (partly as a result of Operation Twist), a smaller increase ($23 billion) in those maturing in from one to ten years, and a decrease of $6 billion in maturities of ten years and over.

Had the cash budget been in balance, short-term government securities in the hands of the public would have declined sharply. This decline, resulting from the flow of funds into government investment accounts, would have made additional savings available to help finance the borrowing demands of individuals and business firms.*

COMMERCIAL BANKS AND DEBT MONETIZATION

In relation to economic activity total borrowing was heavier in the 1960s than in the preceding decade. As a source of borrowed funds commercial banks increased in relative importance. They supplied about 70 percent of the funds required by state and local governments,† about 38 percent of the funds required by

---

* If the cash budget had been in balance many other changes would doubtless have occurred. Inflationary pressures would have been less, gold exports and currency increases smaller, and the deficit in the balance of payments smaller; consequently purchases of government securities by foreign holders and the Federal Reserve banks would have very likely have been smaller.

† Commercial banks purchased municipals by reason of their tax-exempt privilege, the growing availability of shorter maturities and by reason, too, of the fact that commercial banks may underwrite general obligations. "The Municipal Bond Market, 1960–1968" *Economic Review*, (Federal Reserve Bank of Cleveland September 1969), pp. 17–27.

business firms, 47 percent of the increase in consumer credit, and 15 percent of the increase in residential mortgages.[11]

From the beginning of 1960 to the end of 1969, when total bank loans and investments had risen about $213 billion, holdings of municipal obligations had increased by $42 billion, short loans to business $52 billion, and term loans $23 billion, (reflecting a decline in corporate liquidity, as well as growing tensions in the capital markets). Consumer credit on the books of commercial banks increased by $30 billion and mortgage credit increased by $42 billion. Loans on securities had risen $6 billion and other loans $16 billion.[12]

As commercial banks found it more difficult to meet loan requirements toward the end of the decade, business firms turned increasingly to the commercial-paper market. The volume (nonbank related) began to accelerate rapidly in 1966, reaching $27 billion at the end of 1969, as compared with $3.2 billion at the end of 1959. The sharp increase caused concern that commercial banks had become involved in huge "back up" lines and that the quality of the paper had deteriorated.

The change in the structure of bank assets lengthened their average maturity and rendered the banking system increasingly vulnerable to economic change. This vulnerability was further enhanced by a decline in loan quality, particularly in mortgage loans and consumer credit, to which we shall now turn our attention and by a decline in the financial liquidity of commercial banks, which we shall discuss later.[13]

The Quality of Mortgage Credit*

The rapid increase in mortgage debt, which carried the total in terms of GNP far above the levels reached in 1929, resulted from several factors: a high level of building activity accompanied by a sharp increase in construction costs; the sale of existing houses at rising prices; rapid increases in land prices; and aggressive lending practices by commercial banks and other lending institutions. From the end of 1959 to the end of 1969 aggregate mortgage debt rose from $191 billion to $425 billion.

Aggressive lending practices brought about a reduction in down payment requirements, a lengthening of maturities, escalation in appraisals of the real estate underlying mortgage loans, and a tendency to increase the amount of credit

---

* In this discussion of credit quality the author has relied greatly on the assistance of Robert G. Link, Vice President, Federal Reserve Bank of New York, and George W. McKinney, Jr., Vice President, Irving Trust Company. The conclusions do not, however, necessarily reflect their opinions.

granted in relation to the annual incomes of borrowers.[14] Some bank examiners observed a tendency among lenders to reach out for higher-yielding loans, offering more liberal terms and accepting greater risks.† The eagerness of lenders to solicit mortgage loans resulted from the rising overhead costs of financial institutions and from higher rates paid on savings and time deposits.

Collection difficulties became common, deliquencies rose, and mortgage fore-closures increased. The lengthening of maturities caused the equity of home own-ers to rise more slowly. The greater the equity, the more strongly motivated is the borrower to meet his obligations and the greater is the protection accorded lenders in the event of a decline in market values. When equity rises slowly because of longer maturities, the lender relies for protection upon rising real estate prices.

As money conditions finally tightened, bringing an end to declines in the loan-price ratio and to further increases in maturities, some observers suggested that the mortgage market should somehow be insulated from other credit markets so that it would not be subject to changes in Federal Reserve policy and to money market pressures.* When insulation has been tried in other countries, it has been found that the market cannot and should not be insulated. Attempts to do so are frustrated by the flow of funds among various financial markets and by the lend-ing and investment policies of institutions that operate in all markets. As indicated, the market should not be insulated, even if this were possible, since the purpose of restrictive credit policies is to curb demand in all sectors of the economy not only in the mortgage market but also in other markets including that of consumer durables.‡

Consumer Credit

In commenting on the rapid growth in consumer credit, President Allan Sproul of the Federal Reserve Bank of New York said: "I am disturbed not by the total amount of consumer credit but by the fact or the indication that succes-sive relaxations of terms have been largely responsible for keeping the ball in the air. This is a process which cannot go on indefinitely." [15] The relaxation of terms during the 1960's resulted partly from vigorous efforts by commercial banks to in-

† The consequence of these policies is that only after the lapse of some years do monthly repayments of principal exceed monthly payments of interest.

* The United States has recently adopted such measures as liberalization of FHA insurance programs and market support by the FNMA through its mortgage commitment arrangements.

‡ Mr. E. Hoffmeyer, Governor of the National Bank of Denmark, stated in mid-1968, in a speech before the Savings Bank Association of Denmark, that attempts to hold down interest rates on mortgage loans place the interest burden on undertakings vital to economic progress: industry, agriculture, trade, and transport. See Bank for International Settlements, *Press Review* No. 115 (Basle: June 17, 1968), for a summary.

crease their share of the market. They were particularly successful in penetrating the automobile instalment market and pushed the use of instalment credit to finance travel, education, and such high-priced items as mobile homes. The use of revolving credit arrangements and credit cards rose sharply.

The quantity of consumer debt rose from $51.5 billion at the end of 1959 to $122.5 billion ten years later. Until the credit squeeze of 1966 down payments and maturity terms for both new and used cars were steadily liberalized.[16] Younger borrowers, wage and salary earners, and low income groups (all borrowers of greater risk) generally obtained more liberal credit terms.

The proportion of automobiles sold on credit rose, as did the proportion of new car contracts written for thirty-six month terms. The average size of instalment contracts increased. Total instalment credit as a percentage of disposable income rose sharply. Debt repayments grew more slowly. Delinquencies increased. Borrowers began to seek refuge in personal bankruptcy. Those who did so were often younger people who had only recently been employed at their current jobs, were relatively new in their communities, and were often already heavily in debt. Their attitude toward incurring and repaying debt was often more irresponsible than was that of older residents of a community.[17] Lending institutions endeavored to offset the growing risks by charging higher interest rates.

As credit terms are significantly related to subsequent collection or repayment experience, the conclusion is warranted that the quality of consumer credit had declined and a recession of mild proportions would carry the threat of widespread repossessions and bankruptcies. Had the Reserve System still retained powers of selective credit control and had it been willing to use these powers, this deterioration in quality might have been checked.*

It was inevitable that the rise in the volume of private debt, in a period marked by keen competition among commercial banks and financial intermediaries, would be accompanied by a decline in quality. Only by reducing standards could the volume be made to rise sharply. Data does not exist for all debt sectors, but in the case of two sectors, mortgage and consumer debt, for which some data is available, the decline in quality was clearly evident. It was in these sectors that competition among commercial banks and financial intermediaries was particularly keen. The increase in debt quantity and the decline in quality, by intensifying price pressures, had a direct impact upon the deficit in the balance of payments.

---

* An act approved on December 23, 1969, granted the President standby authority to institute selective credit controls to curb inflation.

As Louis Rasminsky, Governor of the Bank of Canada, pointed out, one does not have to wait for a "chill economic breeze" to determine whether or not the quality of credit has fallen.

> A period of sustained economic expansion, involving a substantial increase in the amount of credit outstanding brings with it the risk of a deterioration in credit standards through the use of credit to finance basically unsound positions, or positions involving an inadequate margin of equity, or through the use of excessive amounts of short-term credit for purposes for which long-term borrowing is appropriate.

The central banker, he indicated, must do what he can to remind credit lenders of the necessity for prudence and to encourage investors, particularly during prosperity, to use searching and sophisticated judgment in their appraisal of credit risks.[18]

DECLINE IN COMMERCIAL BANK LIQUIDITY

Speaking before the Illinois Bankers Association in St. Louis in May 1968, President Scanlon of the Federal Reserve Bank of Chicago decried the decline in liquidity:

> In efforts to maximize profits and [in] the mistaken belief that all problems of achieving economic stability have been solved, some banks and other establishments (financial and non-financial) have become accustomed to operating with very low margins of liquidity and limited ability to adjust to unexpected changes. These establishments have become more vulnerable both to normal economic fluctuations and to changes in monetary and fiscal policy. Concern about the impact of policy changes on such institutions may, under some circumstances, restrain proper execution of [credit] policy.[19]

Holdings of government obligations by all commercial banks, which would be expected to provide a measure of liquidity, fell from about 26 percent of total deposits at the end of 1959 to 13 percent at the end of 1969. The average maturity increased sharply until 1966, when, under pressure of the credit crunch, commercial banks began to increase their holdings of short-term government obligations. Through the decade total loans and discounts rose from 50 to 70 percent of total deposits. Holdings of municipal obligations rose sharply, from about

8 to 14 percent of total deposits. These obligations, however, provided minimal financial liquidity; one-third of the obligations held on June 30, 1967, had maturities of ten years or more and 57 percent of five years or more.[20] A breakdown of the data reveals that the lengthening was concentrated to a considerable extent in the municipal obligations held by New York City Banks.

Apparently commercial bankers were convinced that the economy would experience no setback in its rapid growth and that the Reserve System would provide the cash reserves required for further credit expansion. They, therefore, stood ready to respond to loan demands, despite the decline in their financial liquidity reflected in decreased holdings of readily transferable assets, the rise in the loan deposit ratio, the lengthening maturity of assets, and the decline in asset quality. As time went on and as the Reserve System began to shift its policy (see Chapter 15), bankers were forced to seek other means of financing additional loan and investment expansion and of meeting deposit withdrawals; in short, of finding substitutes for the liquidity that would naturally have resulted from marketable assets of short maturity. Large banks consistently sought funds in the Federal funds market, vigorously pushed sales of negotiable certificates of deposit, sold commercial paper, and borrowed in the Eurodollar market.

Federal Funds Market

Through the 1960s commercial banks in metropolitan areas customarily borrowed in the Federal funds market, using the excess reserves of smaller banks to support their loan and deposit expansion and to provide a measure of liquidity. Few were the occasions when the basic reserve position of large member banks was positive; usually it was negative. Borrowings from the Reserve banks and the Federal funds market often equaled substantial proportions of the required reserves of the larger banks. Short-run operations of this type do have the advantage of increasing the fluidity and flexibility of commercial bank funds. However, if long continued, they give evidence of an imbalance in the domestic balance of payments and warrant restrictive credit policies on the part of credit institutions in deficit areas.

Negotiable Certificates of Deposit

In February 1961 a large New York City bank, after having made arrangements for a secondary market, began to sell large denomination negotiable certificates of deposit, an example that was quickly followed by other New York City banks.[21] Through the sale of such certificates they hoped to check the relative decline of New York City as a financial center to counteract deposit instability, and to better compete with financial intermediaries.

Certificates of about thirty-five banks in all parts of the country now constitute the bulk of this market. The total amount issued by large commercial banks increased from $1 billion in 1961 to $26 billion at the end of 1970, when it equaled 9.8 percent of the aggregate deposits of these banks. Those issued by New York City banks at the end of 1970 totaled 7.8 billion and equaled 12.4 percent of their own deposits. As certificates increased, so did holdings of long-term tax-exempt municipal obligations.

As of yet, certificates have not evolved into a first-rate money market instrument. The trading market has limited "depth, breadth and resiliency." Dealers often experience difficulties in matching demand and supply, the principal buyers and sellers are concentrated among corporations, and the market is slow to adjust to rapid rate changes. Participants in the market are quoted as saying that the certificates are a clumsy market instrument and might perhaps have greater appeal if issued on a discount basis.

Certificates of deposit all of which were subject to Regulation "Q" until mid-1970, are in essence, if not in form, a demand deposit and are particularly vulnerable to money market forces. This vulnerability was vividly illustrated during the credit crunch from August to December 1966, when the large banks lost $3.2 billion of large certificates and were forced to borrow $2 billion in the Eurodollar market. Again, during the credit crunch of 1969, large certificates became noncompetitive with other money market instruments and fell $12 billion between December 4, 1968, and September 10, 1969. This huge loss caused the banks, in the absence of an appropriate volume of readily transferable assets, to increase their borrowing in the Eurodollar market by $8 billion.[22]

In order to make certificates of deposit competitive with other money market instruments, the Board of Governors of the Federal Reserve System suspended, effective June 24, 1970, maximum limitations on rates of interest that member banks may pay on single maturity deposits of $100,000 or more that mature 30 days or more but less than 90 days after the date of the deposit. Prior to this change, certificates of deposit maturing in 30 to 59 days were subject to a maximum limitation of 6¼ per cent and those maturing in 60 to 89 days, to a maximum limitation of 6½ per cent. Now able to compete effectively in the money market, commercial banks rapidly increased their outstanding volume of certificates and used the proceeds to reduce their Eurodollar borrowing.

The credit crunch of 1966, which affected not only commercial banks but also financial intermediaries, caused both financial and nonfinancial institutions to recognize the need to improve their liquidity positions. Commercial banks and savings institutions began repaying debt and buying short-term money-market instruments and marketable bonds. Corporations began issuing long-term bonds, converting open lines of credit to committed lines, and building up deposit balances. The improvement in liquidity had just begun when, with a change in Federal Reserve policy (see Chapter 15), the financial markets confronted the credit crunch of 1969.

Sale of Bank Related Commercial Paper and Bank Loans

Other means of obtaining funds through liability management included the sale of bank related commercial paper, which at the end of July 1970 totaled $7 billion, and the sale of bank loans, which totaled another $10 billion. The two together amounted to about 7 percent of the loans and investments of the large commercial banks.

With the commercial paper which they issued directly, subject to the same reserve requirements and interest rate limitations as time deposits, member banks began developing circuitous routes to tap the commercial paper market and did so through use of their holding companies and subsidiary affiliates. The paper sold in this fashion is termed bank-related commercial paper which, as we have stated above, amounted to $7 billion at the end of July 1970.

The growing practice of commercial banks to seek funds in this manner led the Board of Governors to issue various regulations in order to discourage this practice and to make monetary policy more effective. On October 29, 1969, the Board ruled that commercial paper issued through the use of subsidiaries was subject to Regulations D and Q on the same basis as time deposits. The Board gave member banks until February 26, 1970, to make the necessary adjustments. Acting under authority of an Act of Congress of December 23, 1969, the Board, effective September 17, 1970, also subjected the commercial paper issued by bank holding companies to time deposit reserve requirements.*

---

* In drafting this paragraph the author wishes to acknowledge his indebtedness to Mr. Robert G. Link, Senior Vice President of the Federal Reserve Bank of New York, who very graciously in letters, dated January 16 and 30, February 18 and May 12, 1970, discussed the problem of bank-related commercial paper and correlative actions by the Board of Governors. Also see *Federal Reserve Bulletin* (September 1970), p. 721.

The practice of commercial banks in obtaining funds, directly and indirectly, from the commercial paper market and, as we shall see in the next section, from the Eurodollar market represented new and untried developments in American banking. Unless these practices were somehow brought under controls similar to those applicable to bank deposit liabilities, the Federal Reserve System would be handicapped in its efforts to limit the expansion in bank loans and investments. Rapidly changing banking practices call forth equally rapid counter-moves by a central bank. Otherwise, it will not be able to exercise effective credit control.

The Eurodollar Market [23]

The continuing liquidity gap, forced American banks to turn increasingly to the Eurodollar market. This market found its origins in the removal by European nations of exchange restrictions in the late 1950's, in the rapid rise of short-term dollar liabilities resulting from the United States' continuing balance-of-payments deficits, and in the foreign-exchange controls imposed with increasing scope and vigor by the American government on the outflow of short- and long-term dollar funds.† Still other factors were the decision of the British government to curb the use of sterling in the financing of nonsterling trade and the widening differentials in interest rates among national credit markets. These differences themselves resulted largely from the exchange controls of the United States and from such artificial barriers to the flow of funds as the interest rate limitations of Regulation Q.[24]

Although the factors that brought the market into being may be temporary (for example the balance-of-payments deficit of the United States), the market itself has come to play such as important role in international finance that it may well continue even if the deficit in America's balance-of-payments disappears. To be sure, it may function on a diminished scale and in currencies other than dollars, but as Sir George Bolton, Chairman of the Bank of London and South America, has stated:

> In the absence of a "world" central bank . . . the international currency market built up over the last 10 to 15 years represented not a second-best alternative, but the only practical basis on which a viable world future could be built. By building an apparatus in an amazingly short time for the collection and redistribution of the world's surplus cash and capital resources, the commercial banks produced a unique machinery for servicing the

---

† Eurodollars result from credit expansion in the United States, initially; and their ownership by foreign holders results from deficits in the American balance of payments.

financial needs of the whole world. The growth of international money markets followed the virtual closure of the world's two major capital centres, New York and London, to foreign borrowers. By mobilising resources formerly sterilised, and accelerating the velocity of circulation of these funds, commercial bankers had succeeded, for the time being, in averting a major breakdown in the provision of finance for international settlements.[25]

Rejecting the view that the international money market would disappear paripassu with the diminution of the U.S. balance-of-payments deficit, Sir George argued that even if the American administration reduced the deficit when the Vietnam war ended, other currencies, Japanese yen, French francs, German marks, and so on would be perfectly acceptable to the market machinery as it was, and little or no adjustment would be needed. Now that the United States has suspended convertibility (see Chapter 17), these currencies should be even more acceptable.

As we shall endeavor to demonstrate later, however, the market, despite its contributions, is not without its serious threats to the effective implementation of central bank policy and to the stability of international monetary arrangements.

As defined by the BIS in 1965, Eurodollars "are dollars acquired by banks located outside the United States and used for lending to ultimate borrowers, either directly in dollars or, after conversion, in another currency." [26] Because currencies other than dollars are also used, the market might be better called the "Eurocurrency" or even the world-currency market. Dollars (as of December 1970) constitute about 80 percent of the currencies used. They are dollars held in London, Milan, Frankfurt, Zurich, Paris, Tokyo, and Montreal; dollars that have gone abroad to live and work under foreign jurisdiction, earning interest for their owners.[27]

Thus an Arab sheik might deposit his oil royalties from the United States, amounting perhaps to $1 million, with a bank in Zurich. This deposit consists of dollars, a dollar liability of a Swiss bank, on which it pays interest. The Swiss bank now has a deposit in New York: the proceeds of the check deposited by the Arab. It may redeposit the dollars with an Italian bank, which may then lend them to a Japanese businessman. The combinations are infinite. Although enlarging the total volume of dollar deposits held by various foreign banks, the "swinging" Eurodollars do not alter the basic deposit of $1 million in New York. When all intermediate transactions have been canceled, the final result is the dollar-deposit liability of the American bank and the dollar-loan liability of the Japanese businessman.

The "swinging" dollars are not devoid of risk. There is first of all the credit risk inherent in all loans. Added to this is a temptation to extend long-term loans on the basis of short-term borrowings. And, finally, as always, there is the political risk, the threat of central-bank restrictions on the market and of foreign-exchange controls.

The expansion of the Eurodollar total in European money markets could theoretically be infinite.[28] They were not subject, until recently, to reserve requirements,* to interest-rate limitations, or even assessments by the FDIC. What prevents infinite expansion is that Eurodollars do not serve as a local medium of exchange and are usable only when converted into local currencies. Conversion reduces the total of Eurodollars, as would their use to purchase American securities or to import goods from the United States. These transactions represent the leakages in the market.†

London is the center of the market with banks located there accounting at the end of 1970 for nearly 50 percent of all transactions.‡ Next come banks located in Italy and Switzerland for about 12 percent and 8 percent respectively. Banks in France account for, as those in Switzerland, about 12 percent and banks in Canada for about 7 percent. The intricate web of interrelations serves to integrate European money and capital markets and to help equalize interest rates. The web is delicate, however, and could conceivably be destroyed by cataclysmic developments in any one participating nation.

According to data compiled by the BIS the estimated size of the Eurodollar or currency market (net of duplications) increased from $9 billion at the end of 1964 to $57 billion at the end of 1970.[29] Fragmentary data suggest that the market grew slowly in the late 1950's and began to accelerate rapidly about 1960.

Sources and Uses

The Russians played a catalytic role in the original development of the market. Fearful that the United States might block their dollar accounts, they placed dollar balances with banks in Western Europe, becoming a lender to and a borrower from the capitalistic world.

Commercial and central banks in West Europe have also all placed dollars in the market. They have been joined by the BIS and by firms and individuals in Africa, Asia, the Middle East, Latin America, and Canada.[30] Heaviest borrowers have been residents, mainly banks, in the United States and Japan. In December 1966

---

* Eurodollar borrowings, beginning October 16, 1969, became subject to marginal reserve requirements.

† It should also be pointed out that the transfer of dollars from one money market to another involves certain costs that would eventually wipe out the gains to be derived from interest differentials.

‡ One reason for this preeminent position is the location there of branches of American banks, which can collect Eurodollars from multinational companies and their own continental banking connections.

American net borrowings totaled $3.3 billions, rising to $12.7 billions in December 1969 and falling to $8.6 billion a year later. In 1966 American borrowers absorbed 75 percent of the new funds in the market, in 1967 about 25 percent, and in 1968 about 55 percent. As domestic interest rates rose, more was absorbed, and less as they fell. In 1970 American banks repaid about $6 billion of their borrowings and in 1971 about $3 billion. As the U.S. withdrew from the market its place was taken by Europe and the rest of the world.[31]

The United Kingdom has served as an entrepôt, reflecting in this respect the expanding role of the London branches of American banks. Canadian banks, from the first, have played a significant role, frequently funneling American dollars to London and other European centers.[32]

During the time that American banks were making heavy use of the market, Eurodollars became a major source of funds for the loans and investments of large banks. Head offices' dollar liabilities to overseas branches exceeded, or closely approached, outstanding certificates of deposit. Some large banks borrowed continually to enlarge and maintain their own reserve balances. Others borrowed sporadically to make short-term adjustments in their reserve positions, to acquire funds for the liquidation of certificates of deposit or for the withdrawal of domestic deposits, and finally to accommodate adjustments between head-office and London branch accounts.[33]

Eurodollars have been used for various purposes; to bridge financing periods in foreign trade (about one-fourth of world trade is so financed); to finance the working capital requirements, the medium and long-term credit needs of business firms, the credit and liquidity requirements of banks, security dealers and government; and finally for speculative activities in the gold and security markets.[34]

As a rule only very credit-worthy customers have entry into the market and security is not usually required. Risks are considered small, so that margins between deposit and loan rates are meager, about one-quarter of one percent for internationally operating banks and one-half of one percent for industrial and trading companies.[35]

Interest rates in the Eurodollar market are heavily influenced by American credit conditions, a result of intimate working relationships between the head offices of United States banks and their London branches. The *1971 Annual Report* of the I.M.F. pointed out that this has created a number of difficult policy questions for other industrial countries which have capital markets that are closely integrated with the Eurodollar market.[36] In 1969 when Eurodollar rates rose sharply (reflecting increases in American interest rates), industrial nations were forced to allow their own interest rates to rise, both to fight domestic inflation and to moderate the outflow of capital. Banks in Italy, France, the Netherlands, Denmark and Belgium were directed to reduce their net foreign asset position. Italian enterprises were encouraged to borrow abroad.

During 1970 and 1971, when Eurodollar rates were falling, often more rapidly than domestic money rates, again by reason of American monetary policy, nations were compelled to adopt measures to discourage capital inflows. Banks fell subject to special marginal reserve requirements on increases in foreign liabilities and were often prohibited from paying interest on non-resident deposits in excess of specific amounts. Limitations were placed on the sale of money market paper to non-residents. In the United Kingdom, foreign borrowings were restricted to maturities of five years or more.[37]

Banks often rely on "call" or short-term Eurodollars to finance longer-term credit needs. They are induced to do so by the rising yield curve on Eurodollar loans, and they do so with little reluctance, convinced as they are that the supply of funds in the Eurodollar market is elastic and will respond quickly to increases in interest rates. The result is that interest rates in the Eurodollar and the Eurobond markets are often closely related.[38]

Advantages and Disadvantages

The Eurodollar market possesses advantages in creating a closely-knit international money market, in helping to equalize the liquidity of nations between those with liquidity surpluses and liquidity deficits, and in serving as the basis for the Eurobond market. It has enabled American corporations and their affiliates to continue foreign operations despite the exchange controls of the American government and to raise substantial sums abroad in excess of the amounts that they could borrow in local currencies in foreign credit markets.

The market, however, has not been without its risks. As E. Stopper, President of the Directorium of the Swiss National Bank, has pointed out, the Eurodollar market by providing credits has delayed effective action against balance-of-payments deficits, has hampered the efforts of central banks in their struggle against inflation and has forced them to take countervailing measures.[39] These include not only the measures cited in an earlier paragraph but also restricting the use of dollar loans to domestic corporations, limiting the ability of banks and corporations to place dollars in the market and restricting the conversion of dollars into local currencies.

Also, commercial banks have been required to transfer foreign currency assets to central banks.

When the Eurodollar market came under stress toward the end of 1966, central banks and the B.I.S. found it necessary to intervene on a massive scale to prevent an excessive rise in interest rates and to stabilize money market conditions. Swap agreements between the reserve banks, the B.I.S. and foreign central banks sharply increased.

Developments in the Eurodollar market have a direct bearing on central bank action and policy and could at times dominate both. Continued insistence of European central banks that the Reserve System take action to curtail the growth of the market finally forced it to place, effective October 16, 1969, a 10 percent marginal reserve requirement on that portion of U. S. bank Eurodollar borrowings above the daily average of these liabilities in the four weeks ending May 28, 1969.

Later on as interest rates, under pressure of Federal Reserve policy, began to ease in the American market, U. S. banks turned to domestic sources of funds and used the funds so obtained, largely through the sale of Certificates of Deposit, to repay their Eurodollar borrowings, although, in doing so they eroded their reserve free Eurodollar base. The easing of interest rates in the Eurodollar market induced European firms to borrow in the market at a time when European central banks were endeavoring to follow a restrictive monetary policy.

In order to reduce repayments of Eurodollar borrowings and afford support to European central banks in their restrictive policies, the Reserve System in November 1970, moved to moderate the pace of repayment. Effective on January 7, 1971, the reserves to be required against Eurodollar borrowings that exceeded the reserve free base were raised from 10 to 20 percent, and at the same time the reserve free base was redefined. These changes alerted banks to the desirability of preserving their reserve free base and to the possible cost of future borrowings, should they need to have recourse to the Eurodollar market and should they have allowed their reserve free base to decline through repayment of Eurodollar borrowings. In order to give additional support to the restrictive policies of European central banks, the reserve free base in January, 1971, was redefined to include securities of the Export-Import Bank and in March to include U.S. Treasury obligations.[40] Despite these measures, repayment continued, although perhaps in smaller amount that would have been the case had the action not been taken. Measures adopted to slow down the flow of dollars to Europe were shortly thrown into total eclipse by a huge outward flight, as Americans, having lost confidence in the dollar, rushed to convert their dollars into foreign currencies. Foreign monetary authorities were inundated; the "Nixon shock" was the inevitable result. (See Chapter 17).

SOME EVALUATIONS

The environment within which the Reserve banks functioned in the 1960s included continued depreciation of the dollar in terms of consumer buying power, a very rapid increase in debt, a decrease in the liquidity of commercial banks and, consequent growing reliance on the Federal funds market, on issues of certificates of deposit, on sales of commercial paper and loans, and on heavy borrowing in the Eurodollar market. American commercial banks, particularly the large ones relied increasingly on "liability management" instead of on "asset management" to resolve their liquidity problems.

The balance of payments, reflecting inflationary domestic developments and the foreign expenditures of the United States became heavily adverse. The urgent need to strengthen the dollar at home and abroad was not fully recognized until late in the decade, when the premises of the New Economics began to be seriously questioned.

Notes

1. *Economic Report of the President.* Transmitted to the Congress, January 18, 1961 (Washington, D.C.: Government Printing Office, 1961), Chapter 3.

2. *Economic Report of the President.* Transmitted to the Congress, January 1962 (Washington, D.C.: Government Printing Office, 1962), pp. 3–27.

3. *The Measurement and Interpretation of Job Vacancies* (New York: National Bureau of Economic Research, Inc., 1966).

4. *The United States Balance of Payments—Perspective and Policies* (Washington, D.C.: Government Printing Office, 1963), pp. 125–126.

5. *Economic Report of the President.* Transmitted to the Congress, January 1966 (Washington, D.C.: Government Printing Office, 1966), Chapter 7.

6. *Economic Report of the President.* Transmitted to the Congress, February 1968 (Washington, D.C.: Government Printing Office, 1968), pp. 4, 8.

7. Lawrence S. Ritter, "How Fast Does Money Run?" (Manufacturers Hanover Trust Company, March 1967), pp. 1–4.

8. D. W. Pearce and J. Taylor. "Spare Capacity: What Margin is Needed?" *Lloyd's Bank Review* No. 89. July 1968, pp. 1–11.

9. See F. Hartog, "Wage Rise as an Inflationary Factor," *Economic Quarterly Review* (Amsterdam Rotterdam Bank, June 1969), pp. 13–18. See also M. W. Holtrop, "Rising Prosperity and Inflation," Basle Statistical and Economic Society, December 9, 1963.

10. *The Budget of the United States Government Fiscal Year 1971* (Washington, D.C.: Government Printing Office, 1970), p. 584.

11. *Monthly Review* (Federal Reserve Bank of Kansas City, June 1969), pp. 11-16.

12. The data reported here are to be found in the excellent study, *The Investment Outlook* (New York: Bankers Trust Company, 1969).

13. "Commercial Paper: 1970," *Monthly Review* (Federal Reserve Bank of San Francisco, March 1971).

14. Robert Moore Fisher, "The Quality of Real Estate Credit," *Business and Economic Statistics Section, Proceedings of the American Statistical Association, (1966); Monthly Review* (Federal Reserve Bank of Minneapolis, March 1965); *Federal Reserve Bulletin* (June 1963, May 1965 and June 1966); *Business Conditions* (Federal Reserve Bank of Chicago, September 1963); *Monthly Review* (Federal Reserve Bank of San Francisco, July 1967).

15. Allan Sproul, "Reflections of a Central Banker," *Journal of Finance*. Vol. XI, No. 1, (May 1956), p. 11.

16. *Federal Reserve Bulletin,* (May 1963, June 1965, June 1966, and March 1967). See the definitive study by Geoffrey E. Moore and Philip A. Klein, *The Quality of Consumer Instalment Credit* (New York: National Bureau of Economic Research, 1967).

17. *Monthly Bulletin* (Federal Reserve Bank of Atlanta, November 1966); *Business Conditions* (Federal Reserve Bank of Chicago, September 1969).

18. Louis Rasminsky, "The Role of the Central Banker Today," *Supplement to International Financial News Survey*. International Monetary Fund. Vol. XVIII, No. 46 (November 18, 1966). Also, in the area of credit quality, reference should be made to an outstanding work by Edgar R. Fiedler, assisted by Maude R. Pech, *Measures of Credit Risk and Experience* (New York: National Bureau of Economic Research, 1971).

19. *Business Conditions* (Federal Reserve Bank of Chicago, June 1968).

20. These data was kindly supplied by George W. McKinney, Jr.

21. Parker B. Willis, *The Secondary Market for Negotiable Certificates of Deposit* (Washington, D.C.: Board of Governors, 1967).

22. The inverse relationship between fluctuations in certificates of deposit and Eurodollar borrowings at eight individual New York City banks is set forth in Dolores P. Lynn, *Reserve Adjustments of the Eight Major New York City Banks During 1966* (New York: Federal Reserve Bank, August 1967).

23. Discussion of the Eurodollar market are to be found in the following bank publications: *The Euro-Dollar Market* (New York: Bankers Trust Company, 1964); Norris O. Johnson, *Euro-Dollars in the New International Money Market* (New York: First National City Bank, undated); *The Financing of Business with Euro-dollars* (New York: Morgan Guaranty Trust Company, 1967); *Euro-Dollar Financing* (New York: Chase Manhattan Bank, 1968); Fred H. Klopstock, "Euro-Dollars in the Liquidity and Reserve Management of United States Banks," *Monthly Review* (Federal Reserve Bank of New York, July 1968), pp. 130–38.

24. See Jane Sneddon Little, "The Euro-dollar Market: Its Nature and Impact," *New England Review* (Federal Reserve Bank of Boston, May-June 1969), pp. 1–31.

25. George Bolton, "The Ernest Sykes Memorial Lectures for 1968," *The Financial Times* (London), February 14, 1968.

26. Bank for International Settlements, *Thirty-fifth Annual Report,* April 1, 1964–March 31, 1965 (Basle: June 14, 1965), p. 132.

27. Johnson, *op cit., Euro-dollars in the New International Money Market,* p. 4.

28. Fred H. Klopstock, *The Eurodollar Market: Some Unresolved Issues,* International Finance Section, Department of Economics (New Jersey; Princeton University Press, No. 65, March 1968).

29. Bank for International Settlements, *Thirth-Ninth Annual Report,* 1st April 1968–31st March 1969 (Basle: June 8, 1969), p. 149; also, *Forty-First Annual Report,* 1st April 1970–31st March 1971 (Basle: June 14, 1971), p. 157.

30. *Euro-Dollar Financing*. The Chase Manhattan Bank, *op. cit.,* p. 8.

31. Bank for International Settlements, *Thirty-Eighth Annual Report,* 1st April 1967–31st March 1968 (Basle: June 10, 1968), p. 145; *Thirty-Ninth Annual Report,* 1st April 1968–31st March 1969 (Basle: June 9, 1969), p. 140; and, *Federal Reserve Bulletin* (December 1971), p. A88.

32. *Monthly Review* (Bank of Nova Scotia, September 1968).

33. Fred H. Klopstock, "Euro-Dollars in the Liquidity and Reserve Management of United States Banks," *op. cit.,* p. 130.

34. Little, *op. cit.,* p. 11.

35. *Index* (Svenska Handelsbanken), No. 7, 1969.

36. See International Monetary Fund, *1971 Annual Report* (Washington, D.C.) p. 104; and Edward M. Bernstein, "The Eurodollar Market and National Credit Policy," *Quarterly Review and Investment Survey* (Model, Roland and Co.), Second Quarter, 1969.

37. See "C.D.'s Euro-dollars and Monetary Policy," *The Morgan Guaranty Survey,* February 1969; Little, *op. cit.,* pp. 23–24, and Andrew F. Brimmer, "Euro-Dollar Flows and the Efficiency of U.S. Monetary Policy," *address* dated March 8, 1969.

38. Martin Barrett, "Euro-Bonds: An Emerging International Capital Market," *Monthly Review* (Federal Reserve Bank of New York, August 1968), pp. 169–174.

39. E. Stopper, speeches in Zurich on March 17, 1967, and March 21, 1969.

40. *Federal Reserve Bulletin* (December 1970), pp. 940–942, (February 1971), pp. 121–122, and *Fifty-Seventh Annual Report of the Board of Governors of the Federal Reserve System Covering Operations for the Year 1970* (Washington, D.C.: May 21, 1971), pp. 81–82.

CHAPTER 14

$\mathcal{A}$ $\mathcal{M}atter$ of $Priority$

UNHAPPY CHOICES

Through much of the decade of the 1960s, the Federal Reserve System was caught, as the Federal Reserve Bank of Atlanta has pointed out, between the devil and the deep blue sea.[1] Compliance with the wishes of the administration (the devil) nudged policy in the direction of credit expansion; the deficit in the balance of payments (the deep blue sea) finally forced Federal Reserve officials to face the hard realities of their international responsibilities as guardians of the principal reserve currency of the world.

The choice for each nation, as balance-of-payments difficulties continue, can be summarized briefly: First, retention of the par of exchange by adopting deflationary measures which, by reducing incomes, costs, and prices, will check imports, discourage foreign travel, improve labor productivity and managerial efficiency, restore the nation's competitive position in foreign trade, and reallocate productive resources to export industries. The increase in interest rates resulting from this policy will have a direct impact on capital movements.

The foreign exchanges would be left uncontrolled and no new trade barriers imposed. Existing trade barriers might well be lowered or removed in order to expose domestic industry to the exhilarating influence of foreign competition.* A re-

---

* Selective tax policy might also be directed toward encouraging industry to increase its investment in advanced designs of machinery and equipment. This was the purpose of the investment tax credit of 1962. Other nations have used similar means. In August 1968 the Italian Council of Ministers recommended, as a means of increasing productivity, a substantial tax credit (50 percent of the investment increase) to firms that increased their investments above the average level of 1963–1965.

serve-currency nation that seeks to promote world trade free of exchange controls and protectionist devices would appropriately follow this course of action.

Second, retention of the par of exchange by adopting deflationary measures, of greater or less severity, accompanied by controls on the foreign exchanges, foreign trade, and the domestic economy. This epitomized the policy followed the United States in the 1960s.†

Third, the abandonment of the current rate of exchange and the adoption of a floating rate not tied to gold. Those who espouse this action point out that if there were no government intervention in the foreign-exchange markets, rates of exchange would respond to changes in the balance of payments. A deficit would cause rates to decline, encouraging exports and discouraging imports. The corrective influences so engendered, proponents declare, would eliminate the deficit, and at the same time the nation could follow its own domestic economic policies without deference to its balance of payments. Obviously these corrective influences would prevail only if the nation also checked internal inflationary pressures, which means that its own economic policies could not be absolutely independent.

Opponents of this policy contend that government intervention would inevitably take place to prevent disturbances in international trade and finance arising from widely fluctuating exchange rates. In other words, exchange rates would not be permitted to fluctuate freely. No nation lives unto itself. Opponents also point out that fluctuating exchange rates invite economic retaliation, weaken the will of nations to combat internal inflation, thereby leading to further declines of the local currency in terms of foreign currencies, and finally are wholly unsuited for use by a reserve-currency nation. A reserve currency cannot, it is concluded, fulfill its basic functions if it fluctuates beyond the limits permitted by the IMF. Otherwise it will not command confidence, will not contribute to the stability of international monetary arrangements, will not serve efficiently as a world-wide trading currency, and will not promote capital exports.[2] At the annual meeting of the IMF (September 30, 1969), R. Jenkins, British Chancellor of the Exchequer declared, "No recent argument or event has persuaded me that a system of total freedom, with all rates floating freely without Government intervention, is either desirable or durable." He then pointed out that in the past twenty-five years the IMF had witnessed sixty devaluations and only three revaluations, concluding that movements upward are stickier than movements downwards.

---

† President Lyndon B. Johnson set forth his program, which included many types of economic controls, in his New Year's message, January 1968. Gottfried Haberler of Harvard University found the control features of the program "absolutely shocking," embodying many features of the totalitarian system devised by the Nazi "economic wizard," Hjalmar Schacht. *Congressional Record,* February 5, 1968, p. 2136.

And last, the abandonment of the existing par of exchange and the adoption of a new par. The currency is devalued; the price of gold in terms of the local currency is raised. A reserve currency in fundamental disequilibrium cannot escape being devalued. Devaluation should be a well-considered act and not forced by outside pressures. A reserve-currency nation might be able to withstand one devaluation, as Britain did in 1949, and still retain its status. Repeated devaluations may prove fatal. Reserve currency nations have an obligation in the furtherance of world progress and unity to so direct their policies that the internal and external economic forces which might lead to devaluation, are checked. The Articles of Agreement of the IMF provide an orderly procedure for devaluation, should such action prove inescapable.

These measures may, of course, be grouped into many variations and combinations. The United Kingdom experimented with floating rates of exchange from 1919 to 1925 and again from 1931 to 1940. Finally, in 1949 it devalued the pound by 40 percent and again in 1967 by 14.3 percent. From time to time since 1914 the United Kingdom has applied controls of varying rigor on foreign exchange. Except for a short period of 1933, and later in 1971-72, the United States has not experimented with floating exchange rates, but it did devalue the dollar substantially in 1934 and again, by a lesser amount in 1972, (see Chapter 17). Only since 1961 has the United States applied foreign-exchange controls in a period not dominated by world war.

The particular method employed (of the four listed) depends partly upon the reasons for the imbalance but, in the main, it depends upon the temper of a people. Most imbalances result from inappropriate levels of internal demand, from deficient competitive strength, and from excessive capital movements.

More often than not, the appropriate action is the retention of the par of exchange accompanied by deflationary measures.* The adoption of controls nullifies the benefits to be derived from the stimulating and equilibrating operation of the market-price mechanism. The adoption of a floating rate of exchange carries the threat of continuous depreciation and may force other nations to adopt retaliatory measures. Devaluation often ignores or conceals basic economic weaknesses. Once a nation initiates devaluation it all too easily falls prey to the temptation to devalue again.[3]

Occasionally, but very rarely, nations revalue their currencies upward, that is,

---

* It must be recognized that immediately after World War II, permanent exchange rates could not be established until the excess liquidity of wartime inflation had been eliminated through price inflation or through forcible reduction of currency volume.

increase their value in terms of other currencies. Such action was taken by West Germany and the Netherlands on March 5 and 7, 1961, when the two nations revalued their currency upwards by 5 percent and again by West Germany on October 24, 1969, when it again increased the value of its currency, this time by 9.2896 percent. The two actions by West Germany raised the parity of the mark from 23.8095 to 27.3224 cents. Again in 1971 a group of nations, including West Germany, increased the value of their currencies (see Chapter 17). Upward revaluation of currencies by nations with strong balance-of-payments surplus helps to relieve nations, at least temporarily, with a large deficit from having to devalue their currencies. The strong-currency nations, however, bear the main burden of adjusting their trading accounts, through the effect of this action causing exports to decline and imports to increase.*

Minimizing the importance of the warning signals raised by the deficits in the balance of payments, the Kennedy administration directed its efforts toward stimulating a more rapid rate of growth, relying mainly on fiscal policies to achieve this purpose. Although favoring an expansionist monetary policy, it tended to minimize its effectiveness, not regarding it as effective or appropriate as fiscal policy. Reliance on fiscal policy to spur growth caused the administration to turn to foreign-exchange controls to reduce the deficit in the balance of payments, thereby making a significant break with the "one-world concept" that had governed American foreign economic policy since the end of World War II.

FISCAL POLICY AND THE NEW ECONOMICS

The Tax Cut

> I believe', President Johnson declared in his *Economic Report for 1965,* 'that 1964 will go down in our economic and political history as "the year of the tax cut" . . . it was the first time our Nation cut taxes for the declared purpose of speeding the advance of the private economy toward "maximum employment, production and purchasing power" . . . the tax cut was an expression of faith in the American economy.[5]

In the same report, the Council of Economic Advisers attributed the great achievements of the American economy from 1961–1965 to the major and continuing contribution of Federal policies, the most important of which was the tax cut. "These policies," the Council explained, "were not laid down in one master

---

* The upward revaluation of the mark on October 24, 1969 was accompanied by elimination of the 4 percent border-tax adjustment on industrial products, which had been imposed in mid-November 1968 and which was equivalent to a revaluation limited to trade in industrial products.[4]

plan early in 1961 and then carried out on a predetermined schedule. There have been delays, surprises . . . but policies . . . have consistently reflected a number of basic ideas shared by those responsible for Federal economic policies". [6]

The Kennedy and Johnson administrations were convinced that the basic task of fiscal policy was to help provide a total market demand for goods and services that neither exceeds nor falls short of the economy's productive capacity at full employment.[7] Fiscal policy had to go beyond the passivity of the automatic stabilizers and actively promote a continuous high growth rate. "Gone," wrote Walter Heller, Chairman of the Council of Economic Advisers at the time of the tax cut, "is the countercyclical syndrome of the 1950s." [8] This statement by Professor Heller constituted an attack on the policies of the Council of Economic Advisers in the 1950s, chairmaned by Professor Arthur F. Burns, which, while emphasizing the need to promote economic growth, aimed to do so without accentuating cyclical fluctuations or causing inflation. Only occasionally in the postwar period, reported the Council of Economic Advisers, had Federal fiscal policy been used as a positive stabilization device. (1965 *Report,* pp. 101-104) Corporate and individual tax rates had been raised sharply in 1950-1951, at the time of the Korean war; certain tax rates were allowed to decline in 1954 and increases in Federal expenditures occurred in 1958. Otherwise the automatic stabilizers had been relied upon to reduce cyclical fluctuations.

Measurement and Variability

Total economic growth is conventionally measured by changes in GNP at constant prices. To allow for population increases, per capita GNP is often used, and, in order to ascertain more precisely the contribution to human welfare of increases in GNP, military expenditures are frequently excluded. The effect of reductions in military expenditures in raising living standards has been vividly illustrated in the economies of postwar Germany and Japan. If possible, data of GNP should also be adjusted to take account of the effects of increases in environmental pollution.

Over long periods of time great variability in growth rates has been experienced in all industrial nations. In fourteen overlapping decades in the United States, annual rates of increase in GNP, adjusted for price changes, varied from − 0.35 to + 7.02 percent and GNP per capita from − 1.33 to + 6.00 percent.[9] The average growth rate in these fourteen decades, which included the severe depressions of the 1890s and the 1930s, was 3.6 percent. The increase from

1961–1967, when efforts to increase the rate of growth dominated economic policy, was about 5 percent, only slightly higher than the growth rate from 1869–1879 (which began at a business-cycle peak and ended in a trough). Not only had fiscal action comparable to that of the Kennedy and Johnson administrations not been taken, but the national debt had actually been reduced about 10 percent as well. Reduction in the Federal debt, by providing savings for investment may have stimulated growth, as well as the fact that Federal revenues were then derived largely from indirect taxes. Although the regressive nature of these taxes was doubtless inequitable, the tax system did curb consumption at a time of great investment need. This particular decade was marked not only by a rapid growth rate but also by declining prices.

Again in the 1880s, a decade characterized by a fairly rapid growth rate and declining prices, the Federal debt was sharply reduced. Another example of rapid growth accompanying sharp Federal debt reduction occurred from 1922–1929. It is not easy to find reasons for the great variability in growth rates in American history. Some of the most rapid increases occurred in periods when the Federal budget was in surplus, Federal debt declining, and prices falling. These examples illustrate the great complexity of the problem and also indicate that growth may occur under widely disparate economic conditions.

Growth and the Cycle

The New Economics was convinced that, with growth promoted, cyclical fluctuations would be submerged in rapidly rising secular trends. Problems of economic growth cannot, however, be separated from those of the cycle. Impetus to growth occurs on the upward sweep of the cycle. Growth is sustainable only if the measures taken to promote it do not also produce imbalances between costs and prices and between consumption and investment, which are apt to terminate the upward cyclical movement as an economy moves into full employment.[10] Similarly, growth can be sustained only if the action taken does not generate inflationary pressures, a deterioration in credit quality, or heavy pressures on the balance of payments, which eventually force a reversal of policy in order to safeguard the internal and external value of a currency.

Problems of growth and economic progress have long occupied the attention of economists. Adam Smith centered his work "An Inquiry into the Nature and Causes of the Wealth of Nations" largely around conditions needed for economic opulence and has a section called: "Of the Different Progress of Opulence in Different Countries." It was a dynamic, not a static concept. John Stuart Mill was not unmindful of the problem, and Alfred Marshall gave it continued emphasis through his treatise.[11]

On numerous occasions American economic policy has been directed toward this goal. One has only to recall the encouragement given to education; government participation in the establishment of banks and in the building of canals and railways; measures taken to prevent the establishment of a feudal class through the sale of public lands in relatively small parcels; action taken from time to time to strengthen competition; and the willingness of the central government to finance such public works as the Panama Canal and the Tennessee Valley Authority. These are but a few of the many examples which might be cited of the contribution of government in directing expenditures toward self-perpetuating opulence.

Proponents of the New Economics maintained that the novelty of their approach lay in its exclusive emphasis on full employment and on the use of fiscal policy to accomplish this goal. Fiscal policy, they declared, could and should be so directed and so fine-tuned as to ensure sustainable growth. Monetary policy could serve as a handmaiden; fiscal policy must carry the main burden. Fiscal policy thus became "fiscal activism" and as such had to be altered as frequently as necessary to achieve the economic goals of the administration.[12]

Theoretical Underpinnings

The theoretical underpinnings of the New Economics depended upon such concepts as the full-employment surplus or deficit, fiscal drag, fiscal dividends, and the production gap. The vaunted built-in flexibility of the Federal tax system, asserted Professor Heller, is a mixed blessing. It cushions recessions but retards recovery by cutting into private income. Federal tax revenues depend largely upon the level of economic activity, Federal expenditures do not, save for unemployment insurance, change automatically with incomes. The Federal tax system "produces a built-in average increase of $7 to $8 billion a year in Federal revenues." Unless offset by "fiscal dividends" in the form of planned tax cuts or expenditure increases, the automatic rise in revenues becomes a fiscal drag, "siphoning too much of the economic substance out of the private economy and thereby checking expansion."*

---

* The term "fiscal drag" is, in a sense, an indictment of a progressive tax system. The drag arises from the fact that tax payments increase as incomes rise in a period of economic expansion. Aggregate taxes, however, do not rise as much as incomes, and tax receipts are not impounded. They are either spent or can be used to reduce debt. If by reason of the rise in tax receipts, the budget moves into cash surplus, the additional available cash can reduce publicly-held debt, thereby placing savings at the disposal of the investor or entrepreneur. The savings generated will also tend to offset the possible inflationary effects of deficit financing on the part of consumers, businessmen, and local and state governments.

This approach interested itself not so much in the details of Federal expenditures and taxes and their effects on growth but rather in an overall global approach. The Federal budget, it was contended, should be balanced only at those levels of GNP associated with a 4 percent unemployment rate.[13] Unemployment, as we have pointed out earlier, was held to be the result of deficient demand not of structural imperfections.[14] Recent recognition of the importance of structural imperfections has caused the proponents of the New Economics to suggest that full employment must be redefined as a figure higher than 4 percent unemployment. A good illustration of the impreciseness of quantitative economics.

The expansionary or deflationary thrust of the Federal budget on a national income basis was not to be judged by the actual deficit or surplus. Rather it was to be measured by the surplus or deficit which would have been achieved at full employment levels on the basis of existing prices and tax rates.† Adopting the tenets of the New Economics, President Richard Nixon in his budget message of January 25, 1972, stated that the "full employment budget concept is central to the budget policy of this Administration."

The Full-Employment Surplus

The Council pointed out that, even though the actual deficit had amounted to $6.8 billion (cash basis) in 1961, nevertheless, Federal finances had had a deflationary, rather than an inflationary, effect. The surplus at full employment would have been about $9 billion. The production gap, the difference between actual and potential GNP, was estimated at $50 billion.[15] To eliminate the alleged deflationary effects of a hypothetical surplus of $9 billion, as well as of a hypothetical production gap of $50 billion, fiscal action in the form of reduced tax rates or increased expenditures should have been taken, and, if such action had been taken, full employment would have resulted, and the production gap could have been eliminated. The drag resulting from the hypothetical surplus would also have been eliminated.*

---

† The suggestion that the Federal budget be balanced only at high employment levels was proposed by the Committee for Economic Development in 1947. It then suggested that tax rates be set so that a modest surplus would be realized at "high level employment national income." Increases in expenditures were to be accompanied by increases in tax rates which would cover expenditures at this level. *Taxes and the Budget: A Program for Prosperity in a Free Economy* (November 1947).

* The doctrine assumed that economic equilibrium could be attained at full employment if gross private investment equaled personal and corporate savings and if tax revenues (minus full-employment transfer payments) equaled Federal expenditures. To know what action to take to establish this equilibrium, it would be necessary to forecast all the elements in the equation and then to make necessary adjustments in taxes and expenditures, keeping in mind the effect of these adjustments on psychological attitudes. A truly formidable task. See Robert Solomon, "The Full Employment Budget Surplus as an Analytical Concept." *American Statistical Association, 1962,* Proceedings of the Business and Economics Statistics Section.

Uncertain Hypotheses and Assumptions

In its 1968 report, the Council of Economic Advisers acknowledged that the hypothetical measure of the full-employment surplus is "abstract and imprecise."* And so it is, but this admission was very important, for the full-employment surplus had been used as the basis for determining and fine-tuning fiscal policy. Estimates of unemployment, one of the important building blocks in this analysis, as Arthur F. Burns pointed out, are "incomplete and in some respects misleading." [16] For various reasons the actual amount of employment is underestimated, with the consequence that policy makers may overreact and breed inflationary pressures. Furthermore, estimates of what the economic system can produce at a 4 percent unemployment level depend upon various arbitrary assumptions about labor productivity, managerial efficiency, man hours worked, and availability of skilled labor and raw materials.

Even estimates of future Federal expenditures are subject to quick and drastic changes. The Council of Economic Advisers grossly underestimated the rising cost of the Vietnam war. The business community did not make the same error, but it was the Council that had taken on the task of recommending changes in taxes and expenditures to promote growth. Chairman Gardner Ackley, in an address to the American Statistical Association in September 1965, estimated that the rise in spending during the first year of our major commitment in Vietnam was likely to be only $3.5 billion and that press estimates of $10–14 billion were simply figments of someone's imagination. The figments, however, proved to have a hard core of reality. Defense outlays actually rose $13 billion.[17]

Not only are measures of the full-employment surplus imprecise, but the fiscal action chosen to eliminate that surplus is based on various imprecise assumptions relating to the response of consumers and businessmen to the fiscal policies which are adopted and their timing. The Council assumed that the individual response to a reduction in income-tax rates would generate an increase in GNP twice the amount of the tax reduction. The "multipler" would thus be two. The economist of the Joint Economic Committee on the Economic Report calculated a somewhat higher multiplier. Witnesses before the committee confessed their inability to compute the extent to which a reduction in corporate income-tax rates would be translated into higher GNP.[18]

Responses to changes in fiscal policy (and in monetary policy) are not gov-

---

* Nevertheless the Council maintained that the full-employment surplus is a useful way of "distinguishing between the passive operation of automatic stabilizers and discretionary shifts in the budget." (*1968 Report*, p. 65) It is doubtful whether the full employment surplus itself can and does make this distinction. See also Robert Solomon, *op. cit.*

erned by immutable laws. Changing psychological attitudes of businessmen and consumers govern the effectiveness of changes in tax rates. A reduction in tax rates that is expected to be in force for some time will have a much greater impact than will a "quickie" change.[19] A reduction while state and local taxes are rising will have a smaller effect than when these tax rates were stable. A reduction while resources are increasingly employed in the private sector may overstimulate the economy.

An increase in tax rates, when consumers and businessmen are convinced that inflation cannot be suppressed and are drawing upon savings or incurring debts to continue their purchases will have a much slower impact than if the public is convinced that fiscal measures can bring a speedy end to the erosion of purchasing power. A reduction in tax rates accompanied by a deficit financed by the commercial banking system will have a greater impact than when the deficit is financed by savings. The New Economics tends, however, to neglect the monetary aspects of fiscal policy and to concentrate mainly upon the income effects; it tends, also to neglect the importance of the psychological climate within which fiscal and monetary policy function. It needs to be borne in mind that a full employment deficit, like any deficit, has to be financed.

FISCAL ACTION

In his first annual report, Secretary of the Treasury C. Douglas Dillon stated:

> When the present Administration assumed office in January 1961, the nation faced two serious economic problems: a recession at home which had continued for eight months; and a persistent deficit in this country's international balance of payments which had shaken confidence in the stability of the dollar. . . . There is no conflict between our domestic and our foreign economic programs. . . . We must disavow any philosophy and reject all programs that support one exclusively at the cost of the other.[20]

Time demonstrated that priorities had to be established. Fiscal action to stimulate growth eventually conflicted with monetary action to correct an imbalance in the balance of payments. In the early 1960s, however, the administration appeared confident that the future posed no such problem.

Believing that fiscal policy was inappropriately restrictive in 1960, the administration moved vigorously to invoke the fiscal powers of the Federal government.[21] The action initially taken, which was designed merely to support rather than to spur the economy's expansion,[22] included accelerated procurement and construction, speeded up tax refunds, advance payment of veterans' life-insurance dividends, increases in farm price supports, expanded distribution of free food, and increases in the availability of construction credits.

These measures were reflected in rapidly expanding Federal cash payments, which in 1961 increased $10 billion over those in 1960. Cash receipts fell slightly. A surplus of $3.6 billion in 1960 turned into a deficit of $6.8 billion in 1961. If fiscal policy is to prove fully effective in reducing unemployment, all tax rates, the Council declared, had to be reduced. Reduction of some would increase investment. Reduction of others would increase consumption. The main deterrent to investment was held to be inadequate demand. The most important single action, therefore, said President Kennedy, was to raise consumption. Actually, total personal income was at a high level and had increased without interruption throughout the entire postwar period. Expenditures on automobiles and parts alone had undergone a fairly sharp cyclical decline in 1958 and a milder one in 1961. The situation did not seem to call for a crash program of stimulation.

The First Stage

The initial step, which required no new legislation, was the July 1962 revision of depreciation schedules and procedures by the Treasury.[23] The Revenue Act of 1954 marked, as Secretary Dillon pointed out, a new direction in Treasury policy on depreciation. New, liberalized methods—the declining-balance at twice the corresponding straight-line rate and the sum of the years-digits,—were specifically authorized. As important as these changes were in permitting acceleration of depreciation deductions, they did not deal with the basic problem of the duration of the useful lives of machinery and equipment. Rapid increases in obsolescence had in many cases substantially shortened the period of usefulness.

After lengthy investigations beginning in 1956 and continuing through 1962 the Treasury issued a new set of guidelines (a revision of Regulation F), which effected, for tax purposes, a substantial shortening in the estimated useful lives of machinery and equipment. The new guidelines (superseded in 1965) took into account not only increased rates of obsolescence but also increasingly intensive international competition.[24]

Other nations—Sweden, for example—had made extensive use of depreciation deductions and incentive allowances as a means of encouraging investment in productive equipment. Tax benefits of this character enable industrialists to keep abreast of rapid technological changes and are extremely important in furthering "the opulence of nations."

The Second Stage

A second step was provision in the Revenue Act of October 1962 for an investment tax credit of 7 percent (3 percent for certain utilities) on funds spent on depreciable machinery and equipment and used in the United States.* The Treasury estimated that the annual revenue loss (not allowing for the possible stimulating effect of the tax credit) would be $1 billion 20 million. After allowing for the possible stimulating effect, the revenues loss would be an estimated $580 million.

Four years later, when it became apparent that restraint was imperative, the investment tax credit and regulations permitting accelerated depreciation on certain industrial and commercial buildings were suspended (October 10, 1966). This action was regarded as a key element in President Lyndon B. Johnson's anti-inflation program.[25] Five months later the President reported that the suspension had achieved its objectives and requested reinstatement of both the investment tax credit and accelerated depreciation. This was done effective March 10, 1967. Once again, as the Washington merry-go-round whirled about, a bill providing *inter alia* for the repeal of the investment tax credit was signed by President Nixon on December 31, 1969.

Investment tax credits and depreciation allowances are hardly suitable for use as short-run stabilization devices. Business firms make long-run plans for plant and equipment expenditures, which cannot be changed on short notice. If the projected cash flow is suddenly reduced, corporations may be forced to borrow to complete their projects. They cannot operate most effectively in this type of uncertain climate. To employ tax policy "as an alternate whip to speed up the economy and rein to pull it in—and to do this on a short-term basis—is sure to upset and hamper business operations." [26]

The Third Stage

The third and most important step was the Revenue Act of 1964, which was enacted about one year after the President's recommendations and which, the Secretary of the Treasury declared was "the most important domestic economic legisla-

---

* *Annual Report of the Secretary of the Treasury on the State of the Finances for the Fiscal Year Ended June 30, 1962* (Washington, D.C.: U.S. Government Printing Office, 1963), p. 62. The effect of the revision of Regulation F and the adoption of the investment tax credit, according to the Council of Economic Advisers, was to increase by $2½ billion the annual cash flow to corporations, (*Report*, 1965, p. 63). The amount of the investment-tax credit was based upon the full cost of the property with a useful life of eight years or more, two-thirds of the cost of that with a useful life of six to eight years, one-third of the cost of that with a useful life of four to six years. A three-year "carry-back" and a four-year "carry forward" were provided for unused credits. The law initially required a reduction in the depreciable basis of the assets by the amount of the investment credit, (*Report*, 1962, p. 68).

tion since World War II," and the largest tax cut ever enacted.[27] The Treasury estimated that when it became fully effective in 1965 it would reduce the tax liabilities of individuals $9.2 billion and of corporations $2.4 billion.[28]

The Revenue Act reduced corporate income-tax rates in two stages from 52 to 48 percent. In 1966 corporate tax payments, paradoxically enough, were accelerated, with the result that cash payments by corporations as a percentage of income, rose from 51.4 percent in 1963 to 57.4 percent in 1967.[29] Individual income tax-rates were reduced about 20 percent, according to Treasury estimates. Half the reduction took effect January 1, 1964, and the balance a year later. Withholding rates were immediately dropped to 14 percent. The act reduced the top surtax rate from 91 to 70 percent and accorded substantial relief to low-income taxpayers. The dividend credit of 4 percent enacted in 1954 as a means of reducing the double taxation of corporate dividends was repealed. The dividend exclusion was increased from $50 to $100 per person.

Full tax relief for individuals in the lower- and middle-income ranges proved short-lived. Payroll taxes were increased sharply to pay for huge increases in social-security benefits and the medicare programs. The taxable wage base jumped from $4,800 in 1965 to $6,600 in 1966 to $7,800 in 1968, and to $9,000, effective January 1, 1971. The combined employer-employee social-security tax rose from 7.25 percent in 1965 to 8.8 percent in 1967, to 9.6 percent in 1969, and to 10.4 percent on January 1, 1971.[30]

The Record

Except for slight surpluses in fiscal 1960 and 1969, the Federal budget was chronically in deficit through the 1960s (see Table 14.1). The deficit from 1960 through 1971 (fiscal years) totaled $82.8 billion, to which might be added the estimated deficits of 1972 and 1973 of $64.3 billion, making a grand total of $147.1 billion. The deficits in the "full employment" years 1966-1969 totalled 70 percent of all deficits of the 1960s. Full employment surpluses failed to materialize.

Tax policy should have been reversed in 1966.[31] From the fourth quarter of 1960 to the second quarter of 1965 increases in Federal expenditures totaled $27 billion and Federal tax reductions totaled $13 billion. The increase in expenditures was at least twice as potent in stimulating the economy as was the reduction in taxes—and probably even more potent, for the multiplier is thought to be greater. The upward trend in consumer prices accelerated, and wholesale prices began a rapid advance. Defense obligations rose sharply as expenditures on the Vietnam war

Table 14.1

Federal Receipts, Expenditures, Net Lending, and Total Budget Surplus or Deficit
(Billions of Dollars)

Fiscal Year	Receipts	Expenditures	Net Lending	Total Surplus or Deficit	Gross Public Debt (End of Year)
1960	$ 92.5	$ 90.3	$1.9	$+0.3	$290.9
1961	94.4	96.6	1.2	−3.4	292.9
1962	99.7	104.5	2.4	−7.1	303.3
1963	106.6	111.5	−0.1	−4.8	310.8
1964	112.7	118.0	0.5	−5.9	316.8
1965	116.8	117.2	1.2	−1.6	323.2
1966	130.9	130.8	?.8	−3.8	329.5
1967	149.6	153.3	5.1	−8.7	341.3
1968	153.7	172.8	6.0	−25.2	369.8
1969	187.8	183.1	1.5	+3.2	367.2
1970	193.8	194.5	2.1	−2.8	382.6
1971	188.4	210.3	1.1	−23.0	409.5

Source: *Economic Indicators*, November 1971.

soared. Federal spending on domestic programs began to rise. The deficit in the balance of payments worsened. Rising unit labor costs exerted upward pressure on prices. Wage agreements, particularly those in the second half of 1966, toppled the President's voluntary guidelines. Despite increasing inflationary pressures, an excise-tax reduction was enacted on June 30, 1965. Tax repeals and reductions under this act reduced revenues an estimated $4.7 billion.[32] A modification of the 1962 depreciation guidelines increased tax benefits $600 million. Old-age benefits were liberalized, but the increase ($2 billion) was much more than offset by a rise ($6 billion) in social-security and medicare payroll taxes.

The President continued to be optimistic, and in his report issued in early 1966 declared that bottlenecks in production could be averted, wage-price spirals avoided, the Great Society program could move ahead and all defense requirements met. As a gesture of fiscal prudence, he recommended temporary restoration of certain excise taxes and the placing of income- and self-employment tax payments closer to a pay-as-you-go basis. These changes were incorporated into the Tax Adjustment Act of 1966.

The IMF had recommended to the American government in 1966 that tax increases be legislated. The spring or early summer of 1966 would have been the right time—as Robert T. Elson pointed out, the only right time—for a tax increase.[33] Fall elections precluded such legislation, however. The BIS castigated American government inaction: "To tax or not to tax; that was the question. And the indecisive way it was answered gives the key to what happened in the United States economy over the last eighteen months. On the one hand it allowed the forces of excess demand to gather momentum, and, on the other, it left the task of restraint to monetary policy." [34]

Not until his State of the Union Message on January 10, 1967, in which he recommended a 6 percent surcharge, did President Johnson advocate a rise in individual and corporate income taxes. On August 3, 1967, the President, prompted by the IMF, recommended raising the surcharge to 10 percent. But Congress would not act until the President accepted a mandatory reduction in Federal expenditures. He finally agreed. Legislation providing for a 10 percent surcharge on incomes paid by individuals and corporations and setting a ceiling on expenditures of $180.1 billion, $6 billion less than the outlays initially projected for fiscal 1969, was finally enacted on June 30, 1968. (Congress shortly began to whittle away at the mandatory reduction of $6 billion. On September 24, 1968, the Senate exempted from the $180.1 billion expenditure ceiling, an unexpected increase of $960 million in farm-price supports. Certain categories, including spending related to Vietnam, interest, veterans' affairs, and social-security payments were exempted from the ceiling. The 10 percent surcharge, which expired on June 30, 1969, was extended on August 7, 1969, to the end of the year.) [35] The Federal Reserve Bank of New York declared in 1968:

> The passage of the Revenue and Expenditure Control Act of 1968 was the culmination of a prolonged struggle to bring fiscal restraint to bear on the inflationary problems at home and the weakening position of the dollar abroad . . . it was not until international speculation threatened the dollar that the margin of extra support needed to pass a tax bill developed.[36]

The President's recommendation for a tax increase, though clearly needed, was opposed by the Joint Economic Committee. Its arguments were that Congress should first reduce expenditures, that the contingencies envisaged by the President might not occur, that forecasts of Federal receipts and expenditures were notoriously inaccurate (perhaps unavoidably so), and that the Federal budget should first be revised and reformed.[37] Some members argued that the second half of 1967 might prove sluggish in view of the overhang of inventories. Action, they argued, should be taken only when a rational judgment was possible. The opposition of this group, presumably better informed on economic problems than was the average congressman, affords a good illustration of the political difficulties involved in reversing tax reduction, even when reversal is warranted.

Disadvantages

The events of the 1960s demonstrated that fiscal action does not prove a particularly effective fine-cutting tool, partly because of delays in political action, partly because of failure to forecast the effects of fiscal legislation accurately. The President procrastinated in recommending a reversal of the 1964 law. Congress, buffeted by political pressures and confused by the administration's evasive and secretive attitude on war costs, delayed action. When fiscal action was finally taken and the Revenue and Expenditure Control Act of 1968 enacted, the restraining impact turned out to have been grossly overestimated. An immediate slowdown of the economy and the possibility of "overkill" in 1969 had been forecast. Studies by the staff of the Federal Reserve Board of Governors had supported these forecasts. In consequence, a majority of the members of the Federal Open Market Committee were unwilling, particularly in view of Treasury financing needs, to move toward firmer market rates. Not until December 17, 1968, when it had become clear that fiscal action had not achieved expected results, did the Open Market Committee vote to encourage firmer conditions in the money and short-term credit markets.[38]

The next important finance measure was the Tax Reform Act of 1969, signed by President Nixon on December 30. This not only eliminated the investment tax credit but provided also for an increase in social security benefits, an increase in personal income tax exemptions, an extension of the income tax surcharge at a 5 percent rate through June 1970, a reduction in the oil depletion allowance, and a postponement of scheduled reductions in telephone and automobile excise taxes. On balance it is estimated that the Act had the effect, if business activity remained at a high level, of increasing revenues in fiscal 1970 by $3.8 billions and in fiscal 1971 by $2.4 billions.[39] Business activity declined and total revenues fell sharply. President Nixon was not able to fulfill his pledge of a balanced budget and as unemployment tended to increase, he was probably pleased that economic developments had themselves unbalanced the budget. At least nothing was said, as it was in the Great Depression, of the imperative need for a balanced budget. Subsequent fiscal developments are discussed in Chapter 17, along with other measures taken at the time of the suspension of convertibility.

Even at best, fiscal policy is an awkward and cumbersome tool. It cannot, as monetary policy can, respond quickly to unexpected events. It cannot change direction speedily, when initial action turns out to have been based on erroneous forecasting. Monetary policy is thus more flexible and responsive.

In order to change tax rates quickly and without lengthy congressional debate, President Kennedy had suggested that Congress delegate some of its fiscal authority, subject to various limitations, to the President.[40] The rationale for this suggestion was that the President would act promptly to change tax rates in the direction and by the amounts considered desirable.

Even if the Congress were to delegate this power, which it has shown no disposition to do, there is no reason to believe that the executive would show great wisdom in its exercise. He would be faced with the same problems that confront all fiscal and monetary authorities: recognizing the need for change, forecasting the effects of change, deciding when to act, and deciding the amount of action to be taken. Furthermore, the President is subject to political pressures similar to those acting on other politicians and political agencies. He would always have to include the electorate in his calculations. Tax reductions would probably occur quickly, increases more slowly. Although the Federal Reserve System cannot completely disregard political currents in its credit policies, it is somewhat freer of such pressures than are Congress and the President. And, if it so desires, it can move quickly.

Experience with fiscal policy in the 1960s carries little promise of its future effective use. To be sure, the adoption of an investment tax credit benefited the economy by encouraging investment of corporate funds in productive equipment. Its later elimination, subsequent reinstatement, and elimination once again proved upsetting to business plans. Reduction of the corporate income tax was itself offset on a cash flow basis by the acceleration of tax payments and at best has a long-delayed impact. The reduction of individual income taxes was, even at the time of its enactment, regarded by many as a mistake.[41] Unemployment was structural, rather than cyclical, and inflationary pressures were beginning to build up. Reversal proved difficult and might never have occurred without the intervention of the IMF.

GROWTH AND FISCAL POLICY RECONSIDERED

For the remainder of the twentieth century, consumer, business, and public sectors of the economy seem likely to need vast amounts of savings: for machinery and equipment, transportation expansion and improvement, development of natural resources, water provision and elimination of pollution, commercial and housing construction, education, and research and development. The Federal tax system might well be directed toward encouraging corporate, business, and personal savings.

Along with carefully considered changes in tax policy, Federal expenditures might be redirected, to the greatest extent possible, into those areas that stimulate self-perpetuating growth in GNP and away from military involvement and support of such vested interests as corporate agriculture. Also important is the need to develop and conserve natural resources and to advance education and research. In the budget for fiscal 1969, estimated expenditures for education totaled $12 billion and for basic and applied research (most of which was associated with military needs) another $5.7 billion. The two totaled $17.7 billion out of estimated total expenditures of about $186 billion.[42] It may not be politically possible to redirect expenditures from the military to education, research, and social betterment, but if it is not, heavy military outlays carrying the menace of competitive nuclear weapons make discussion of policies of economic stabilization and growth seem trifling and irrelevant.

A Federal budget that is greatly shaped by military expenditures can be inflationary even when in balance. Goods produced on government order are not those desired by civilians. An "inflationary gap," (a term used during World War II), emerges, justifying an overbalanced budget and debt reduction even at levels of unemployment that the Council of Economic Advisers might consider excessive.

Notes

1. *Monthly Review* (Federal Reserve Bank of Atlanta, May 1964).

2. For a defense of floating exchange rates, see Gottfried Haberler and Thomas D. Willett, *U.S. Balance of Payments and International Monetary Reform: A Critical Analysis* (Washington, D.C.: American Enterprise Institute, 1968).

3. See Sir George Bolton (Chairman of the Bank of London and South America), *The Times* (London), September 12, 1967.

4. See Bank for International Settlements, *Thirty-Ninth Annual Report,* 1st April, 1968–31st March 1969 (Basle: June 9, 1969), p. 11.

5. *Economic Report of the President.* Transmitted to the Congress January 1965 (Washington, D.C.: Government Printing Office, 1965) p. 5.

6. *Ibid.,* p. 61.

7. *Ibid.,* p. 62.

8. Walter W. Heller, *New Dimensions of Political Economy* (New York: W. W. Norton & Company, Inc., 1967), preface.

9. Simon Kuznets, *Economic Growth and Structure: Selected Essays* (New York: W. W. Norton & Company, Inc., 1965), p. 305.

10. Arthur F. Burns, "Heller's New Dimensions of Political Economy," *The National Banking Review,* Vol. 4 (June 1967), pp. 371–375.

11. Adam Smith, *An Inquiry into the Nature and Causes of the Wealth of Nations* (New York: The Modern Library, edition 1937), Book III; John Stuart Mill, *Principles of Political Economy* (New York: The Colonial Press, edition 1900); Alfred Marshall, *Principles of Economics,* Seventh Edition (London: MacMillan and Co., 1916). The importance of growth was emphasized by the Council of Economic Advisers in the Eisenhower Administration, *Report* (1954), p. 112.

12. George Terborgh, *The New Economics* (Washington, D.C.: Machinery and Allied Products Institute, 1968).

13. Heller, *op. cit.,* p. 65.

14. A good discussion of structural unemployment is to be found in the *Fifty-First Annual Report for the Year Ended December 31, 1965* (Federal Reserve Bank of New York, 1966) pp. 15–17.

15. *Economic Report of the President* (Washington, D.C.: Government Printing Office) January 1963, pp. 18, 26–28; January 1965, p. 64; and February 1968, pp. 60 and 65.

16. *Twentieth Anniversary of the Employment Act of 1946: An Economic Symposium.* Joint Economic Committee, Congress of the United States, 89th Cong., 2nd Sess., February 23, 1966 (Washington, D.C.: Government Printing Office, 1966) p. 31.

17. *Monthly Economic Letter* (First National City Bank of New York, June 1968).

18. *January 1963 Economic Report of the President,* Part I, Joint Economic Committee, 88th Cong. 1st Sess., 1963, (Washington, D.C.: Government Printing Office, January 28, 1963), pp. 1–44.

19. Burns, "Heller's New Dimensions of Political Economy," *op. cit.,* p. 375.

20. *Annual Report of the Secretary of the Treasury on the State of the Finances* (Washington, D.C.: Government Printing Office, 1961), p. 3. For an excellent review of Federal fiscal policy in the 1960s, see *Federal Reserve Bulletin* (September 1968), pp 701–718.

21. *Economic Report of the President.* Transmitted to the Congress January 1962 (Washington, D.C.: Government Printing Office, 1962) p. 82–84.

22. *Economic Report of the President.* Transmitted to the Congress January 1963 (Washington, D.C.: Government Printing Office, 1963) p. 18.

23. *Ibid.,* p. XVII–XVIII.

24. For a discussion of some of these changes, see *Annual Report of the Secretary of the Treasury on the State of the Finances for the Fiscal Year Ended June 30, 1962* (Washington, D.C.: Government Printing Office, 1963), pp. 297–304. Also see *Depreciation Guidelines and Rules* (rev. ed; Internal Revenue Service Publication No. 456 [Washington, D.C.: Government Printing Office, 1964]); and *Internal Revenue Bulletin* (May 17, 1965).

25. *Special Message,* September 8, 1966. *Annual Report of the Secretary of the Treasury on the State of the Finances For the Fiscal Year Ended June 30, 1967,* (Washington, D.C.: Government Printing Office, 1968), p. xx.

26. William Proxmire, *Tax Changes for Shortrun Stabilization* printed for the use of the Joint Economic Committee, (May 27, 1966), p. 20. See *Capital Goods Review, No. 75,* Machinery and Allied Products Institute (September 1968).

27. *Annual Report of the Secretary of the Treasury on the State of the Finances for the Fiscal Year Ended June 30, 1964.* (Washington, D.C.: Government Printing Office, 1965), p. 36.

28. *Ibid.,* p. 37.

29. *Monthly Economic Letter* (First National City Bank of New York, June 1968), p. 67.

30. *Monthly Economic Letter* (First National City Bank of New York, June 1968), and *The Budget of the United States Government Fiscal Year 1971* (Washington, D.C.: Government Printing Office, 1970), p. 69.

31. *Fiscal Policies of the Coming Decade* Hearings before the Subcommittee on Fiscal Policy of the Joint Economic Committee, 89th Cong., 1st sess. 1965, (Washington, D.C.: Government Printing Offie, 1965).

32. *Annual Report of the Secretary of the Treasury on the State of the Finances for the Fiscal Year Ending June 30, 1965* (Washington, D.C.: Government Printing Office, 1966), pp. XX–XXI.

33. Robert T. Elson, "How the Old Politics Swayed the New Economics," *Fortune* (September 1, 1968), pp. 75–77, 168–172.

34. Bank for International Settlements, *Thirty-Seventh Annual Report,* 1st April 1966–31st March 1967 (Basle: June 12, 1967), pp. 3–4.

35. *The New York Times,* September 25, 1968, pp. 1 and 24.

36. *Fifty-Fourth Annual Report for the Year Ended on December 31, 1968* (Federal Reserve Bank of New York, February 28, 1969), pp. 15–16.

37. *1967 Joint Economic Report,* March 17, 1967, 90th Cong., 1st sess., Report No. 73 (Washington, D.C.: Government Printing Office, 1967), p. 10–11.

38. *Review* (Federal Reserve Bank of St. Louis, May 1969).

39. *The Budget of the United States Government Fiscal Year 1971* (Washington, D.C.: Government Printing Office, 1970), p. 67.

40. *Economic Report of the President* (Washington, D.C.: Government Printing Office, 1962), p. 18. See *Annual Report of the Secretary of the Treasury on the State of the Finances for the Fiscal Year Ended June 30, 1961* (Washington, D.C.: Government Printing Office, 1962), p. 25.

41. See E. B. Schwulst (President of Bowery Savings Bank) letter to *The New York Times,* January 26, 1964.

42. *Special Analyses, Budget of the United States, Fiscal Year 1969* (Washington, D.C.: Government Printing Office, 1969), analyses H and J.

The Moment of Truth

CHAPTER 15

TWISTING THE INTEREST RATE CURVE

The Federal Reserve System, in close cooperation with the administration, in the early 1960s adopted policies that, in its opinion, would prevent even a temporary lull in growth and would at the same time reduce, if not eliminate, the deficit in the balance of payments. The twofold objective was to be accomplished by Operation Twist.

The interest-rate curve was to be twisted. Short-term rates were to rise, and long-term rates were to remain stable or perhaps even to decline. The increase in short-term rates, it was thought, would check the flow of interest-sensitive funds abroad, and stability in long-term rates would promote construction activity, heavier investment in capital goods, and flotation of municipal obligations. The first would tend to correct the imbalance in the balance of payments, and the second would facilitate growth.[1]

The twist in the interest-rate curve would result from Federal Reserve purchases of intermediate- and long-term securities and Treasury sales of short-term debt.[2] The demand for the one would stabilize intermediate- and long-term yields, and the supply of the other would increase short-term yields.

Operation Twist was made possible by a directive of the Federal Open Market Committee issued on February 7, 1961.[3] Abandoning the "bills-only policy," this directive authorized the Federal Reserve Bank of New York to conduct open-market operations in intermediate- and long-term securities with maturities not exceeding ten years. Reserves would thus continue to be supplied to the banking system, and simultaneously the interest-rate curve would be twisted in the desired direction.

In twisting the curve in the early years of the decade, the Reserve System planned to proceed cautiously. Initially it intended to confine purchases of government obligations within the one to five and-a-half year maturity range. Once the market had become accustomed to the change in policy, it would then undertake operations within the five and-a-half to ten year maturities. Even before the adoption of Operation Twist, in the fall of 1960 the System had extended its open-market operations to include issues in the 9- to 15-month maturity range.

In 1961 the Federal Reserve purchased on balance $2.6 billion of U.S. securities maturing in more than one year. More than half had maturities of two to six years. In addition, the Treasury, reinforcing Federal Reserve action, purchased for its agency and trust accounts $900 million of long-term securities, mostly with maturities of more than ten years.

The same policy was followed in 1962. Nearly all the increase in the System's holdings of securities, $1.9 billion, represented net purchases of issues maturing in more than one year. Purchases of such securities in 1963 fell to $1.5 billion and in 1964 to $1 billion. The bulk of the System's operations in 1965 was in Treasury bills. Through these years the Treasury raised most of the cash that it required through the sale of Treasury bills and purchased moderate amounts of long-term securities in the market.

The decline in Federal Reserve purchases of longer-term securities represented growing disillusionment with Operation Twist, for the following reasons. First, short- and long-term interest rates tend to move in the same direction over the long run. Short-term rates cannot increase by any significant amount without market arbitrage producing a sympathetic rise in long-term rates.

Second, attempts to keep long-term rates stable while short-term rates are rising involve the Federal Reserve System in pegging operations. Its ability to exercise credit control is thus impaired. Renewed pegging operations in this period proved disturbing to those who recalled the results of the pegging of the yield curve in 1941–1953 and the enormous political difficulties involved in withdrawing the peg.

Third, twist operations interfere with appropriate Federal debt management. When the government must finance its operations through the issuance of short-term obligations, a large increase in the floating debt occurs, thus producing an imbalance in debt maturities. From 1960–1964, when Operation Twist governed Federal Reserve and fiscal policies, debt maturities of less than one year increased from $70 billion to $81 billion. Despite this increase, the average maturity of the · marketable debt, because of advance refunding, rose from four years and four months to five years. Had the short-term debt not risen, the average maturity would have increased even more than it did.

Fourth, and finally, the effectiveness of increases solely in short-term interest rates in resolving balance of payments difficulties is questionable. Long-term capital flows are frequently larger than short-term flows and are not unaffected by measures specifically designed to raise short-term rates.

It is not the absolute level of interest rates that controls the international flow of funds but rather their level relative to those in other nations. With short-term rates, it is this differential plus or minus a forward premium or discount on the currency into which funds are moved that is controlling.[4]

Operation Twist was abandoned when it became apparent that credit availability in both the money and capital markets had to be reduced if inflationary pressures were to be checked. A significant step in this direction was the increase in the rediscount rate from 4 to 4.5 percent on December 6, 1965, which, as we shall see later, was vigorously opposed by the administration.

Despite its failure in the early 1960s, the Federal Reserve System revived Operation Twist in the first months of 1971. Again its policy was to raise short-term and lower long-term interest rates. The revived experiment was abandoned at the time of the debacle of the dollar (Chapter 17).

On the basis of the two experiments, it is coming to be recognized that long-term interest rates can not be substantially reduced by money market gimmicks. A lasting decline will be achieved only if people gain confidence in the long-term purchasing power of the dollar.

The Seductive Lure of Controls

Dominated in the early 1960s by the desire to prevent increases in the long-term rate of interest and later entangled in the web of the rising foreign exchange costs of the Vietnam war, the Kennedy-Johnson administrations, as goverments are wont to do under similar circumstances, fell back on a whole gamut of controls, directed particularly against foreign lending and investing. Controls which were initially voluntary became mandatory, those which were "strictly" temporary tended to become permanent, and those which were applied only to parts of the market were extended to the entire market. The elimination of controls, once they are established, proves politically difficult. Not only do nations hesitate to administer the bitter medicine of restrictive monetary and fiscal policy but the controls themselves often engender vested interests that battle for their continuation. A weak currency invites an ever expanding network.

Controls Adopted

The controls adopted in the 1960s were mainly directed towards curbing the use of American funds in foreign loans, in portfolio and direct investments. The foreign exchange costs of the Vietnam war, the maintenance of American troops abroad and tourist expenditures all continued to swell the growing volume of dollars held in foreign nations. To this total were added those dollars, in increasing amounts, seeking havens of monetary refuge.

Among the controls adopted were an Interest Equalization Tax, guidelines on foreign loans, and controls over direct investments. Initially recommended by President Kennedy on July 18, 1963, an Interest Equalization Tax was adopted by Congress as a "temporary" measure in September 1964. The tax was applied retroactively to July 19, 1963, to bonds issued, and to August 17, 1963, to securities listed on the national exchanges.[5] The law has been extended on various occasions but, unless extended again, will expire on March 31, 1973.

The Interest Equalization Tax applies to securities sold in the United States, capital markets by developed nations (except new Canadian issues),* and to long-term bank loans with a similar exemption. Initially, purchases by American citizens or residents were subject to a tax equivalent borrowing charge of 1 percent per annum. This was reduced in November 1969 to 0.75 percent. The rate of tax now ranges between 0.79 percent and 11.25 percent, depending on maturity, for acquisitions of debt obligations, including bank loans, with a period remaining to maturity of one year or more.

---

* The Canadian authorities vigorously opposed the application of the tax to Canada, pointing out that Canada must be exempt if trade and financial payments were to continue unimpeded between the two countries. Otherwise Canada might be forced to take retaliatory measures. An understanding was quickly reached with the Canadian government, exempting Canadian issues, provided that Canadian authorities agreed not to increase Canada's official reserves through borrowings in the United States. This in effect placed Canadian monetary reserves under the control of United States authorities, a result not altogether pleasing to Canadians. Mr. Donald B. Marsh of the Royal Bank of Canada pointed out (February 24, 1965) that if the reserves of Canada were to remain fixed in amount, Canada should of necessity adopt a floating rate of exchange. A nation could have flexible rates and fixed reserves, fixed rates and flexible reserves, but not fixed rates and fixed reserves.

The purpose of the measure was to raise the costs of borrowing intermediate- and long-term funds in the United States by the residents of developed nations, with the Administration selecting the nations to be considered developed and developing. Interest charges on foreign borrowings in the United States were to be raised and to be made equivalent to rates prevailing in Europe not through credit restriction, but by a tax levy. In consequence, it was believed that long-term rates in the domestic market would remain unchanged and the twisted interest rate curve would not change.

The same act that embodied the Interest Equalization Tax initially imposed a 15 percent purchase tax on the equities of firms located in the developed nations and sold in the United States. Subsequently the tax was raised to 18.75 percent and still later (April 4, 1969) it was lowered to 11.25 percent.

Major exemptions from the Interest Equalization Tax and the stock purchase tax included direct investments; investments in less developed nations; purchases from other U.S. holders; debt obligations acquired in connection with exports; and the purchase of original or new issues when the President of the United States determined that the application of the tax would have such consequences for a foreign nation as to imperil or threaten the stability of the international monetary system. Pursuant to this provision Canadian obligations were exempt, as were those bank loans made by foreign branches of U.S. banks to foreign borrowers.

Although Paul A. Volcker, Under-Secretary of the U.S. Treasury for Monetary Affairs, stated that the law provided important protection for the American balance of payments position, in particular when interest rates were relatively low in the United States,[6] it would be difficult to prove that it had had any but a minuscule effect. Foreigners were able to borrow American dollars in the Eurodollar market, swollen to gigantic size by the flight of funds from the United States. The Tax did not prove to be a substitute for monetary and credit policy, it simply created a psychological atmosphere in which action was postponed and inflationary pressures gained greater momentum than otherwise would have been the case. Nor did it succeed in holding down interest rates; domestic long-term rates in 1969 reached levels never before attained in the United States.

Lending and investment guidelines for banks and non-bank financial institutions were also issued. Although the Federal Reserve Bank of New York reported that the Interest Equalization Tax had held back some outflows of private capital, others accelerated.[7] In order to achieve a "decisive improvement," a new "temporary" program initiated by President Lyndon B. Johnson on February 19, 1965, put special emphasis on reducing capital outflows by use of voluntary restraints. Administration of the program was shared by the Reserve System and the U.S. Department of Commerce. The System, in cooperation with the Treasury, was made responsible for working with banking institutions. The Department of Commerce, also in cooperation with the Treasury, was given the task of working with non-bank financial institutions.

The purpose of the guidelines was not only to check the outflow of funds and to induce an inflow but also to promote American exports and to enhance opportunities for U.S. financial institutions to compete for export credits and foreign loans. In the attempt to accomplish these many purposes, a few initial rules have proliferated into lengthy and complicated regulations shot through with many exceptions. The guidelines for commercial banks, as revised on November 11, 1971, exempted export credits from control and, under a series of complicated rules, established a ceiling on non-export credits of about $9.7 billion.[8]

Funds advanced to residents of Canada continue to be exempt from the program, in return for which the Canadian Government has taken steps to ensure that Canadian financial institutions will not serve as a "pass through" for U.S. funds. In the granting of loans and the making of investments, banks and non-bank financial institutions, as well, were expected to give priority to developing countries. Banks were urged, too, to discourage customers from placing liquid funds outside the United States.

Regulations covering foreign direct investments have increased in length and complexity and have become progressively more rigid. These were initially part of a voluntary restraint program, but became mandatory on January 1, 1968. Three restraints are now placed on direct investments: annual limits on capital outflows plus reinvested earnings; limits on the total amount of investment each year to a percentage of the amount invested in the base period; and limits on the amount of short-term financial assets held abroad by direct investors.[9]

Finally, controls were extended to wages and prices. The issuance of wage and price guidelines to achieve the best of all possible worlds—rapid growth, low unemployment, low interest rates, and stable prices was proposed by the Council of Economic Advisers in 1962. The wage guidelines recommended that increases in hourly compensation be limited to the trend rate (3.5 percent a year) of the growth in productivity for the economy as a whole. The price guidelines called for stable prices in industries in which the productivity trend approximated the average rate for the economy. It called for price declines when productivity gains exceeded the average and it recognized the need for price increases when improvement was lower than average. The guideline proposals, which were "only rhetoric" in the President's 1962 *Economic Report,* had been translated into a specific formula in the 1964 report.[10] Violated with impunity by major industrial unions, battered by the airline strike settlement and by the general increase in steel prices in 1966,[11] the guidelines became a dim memory in Washington's political life. Even the Council of Economic Advisers admitted in its 1968 report that the guidelines had not been intended as a criterion of how the economy should behave, but rather, as reflection of how it was behaving.[12]

Unwilling to revive the guidelines that it regarded as ineffective, the Nixon Administration initially relied upon "inflation alerts." These were pronouncements deploring certain wage and price increases that had little value other than to subject the "guilty parties" to a type of moral suasion. Only when accompanied by an easing of import quotas, as in the case of oil, were such alerts important. But it was the easing of the quotas and not the alert which helped restrain inflation. Proving completely ineffective, inflation alerts were not revived when the dollar was in deep trouble in 1971. Instead, the Administration invoked direct controls over wages, prices and dividends (see Chapter 17).

Guidelines, income policies, and inflation alerts are effective only in a restrictive credit and fiscal environment. And then, as a British committee has pointed out, they are not necessary. Otherwise they are simply a form of incantation.[13]

Other Measures

Other efforts to reduce the deficit in the balance of payments included a long list of activities directed toward increasing exports, reducing imports and foreign travel, encouraging tourism in the United States, increasing domestic procurement by the military and economic-aid programs, encouraging foreign investments in the United States, and inducing foreign nations to pre-pay debts to the U.S. government. Some of the measures were frankly protectionist, for example, those that reduced the duty-free allowance on goods brought in by American tourists and tied American government overseas expenditures to American industry. The end result was to devalue the investment dollar, the foreign aid dollar, and the tourist dollar.

Protectionism, taking the form mainly of quota restrictions, resulting either from unilateral action or bilateral agreements, gained popular support among manufactures and trade unionists. The result was that in 1971 about 22 percent of the value of agricultural imports in the U.S. were subject to quotas, and about 17 percent of industrial imports. A discouraging feature of American trade policy is that the use of quantitative restrictions by the United States has been increasing, while their use by Japan and the European community has been declining.[14]

Some Observations

Reliance on economic controls represented a sharp departure from the liberal trading and investment policies of American administrations in the early postwar years. The policy then was to free currencies from the entangling web of exchange restrictions and to free trade from stultifying protectionism.

Controls imposed on one item act upon others. For example, controls imposed on investment operations reduce exports, causing nations to seek other sources of supply. They also result in declines in royalty payments, in the demand for replacement parts associated with particular investments and in the demand for services of American personnel. For purposes of formulating the regulations, the administration divided the nations of the world into three classes: the less developed, developed nations dependent upon capital inflow, and others. A glance at the nations included in each category convinces one that political considerations were not entirely absent in the classifications.[15]

Direct controls on international capital flows, warned the Joint Economic Committee in 1968, "should be ended, the sooner the better, since the very existence of such controls, whether mandatory or voluntary, kill the goose of investment that lays the golden egg of future investment earnings remitted to the United States." Furthermore, these controls, the committee pointed out, discriminate in favor of firms already heavily invested abroad as against new competitive investment. They build a wall to keep American capital from flowing into a more favorable investment climate. As each new loophole is discovered, a new restrictive measure, a new sentry, a new guardhouse, a new barbed-wire fence, has to be added.[16]

The interest equalization tax forced subsidiaries of American firms to obtain the funds that they required in foreign money markets, particularly in the Euro-dollar market. It forced development in the United States of a second securities market for new foreign securities. Until it was amended it impaired the competitive position of foreign branches of American banks. The overall net effect on the balance of payments was probably small. Europeans often sold existing holdings of American securities in order to purchase new issues of comparable American securities sold abroad at higher interest rates.

Controls on direct private investment and foreign lending were aimed at those items in the balance of payments that had over the years yielded a handsome return flow to the American economy. Earnings, management fees, and royalties—the results of the innovative dynamism of many American concerns—flowed back, strengthening the American dollar. Controls, however, weakened confidence in the dollar. Foreigners recognized that it was but a short step from controls on American-owned dollars to controls on foreign-held dollars. The "equilibrium in the U.S. balance of payments," declared the I.M.F. in 1968, "should, in the longer term, encompass a removal of capital controls in line with the necessary enlargement of the current account surplus." [17] The close relationship between capital movement and trade implies that as capital movements are freed from the shackles of control, so trade must also be freed.

ZIGZAGGING TOWARD HIGHER RATES

During the period when Operation Twist dominated Federal Reserve thinking, overall credit policy was quite expansive and continued so until 1965, when, as shown in Chart 15.1 the Reserve System began to move hesitantly and sporadically toward credit restriction. In the first half of 1965, 1966, and 1968, net free reserves were turned into net borrowed reserves of modest amounts in order to restrain the increase in bank credit, to moderate inflationary pressures, and to strengthen the dollar in the foreign exchanges.* The less restrictive policies which followed in the second halves of 1965 and 1966 and through 1967 were adopted in the effort to maintain Treasury financing on an even keel, to check possible recessionist tendencies, to support the mortgage market, to promote consumer buying, to mark time while awaiting the effects of a possible increase in tax rates, to escape the threat of a severe money-market crisis resulting from disintermediation, and to relieve occasional heavy pressures on pound sterling. Not until about May 1969 was pronounced restraint applied.[18] Even then the volume of member-bank borrowings was quite low in comparison, for example, with the totals attained in 1920.

Credit pressures through these years cannot be judged solely by the volume of net free and borrowed reserves (Chart 15.1). Commercial banks, in the face of

---

* In mid-1968 the Reserve System moved toward an easier policy in order to assist Treasury financing, which had the unfortunate result of stimulating a very rapid increase in the loans and innvestments of commercial banks. See *The Morgan Guaranty Survey*, October 1968.

Chart 15.1

EXCESS RESERVES AND BORROWINGS OF MEMBER BANKS

WEEKLY AVERAGES OF DAILY FIGURES

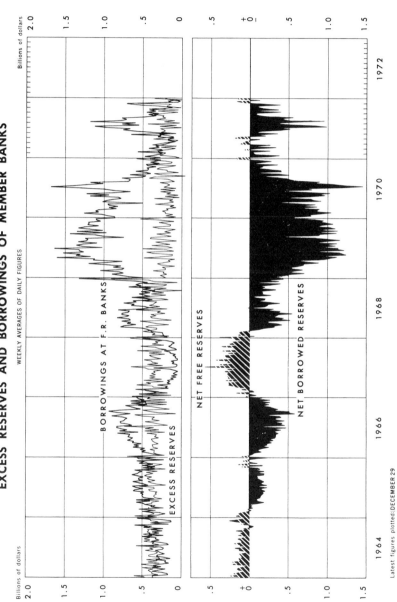

Latest figures plotted:DECEMBER 29

BOARD OF GOVERNORS OF THE FEDERAL RESERVE SYSTEM

heavy credit demands as customers activated unused lines of credit, were becoming increasingly dependent upon liability as opposed to asset management.

Through 1969 the reserve aggregates in the form of nonborrowed and total reserves, fell; the growth in bank credit and the money supply came to a virtual halt. The growing illiquidity of the banking system, reinforced by Federal Reserve restraint, forced interest rates in 1969 to probably the highest levels in the history of the United States. The prime lending rate rose to 8.5 percent which meant that, once adjustment was made for the cost of carrying compensating balances, the finest commercial risks paid as much as 10.5 percent on their borrowings.

In action taken on February 10, 1970, the Federal Open Market Committee broke with its tight money policy. By a vote of nine to three, the Committee directed that open market operations "until the next meeting . . . be conducted with a view to moving gradually toward somewhat less firm conditions in the money market." [19] This directive replaced the one adopted on January 15, which called for the maintenance of firm conditions in the money market.[20] Short-term money market rates responded fairly quickly to the change in policy; long-term rates responded only after a considerable lag (Charts 15.2 and 15.3). On July 27, 1971, in view of the extraordinarily large balance of payments deficit, the Federal Open Market Committee adopted a directive for a more moderate growth in monetary aggregates. This directive remained in force until the close of the year when the Reserve System, believing that the new economic controls would check inflation, once again veered towards an easier money policy, (see Chapter 17).

Not since the latter part of the decade of the 1920s had monetary policy shifted so rapidly from ease to restraint and back again. Monetary policy, as reflected in changes in net free and net borrowed reserves, shifted in late 1965, again in 1966, 1967, 1968, 1970 and in 1971 (see Chart 15.1).[21] The reasons for the policy shifts and the impact of these shifts on discount-rate policy form the discussion of the succeeding sections of this chapter.

The Discount Rate

Changes in the discount rate from 1964 to 1971, along with fluctuations in long- and short-term interest rates, are shown in Charts 15.2 and 15.3. The first increase in the discount rate became effective on July 17, 1963, when seven Federal Reserve banks were permitted, by a vote of three-to-one of the Board, to increase their rates from 3 to 3.5 percent. The other Federal Reserve banks quickly followed.

Chart 15.2

SHORT-TERM INTEREST RATES

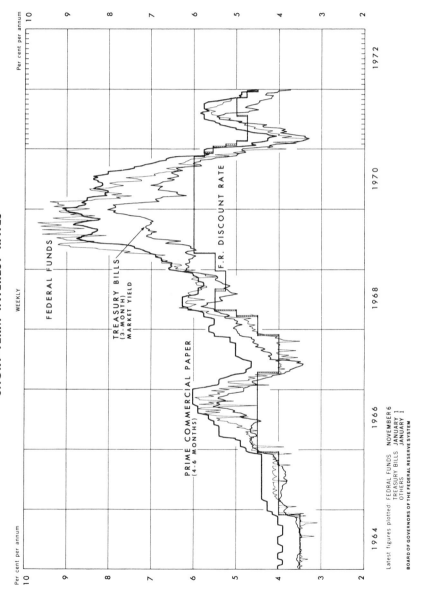

WEEKLY

Per cent per annum

Per cent per annum

FEDERAL FUNDS

TREASURY BILLS
(3-MONTH)
MARKET YIELD

PRIME COMMERCIAL PAPER
(4-6 MONTHS)

F.R. DISCOUNT RATE

1964   1966   1968   1970   1972

Latest figures plotted FEDERAL FUNDS   NOVEMBER 6
                        TREASURY BILLS   JANUARY 1
                        OTHERS   JANUARY 1
BOARD OF GOVERNORS OF THE FEDERAL RESERVE SYSTEM

Chart 15.3

BOND YIELDS

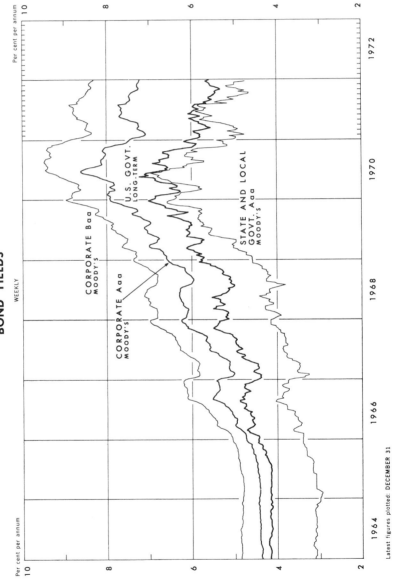

WEEKLY

CORPORATE Baa
MOODY'S

CORPORATE Aaa
MOODY'S

U.S. GOVT.
LONG-TERM

STATE AND LOCAL
GOVT. Aaa
MOODY'S

Per cent per annum

1964   1966   1968   1970   1972

This step, which was really part of Operation Twist, had been anticipated when the Federal Open Market Committee on December 18, 1962, by a vote of seven to five, directed the Federal Reserve Bank of New York "to accommodate moderate further increases in bank credit and the money supply, while aiming at money market conditions that would minimize capital outflows internationally." [22] The System hoped that this action, plus a modest reduction in net free reserves, would stay the outflow of short-term funds without putting pressure on long-term rates or restraining domestic growth. The action was mild. Net free reserves continued to exceed the levels prevailing at comparable periods of cyclical expansion in the 1950s.

The next rise became effective November 24, 1964, when five Federal Reserve banks increased their discount rates from 3.5 to 4 percent. By the end of the month all the other Reserve banks had taken similar action. This increase followed by a matter of hours an announcement by the Bank of England of an increase in its rate from 5 to 7 percent and was designed to preserve the strength of the dollar internationally and to counter possible capital outflows from the United States.

The increase in the balance-of-payments deficit in the second and third quarters of 1964 caused the Federal Open Market Committee, as early as August 18, to direct the Federal Reserve Bank of New York to maintain slightly firmer conditions in the money market. The directive, adopted by a vote of six to five, followed increases in the sensitive price indexes, a rapid rise in the money supply, and a deterioration in the international economic situation. The increase in the loans of commercial banks had accelerated. Their holdings of short-term government securities had fallen, and their liquidity had been reduced.

It was the next increase, from 4 to 4.5 percent, effective December 6, 1965, at the New York and Chicago Federal Reserve banks, that aroused the ire of the administration. The request for the increase had been approved by the Board by a vote of four to three and was followed shortly by similar requests from other Reserve banks. Within hours after the rate increase, President Johnson expressed regret that action had been taken "that raises the cost of credit, particularly for homes, schools, hospitals and factories." A week earlier Secretary of the Treasury Henry H. Fowler, had publicly warned against a rise in interest rates.[23]

President Johnson charged that the action was premature and should have been deferred until one had the "full facts on next year's budget, Vietnam costs, housing starts, state and local spending and other elements in the economic outlook."

In an unprecedented press release, the Board (or at least a majority of the

Board) explained that its action had been taken because of rapid increases in debt (particularly in the form of business loans) rising money-market pressures, growing tightness in manpower and productive capacity, and increasing military demands. The Board's action would, it was hoped, counter inflationary pressures, bolster the government's program to overcome persistent deficits in the balance of payments, and demonstrate anew the determination of the United States to maintain the international position of the dollar.*

The minority had voted against the rise on the ground that the Federal fiscal position would prove less stimulating than anticipated, that balance-of-payments pressures were receding, that monetary policy was already sufficiently tight, and that action should be delayed pending better coordination of monetary and fiscal policy. The majority pointed out that every effort had been made to obtain policy coordination, that all of the facts on fiscal developments in early 1966 were available, and that an independent Federal Reserve System should use its best judgment.

The discount rate remained at 4.5 percent until April 7, 1967, when it was lowered to 4 percent. An attempt on July 14, 1966, by four Federal Reserve banks, including the New York bank, to break away from the pegged rate of 4.5 percent, when all interest rates were rising sharply, and to increase the discount rate to 5 percent was vetoed by the Board of Governors. Subsequent recommendations by as many as seven Reserve banks were disapproved by the Board. Two would have raised discount rates to 5.5 percent. Concern about rising inflationary pressures, the international position of the dollar, and the absence of fiscal restraint had prompted these recommendations. Refusal to permit increases by the Board of Governors followed within a few months its severe castigation by President Johnson. The Reserve banks were closely in tune with economic developments; the Board felt the full brunt of political pressures. The gap between discount and market rates widened, contributing to uncertainties in the credit markets and generating difficulties in discount-window administration.

Business Loans the Culprit

The Board of Governors, unwilling to sanction an increase in discount rates, fell back on moral suasion in an attempt to reduce inflationary pressures. It seemed to regard business loans, regardless of purpose, as the chief inflationary

---

* The possibility of an increase in the discount rate had been discussed at a meeting of the Federal Open-Market Committee on the 23rd of November.

culprit. This point of view was quite opposite to that held during the price inflations of 1919 and the Korean war. Then business loans were encouraged, and other loans were discouraged.

Despite three increases in the prime rate, business loans increased during the first seven months of 1966 at an annual rate of more than 20 percent. This rapid rise resulted from an acceleration of corporate income-tax payments in March 1966 and from anticipatory borrowing by business firms in an environment marked by credit uncertainties. In an effort to moderate this expansion, Reserve bank presidents, in a letter dated September 1, 1966, urged member banks to hold down the rate of business-loan expansion, apart from normal seasonal needs, and to use the discount window in a manner consistent with this goal.[24] Cooperating member banks, the statement implied, would receive sympathetic treatment at the policed discount window.

The Board's displeasure with the increase in business loans was intensified by the fact that it was being financed partly through liquidation of municipal securities and curtailment of nonbusiness lending. A Board member described loans on securities, loans to sales-finance companies and to consumers for durable-goods purchases, along with construction and mortgage loans as types of lending that had suffered in competition with business borrowers. The letter, which had little or no effect and which must be regarded as a curious aberration in credit policy, was withdrawn on December 27, 1966. The monetary authorities, in adhering rigidly to a 4.5 percent rate, had really "discarded the discount rate as an instrument of quantitative credit policy and as an indicator of Federal Reserve objectives." [25]

Reserve Requirements

Unwilling to allow discount rates to be increased in the middle of 1966, the Reserve System took refuge in various substitute measures. One of these which we have mentioned was the pressure brought to bear on member banks to reduce the volume of their business loans. Another consisted of increases in reserve requirements. On June 24, 1966, the Board acted to increase reserve requirements from 4 to 5 percent on time deposits in excess of $5 million, thus sequestering $420 million of reserve funds. Again on August 17, it announced a further increase, from 5 to 6 percent, impounding an additional $450 million. Both increases were designed to restrain issues of time certificates of deposit, to discourage reliance upon such certificates as a basis for credit expansion, and to induce member banks to restrict consumer loans and to husband their liquid assets. This action, in effect, recognized the money market character of the certificates. Not over a thousand banks fell subject to these requirements—namely those which had been most active in issuing large-denomination certificates.

Disintermediation

The sharp increase in open-market interest rates in 1966, coupled with controls imposed on interest rates allowed to be paid by commercial banks and savings institutions on time and savings accounts gave rise to a phenomenon known as "disintermediation." Strictly defined, "disintermediation" is the reversal of intermediation and is a term used to describe the process of withdrawing savings funds from financial intermediaries for direct placement in the securities markets. Its usage has been broadened to include the shifting of funds from one type of financial institution to another in order to benefit by differences in interest rates and to include, too, the short-circuiting of financial institutions in order to place funds directly in the security markets.

Disintermediation caused an absolute decline in the funds available to savings-and-loan associations and to mutual-savings banks. Contractual-savings institutions did not suffer to the same extent. The inflow of funds to life-insurance companies continued, although policy loans rose rather sharply. The Reserve System made special arrangements which were not used, to provide emergency credit assistance to nonmember depository-type financial institutions that might experience large deposit drains.[26]

The eight large money-market banks in New York City were acute victims of disintermediation. Through the postwar period their share in the total deposits of all member banks had declined; their share in business loans had remained about the same. Their share in deposit totals would have fallen even more had they not vigorously pushed the sale of negotiable certificates of deposit. As liquidity fell to a "historically low point," they were "less well-equipped to handle an oncoming barrage of credit requests than they had been at any previous time during the postwar period."[27]

Negotiable certificates of deposit remained the larger banks' major source of new lendable funds. The maximum interest rate under Regulation Q had been increased in December 1965 to a flat 5.5 percent for all maturities of more than thirty days. This rate remained competitive with open-market rates until about August 1966, when, because of soaring open-market rates, the CDs lost their investor appeal and did not regain their competitive position until the end of the year.

In the interim, the CD liabilities of the large New York City Banks fell $2.1 billion. To meet the double drain of deposit loss and loan demand these banks were compelled to reduce their security holdings, to borrow heavily in the Federal-funds and Eurodollar markets, and to sell certificates of deposit in Europe. They made little use of the discount window, for they were unwilling to have their lending and portfolio adjustments subjected to Federal Reserve scrutiny. The Federal-funds rate soared far above the discount rate.*

In its *Report for 1966,* the Federal Reserve Bank of New York stated:

> Against this background of sharply rising interest rates, falling bond prices, and a heavy calendar of forthcoming issues, there developed something of an atmosphere of impending crisis. Sellers in the securities markets found dealers very reluctant to bid, and new issues moved very slowly even at sharply higher offering yields. Market participants were increasingly concerned over the chance that even more severe pressures might develop—especially if banks began to experience, at the September tax rate, a sizable loss of CD funds.[28]

To prevent a money-market crisis, the Reserve banks purchased securities in sufficient volume to cause a sharp decline in net borrowed reserves during the second half of 1966 (see Chart 15.1). After reaching a peak in the early autumn, open-market rates declined rapidly. Interest rates would not have soared had the Federal Reserve System shifted toward restraint in 1964, a year marked by a sharp increase in the deficit in the balance of payments. But 1964 was the year of the tax cut. The increase in the discount rate as late as December 1965 was condemned so vigorously by the administration that in 1966 the Board did not permit a majority of the Reserve banks, that wished to do so, to raise discount rates as open-market rates escalated (see Chart 15.2). The System continued to underwrite rapid credit increases in an overheated economy.

The credit crunch would have been less severe had the Federal Reserve Board raised the maximum permissible rates on CDs. During the crisis itself the Board not only refused to raise the 5.5 percent ceiling on large CDs, but actually lowered to 5 percent the ceiling on time deposits of less than $100,000 as well. The refusal to raise rates on large CDs was intended to "cool" the inflationary boom in plant and equipment expenditures, and the lowering of the rate on small CDs was

---

* In the second half of 1965 heavy defense orders were superimposed on a capital-goods boom. Corporate income-tax payments accelerated, and corporations were required to speed up payments of taxes withheld to the Treasury. Banks had to borrow heavily over the tax payment dates in 1966, thus in effect borrowing on behalf of the United States Treasury.

intended to ease the pressure on savings-and-loan associations and mutual-savings banks. Not until April 19, 1968, under threat of another sharp disintermediation, were maximum rates on large CDs raised as high as 6.25 percent.

Many observers concluded that the regulation of interest rates paid by various competing institutions in order to govern their relative growth or the ultimate use of their funds is undesirable. Better leave these determinations to the impersonal forces of the market place! [29]

Expansionist Policy in 1967

Inventory liquidation, a leveling-off in consumer demand for durable goods, a decline in residential construction and capital expenditures induced the Reserve System to follow a less restrictive policy in 1967. During this minirecession net free reserves were increased sharply and discount rates beginning in April were lowered to 4 percent. Reinforcing this action, reserve requirements against all savings deposits and against the first $5 million of time deposits were lowered in two stages from 4 to 3 percent, thus releasing $850 million of reserve funds. In view of continued inflationary pressures, high employment, cost-push escalation, a worsening deficit in the balance of payments, and a sharp increase in the Federal deficit, the easier money policy scarcely seemed justified. A shift to a more restrictive monetary policy after the middle of the year was made difficult, the Federal Reserve Bank of New York explained, by the Treasury's very heavy financing program for the second half of the year. In addition, the Reserve System sought to avoid hindering passage of the proposed tax surcharge and putting further pressure on the pound.[30]

In any event, the lower rate proved shortlived. Within two to nine days after the devaluation of the British pound (November 18, 1967), the Board approved increases from 4 to 4.5 percent in the discount rates at all Reserve banks.* This action was followed in January by an increase ordered by the Board of Governors, on December 27, 1967, in reserve requirements against demand deposits in excess of $5 million; from 16.5 to 17 percent at reserve-city banks and from 12 to 12.5 percent at other member banks. These changes impounded $550 million of reserve funds. The purpose of this action was to reduce the volume of bank funds available for loans and investments, to check inflationary pressures, and to help restore equilibrium in the balance of payments.

---

* The Bank of England increased the Bank rate to 8 percent, the highest level in fifty-three years. Following the devaluation of sterling, the Federal Reserve System purchased a substantial volume of government securities to remove the overhang from the market. The Federal Reserve Bank of New York recommended an increase to 5 percent.

With the dollar falling subject to increased pressures and with waning expectations of the adoption of the President's fiscal program, discount rates were raised to 5 percent at all Reserve banks in March 1968 and to 5.5 percent in April. (The gold crisis induced the Federal Reserve Bank of New York to recommend an increase to 6 percent.) These increases were accompanied by a more restrictive open-market policy. Against the background of the weakening position of the dollar abroad and its loss of purchasing power at home, a gold "hemorrhage," rapidly rising interest rates, and IMF insistence that the United States take remedial action, the administration was in no position to offer opposition. It contented itself with the belief that once tax rates had been raised interest rates might stabilize or even decline.

Convinced that the passage of the Revenue and Expenditure Control Act in June 1968 would reduce consumer spending, check the increase in bank credit, and ease inflationary pressures—and wishing to avoid action that would lead to an economic "overkill"—the Board of Governors approved a reduction in discount rates to 5.25 percent in late August 1968. (The Federal Reserve Bank of New York opposed this decrease and continued during October and November to urge a more restrictive policy.) This action, preceded by an expansive open-market policy, reflected expectations that the tax surcharge would lead immediately to lower interest rates. But, to the consternation of many forecasters, bank loans, interest rates, and prices continued to rise, with the result that, after some hesitation, the Open-Market Committee finally decided at a meeting on December 17, 1968, to move toward monetary restraint,[31] an action which was marked by an increase in discount rates from 5.25 to 5.50 percent.

SKYROCKETING INTEREST RATES

An initial policy of moderate restraint yielded to action placing member banks under greater pressure in 1969 than in 1966. Net borrowed reserves (Chart 15.1) rose as high as $1.1 billion, more than twice the amount attained in the earlier year. Pressures were quickly communicated, through the Federal-funds market, to banks in all parts of the country.

The pressures would have been much greater had the Reserve System not engaged in large open-market operations. The increase in open-market holdings from January 1 to December 24, 1969, amounted to $4,410 million, which was sufficient to offset the effect on member-bank reserves of the increase of money in circulation ($3,019 million), of a substantial rise in Treasury deposits with the Federal Reserve banks ($826 million), and of a decline in other Federal Reserve assets ($487 million)—mainly holdings of sterling exchange. Member-bank borrowings at Reserve Banks, which rose as high as $1.6 billion in the summer of 1969, were still slightly less than the total at the end of 1952 and considerably less than the total at the end of 1920 ($2.7 billion).* The total volume of member-bank borrowing is, of course, not the sole measure of the restrictiveness of Federal Reserve policy. We must also consider other policies currently in force including the administration of the discount window, which was apparently more restrictive in 1969 than it had been in 1920.

Skyrocketing interest rates not only reflected Federal Reserve credit policies, but also the continued rapid increases in loan demand and concurrent declines in total deposit liabilities. The two in combination subjected commercial banks, which lacked shiftable assets in large volume, to an unprecedentedly severe drain. In consequence the resulting credit crunch was much more severe than that of 1966. The sale of $10 billion of U.S. securities by commercial banks equaled only one-third of the increases in loans. The balance of the funds required to meet the loan demand was obtained by increases in nondeposit liabilities which the Reserve System endeavored to limit by various restrictive measures. In order to obtain nondeposit funds, commercial banks established numerous foreign branches and organized one-bank holding companies.[32]

Supporting Measures

In addition to an open-market policy, which increased member-bank indebtedness, other actions by the Reserve System in 1969 included, first an increase early in April 1969 in discount rates to 6 percent, the highest in forty years. Despite this rise the discount rate in the United States remained equal to or below those in a number of industrial nations. At the end of 1969 the discount rate in Belgium was 7.5, in Canada 8 percent, in France 8 percent, in Germany 6 percent, in Japan 6.25 percent, in Sweden 7 percent, and in the United Kingdom 8 percent. A higher discount rate would seem to have been justified in the United States in view of continued inflationary pressures and the grave liquidity deficit ($7.2 billion) in its balance of payments in 1969. Actually, because of controls at the discount window, the Federal Reserve discount rate lost importance as a credit-rationing instrument. The Federal funds rate, which averaged 8.2 percent, and

---

* It was much lower in relative terms. At the end of 1920 member-bank borrowing had been 16 percent of total loans and investments. Had the same relationship prevailed in 1969, member-bank borrowing would have risen to $51 billion. We are not suggesting that they should have been forced to this level but include the figure simply as a crude measure of the relative severity of Federal Reserve policy.

borrowing rates on Eurodollars, which rose as high as 13 percent, became the effective "discount rate."

Several Federal Reserve Banks through 1969 requested still further increases in their discount rates. The Federal Reserve Bank of Boston requested an increase to 6.5 percent (June 16, 1969); the Federal Reserve Bank of St. Louis to 7 percent (May 22); the Federal Reserve Bank of Chicago to 7 percent (June 12, June 26 and July 24); and the Federal Reserve Bank of Kansas City to 7 percent (July 10). All requests were denied. Requests by the Federal Reserve Banks for higher discount rates and refusal by the Federal Reserve Board had occurred under similar circumstances in 1929. In each year, 1929 and 1969, the requests seemed amply warranted. Their denial forced recourse to other less appropriate action.

The second action was a rise of .5 percent in member-bank reserve requirements against demand deposits, effective April 17, 1969. This step increased the required reserves of member banks by $650 million, "with about $375 million of that total occurring at large city banks where pressures from CD drains were already causing strains on liquidity positions." [33]

The third action of the Reserve System was the inclusion of "London checks" in gross demand deposits. In a ruling effective July 31, 1969, the Board of Governors redefined gross-demand deposits to include certain bank-deposit liabilities arising from Eurodollar transactions. In other words, the Board made it clear that gross-demand deposits, as redefined, included checks and drafts drawn by or on behalf of the foreign branches of member banks on accounts maintained by such branches with the domestic offices of the parent bank. It was estimated that this action increased gross demand deposits by $3.3 billion and required reserves by about $600 million." [34]

The fourth action, also effective October 16, 1969, was a 10 percent marginal reserve requirement placed on the net borrowings of member banks from their own foreign branches to the extent that such borrowings exceeded the amount outstanding in a base period. The purpose of this amendment to Regulations D and M, which increased required reserves by an estimated $415 million,[35] was to limit the special advantage that banks with access to Eurodollars had in adjusting to domestic credit restraint.[36] Later, effective on December 23, 1970, the Board of Governors raised from 10 to 20 percent the reserves that member banks must hold against Eurodollar borrowings that exceeded the reserve-free base.[37] The purpose of this stipulation was not to discourage Eurodollar borrowings (the reason for the earlier regulations), but rather, to discourage their repayment below the reserve-free base. The repayment of Eurodollar borrowings increased the dollar assets of foreign central banks and their claim on the reserve assets of the U.S. Treasury (see Chapter 14).

The fifth action, effective September 4, 1969, saw the term deposit redefined to include with exceptions, any promissory note acknowledgement of advance, due bill, or similar instrument that was issued by a member-bank principally as a means of obtaining funds to be used in its banking business.[38] This action increased required reserves by about $180 million.

The final action, following the enactment of appropriate legislation by the Congress (December 23, 1969), permitted the Board of Governors to apply reserve requirements to the funds received by member banks resulting from the sale of commercial paper issued by bank affiliates. Although a few banks had issued such paper in 1968, it was not until the credit crunch of 1969 that the development gained rapid momentum, when nearly 50 banks were active in the market. In early June 1969, the outstanding amount of bank-related commercial paper was estimated by the Board of Governors at $860 million. By the end of October, the amount had grown to $3.7 billion and by July 1970, to $7.8 billion. With the suspension on June 24, 1970, of interest rate ceilings on CDs, the volume declined rapidly, falling to about $1.9 billion by the end of 1971.

Believing that "commercial bank exploitation of non-deposit funds . . . could subvert the System's policy of restraint," and concluding that the issuance of such paper "represented a blatant evasion of Regulations D and G by the banks," besides leading to a "fragmentation of the banking system," the Board decided, once authorization had been granted by Congress, to apply reserve requirements to bank-related commercial paper.[39]

The imposition of a 5 percent reserve requirement on bank-related commercial paper, effective September 17, 1970, was accompanied by a reduction in member-bank reserve requirements on time deposits in excess of $5 million from 6 to 5 percent, effective October 1, 1970. The inconsistency of these actions, which released about $350 million of reserve funds, arose from the desire to increase over a long-term the basic effectiveness of reserve requirements, while in the short-run, to release funds to a market beset by money market uncertainties resulting from a gigantic bankruptcy.

The unexpected collapse of the Penn Central Transportation Company (June 31, 1970) provoked a run on the commercial paper market. In three weeks non-bank paper fell by $3 billion or by almost 10 percent. Federal Reserve discount policy was immediately liberalized to assure the availability of funds to banks and their customers. Banks were informed that "as they made loans to enable their customers to pay off maturing commercial paper, and thus needed more reserves, the Federal Reserve discount window would be available." [40]

The restrictive measures adopted by the Reserve System were doubtless responsible for the leveling-off of total loans and investments on the books of large commercial banks, following a strong upward trend over the preceding eight years. This leveling-off was accompanied by significant changes in asset composition. Total loans in 1969 increased $11 billion, or about 7 percent, and investments fell $8 billion, or about 12 percent. The increase in loans resulted mainly from a rise in commercial and industrial loans (about half of which were term loans) and by a lesser rise in real-estate loans, consumer instalment loans, and loans to financial institutions.

The increase in commercial and industrial loans resulted from a rise in inventory investment and from expenditures on producers' durable equipment. A decline in corporate liquidity forced business firms to rely heavily on borrowed funds obtained from banks, insurance companies, or the commercial-paper market.

Not only the commercial banks, but financial intermediaries as well felt the pressure of monetary policy. Increases in the savings capital of savings-and-loan associations slowed perceptibly, with the result that they had to rely heavily on borrowed funds to meet their mortgage commitments. Mutual-savings banks experienced slowdowns in deposit totals. Life-insurance companies were forced to devote increasing amounts of their cash inflow to policy loans.[41]

Reliance on liability management, a characteristic feature of the late 1960s, not only tended to remove bank operations from the control of the regulatory authorities, which weakened the power of the Reserve System to control the volume and use of credit, but also undermined the confidence of those who relied on the money supply as a precise determinant of monetary policy. Definitions of money changed as banking practices altered.

DESCENDING FROM THE ALPINE HEIGHTS

The expansion phase of the business cycle of the 1960s, 105 months, was the longest on record. It began in February 1961 and ended in November 1969. The contraction which then set in, lasted, according to present estimates, but 12 months, terminating in November 1970.

Except for a decline in 1967, the Treasury bill rate rose steadily in the expansion phase, from 2.4 percent in 1961 to 6.7 percent in 1969. Corporate bond yields, reflecting the effect of Operation Twist, did not begin to increase until

1964. Once the increase set in, they rose rapidly, overtaking the bill rate in the middle of 1970 (Charts 15.2 and 15.3). By December 1971, the Treasury bill rate had fallen to 4 percent and the corporate bond rate (Aaa) to 7.25 percent. This disparity reflected the deep-rooted conviction of continuing inflation.

Aside from the steepness of both the rise and the subsequent decline, short-term interest rate behavior was quite similar to that in other cycles. This, however, was not true of all indexes. The consumer price index, which in other post-war recessions had stabilized or risen slowly, continued a sharp increase. Wholesale prices followed a similar course. Wages and salaries, which fell in other recessions, stabilized in the contraction phase (1970) and then renewed the previous sharp increase. Per capita disposable personal income continued to rise. In other recessions it had leveled off. Compensation of employees as a percent of national income continued on a high plateau. Labor cost per unit of output continued the rise which began in 1965. These few indexes reflected the persistence of cost-push as an inflationary factor, which itself was abetted by huge federal deficits, greatly exceeding those of other post-war cycles.

The overriding differences between this and previous periods of contraction and expansion were not only the persistence of cost-push, but also, as an accompanying phenomenon, the decline in net exports of goods and services and the huge deficits which resulted from trade and other factors in the balance of payments. The weakening of the dollar at a time when employment, contrary to the situation in previous post-war periods of contraction and expansion, had shown no cyclical increase (1971-1972) confronted the Federal Reserve System with some of the most difficult policy decisions in its history. The dilemma was finally "resolved" by suspending convertibility and adopting price and wage controls (Chapter 17).

The directives of the Federal Open Market Committee through 1970, although often ambivalent and subject to diverse interpretations, were pointed in the direction of less firm conditions in the money market. The first such directive was issued on the 10th of February 1970. Despite the fact that prices and costs were rising at a rapid rate and the balance of payments had been in substantial deficit, the majority of the Committee voted to move towards less firm money market conditions and to promote a moderate growth in money and credit. Those who opposed the resolution (including Mr. Alfred Hayes, President of the Federal Reserve Bank of New York), felt that any easing of interest rates was premature, mindful as they were of the strength of inflationary expectations and the prospectively large balance of payments deficit.

Through the remainder of 1970 much the same type of directive was voted. That of March 10, 1970, which advocated an "orderly reduction" in the rate of inflation, "sustainable" economic growth and "reasonable equilibrium" in the balance of payments may be taken as typical. Occasionally, directives as that of April 7, 1970, called attention to the need to support Treasury financing. The directive issued on the 18th of August, with three dissents, called for even more vigorous expansion, as did that of the 15th of September.

The directives, as indicated above, did not enlist unanimous support. Mr. Alfred Hayes dissented on four occasions, Mr. Darryl R. Francis, President of the Federal Reserve Bank of St. Louis, on three, Mr. Andrew F. Brimmer, a member of the Board of Governors, on two. At the meeting held on October 20, Mr. Hayes opposed further easing of conditions in the credit markets because it implied a persistent push towards lower interest rates, irrespective of market forces. Mr. Francis also dissented apparently on the ground that the proposed policies put misguided emphasis on the importance of increases in bank credit and would not achieve what he regarded as an optimum increase in the money stock. Mr. Brimmer dissented mainly by reason of the inflationary pressure which might result from the policies proposed.

In its *Annual Report for 1970* the Board of Governors admitted that progress toward containing the rate of inflation had been slow (p. 15), and that wage pressures continued strong despite "a weakening in demand for labor" (p. 14). The long-term investment boom which "had persisted with only minor interruptions since the early 1960's" had ended (p. 9); the consumer continued bearish (p. 34); "the traditional U.S. trade surplus had weakened" (p. 53).

In the early part of 1971, the Federal Open Market Committee emphasized the need to further expand monetary aggregates and to reduce interest rates particularly long-term rates. To do so the Reserve Banks began buying intermediate and long-term obligations.[42] The directive for April 6, 1971, continued this policy. It was opposed by Mr. Hayes who, in view of the international financial situation, saw the desirability of higher short-term rates.

European developments caused the Committee, beginning with its meeting on May 11, 1971, to direct more attention to the international situation. The German mark and the Dutch guilder had been permitted to float, the Swiss franc and the Austrian schilling were revalued (Chapter 17). In consequence the directive called for a "moderate" growth in monetary and credit aggregates.[43] The same directive was adopted on June 8 and June 29. To support this newer, more restrictive policy, discount rates were increased in mid-July by one-fourth of a percentage point to 5 percent.

Following the legal suspension of convertibility of the American dollar in August and the adoption of the freeze on wages and prices (see Chapter 17), the Reserve System once again began to move towards easier conditions in the money market. Open-market operations converted net borrowed reserves, which totaled $658 million in July 1971, to net free reserves of $48 million in December. Discount rates were reduced in two steps, on November 19 and December 13, from 5 to 4.5 percent.

The Government's new economic program (Chapter 17) had, according to the Federal Open Market Committee, "reduced inflationary expectations" [44] and presumably relieved the Reserve System of the need to direct its monetary policy towards this goal. Federal Reserve policy, in consequence, veered sharply towards easier money market conditions. In testifying before the Joint Economic Committee, Dr. Arthur F. Burns stated that the Reserve System had in recent months sought a faster rate of monetary expansion and did not intend to allow the present recovery to falter for want of money and credit.[45] He took exception to those who asserted that higher short-term rates were needed to encourage a reflux of dollars from Europe.

During the months (December 1969 to December 1971) that the Reserve System, with temporary interruptions, followed an easy money policy, their holdings of U.S. Securities increased by $12 billion. This increase financed the rise of money in circulation, ($7.5 billion) and brought about an increase in total member-bank reserves of over $3 billion. Moreover, the process reduced member-bank borrowings at the Reserve Banks by almost $1 billion. Net excess reserves emerged in modest amount.

Commercial banks expanded their loans and investments by $90 billion or by nearly 21 percent in two years. The increase took the form mainly of a rise in holdings of U.S. and municipal securities, and of consumer and real estate loans. Commercial and industrial loans reflected a much smaller rate of increase, about 6 percent.

The offsetting liabilities to the large increase in earning assets ($90 billion) consisted of an increase in demand deposits of $18 billion, of CDs of $22 billion and of other time deposits of $53 billion. The increase in demand deposits, through 1970 and 1971, of about 11 percent, plus a continuing rapid increase in deposit turnover did not justify a pronounced easy money policy. Ample purchasing power was available to finance a large increase in business activity.

The year 1971 ended with basic economic problems unresolved. This situation was the result, in part, of the insistence of the majority of the Federal Open Market Committee, that downward pressure be applied to interest rates. Overlooked was the fact that basic conditions had changed. Unemployment was more structural than cyclical. Trade unions had become instruments of great monopolistic economic power. Cost push proved a dominating force. The money supply was increased to validate resulting wage and price escalations. American management had lost its innovative drive, and workers seemed no longer imbued with the "Puritan ethic." Psychological attitudes boded ill for sustainable economic expansion. These attitudes found reflection in the benign neglect accorded the deficit in the balance of payments. Among the members of the Federal Open Market Committee, Mr. Alfred Hayes was virtually alone in accentuating this weakness in American economic development. In general, Washington opinion seemed to hold that foreign central banks had no choice but to support the dollar.

SELECTIVE CREDIT CONTROL

Margin Requirements

Margin requirements, the only type of selective credit control now used by the Board of Governors, fluctuated between 50 and 90 percent through the 1960s. Following a sharp drop in stock-market credit and an abatement of speculative psychology, initial margin requirements were reduced from 70 to 50 percent on July 10, 1962. Somewhat more than a year later (November 6, 1963), following a sharp increase in customers' debit balances, initial requirements were again raised to 70 percent. Debit balances fluctuated without showing a definite trend until 1967, when sharp increases brought a further rise in margin requirements, to 80 percent on June 8, 1968. The increase would doubtlessly have been ordered earlier were it not for the fact that customers' debt balances in 1967 were being financed not so much from bank borrowing but rather from the use of customers' free credit balances. On March 11, 1968, a new margin requirement of 50 percent on convertible bonds was established; it was raised to 60 percent three months later. A very sharp decline in stock prices and in the use of credit for stock purchases, caused the Board of Governors, effective May 6, 1970, to reduce margin requirements on purchasing or carrying stocks from 80 to 65 percent and on purchasing, or carrying convertible bonds from 60 to 50 percent. On December 3, 1971, margin requirements on stocks were further reduced to 55 percent. Total customer credit had been declining and stock prices were sluggish.

Although beginning in November 1963 and continuing through the 1960s, initial margin requirements were 70 percent or higher; the proportion of margin debt in accounts with margins below this level has been substantial. Even in periods when stock prices have been rising rapidly, nearly half of the outstanding debt was margined at less than 70 percent.[46] Regulations of the New York Stock Exchange prevent firms from allowing such customers' equity to fall below 25 percent (the maintenance margin). Most brokers require additional margin before that level is reached.

Accounts with thin margins have always been a danger to the market. Slight declines in stock prices can lead to margin calls, which if not met cause forced sales of securities, which in turn may cause a collapse in stock prices, thereby triggering widespread demand for additional margin. These developments may have strong adverse effects on consumer and business sentiment and may be reflected in cyclical declines in consumer buying and industrial activity, as in 1929.

After many years of experience with enforcement of margin requirements, the Board of Governors is convinced that this credit sector is a particularly appropriate one for selective credit control. It is an area that is reasonably definable in terms of the purposes of loans, the collateral used, and the nature of loan contracts. It is important enough in terms of size and volatility so that regulation can help to reinforce general credit controls.*

The Board of Governors has, on the whole, administered the requirements not only flexibly but also in sympathetic understanding of stock-exchange needs and of the whole complex of monetary controls. Changes in margin requirements have, over a period of time, exerted definite and substantial influence on stock-market credit. If initial margin requirements (now 55 percent) were accompanied by a maintenance or retention requirement of say 40 percent, the regulations could prove even more effective in influencing the volume of stock-market credit. High initial margin and maintenance requirements in combination might have restrained the rapid increase in customers' debit balances through 1967 and 1968.†

---

* On July 8, 1969, pursuant to Section 7 of the Securities and Exchange Act, as amended on July 29, 1968, the Board of Governors extended its regulations governing margin requirements for securities transactions to the purchase and carrying of certain securities traded over the counter. See *Federal Reserve Bulletin* June 1969, pp. 519–547; July, 1969, pp. 625–630.

† It may be of historical interest that, effective January 21, 1946, the Board of Governors ordered initial margin requirements of 100 percent along with a retention requirement of 100 percent. By placing stock exchange transactions on a cash basis, this regulation brought about a sharp decline in stock-market credit, which, of course, was its purpose.

The Credit Control Act of 1969 provided that the President might authorize the Board of Governors to institute selective credit control when necessary to control inflation.[47] This grant of power was not used and extensions of consumer credit, for example were left uncontrolled.

CONCLUDING OBSERVATIONS

Many of the economic problems of the late 1960s arose from adoption in the early part of the decade of a single overriding goal for fiscal and monetary policy. Growth, measured simply by increases in GNP, of whatever origin, took precedence over all other goals. The promotion of growth, it was believed, would reduce unemployment, eliminate the deficit in the balance of payments, and increase productivity, thus stabilizing prices.

Government expenditures rose, tax rates were cut, and Federal Reserve action enlisted. The "bills only" policy was suspended, the interest rate curve twisted, and long-term rates were initially pegged. Federal Reserve operations relieved the economy from the discipline of the balance of payments. On various occasions it also relieved the Treasury of the threat of rising interests rates and maintained Treasury financing on an even keel. The fundamental principles of the Federal Reserve Treasury accord of 1951 were ignored.

For the first few years the policy seemed to work. Aggregate unemployment was reduced, and wholesale prices and labor costs per unit of output were stable. On the other side of the ledger, the deficit in the balance of payments continued, foreign short-term liabilities of the American economy soared, consumer prices rose, individual and noncorporate debt increased rapidly, the quality of credit declined, and the liquidity of financial and nonfinancial corporations diminished. The Federal budget showed a continuous deficit, which became very large once Vietnam war costs began to rise. The floating debt rose more than 50 percent.

According to many observers, including IMF experts, the debit entries warranted a sharp increase in tax rates in 1966. Had such an increase been enacted, and had it produced a budget surplus of perhaps $10 billion in conjunction with a consistently restrictive monetary policy (which was favored not only by the IMF but also by the BIS), it is probable that the deficit in the balance of payments would have fallen and skyrocketing interest rates would have been avoided. The longer that restrictive action is postponed, the more deeply rooted will be the conviction that inflation is irreversible. Further, the more deeply rooted this conviction, the severer will be the measures required to end inflation, and more serious, the consequent rise in unemployment.[48] If the market economy is to be preserved and totalitarian controls avoided, fiscal and monetary action must bring an end to inflation. It does so by reducing aggregate demand. There is no alternative.

Notes

1. For a discussion of the interest sensitivity of capital investments, see Benjamin J. Cohen, *A Survey of Capital Movements and Findings Regarding Their Interest Sensitivity*. (New York: Federal Reserve Bank, July 5, 1963).

2. As the Treasury increased its short-term debt, there was danger that the Board of Governors might revive its proposal for a secondary reserve requirement, which it had set forth in its *Thirty-Second Annual Report* (Washington, D.C.: Board of Governors, June 14, 1946), p. 8.

3. *Forty-Eighth Annual Report of the Board of Governors of the Federal Reserve System Covering Operations for the Year 1961*. (Washington, D.C.: March 8, 1962), p. 40.

4. J. Herbert Furth, "International Developments and Monetary Policy" *Business Conditions* (Chicago: Federal Reserve Bank, October 1964).

5. For a resume of foreign-exchange controls in the United States, see *Twentieth Annual Report of Exchange Restrictions*, International Monetary Fund, (Washington, D.C.: 1969); *Twenty-First Annual Report on Exchange Restrictions*, International Monetary Fund, (Washington, D.C.: 1970) and *Twenty-Second Annual Report on Exchange Restrictions*, International Monetary Fund (Washington, D.C.: 1971).

6. *Annual Report of the Secretary of the Treasury on the State of the Finances for the Fiscal Year ended June 30, 1972* (Washington, D.C.: Government Printing Office, 1971), p. 492.

7. *Fifty-first Annual Report for the Year Ended December 31, 1965* (Federal Reserve Bank of New York, February 28, 1966), p. 30.

8. *Federal Reserve Bulletin* (November, 1971), pp. 906–916.

9. See *Euro-Dollar Financing* (New York: Chase Manhattan Bank, April 1968), Part V. Tax incentives to invest in developed nations were removed by the Revenue Act of 1962. Also see *Foreign Direct Investment Regulations* (Washington, D.C.: Department of Commerce, 1969).

10. *The Wage-Price Issue: The Need for Guideposts* Joint Economic Committee, 90th Cong. 2nd sess., January 31, 1968 (Washington, D.C.: Government Printing Office, 1968).

11. *Monthly Economic Letter* (New York: First National City Bank, September 1966).

12. *Economic Report of the President*. Transmitted to the Congress, February 1968 (Washington, D.C.: Government Printing Office, 1968), p. 122.

13. *Council on Prices, Productivity and Incomes:* First Report (London: H. M. Stationery Office, 1958). See Arthur F. Burns, *The Business Cycle in a Changing World* (New York: National Bureau of Economic Research, 1969), chaps. 7–10. Also see Robert H. Floyd, "Income Policies: A Quiet Critique." *Monthly Review* (Federal Reserve Bank of Atlanta, December 1970), pp. 174–181.

14. See *The United States Balance of Payments—Perspective and Policies* (Washington, D.C.: Government Printing Office, 1963), pp. 35–38 and a speech by John C. Renner, Director Office of International Trade, Department of State, at the Foreign Policy Conference, sponsored by the Dayton Council on World Affairs, January 30, 1971.

15. The nations are listed in *Euro-Dollar Financing, op. cit.,* p. 40. See an excellent study by Nicholas K. Bruck and Francis A. Lees, "Foreign Investment, Capital Controls and the Balance of Payments," *The Bulletin,* (New York University Graduate School of Business Administration, April 1968).

16. *1968 Joint Economic Report* 90th Congress, 2nd session. Report No. 1016 (Washington, D.C.: Government Printing Office, 1968), pp. 19, 72, 73.

17. *1968 Annual Report.* International Monetary Fund (Washington, D.C.: 1968) p. 10.

18. See Memorandum by Roy L. Reierson, Bankers Trust Company of New York, December 8, 1969, p. 7.

19. *Federal Reserve Bulletin* (May 1970), pp. 442–443.

20. *Federal Reserve Bulletin* (April 1970), p. 339.

21. *1969 Annual Report* (Federal Reserve Bank of Cleveland, 1969), pp. 8–9.

22. *Forty-Ninth Annual Report of the Board of Governors of the Federal Reserve System Covering Operations for the Year 1962* (Washington, D.C.: Government Printing Office, March 6, 1963), p. 109.

23. For discussion see *The New York Times,* December 6, 1965, pp. 1 and 61.

24. The statement appears in *Monthly Review* (Federal Reserve Bank of New York, September 1966), p. 209.

25. Roy L. Reierson, address to the Money Marketeers of New York University, New York, October 19, 1966.

26. *Fifty-Second Annual Report for the Year Ended December 31, 1966* (Federal Reserve Bank of New York, March 6, 1967), p. 27.

27. Dolores P. Lynn, *Reserve Adjustments of the Eight Major New York City Banks During 1966* (Federal Reserve Bank of New York, July 1968), p. 10. Also see *Monthly Review* (Federal Reserve Bank of Richmond, April 1968), and *New England Business Review* (Federal Reserve Bank of Boston, December 1967).

28. *Fifty-Second Annual Report for the Year Ended December 31, 1966* (Federal Reserve Bank of New York, March 6, 1967), p. 27–28.

29. *Business Conditions* (Federal Reserve Bank of Chicago, March 1968).

30. *Fifty-Third Annual Report for the Year Ended on December 31, 1967* (Federal Reserve Bank of New York, February 28, 1968), p. 26.

31. An account of policy changes in 1968 can be found in the *Review* (Federal Reserve Bank of St. Louis, May 1969), pp. 3–15.

32. *Business Conditions* (Federal Reserve Bank of Chicago, May 1970), p. 8.

33. *Fifty-Fifth Annual Report for the Year Ended on December 31, 1969* (Federal Reserve Bank of New York, March 2, 1970), p. 23.

34. *Weekly Money Market Bulletin* (Morgan-Guaranty Trust Company, August 8, and August 22, 1969). *Fifty-Fifth Annual Report for the Year Ended on December 31, 1969* (Federal Reserve Bank of New York, March 2, 1970), pp. 25–26. The exclusion of checks issued by a member-bank in repayment of Federal funds borrowed (*Federal Reserve Bulletin,* 1928, p. 656) did not, the Board explained, apply to other transactions.

35. *Federal Reserve Bulletin* (December 1969), p. A 17.

36. *Federal Reserve Bulletin* (August 1969), p. 656.

37. *Monthly Review* (Federal Reserve Bank of New York, December 1970), p. 278.

38. *Federal Reserve Bulletin* (August 1969), p. 656.

39. Frederick C. Schadrack and Frederick S. Breimyer, "Recent Developments in the Commercial Paper Market," *Monthly Review* (Federal Reserve Bank of New York, December 1970), pp. 287–290. Also see *57th Annual Report 1970, Board of Governors of the Federal Reserve System* (Washington, D.C.: May 12, 1971), pp. 75–76.

40. Schadrack and Breimyer, *op. cit.,* p. 289.

41. *American Banker* (New York), October 13, 1970, p. 16.

42. *Federal Reserve Bulletin* (May 1971), p. 397.

43. *Federal Reserve Bulletin* (August 1971), p. 670.

44. *Federal Reserve Bulletin* (January 1972), p. 38.

45. *The Wall Street Journal,* February 10, 1972, p. 3.

46. *Federal Reserve Bulletin* (June 1968), pp. 470–481.

47. *56th Annual Report 1969 Board of Governors of the Federal Reserve System* (Washington, D.C.: May 6, 1970) p. 298.

48. The Phillips' curves move to the right. See *Monthly Review* (The Bank of Nova Scotia, September 1969).

The Federal Reserve System and International Monetary Cooperation

Central banks have long cooperated, at times successfully, at times unsuccessfully, strengthening, bolstering and maintaining the international monetary system. Prior to World War I, the Bank of England and the Bank of France, occasionally joined by other central banks, cooperated sporadically at various critical periods. In the 1920s those two banks joined regularly by the Reichsbank and the Federal Reserve System, frequently conferred in attempts to evolve policies in their mutual interest. In the 1930s cooperation took place through the newly established institution, the Bank for International Settlements, or directly among the central banks of the tripartite countries, the United States, Great Britain, and France. The Reichsbank had by then become involved in financing the rearmament of Adolf Hitler's Germany. The Bank of Japan was engaged in "promoting" the "co-prosperity sphere" in the Pacific. The world had split into economic and political frag-

* In preparing this chapter the author had major assistance from the late Ivar Rooth, former Governor of the Sveriges Riksbank and former Managing Director of the International Monetary Fund, and from W. Lawrence Hebbard, Secretary of the IMF.

ments, and the international monetary system was functioning imperfectly. (See chapter 10)[1]

The decline in economic activity in the industrial nations during the 1930s brought about a sharp reduction in imports, with a devastating effect upon international trade. To protect their reserves, nations instituted trade barriers and foreign-exchange controls, introduced multilateral systems of exchange rates, devalued currencies unilaterally, and engaged in competitive currency depreciations. It was soon recognized that these expedients were mutually self-defeating, that international payments in the postwar period should be liberalized, and that institutional arrangements for close monetary cooperation should be established.

In the years following the end of World War II, monetary cooperation has been close and continuous. The BIS has provided a forum for representatives of central banks; the newly organized IMF a forum for representatives of finance ministries, central banks, and various other government agencies. Cooperation has not only been on a collective basis, but, bilateral arrangements have also frequently evolved.

Continuous cooperation has been facilitated by rapidity in travel and communication. In the 1920s nations had to depend upon ocean liners and cables.* In the 1960s air travel and telephones made all central bankers close neighbors.

The aim of long-continued cooperative efforts is to exchange information and points of view; to facilitate multilateral surveillance; to improve the functioning of the international monetary system; to prevent its collapse in periods of crisis; to harmonize domestic monetary policies as much as possible; and to adjust the monetary system to a continuously evolving world economy. Cooperation is essential, as Karl Blessing, former President of the Deutsche Bundesbank has pointed out, for the preservation of the capitalist system. Capitalism can be maintained only as long as national and international monetary systems function satisfactorily: "Capitalism and sound money are twins." [2] It is doubtful, he added, that capitalism could survive another monetary collapse like that of the 1930s. Another such collapse would probably plunge the world into totalitarianism.

BASIC CONDITIONS FOR A SMOOTHLY FUNCTIONING INTERNATIONAL MONETARY SYSTEM

The problems faced by central banks in the development of financial cooperation are innumerable. These concern the means and aims of cooperation, the

---

* In the 1920s the Bank of England and the Federal Reserve Bank of New York exchanged daily cablegrams on financial developments in the London and New York markets.

amount of assistance to be granted to deficit nations, and the adjustments expected of deficit and surplus nations. Successful policy must combine international assistance with national discipline.[3]

Conditions for a smoothly functioning international monetary system, in which nations need a minimum of external assistance can be summarized somewhat as follows:

The first, is an absence of exchange controls and trade barriers. Total elimination of such controls and barriers on the part of all nations in the free enterprise world is doubtlessly an ideal not soon to be achieved. Even so, the key-currency nations, and those that aspire to such status, should rid themselves of barriers to the free flow of funds and commodities.* The rapid economic growth of the European Common Market countries has vividly demonstrated the value of the orderly adoption of free-trade and- exchange policies.

Even the developing nations would benefit from the absence of exchange and trade barriers; controls in India, for example, lead to economic mismanagement, waste of resources and manpower, and infestation of the whole economy with black markets. The absence of controls in Hong Kong acts as a powerful stimulus to economic growth.

The second condition is avoidance of deficits, except for short periods, in the balance of payments of key-currency nations. The basic reason for this exhortation is that part of the deficits, as these are incurred, will be financed over time by an accumulation of short-term liabilities owed to foreign official monetary holders. These liabilities serve as the monetary reserves of the accumulating nations, fostering credit expansion there, without requiring parallel credit contraction in the key-currency nation. This is, of course, the basic weakness of the gold-exchange standard.

Should the accumulation of liabilities cause confidence to wane, the reserve centers may be exposed to unbearable pressures as their currencies are shifted into other currencies, gold, or SDRs.

The imbalance in the United States' balance of payments from 1947 through 1957 on a liquidity basis (which amounted to about $5 billion), has been justified on the grounds that it provided foreign nations with needed dollars for use in international transactions. This argument is supported by the willingness of foreign nations to hold dollars. The deficit from 1958 through 1971, which occurred after the economic reconstruction of Europe and Japan and which, on a liquidity basis

---

* A barrier used by the United States is that of persuading exporting nations to limit the sale of competing products to the United States. A quota is thus imposed not by the United States but by exporting nations at the request of the United States.

amounted to about $66 billion, carried, on the other hand, the constant threat of widespread monetary disturbances and eventually resulted in dollar devaluation.

Third; key-currency nations must be willing to suppress inflation. This willingness demonstrates the readiness of such nations to submit to the discipline of the balance of payments. It supports the status of the currency as an acceptable standard of deferred payments and reduces the threat of currency crises. The other side of this coin is the willingness of key-currency nations to counteract deflationary tendencies. Inflationary pressures are emphasized here because acute depression has not been a problem since 1930.

Fourth; all nations must be willing to promote free and efficient financial markets and to maintain high qualitative standards in domestic and foreign lending. The maintenance of qualitative lending standards implies that short-term funds will ordinarily not be used for long-term investment needs; that credit standards will not deteriorate; and that only those foreign investment needs will be financed commercially, which, in increasing the exports of borrowing nations, will enable them to earn the foreign-exchange necessary to repay funds borrowed.

Departure from these criteria has, in the postwar period, led to a whole series of monetary crises. Short-term funds generated largely by the deficit in the American balance of payments have moved from one currency center to another in search of security. Failure to correct the deficit in its balance of payments by monetary and fiscal policy has led the United States to impose a whole array of exchange controls. Failure to check domestic inflationary pressures has induced investors to rush into land and equities to protect savings. Failure to maintain high qualitative credit standards has intensified domestic inflationary pressures and has burdened many· of the developing nations with debts that they can repay only with great difficulty. Originating in a surfeit of liquidity, these developments have caused prices to rise in the leading industrial nations and have generated widespread demand for even more liquidity and additional supplements to existing monetary reserves.

The need for financial cooperation on a broad scale among central banks would seldom arise if nations were to abide by the criteria for a smoothly functioning international monetary system that we have listed. Departure from these criteria have led to one crisis after another, to hurried international conferences, and to loans by nations that have adhered to the criteria to those that have deviated.[4]

Frequent monetary conferences, as E. Stopper, President of the Swiss National Bank has pointed out, are a manifestation not of basic technical defects in the international monetary system, but rather, of the high priority that most nations have given to what is termed full employment, even at the cost of continuous currency depreciation. The elimination of payments imbalances resulting from the policies followed has been delayed in some nations by the existence of large reserves and huge grants of credit. Inflationary tendencies have thus spread throughout the world.[5]

INTERNATIONAL RESERVES AND LIQUIDITY

"International liquidity," as defined by the IMF "consists of all the resources that are available to the monetary authorities of countries for the purpose of meeting balance of payments deficits." [6] The resources may take many forms:

1. Gold holdings of treasuries, central banks and even commercial banks that belong to the "official family"; gold holdings of individuals may be included, if they can be quickly mobilized;

2. Foreign-exchange holdings of central banks, treasuries, commercial banks, and individuals, provided that they can be readily mobilized and converted into gold or other fully convertible foreign currencies;

3. Reserves in the IMF;

4. Ability of nations to use their allotments of Special Drawing Rights;

5. Conditional borrowing from the IMF or under bilateral arrangements from other central banks;

6. Holdings of short-term government securities, private securities, or bankers' acceptances denominated in convertible currencies;

7. Stocks of silver, precious stones, and readily salable commodities under certain circumstances.[7]

The volume of liquid resources which are not subject to precise measurement, may be stated as a gross amount or simply as a net amount (after subtracting short-term debts owed to foreigners). Liquid resources may also be divided between owned reserves and borrowing facilities. Borrowing facilities may in turn be available automatically or usable only under certain prescribed negotiated conditions. Liquid assets for settling balance-of-payments deficits are extremely heterogeneous and subject to changing conditions. (The impositions placed by Great

Britain in 1967 on the use of sterling balances owned by foreign monetary authorities thus impaired the usefulness of these balances as monetary reserves as indeed did the suspension in 1971 of the convertibility of the American dollar.) Those that are normally included in monetary reserves and represent the "first line of defense" are holdings of gold, SDRs, reserve positions in the IMF and convertible foreign exchange. These components will be held and used only as long as they command the confidence of nations. Once a component, whether it be American dollars, SDRs or gold, suffers a loss of confidence, it will cease to be held and used by nations.

Reserves are needed to settle balance-of-payments deficits. The smaller the imbalance, the less liquidity is required. No amount of reserves will prove adequate if a nation fails to counter energetically a continuing deficit in its balance of payments, to establish appropriate exchange rates, to check domestic inflationary pressures, and to maintain its competitive position in international trade.

No amount of reserves will prove adequate if developing nations, for example, fail to relate realistically their foreign debt service to their exports of goods and services. In the postwar period, external debt-service liabilities have increased considerably more rapidly that have net exports.[8]

Inappropriate policies result in loss of confidence in a currency and lead to domestic and foreign action that sooner or later causes adequate reserves quickly to become inadequate. Funds are shifted into strong currencies, importers speed up imports of goods and expedite payments, exporters delay receiving payments for goods sold abroad. The effect of confidence, as a Staff Report of the IMF once pointed out, is more important in determining the adequacy of reserves than is the effect of adequate reserves upon confidence. The need for additional liquidity is diminished as internal economic equilibrium is attained in individual nations.

A few years ago the ministers and governors of the Group of Ten, participating in the General Arrangements to Borrow, concluded that there was then no general shortage of reserves.[9] As large United States deficits were not regarded as a satisfactory source of future reserves, it was concluded that at some time existing reserves might have to be supplemented by the deliberate creation of additional reserve assets. Reserves should be deliberately created, the committee concluded, only if there were clear evidence of a worldwide reserve deficiency.* In the meantime, according to many students of the subject, gold remains as the principal reserve medium, and is irreplaceable as a disciplinary element in the adjustment process.

---

* Price increases in leading industrial nations seem to indicate that there is no global shortage of liquidity.

International Trade and Liquidity

The adequacy of reserves depends so heavily on qualitative factors that it is not subject to precise quantitative determination. Thus, there is no necessary relationship between increases in world trade on one hand and volume of required reserves on the other. The flow of goods and services in a world without exchange and trade barriers would cancel indebtedness in multilateral clearance. International trade, financed by commercial banks, creates its own credit.[10] The volume of credit rises as trade needs increase. Only when confidence in a currency is lacking do the leads and lags in trade affect reserves.

As the BIS pointed out in one of its annual reports, there is no simple functional relationship between liquidity needs and the volume of world trade; there is, indeed, no simple functional relationship between the need for liquidity and such other statistics as the domestic money supply or total external transactions. The need for liquid resources, the BIS emphasized, is now related mainly to the instability resulting from increased international movements of short-term funds.[11] These funds are generated by domestic inflationary pressures that have themselves resulted from excess domestic liquidity.

Payments Fluctuations and Reserves

Although adequate reserves for an individual nation cannot be determined mathematically, some of the items in the balance of payments which have an important bearing on this problem follow:

First, is seasonal variations in imports and exports. These variations do not usually engender serious difficulties and can be readily financed by commercial banking systems or the IMF. American seasonal variations in foreign trade, which were very pronounced before 1914, were financed by the British banking system. The agricultural seasonal variations of the Latin American nations induced the framers of the Federal Reserve Act to permit American banks to accept special bills of exchange to enable these nations to borrow dollars to tide over seasonal spans.

Second, is variability in the prices of imports and in the prices of and demand for exports. Variability in export prices particularly affects the raw-material-producing nations. This variability can be diminished by policies on the part of industrial nations which seek to reduce the amplitude of their own business cycles. The demand for raw materials by industrial nations is closely related to income, which in turn is related to cyclical fluctuations.

Cycles in the industrial nations are quickly communicated to raw-material nations. As the volume and prices of the latter's exports rise, monetary reserves increase, and domestic credit expansion is stimulated. The resulting prosperity causes foreign investors to invest in the securities of the raw-materials nations, often in amounts beyond the capacities of the nations to repay even in prosperous times.

The opposite sequence occurs when a decline in foreign demand causes a drop in export prices and volume. Monetary reserves are depleted. The foreign-exchange value of a currency is threatened. Either deflationary policies must be adopted to protect the currency, or the currency itself, must be devalued. Unless deflationary policies are quickly adopted, there will be an outward flight of currency, inducing the nation to impose foreign exchange controls.*

Third is crop failures. In recent years they have occasionally caused heavy drains on reserves. The failure of the Russian wheat crop in 1963–1964 forced the USSR to draw upon its own gold stock to import Canadian wheat.

Fourth, is changes in demand for particular products owing to the appearance of competing materials. Two examples are the displacement of Japanese silk by nylon and the displacement of British coal by oil and hydroelectric power. A nation whose entrepreneurial class is flexible and imaginative can make a reasonably rapid adjustment. Monetary reserves, however, may be depleted, and a nation so affected may need outside help until adjustment can be accomplished.

Fifth, is a decline in the competitive strength of a nation's export trade. This is usually as a result of domestic inflation, accompanied by a decline in labor productivity and by passive managerial attitudes. It may, too, result from economic controls which cause an economy to become subject to bureaucratic direction.

Sixth, is foreign political policy. A nation must tailor its foreign policy to its own economic capacity. Failure to do so, as in the American intervention in Vietnam, can lead to a serious drain on reserves.

Seventh, is short- and long-term capital movements. Over the past decade the most important factor influencing monetary reserves has been the heavy flows of funds across frontiers. Finding their origin mainly in the payments imbalance of Britain and the United States, and in the gold exchange standard, they have subjected currencies to massive tidal movements.

The greater the stock of reserves owned by an individual nation, the greater is its confidence that it can weather an emergency. Reserves, either owned or capable of being borrowed, should be large enough to tide a nation over seasonal

---

* The developing nations frequently rely on industrial nations to restore their depleted reserves and to maintain investment growth. Although problems of economic growth are beyond the scope of this volume, we note that South American nations have handicapped themselves by not providing educational opportunities for their people, by failing to end the concentration of land ownership, and by refusing to adopt and enforce equitable tax systems.

fluctuations and to maintain, barring a severe depression, external debt payments and currency convertibility. Beyond prudent need, accumulation ties up the resources of a community in unproductive use.

Reserves buy time, but the time must be used effectively through appropriate internal monetary and fiscal policies. Unfortunately, the greater a nation's liquidity, the greater is its tendency to defer remedial action. Similarly, the greater a nation's access to international credits, the greater is its tendency to defer basic economic adjustments.

Global Reserves

Total international monetary reserves amounted to $62.7 billion at the end of 1960; they had increased, with important intermediate fluctuations, to an estimated $98.5 billion by the end of March 1971.[12] The amount and proportion of gold fell and the amount and proportion of foreign exchange (dollars and pounds made available through the balance-of-payments deficits of the United States and the United Kingdom) rose sharply. The reserve position in the IMF increased slightly; SDRs appeared first in 1970.

Table 16.1
International Monetary Reserves
(Billions of Dollars)

	End of December 1960	End of March 1971	Change
Gold	$38.0	$36.9	−$ 1.1
Foreign exchange	21.1	48.5	+ 27.4
Reserve positions in IMF	3.6	7.3	+ 3.7
SDRs	—	5.8	+ 5.8
Total	$62.7	$98.5	+$35.8

Source: International Monetary Fund, 1964 Annual Report (Washington, D.C.), p. 82; and International Monetary Fund, 1971 Annual Report (Washington, D.C.), p. 28.

Between 1960 and 1971 increased holdings of foreign exchange (dollars and pounds) made the most important contribution to international liquidy; holdings of SDRs and reserve positions in the IMF followed next, while holdings of gold actually declined.

Of the total resources included in international liquidity ($98.5 billion) the United States held $14.1 billion, the United Kingdom $3.3 billion, industrial Europe $42.0 billion, Canada $4.8 billion, Japan $5.9 billion, other developed areas $9.3 billion, Latin America $5.7 billion, the Middle East $3.4 billion, the rest of Asia $5.3 billion, and other Africa $4.4 billion.

Significant changes occurred in the geographical distributions of reserves from 1960 to 1971. The most important were the declines in the reserve holdings of the United Kingdom and the United States, and the sharp increases in Continental Europe, Canada, and Japan. Reserves fluctuated mainly in response to changes in the trade balance and to the shift of funds from one center to another.

About 37 percent of the international monetary reserves of the free world are in gold. The opportunity to add to gold assets from massive sales by the United States, the IMF, and occasionally France, has been seized by many nations. Gold continues to be the basic element in the world monetary system. The preference for gold arises from its immunity to control by any one nation, to its universal acceptance as a payment of last resort, and to its protection against the hazards of depreciation. "Currencies," as Sir Leslie O'Brien, Governor of the Bank of England has stated, "cannot stand comparison with it." *

So great is the prestige of gold that credit arrangements, in order to protect creditors, are stated in terms of gold or its equivalent. The accounts of the BIS are kept in Swiss gold francs. Obligations of nations to the IMF carry a maintenance-of-gold-value clause. SDRs are guaranteed in terms of a weight of gold. The swap network of the Federal Reserve System is protected against an adjustment of the dollar-exchange rate. Borrowings by the- U.S. government are frequently denominated in local currencies. A large part of official foreign-exchange reserves is protected against devaluation. These protective devices are essential in an international monetary system based on national currencies, which often seem unable to resist inflation.[13]

SHORING UP THE SYSTEM

Weaknesses in the System

The international monetary system, buffeted by a series of crises in the 1960s, was in danger of collapse. The British pound, once the impregnable reserve currency of the Victorian period, was subject to periodic runs. A fairly high

---

* *Quarterly Bulletin* (Bank of England) Vol. 8 No. 4, December 1968, p. 408. Until a few years ago the position of the Bank of England was that one reserve currency should not be held in terms of another currency. Although understandable and justifiable, this position was abandoned when sterling was attacked in the middle and late 1960s.

current-account surplus in 1958 was followed by a heavy current-account deficit in 1960, by a still larger deficit in 1964, and by an even larger deficit in 1967.

The fact that sterling was weak in the post-World War II period is attributed by the BIS to Great Britain's unwillingness to come to grips with price inflation. Britain did not introduce far-reaching monetary reforms as did Germany and the Netherlands. Unlike Italy, she did not accept the price inflation implicit in wartime expansion of domestic liquidity. Price controls and rationing were maintained. Balance-of-payments deficits were met through foreign aid and borrowing. "A low rate of private saving and rapid institution of a comprehensive welfare programme," concludes the BIS, "aggravated the ajustment problems." [14] Sterling was not reestablished as a strong currency.

But sterling was not alone in provoking monetary crises. The dollar, which had commanded worldwide confidence in the middle 1950s, ended the 1960s subject to suspicion and mistrust. The United States emerged as a heavy debtor on short-term account and as an illiquid banker. The net result was first the suspension of gold payments to nonofficial claimants, and later to all claimants, termination of the gold pool, adoption of foreign-exchange controls and trade quotas, and heavy reliance on other currencies, notably those of Germany, Switzerland, Italy, the Netherlands, Belgium and Japan. These were the strong currencies of the Western and Eastern World which, on various occasions, included the French franc.

Failure of Britain and the United States to follow policies that would have strengthened their currencies forced them to rely heavily on foreign loans, borrowing from IMF, bilateral borrowing under the Basel Arrangements and swap transactions among central banks.

THE INTERNATIONAL MONETARY FUND

According to its Managing Director, Pierre-Paul Schweitzer, the IMF has continuously endeavored to foster international cooperation, to promote stable and orderly exchange arrangements and adjustments among member nations, and to assist in eliminating discriminatory currency practices and foreign-exchange restrictions.[15] The IMF has regularly consulted with members and has developed a large and varied program of technical assistance.†

---

† Many nations first joined the IMF in order to be able to borrow from the International Bank for Reconstruction and Development; inasmuch as membership in the IMF is a prerequisite to membership in the World Bank. As Governor Rooth pointed out in a memorandum, many nations at the time they joined the Fund were actually insolvent and should not have been admitted to membership.

Quotas

Each of the 120 members of the IMF is assigned a quota based on general "economic power." The quota serves three main functions: determining within approximate limits the voting rights of the members, setting the subscription of each member to IMF resources, and determining the borrowing rights of each member. Each member is entitled to 250 votes plus 1 additional vote for each part of its quota equivalent to 100,000 SDRs; the quota of the United States, the largest of all, is 6.7 billion SDRs, entitling it to 67,250 votes, or 21.9 percent of the total.

Subscriptions are payable partly in gold and partly in the member's currency. Normally the gold subscription is 25 percent of the quota and when a quota is increased, 25 percent of the increase must usually be paid in gold. The assets of the IMF consist of gold, member-nations' currencies, and recently added SDRs. On January 31, 1972, holdings of gold amounted to 5.3 billion SDRs, of member currencies to 23.6 billion SDRs, and holdings of SDRs to 504 million.

Following the suspension of convertibility by the United States, the IMF began to present its data in terms of SDRs rather than in terms of dollars, as was its previous practice. Conversions of dollars into SDRs were calculated at the cross rates reflecting the actual and prospective parities that were agreed to on December 18, 1971 and subsequently, with gold at its future price of 38 U.S. dollars an ounce (Chapter 17).[16]

Financial Assistance

Each member-nation is entitled, under various rules and regulations, to draw upon the assets of the IMF. The right of a member to purchase gold or the currency of another member has been called a "drawing right." Actually, because credit considerations are often involved, the term "borrowing right" or, from the point of view of the Fund, "credit grants" would be more appropriate.

A member-nation may draw virtually automatically an amount equal to its reserve position. Its reserve position equals its quota minus the IMF holdings of its currency plus loans that it has made to the IMF. On January 31, 1972, Germany's IMF quota was 1600 million SDRs and IMF holdings of German currency were 502 million SDRs. Also, on this date Germany had no loans outstanding to the IMF. Its reserve position was, therefore, 1,098 million SDRs (1,600 million SDRs minus 502 million SDRs). It could borrow this amount virtually automatically in gold or other currencies.

Nations seeking to borrow amounts equal to but not exceeding 125 percent of their quotas can "confidently expect a favorable response," provided that they are making reasonable efforts to solve their economic problems.

Borrowing between 125 percent and 200 percent of a quota is subject to increasingly severe restrictions. The nation must send a letter of intent to the IMF outlining the measures that it plans to adopt to check inflation and to eliminate a deficit in its balance of payments.

Some nations borrowing large amounts in terms of their quotas at the end of January 1972 included Ceylon 186 percent, Chile 125 percent, Colombia 134 percent, Ghana 120 percent, Mali 137 percent, Morocco 113 percent, the Philippines 154 percent, Indonesia 148 percent, Israel 163 percent, the United Arab Republic 132 percent, and Yugoslavia 130 percent.

Unless the rules are waived, a member-nation is not allowed to draw upon the IMF for amounts that will raise IMF holdings of its currency more than 25 percent in any twelve-month period or above 200 percent of its quota. Member nations repay their borrowing by repurchasing their own currencies with gold, other currencies or SDRs. A member's debts are also reduced when IMF holdings of its currency are purchased by another member.

As a general rule, member nations undertake to repay their debts within periods not exceeding three to five years. They can be considered out of debt when IMF holding of their currency fall to 75 percent or below of their quota. On debts greater than 100 percent of its quota a member-nation pays interest or a service charge, increasing with the amount and duration of the debt and rising to a maximum of 5 percent.[17] Beginning the third year on relatively small loans and the second year on large loans, the Fund enters into consultations with a member respecting debt repayments.[18]

Beginning in 1952 the IMF began to enter into Standby Arrangements with member nations. Such arrangements assure members that they may purchase during a fixed period of usually one year the currencies of other members, up to stipulated amounts.

In January 1972, Standby Arrangements with fourteen nations were currently in effect. The amounts ranged from 83.5 million SDRs for Yugoslavia to 3.0 million SDRs for Haiti. The total amount agreed upon was 401.5 million SDRs and the amount drawn was 154.7 million SDRs. Most fund drawings are against such Arrangements.

Activities of the IMF

Ability of the IMF to render assistance to currencies under attack, particularly those with large short-term debts,* is contingent upon its holdings of gold and usable currencies and upon the revolving character of its outstanding loans. The IMF unlike central banks within individual nations, cannot itself create credit. It can lend only those assets that it has on hand and in this respect it resembles a financial intermediary. Its lending power is no greater than the amount and quality of its assets. Holdings of gold, usable currencies,† and SDRs are now (January 31, 1972) relatively small, totaling no more than 11 billion SDRs.

Through its history the IMF loans have been extended consistently and in large amount to relatively few nations. They have included South American nations long beset by inflation, for example, Argentina, Brazil, Chile, and Colombia, developing nations struggling to finance ambitious economic plans and rearmament, including India, Indonesia, the Philippines, the Sudan, Turkey, Iran, the United Arab Republic, and Yugoslavia, and key-currency nations, notably the United Kingdom. Many of these credits have been investment credits and should more appropriately have been extended by the World Bank.‡

Consequently the IMF holds a fairly large volume of currencies that we shall, perhaps somewhat arbitrarily, call "non-usable." A sample of such currencies is set forth in Table 16.2.

It is possible that some non-usable currencies may become usable because of loan refundings and shifts in the balance of payments. If, however, to this sum the currencies of the United Kingdom and the United States are added, the total becomes 13,055 million SDRs.

An increase in the amount of loans to inflation-oriented and developing nations has been accompanied by a rise in loan maturities. Although no decision was reached when the IMF was established, the consensus seemed to be that credit extensions should be limited to fairly short maturities. Loans now are granted for up to five years and can be renewed.

---

* Although Article XIV, Section 11 of the IMF Articles states that the "Fund is not intended . . . to deal with international indebtedness arising out of war," actually, as Governor Ivar Rooth pointed out, the existence of Britain's overseas debt was an important consideration in the establishment of IMF.

† On January 31, 1972, the currencies of Austria, Belgium, Canada, Finland, France, Germany, Italy, Japan, Mexico, the Netherlands, Norway, and Venezuela, only 12 nations out of a total of 120 were included. We define usable currencies as IMF's holdings of currencies in amounts less than 75 percent of each nation's quota and of currencies that enjoy a relatively wide market in the foreign-exchanges.
Since the establishment of the IMF in 1947, through December 1971, total drawings have amounted to 23.9 billion SDRs. Of this amount 13.7 billion were in the currencies listed. If we add the currencies of the United Kingdom (1,056 million SDRs) and the United States (7,911 million SDRs) which were used when they were strong, the total rises to 22.7 billion SDRs. Other currencies were employed in insignificant amounts.

‡ It is questionable that the IMF should purchase the currency of a nation engaged in rapid rearmament.

Table 16.2
IMF Holdings of Non-Usable Currencies
(Millions of SDRs) (January 31, 1972)

Burma	78	Pakistan	277
Ceylon	182	Peru	126
Chile	197	Philippines	239
Colombia	210	Sudan	85
Ghana	105	Turkey	213
India	864	United Arab Republic (Egypt)	249
Indonesia	385	Yugoslavia	269
Israel	163		
		Total	3,642

Source: *International Financial Statistics* (Washington, D.C.: International Monetary Fund, February 1972), pp. 8 and 9.

The Fund is not particularly liquid. This is a condition which has resulted from the political influences which have come to bear on credit operations, from the unwillingness of nations to put their own houses in order, and from loans which indirectly have financed long-term requirements.

Efforts to Strengthen the IMF

The small total of really usable assets has led to several attempts to strengthen the IMF. In September 1959 and succeeding months, most quotas were increased 50 percent, and some by even larger percentages. Again in February 1966 and succeeding months quotas were increased a further 25 percent, somewhat more for sixteen nations. These two increases provided the IMF with about $2.4 billion in gold and an increase of about $12 billion in local currencies. Had the additional currencies proved fully usable, the Fund would have had ample resources to deal with most contingencies.*

A further increase in quotas, totaling $7.1 billion, or about 30 percent, occurred in 1970. The purpose of this increase was not only to adjust the quotas of individual nations (particularly the developing nations) but also to strengthen the financial resources of the IMF "compatible with increases in world trade" and to increase conditional liquidity (borrowing from the IMF) in order that it parallel the increase in unconditional liquidity (SDRs). The increase in gold holdings (stated in dollars) amounted to only $1,180 million and in currency

---

* Monetary cooperation among member nations is paralleled by cooperation among members of the European Economic Community (the Common Market nations). Policies on exchange rates are regarded as matters of common concern. Mutual assistance is envisaged in the event of balance-of-payments difficulties. (The *New York Times*, January 27, 1970.)

holdings to $5,926 million, of which only a relatively small amount could be counted as usable.

General Arrangements to Borrow

To enlarge its holdings of lendable currencies further, the IMF entered in 1962 into borrowing arrangements with eight members and with the central banks of two others. The participants agreed to lend the IMF an aggregate amount of $6 billion in their currencies at the par value in effect at the time that the arrangements were made. These loans were to be repaid within five years and contained an absolute gold guarantee. The gold guarantee is absolute in that it cannot be rescinded by the IMF board of directors in the event of a uniform rise in the price of gold. The same guarantee applies to the SDRs.[19]

The nations that entered into these arrangements and their commitments are shown in Table 16.3.*

Between December 1964 and August 1971, total IMF borrowing from these nations amounted to 2.2 billion SDRs and repayments to the same amount, leaving 5,959 million SDRs available. The pound and the dollar have not been drawn upon since the inception of the arrangements. In fact, they have been the currencies that have needed help and have been aided by IMF borrowings mainly from Germany, Italy, France, the Netherlands, and Japan.

---

* The Fund has also borrrowed from Italy outside the General Arrangements to Borrow.

Table 16.3
General Arrangements to Borrow
Lending Commitments
(Millions of SDRs)

Belgium	154
Canada	198
France	485
Germany	1,147
Italy	545
Japan	269
The Netherlands	206
Sweden	99
United Kingdom	857
United States	2,000
Total	5,960

The initial total was $6,000 million, but has been altered since by changes in the par value of currencies or exchange rates.

Source: *International Financial Statistics*. (Washington, D.C.: International Monetary Fund, March 1972), p. 16.

BASEL ARRANGEMENTS

The growing inability of the IMF to cope with international monetary crises led to supplementary arrangements: the Basel arrangements and swap transactions. The Basel arrangements, so-called because they are negotiated by or through the Bank for International Settlements, are ad hoc lending arrangements among central banks. Much the same group of central banks participates as was included in the General Arrangements to Borrow.

An example of the use of such credits is provided by the sterling crisis of the fall of 1964. Sterling began to weaken at the end of May and continued to fall from August to October. The causes were the continuing deficit in the balance of payments and uncertainties associated with the general election and the adoption of new tax measures. By November a very severe confidence crisis had developed. The Bank of England reported that sales of sterling, "were massive and growing." [20] The discount on forward sterling widened rapidly, and authorities began to support the forward market.

Short-term facilities were obtained from overseas central banks. A $500 million swap arrangement with the Federal Reserve System was already in effect and a small drawing was made at the end of August. In September additional credits totaling $500 million were arranged with the central banks of Belgium, Canada, France, Italy, the Netherlands, Switzerland, and West Germany. Toward the end of November further assistance was obtained from these banks and also from the central banks of Austria, Japan, and Sweden and from the BIS and the Export-Import Bank of the United States.

On December 2 the United Kingdom drew the full amount, equivalent to $1 billion, under its standby arrangement with the IMF. The drawing, which was repayable in three years, was made in eleven currencies. To obtain these currencies the IMF drew upon its own holdings for $345 million, sold $250 million of gold, and borrowed $405 million under the General Arrangements to Borrow.[21] In all, about $2.5 billion of aid were obtained by the United Kingdom to avert sterling devaluation (See Table 16.4). Devaluation did come three years later, and it might have been wiser to devalue in 1964 for sterling was in fundamental disequilibrium.

Short-term credits provided by the central banks were repaid through additional borrowing of $1,400 million from the IMF. To obtain these funds the IMF drew upon its own currency holdings for $475 million, sold $400 million of gold, and borrowed $525 million under the General Arrangements to Borrow.[22] Special

Table 16.4

Outstanding Short-term
Aid Received by
the United Kingdom
(Millions of Dollars)

	December 1964	April 1965	May 1965
Federal Reserve Bank of New York	$ 200	$ 280	$ –
Other short-term assistance	325	817	–
Total	$ 525	$1,097	–
IMF	$1,000	$1,000	$2,400
Swiss bilateral credits	80	80	120
Total	$1,605	$2,177	$2,520

credits have on occasion been extended by commercial banks to the Bank of England. On October 25, 1967, three large Swiss banks extended a one-year credit (denominated in Swiss francs) of $450 million Swiss francs.

Credits extended through this period resembled a rapidly moving merry-go-round. Central banks sometimes lent directly to the Bank of England, sometimes to the IMF. The creditors remained the same, but the debts revolved. As Karl Blessing pointed out, "The responsibility of creating additional liquidity can only be borne by a group of countries with strong currencies." [23]

SWAP TRANSACTIONS

On February 13, 1962, the Board of Governors of the Federal Reserve System authorized open-market operations in foreign currencies, thus initiating central bank swap transactions to supplement the dwindling lending facilities of the IMF. These transactions have come to play a significant role in international monetary cooperation. The resumption of foreign-exchange transactions by the System in February 1962 and by the U.S. Treasury in March 1961 was part of the cooperative effort by treasuries and central banks on both sides of the Atlantic to create "a first line of defense against disorderly speculation in the foreign-exchange markets." [24] The broad purposes of the new arrangements, as officially stated, were to help safeguard the value of the dollar by offsetting, when deemed appropriate, the flow of gold and payments across international frontiers; to moderate changes in spot and forward exchange rates; to aid in making the existing system of international payments more efficient and to further monetary cooperation among central banks; and to facilitate growth in liquid assets available in international money markets in accordance with the needs of an expanding world economy. Actually the basic justification for the swap arrangements was not that of meeting international liquidity needs, but simply to offset for brief periods the effects of the international flow of gold and payments.*

The Mechanics

A swap consists simply of a reciprocal credit facility under which a central bank agrees to exchange on request its own currency for the currency of another central bank up to a maximum amount over a limited period of time. Each swap agreement is renewable. Many are renewed, sometimes for larger sums and longer maturities.[25]

The Federal Reserve Bank of New York has charge of American swap agreements and is authorized to purchase and sell foreign currencies in the form of cable transfers through spot or forward transactions in the open market at home or abroad, including transactions with the Stabilization Fund of the U.S. Treasury.

If the Reserve System and the Bank of England were to enter into a swap agreement for perhaps $50 million (which they could do by telephone) at the rate of $2.60 per pound sterling, the Federal Reserve Bank of New York would credit the Bank of England on its books with $50 million, and the Bank of England would credit the Federal Reserve Bank of New York with about £19.2 million. In order to support the pound, the Bank of England would be in a position to sell dollars in London or to buy pounds in New York up to the prescribed amount. The transaction would be subject to reversal on a specified date. Repayment is made at exchange rates prevailing at the time the swap line is drawn upon. The lending nation is thus protected against losses arising from devaluation.[26]

In our example the Reserve System could place its idle sterling balances in the interest-bearing time deposits in London or invest them in bills of exchange and acceptances arising from actual commercial transactions and maturing in not more than ninety days. If, on the other hand, the Reserve bank had itself made the swap drawing, the Bank of England could invest its dollar balances in non transferable U.S. Treasury certificates of indebtedness. Invested funds on either side of the Atlantic bear interest at equal rates. Swap drawings have no effect on

---

* On March 20, 1962, the central banks of the Nordic countries, i.e. (Denmark, Finland, Iceland, Norway, and Sweden) entered into a swap arrangement. Requests for credits can be made only after a country has drawn on its own holdings of foreign exchange to a ''reasonable'' extent. *Economic Bulletin* (Norges Bank), Volume 38, No. 3, 1967.

the American balance of payments since the addition to official reserves offsets the short-term liability due to the central bank partner.

A sale by the Bank of England as the result of a swap transaction of dollar balances on the books of the Reserve bank increases member-bank reserves. This increase could, of course, be offset by a sale of government securities on the part of the Reserve System but, unless offset, it would increase member-bank reserves and is tantamount to an open-market operation.

Assets denominated in foreign currencies are included among "other assets" on the Federal Reserve statement. On October 29, 1969—"other assets" amounted to $2,906 million, of which $1,918 million consisted of foreign currencies.[27] Although this amount is not large in comparison with open-market securities holdings, changes at certain critical periods, for example, in the final quarter of 1967, have had significant impacts on member-bank reserves.

Growth in Reciprocal Arrangements

The first reciprocal currency agreement, for a term of three months and for $50 million was entered into with the Bank of France on March 1, 1962. Since that time, as Table 16.5 shows, the agreements have increased in size and have included a larger number of central banks.

Starting with seven central banks and the BIS, the arrangement now includes fourteen central banks and the BIS. The total amount which can be employed has risen from $700 million to $11,730 million. The increase has been accompanied by a rise in the maturities of the arrangements. Initially, maturity was set at three months except for a six months' swap with the Bank of Canada, but, it has subsequently been increased with the understanding that the credits may be rolled over under mutual agreement.

The increase in swap arrangements resulted from the weakness of the pound and the dollar and from possible disturbing effects of the Eurodollar market. Had it not been for the large short-term liabilities of the United Kingdom and the United States and, in the case of the United States, an increasing volume of such liabilities, reciprocal currency arrangements could probably have been held to a total of not more than $1 billion.

The Use of Swaps

From the inception of the Federal Reserve swap network in March 1962 to December 1970 total drawings amounted to more than $23 billion, of which about

Table 16.5

Data of Federal Reserve Reciprocal Currency Arrangements (Millions of Dollars)

	Arranged March 1–August 2, 1962	In Effect October 14, 1971
Austrian National Bank	$ –	$ 200
Bank of Canada	250	1,000
Bank of Denmark	–	200
Bank of England	50	2,000
Bank of France	50	1,000
Bank for International Settlements	100	1,600*
Bank of Italy	–	1,250
Bank of Japan	–	1,000
Bank of Mexico	–	130
Bank of Norway	–	200
Bank of Sweden	–	250
Deutsche Bundesbank	50	1,000
National Bank of Belgium	50	600
Netherlands Bank	50	300
Swiss National Bank	100	1,000
Total	$700	$11,730

* Dollars against Swiss francs $600 million and dollars against authorized European currencies other than Swiss francs $1,000 million.

Source: *Federal Reserve Bulletin* (September 1962), p. 1147 (December 1969), p. 937; *Monthly Review* (Federal Reserve Bank of New York), September 1970, p. 199, and October 1971, p. 217.

$8 billion were drawn by the Federal Reserve System and roughly $15 billion by other central banks (mainly the Bank of England) and the BIS.[28] The Federal Reserve System has made fairly continual use of swap arrangements, drawing upon central banks in Belgium, Germany, Italy, the Netherlands, and Switzerland and upon BIS. Outstanding drawings by the System reached a peak of $3 billion on August 13, 1971. Much of this debt was incurred to offset a speculative outflow of funds which, it was hoped, would reverse itself. Up to the present time (March 1972) this has not occurred. (See Chapter 17.)[29]

Only occasionally have central banks other than the Bank of England and the Federal Reserve System used the swap arrangement. The Bank of Canada did so in 1962 and again in a large amount in 1968. The Bank of Italy used it briefly in 1964. Not until 1968 did the Bank of France, the National Bank of Denmark, and the Netherlands Bank draw on their credits. The Bank of Japan did so for a small amount in 1964.

Swap transactions are usually negotiated in terms of two currencies, dollars and pounds, as in our illustration. The BIS has, however, entered into swap agreements involving more than two currencies. On an *ad hoc* basis the Reserve System itself has engaged in third currency swaps, using balances in one foreign currency to acquire balances in another. These swaps are not part of the ordinary network and remain outstanding longer than do the usual swaps.

A dramatic illustration of the use of swap agreements occurred immediately after the assassination of President John F. Kennedy on Friday, November 22, 1963:

> The initial shock of the news from Dallas temporarily paralyzed the New York exchange market and as ominous rumors concerning the condition of both the President and Vice President began to flood the financial markets, there was a clear risk that the panic selling which had hit the stock market might spread to the gold and foreign exchange markets as well.[30]

The Federal Reserve System activated its swap arrangements and immediately placed sizable purchase orders for most major currencies at rates prevailing just before the tragedy. Speculative fears subsided. The actual amount of funds used was small, but the existence of previously established lines of communication proved decisive.

Still another illustration of the use of swap agreements is the support given to the French franc after the disorders of May 17, 1968. Student rioting was followed by labor strikes which paralyzed the French economy and forced nearly all French banks to close. For all practical purposes labor disturbances also closed the Paris exchange market.[31] Speculative flows from France, swelled by a precipitous reversal of commercial leads and lags, grew substantially.

Official support of the franc through May and June is estimated at $1.5 billion. Part of that support took the form of sales of gold while other consisted of sales of credits from the IMF and central banks. For the first time since its inception in March 1962 the Bank of France drew the full $100 million then available under the swap agreement; subsequently, it drew an additional $600 million, which became available when the swap line was increased from $100 million to $700 million.

Upon the termination of the disorders, accompanied by the adoption of foreign-exchange controls and restrictive credit and fiscal policies, the franc regained strength. The Bank of France and the French government began to repay their borrowing.

Swap transactions have been successful in offsetting the effects on national and international money markets of seasonal requirements. Swiss commercial banks, for window dressing purposes increase by substantial amounts their balances at the end of June and December with the Swiss National Bank. Before the swap arrangements they did so by selling dollar assets on Swiss markets, invoking wide fluctuations in dollar-exchange rates. Now, the large Swiss banks sell dollars on a swap basis to the Swiss National Bank, which in turn sells the dollars to the BIS for gold, also on a swap basis. In this way the dollar holdings of the Swiss National Bank do not exceed their traditional proportions to gold, and a call upon the gold stock of the United States is avoided. The BIS in turn invests the dollars in short-term securities in the United States. The seasonal liquidity requirements of the large Swiss banks are thus neutralized.

The Eurodollar Market and Swap Agreements

Although central banks have long been accustomed to deal with periods of temporary stress in their own money markets, only in recent years have they been faced with similar responsibilities in the international money and credit markets, by reason of the development of the Eurollar market. The BIS has assumed the major responsibility for easing tensions in this market.

During the Middle East crisis in 1967, for example, and on various other occasions during the fourth quarter of the same year the BIS activated its dollar swap line with the Federal Reserve System and invested the proceeds in the Eurodollar market. The market was thus stabilized and continued to play its role as an international money and credit market.[32] The BIS was assisted in its operations by the Deutsche Bundesbank which offered dollar swaps to commercial banks at preferential rates, which they in turn were permitted to lend in the Eurodollar market.

Following the devaluation of sterling in November 1967, Eurodollars moved into other currencies and gold. This development, which coincided with the usual seasonal peak prompted further intervention in the market by the BIS and by central banks of the gold-pool nations.

Recycling

Evolving from the swap agreements is a recent suggestion for a general European swap agreement. The purpose would be to enable nations undergoing large flows of funds to continue to count them in their reserves. A movement of gold from the Bank of France to the Deutsche Bundesbank would thus simply change the character of French reserves. The decline in gold assets would be matched by an increase in foreign-exchange assets. Similarly the flight of funds from commercial banks in France to those in Germany, once the various bookkeeping operations had taken place, would give the Bank of France a credit on the books of the Deutsche Bundesbank. The former would not be compelled to ship gold or to use dollar reserves.

This proposal was discussed at the Group of Ten meeting at Bonn in November 1968. Central bankers from the surplus nations, Germany, the Netherlands, and Switzerland, expressed fears that the automaticity involved in recycling, what has been called "mirror liquidity," would amount to an open-end agreement by them to finance the deficit nations, which would then not have to take necessary corrective action.[33]

Forward Transactions

On frequent occasions in the 1960s central banks, including the Federal Reserve System, intervened in the forward exchange market. In its operations the Reserve System has received assistance from the Stabilization Fund of the U.S. Treasury.

Normally the forward premium or discount on one currency in terms of another is directly related to the interest-rate differentials between the countries concerned. Forward rates, however, may deviate widely from their "interest parities."[34] Central-bank intervention in forward markets is designed to bring forward rates closer to interest parities in order to dampen speculation against expected currency depreciation, to tide over short, very short imbalances, in the balance of payments, and to shift liquid funds between domestic and foreign money markets. Official support of the forward exchange value of a currency is analogous to borrowing abroad on a short-term but renewable basis.[35] It proves successful in those cases in which a currency is temporarily depressed by reason of lack of confidence.

In his Eighth Report on Treasury and Federal Reserve Exchange Operations, Charles A. Coombs, in charge of the Foreign Department of the Federal Reserve Bank of New York, described the success of the Bank of England's operations in the forward-exchange market:

> While short-term central bank credits . . . provided the basic defense line for sterling during this troubled period [September 1965–February 1966], inadequate recognition has been given to

the success of Bank of England operations in the forward market that were conducted forcefully and with great technical skill during the course of the year. Such large-scale operations in the forward market not only exerted at critical moments a highly salutary influence on market confidence, but also had the vitally important effect of relieving pressure on the spot market and British dollar reserves by providing at reasonable cost the alternative of hedging in the forward market. In the absence of such forward operations it seems all too clear that the drain upon British reserves and utilization of central bank credits would have been much heavier and consequently would have aggravated still further an already dangerous crisis.[36]

One of the major decisions at the Frankfurt meeting of central bankers (November 26, 1967) after devaluation of the pound was to launch coordinated central-bank activity in the forward market. Sizable operations were specifically designed to induce reflows into the Eurodollar market of "hot" money that had gone into Continental European financial markets after sterling devaluation.[37] Forward operations by the Deutsche Bundesbank in November and December alone totaled $850 million. Similar forward operations by the central banks of Switzerland, the Netherlands, and Belgium on behalf of the Federal Reserve System and the U.S. Treasury also helped to arrest speculative inflows to Continental currencies at that time.

Severe tensions in the gold market in March 1968 evoked a strong demand for forward Swiss francs. In order to dampen speculative ardor, the Swiss National Bank, acting for the Federal Reserve System, and the U.S. Treasury jointly sold the equivalent of $56 million in Swiss francs.[38]

Transactions in forward exchanges have come to play and doubtless will continue to play a significant role in central bank cooperation.

Roosa Bonds

When a swap transaction had not been retired by a reverse flow of funds, repayment by the United States had, prior to the suspension of dollar convertibility, been made by means of gold sales, drawings on the IMF, and sales of so called Roosa bonds. Beginning in 1962 the United States initiated sales of non-marketable government securities, denominated in dollars or foreign currencies, to foreign central and commercial banks. The purpose was to fund short-term dollar liabilities and to dissuade foreign nations from drawing on the American gold stock. As of December 1971 these securities totaled $9.7 billion; of this amount, $7.8 billion were payable in dollars owed principally to Germany and Canada and $1.8 billion were denominated in foreign currencies issued in Switzerland and Germany.[39] The amount denominated in foreign currencies should be deducted from the gold stock to arrive at a figure more indicative of the American gold position.

A Few Observations

Swap transactions have come to play an exceedingly important role in helping leading industrial nations meet heavy temporary foreign drains without suffering loss of gold or exchange reserves. They multiplied rapidly because of the huge volume of liquid funds unleashed by the American balance-of-payments deficit. Their use, as important as it was in past crises, however, should, as most students recognize, be confined to very short seasonal or crisis periods and should not be used as a substitute for the fundamental adjustments that deficit nations must endure. Their future use awaits the reestablishment of convertibility by the United States.

SPECIAL DRAWING RIGHTS

"The mechanisms of international payments are shaped by two processes: spontaneous evolution and deliberate construction," so wrote L. P. Thompson-McCausland in the Bank of England *Quarterly Bulletin*.[40] Spontaneous evolution over many centuries gave rise to the many variants of the gold standard, to the development of London and New York as international banking centers, and to the use of the pound and the dollar as transaction and reserve currencies. Deliberate construction led to the rejection of bimetallism in the last century, to the many instances of central-bank cooperation after World War I, to the establishment of the BIS and the IMF, and, finally, to the proposal for Special Drawing Rights. This proposal was adopted unanimously by the Board of Governors of the IMF at the conclusion of their annual meeting held in Rio de Janeiro on September 29, 1967.

In its resolution the Board requested the executive directors to draft amendments to the Articles of Agreement of the IMF implementing the proposal for SDRs. The executive directors sent the proposed text of the amendments to the Board of Governors on April 17, 1968, which approved it on May 31, 1968. The amendments were to become effective when accepted by three-fifths of the members having four-fifths of the total voting power, as they were at the IMF annual meeting in September 1969.

Even then, the SDRs were not to be activated unless or until members with

75 percent of the total quotas had deposited with the IMF instruments of participation pledging that they would undertake all of the obligations of the participants. Finally, a decision to issue SDRs both as to timing and amount, required a majority of 85 percent of the total voting power of the participants in the special drawing account. This requirement gave both the Common Market nations and the United States effective veto power. According to initial plans, decisions to issue or cancel SDRs were to be made for basic periods of five years. In the interests of prudence, the IMF declared, the initial period was limited to three years.

The various legal steps required to implement the plan reflected the desire for careful consideration at each separate step and to ensure the fullest possible understanding and support of the provisions.

Arguing from the analogy of domestic central banks, many students have envisaged the establishment of an international central bank, evolving from the adoption of the SDRs. In time, perhaps, an international central bank may be organized. That time, however, seems far distant. It presupposes the establishment of a world government or a federation of governments. An international central bank will be one of the final, not one of the initial, stages in the evolutionary process of world unification.

In the meantime regional central banks may be established. One might be centered in the Common Market nations, another in Japan and South East Asia, another in the "dollar world." Their establishment also would presuppose the surrender of some national sovereignty. At the moment monetary and fiscal authorities, whether in deficit or surplus nations, seem to prefer to make their own fateful decisions, rather than to be governed by an international or fiscal authority.[41]

Paper Gold

The SDRs are an ingenious device permitting the IMF to increase the reserves of central banks not through the conversion of the IMF into a central bank, but by the allocation, under relatively strict regulations, of what has colloquially been termed "paper gold." Gold entering the vaults of central banks can be used to buy currencies from the IMF or from other central banks. Similarly, the SDRs can be used to buy currencies from the IMF or from other central banks. They are to be issued only to governments and exchanged only among governments.*

In this respect the SDRs have the attributes of gold. Unlike gold, which in-

---

* Some participants have designated their central banks as participants, others have designated their Treasuries.

creases monetary reserves only as new production exceeds non monetary demand, the SDRs presumably will increase world reserves by a certain fixed amount each year. Unlike gold, which may swell the reserves of those nations that do not "need" additional reserves, SDRs will be allocated as a fixed percentage of each nation's quota, to all participants.† Also unlike gold, the SDRs will not fall subject to hoarding or industrial demand.

The basic reason for instituting the SDRs as the President stated in a message to Congress, was to provide nations with acceptable international reserves to supplement existing reserves.* Gold, he explained, had become less and less dependable as a source of regular additions to reserves. Dollar exchange itself would be reduced as the United States moved toward a balance-of-payments equilibrium. He concluded that the SDRs are a landmark in the long evolution of international monetary arrangements. For the first time a reserve asset would be created by the joint decision of many nations.

Ministers and Central Bank Governors in the Group of Ten participating in the General Arrangements to Borrow were not nearly as optimistic as was President Johnson. Although they expressed satisfaction with the action taken at Rio de Janeiro and thought that the SDRs would make a substantial contribution to the strengthening of the international monetary system,§ they concluded that the SDRs could not solve the balance-of-payments problems of individual countries and could not, of course, fund the huge floating liabilities of the United States and the United Kingdom.

The SDRs were viewed by the Deutsche Bundesbank as a "reform for the longer run." [42] Many years would have to elapse, it declared, before this innovation had significant results or indeed had even proved itself, and present proposals might have to be seriously modified in the light of subsequent developments. A substitute had to be found, the Bank continued, for the very "irrational and arbitrary ways in which the world economy was supplied up to now with gold and foreign-exchange reserves." [43] The irrationality of the first could be resolved if gold were relegated to the status of a commodity, and the irrationality of the second could be eliminated if the United States were to eliminate the deficit in its balance of payments.

---

† This percentage may change because a nation, which did not vote for the decision to allocate, may opt out of the allocation. A change in amount of quotas may alter the total amount to be allocated and members which become participants during a basic period may have SDRs allocated to them only for the remainder of the period if the Fund so decides.

* April 30, 1968. On June 19 President Johnson signed a bill giving him the authority to accept the amendment and to deposit an instrument of participation on behalf of the United States.

§ Meeting held on March 29 and 30, 1968. France remained completely skeptical and would not give its endorsement to this statement.

The Issuance of SDRs

Issues of Special Drawing Rights are administered by the IMF which must decide whether or not there is a "global need to supplement reserves." The proposal itself does not pass judgment on this critical problem, nor does it suggest any criteria, other than that the need must be global and unrelated to the requirements of a single country.

In a report submitted to the board of directors of the IMF in 1969, the Managing Director Schweitzer declared somewhat ambiguously that there was a global need for increased liquidity. The ambiguity possibly arose from the fact that SDRs were apparently not be activated until the United Kingdom and the United States had overcome their payments imbalances. It may also have reflected a widespread belief that there was actually a surfeit of liquidity rather than a shortage. This was evidenced by rising consumer prices in the leading industrial nations.

In the 1950s and early 1960s there was little doubt, Schweitzer concluded, that global reserves were adequate. Since 1964 basic criteria had come into conflict. The main indications of reserve inadequacy were increased reliance on trade and payments restrictions, and increased recourse to international financial assistance. In part, this situation resulted from the unwillingness of deficit nations to suppress domestic inflationary pressures. He noted, however, that both the United Kingdom and the United States were taking energetic measures to prevent further currency depreciation. He added that IMF keeps international payment developments constantly under review and stands ready to suggest appropriate measures to prevent currency erosion.

After weighing pros and cons and after estimating the probable demand for and supply of international reserves resulting from various sources, Schweitzer concluded that Special Drawing Rights approximately equivalent to $3.5 billion should be allocated at the beginning of 1970, $3 billion at the beginning of 1971, and $3 billion at the beginning of 1972. All amounts are now stated in SDRs, defined as equivalent to 0.888671 grams of fine gold.

The rate of allocations at the beginning of 1970 was 16.8 percent of the quota of each of the 104 participating nations; at the beginning of 1971, 10.7 percent of the quota of each of the 109 participating nations; and at the beginning of 1972 10.6 percent of the 112 participating nations. Some of the more important allocations are shown in Table 16.6.

In order to illustrate the role of the SDRs in Federal Reserve operations, let us assume that the U.S. Treasury wishes to activate 200 million SDRs of its allot-

Table 16.6

Allotments of Special Drawing Rights Received by Certain Participants
(Millions of SDRs)

Participants	January 1, 1971
Belgium	209.3
Australia	225.6
The Netherlands	236.5
Italy	318.0
Japan	377.4
Canada	358.6
India	326.2
France	485.0
Germany	542.4
United Kingdom	1,006.3
United States	2,294.0
Total	6,379.3
All other nations	2,935.7
Grand total	9,315.0

Source: *International Financial Statistics*, Vol. 25, No. 3 (March 1972), p. 7.

ment, placing these with the Federal Reserve banks. The effect on the combined statement is shown in Table 16.7.

Table 16.7

Hypothetical Combined Statement for All Federal Reserve Banks
(Millions of SDRs)

Assets		Liabilities	
SDR certificates	200	Due to U.S. Treasury	200

The SDRs like gold, increase the reserve assets of the Federal Reserve banks and the monetary reserves of the nation. The Treasury can use its deposit account in any manner that it pleases. If it were to draw upon its deposits, member-bank reserves would, of course, rise.

The U.S. Treasury now requests the IMF to find a purchaser of the SDRs held by the Reserve Banks. The Fund, in accordance with Article 25 (Section 2b) of its Articles of Agreement, shifts the SDRs to Germany, a designated recipient, which in turn, places them with the Deutsche Bundesbank. The effect of this hypothetical example upon the balance sheets of the two central institutions is:

Table 16.8

Hypothetical Statements

Federal Reserve Banks		Deutsche Bundesbank*	
(Millions of SDRs)			
Assets	**Liabilities**	**Assets**	**Liabilities**
SDR certificates −200	no change	SDR certificates +200	Due to Federal Reserve
Due from Deutsche Bundesbank +200			Banks +200

* It is assumed that the Deutsche Bundesbank would supply German marks. Actually, it has the right to supply any convertible currency.

The Federal Reserve banks would then be in a position to sell 200 million SDRs worth of German marks in the U.S. market. Being tantamount to an open-market sale, unless offset, this move would reduce member-bank reserves. The transfer of marks from the books of the Deutsche Bundesbank to those of local German banks increases the reserves of the latter. In other words, unless offset, this operation has the same effect on the banking systems of the two nations as would an export of gold from the U.S. to Germany. Actually, the transactions set forth in the example would probably take place directly between the Treasuries of the two nations, but even so, the final result would be that which we have depicted.

It is assumed that Germany has been designated by the Fund as a participant qualified to receive SDRs. (A qualified participant is one with a strong balance of payments position and adequate gross reserves.) In this instance the Fund served the function of a railway switching yard in shunting SDRs to the appropriate recipient.

A participant may use its holdings of SDRs to obtain, in direct agreement with another participant, an equivalent amount of its currency. A participant may also transfer its holdings of SDRs to the general account of the Fund in repurchases of its own currency and in the payment of charges. The Fund itself may use its own holdings of SDRs to replenish its holdings of a member's currency.

In being designated as a recipient of SDRs, Germany, in the above illustration, is not required, unless it agrees otherwise, to take an amount of SDRs in excess of twice its initial allotment (i.e. 1,084.8 million SDRs). In other words, it is limited in its total holdings of SDRs, to its initial allotment (542.4 million SDRs), plus twice that amount (1,084.8 million SDRs) or to a grant total of 1,627.2 million SDRs. The U.S. in turn cannot make use, on the average, of more than 70 percent of its initial allocation of SDRs. If its average use should exceed this total, the U.S. must retire the excess by the use of gold or currencies acceptable to the Fund. The U.S. representatives opposed the requirement that credit lines be reconstituted. This provision is, however, very important in preventing an undue use of SDRs by any one participant.

A participant desirous of using SDRs to meet a balance of payment need, will be entitled to obtain currency convertible in fact from a designated participant and the Fund may not prevent this transaction. If a participant persists in using SDRs in the absence of a legitimate need, its right to use the SDRs still in its possession may be suspended by the Fund. The Fund also has the right to reverse any transaction which was not based on a legitimate need.

The Fund establishes quarterly plans, which designate the participants to receive SDRs during the ensuing quarter, and, in so doing, the Fund is directed to select participants in such a manner as will promote a balanced distribution. From January 1, 1970 to April 30, 1971, the number of designated participants varied each quarter from 22 to 28. All participants so designated came to 37 out of a total of 108 nations participating in the SDR arrangements. Nations that hold SDRs beyond their net cumulative allocations, (allocations minus cancellations) receive interest on the excess; those that hold SDRs less than their net cumulative allocations, pay interest on the deficit.

SDRs can, with proper and strict safe guards, significantly contribute to monetary integration in the capitalist world. They do not represent claims on individual nations but are rather reserve assets, which participants know that they can use to obtain currencies for other participants in accordance with the provisions of the IMF.

Their use should be dictated by strictly economic, rather than political, considerations. The reason for this obvious interjection is that the executive directors of the IMF have in the past, according to Lord Cromer, one-time Governor of the Bank of England, tended, on major issues, "to represent positions which are ultimately political." This tendency has prevented the IMF from exercising sufficient surveillance over major countries.[44] Unless there is meticulous surveillance (as must be the case over any extension of credit) this proposal is doomed to failure, especially as many provisions of the agreement seem ambiguous or weak.

Use of the SDRs

From January 1, 1970 to January 31, 1972, 62 participating nations made use of their SDR allotments. Total net use amounted to 1,530.1 million SDRs, of which 1,026 million were sold to other nations, and 504.1 million paid to the IMF. Important users of SDRs were Colombia, Argentina, India, Indonesia, Israel, Morocco, New Zealand, Pakistan, the Philippines, Turkey, United Arab Republic, United States, and Yugoslavia. Important purchasers of the SDRs were Australia, Austria, Belgium, Canada, Germany, Japan, and the Netherlands. Nations using the SDRs included those which had commonly borrowed abroad to finance deficits in their balance of payments resulting from a weakening of their international competitive ability, from development programs, and from rearmament.

It has been suggested that the SDRs be used to finance economic development. This would not seem a legitimate use of a reserve asset. Economic development would most appropriately be financed by the World Bank. As an investment banking institution, it assists in formulating development projects, in appraising their utility to the borrowing nation, and their value in generating foreign-exchange for loan repayment. The IMF cannot and does not exercise this type of control over the SDRs. Little wonder that some nations look upon the SDRs as manna from heaven.

MONETARY TURBULENCE

Monetary turbulence in its many forms was illustrated by the hectic developments through the two years from November 1967 to November 1969. This period witnessed the devaluation of sterling (November 18, 1967), the temporary closing of the London gold market (March 15, 1968), the devaluation of the French franc (August 8, 1969) and the revaluation of the German mark. (October 26, 1969).* The dollar was involved in all developments, either directly by reason of the massive outflow of funds from the United States or indirectly by reason of the equally massive flow of funds through the United States from one country to another.

The Demise of Sterling

No development in this period was more important that the demise of sterling. A currency which, in the hundred years after the Battle of Waterloo, had risen to

---

* The devaluation of sterling by 14.3 percent had been preceded by intense consultation among the industrial powers. One result was that no industrial nation followed Great Britain's example, as none wished to weaken the position of sterling as a key currency. This decision affords an outstanding example of monetary solidarity.

what seemed an impregnable position was critically weakened by the economic policies of the 1950s and 1960s and became even more overvalued in 1963 after the adoption of an inflationary program, the purpose of which was to stimulate growth and ostensibly to improve the competive position of British industry. Devaluation, which probably should have taken place in 1964, was an inevitable consequence of inadequate past performance and of government policy vacillating between the desire to create a welfare state and to sustain the international acceptability of sterling.[45] The large government expenditures demanded by a welfare state caused foreigners to lose confidence in its currency.

Beginning in May 1967, shortly after a third cut in the British bank rate from 6 to 5.5 percent as part of a current "reflationary" program, confidence in the pound began to wane. The British trade deficit rose, exports failed to expand and imports continued high, reflecting a sharp rise in domestic demand. These trends were aggravated by the Middle East crisis, which caused Arab countries to shift their sterling balances to Paris. The market became concerned about the effects of closing the Suez Canal on the British balance of payments. Rising government expenditures and dock strikes caused additional fears, leading to heavy withdrawals of sterling by nations outside the sterling area. The demand for gold increased, and the premium on investment dollars exceeded 30 percent.

Toward the middle of November the market became convinced that devaluation was imminent, and the pound, spot and forward, was sold on a massive scale. A governor of the Bank of England declared:

> Much has been made of the part played by speculators in bringing the pound down. Speculators were there, of course, particularly at the end, but it is a travesty of the facts to put the blame on them . . . for many years past it has been our inadequate performance that has undermined confidence in us and in ourselves. We all too thoroughly provided the raw material for a bearish view of sterling.[46]

Devaluation, he continued, is not an escape from reality. It can succeed only if costs are kept under control and prevented from whittling away the immediate competitive advantage arising from devaluation.

In order not to whittle away the immediate competitive advantage of devaluation, Britain raised Bank rate to 8 percent, the highest since 1914, and put "severe but selective restrictions" on bank lending.[47] At the time of the 1949 devaluation Bank rate had been held to 2 percent. Monetary policy was not then invoked. The result was that the devaluation was largely wasted; prices rose quickly to nullify the competitive advantage.[48]

During these critical months of 1967 the heavy deficit in the balance of payments, plus the flight of funds from Great Britain, was financed by equally massive foreign borrowing. (See Table 16.9).

Table 16.9 *

The Need for External Borrowing from July 1, 1967–March 31, 1968 (data in millions of dollars)

Goods, services, and transfer payments		−$1,385
Long-term capital movements		− 438
Net errors and omissions		− 329
Short-term capital movements		− 1,526
Exchange adjustments		− 298
		−$3,976

Sources of External Borrowing

IMF accounts	(decline)	$ 319
Sterling liabilities to central monetary institutions and BIS	(increase)	3,016
Official liabilities in non sterling currencies	(increase)	767
Transfer of securities (for sale) from dollar portfolios to reserves	(increase)	490
Gold and convertible currency reserves	(decrease)	112
		4,066
Discrepancy		− 90
		$3,976

* International Monetary Fund, *1968 Annual Report*, (Washington, D.C.), p. 120.

The bulk of the funds borrowed (perhaps $2 billion) were obtained from central banks under swap agreements. To reduce these credits Britain drew on the IMF for $1.4 billion in June 1968.

As *The Economist* (London) pointed out, London faced the danger of losing sterling-area reserves at each successive sterling crisis. Fearful that this would happen after the end of World II, the balances were blocked and were only gradually released. The total remained remarkably stable but the geographical composition changed greatly. India and Pakistan used up their balances but the Middle Eastern and Far Eastern sterling countries increased their holdings. Before the 1967 devaluation the sterling-area nations refrained from reducing their balances in London. They did so through "loyalty to the club," by the persuasion of high interest rates and by an unwillingness to break the bank.*

---

* In 1949, the currencies of the sterling area, together with many other currencies, followed sterling in devaluing against the U.S. dollar. In 1967 the great majority of sterling-area nations made no move, so that devaluation meant losses in terms of their own currencies and induced shifts into gold or dollars. The financial links between Great Britain and the sterling area were thus loosened still farther. It was thought that a dollar guarantee would give greater stability to the sterling area.

After devaluation, the nations of the sterling-area, in order to diversify their reserves, began to draw upon their balances, reducing them from £1.7 billion on March 31, to £1.5 billion on June 30, 1968. A continuation of this trend would have forced Great Britain to devalue once again.

To avoid this threat and to give greater stability to the sterling system, the Bank of England in the spring of 1968 arranged through the BIS for a $2 billion credit from central banks in twelve nations.† The credits could be drawn upon and used to meet declines in both official and private balances, but could not be used to finance deficits in the balance of payments. Drawings could be made over three years and repayments were due within ten years.

The credits negotiated by the United Kingdom enabled it to guarantee the dollar value of a substantial part of the reserves of the sterling area which it was willing to do provided that each member nation maintained a certain proportion of its reserves in sterling.‡ In effect this action blocked those balances and prevented sterling-area nations from switching their sterling reserves into other currencies or gold. It also dissuaded other nations from establishing or increasing sterling balances. The British government described the arrangement as "a unique opportunity to give sterling a new stability." Actually it came close to ending the role of sterling as a reserve currency and strengthened for the time being the position of the dollar as an anchor currency.

Like the United States, the United Kingdom is a heavy debtor on short-term accounts and a large creditor on long-term accounts. At the end of 1968, net official short-term liabilities to the IMF and to monetary authorities in both sterling and non sterling areas totaled about $10 billion. These liabilities had increased by $7.4 billion since 1962. Total official and non-official long-term assets exceeded long-term liabilities by more than $13 billion and had increased about $7 billion since 1962.

If Great Britain could use its excess long-term assets to discharge its short-term liabilities, it would be in a satisfactory financial condition. A large part of the long-term assets, however, are in the form of direct investments, which might be difficult to liquidate without considerable sacrifice and which are not necessarily located in nations to which Britain is obligated.

---

† To meet its commitment the BIS could borrow on short and medium terms in the international markets, use the funds placed on deposit by overseas sterling area central banks, and draw upon the stand-by arrangements totaling $2 billion with twelve nations.

‡ The proportion varied from country to country; for Australia and Malaysia it was 40 percent, but for others it has not been published. Provided that the agreed proportion is maintained, the British government guarantees the value, in U.S. dollars, of that part of the official sterling reserves held by each overseas sterling-area country that exceeds 10 percent of its total official reserves. *Midland Bank Review,* (London: Midland Bank Ltd., November 1969), p. 17.

Britain's basic problem, like that of the United States, arose from the fact that it borrowed short and loaned long. The problem, therefore, centers on the short- and medium-term debt, which calls for total repayments of about $5 billion from the beginning of 1970 to the end of 1975.[49] Some part of the debt can be discharged by a favorable trade balance, which recently has been increasing, part might be repaid by use of Britain's alloment of SDRs and part by refunding.

On February 7, 1972, the Right Honorable Edward Heath, Prime Minister of the U.K. stated that Britain was ready to repay the last instalment of its debt to the IMF amounting to £415 million. For the first time since 1964 the nation would be free of all short-term international debt.[50]

Pressure on the Dollar

In the first two weeks of March 1968, belief that the price of gold could not be held gained ground. The American trade balance suffered a sharp decline and pressure on the dollar became severe. Shifts from currency into gold became disturbingly large. A conference of central bankers, hurriedly convened in Washington, took action to end the gold pool. Between the devaluation of the pound on November 18, 1967, and the termination of the gold pool on March 16, 1968, the United States lost about $2.3 billion in gold, an amount equal to 18 percent of its stock. In addition, the U.S. Treasury drew $200 million in foreign currencies from the IMF and sold $396 million of non marketable obligations to official institutions in foreign countries. The loss of gold led to further intensification of American foreign-exchange controls over capital movements.

The problems now facing the United States are very severe. They include, as will be pointed out in Chapter 17, elimination of exchange controls, the attainment through increased competitive power in foreign trade of very large favorable annual trade balance put by some students at $10 billion and the funding of a large part of the short-term liabilities owed to foreigners.

France

The French currency crisis of November 1968, unlike the British crisis of November 1967, and the gold crisis of March 1968, did not subject the dollar or the American gold stock to strong pressures.

After the political and social unrest of June 1968, France legislated large increases in wages, salaries, and social welfare outlays and endeavored to find a way out of its difficulties by spurring economic expansion. Such forced expansion caused fear that the franc would be devalued and led to a sharp capital flight which was itself aggravated by an announced increase in income and inheritance taxation.

A massive flight of funds, mainly to Germany, took place. German credit institutions placed most of the incoming liquid funds on foreign money markets in response to a favorable foreign-exchange cover offered by the Deutsche Bundesbank. France lost 50 percent of its reserves, which declined from $6 to $3 billion; borrowed $700 million under a swap agreement with the Federal Reserve banks; and drew $745 million from the IMF.* Contrary to general expectations, the franc was not devalued at that time. Instead, France reduced the budget deficit from $2.3 to $1.3 billion, froze prices and wages, provided tax relief to stimulate exports, and imposed far-reaching foreign-exchange controls.

During the French crisis the pound was under very severe pressure, causing the British government to impose severe restraints on bank lending and to require importers to deposit amounts equal to 50 percent of the value of imported goods with British customs for six months. At one stroke imports were thus discouraged and lendable funds impounded.

Despite tight exchange controls the French franc remained exposed in the early months of 1969. Inflationary pressures continued, heavy wage demands persisted and the political situation deteriorated resulting in President Charles de Gaulle's defeat on April 27. A heavy volume of funds again flowed into Germany.

Georges Pompidou's impressive election victory gave temporary relief to the franc. Rising Eurodollar rates, however, again placed it under heavy pressure. Faced with continued attrition of official reserves, the French government announced on August 8, 1969, that it had decided to devalue the franc by 11.1 percent to $0.180044, rather than impose too severe a deflation on the French economy. Although devaluation came as a distinct surprise to many people, the possibility had been discussed with the group of Ten as early as November 1968.[51]

Germany

Through these two convulsive years the German mark commanded universal confidence. Labor productivity remained high, wages and salaries fell in terms of sales, industrial-export prices continued competitive, and the trade balance was highly favorable. The German people are noted for their thrift and their opposi-

---

* France was also granted central-bank credit of $2 billion (text of communique of Group of Ten Meeting, November 22, 1968).

tion to government action that might provoke inflation. The result was that monetary and political disturbances in other nations quickened a huge inflow of short-term funds and heightened the conviction that Germany would revalue the mark. The inflow of foreign money was concentrated in certain critical periods. From the beginning of February to the end of September 1969, when convictions grew that the mark would be revalued the gross inflow totaled about 20 billion marks.[52] The funds flowing into Germany were either owned by foreign firms and individuals or had been borrowed in order to purchase German goods or to speculate in German currency. Expectations that the mark would be revalued generated important leads and lags. Firms were anxious to buy marks and to purchase German products, but not anxious to receive payment for products sold to Germany.

The inflow would have provoked rapid credit expansion had it not been for countermeasures by the Deutsche Bundesbank, including imposition of a 100 percent reserve requirement on new deposits owed to non residents. Other measures included the resale, by means of swap transactions, to credit institutions for use abroad of a certain proportion of the dollars acquired in spot dealings,[53] reductions in the open-market portfolio of the Deutsche Bundesbank, and increases in discount rates.

During September 1969 the world became convinced that the mark would be revalued soon after the German parliamentary elections. Funds began flowing into German in even greater amounts. In the first seventeen days the Bundesbank purchased $625 million and during the following week a further $875 million. On September 24 alone it bought $250 million. To dam the inflow the Bundesbank requested that the West German government close the foreign-currency exchanges on September 25th. On the day after the German elections (September 29) there were indications of a renewed inflow and the exchanges were closed; the Bundesbank received permission to let the mark float. It was no longer required to buy dollars at the stipulated rate.

This action was a prelude to the upward revaluation of the mark by 9.3 percent, which took place October 26 and which raised the new parity from 25 to 27.3224 cents. This revaluation exceeded by a wide margin the earlier revaluation of 5 percent on March 6, 1961. Compared with the parities at the beginning of 1958, the value of the mark at that time in relation to the dollar and most of the currencies of Western industrial nations was raised 14.75 percent, in relation to the pound sterling 34 percent, and in relation to the French franc 52 percent.[54]

The 1969 revaluation rate was set relatively high in order to help eliminate the cost and price differentials between Germany and other countries and to allow for any new price disparities that might occur. It was followed by a rapid drain of "hot" money from Germany, which eliminated the excess liquidity in the banking system.

In revaluing the mark, Germany assumed then, as it did in 1971, a heavy share of the burden for making the price and cost adjustments necessitated by realignment of exchange rates. The need for realignment itself resulted from the unwillingness of various nations, France, the United Kingdom, and the United States to suppress domestic inflationary tendencies. The burden was thus shifted to the nation that had kept its house in order.

No exchange techniques, no matter how carefully thought out, can compensate for defects in national policies. In the 1960s such defects gave rise to massive movements of "hot" money; to the countervailing use of swap arrangements; to dependence on the IMF (handicapped as it was by large holdings of non-usable currencies); to various types of outside assistance; and finally to the proposal for the SDRs. These measures are only short-run palliatives. Lasting reform awaits action by leading nations in providing a satisfactory standard of deferred payments. Once this is provided, "hot" money will then be quickly invested in long-term obligations, thrift will be encouraged, and savings will be used in ways that will contribute to self-generating increases in national income.[55]

Notes

1. An historical review of the relations of the Bank of England with other central banks is to be found in *Quartely Bulletin* (Bank of England, December 1967), VII, No. 4, 374–380; also see Stephen V. O. Clarke, *Central Bank Cooperation 1924–31* (New York: Federal Reserve Bank, 1967); and William Adams Brown, Jr., *The International Gold Standard Reinterpreted 1914–1934,* 2 Vols. (New York: National Bureau of Economic Research, 1940).

2. Karl Blessing to the National Industrial Conference Board, New York, September 21, 1966.

3. See Pierre-Paul Schweitzer (Managing Director of the International Monetary Fund) address to the Canadian Council of the International Chamber of Commerce, Montreal, January 21, 1965.

4. See Roy L. Reierson, *The Question of International Liquidity* (New York: Bankers Trust Company, November 1965).

5. E. Stopper address to the Association of Swiss Holding and Finance Companies, December 11, 1968 quoted in *Press Review,* Bank for International Settlements (Basle: December 12, 1968).

6. International Monetary Fund, *1964 Annual Report* (Washington, D.C.), p. 25.

7. International Monetary Fund, "The Adequacy of Monetary Reserves", *Staff Paper,* Vol. III, No. 2, (October 1953) pp. 181–227.

8. OECD Information Service, press release, July 13, 1965. See Pieter Lieftinck, *External Debt and Debt-Bearing of Developing Countries* ("Essays in International Finance No. 51, International Finance Section" [Princeton, New Jersey: Princeton University Press, March 1966]).

9. *International Financial News Survey* (International Monetary Fund, Volume XVIII, No. 30, July 29, 1968).

10. See Karl Blessing, "International Monetary Problems," *Progress* (Unilever Quarterly), II, No. 288, 1966.

11. Bank for International Settlements, *Thirty-Third Annual Report,* 1st April, 1962–31st March, 1963 (Basle: June 10, 1963), p. 30.

12. For discussion see *The Economic Review* (Federal Reserve Bank of Cleveland, July 1968).

13. See *Monthly Economic Letter* (First National City Bank of New York, November 1968), pp. 128–131.

14. Bank for International Settlements, *Thirty-Eighth Annual Report,* 1st April 1967–31st March 1968 (Basle: June 10, 1968), p. 7.

15. *International Financial News Survey* (International Monetary Fund, Volume XX, No. 49, December 13, 1968). Each member-nation appoints a member of the Board of Governors of the Fund: Six members, the United States, the United Kingdom, Germany, France, Japan, and India, each appoint an executive director. Other member nations are divided into fourteen groups, each of which selects one executive director. Members of the board of directors and the board of executive directors come from ministries of finance, central banks, government banks, and government agencies or departments interested in economic affairs. The IMF operates largely through its executive directors, to whom the board of directors has delegated all its powers, except for some that it cannot legally delegate. The extent to which any director consults with his home government on pending issues depends upon domestic arrangements. The annual meetings of the IMF and the World Bank provide a forum for ministers of finance, their staffs, and other interested parties, including representatives of central banks.

16. See International Monetary Fund, *International Financial Statistics,* Volume 23, No. 1 (January 1970), p. 6, and Volume 25, No. 3 (March 1972), p. 19.

17. For a schedule of these charges see *1969 Annual Report* of the International Monetary Fund (Washington, D.C.), p. 181.

18. For a complete discussion of IMF lending policies including compensatory financing of export fluctuations see Hans Aufricht, *The Fund Agreement: Living Law and Emerging Practice* ("Princeton Studies in International Finance No. 23, International Finance Section, Department of Economics." [Princeton: Princeton University Press, 1969]).

19. See Address by Miroslov Kriz., "The Future of Gold," at the Annual Meeting of the American Economic Association, Chicago, Illinois, December 30, 1968 in *The American Economic Review,* Vol. LIX, No. 2, (May 1969) pp. 353–356.

20. *Quarterly Bulletin* (Bank of England), Vol. V, No. 1, March 1965, p. 3.

21. *Quarterly Bulletin* (Bank of England), Vol. IV, No. 4, December 1964, pp. 257–259.

22. *Quarterly Bulletin* (Bank of England), Vol. V, No. 2, June 1965, p. 109.

23. Quoted in the *Financial Times* (London), September 3, 1966.

24. *Federal Reserve Bulletin,* (March 1962), p. 289, (September 1962), p. 1138. A detailed discussion of current swap transactions can be found twice yearly in this bulletin.

25. See "Central Bank Swaps", *Monthly Review* (Federal Reserve Bank of Atlanta, December 1967).

26. *New England Business Review* (Federal Reserve Bank of Boston, December, 1968).

27. *Federal Reserve Bulletin,* (December 1969), p. A12.

28. *Federal Reserve Bulletin,* (September 1968), p. 724; (September 1969), p. 699; and (March 1971), p. 191.

29. *Federal Reserve Bulletin,* (September 1967), p. 1520; (March 1971), pp. 189–192; and *Monthly Review,* (Federal Reserve Bank of New York, October 1971), p. 217.

30. *Federal Reserve Bulletin,* (March 1964), p. 295.

31. *Federal Reserve Bulletin,* (September 1968), p. 729.

32. Bank for International Settlements *Thirty-Eighth Annual Report,* 1st April 1967–31st March 1968 (Basel: June 10, 1968), p. 145.

33. See *Midland Bank Review,* (London: Midland Bank Ltd., November 1969), p. 17.

34. Ekhard Brehmer, "Official Forward Exchange Operations: The German Experience" *Staff Papers* Vol. II, No. 3 (Washington, D.C.: International Monetary Fund, 1964).

35. J. Marcus Fleming and Robert A. Mundell, "Official Intervention on the Forward Exchange Market" *Staff Papers* Vol. 11, No. 1 (Washington, D.C.: International Monetary Fund, 1964).

36. Charles A. Coombs, "Treasury and Federal Reserve Foreign Exchange Operations," *Federal Reserve Bulletin,* (March 1966), p. 319.

37. *Federal Reserve Bulletin,* (March 1968), p. 269.

38. *Federal Reserve Bulletin,* (September 1968), p. 734.

39. *Federal Reserve Bulletin,* (November 1970), p. A 81; and (February 1972), p. A 83.

40. "The Place of Special Drawing Rights in the International Monetary System," *Quarterly Bulletin* (Bank of England) Vol. 8, No. 2, June 1968, p. 146. Also see "Experience with Special Drawing Rights." *Economic Review,* (Federal Reserve Bank of Cleveland, March 1971), pp. 3–14.

41. See *Central Banking and Economic Integration* lecture by M. W. Holtrop, to the Per Jacobsson Foundation, May 16, 1968, at Konserthuset-Stockholm.

42. *Report of the Deutsche Bundesbank for the Year 1967,* p. 45.

43. *Ibid.*

44. See commentary by the Earl of Cromer, on *Central Banking and Economic Integration* to the Per Jacobsson Foundation, May 16, 1968 at Konserthuset-Stockholm.

45. Bank for International Settlements, *Thirty-Eighth Annual Report.* 1st April 1967–31st March 1968 (Basle: June 10, 1968), p. 7.

46. *Quarterly Bulletin* (Bank of England), June 1968, p. 171.

47. See *The Midland Bank Review* (London: Midland Bank Ltd., February 1968).

48. A good comparison of economic conditions in Britain in 1949 and 1967 and the results of the two devaluations can be found in *Economic Commentary* (Federal Reserve Bank of Cleveland, December 9, 1967).

49. Benjamin J. Cohen, *The Reform of Sterling* ("Princeton Studies in International Finance, No. 77, International Finance Section, Department of Economies", [Princeton, New Jersey: Princeton University Press, December, 1969]); The Right Honorable Roy Jenkins (Chancellor of the Exchequer) address to the House of Commons, London, February 27, 1968.

50. *The Financial Times* (London) February 8, 1972.

51. "Treasury and Reserve Foreign Exchange Operations," *Federal Reserve Bulletin* (September 1969), pp. 706–708.

52. *Monthly Report of the Deutsche Bundesbank*, December 1969, pp. 35, 65.

53. See *Monthly Report of the Deutsche Bundesbank*, October 1969, p. 5. (The Deutsche Bundesbank assumed the exchange risk).

54. *Monthly Report of the Deutsche Bundesbank*, November 1969, p. 37.

55. See Lord Robbins, "Issues and Alternatives," *Monetary Reform and the Price of Gold: Alternative Approaches* edited by Randall Hinshaw (Baltimore: Johns Hopkins Press, 1967); and Louis Rasminsky (Governor of the Bank of Canada), address to the Annual Banquet of the Overseas Bankers Club at Guildhall, London, February 3, 1969.

CHAPTER 17

Bretton Woods Revisited

Convened upon the initiative of the United States, the United Nations Monetary and Financial Conference, meeting at Bretton Woods, New Hampshire, from July 1-22, 1944, drafted the Bretton Woods Agreement. This provided not only for the establishment of the IMF but also for its sister institution, the International Bank for Reconstruction and Development.[1]

The Articles of Agreement of the IMF were adopted against the background of pervasive and mutually destructive economic anarchy of the 1930s. In endeavoring to build a better world, the Articles of Agreement not only provided for the lending activities of the Fund, discussed in previous chapters, but also laid the basis for the elimination of exchange restrictions, for the establishment of par values for currencies and stable exchange rates and for frequent consultations among members and the officials of the Fund. The last function is one of the most important inasmuch as "regular consultations between the Fund and the member provide the Fund with an opportunity to review and to criticise the monetary and financial policies being pursued by the member."[2] Certain actions, such as changes in exchange rates or the imposition of exchange controls must receive the concurrence of the Fund. Willingness of member nations to consult with the Fund and to abide by its decisions implies a readiness to surrender some of their sovereign rights. In the absence of a readiness to do so, no international organization can succeed.

The Bretton Woods agreements envisaged the dollar as the linchpin of the new international monetary system. The United States then possessed large gold reserves and dominant economic power. There was promise of a strong, perhaps overly strong, balance of payments position. The larger part of world trade was conducted in dollars, most export and import contracts were stated in dollars and the bulk of long-term bonds was floated in dollars.

The par values of currencies were expressed in terms of gold or in terms of the U. S. dollar of the weight and fineness in effect on July 1, 1944. Each member was obligated to keep the maximum and minimum exchange transactions of its currency within one percent of parity. A member agreeing freely to buy and sell gold (the United States) was deemed to have abided by this undertaking. The monetary system thus established was in reality the dollar exchange standard. Nations linked their currencies to the dollar and the dollar, alone among currencies, assumed the obligation of gold convertibility.

The deficit in the balance of payments of the United States, resulting largely from the Vietnam war and the inflation it engendered, brought the Bretton Woods system to an end.[3] The United States tried unsuccessfully to stave off the inevitable debacle by foreign exchange controls and trade restrictions, by bringing pressure on foreign holders of dollars not to redeem their holdings in gold, by favoring a two-tier gold market, by arranging foreign loans and swap agreements, by drawings upon the IMF and by frantic sponsoring of the SDRs.

On August 15, 1971, the dollar link to gold was finally broken and the international monetary system was cut loose from its moorings and is now adrift in uncharted seas. This could have been prevented had the United States followed "the rules of the game." Heavy deficits in the balance of payments called for restrictive fiscal and monetary policies and a sharp reduction in foreign military commitments and expenditures.

Restrictive monetary and fiscal policies might have been inaugurated not later than 1965. Thereafter inflation gained momentum, labor costs per unit of product rose sharply and consumer and wholesale prices escalated. Adopting restrictive policies at that time as urged by the IMF and the BIS, might have enabled the United States to avoid the credit crises of 1966 and 1969 and might have made the recession of 1970 less severe. The dollar exchange standard permitted administrations to view the deficit in the balance of payments with "benign neglect." Nations whose currencies were tied to the dollar were saddled with the task of financing the deficit. Theirs was the responsibility to buy dollars in order to peg exchange rates. This situation would persist as long as other nations refrained from redeeming dollar holdings in gold or in other reserve assets.[4]

At an extraordinary meeting of the France-U.S. Association in Bordeaux on March 21, 1972, M., O. Wormser, Governor of the Bank of France, stated that the dollar crisis had existed for over ten years. The crisis was due not to the Bretton Woods agreements, but, to the fact that member nations did not abide by these agreements. If, instead of accumulating dollars they had demanded that they be redeemed in gold, the U. S. would have realized that it must take corrective action and that it could not continue to live on the largess of its friends.[5]

The Background of the Crisis

Developments at home and abroad, reinforcing one another, combined to make 1971 one of the most critical years in the monetary history of the United States. The pace of domestic economic recovery was "unacceptably slow," too slow to make any dent in the margin of idle men and machines.[6] Industrial production was weak, inventory spending lagged, and productivity gains were disappointingly small. A sizeable retrenchment took place in plant and equipment expenditures. The capital markets were subject to severe strains. Consumer savings were large and consumer spending relatively small.

Unemployment continued large, especially in those parts of the country affected by defense contracts. The unemployment rate (seasonally adjusted) reached 6 percent by the end of 1971, and exceeded this by a wide margin through 1971 in certain areas, notably in Washington, Connecticut, Michigan, and Maine. Average weekly earnings continued to rise, particularly in manufacturing and contract construction. Wage rate increases in collective bargaining agreements (for the first year) in construction came to about 14 percent; in all industries to about 12 percent.[7]

The coexistence of high unemployment and rising prices served to undermine public confidence in the ability of the country to cope with domestic problems. The consumer felt the full impact of rapidly rising food prices. This the government could have checked in part, had the farmer not possessed great political power, by ending "voluntary" quota restraints on meat imports and by permitting the free importation of fruits and vegetables from Mexico.[8]

Foreign Developments

"The period since the mid-1960s," reported Pierre-Paul Schweitzer, Managing Director of the IMF before the Economic and Social Council of the United Nations, "had been marked by recurrent crises in gold and the foreign exchange markets evidenced by enormous shifts of capital among the major financial centres." [9] Short-term funds, resulting mainly from the balance of payments deficit of the United States, exceed $64 billion by the end of 1971. At the end of 1958, when currency convertibility first became common, they had amounted to only $17 billion.

In the meanwhile the country's gold stock fell from about 120 percent of these liabilities to 16 percent. Fear of a continuous erosion of the purchasing power of currencies, of the devaluation of currencies, of rising long-term interest rates, caused short-term funds to grow ever larger. The closer integration of money markets through the 1960s, the rise of the Eurodollar market, the growth of multinational corporations, along with an increased sensitivity to possible interest and exchange rate changes, lay at the basis of gigantic money flows. Never had the world witnessed such hectic phenomena.

The magnitude of the potential movement of short-term funds was revealed in 1970 when for the first time in several years monetary policies in Europe and in the United States moved in opposite directions.[10] In 1970 American monetary policy had eased. Real output was stagnant and unemployment was rising. These developments, rather than the continued increase in unit labor costs and in consumer and wholesale prices, formed the rationale of Federal Reserve policy. Beginning about the middle of the year, the Reserve System took action to bring about a sharp reduction in net borrowed reserves. Short-term rates collapsed. European nations on the other hand continued to follow a policy of restraint. Short-term rates in Germany and the United Kingdom remained at high levels. The dollar flow to Europe was massive. Much was used by American banks to repay Eurodollar borrowings from their foreign branches. Repayment of these borrowings enabled European banks to shift dollars into home currencies for local use. To provide the local currencies required, European central banks had to purchase massive amounts of dollars. United States short-term liabilities to official institutions grew by $8 billion.

The inflow of funds undermined policies of restraint in a number of European countries. Accordingly, various measures were introduced by foreign governments and central banks to discourage use of Eurodollar credits by their residents. Cyclical fluatuations in the United States and other European nations began to be more closely aligned.

At the end of 1970, confidence in the dollar was relatively well sustained. The situation however, changed quickly; early in 1971 international financial markets began to sense an impending crisis. Outflows of short-term funds from the United States continued in large volume. A substantial amount ($6 billion from December 30, 1970 to June 30, 1971) was used to reduce Eurodollar borrowings. A still larger amount represented the flight of funds seeking security. The decline in the trade surplus of the United States aroused fears of a continued loss of funds and of a decline in its competitive strength in international markets.

The German mark was particularly exposed to speculative buying pressure in view of Germany's large trade surplus and its restrictive credit policy. Interest rates were kept above international levels and German firms borrowed heavily abroad. The German government was confronted with the dilemma of making "its restrictive policy effective while simultaneously allowing its business corporations unfettered access to the Euro-dollar market." [11]

Following an increase in German official reserves by $3 billion in the first four months of the year, German economic institutes early in May recommended the floating of the German currency or its revaluation. Speculative funds flooded into Germany. The Deutsche Bundesbank was forced to buy increasing amounts of dollars, more than $1 billion on May 3-4 and a further $1 billion on May 5, when it withdrew from the market. To protect themselves against a speculative inflow of funds, the central banks of the Netherlands, Switzerland, Belgium and Austria simultaneously terminated official support of the dollar. Over the following weekend, the Swiss franc and the Austrian schilling were revalued by 7.07 percent and 5.05 percent respectively. The German mark was allowed to float, as was the Dutch guilder. As they floated upwards they tended to become barometers of weakening confidence in the dollar. On May 11, Belgian authorities announced that they would support the dollar at previous exchange rate levels for commercial transactions but not for non-commercial transactions. These various decisions destroyed confidence in the continued viability of the Bretton Woods system.

In the meanwhile the American economy performed badly. The foreign trade balance slipped into a deep deficit in April and following months. The trade deficit for the entire year (1971) was $2 billion, which was the first annual deficit recorded since 1895. The net liquidity deficit for the entire year is estimated at $23 billion and for the first three quarters it amounted to $18 billion. "In July and early August, events moved inexorably toward their climax as speculative anticipations reached throughout the full range of trade and investment decisions in the market." [12]

On Friday, August 6, a Congressional subcommittee report asserted that the dollar had become overvalued and called for corrective action.[13] The same day the U. S. Treasury reported a loss of reserve assets of $1 billion. Over the following week $3.7 billion moved into the coffers of foreign central banks. On Sunday, August 15, the President bowed to the inevitable and announced the de jure suspension of the convertibility of the dollar.

The drain on U. S. reserve assets through the years of crisis is shown in the table below. In addition to the loss of 28 percent in reserve assets, in these years the U. S. sold non-marketable Treasury bonds to foreign official institutions totaling $6.2 billions and the Reserve Banks increased their swap liabilities by about $2.5 billion. As had been so often predicted, the gold or dollar exchange standard, unless nations were willing to submit to the discipline of the balance of payments, carried the seeds of its own destruction.

Table 17.1

U.S. Reserve Assets
(In Billions of Dollars)

End of	Total Reserve Assets	Gold	Convertible Foreign Currencies	Reserve Position in IMF	SDRs
1969	17.0	11.9	2.8	2.3	0
1970	14.5	11.1	.6	1.9	.9
1971	12.2	10.2	.3	.6	1.1
Change	− 4.8	− 1.7	−2.5	−1.7	+1.1

Source: *Federal Reserve Bulletin* (March 1972), p. A77.

The Ides of August • On Sunday evening August 15, in a nationwide television broadcast, President Nixon stated that, to achieve prosperity without war, he planned to create more and better jobs, to stop the rise in living costs and finally to protect the dollar from the attacks of "international money speculators." [14]

The President pointed out that in the past seven years there was an average of one international monetary crisis every year. The gainers, he declared, were the international money speculators, "they thrive on crises, they help to create them." Accordingly he had directed the Secretary of the Treasury to "defend the dollar against the speculators." In fulfilling this mission Secretary John B. Connally was directed to suspend "temporarily" the convertibility of the dollar into gold or other reserve assets. The effect of this action, the President concluded, would be to stabilize the dollar. Finally in cooperation with the IMF and those who trade with us, the United States would "press for the necessary reforms to set up an urgently needed new international monetary system." And he added, "I am determined that the American dollar will never again be a hostage in the hands of international speculators." [15]

The President's remarks were reminiscent of those of President Roosevelt 38 years earlier when he brought the London Economic Conference to an untimely and tragic end (Chapter 11). Speculators are always blamed for the results of superficial, erroneous and misguided policies, engineered by governments themselves. Speculators there are in such instances, but they are not the root cause of difficulties.

In taking the action he did, President Nixon violated the Articles of Agreement of the IMF. Member nations are required "to collaborate with the Fund" to promote exchange stability, to maintain orderly exchange arrangements with other members, and to avoid competitive exchange alterations (Article IV, Section 4(a), Articles of Agreement of the International Monetary Fund).

Not only did the Administration not consult with the Fund, but, it was guilty of gross discourtesy in not informing the Fund of its intended action. Thirty minutes before the President's broadcast, Messrs. Pierre-Paul Schweitzer and Frank A. Southard, Jr., Managing Director and Deputy Managing Director respectively of the IMF, were invited to the Treasury and were then, and only then, informed of the contents of the address, save for the imposition of the surcharge. They then were "privileged" to listen to the President's televised remarks and in this fashion to learn of the surcharge.

By imposing "temporarily" an additional tax of 10 percent on goods imported into the United States, the Administration also violated the General Agreement on Tariffs and Trade (GATT). On August 24, nine days after the broadcast, officials of GATT meeting in Geneva declared that the import surcharge was not in conformity with the Articles of Agreement [16] and later (September 11) a report by a 25-nation working group stated that members were entitled to take counter action against the United States.[17]

The day following the President's speech, the Secretary of the Treasury declared that the President had no intentions of altering the monetary price of gold from its parity of $35 an ounce.[18] Representative Henry S. Reuss of Wisconsin disagreed, pointing out that a modest increase in the price of gold "may now be wise." [19]

Importance of Compliance and Consultation • Nations sponsoring and joining international organizations such as the IMF, GATT and the U.N. must be prepared to surrender some part of their sovereign rights and abide by the rules formulated and adopted by these organizations. In failing to consult with the IMF, the United States sabotaged the Articles of Agreement, alienated its administrators and established an unfortunate precedent for other nations to follow.

Moreover by not consulting with and not notifying those nations which had loyally supported the dollar (Germany and Japan), American policy once again tended to divide the world into monetary blocs as it had in the 1930s. The most powerful and enduring of these blocs includes the nations of the Common Market, together with their trading partners in Africa. Japan, along with the nations of South East Asia and possibly China, may comprise another bloc. This bloc has fairly close ties with Australia, New Zealand, South America and Canada. The dollar bloc consists of the United States, with Canada and Mexico as uneasy members, and with ties more or less clearly defined with various other nations. Still another bloc, of course, is the Soviet bloc, consisting of the U.S.S.R. and the satellite nations. Here relationships are very rigid and well defined.

Should the U. S. move toward protectionism and trade restrictions, envisaged for example in the Hartke-Burke bill (S. 2592, 92d Congress, 1st Session), currency blocs will become increasingly delineated and rigid. Foreign exchange controls, so characteristic of Nazi economic policy, will in all likelihood be revived and come to dominate, distort and pervert international economic relations. The majority and minority members of the Joint Economic Committee on International Economic Issues were in agreement in opposing quotas or similar restrictions limiting imports. "Any suggestion to adopt such techniques as a general solution should be emphatically rejected." The appropriate solution to U.S. trade and balance-of-payments problems "lies in the prompt adjustment of exchange rates and in effective policies to strengthen competitiveness through efficient management, increased worker productivity, and shifts in the composition of output towards those industries in which the United States has a comparative advantage." [20]

The purpose of such international economic organizations as the IMF is to integrate economic policy and in so doing to substitute internationalism for nationalism. No nation can willfully follow its own economic policies any more than it could have done so under the pre-1914 gold standard. Only behind the iron wall of totalitarian controls are nations relatively free to follow their own dictates.

Controlled Floating • Following the suspension of convertibility by the United States on August 15, 1971, the major European governments "kept their exchange markets closed all the following week, as they sought to develop some joint policy response to the United States measures." [21] These efforts failed and on Monday, August 23, they opened their exchange markets on an uncoordinated basis. All governments but the French suspended their commitments to peg, in terms of the dollar, the previous upper limits of their exchange rates. Continuing intervention by the Bank of France was confined simply to commercial transactions; other transactions were allowed to follow their own level. The Japanese government initially sought to maintain the rate for the yen, but after being swamped by an inflow of $4.4 billion, allowed the yen to float.

By October 8 the major trading currencies stood at a premium over their former official ceilings. The premium varied from 1.1 percent in case of the Swiss franc to 9.5 percent in case of the German mark. The exchange rate structure which emerged was "the product of controlled rather than free floating." Almost every country "attempted to minimize the appreciation of its own currency in terms of the dollar through *ad hoc* purchases of dollars . . . or by more intensive use of direct and indirect measures to inhibit capital inflows." [22] The exchange rate patterns which emerged, after the middle of August, were largely the by-product "of outright official purchases of dollars and of an extensive network of official regulations." [23] In other words, there were no freely floating exchange rates and the effects of normal demand were "swamped by the impact of rumors and conflicting reports of official agreement—or disagreement—on appropriate exchange rate levels." [24]

Negotiations • This situation could not long endure if the nations of the world were to resume normal trading relationships. In the words of the Honorable Karl Schiller, Co-Chairman of the Boards of Governors of the International Monetary Fund and the International Bank for Reconstruction and Development:

> The need to re-establish orderly conditions in the world monetary system and put it on a sounder basis is widely recognized. . . . The problems we are facing are not problems of any one country or group, let alone any particular institution. They concern the international community at large—all the governments, the banking groups, and other financial communities . . .[25]

To resolve these problems conference followed conference, often characterized by a spirit of confrontation rather than compromise. The bases of disagreement concerned the devaluation of the dollar, the removal of the 10 percent import surcharge, the restriction of the investment tax credit to purchases of American machinery and the proposed tax relief to Domestic International Sales Corporations to stimulate exports.

One of the first of many conferences was held in London on September 15 and 16. The meeting was attended by the Finance Ministers of the Group of Ten, whose members include Belgium, Britain, Canada, France, Italy, Japan, the Netherlands, Sweden, the United States, West Germany—and with Switzerland as an observer. On the first day, Secretary Connally told the trading partners that they must help produce a $13 billion improvement, presumably in current account, in the American balance of international payments. He reiterated the statement he made on August 19th that the United States had no intention of altering the monetary price of gold (although the other nations favored this) and defended the application of the import surcharge. The meeting "sputtered to an inconclusive close." [26]

On September 13, the Council of Ministers of the European Communities agreed on a common position for the annual meeting of the IMF in Washington, September 27-October 1. This position included: the reform of the international monetary system, a return to realistic exchange rates, agreement on the extent to which currencies should be allowed to fluctuate around par, the constitution of international reserves which should consist of gold, a gradually increasing share of SDRs, a declining proportion of foreign exchange and the observance of international trade treaties.[27] Despite these preparations nothing was accomplished at the IMF meetings. The U. S. Secretary of the Treasury, John B. Connally, said that the U. S. objective was "to reduce, if not to eliminate the role of gold in any new monetary system." Only if governments were willing to make tangible progress towards dismantling specific trade barriers and to allow market forces to determine exchange rates, for a transitional period, would the U.S. be prepared to remove the import surcharge. An increase in the price of gold, the Secretary stated, was "of no economic consequence and would be patently a retrogressive step." [28] Meanwhile a resolution was introduced in Congress by Representative Henry S. Reuss and Senator Jacob Javits calling for a "fair and realistic change in the dollar-gold parity." [29]

The Group of Ten met in Paris on October 17-20, but were so divided that serious negotiations were not possible. The principal obstacle was the refusal of the United States to devalue the dollar. France was a vigorous advocate of dollar devaluation.

The third meeting held by the Group of Ten (Rome, November 30-December 1) to discuss international monetary problems was attended by the Managing Director of the IMF, the President of the Swiss National Bank, the Secretary-General of the Organization for Economic Cooperation and Development, the General Manager of the BIS and the Vice-President of the Commission of the European Communities.

Prior to this meeting the Finance Ministers and Central Bank Governors of the Group of Ten decided to force the United States to declare categorically whether or not it planned to devalue. Earlier, on November 4, the United States had declared it had no intention of devaluing the dollar.[30] This statement was made despite the fact that IMF studies showed that for each one percentage point of weighted devaluation against the rest of the world the American balance of payments would improve by $800 million.[31] While no communique was issued after this conference, Secretary Connally said that progress had been made. In fact, the realignment of currencies did not get started until this conference. The reason was that the American position had softened on the question of dollar devaluation.

Following this conference, President Richard Nixon of the United States and Georges Pompidou of France met at Angra do Heroismo in the Azores on December 13 and 14 and reached agreement on a number of important issues. These included the devaluation of the dollar, the realignment of exchange rates, a return to fixed parities, a widening of the margins of fluctuation and a study of the international monetary system.[32] These decisions formed the basis of the agreements reached at meetings held from December 16-18 at the Smithsonian Institution in Washington. At that time the Ministers and Central Bank Governors of the Group of Ten agreed on an interrelated set of measures to restore stability to international monetary arrangements, and to provide for expanding international trade. These measures included: (1) agreement on exchange rate relationships among the nations attending the Conference; (2) urgent recommendation that those not attending the Conference reach quick decisions respecting their exchange rates; (3) pending agreement on longer term reforms, a widening of the margin of possible exchange rate fluctuations by $2\frac{1}{4}\%$ below and above the new exchange rates; (4) avoidance of competitive exchange rate warfare. The United States agreed to devalue the dollar in terms of gold to $38 an ounce; to suppress the recently imposed 10 percent import surcharge and related provisions of the Job Development Credit. Those attending the Conference urged that trade negotiations be pushed ahead vigorously, that studies be made relative to the reform of the international monetary system, and that attention be directed to such questions as convertibility, the proper role of gold, of reserve currencies and SDRs and the appropriate volume of liquidity.[33]

Shortly after the Conference 24 countries decided not to change the par values of their currencies, which meant that the change in terms of the U. S. dollar represented an appreciation of 8.57 percent, 10 countries changed the par value of their currencies (6 lowered the par value and 4 kept it unchanged); the majority of nations (32) established central rates, the percentage change in U.S. dollars varied from −16.67 percent to +16.88 percent. Most of the remaining countries did not change the parity of their exchange rates in terms of the U.S. dollar, the French franc, pound sterling or Spanish peseta. A few adopted flexible exchange rates (the most important was Canada) or multiple exchange practices.[34] Exchange rates were to be maintained by purchase and sale of intervention currencies principally the U.S. dollar. Holdings of U.S. dollars by official institutions continued to increase as they intervened in the market to keep the dollar from falling below the minimum exchange rate.

The Gold Dollar • As indicated earlier the "Par Value Modification Act," (Senate Bill 3160, signed by President Nixon April 3, 1972) devalued the dollar by 8.57 percent. Why this percentage was agreed upon, instead of some other, has not been explained. Actually, in view of the market price of gold, the devaluation probably should have been larger. The modest amount of the devaluation means that more may impend unless the U.S. makes strenuous efforts to reduce its payments deficit. Dollar devaluation required appropriations of about $1.6 billion to maintain the gold value of its obligations in the IMF and other international institutions.[35]

The Aftermath • Relying upon wage and price controls to check inflation, the Federal Reserve System, following the measures taken on August 15, took action to reduce interest rates. The yield on 3-month Treasury bills fell from 5.405 percent in July 1971, to 3.180 percent in February 1972. The yield on long-term Aaa corporate bonds, reflecting continued inflationary expectations, fell substantially less, from 7.64 to 7.27 percent.

The confidence placed by the Administration in price and wage controls proved ill-founded. Following a dip in the third quarter of 1971, wholesale prices surged forward rapidly. In the three months after the freeeze the Consumer Price Index rose at a faster rate than in the preceding year. The increase was particularly marked in the case of farm products which had been left uncontrolled (although they were subject, beginning in October 1942, to controls in World War II). Average hourly earnings from August to February in nonagricultural employment rose by 2.6 percent. Continued price and wage increases, plus the resignation of the labor representatives on the Pay Board, generated lack of confidence in the efficacy of the Administration's control measures. The lack of confidence was reinforced by the continued rise in the money supply resulting from the Federal Reserve easy money policy and by the current and prospective heavy Federal deficits.

The Federal Reserve System continued to follow an easy money policy in order to reduce the rate of unemployment, which, for all workers, hovered around 6 percent. The average for 1971 was 5.9 percent as contrasted, for example, with 4.9 percent for 1970 and 3.5 percent for 1969. The average for the first two months in 1972 was 5.8 percent.

Federal Reserve policies directed toward domestic developments forced short-term interest rates below those in Europe with the result that the dollar continued weak, despite the measures taken on December 19, and, instead of a reflux of dollars from Europe, the outflow increased. The conviction grew that the December agreements had solved none of the basic international monetary problems. The market nervousness was reflected in a continued high price for gold and a weak dollar. This forced foreign monetary authorities to give continued support to the dollar. In fact, from December 29, 1971 to March 29, 1972, the volume of marketable U.S. Government securities held in custody by the Federal Reserve Banks for foreign and international accounts, increased from $27.5 billion to $30.8 billion, a measure of the support that was accorded. The foreign implications of Federal Reserve policy received emphasis at the January 11 meeting of the Open Market Committee when three members dissented from the majority opinion, which called for an increased growth of the money supply.

The Federal Reserve System began to move toward a firmer monetary policy by the end of February 1972. Rates in European markets started to decline. Had Federal Reserve interest rate policy been firmer and had the markets not been disturbed by the prospect of huge fiscal deficits in the U.S., funds might have moved in large volume towards the United States. But as the Deutsche Bundesbank pointed out, the policy of cheap money was pursued in the United States contrary to the requirements of the balance of payments. The Bundesbank was forced to rely on direct controls to sever its credit system from that of the United States.[36]

Unresolved Issues • There are many unresolved issues in domestic and international monetary relationships. As William McChesney Martin, former Chairman of the Board of Governors of the Federal Reserve System stated: "We are suspended in a euphoria of belief that the realignment of currencies achieved on that occasion [December 1971] has settled all of our troubles. This is certainly not the case." [37] Simply to enumerate the issues involved conveys an idea of the magnitude of the task.*

The first task is to bring the balance of payments of the United States (liquidity basis) into equilibrium. Until this is achieved progress towards international monetary reconstruction is not possible. If central banks, by reason of a continued deficit in our balance of payments, find themselves accumulating more dollars than they are willing to accept, they must either allow their currencies to float or to apply foreign exchange controls. In all probability they would resort to controls. Trading blocs would coalesce behind various types of discriminatory exchange and trade practices.[38]

The imbalance in the balance of payments of the United States will not come to an end unless domestic inflation is checked. Inflation taking place in a free market economy can be checked only by use of restrictive monetary and fiscal policies. Should a nation not be able to institute such policies, by reason of the resulting unemployment, there is no alternative but to fall back on price, wage, and foreign exchange controls. A heavily travelled road to serfdom looms ahead.

To assist in the balancing of its foreign accounts, the United States must be prepared to withdraw its armed forces from Western Europe and South East Asia. Foreign economic aid will need to be reduced to modest amounts relayed through international organizations. The huge volume of dollar liabilities owed to foreign official institutions will have to be funded or blocked, as were comparable sterling balances after World War II, to be released gradually in response to demand. A return flow of dollars would be prompted by interest rates in American money markets exceeding those in Europe. Higher domestic interest rates would, of course, be expected to result from restrictive monetary policies.

Along with these measures, the American businessman, through innovative zeal and constructive salesmanship, should work vigorously to increase export trade. At the same time, the United States must refrain from trying to take refuge behind protective tariff or quota barriers. Instead, present foreign exchange controls should be dismantled, quota restrictions and other non-tariff distortions to trade eliminated and tariff barriers further lowered.[39] The United States cannot expect foreign nations to adopt free trading policies unless it provides essential leadership.

Once the United States and other nations beset by inflation put their houses in order, attention could then be directed towards needed changes in international

---

* For a discussion of the issues by the present Chairman of the Board of Governors, see remarks by Arthur F. Burns, "Some Essentials of International Monetary Reform," International Banking Conference, Montreal, Canada, May 12, 1972.

monetary relationships. The more important problems concern the termination of the dollar or any other type of foreign exchange standard and its replacement by reserve assets which are not controlled by the monetary or political policies of any one nation. In the past, gold served an extremely useful function in this respect; it is conceivable it could do so in the future along with the SDRs. But if the SDRs are to serve as an international reserve asset, it is important that they be issued only when there is clear indication of need for greater world liquidity. And then they could be issued, as now, as a percentage of each member bank's quota in the IMF. Above all, they should not be issued to finance economic development. This is not the function of a reserve asset, but rather, of long-term loans granted and administered by the World Bank.

The IMF itself would seem to need no basic change; it has on the whole functioned well and effectively. It has sufficient assets in terms of local currencies to care for any foreseeable international monetary need, provided, of course, that local currencies are usable, which will be the case if nations follow prudent domestic policies. Prudent domestic policies would make all currencies usable. And if domestic policies are not prudent, i.e., are inflationary, the IMF cannot conceivably possess assets sufficiently large to cope with the resulting international disequilibria.

The phasing out of the dollar as an international reserve asset does not imply its complete dethronement. It would still be used as an important trading currency, along with the yen and the projected currency of the Common Market. The volume of dollars required for trading purposes might, to hazard a guess, be in the neighborhood of $10 billion. These dollars circulate at high velocity.

Following a decade in which the United States failed to check domestic inflation and spent lavish amounts abroad, the road back to a viable international monetary system will not be easy. The international monetary system is no stronger than the supporting domestic base. Only when fears of further dollar devaluation have been eradicated will the IMF, in close collaboration with the Group of Ten, be able to deal with the problems raised at the Smithsonian meeting. In the ensuing discussions, the Federal Reserve System will be expected to play a leading role.

Notes

1. A history of the International Monetary Fund is to be found in the following work: J. Keith Horsefield *et al., The International Monetary Fund 1945–1965* (3 vols.; Washington, D.C.: International Monetary Fund, 1969).

2. *Ibid.*, Vol. II, p. 3.

3. See Frank A. Southard, Jr., "Developments in the International Monetary System," remarks at the National Foreign Trade Convention, November 15, 1971, mimeographed release; "The Retreat from Bretton Woods," *Midland Bank Review* (London: Midland Bank Ltd., November 1971), pp. 12-20; and speech by Pierre-Paul Schweitzer, "International Aspects of Monetary Policy," at the University of Wales, printed in *International Financial News Survey* (International Monetary Fund, November 17, 1971).

4. See speech by Dr. Guido Carli in Rome on October 30, 1971, reprinted in *Press Review,* Bank for International Settlements (Basle: November 4, 1971).

5. *Press Review,* Bank for International Settlements (Basle: March 23, 1972), p. 2.

6. *Fifty-Seventh Annual Report for the Year Ended December 31, 1971* (Federal Reserve Bank of New York, March 3, 1972), p. 5.

7. *Economic Report of the President.* Transmitted to the Congress January 1972 (Washington, D.C.: Government Printing Office, 1972), pp. 38–49.

8. *The New York Times,* April 7, 1972, Editorial, p. 34.

9. *Press Review,* Bank for International Settlements (Basle: October 27, 1971).

10. *Fifty-Seventh Annual Report for the Year Ended December 31, 1971* (Federal Reserve Bank of New York, March 3, 1972), p. 33.

11. *Monthly Review* (Federal Reserve Bank of New York, October 1971), p. 215.

12. *Loc. cit.*

13. *Loc. cit.*

14. *The New York Times,* August 16, 1971, p. 14. Also, the Ides of August is actually the 13th.

15. Other proposals included endorsement of the Job Development Act of 1971, a 10 percent job development credit for one year effective August 15, 1971, to be followed by a

5 percent credit after August 15, 1972, repeal of the 7 percent excise tax on automobiles, a speeding-up of personal income tax exemptions scheduled for January 1, 1973, to January 1, 1972, a cut of $4.7 billion in Federal spending, a postponement of government pay increases and a 5 percent cut in government personnel, 10 percent cut in foreign economic aid and a 10 percent surcharge on imports. Additionally, a freeze was ordered on all prices and wages in the U.S. for a 90 day period and a cost-of-living Council was appointed to prepare plans for achieving continued price and wage stability upon the termination of the 90 day freeze. (*The New York Times,* August 16, 1971, p. 14.)

16. "GATT Meeting on U.S. Trade Measures," *International Financial News Survey* (International Monetary Fund, September 8, 1971), XXIII, No. 35, 277.

17. *The New York Times,* September 12, 1971, p. 13.

18. *Press Review,* Bank for International Settlements (Basle: August 19, 1971).

19. *The Wall Street Journal,* September 22, 1971, p. 9.

20. *1972 Joint Economic Report.* Report of the Joint Economic Committee, Congress of the United States, on the January 1972 Economic Report of the President together with Minority and Other Views. 92d Cong., 2d sess. (Washington, D.C.: Government Printing Office, 1972), pp. 61-62.

21. *Monthly Review* (Federal Reserve Bank of New York, October 1971), p. 215.

22. *Ibid.,* pp. 217 and 222.

23. *Fifty-Seventh Annual Report for the Year Ended December 31, 1971* (Federal Reserve Bank of New York, March 3, 1972), p. 43.

24. *Loc. cit.*

25. *Supplement to International Financial News Survey* (International Monetary Fund, September 29, 1971), Vol. XXIII, No. 38.

26. For a discussion of these meetings see *The New York Times,* September 15, 1971, p. 61; September 16, 1971, pp. 1 and 34. Also *The Wall Street Journal,* September 16, 1971, p. 2; and September 17, 1971, p. 4.

27. *European Community* (European Community Information Service, October 1971), No. 149, p. 10.

28. *The New York Times,* October 1, 1971, p. 1.

29. *Ibid.* p. 22.

30. *The New York Times,* November 5, 1971, pp. 59 and 68.

31. *The New York Times,* November 8, 1971, pp. 63 and 65.

32. *Service de Presse et l'Information,* January 1972, pp. 3–4. (Available from the French Embassy, 972 Fifth Avenue, New York, N.Y. 10021.)

33. *International Financial News Survey* (International Monetary Fund, December 22, 1971), Vol. XXIII, No. 50; and *Press Review,* Bank for International Settlements (Basle: December 21, 1971).

34. *International Financial News Survey* (International Monetary Fund, February 2, 1972), XXIV, No. 4, 28–32.

35. *Background Material on Legislation Modifying the Par Value of the Dollar* Committee on Banking and Currency, House of Representatives, 92d Cong., 2d sess. February 15, 1972 (Washington, D.C.: Government Printing Office, 1972); *International Financial News Survey* (International Monetary Fund, April 12, 1972), Vol. XXIV, No. 14.

36. *Monthly Report of the Deutsche Bundesbank,* XXIV, No. 2, 8.

37. *The New York Times,* February 25, 1972, p. 53.

38. William S. Ogden, "The International Monetary Scene," *International Finance* (New York: The Chase Manhattan Bank, April 10, 1972), p. 7.

39. See Robert E. Baldwin, *Non-Tariff Distortion of International Trade* (London: Allen and Unwin, 1971).

CHAPTER 18

Monetary Instruments: Review and Analysis

IMPORTANCE OF THE FINANCIAL INFRASTRUCTURE

The older central banks evolved slowly in line with the changing needs of growing economies. Initially established as commercial banks, they have gradually, as other financial institutions came into being, restricted their clientele to governments and commercial banks. Many of the newer central banks, like those of Canada and the United States, have been superimposed upon developed financial structures. Central banks in the developing nations, on the other hand, often represent the first rather than the final stages in financial evolution.

A well-functioning financial infrastructure is a prerequisite for a well-functioning central bank—and indeed for economic growth. The infrastructure includes such institutions as cooperative banks, savings banks, industrial-development banks, urban- and agricultural-mortgage banks, and commercial banks. Cooperative banks, owned and managed by the citizens themselves, permit a local testing of credit and enable the members to become acquainted with credit techniques, and accounting and business principles. They thus provide basic education in the principles of entrepreneurship. Mortgage banks are essential in real-estate finance and in the promotion of agriculture: industrial banks are equally essential in financing new ventures and industrial innovations. Thrift institutions serve as catalytic agents in economic growth.[1]

In the absence of such a financial infrastructure, a central bank is often established by a developing nation not from any vital need but simply as a status symbol.[2] The old currency boards that had previously served such nations in a passive way, tying local currency issues to reserves held in the mother countries, were replaced by central banks that, the new nations naively expected, would enable them to throw off the chains of financial dependence and accelerate economic progress. Once the umbilical cord was cut, such central banks, often located in nations lacking other financial institutions and devoid of traditions of fiscal responsibility, were usually enlisted in the service of national financial needs and became instruments for financing budgetary deficits. With alarming frequency the purchasing power of currencies quickly eroded.

In the absence of a financial infrastructure, a central bank is often expected to finance not only government deficits, but also a medley of financial needs. Thus, in Pakistan, for example, the central bank may purchase, hold, and sell shares and debentures of any banking company or any corporation established to promote economic development. Saddled with a host of financial tasks, such central banks take on the character of a state bank (Gosbank) in a communist nation, whose function is to finance the economic plan, as this has evolved from the planning apparatus of a totalitarian state. In the modern age a central bank should probably represent the final, and not the initial phase of financial evolution.*

Asset Quality and Balance Sheet Ratios

The ability of a central bank to function effectively and to achieve its policy goals is contingent upon the strength of the underlying financial structure, which in turn depends upon the quality of assets and upon balance-sheet equilibrium. Asset quality tends to deteriorate and imbalances begin to develop on the upward sweep of the business cycle. Credit standards in the granting of business loans, consumer and morgage credits, and bond purchases tend to fall. The loan-deposit ratio increases rapidly. At the same time financial institutions tend to borrow short

---

* Some students argue that a central bank in a developing nation can play an important role in economic development by itself promoting the establishment of a financial infrastructure and by a well-considered monetary policy. And so it can if the central government follows a prudent budgetary policy.

and lend long and to allow ratios of financially liquid assets to deposit liabilities and of capital funds to risk assets to fall.

A central bank must keep itself informed of changes in the balance sheets of financial institutions and of developments in the security markets. Its task is rendered easier to the extent that financial institutions specialize in certain lending fields. If savings-and-loan associations, savings banks, and mortgage banks finance urban mortgage needs; if finance companies, savings banks, and cooperative banks finance consumer credit needs; if cooperative banks and special agricultural banks finance the intermediate- and long-term credit needs of agriculture; and if industrial banks and capital markets finance the long-term credit needs of business enterprise and government, then the central bank can direct its attention more specifically to change occurring in the loan and investment portfolios of the money-creating institutions: the commercial banks. It can often achieve its goal through general, rather then selective, credit controls.

Not that a central bank should be oblivious to developments in other financial markets. It must be prepared, for example, by increases in margin requirements, to take early action against speculative excesses in the security markets, and by changes in lending terms, to safeguard the quality of instalment and mortgage credit (provided, of course, that it has powers of selective credit control). It must be aware of a decline in lending standards in noncommercial bank financial institutions and must be prepared to take appropriate action within its powers.

Commercial banks have long been multipurpose institutions in many European nations and have tended to become so in the United States, particularly since World War II. A multipurpose commercial bank, more than one that concentrates on commercial business loans, must watch balance-sheet ratios with great care. Long-term assets should be balanced with genuinely long-term liabilities. Mixed banking (a European term describing commercial banks engaged in financing the short-, medium-, and long-term credit needs, as well as the equity needs ·of business) requires an adequate ratio of financially liquid assets to deposit liabilities. The adjectives "adequate" and "substantial" cannot be defined in precise mathematical terms. They can be judged only in the light of past experience. If commercial banks are historically-minded, if they are aware of developments in past critical periods, if they profit by this experience, and if they are not carried away by the euphoria of the moment, they will probably establish what prove to be adequate ratios.

When the financial infrastructure breaks down, as it did in Germany and the United States in the 1930s, the central bank is powerless to halt currency devaluation and foreign-exchange and other types of economic controls.

IMPORTANCE OF THE ENVIRONMENT

A central bank cannot escape its financial, psychological, political, and economic environment. The financial environment may lack the underpinning provided by other institutions. The psychological environment may be one in which the bank is expected to perform miracles. The political environment may be such that the state looks upon the central bank as its servant and appoints administrators who can be counted upon to carry out its orders. The economic environment may hamper or expedite central-bank operations. A free market economy characterized by an absence of exchange controls and tariff barriers, price supports, and subsidies and by freedom of wages and prices to respond to market forces facilitates its operations; a controlled economy, by definition, inevitably forces it to be a servant of the state.

Unfortunately, the American environment has not always been conducive to the best functioning of the Federal Reserve System. Broad changes resulted from two world wars and the economic dogma of government. During both wars the System was the captive of the state. After World War II it extricated itself from Treasury control in the early 1950s, only to fall subject again a decade later; the country paid in the degree of inflation from which it suffered.

In the 1930s the Federal Reserve System was thrust aside, and the Treasury took over. The administration had fallen prey to the doctrines of certain monetary economists. Again in the 1960s the Reserve System was dominated by conviction on the part of the administration that growth would be promoted by low, long-term interest rates. Other considerations were brushed aside.

The best guardian of independent action by a central bank is an enlightened and educated public opinion. An enlightened public opinion will interest itself in the caliber of the management of a central bank, will endeavor to protect a central bank from the onslaughts of politicians and will support monetary policies geared to protecting the domestic and foreign value of a currency. A public ready to defend the independence of a central bank is usually one which, by reason of tragic monetary experience (Germany) or by reason of maturity of judgment (Switzerland) is convinced that economic welfare can best be promoted by a vigorous defense of the purchasing power of a currency.

MONETARY POLICY

Monetary policy is, of course, the term descriptive of the action of central banks in achieving particular objectives. It may be defined narrowly as action designed to influence the supply and use of money. Money in this sense includes simply the final means of payment: currency plus deposits subject to check or to immediate transfer. These deposits include not only demand deposits but also the gyro accounts of post offices and savings banks and even time deposits when subject to check.

Money in this sense is "created" by central and commercial banks. A commercial bank may itself be defined as any financial institution, whether it is called a commercial bank or not, which has deposit liabilities subject to check or gyro transfer. Central banks issue currency and, in addition, provide the bulk of the reserves to commercial banks on the basis of which credit expansion takes place. In making loans and buying securities, commercial banks create money—that is, they create demand-deposit liabilities against themselves, which add to the final means of payment of the total community.

Monetary policy as narrowly defined is the primary responsibility of central banks. It is not their exclusive responsibility, as governments may influence the money supply by buying and selling SDRs and foreign exchange, by changing the price of gold, by controlling gold exports and imports, and by issuing paper money. All governments have the power (subject to IMF regulations) to change the price of gold and to control their own gold imports and exports. The issue of paper money directly by governments, which at one time was very common, now occurs rarely.

Monetary policy may also be defined more broadly, to include all actions designed to influence the use of lendable funds, in the form of loans or investments, extended by commercial banks and other lending institutions. Monetary policy in this broader context includes not only the action of central-banks respecting the issuance of currency and changes in commercial bank-reserves, but also rules and regulations respecting the loans and investments of savings banks, insurance companies, investment trusts, pension funds, and other financial intermediaries. In the United States it also includes the work of such agencies as the Federal Housing Administration, the Farm Credit Administration, and the Veterans Administration.

Economic policy, of which monetary policy is an important ingredient, is geared to the level of a nation's expenditures: the total of consumer, business, and government spending. Efforts to influence the total volume of spending include not only monetary policy in its broader sense, but also policies respecting public expenditures, taxation, and the management of the public debt.

The differences underlying our two definitions of monetary policy—the one restricted to the supply and use of money and the other including as well the use of all loanable funds—are set forth in two recent reports. The first was by an American private group, the Commission on Money and Credit, the other, by a British official group, appointed by the government, entitled the Committee on the Working of the Monetary System, often referred to as the Radcliffe Committee, from the name of its chairman.[3]

Monetary policy, according to the Commission on Money and Credit, is directed at the money supply: the quantity of demand deposits and currency. A central bank exercises control over the volume of money by influencing the cash reserves of the commercial banks and by issuing paper money. Fluctuations in cash reserves or, in the United States, more specifically in net free and net borrowed reserves bring about expansions and contractions in commercial-bank credit and thus in demand deposits.

The Radcliffe Committee abandoned this "traditional" approach to monetary policy for a broader definition. It did not regard control of the money supply as unimportant, but, viewed money (demand deposits plus currency) as only "part of the wider structure of liquidity in the economy." [4] The level of total demand is influenced by the "lending behavior of an indefinitely wide range of financial institutions." [5] Commercial banks are only one of many types of such institutions. The borrower may quickly substitute one for another. The interchangeability is so great that a restrictive credit policy may simply lead borrowers, temporarily at least, to seek accomodation from lending institutions other than commercial banks.

Although its definition of monetary policy was narrower than that of the Radcliffe Committee, the Commission on Money and Credit was not unaware of the spreading effects of monetary ease or restraint. Monetary restraint, it declared, not only increases interest costs but also reduces the availability of credit. Its effects spread through the community to all holders of financial assets, influencing the decisions of all borrowers and lenders. It has an important impact on the availability of mortgage credit and on borrowing by states and municipalities.

The major implications of the Radcliffe Report are that central banks should go far beyond attempts simply to control the volume of money per se. Central banks must be aware of the manner in which borrowing needs in all credit markets are being met, of lending terms in various markets, and of the sources of funds for consumer and business finance. They must be cognizant of changes in the amount of savings, of developments in domestic and foreign capital markets, and of changes in the quality of credit. They must also interest themselves in problems of development credits and in possible credit gaps in the economy. In other words, central banks must follow changes in all credit sectors and, indeed, in all phases of economic life.

In this study, our point of view has been more closely related to that of the Radcliffe Report than to that of the Commission on Money and Credit. The British report reflects a breadth of view and an analytical insight not present in the American report.

INSTRUMENTS OF MONETARY POLICY

Whether they accept the point of view of the Commission on Money and Credit or that of the Radcliffe Committee, central banks employ a variety of instruments to achieve their particular objectives. Instruments used to influence the money supply include use of the discount rate, open-market operations, and changes in reserve requirements. Instruments employed principally to affect the loans and investments of commercial banks and other lending institutions include definitions given to paper eligible for discount and purchase, the use of moral suasion, liquidity ratios, controls exercised over interest rates paid on savings and time accounts, selective credit controls, the imposition of credit ceilings, and the issuance of lending directives. It is difficult to separate the effects of these different instruments. Reliance on instruments directed primarily at influencing the money supply not only affects the money supply itself but also influences the loan and investment policies of lending institutions. The use of instruments directed at influencing the loans and investments of commercial banks also affects the money supply.

Certain of the instruments listed, such as action respecting the open-market portfolio of the Reserve Banks and the reserve requirements of member banks, affect the volume of credit by influencing its cost (the level and structure of interest rates); others like selective credit controls and lending directives affect the volume of credit by influencing its availability. Again a clear-cut distinction cannot be made. An increase in the cost of credit affects its availability, and a reduction in availability affects its cost.

Discount Rates

The discount rate, which is simply the cost at which cash (notes and deposits) may be obtained for temporary periods from a central bank, was and still remains one of the most important instruments of general credit control. The discount window has a time as well as a rate dimension, for credits are granted at a certain rate for a minimum or maximum period.⁶ Alterations symbolize a change in policy or a change in the appraisal of current and impending economic trends. Such changes always have an important psychological effect, as well as a very direct impact when bank lending rates are tied to the discount rate (as in England).

Discount rate policy first developed as an instrument at the Bank of England in the nineteenth century. It began to be governed by certain basic rules: the maintenance of Bank rate above the market, that is, above the rates prevailing on those types of paper which the Bank of England stood ready to discount or purchase; the charging of penalty rates on paper of lower quality and on Lombard loans (for which securities serve as collateral); willingness in crises to extend credit freely but at high rates; and readiness to alter the rate frequently in response to changes in economic conditions.

In Victorian Britain, open market operations were used to adjust money-market rates to the changed level of Bank rate. Sales of securities increased, and purchases decreased open-market rates. In this way Bank rate was made effective. At the present time in the United States, open-market operations are a prelude to discount-rate changes. Changes in discount rates respond to changes in open-market rates brought about by open-market operations.

Readiness by a central bank to make frequent and, if necessary, sharp changes in discount rates, whether they lead or follow the market, is a hallmark of its independence and a reflection of its willingness to influence economic change. It is also a reflection of the willingness of governments to adjust the interest rates on their obligations to market forces.*

The psychological impact of changes in the discount rate is so important that changes should occur in distinct steps, small or large; the discount rate should not, as it did for a number of years at the Bank of Canada, merely fluctuate above market rates by a constant interval. From November 1956 to June 1962 the Canadian discount rate was pegged at .25 percent above the weekly average tender rate on Canadian ninety-one day treasury bills.† It also robbed the discount rate of the psychological impact of distinct and abrupt change and placed it under the indirect control of the market.

---

* It should be borne in mind that though responsibility for setting discount rates ordinarily rests with the board of directors of a central bank, prior consultation with treasury officials is customary.

† Report of the Royal Commission on Banking and Finance (Canada, 1964), pp. 411–413. This policy was adopted to quiet political criticism that the Bank of Canada, by raising discount rates, had caused high interest rates in Canada. The Board of Governors of the Federal Reserve System has opposed use of this technique, which would deprive the discount rate of its "signal effect." The Federal Reserve and the Treasury: Answers to Questions from the Commission on Money and Credit (Englewood Cliffs, N.J.: Prentice-Hall 1963), p. 123.

Nearly all nations have multiple rate structures. Rates rise above the basic rate, depending upon the type of paper discounted or offered as collateral or upon the amount and duration of the accomodation desired, or upon types of institutional borrowers. The rate structure may be a progressive one, with preferential rates for certain types of paper and progressive penalty rates geared to the type of paper or to the amount of borrowing. The National Bank of Belgium thus had a total of ten different rates on discounts and advances in 1966. Its rates varied both with the quality of the paper discounted and with the maturity of the advances.[7]

As George Garvy has pointed out, progressive rate structures reduce administrative problems at the window.[8] They are often used to enforce discount quotas and liquidity ratios, to penalize continual borrowing and borrowing for a profit, and to discriminate against noncooperative banks.*

In comparison with foreign central banks, the Reserve System has a fairly simple rate structure. The basic rate (February 1972) of $4\frac{1}{2}$ percent applied to discounts of eligible paper and to loans collateralled by U.S. direct and guaranteed obligations, by any other obligation eligible for purchase by the Reserve banks, or by Federal intermediate credit bank debentures maturing in six months. A higher rate, 5 percent, applied to advances with maximum maturities of four months secured to the satisfaction of the Reserve banks. If proposals of the steering committee concerning the discount window are adopted, the System may once again adopt a progressive rate structure, with rates varying according to the amount and duration of the borrowing.

In the early days of the Federal Reserve System, much attention was given to the appropriate relation of the basic discount rate to market rates.[9] Many students, arguing from British experience, insisted that the basic discount rate must be above the market rate to discourage borrowing for profit and to restrict borrowing to actual need. In Great Britain the market rate was easily identifiable, that is, the rate on bills of exchange that the Bank of England stood ready to discount. But what was the market rate in the United States? Some suggested the prime lending rate of commercial banks, others the yield on Treasury bills, which commercial banks usually employed to adjust their cash position. If borrowing becomes a

---

* Their early use in the United States did force Reserve officials to keep a close tab on borrowings. Clay J. Anderson, *Evolution of the Role and Functioning of the Discount Mechanism* (Federal Reserve Bank of Philadelphia, November, 1966), p. 7. A memorandum prepared by Mr. John J. Balles, Senior Vice President and Chief Economist, Mellon National Bank and Trust Company, Pittsburgh, Pennsylvania, proposed that "serious consideration be given to the possibility of a plan which would incorporate a progressive set of discount rates, above the prevailing discount rate, to apply to borrowing above the basic line." This suggestion was made with reference to the proposal of a steering committee of the Federal Reserve System (July 1968) that the discount mechanism be revised. John J. Balles "The Proposal and New Legislation." *The Discount Mechanism: Another Look,* A Collection of Working Papers written for the Banking and Financial Research Committee of the American Bankers Association, February, 1969, p. 32.

"right" and ceases to be a privilege, the discount rate will probably have to be set above the prime lending rate of the commercial banks to discourage borrowing for profit.

In comparing discount and open-market rates, we must keep in mind that since the establishment of the Federal Reserve System interest rates have been subject to control for long periods. Even in years when the discount rate was free to fluctuate the rate on prime commercial paper has ruled above the discount rate except for rare occasions. Even the yield on Treasury bills has been either equal to or above the discount rate, except during recessions. The discount rate has not been a penalty rate. The less conservatively managed banks, unless checked by their own inhibitions or by Reserve officials, have been able to exploit the credit facilities of the Reserve System for profit.

The individual bank facing a deficiency in its legal reserve position may borrow from a Reserve bank; draw down balances with other banks; borrow from correspondent banks or on the Federal funds market and Eurodollar markets; issue negotiable certificates of deposit; sell money-market assets like Treasury bills and other government obligations, municipal securities, bankers' acceptances, and commercial paper; sell participations in its loan portfolio or commercial paper issued by one-bank holding companies; or refuse to renew existing loans and to extend new loans. Only borrowing from a Reserve bank will increase the reserves of the whole banking system. The other methods (except for loan liquidation) simply redistribute reserves among the units in the banking system.*

Which of the methods listed are used depends upon opportunity costs, the strength of the reluctance to borrow from the Reserve banks, and the manner in which the discount window is administered. Banks do not always select the method involving the lowest cost. Banks may be reluctant to borrow, since they do not have equal access to the money market; customer relations may influence the choice of the method used.

The Alleged Tradition Against Borrowing • Traditionally the Reserve System has assumed that member banks, or at least a majority of them, are reluctant to become indebted to the Reserve banks.† This reluctance has been explained by a widespread tradition against borrowing and by a belief on the part of member banks that borrowing from the Reserve banks is not sound banking procedure.

---

* Loan liquidation is a tedious and highly deflationary method of freeing reserves, inasmuch as loans and the offsetting deposits would have to be reduced by about eleven times the amount of the desired reduction in required reserves.

† The reluctance apparently increases with the size of borrowings; Murray E. Polakoff. *Federal Reserve Discount Policy and its Critics*. Reprint Series No. 14, Schools of Business, New York University, December 1964, p. 207.

The assumption that there is a tradition against borrowing is comforting when Reserve banks are reluctant to increase the bank rate, but does not, as Robert C. Turner pointed out years ago, stand up to close scrutiny. In 1922–1936 he found a positive correlation between the level of discounting and profit spreads on open-market loans.[10]

Once the discount rate was free to move in the early 1950s, officials of the Reserve System began to devote considerable thought to the validity of this "tradition" and to the basis of an effective discount policy. If the tradition were strong, the Reserve banks would be forced to make only occasional changes in the discount rate*. According to Murray E. Polakoff, the rise of daily member-bank borrowing to $1.5 billion in the final quarter of 1952, when the Treasury-bill rate stood .5 percent above the discount rate, caused great consternation in the Reserve System. Apparently the "tradition" needed to be strengthened. This was accomplished in 1955 by a revision of Regulation A which, in setting forth rules respecting loans to member banks, relied on nonprice criteria to influence total member-bank borrowings.

These nonprice criteria have apparently been important, for how else can the readiness of New York City banks to borrow heavily in the Eurodollar market at interest costs far above the bank rate be explained? [11] Not only the Reserve banks, but also central banks in all nations rely on criteria other than price to supplement discount rate policy. This reliance will undoubtedly continue. Credit is not a homogeneous commodity like wheat, which can be neatly graded and classified. It has a qualitative dimension as well. Qualitative considerations like the credit worthiness of borrowers and cyclical changes in credit standards lend themselves to nonprice rationing at the discount window.

Open-Market Operations

Open-market operations, which are the most important instrument of credit policy in the United States, are conventionally defined as those credit activities initiated by a central bank. They include the purchase and sale of government obligations and other securities, bankers' acceptances, and commercial paper. They may

---

* In a recent study (Jack L. Cooper "Continuous Borrowing from The Federal Reserve System: Some Empirical Evidence," *The Journal of Finance,* Vol. XXIV, No. 1, March 1969) the author concludes that a significant proportion of reserve-city banks have engaged in continuous borrowing. In 1966 in the Seventh Federal Reserve District almost 27 percent of all banks were in debt at one time or another, among them was a group of chronic borrowers. Banks borrowed to take advantage of the difference between the discount rate and market rates. Cooper also found, as have others, marked differences in the administration of the discount window among the Reserve Banks. Member bankers believe that there is "a substantial lack of uniformity from district-to-district in discount administration." (Letter by Wesley Lindow (Chairman, Banking and Financial Research Committee of American Bankers Association), to Senator William Proxmire, September 17, 1968.)

also include purchases and sales of foreign exchange and gold, although such purchases do not usually result from the initiative of the central bank itself.

Central banks' open-market operations are often distinguished from lending operations, which allegedly result from the initiative of borrowers, including commercial banks, other financial institutions, and the government. It is not easy to determine initiative in all instances. Financial institutions may be forced to borrow from a central bank because it has engaged in open-market operations—has sold securities—or because it has increased reserve requirements. The initiative of the borrower then results from the initiating action of the central bank.

The relative importance of open-market operations varies widely among central banks of the world.[12] They are apt to be most important in nations with well-developed capital markets, like the United States, the United Kingdom, and Canada. In the absence of such markets, central banks may buy and sell money-market securities directly from and to financial institutions, national-debt offices, social-security funds, and the like. Sometimes central banks may issue their own securities in order to soak up lendable funds in the community. Occasionally open-market operations, like those of the Swiss National Bank, have been conducted in gold coins and bars. If the selling price exceeds the mint price this type of open-market operations helps to meet bank expenses, as well as to exert control over the credit volume.

Even though freely functioning well-developed money and capital markets exist in only a few nations, practically all central-banking statutes provide for open-market operations. The Reserve Bank of India may, subject to regulations, buy and sell gold coin and bullion and foreign government securities, and shares in financial institutions. The Bank of Mexico is authorized to buy and sell gold and silver, foreign exchange, Treasury certificates and debentures, and other securities (with the exception of shares) having a "constant market value."

The Central Bank Act of the Philippines directs the central bank to refrain from open-market purchases "in periods of inflation or as long as inflationary dangers exist." Conversely, when national monetary policy requires an expansion of the money supply, the central bank may purchase certificates of indebtedness issued by the government or by its political subdivisions. In purchasing such obligations the central bank should give preference to short-term obligations, in order to be free to reduce the money supply should subsequent conditions require this action.

In recent years open-market activity has been promoted by various institutional changes. In Australia, there has been an effort to establish short-term money markets. In other nations laws have been changed to permit central banks to buy other than government securities—for example, private bonds including mortgage bonds. Laws have also been liberalized to permit central banks to issue their own securities. Some governments have attempted to coordinate their debt-management policies with open-market operations, which may take the form of sales of securities by the Treasury and the impounding in the central bank of the funds realized.

Preferences for maturities in which the open-market operations are conducted differ among central banks. The Bank of England and the Bank of France usually concentrate on short-term securities. The Bank of Canada and the Scandinavian central banks, subject to limitations and exceptions, conduct operations in all debt maturities. The Federal Reserve System has not followed a consistent policy. In the 1920s it purchased certificates, notes, and bonds; in 1930–1931 it purchased bonds; and in 1932–1933 it purchased notes. At the end of 1941 the open-market portfolio consisted largely of bonds; whereas at the end of World War II it consisted mainly of Treasury bills. The Reserve System had purchased the securities that no other buyer wanted.

In order to avoid being drawn again into the pegging operations that had dominated open-market operations from 1941 to 1951, the Reserve System, once it regained freedom of action, began conducting open-market operations in Treasury bills. Such action resulted from a directive of the Federal Open Market Committee, which restricted open-market purchases and sales to short-term government obligations. As such operations were confined in practice to Treasury bills, this policy became known as the "bills only" policy. The policy was initiated in 1953 and ended in 1961. (For further discussion, see Chapter 8.) Those who favored the "bills only" policy noted that open-market operations in short-term obligations have the advantage of reducing to a minimum the discretion of the Reserve officials. Decision was confined to the amount of securities to be purchased or sold and did not involve judgments relative to maturities or types. Large operations could be conducted with minimum effects on price; the shorter the maturity, the smaller are the price changes resulting from either a rise or a decline in interest rates. Because markets in short-term obligations are very active, reversals can quickly occur. Confining open-market operations to the "short end" of the interest curve also convinces dealers that the long-term markets are free of the artificial effects of direct intervention; they are thus more willing "to take a position."

Those who opposed confining open-market operations to Treasury bills asserted that the structure of interest rates is the center-piece of monetary action and that Reserve banks should be prepared, in the interests of monetary stabilization, to influence long-term rates directly. They declared that the transmission effect—

the transmission along the interest rate curve of developments in the short- to the long-markets—could not be counted upon to influence long-term rates either at the desired time or in the desired amount. Only when operations in the short-term market are conducted on a massive scale can one be certain that the effects will be quickly transmitted.

The proponents of the "bills only" policy replied that there is no ideal structure of interest rates, adding that the ascending interest rate curve was a phenomenon of the Great Depression and that, prior to 1930, a descending or a level interest rate curve was most commonly experienced. The ascending interest rate curve, the result of a special series of events, could not be expected to continue indefinitely. The proponents also asserted that changes in one market are quickly transmitted to other markets through arbitrage. Above all, confining operations to those securities closest to money enforces the independence of the Reserve System and helps to neutralize the danger that it will become involved once again in pegging bond yields.

Targets of open-market operations in the United States, as set by the Federal Open Market Committee now include such statistical goals as: total member-bank reserves, required reserves, borrowed reserves, net borrowed and net free reserves, the money supply, commercial bank credit, and money-market interest rates. To the extent that these targets or some of them can be achieved by the manager of the open-market account, it is expected that the more basic objectives of policy can be attained.*

In the 1920s and the 1950s the basic objective of open-market operations was to moderate the amplitude of cyclical fluctuations; in the 1930s it was to overcome economic stagnation; in the 1940s it was to finance the requirements of war finance; and in the early 1960s it was to offset the effects of gold losses and currency increases on member-bank reserves and to provide the reserves necessary to maintain low long-term rates, accompanied as this policy was by rapid credit expansion (see Chapters 12—15).

As a result of heavy open-market operations in the past thirty years, holdings of government securities by the Federal Reserve banks have risen from $2.5 billion to $71 billion, or from about 5.3 to about 17 percent of the total public debt. The interest subsidy received by the Federal government on holdings of its obligations by the reserve banks has been advanced as an argument in favor of open-market operations as opposed to changes in reserve requirements as an expression

---

* An important recent study of open market operations entitled "Open Market Operations and the Monetary and Credit Aggregates—1971" is to be found in the *Monthly Review* Vol. 54 No. 4 of the Federal Reserve Bank of New York, April 1972.

of Federal Reserve policy. In 1970 Federal Reserve interest income on holdings of U.S. government securities was $3.6 billion, of which $3.5 billion was remitted to the Federal government.

During the period of heavy gold exports in the 1960s open-market operations relieved the American economy from making the adjustments dictated by the international situation. Reliance on open-market operations to escape adjustment caused one French economist to dub these operations and the gold-exchange standard "an Anglo-Saxon error." But open-market operations do not offer a genuine escape from adjustment, for by prolonging fundamental disequilibrium, they make later adjustment more difficult. Their use might well be confined to moderating cyclical swings in business activity and to financing secular increases in the currency. They should not be used to offset losses in international reserves, whether in gold, SDRs, or official holdings of foreign exchange.

Variable Reserve Requirements

By either law, custom, tradition or regulation, commercial banks and (in some nations) other financial institutions, maintain minimum reserves against deposit and other liabilities. These reserves may take the form of cash on hand or deposits with the central bank. The minima may differ by type of deposit liability and by the geographical location of the bank. Minimum requirements may be higher for increments in deposits than for the basic level. Central banks or governments usually have the power to change these requirements and have done so frequently in the postwar period.† In England increases in reserve requirements may be effected by requiring commercial banks to establish special deposits with the central bank separate from but in addition to their usual reserve deposits.

Reserve requirements are traditionally based on deposit volume rather than on deposit turnover. Some years ago a committee of the Reserve System departed from tradition to suggest that both volume and turnover be used as the basis of reserve requirements. This proposal acknowledged the importance of velocity in bringing about changes in the effective money supply. Over the past two decades deposit turnover has increased more rapidly than has the volume of demand deposits and has exerted a correspondingly greater influence on prices. Had the suggestion been adopted, required reserves would have risen along with the rise in

---

† The Federal Reserve System was apparently the first central bank to be given the power to alter member-bank reserve requirements.

deposit turnover. Had the additional rise in required reserves not been offset by open-market operations, inflationary pressures would have been under greater restraint.

Beginning with its *Annual Report* of 1964,[13] the Board of Governors recommended elimination of the two-way classification of member banks (reserve-city and country banks) and proposed that it have the power to fix graduated reserve requirements according to the amount of each bank's demand deposits and, that all insured commercial banks be subject to such requirements. Basing reserve requirements on the amount of a bank's demand deposits would eliminate the traditional, but not wholly logical, requirement that they be related to the size of the town in which the bank is located. Subjecting the deposits of all commercial banks to reserve requirements give recognition to the monetary character of all deposits whether member or nonmember.

The first administrative change in member-bank reserve requirements, following the passage of the Banking Act of 1935, occurred in 1936. This and subsequent actions doubled requirements. Increases were ordered (except for a temporary decrease during the 1938 depression) to absorb part of the flood of gold inundating the country before U.S. entry into World War II. During the war itself, reductions in the reserve requirements of the central reserve-city banks helped to offset the drain of funds to centers of military production. In 1948 general increases were ordered to fight inflation. Beginning in 1949 and continuing through the 1950s, changes were intended to moderate cyclical fluctuations and to reduce the reserve requirements of central reserve-city banks to the declining level of those for reserve-city banks. Reductions on the downward sweep of the cycle were not offset by increases on the upward sweep, however, so that decreases through the decade represented a secular downward trend. This action responded to a common belief among commercial bankers that reserve requirements were not only "too high" but that reductions were needed to finance secular increases in the money supply.

Important changes in member-bank reserve requirements ceased with the 1950s. Changes since then have been marginal, affecting only large aggregates of demand and time accounts, Eurodollar borrowing, "London checks," and commercial paper issued by bank holding companies (see Chapter 15). The Board of Governors apparently has concluded that member-bank reserve requirements are near rock bottom.

Liquidity Ratios

A relatively new instrument of monetary policy is the liquidity ratios introduced in many nations during the past twenty years. Commercial banks and, in certain instances, other financial institutions, are required to maintain in proportion to deposits or other liabilities a certain volume of assets not only in the form of cash but also in call loans, commercial paper, government securities, various types of business loans, and so on. Often the purpose of these requirements in the immediate postwar period was to find a home for the floating debt of governments. It was mainly for this reason that the Board of Governors proposed their introduction in the United States in 1948.

In the United Kingdom the reserves of the commercial banks on January 15, 1969, consisted of liquid assets equal to 32.1 percent of total gross deposits. Cash on hand and deposits with the Bank of England equaled 7.8 percent of gross deposits, money on call and short notice 13.6 percent, and bills discounted 10.6 percent.[14] The ratio of total liquid assets to gross deposits is the clearing banks' conventional measure of their liquidity. The exact proportions of these different assets vary from bank to bank and from day to day, according to the views of the managers of the money market position of the particular bank. The bulk of liquid assets represents credits to the public sector.

Liquidity ratios have been established not only to give monetary authorities the power to influence fluctuations in credit volume, but also to channel credit into specific use. As public deficits rise and government obligations increase, liquidity ratios may be raised. As long as liquidity ratios can be raised in this way, they will not prove effective in dampening inflationary pressures. It is not the particular ratio which dampens inflationary pressures but rather the quantitative limitations imposed on the assets which comprise the reserves of commercial banks.

From an overall point of view, it is preferable that the reserves of commercial banks be held solely in the form of cash on hand and deposits with the central bank. Excluding other assets reduces the danger that liquidity requirements will be directly used to finance Government deficits or to channel funds into uses thought desirable by the state.

Eligibility Requirements and the Discount Window

Access to the discount window is "traditionally based on eligibility requirements with regard to the purpose, maturity and credit standing of the drawer and endorser."[15] The requirements are important in establishing the degree of access to the window and in conditioning commercial-bank attitudes toward the loan applications of their own customers. Even if the requirements are quite liberal, access to the discount window is invariably subject to restraint. Nowhere is discounting an absolute right.

Central banks have the power to refuse accomodation to a commercial bank even when it submits eligible paper. If the paper is genuinely self-liquidating there is less disposition to question the purpose of the loan, and, at least in Belgium self-liquidating paper is never rejected. Changes in eligibility requirements are often used as a tool of monetary policy, and access to the discount window is usually contingent upon a bank's compliance with the objectives of monetary policy. Prior to World War I central banks limited extensions of credit principally to short-term self-liquidating paper. In testimony before the U.S. National Monetary Commission, officials of the Bank of England declared that they stood ready to discount bills signed by two British citizens (one of whom had to be the acceptor) with a usual maturity of four months. In exceptional cases the maturity could run six months. Trade bills, drawn to liquidate actual commercial transactions, would be discounted at or below Bank rate. Finance bills were discounted only at a penalty rate. The Bank of France explained that it discounted bills of exchange that had no more than three months to run and bore signatures of three individuals known to be solvent (securities could be substituted for one signature). The Reichsbank stood ready to discount bills not exceeding three months' duration and bearing the names of two parties known to be solvent. Only agricultural paper was subject to renewal. The Reichsbank extended Lombard loans (which were small relative to discounts) at a rate above the bank rate.

The effect of two world wars on the portfolios of central and commercial banks, the universal invasion into medium-term financing by commercial banks, and growing faith that shiftable assets are equal (if not superior) to self-liquidating assets have wrought great changes in the portfolios of central banks. Credit extensions by the Federal Reserve banks now consist mainly of loans against government securities. Discounts of eligible paper are negligible and have not been important since the 1920s.

Limiting credit extensions to self-liquidating paper, though considered antiquated in the present world, has the following advantage: The central bank has a short-term liquid asset that can be discounted with a minimum of credit investigation, which is payable at maturity and which is related to the flow of trade. Opening the discount window to all types of paper not only widens access to central-bank credit but also forces the central bank to follow the lending and investing policies of individual banks more meticulously than it otherwise would. Broad access to the discount window may lead, as it has in Japan, to some direct control over the loans and investments of commercial banks. In fact, the central bank may be compelled to adopt a "window guidance" policy, in order to prevent a deterioration in the quality of commercial banks' loans and investments and to guard itself from being inundated with low-quality paper with all its inflationary potential.

Broadened access to the discount window inevitably entails close scrutiny of reasons for applying to the central bank. At the present time, when a member banks appears to be using Federal Reserve credit for other than temporary, seasonal, or emergency needs and beyond requirements "which can reasonably be met from the bank's own resources, administrative contacts with the bank are made." [16] Prospects for debt retirement are reviewed, and a positive program for adjusting earning assets may be developed.

An initial request for accommodation is usually not questioned by the Reserve banks. Because the notes mature in fifteen days and are then automatically debited to the borrowing bank's account, the question of renewal cannot long be deferred. The Reserve bank may then intervene to suggest to the borrower that it make appropriate adjustments in its portfolio.

It is highly questionable whether borrowing from a central bank should be a right even for a limited time and amount. No individual or corporation has a right to credit from any lending institution, and no commercial bank should have a right to credit from a central bank. Once a right is granted, politics will force continuous extension until finally the central bank loses total control of the discount window.

Moral Suasion and Gentlemen's Agreements

Frequently in this and other nations central banks, unable or unwilling to raise discount rates in order to tighten credit, have relied on what is termed "moral suasion" to check increases in bank loans and investments. Central banks have exhorted commercial banks to limit their loans to productive purposes (as defined by the central banks), to avoid speculative loans and loans to enlarge plants when plant capacity is not being fully used, to avoid loans for nonessential construction, to avoid participating in call and mortgage loans outside the normal business area, to refrain from lending at a faster pace than can be financed by liquidation of assets or receipts of deposits. The response to these recommendations involves subjective judgments at lending institutions, which are not necessarily disinterested.

Moral suasion has not proved effective as an instrument of central-bank policy. It is apt to work inequitably upon those bankers who are sensitive to public opinion or who hold conspicuous community positions and those who do not have these characteristics. As the Royal Commission on Banking and Finance in Canada has pointed out, moral suasion cannot be relied upon to carry much of the weight of policy in normal situations, for market participants cannot be expected to act against their own interests except temporarily and in exceptional circumstances. The conclusion of one Governor of the Bank of Canada, Mr. Graham Towers, was that ultimately monetary and fiscal policy must do the job.[17]

"Gentlemen's agreements" have frequently been invoked in nations where the central banks are unable for one reason or another to use classical methods of credit control. This is particularly true in Switzerland, where the worldwide prestige of Swiss currency has generated large capital imports, affecting the money supply and increasing the liquidity of the economy. The Swiss National Bank has had the problem of holding liquidity in check at a time when its securities portfolio was miniscule. To help resolve such difficulties, the central bank has acted to check the inflow of funds by limiting the conversion of dollars into Swiss francs, by encouraging the export of capital, and by selling securities on treasury account and impounding the proceeds. As far back as 1927 it began entering into "gentlemen's agreements" in an effort to deal with some of these problems. The agreements cover not only commercial banks but also financial intermediaries.

In order to discourage the inflow of foreign funds, the agreements have often provided that demand deposits owed to foreigners earn no interest, that new foreign deposits be accepted only if subject to notice, that short-term foreign deposits be subject to commission charges, and that foreign funds not be invested in Swiss securities and mortgages. The main features of the agreements, frequently revised, were the nonpayment of interest on foreign demand deposits and the requirement of notice prior to withdrawal. These restrictions have not proved a serious barrier to the inflow of funds impelled by fear of war and currency devaluation. Certain transactions sidetracked the banks, others were exempt, and still others represented repatriation of Swiss funds not subject to the agreements.

Selective Credit Control

Selective credit control is a modern technique used in relatively homogeneous loan areas and in areas where the demand for credit is relatively insensitive to interest-rate changes. The area must be one which is reasonably definable in terms of the purpose and the nature of the loan, and important enough in terms of size and volatility that regulation can help enforce general credit controls.

In the United States, selective credit control has been applied to stock-exchange loans, consumer credit, and mortgage loans. Monetary authorities have tried to control stock-exchange loans by regulating the loan-to-value ratio (mainly under the authority of sections 7 and 8 of the Securities Exchange Act of June 6, 1934); consumer credit by governing down payments and maturity terms; and mortgage credit by governing maturity terms and the loan-to-value ratio.

Consumer credit, which is relatively insensitive to interest control, has been placed under selective controls in most nations. In the United States such controls (Regulation W) were first instituted on September 1, 1941; they were terminated on November 1, 1947. Over the next five years they were reinstated twice (on September 30, 1948, and September 18, 1950) and suspended twice (on June 30, 1949, and May 7, 1952). Even though the war experience was not normal, the Board of Governors was sufficiently satisfied with the results to recommend, in 1945, permanent selective control of consumer credit. The proposal was not, however, favorably received by the administration or Congress.

Experience with consumer-credit controls, wherever they have been applied, has been generally favorable. The Board of Trade in the United Kingdom, whose job it is to administer such controls, stated that they are easy to administer and take effect quickly.[18] The Radcliffe Committee supported the use of selective controls as did an earlier study prepared by the New York Clearing House Association.[19] Neither group looked upon selective controls as a substitute for general credit controls. Unlike consumer credit, mortgage credit is more responsive to general credit controls. Selective controls are often employed to encourage rather than to discourage lending operations, and at times, are used to nullify the effects of general credit control on the mortgage markets.*

The experience of the Reserve System in applying selective credit controls to security loans has been favorable. It is a credit area which is reasonably definable in terms of the purpose of the loans, the collateral used, and the nature of the loan contract. Trade practices are specialized and sufficiently standardized so that

---

* Following the outbreak of the Korean War, President Harry S. Truman, under the Defense Production Act of 1950, was given temporary authority to regulate real-estate credit. He delegated control of the terms of conventional mortgages (Regulation X) to the Board of Governors, control of the terms of insured mortgages to the Federal Housing Administration, and control of the terms of guaranteed mortgages to the Veterans Administration. Regulation X broke new ground. It represented the first attempt, in this country or abroad, to restrain inflationary pressures through comprehensive regulation of mortgage terms. In the spring of 1952 the administration rescinded the authority that it had delegated, apparently just as it was proving effective.

regulation can be applied as a continuation or an extension of these procedures rather than as a drastic disruption. The flow of credit has responded to the terms established. Restrictive action is shortly followed by a decline in credit volume and easing action by a rise.

Lending Directives

Closely allied to selective credit controls is the use of lending directives. These are directives issued by a central bank, a minister of finance, or both, to commercial banks or other financial institutions, respecting permissible increases or required decreases in total loans, and/or in the amount of loans to be extended to particular industries.

Nations generally resort to lending directives either to avoid the higher interest rates resulting from general credit controls or to direct credit into channels regarded as socially productive. In the United States lending directives have been used to check the flow of commercial-bank credit abroad; in Norway [20] and Great Britain, they have been used to place ceilings on increases in commercial-bank loans. Other nations, (like France and Italy) have subjected loans by commercial banks to prior approval by the central bank.* Other countries have influenced the management of bank funds through window guidance (Japan) or establishment of various asset and liquidity ratios (West Germany). Still others have permitted only part of new deposit increases to be used in loan expansion. An endless variety of measures has been used, resulting in a complex system of controls, which try to substitute government direction for the impersonal action of market economy. India in a recent law empowered its central bank to direct all commercial-bank credits to "socially desirable purposes."

Action by the Bank of England, following sterling devaluation in November 1967, affords a good case example of the imposition of lending directives and ceilings. Banks were asked to limit lending for most purposes to the levels then current after allowance for seasonal fluctuations. The ceiling applied to all sterling lending to the private sector and to foreign borrowers, with the specific exceptions of export transactions and shipbuilding. Within the ceiling, priority was to be given to lending categories necessary to improve or sustain the balance of payments. Equivalent restrictions were applied to lending by instalment-finance houses.

---

* In France prior submission of individual applications is part of the general reporting arrangements involved in planning; and in Italy prior approval is exercised only on a general not a specific level.

Further restrictions were adopted in May 1968, when all sterling lending by banks was brought under control. Total lending was not to exceed 104 percent of the November 1967 figure. Banks were again asked to give priority to loans directly related to improving the balance of payments. In November 1968 credit for less essential purposes, particularly for consumption, was further restrained.

This program was accompanied by an import-deposit scheme, which affected about a third of total imports, mostly manufactures. Importers were required to deposit with Her Majesty's Customs an amount in sterling equal to 50 percent of the value of the imported goods before they could be withdrawn from the port area. The deposits, which bore no interest were to be repaid 180 days later. The plan was intended to reduce imports by raising their cost and reducing the liquid funds available to importers. Banks were cautioned to be very restrictive in lending for import deposits. The scheme was reinforced on December 18, 1968, when importers were forbidden to borrow foreign currency to comply with these deposit requirements.[21]

TRANSMISSION EFFECTS OF RESTRICTIVE MONETARY POLICY

The preceding sections of this chapter have included discussion of various techniques used by central banks to control credit. The effects of a restrictive credit policy, if this is the policy adopted, upon commercial banks cannot be accurately foretold. Neither the precise effect nor the timing can be predetermined. Much depends upon the financial condition of commercial banks, the absence or presence of liquid assets, the ability of commercial banks to borrow at home or abroad (Eurodollars), the speed with which the policy is adopted, and changing psychological attitudes.

Initially a restrictive policy forces changes in the composition of commercial-bank assets. The sale of securities or an increase in reserve requirements by the Reserve banks, if net excess reserves are negligible, will force member banks into debt. Net borrowed reserves will rise. Because they are unwilling or not permitted to remain long in debt to the Reserve banks, individual member banks will begin to buy Federal funds, to reduce their holdings of open-market paper and security loans, and to sell government obligations. They will strive to increase their outstanding volume of CDs; they will also borrow in the Eurodollar market.

The redistribution of assets among commercial banks permits individual units to reduce their indebtedness to the Reserve banks. The net indebtedness of the entire banking system remains the same and can be reduced only if the central bank reverses its policy, if the nation experiences an increase in its reserve assets, if the currency volume declines, or if there is substantial shifting of assets from commercial banks to other holders.

The forces activated by a restrictive policy may compel commercial banks to reduce holdings of government obligations, particularly in the initial phases of the policy when they attempt to meet loan demands. Cyclical fluctuations in government obligations were important during the 1950s, when the Reserve banks alternated restrictive and expansionist policies in an effort to counteract business fluctuations.[22] Being loan-oriented, commercial banks have not hesitated to sell government obligations at a loss, when necessary, in order to extend loans. The so-called "locked-in effect" has not proved a deterrent.

Sooner or later a restrictive monetary policy exerts a tightening effect on loans. Neither the precise effect nor the lag in that effect can be determined with any precision. It may be delayed by the existence of confirmed lines of credit or, in countries influenced by British practices, by overdraft limits.

A restrictive policy causes commercial banks to screen loan applications with greater care, granting some, weeding out others. Banks become more selective, raising standards of credit worthiness and eliminating marginal risks. They grant preference to regular customers, to those with good deposit balances, and to businesses with good growth potential.[23]

Commercial banks in the course of a restrictive credit policy are apt to avoid loans for speculative purposes, loans with long maturities—especially those with an alternative of capital market financing—loans subject to continuous renewals, loans for nonproductive purposes (if these can be defined), loans to shoppers and transients, loans to retire preferred stock or to pay off other creditors, loans to acquire other businesses and loans outside the normal trade area. A high valuation is placed on established and growing customer relations and on customers with appreciable balances. Lines of credit are carefully watched. Borrowers are required to have more collateral. There is firmer adherence to repayment schedules and to the maintenance of deposit balances.

Lowest on the priority list of loans are mortgage loans, which usually involve no customer relations. Loans to brokers are also likely to be ill favored. Loans to government securities dealers and to non-commercial-bank lenders are reduced. Loans to finance companies, except "captive companies," are curtailed. The volume of consumer-instalment paper acquired from dealers, finance companies, and other banks is reduced. Banks prefer to extend consumer credit directly to borrowers. Standards are tightened, and loans are restricted to good customers.

Term loans are scrutinized with great care. (Maturities are reduced, and volume is decreased.) The highest priority is given to short-term commercial loans, especially seasonal loans. Commercial banks encourage their commercial customers to reduce their borrowing, to intensify collections, to reduce receivables and inventories, and to drop bad customers.

In a period of credit restraint, small business is apt to be more adversely affected than large business. The reasons are that small businesses are generally not as credit-worthy as large businesses and their credit-worthiness tends to deteriorate in periods when credit restraints are applied. The policy of according preferential treatment to old customers tends to discriminate against small businesses, many of which were newly established.

Selective credit controls, if loan terms are quickly tightened and maturities drastically reduced, fairly quickly affect the outstanding volume of credit in particular areas. The impact may be lessened as borrowers evade the regulations. But evasion may be difficult when monetary authorities adopt measures like that successfully used in Denmark: any contract drawn in contravention of the rules is ipso facto void.

A restrictive credit policy affects the amount and distribution not only of commercial-bank assets but also those of financial intermediaries. Restrictive policies restrict a cash inflow. Individuals may invest their funds directly in money-market instruments. Mortgage repayments decline. Depositors borrow from savings banks, and policy loans of insurance companies increase. Insurance companies are less willing to assume a fully committed position and shift emphasis from areas (mortgage loans) where yields are relatively slow to change, to areas where yields are more sensitive (corporate bonds).

The effects of restrictive policy spread to the capital markets. Interest rates, both short- and long-term, rise, and the willingness of investment bankers to undertake new issues weakens. Municipalities often delay bond sales. Interest rates on new corporate issues rise above those on comparable outstanding issues. Commercial banks begin to withdraw from the market. The tightening of credit has a greater impact on the amount of issues publicly placed than on those privately sold, and has a greater impact on small than on large issues.

Trade credit introduces an element of elasticity in the economic system, permitting continued financing, even on a temporary basis, of economic expansion when bank credit is restricted. Business creditors finance business debtors, by reducing cash holdings, by selling marketable securities, and by recourse to the capital markets. The volume of trade credit is largely unaffected by changes in interest rates. If business optimism yields to pessimism, trade credit may be drastically reduced.

In many ways—through affecting business and individual spending, capital markets, and the lending and investment policies of all financial institutions—a restrictive credit policy can check inflationary pressures. How quickly the results become apparent depends, as we have indicated, upon many factors. The economy cannot be "finetuned."

Although the effects of restrictive policy cannot be foretold, still less can those of expansive policy. Much depends upon the psychological reactions of businessmen and consumers, upon what is termed an atmosphere of confidence. For confirmation we need only refer to the lack of response of the business community in the Great Depression to expansive monetary policies.

CONCLUDING OBSERVATIONS

If it is to make a maximum contribution to economic stability and growth, a central bank must necessarily accept a broad definition of monetary policy. Its concern is the whole credit structure: individual, corporate, government, bank, and trade credit, and the whole spectrum of financial institutions. To restrict itself to the narrow definition of monetary policy is to remove itself from the mainstream of financial and economic developments. The whole economic world is its province, and the whole economic world forms the basis of its economic research and policy.

Discount rate policy, opening or narrowing the discount window, open-market operations, changes in reserve requirements, and selective credit controls have been the principal instruments of American credit policy. Changes in the discount rate, combined with open-market operations signal policy changes. Alterations in reserve requirements, particularly in the 1950s, were ordered occasionally by the Reserve System by way of added emphasis. Beginning in 1969 reserve requirements were extended to nondeposit liabilities in order to take account of innovations in banking techniques. Opening or narrowing the discount window, despite the greater liberality at the time of the credit crisis of 1970, has not been as important an instrument of policy as it may become in the future. In order to further dispel the uncertainties prevailing at the time of this credit crisis, the Reserve System lifted interest ceilings on large short-term certificates of deposit. Selective credit controls have, on the whole, functioned well in the security markets and are necessary on a standby basis in the field of consumer credit.

Essential to the implementation of central-bank policy is a well-functioning financial infrastructure. This includes not only commercial banks and financial intermediaries but also capital markets that serve to place the savings of the community at the disposal of those best equipped to promote economic development. Also essential to the implementation of central-bank policy is well-conceived and well-ordered management of the public debt. This topic is discussed in the next chapter.

Notes

1. See B. H. Beckhart, *The Criteria of a Well-Functioning Financial System* (Australia: University of Queensland Press, 1961). Address at the University of Queensland, St. Lucia, Australia, July 28, 1960.

2. See W. F. Crick (ed.), *Commonwealth Banking Systems* (Oxford: Clarendon, 1965), Chap. 1.

3. *Money and Credit: Their Influence on Jobs, Prices and Growth.* The Report of the Commission on Money and Credit. (Englewood Cliffs, N.J.: Prentice-Hall, 1961); *Committee on the Working of the Monetary System, Report.* (London: Her Majesty's Stationery Office, August, 1959).

4. *Committee on the Working of the Monetary System, op cit.,* p. 132.

5. *Ibid.,* p. 134.

6. George Garvy, *The Discount Mechanism in Leading Industrial Countries Since World War II* (Washington, D.C.: Board of Governors of the Federal Reserve System, 1968).

7. *Eight European Central Banks.* Published under the auspices of the Bank for International Settlements, Basle (New York and London: Frederick A. Praeger, Publisher, 1963).

8. Garvy, *The Discount Mechanism in Leading Industrial Countries Since World War II, op. cit.,* pp. 184–5.

9. For a history of discount rate policy, see Clay J. Anderson, "Evolution of the Role and Functioning of the Discount Mechanism," *Fundamental Reappraisal of the Discount Mechanism* (Federal Reserve Bank of Philadelphia, November 1966).

10. Robert C. Turner, *Member-Bank Borrowing* (Columbus: The Ohio State University, December 1938). For an exposition of the traditional view see Winfield W. Riefler, *Money Rates and Money Markets in the United States,* (New York: Harper & Bros., 1930). Clay J. Anderson (*op. cit.,* p. 34) called attention to a study which pointed out that of 250 national banks which failed from 1920 to about 1925, four-fifths were traditional borrowers from the Reserve System prior to failure.

11. Dolores P. Lynn, *Reserve Adjustments of the Eight Major New York City Banks during 1966* (Federal Reserve Bank of New York, August 1967; revised July 1968).

12. Peter G. Fousek, *Foreign Central Banking: The Instruments of Monetary Policy* (Federal Reserve Bank of New York, November 1957).

13. *Fifty-first Annual Report Board of Governors of the Federal Reserve System Covering Operations for the Year 1964* (Washington: March 22, 1965), pp. 200–202.

14. *Quarterly Bulletin* (Bank of England), June 1969, p. 236; also December 1962, "Bank Liquidity in the United Kingdom," pp. 248–256. See *Committee on the Working of the Monetary System, op. cit.,* pp. 49 and 52.

15. Garvy, *op. cit.,* p. 10.

16. *The Federal Reserve and the Treasury: Answers to Questions from The Commission on Money and Credit* (Englewood Cliffs, N.J.: Prentice-Hall, Inc., 1963), p. 130.

17. *Report of the Royal Commission on Banking and Finance* (Canada), 1964, p. 476.

18. *Committee on the Working of the Monetary System, Principal Memoranda of Evidence,* I (London: Her Majesty's Stationery Office, 1960), p. 234.

19. *Committee on the Working of the Monetary System, Report, op. cit.,* p. 187; and *The Federal Reserve Re-examined,* A Study made by the New York Clearing House Association, 1953, p. 126. The Clearing House Study proposed the delegation of standby authority to the Board of Governors of the Federal Reserve System.

20. For a listing of lending directives in Norway, see *Economic Bulletin* (Norges Bank), Vol. 39, No. 1, (1968).

21. *Bank of England Report for the Year Ended 28th February 1969,* pp. 21–22.

22. See Michael E. Levy, *Cycles in Government Securities, Part I, Federal Debt and its Ownership* ("Studies in Business Economics, No. 78," [New York: National Industrial Conference Board Inc., 1962]).

23. See Donald R. Hodgman, *Commercial Bank Loan and Investment Policy* (Champaign, Illinois: The University of Illinois, 1963).

Goals of Monetary Policy: Review and Analysis

CHAPTER 19

THE IMPORTANCE OF UNAMBIGUOUS GOALS

"Central bankers of the world, unite; you have nothing to lose but your currencies." So urged a central banker from a communist nation a few years ago. By this he meant that central bankers or their counterparts have a common interest in protecting the purchasing power of currencies and in opposing inflationary actions by governments, whether in capitalist or communist nations. Throughout history governments have been very adept at adopting policies, often with declared motives of highest altruism, which have debased and depreciated currencies and which finally rendered them worthless.

A central bank, as a creature of the state, cannot easily divorce itself from the current policies and goals of government. The means adopted may, however, destroy the end desired. A central bank in close touch with local and foreign money markets and credit institutions is in a strategic position to appraise current developments and to advise governments on economic policy. It has deep insight into the working of financial institutions and also intimate knowledge of financial processes.*

Central banks cannot be independent from governments but they can be independent within governments. Their independence can be buttressed by the provisions of their charters, which vary greatly in length and content. The statute may be brief as that of the Bank of England or it may be long and complicated, as that of the Federal Reserve System. In a way, conciseness of the charter of the Bank of England and the involved charter of the Federal Reserve Act reflect different approaches of two countries to government problems, one relying upon an unwritten constitution, tradition, and precedents, the other upon a written constitution and statute law.

Whether simple or complex, the charter best protects a central bank when it unambiguously defines the goals of credit policy. This, the charter of the Deutsche Bundesbank does in directing the bank to safeguard the internal and external value of the German currency. Similarly, the Austrian National Bank is to ensure, by all means at its disposal, the value of Austrian currency. The Netherlands Bank has the task of regulating "the value of the Netherlands currency in such manner as shall be most conducive to the country's welfare, and in that connection to stabilize the said value as far as possible." [1]

In these few examples central banks have in the main been entrusted with single responsibilities. In other statutes central banks have been assigned responsibilities that are often in conflict. In the Philippines the central bank is to maintain monetary stability, to preserve the international value of the peso, and to promote rising levels of production, employment, and real income. The Reserve Bank of Australia is to use its powers in such fashion as to best contribute to the stability of the currency of Australia, to maintain full employment, and to advance the economic prosperity and welfare of the Australian people.

American Goals

In the United States, congressional directives on credit policy lack clarity and direction. The Federal Reserve banks are to establish rates of discount with a

---

* In an interview, which appeared in the July 1966 issue of "The Banker," London, Mr. L. K. O'Brien, Governor of the Bank of England, is quoted as saying: "There are times when the Bank feels it right to speak out unasked, even though this may occasionally entail treading somewhat on particular toes. Public expression of disquiet cannot possibly be ruled out, even at the risk of incurring displeasure in some quarters or of accusations that the Bank is stepping outside what some may regard as its proper function . . . Dealing each day in all these [financial] markets gives the Bank technical knowledge and competence which no other branch of the authorities can have any means of acquiring . . . It can see there, as a participator, the real effect of official policies, and this daily contact with real life, is what gives weight to the Bank's advice in the monetary field particularly."

"view of accommodating commerce and business," the Board of Governors of the Federal Reserve System may change reserve requirements to prevent "injurious credit expansion or contraction," and regulate margin requirements in order to prevent "the excessive use of credit for the purchase or carrying of securities." The Federal Open Market Committee is to conduct its operations with a view "to accommodating commerce and business and with regard to their bearing upon the general credit situation of the country." [2] These goals are extremely ambiguous and subject to many interpretations. Equally ambiguous is the Employment Act of 1946, which the Reserve System has indicated its readiness to accept, provided that its own responsibility is limited to promoting growth within the framework of a stable price level:

> The Congress hereby declares that it is the continuing policy and responsibility of the Federal Government to use all practicable means consistent with its needs and obligations and other essential considerations of national policy, with the assistance and cooperation of industry, agriculture, labor and State and local governments, to coordinate and utilize all its plans, functions, and resources for the purpose of creating and maintaining, in a manner calculated to foster and promote free competitive enterprise and the general welfare, conditions under which there will be afforded useful employment opportunities, including self-employment, for those able, willing, and seeking to work, and to promote maximum employment, production and purchasing power.[3]

Upon concluding a review of congressional directives on credit policy, the Board of Governors replied to the Patman Committee in 1952 that the long-run economic objectives of the System are "to minimize economic fluctuations caused by irregularities in the flow of money and credit, foster more stable values, and thus make possible the smooth functioning of the monetary machinery so necessary to promote growth of the country and to improve standards of living.[4]

Different Approaches

Before World War II a British group, the Macmillan Committee, which was appointed by the government to inquire into banking, finance, and credit, declared that the objectives of monetary policy should include stabilizing the value of the pound sterling in terms of other currencies, adhering to the international gold standard, raising and then stabilizing wholesale prices, once they had been "raised sufficiently." [5] The majority of the committee, with J. M. Keynes concurring, opposed devaluation as a means of accomplishing these objectives, asserting that "the state of affairs immediately ensuing on such an event would be worse than that which proceeded it." [6] The Committee placed main emphasis on the stability of the foreign exchanges and the maintenance of the international gold standard. These were in fact the principal economic objectives of the policies of the Bank of England from the close of the Napoleonic Wars to the outbreak of World War I.

Ideas and attitudes change with time. The Radcliffe Committee and the American Commission on Money and Credit, to which we have already referred, had sought to enlarge the goals of monetary policy. The Radcliffe Committee listed five such goals: a high, stable level of employment; "reasonable" stability of the internal purchasing power of money; steady economic growth and improvement in the standard of living; some contribution to the economic development of the outside world (implying a margin in the balance of payments); and a strengthening of London's international reserves (also implying a further margin in the balance of payments). The Committee made no attempts to define such adjectives as "high," "stable," "reasonable," and "steady." Objectives were stated in qualitative not quantitative terms.

The Commission on Money and Credit viewed national economic policy as "an integrated whole," declaring that "both private enterprise and government have major and complementary roles to play in achieving national objectives." These objectives are a rate of increase in GNP, ranging between 3.5 and 4.5 percent a year; a low level of unemployment; and reasonable price stability. The Commission defined a low level of unemployment as being somewhere near the point at which "the number of unfilled vacancies is about the same as the number of unemployed."

The Commission on Money and Credit, at least by implication, leaves one with the impression that it looked upon price level stability as the monetary goal of lowest priority. The disastrous consequences of inflation, it asserted, arise from galloping inflation, which, it concluded, was not a real threat to the United States.

In discussing international monetary relations the Commission seemed unable to decide whether or not stability in the foreign-exchange value of the dollar was important enough to warrant adoption of corrective measures. The Radcliffe Committee, on the other hand, concluded that preservation of a fixed exchange rate would offer the best prospect of avoiding stresses and strains within the sterling area and would afford a firm basis for international trade and investment.

The Radcliffe Committee emphasized the possibility of conflicting objectives of monetary policy. The pressure of demand implicit in high-level employment, it warned might jeopardize the external and internal value of the pound. The Commission on Money and Credit, on the other hand, optimistically assumed that the objectives of monetary policy which it endorsed were basically compatible.

GREATER SHARING OF POWER

Although the Federal Reserve Act is ambiguous about credit objectives, the Banking Act of 1935 provides a good legal framework for the System. We would suggest no changes in the number of Board members, in their required qualifications (except to add that they be versed in banking and finance by education, training or experience), or in their terms of office. Nor would we suggest that the term of the chairman be synchronized with that of the President of the United States; an unsynchronized term enables the President to learn to know the incumbent chairman of the Board and to avoid the common temptation to "make a clean sweep."

In order to provide for greater sharing power, all of the credit control powers of the System might well be concentrated in the Federal Open Market Committee. In addition to its current power over open-market operations, it would then have authority to approve changes in the discount rate and to order changes in reserve requirements and in margin requirements on security loans. If the Reserve System were to be given power to regulate instalment and mortgage credit, the Open Market Committee would be the proper body to regulate terms.

When changes in the discount rate were to be contemplated, the Reserve banks would not only initiate action as they do now; they also would share in final decisions.* Throughout the history of the Reserve System, Reserve banks have shown greater perspicacity in discount policy than has the Reserve Board itself. The New York Federal Reserve Bank has frequently recommended changes in bank rates, which in the light of later developments were completely justified, only to have its proposals rejected by the Board at the time they were made. Similarly, in ordering changes in member-bank reserve requirements and in margin requirements on security loans, the insight and experience of the Reserve banks should be brought to bear directly on the action taken.†

BASIC OBJECTIVES OF MONETARY POLICY

The basic objectives of monetary policy that we would assign to the Federal Open Market Committee for implementation include moderating the amplitude of

---

* In current practice action is usually initiated at meetings of the Federal Open Market Committee.
† For further discussion of the administrative framework of the Federal Reserve System and possible changes, refer to Chapter 2.

the business cycle, preventing deterioration in the quality of credit, achieving price level stability and rectifying imbalances in the balance of payments. Other frequently mentioned aims, such as full employment and economic growth, are ancillary to these basic objectives. Other aims such as pegged interest rates and fixed percentage increases in the money stock cannot be considered objectives in themselves, but simply as possible means to attain certain economic goals.[7] Still another objective, which requires the close cooperation of the U.S. Treasury, is the management of the public debt in accordance with basic policy aims.

The Business Cycle

According to analyses by the National Bureau of Economic Research, the period from the establishment of the Federal Reserve System in 1914 to 1969 was marked by twelve business cycles, varying greatly in duration and intensity. The longest (measured from peak to peak) began in May 1960 and ended November 1969 covering a period of 114 months. Another long cycle was that which included the years dominated by World War II from May 1937 to February 1945, 93 months in all. The shortest lasted from August 1918 to January 1920, 17 months.

The severest declines in business activity occurred from January 1920–July 1921, August 1929–March 1933, and May 1937–June 1938. They were so severe that they can justly be called "depressions," whereas the others could be characterized as "recessions."

Periods of expansion since the establishment of the Federal Reserve System have generally been longer (average 42 months) than they were from 1854 to 1913 (average 26 months), and periods of contraction have been shorter (average 15 months and 23 months, respectively). Whether this has resulted from Federal Reserve policy or whether it was a result of fortuitous circumstances cannot be established. One would hope that longer expansions and shorter contractions would result from the existence and functioning of the Reserve System.

A central bank succeeds in reducing cyclical amplitudes when it can influence those factors in GNP that are principally responsible for cyclical change: business expenditures on inventories, business expenditures on plant and equipment, consumer expenditures on durable goods, and consumer expenditures on housing.

These particular expenditures have shown great volatility since World War II. Consumer expenditures on nondurables and services have grown with scarcely any interruption, as have state and local expenditures. Federal expenditures, mainly because of changes in defense spending, have fluctuated erratically and have, on the whole, intensified rather than moderated the cycle.

In the 1920s and 1950s more than in other periods, Federal Reserve policy was directed toward tempering cyclical fluctuations. Stimulated by the research work of W. Randolph Burgess, Wesley Clair Mitchell, Carl Snyder, H. Parker Willis, and others, the Reserve System, following World War I, developed various statistical measures of cyclical fluctuations, those "continuous, cumulative and self-reversing changes" in economic activity that are themselves characteristic of an economy dominated by business decisions based on profits.[8] In its attempts to moderate booms and to stimulate activity in recession the System relied mainly upon the discount rate and open-market operations. Lacking powers of selective credit control, it was not able in the 1920s to restrain the use of credit for stock-market speculation. Anxious as it was to reestablish the international gold standard, it was not always able, particularly in 1924 and 1927, to pursue policies most conducive to economic stability: an early example of a basic conflict in objectives!

The efforts of the Reserve System to promote economic stability in the 1920s were, however, reinforced by Federal budgetary surpluses and a decline in the Federal debt. The former, which persisted despite a fairly continuous decline in tax rates, provided savings needed for the financing of capital expenditures. The System's efforts to promote stability were hampered, on the other hand, by the emergence of domestic imbalances resulting from stock-market speculation, the activities of the security affiliates, and a decline in the quality of credit. Its efforts were also hampered by the emergence of foreign imbalances resulting from the protectionist trade policies of the United States, overvaluation of the pound, efforts to collect war debts and reparations, and deterioration in credit standards for foreign bond issues.

In the 1930s interest in cyclical fluctuations yielded to what seemed the deeply rooted problem of economic stagnation. (See Chapter 10.) In the 1940s this problem was superseded by the overriding dominance of war finance, which was in turn displaced in the 1950s by renewed interest in the cycle.

Although problems associated with cyclical fluctuations were dormant in the 1930s and 1940s, they were never completely nonexistent. The sharp decline in economic activity in 1937–1938 was a reminder, as Frank R. Garfield has pointed out,[9] that even in years characterized by a low level of resource exploitation, cyclical elements lurked in the wings ready to dominate the stage.

The economy of the 1950s differed in many respects from that of the 1920s. Total governmental expenditures on goods and services rose from about 8 to 20 percent of GNP. Social security payments underpinned consumer income. High Federal expenditures, including those of social security, accompanied by heavy reliance on the income tax, gave birth to the automatic stabilizers. Of great importance was the fact that the international economic policy of the United States in that decade was more intelligently geared to the world situation than it was in the 1920s.

The Reserve System possessed new weapons in its ability to apply selective credit controls to security loans and to raise member-bank reserve requirements. Success attended their efforts to mitigate cyclical fluctuations, aided as they were by the automatic stabilizers and occasionally by positive fiscal policy (See Chapter 9). The recessions were mild and short-lived.

Emphasis on the cyclical character of economic fluctuations yielded in the 1960s to belief that cyclical fluctuations could be submerged in rapid economic growth. Expansive fiscal and monetary policies designed to promote growth, however, generated domestic and foreign imbalances that demanded corrective action.

It was eventually recognized that the inflationary boom, a byproduct of efforts to stimulate growth as well as the requirements of the Vietnam War, had to be checked if the rise in labor cost per unit of output was to be stopped, imports reduced, exports increased, and output per man hour increased. These purposes could not be accomplished unless the economy accepted recession. Expansive fiscal and monetary policy thus led to necessary corrective measures that have given the business cycle a rebirth.

The most difficult problem encountered by a central bank in trying to reduce cyclical amplitudes is choosing the timing and intensity of its actions. How can it know when to pass from a policy of ease to one of neutrality, and from one of neutrality to one of restriction? How can it know whether its actions should be mild or drastic?

If a central bank were reasonably certain that recession would shortly yield to recovery, it could prepare to shift from a policy of ease to one of neutrality. If it were reasonably certain that prosperity would shortly yield to recession, it could prepare to shift from restriction to ease.

In an effort to forecast turning points in the business cycle, the National Bureau of Economic Research selected, on the basis of past performance, certain indexes that are regarded as leading indicators. They include about thirty series that ordinarily reach peaks or troughs before such aggregate series as GNP, unemployment, the index of industrial production, personal income, and retail sales. Because the list of leading indicators is long, attempts have been made to combine all the items in a single index, which affords a clue to the turning points in the business cycle.

A central bank is helped by the leading indicators in being able to forecast, better than it could in their absence, the turning points in business conditions. They do not, however, help a central bank decide exactly when, on the upward sweep of the cycle, to adopt restrictive measures in order to forestall a boom. Nor do they afford any clue to the amount of restriction or braking that is required.

In deciding "when" and "how much," a central bank must act more as a psychologist than as a statistician. It must try to probe the future buying intentions of businessmen and consumers. It must try to weigh such intangible factors as the acceptance of inflation as a way of life. It cannot neglect study of various statistical indexes, but a time comes when it must ultimately rely upon its "feel" for the markets, on its "intuition," of the meaning and significance of the passing scene.

Even if a central bank were perfectly able to take appropriate action at the right time, it could not by its own efforts entirely eliminate the cycle. The cycle is not simply a "dance of the dollar." It arises partly from business spending on such capital goods as railways, electric-power plants, atomic installations, and irrigation projects, which, when completed, may satisfy demand for some time without need for further enlargement. The role of monetary policy is reduced particularly in periods when business relies upon internal funds for capital improvements.

The business cycle is a continuing phenomenon of modern life. Fluctuations can be reduced by central-bank action, and central banks should look upon their reduction as an important goal of policy. Through the 1920s and 1950s considerable success attended the Reserve System's efforts to reduce cyclical fluctuations. Viewed from the present, it seems that open-market purchases were probably carried too far both in 1924 and in 1927, and that the restrictive credit policies adopted in the first half of 1928 should have been continued through the year (See Chapter 9). But the Reserve System had a very creditable record. It provided leadership in central bank cooperation and in the world's return to the gold standard, and it created innovations in the use of open-market operations. It pioneered in the collection and compilation of statistical data, and in this area became a leader among central banks.

In the 1950s too, the Reserve System, assisted by the built-in stabilizers, made important contributions to economic stability. It may have moved too far toward ease in 1954 and may have been tardy in imposing restraint in 1955. Over the whole period it would have been justified in following a more restrictive policy, in view of the use made of bank credit and, toward the end of the decade, of the growing reluctance of foreigners to hold dollars and of the rise in the con-sumer-price index. Its overall record was, however, creditable. Granted a peaceful world, the policy actions of the Federal Reserve System in future decades may, as in those two periods, be geared toward reducing the amplitude of cyclical fluctua-tions. The cycle has not yet been laid to rest.

Credit Quality

A very important basic objective of monetary policy is to prevent, as much as possible, the decline in credit standards that normally occur on the upward sweep of the business cycle, which lead to a deterioration in credit quality and con-sequently, to its over extension and to subsequent losses and bankruptcies that deepen the recession. The money supply is no stronger than the quality of credit on which it rests. A decline in quality causes an increase in quantity, which, by causing prices to rise, induces a further extension of loans and a further decline in quality.

The existence of a decline in the quality of credit is not something that is as-certained only after the event, that is, after recession has occurred. It can be de-tected on the upward sweep of the cycle, and to the extent that it is then checked the boom may be dampened and the ensuing recession in business activity mini-mized.

The National Bureau of Economic Research has undertaken a number of pi-oneer and exhaustive studies in this area covering developments in such fields as changes in the quality of foreign bonds, trade credit, consumer and agricultural credit, and bank loans. Deterioration in credit quality, according to the pathfind-ing study of Geoffrey H. Moore, can mean a decline in actual quality, as indicated by loss rates, foreclosure rates, and default or delinquency rates determined after the event; a decline in estimated quality, as indicated by loss reserves, interest dif-ferentials, bank examiners' appraisals, and the like; a shift toward types of loan contracts or types of borrowers that may be expected to involve higher delinquency or loss rates; and a change for the worse in the economic prospects of the debtors.[10]

In one of its studies, the National Bureau found that the quality of foreign bonds floated in the United States during the second half of the decade of the 1920s had fallen from those floated in the first half. The bonds in the second half were of poorer quality and, as such, were, to an increasing extent, issued by investment banks other than those that had been particularly active in the first half of the decade. It was not easy for a foreign government or a city to obtain a dollar loan early in the decade. Borrowers on their own initiative had to seek investment bankers who stood ready to persuade their clients to purchase the bonds. In the second half, representatives of investment-banking houses eagerly sought foreign debtors and induced them, by offering low lending rates, by bribery and by chicanery, to issue bonds that often had little relevance to the economic needs of the country and to its ability to repay. That credit quality had declined was recognized at the time.[11]

Much the same experience was encountered in the urban mortgage loans of life-insurance companies. The foreclosure rate on loans extended in the first half of the 1920s was less than that on loans extended in the second half. Optimism dominated the attitudes of lenders and borrowers at a time when caution would have been more appropriate.[12]

The National Bureau uncovered through the 1950s and 1960s similar instances of deterioration in credit quality. The quality of trade credit, which is one of the most important means of financing in the American economy, had been declining since the late 1940s.[13] Its quality "weakens during periods of general economic expansion and is restored during periods of recession." [14] Financial ratios were found to be effective indicators of risk.

The rapid growth in instalment credit after World War II had been marked by a sharp lengthening of maturities and an equally sharp decrease in down payments. Paralleling the easing of terms, changes occurred in borrower's characteristics. Credit terms were found to be significantly related to subsequent collection or repayment experience. Deliquency, repossession, and loss ratios increased to the extent that preceding lending terms had been relaxed.[15]

Similarly, the progressive easing of mortgage terms in the postwar period has facilitated the growth of mortgage debt. Smaller down payments, higher loan-to-value ratios, and longer maturities have enabled many families to qualify for mortgage debt. The repayment rate is reduced, and the borrower accumulates equity slowly.

The demand for mortgage credit responds quickly to reductions in minimum down payments. The easing of lending terms enables many to obtain mortgage credit who would not otherwise be able to do so; the quality of loans is apt to decline. In the postwar period the loan-to-value ratio on FHA insured home mortgages increased from 87 to 95 percent, and the average period to maturity rose from twenty-one to thirty years. Robert E. Knight of the Federal Reserve Bank of Kansas City pointed out that the "foreclosure rate has risen steadily and significantly" and that "the figures leave little doubt that some decline in the quality of credit has occurred." [16]

The decline in the quality of business credit through the 1960s was mirrored in the progressive deterioration of various financial ratios. The current ratio, the quick ratio, the solvency ratio, and the equity debt ratio all declined.[17]

In the early part of the decade, nonfinancial corporations obtained sufficient funds from internal sources to finance their expenditures on inventories and plant and equipment. Beginning in 1965 they were forced to rely to an increasing extent on bonds and mortgages and bank loans. The equity debt ratio fell sharply. The relation of the one to the other became increasingly unbalanced.

The liquidity position of American business corporations had in reality been "deteriorating for a protracted period." The practice of basing depreciation charges on historical cost caused earnings to be overstated. Companies began using up their capital and "compounded their problems by relying extensively upon short-term borrowings, either from the commercial banks or in the commercial paper market." [18]

Business management was convinced that it faced no liquidity problem. Bank loans could be quickly obtained. This continued until commercial banks themselves fell victims to a decline in their own liquidity. This situation threatened to engulf the whole economy until relief was provided by the Federal Reserve System (see Chapter 15).

A central bank that extends credit by the discounting of commercial paper is better able to follow trends in the quality of business loans than one which extends credit mainly against the collateral of government securities, as do the Reserve Banks. In a former case it is able to accumulate and analyze the financial statements of a great variety of business enterprises. In so doing it gains first-hand knowledge of business credit trends.

A central bank has at its disposal a number of clues to declining credit quality: the predictive value of financial ratios, the effects of liberalized lending terms on mortgage and consumer credit, and bank examiners' criticisms of loans. If signs point to deterioration in the quality of credit, which could not only precipitate but could greatly deepen a recession, a central bank needs to inaugurate a restrictive policy. The open-market portfolio could be reduced, the discount window narrowed, the discount rate raised, and selective credit controls tightened. Obviously a central bank, to achieve its purpose, must have the cooperation of such government lending agencies as the FHA and VA (in the field of mortgage credit) and the Export-Import Bank (in the field of foreign credits). The overriding significance of changes in credit quality as a criterion and objective of monetary policy is that they are apt to precede and portend such other changes as cyclical fluctuations in business activity and price inflation.

Price Stabilization

Price stability has long been regarded as one of the most important goals of monetary policy, leading as it does to equitable relations between debtor and creditor, to increased savings, and to rational business and investment decisions.

The most useful measure of price change is the consumer-price index.[19] Stability in this index is compatible with cyclical swings in wholesale prices, provided that the price rise on the upward sweep of the cycle is offset by a price decline on the downward sweep. This counterbalancing movement occurs to the extent that the Reserve banks are able to moderate cyclical fluctuations. Stability in the consumer-price index is also compatible with increases in certain prices, such as those in the service industries, provided that the prices of those products that have enjoyed productivity gains decline. If products enjoying productivity gains loom large in the consumer-price index, a non-inflationary index, according to the late Sir Dennis Robertson, is one which declines.[20] The price declines in the relatively prosperous 1880s enabled consumers to share the benefits of increases in the supply of goods and in productivity. If productivity gains are fully absorbed by wages and profits, the prospect of a decline in the consumer-price index is very dim.

Some economists would define a stable index as one that does not increase more than 2–3 percent a year. But a continued rise of this magnitude results in grave economic injustice. Among those who suffer are holders of fixed interest obligations (whether they do so directly or indirectly through monies they have with savings banks and insurance companies), those on fixed incomes, salaried workers unprotected by strong labor unions, and the owners of rent-controlled buildings.

When price rises are expected to continue, unorganized workers might demand protection against further depreciation in the currency by insisting that their wages be linked to a price index. "Indexation," as this technique is called would of course quickly spread. The purchasers of fixed-interest obligations would also demand protection, as would those on pensions and those with savings and even checking accounts. The spread of indexation would, as European experience has proved, accelerate inflation.

A currency serves a nation best if it fulfills in complete measure the classical functions of money: a medium of exchange, a storehouse of value, and a standard of deferred payments. The inflations that have swept many nations since 1914 give ample proof of the vital importance of these historic functions. When by reason of a prolonged and sharp inflation, a currency no longer serves as a medium of exchange, such articles as cigarettes fill the void. This was the experience in German hyper-inflations. When even relatively mild inflations cause currencies to lose their credibility as a storehouse of value, investors rush to acquire gold, jewelry, land, and equities. When currencies fail as a standard of deferred payments, long-term obligations begin to be stated in terms of foreign currencies, a purchasing unit or even in commodities. Failure on the part of currencies to render basic functions undermines the legal, social, and economic basis of society.

Throughout the entire history of the Federal Reserve System, the consumer-price index has risen from 43 in 1914 (1947–1949 = 100) to 166 in 1970. The principal increases occurred during and after World War I (1915–1920) and II (1941–1948). Superimposed on the increase occurring in World War II was a fairly steady and relatively sharp rise during the Vietnam War.

Sharp declines in consumer prices occurred in the depression of 1920–21 and in the Great Depression. Relative stability was experienced in only eighteen years, from 1921–1929, from 1934–1940, and from 1952–1956. Federal Reserve policy was but one of many factors contributing to the price level stability during those years. In the 1920s and 1950s, the Reserve system was assisted in its policies by a cooperative government and a prudent fiscal policy (see Chapter 9). In the 1930s, the large volume of unemployed served to dampen inflationary pressures (see Chapter 10).

In other periods, the Reserve system frequently fell under Treasury influence and control. This was true during and after World Wars I and II, through the Great Depression, and much of the 1960s.* Treasury goals are not necessarily those of a central bank. Secretaries of the Treasury are usually interested in the maintenance of low interest rates and a favorable climate for the flotation of federal obligations, even at the risk of price inflation, a decline in credit quality and a worsening in the balance of payments. And a central bank, no longer required to maintain minimum gold or other reserve assets, is not in a strategic position to oppose the importunities of government. When it was required to maintain gold reserves, it could point to the effect of the proposed policies of government on its reserve ratios, which in the public mind had an aura of sanctity.

---

* A requirement that money supply increase by no more than a fixed percentage each year would not have prevented the inflation of World Wars I and II or the deflation of the Great Depression. As a barrier to war finance, this limitation would have been brushed aside as was the limit on the outstanding volume of Federal debt and the reserve requirements against Federal Reserve notes and deposits. Nor would this requirement have stayed the Great Depression whose causes, as we have tried to point out, lay much deeper than changes in the volume of money (see Chapter 10).

Peoples of the Western world are convinced that inflation is a way of life. In consequence, the more vigorous are the measures required to bring it to an end. As inflation continues, cost-push becomes more firmly entrenched in the price system. The money supply is apt then to be increased to validate cost-push price pressures. Consumers and businessmen buy equities, land, and real estate to protect themselves against further depreciation of the currency. Expectations may not change unless deflation ensues. Only strong anti-inflationary measures will convince people that the central bank and the government are taking determined action. Ending inflation inevitably involves recession. Acute labor shortages disappear, productivity increases, unit costs of production fall, and managerial efficiency improves.

The unemployment engendered may not be politically acceptable. So once again inflationary measures are adopted and prices rise, causing greater social injustice and more grievous misallocation of resources.

The Balance of Payments

Not until the 1960s did balance-of-payments considerations loom large in the formulation of American foreign economic and Federal Reserve policy. Although other nations had from time to time been subjected to the discipline of the balance of payments, a serious deficit was a unique experience for the United States.

The problem originated in United States' efforts to be both world banker and policeman without the necessary underlying economic strength. The problem was aggravated by the unwillingness of the administration, intent as it was on promoting growth, to support restrictive monetary and fiscal policies in the early 1960s.

Although the trade surplus began to decline in 1965 and finally disappeared at the end of 1968, the principal cause of the deficit through these years was external payments by the Federal government. From 1960 through 1967 the deficit on government account was $23 billion, the surplus on private account $2.5 billion.[21] From 1950–1959 the surplus on private account had equaled 65 percent of the deficit on government account, in 1960–1967 only about 11 percent. The remedy obviously is to increase one and reduce the other. Yet the fiscal and monetary policies followed through the 1960s had the opposite effect.*

---

* In the 18 years from 1950 through 1967, the balance-of-payments surplus in the private sector was $34 billion, and the deficit in the government sector was $71 billion, leaving an overall deficit of $37 billion. To finance this deficit the gold stock fell $12 billion, and liquid liabilities to foreigners rose $26 billion. From 1968 through 1970 the situation had improved with the surplus in private account rising relative to the deficit on government account. The surplus on private account, however, was still not equal to the deficit in government account. The improvement resulted from a heavy capital inflow in 1968. The situation deteriorated rapidly in 1971.

Pax Americana did not have sufficient underlying economic strength to carry the overseas burdens of the 1960s. The United States cannot live off the land as did the Roman and British Empires in the heydays of Pax Romana and Pax Britannica. When the Roman legions could no longer do so, they returned home; when Britain was no longer equal to the tasks of defending its commitments, it began to repatriate its army and navy. As Frank E. Morris, President of the Federal Reserve Bank of Boston has said "As a nation we have found that we could not afford to play an unlimited role both as banker for the free world and as its military protector." [22] The alternatives are scaling down overseas commitments, shifting the burden to our allies, or a continuation and intensification of economic controls.

Although the trade surplus may improve in the future, it is unrealistic to expect increases sufficient to finance the current level of overseas expenditures by the U.S. government, which averaged $2.8 billion, between 1960 and 1967, while the surplus on private account averaged only $310 million.

Changes in merchandise exports and imports during the three years 1966–1968 illustrate the problems facing the United States. Exports, responding to the general upswing in world demand, rose $4.2 billion, while imports, reflecting the intense demand of an overheated domestic economy, rose $7.8 billion. American exports in this period increased less than did the world total; the poorer showing reflected the declining competitive position of the American economy. Beginning in 1965 export prices for American manufactured goods increased sharply, those of Germany increased slightly, and those of Japan and Italy rose moderately.[23] Imports of finished goods particularly automobiles into the United States increased rapidly as a result of lower prices and more attractive styling and design.

The American economy is faced with the need, through reductions in unit costs, through the styling of products and through directing research and development toward the production of new products to improve its competitive position in world trade. In the absence of a sharp decline in U.S. government expenditures abroad, however, the deficit will continue, threatening proliferation of exchange controls, restrictive trade practices, and dollar devaluation.

Nor can the United States extricate itself from its present position by substituting flexible exchange rates for current IMF parity arrangements. A system of flexible exchange rates has considerable theoretical appeal. The arguments are that a nation is then free to pursue those domestic economic policies that it considers advantageous and is not compelled because of balance-of-payments deficits, from whatever their source, to accept socially undesirable adjustments like wage and price deflation. The downward rigidity of money wages and prices creates unemployment that is "both wasteful and socially intolerable." [24] Because unemployment is regarded as intolerable, nations resort to interventionist action, tariffs, trade and exchange controls, and tying of aid.

Those who oppose flexible exchange rates point out that they weaken the will of central banks and governments to suppress inflation and lead to foreign retaliation. Had the American dollar been free to float, it is doubtful whether the Reserve System would, in view of the opposition of the administration, have mustered the courage required to increase the discount rate on December 6, 1965. Had floating exchange rates been allowed to fall, in order to subsidize exports or to encourage foreign tourist expenditures and capital imports, foreign nations would assuredly have retaliated. A fluctuating rate can be violently destabilizing, and because it may be violently destabilizing, a nation may need larger reserves than it would under a regime of stable rates.

Since floating exchange rates aggravate balance-of-payments problems they are not permitted, when used, to fluctuate freely. Exchange flexibility is limited. Under no exchange system is a nation free to ignore international considerations. A highly fluctuating rate would not receive international acceptability. The difference between a fixed and a fluctuating rate is not a difference in kind but in degree. Under a flexible rate system a nation will find that there are implicit if not explicit limits to exchange rate variation.[25] Official intervention is customary and unavoidable. Intervention itself carries the threat of exchange rate manipulation for narrow nationalistic purposes. A system of fluctuating exchange rates has not in practice meant a system of freely fluctuating rates. In other words nations have not been enabled in untrammeled fashion to follow domestic economic policies.

Fluctuating exchange rates, though perhaps preferable to a system of universal exchange controls, nevertheless will in time give way to a system in which exporters and investors demand that contracts be stated in their own currencies. The only escape from this essentially restrictive situation is to begin to state contracts in those currencies that fluctuate least. The tendency toward a universal currency is a basic historical phenomenon in international monetary relations.[26] A system in which all currencies are free to move against one another is not viable, will not long endure, and may (as in the 1930s) lead to the formation of currency blocs.

The IMF rules permit member nations, following preliminary consultation, to change the par values of their currencies up or down as much as 10 percent.* Larger alterations require express permission from the IMF. Since its establishment the foreign exchange values of the overwhelming majority of currencies have been altered. The par values of some currencies have by successive changes, been reduced as much as 99 percent. There has been no difficulty apparently in obtaining the approval of the IMF to changes in exchange rates.† The IMF has functioned in flexible fashion.

ANCILLARY OBJECTIVES

The basic objectives of monetary and fiscal policy (not always to be realized) are the combating of inflation and stabilization of the consumer-price index, the tempering of cyclical fluctuations, checking of declines in the quality of credit, and elimination of imbalances in the balance of payments. Usually there is no conflict among these objectives. An adverse balance of payments is often the result of inflationary pressures, which become pronounced on the upward sweep of the cycle and which result from increases in the quantity and decreases in the quality of credit. Ancillary to these basic objectives are promotion of employment and growth. They are regarded as ancillary because if the basic objectives are achieved, these objectives will, over the long run, be attained.

Employment

From 1947–1970 the employed civilian labor force rose from 57 million to 79 million. The rise was entirely nonagricultural; agricultural employment fell, reflecting dramatic increases in productivity. Those displaced from agriculture found nonagricultural employment or joined the unemployed. Increases in nonagricultural employment have been most rapid in services, in state and local government, in wholesale and retail trade, and in finance, insurance, and real estate.

---

* The IMF rules permit a member nation to make use of the 10 percent rule only once. "Since the great majority of members have changed their parities by more than this amount since they became members of the Fund, this particular provision has lost what little importance it may have had originally." Jacques J. Polak, Economic Counsellor of the IMF in a letter dated May 23, 1969.

† Those who believe that the rules of the IMF are too strict and that even greater flexibility should be permitted propose as substitutes a wider band and a crawling peg. For a discussion see *Review* (Federal Reserve Bank of St. Louis), February 1969, and April 1969; George N. Halm, *Toward Limited Exchange Rate Flexibility* (Essays in International Finance No. 73 March 1969, Princeton University, Princeton, New Jersey); John H. Williamson, *The Crawling Peg* (Essays in International Finance No. 50 December 1957, Princeton University, Princeton, New Jersey). As the Algemene Bank Nederland pointed out in its economic review for February 1969, the proposals offer no better alternative to the present system; the advantages are dubious and the detriments large.

Employment has risen more slowly in transportation, public utilities, and manufacturing; it has fallen in mining.

As the Federal Reserve Bank of Chicago has pointed out, "The labor force is not a fixed number of people even in the very short run." [27] Almost all men between twenty-five and fifty-five are permanent participants. Younger or older men and women participate periodically or not at all. Additions to the labor force come from those reaching the age of twenty-one, which will increase in the 1970s and from those who by reason of special training programs will be available for employment. The predicted rapid increase in the 1970s of those reaching the age of 21, as well as a hoped for diminished demand for military personnel, will tend to dampen inflationary pressures.

The pressure on the labor supply throughout the postwar period, resulting from the rise in civilian employment and intensified by the increase in the armed forces, has accelerated inflationary pressures. Excessive rates of price inflation "have been associated with periods when the unemployment rate has been appreciably below 4.5 percent." [28] In view of the structural character of American unemployment, a rate of 4.5 percent might be regarded as tantamount to full employment. Structural unemployment and changing job opportunities afford little justification, according to the Committee for Economic Development, "for the notion that the target for high employment should be set in terms of a constant fraction of the labor force." It concludes that better insights can be obtained from more careful collection and analysis of statistics on job vacancies and on the characteristics of the unemployed.[29]

Structural unemployment is beyond the central banks' power to correct. It may result from minimum-wage legislation, discriminatory practices by trade unions and employers, lack of educational opportunities and impediments to labor mobility. (Labor mobility could be enhanced by vesting pension rights, relocation assistance, reciprocity in state licensing, and manpower-training programs.) It may also result from technical advances and the economic decay of various regions. It has to be handled on a vigorous ad hoc basis by government, labor and business groups.

There are dangers, as E. Victor Morgan has noted, in "trying to run an economy too close to the absolute limit of its capacity." [30] Extreme labor shortages increase recruitment difficulties, induce firms to hoard labor, put a premium on inefficiency and limit the expansion of new and perhaps more progressive firms. Delivery dates lengthen, and costs are frozen into the price and wage structure. Expectations of continued inflation are reflected in aggressive wage demands and large wage gains relative to unit costs. Inflation spirals and becomes self reinforcing.[31]

The risks that may be involved in using fiscal and monetary means to force high levels of employment were vividly illustrated in the 1960s. That is why we choose to look upon employment goals as ancillary to monetary policy, subordinate to but dependent upon the attainment of basic objectives. To the extent that a central bank interests itself in unemployment, it really is interesting itself in the broad problem of the business cycle, tempered by the need to prevent an inflationary overheating of the economy.

Economic Growth

In recent years Western nations have become very growth conscious, not only in the attempt to provide higher living standards for their citizens but also to ensure that they are not outstripped in the competitive race by communist powers.

Statistics of growth are not only subject to many statistical errors (perhaps inevitably so, for the data are so very complex) but also convey little idea (on an international basis) of the types of goods and services being produced and the distribution of the national product. One nation may decide to build swimming pools, another to construct power plants. Each may, at least for a short period of time, have the same growth rate. One may concentrate on civilian products, another on military. One may divert the results of its productive efforts to a privileged few, as in some South American nations; another may have a more even distribution of product. Some nations may follow policies that seem in the short run to promote growth but, by causing air and water pollution and wasteful use of natural resources, destroy the basis for future growth.[32]

Possibly the most important contribution that a central bank can make to economic growth is to direct its policies toward price stabilization. A stable currency promotes growth by fostering thrift, by making it possible for businessmen to make long-run decisions, by making it unnecessary for the individual to protect himself against inflation by investing his funds in such a way—in land, for example—that they contribute little to general economic welfare.

Inflation confers short-run, largely illusory benefits on business firms and thus seems to promote economic growth. Inventories may initially be sold at higher than expected prices; wages may lag behind prices, and profits may be favored. Debts may be repaid in depreciated currency. But the stimulus, as Morgan has pointed out, is essentially fraudulent and the same goal could be accomplished equally well by reducing the weight of goods sold.[33] Firms must replenish their working capital, and eventually raise wages, usually when productivity is falling and unit costs rising. Interest rates soar; credit is less available; demand falls; book profits become book losses.

A real stimulus to growth, by which is meant a self-sustaining increase in real output over a period of time, results from capital investment by business firms, from public works such as the Australian Snowy River project, from carefully considered tax policies, from abundant risk capital, from improved educational opportunities for all, and from equal employment opportunities. It depends, too, upon the willingness of individuals to work hard and to increase their savings, thus making funds available for capital investment, and upon willingness of governments, individuals and business firms to conduct themselves prudently and honestly.* A stimulus to growth also comes from gains in productivity, particularly those resulting from the transfer of agricultural labor to industry, from economies of large scale production, and from an absence of monopolistic practices, price subsidies, tariffs, and other forms of protectionism. It results, too, from a well-functioning financial infrastructure, including development banks that are able and willing to finance new and young enterprises, and above all, from successful efforts of central banks to check currency erosion.

MEANS TO AN END

Interest Rates

On various occasions in the history of the Federal Reserve System, interest rates have been viewed as a goal of credit policy rather than as a means to reach a basic objective, particularly in World Wars I and II and in the 1930s and 1960s. In these periods interest rates of varying maturities were pegged below the rates that would have obtained in a free market. Pegging worked to the advantage of neither the government nor the nation. The Treasury insisted during the two world wars that interest rates be held down as a means of reducing costs on the public debt. The money saved was more than offset by higher costs resulting from inflation induced by easy-money policies. The transition to a peacetime economy was made more difficult.

---

* The role of integrity in economic growth is a neglected subject. One factor in the recent rapid economic growth of Japan is the integrity of business and political leaders and the confidence which they inspire in foreign bankers and businessmen.

The abnormally low interest rates of the 1930s, in the absence of that intangible factor, business confidence, did not have a particularly stimulating effect upon business activity. In generating a sharply ascending curve, interest policy laid the basis for the highly inflationary financial policies of World War II. The effects of the interest rate policy of the 1960s, in stimulating inflation and thus aggravating the imbalance of payments have been discussed earlier.

Interest rates as a policy goal have perhaps been influenced by medieval doctrines and by doctrines not so old that money is "non-productive" and that banks perform no service in lending money because they lend only what they create. A reflection of this attitude is the 4.25 percent ceiling placed on the coupon rate on government bonds in 1918; while altered, it has never been repealed.

Government policy on interest rates is frequently apparent in the mortgage market. Housing is regarded as an industry with certain "moral" attributes, to be protected against the rising costs of borrowed funds. Pegging rates in this as in other fields has caused building costs to rise; the funds saved in reduced interest costs have been more than outweighed by rising construction costs. Government policy that throws a protective cloak around mortgage markets and other sectors of the economy harms not only those sectors but the whole economy as well.

Interest rates are a price and as such they have an important function to perform. As a price they are not a goal of policy but rather an important means of reaching desired objectives.

Pre-Determined and Fixed Increases in the Money Stock

In the past five-to-ten years, as Richard G. Davis pointed out, economists have come to the fore who espouse the doctrine—which in its extreme form holds that only money matters—that the "behavior of the rate of change of the money supply is the overriding determinant of fluctuations in business activity." [34] Government spending, taxation, and debt-management policies; innovations in the credit system; changes in credit quality; relative reliance on trade as opposed to bank credit; the rise of new international money markets, discriminatory and monopolistic labor and business practices; and the changing importance of cost-push have presumably a relatively small or negligible influence on business fluctuations.

A central bank should, according to the more dogmatic proponents of this doctrine, "maintain a steady rate of growth in the money supply, year in and year out, at a rate which corresponds roughly to the growth in the economy's productive capacity." [35] Discretionary control of the money supply has, it is claimed, resulted in monetary chaos and instability. Economic forecasting is very imperfect and human judgment deficient. A central bank that endeavors to moderate business conditions by exercising its own judgment will produce the very instability that it seeks to avoid. This point of view found expression in a recommendation by the Joint Economic Committee that the "money supply" (currency plus demand deposits adjusted) be increased at an annual rate ranging from 2 to 6 percent. The smaller increase would be appropriate to a period of inflation and the larger to a period of unemployment.

If, however, "only money matters," if changes in the money supply are directly related to increases in a real productive capacity, and if the money volume is all-controlling, why, indeed, should the economy be subjected to such wide variations in rates of increase? As an afterthought the committee recommended that the Federal Reserve System purchase obligations of the Federal Home Loan Bank Board and the Federal National Mortgage Association to avoid imposing an undue share of the burdens of monetary restraint on the housing industry—a very important deviation from the basic rule! [36]

The adoption of the mechanistic rule proposed by the Joint Economic Committee would require radical changes in our banking and monetary systems. Commercial banks would probably fall subject to a 100 percent reserve requirement. They could expand loans and investments only as their reserves with the Federal Reserve banks increased, through purchases of government securities in amounts necessary to generate increases in the money supply at whatever percentage might have been decreed by the Congress. The present "commitment" of the Treasury to buy and sell gold on official account at $38 an ounce would be eliminated and the dollar would be permitted to fluctuate freely in terms of other currencies. In order that permitted increases in loans would be used for "socially productive" purposes, both the commercial and central bankers, would doubtless find their authority largely superseded by state direction.

Many proposals to substitute mechanical rules for the discretion of central bankers have been made in the past. One such attempt in England was the Peel Act of 1844, which was based on the premise that, if Bank of England notes were converted into what were in effect gold certificates, commercial crises could be eliminated. The Bank of England would thus be relieved of the onerous task of deciding when to follow policies of monetary ease and when to follow policies of restraint. All would be determined quite automatically: As gold came into the nation the notes of the Bank of England would increase; as gold left the country they would diminish. Prices would thus be stabilized. The results were disappointing. Bank deposits replaced bank notes, and England was again engulfed in commercial crises.

There is nothing in the current proposals to suggest that a similar substitution would not result. If the commercial banking system and the Federal Reserve System were strait jacketed, other types of "money" would shortly come into use. The business community might use bills of exchange as currency as did British merchants a hundred years ago; its members might begin to finance one another with great vigor; trade credits might be substituted for bank credit; credit cards might be used more heavily; increased reliance might be placed on foreign money markets. Measures might be employed to increase velocity, such as an electronic giro system of money transfer. As the Radcliffe Committee pointed out, there is great interchangeability, ingenuity, and adaptability in the credit system. As various techniques were introduced, the money supply might have to be continuously redefined and new controls initiated.

The proposal gives rise to many difficult practical and theoretical problems, which have not been adequately treated. How, for example, is money to be defined? There is already serious disagreement among economists over the appropriate definition.[37] The inclusion of the Eurodollar float in money-supply figures increased the annual growth rate by 1.6 percent points for the first half of 1969.[38] Are overdrafts and confirmed lines of credit to be included? How is the impact of changes in the money stock to be measured? If interest rates are taken as a measure, the direct link between changes in money and changes in activity will be broken.* What weight is to be given to changes in the availability, as well as in the cost, of credit? to changes in the types of debt being monetized? to changes in the quality of credit?[39] What weight is to be given to changes in deposit turnover and income velocity, which not only fluctuate widely in the short-run but have also increased sharply through the postwar period? What weight is to be given to increased competition among all financial institutions, to the fact that holders of financial assets are being more interest-sensitive? What is the effect of business activity on the volume of credit? What is the effect of changes in credit volume on business activity? What is the effect of restrictive monetary policy on various economic sectors: small businesses, state and local government, residential construction, and the like? What weight is to be given to the effect of the balance of payments on the volume of loanable funds and monetary policy?[40] What weight is to be given to the practice of businessmen and consumers in 1971 of accumu-

---

* 1969 *Joint Economic Report*, p. 23. The Joint Economic Committee has declared quite dogmatically that "the state of financial markets as a reliable indicator of the extent to which monetary policy is restraining or expansionary" should be disregarded by the Federal Reserve System.

lating precautionary balances? Such are some of the problems that would have to be solved before a computer could be substituted for central-bank discretion.

As Davis has pointed out in his article, the money supply is very erratic, partly reflecting shifts between Treasury and private accounts. Based on the flow-of-funds data, swings in the Federal government's demand for funds are frequently large. They have ranged from a repayment of more than $5 billion in the second quarter of 1967 to borrowing of almost $8.7 billion in the next quarter.

> Faced with this sort of situation, is the monetary policy maker to hold the growth in the money supply to a fixed rate (and risk possible serious damage to both the financial system and the economy) or should he cushion the impact by permitting money to grow at a faster or slower pace than might be called a fixed rate? If he does the latter, how much flexibility is possible without returning to discretionary policy? [41]

The money supply gives evidence of no clear-cut cyclical pattern. Leads in the peaks of the money supply are quite variable in relation to subsequent peaks in business, and do not necessarily imply causation. Although economists are generally agreed that money does exert causal influence on business, the relationship seems imprecise and may at times be reversed.

A good case study is afforded by attempts in 1971 to "fine tune" the money supply. Despite its efforts to do so, the Federal Reserve Bank of New York reported that M_1 (currency + demand deposits) "did not respond quickly to the changing impact of open-market operations on reserves and interest rates." On the other hand, the credit proxy (total member bank deposits subject to reserve requirements + Eurodollar borrowings + bank-related commercial paper + certain other non-deposit items) was "reasonably" sensitive to the System's influence. [42]

The aim of this study has been to emphasize the effect of central bank policies on the volume and quality of credit, in all their many manifestations.

To assert that changes in the money supply should be the sole goal of central banking policy is to ignore the effect of multitudinous factors on business activity. As the Federal Reserve Bank of Boston has pointed out "Given the complex and dynamic character of our financial markets, any attempt to describe the impact of policy on these markets (and through these markets on the economy) in terms of a single statistical series is highly likely to lead to analytical errors." [43]

The study of money, as Stephen Colwell pointed out years ago, is in reality a study of credit—its cost, availability, and quality—and of the effects of changes in each of these factors on business and individual spending in different economic sectors.[44] Emphasis on the money supply as such, however defined, is a sterile approach to a problem that involves the lending and investing operations of many credit institutions in all their ramifications. Control over changes in the quantity of money is not to be considered an end in itself but only a means, along with interest rates, of reaching desired objectives.[45]

DEBT MANAGEMENT IN THE SERVICE OF FEDERAL RESERVE POLICY

From the end of 1914 to 1971, the gross Federal debt has increased from $1 billion to $424 billion. Although the bulk of increase occurred during the two great wars, the rise since World War II amounts to about 65 percent of the total. The increase in volume has been accompanied by a disquieting reduction in average maturity.

Before the Great Depression the goal of Federal fiscal policy was an annually balanced budget. Fiscal dividends were used to reduce debt, particularly the floating debt. Although this goal proved unattainable during war and depression (and should not have been attempted in the latter) the Civil War debt was sharply reduced and could have been extinguished had government bonds not been used as the basis of the currency. Similarly the debt incurred in World War I was sharply reduced in the 1920s.

The goal of an annually balanced budget gave way in the 1930s to the doctrine that the budget should be balanced only on the upward sweep and at the peak of the business cycle. Implemented for a short time in the 1950s (the deficits exceeded surpluses by a slight margin),* this cyclical doctrine gave way in the 1960s to the conviction on the part of some economists that the budget should be used to promote growth and should be balanced, if at all, only in a superheated economy.†

The doctrines of the 1960s, plus the fiscal effects of the Vietnam War, resulted in a very sharp rise in Federal debt, paralleling a very substantial quantitative increase and a marked qualitative decline in private debt. In earlier American history, a public debt was regarded as a nuisance, to be reduced as quickly as possible, once a war emergency had passed. This traditional policy was believed

---

* National-income and product surpluses equaled $27 billion and deficits $28.1 billion in 1950–1959.
† The so-called "full employment" budget, rather than the traditional budget, would be balanced, but a full employment budget would probably be experienced only in a superheated economy. As now defined, full employment occurs when 96 percent of the labor force is employed. In view of the structural character of unemployment, employment at this level would imply an overheated economy.

to be justified because a decline in the debt maintained the "credit" of the government, reduced total interest costs, offset the possible inflationary effects of private debt increases, provided savings for economic development, eased problems of refinancing and permitted the government to borrow advantageously from nonbank sources in subsequent emergencies.

Short-Term Debt

These earlier policies of public-debt reduction were supported by the British Colwyn Committee, which concluded in 1927 that the English public debt should be retired at a more rapid rate. John Maynard Keynes concurred with the committee that it was sound policy to repay a certain amount of debt each year.[46] A reduction in debt demands a high degree of fiscal responsibility. It presupposes prudence in expenditures and the use of surplus tax receipts to reduce debt, particularly short-term debt.

Policies of American debt management since World War II have lacked direction. The short-term marketable debt has soared. From the end of 1947 to the end of 1971, "short issues," those maturing within one year, rose from $51 to $119.1 billion. Obligations with maturities of 10 years and above declined from $60 billion to $20 billion. U.S. savings bonds rose slightly from $52 to $55 billion, and special issues rose from $29 to $86 billion. The average maturity of the marketable debt fell from nine years and five months to three years and four months. Short-term issues, which financed the deficit, would have risen more had it not been for frequent recourse to advance refunding. At no time, however, did the Treasury make really significant efforts to lengthen the debt, as did the British and Canadian governments.

Publicly held debt gravitated from investment to liquidity holders. Short-term issues were sold in periods of prosperity and long-term issues, when they were sold at all, were offered in recession—quite the opposite from the usual cyclical criteria of debt management. The Federal Reserve System increased its holdings from $23 to $70 billion as the volume of currency in circulation increased, as member-bank reserves rose, and the gold stock declined. The System has, on frequent occasions, been compelled to support Treasury financing on an "even keel" and has in consequence been forced to postpone its efforts to exercise credit control.

Only rarely and mainly through advance refundings has the Treasury endeavored to lengthen the average maturity of the debt. True, it was handicapped by the 4.25 percent ceiling, imposed by an enactment of April 4, 1918, on the coupons of obligations of five years and more in maturity.* The Treasury has not, however, been willing to use the powers that it possesses. When Senator Robert Kennedy was Attorney General he ruled (April 25, 1961) that this limitation did not preclude the Treasury from issuing obligations with a 4.25 percent coupon at a discount.

The debt management problem is a dual one: a reduction in the total Federal debt by the use of "fiscal dividends" and a sharp absolute and relative reduction in the short-term debt. A reduction in total Federal debt will help to provide savings funds that promise to be in heavy demand in the 1970s. Savings will be needed to finance the demand for housing, for consumer-durable goods, and producers' durable equipment. They will be needed to finance public transportation, elimination of air and water pollution, higher quality education, and medical facilities.

A sharp reduction in the short-term debt would give the Reserve System greater independence in monetary management and would safeguard commercial banks from the threat of secondary reserve requirements. The weakness of a large short-term debt has long been recognized. The Colwyn Report pointed out that it subjects a government to the vicissitudes of the money market, forces the Treasury to make frequent trips to the money market, and compels a central bank to assist Treasury financing operations.[47]

The Radcliffe Committee also favored vigorous leadership by monetary authorities and the Treasury to raise interest rates on long-term obligations in order to promote their sale; it pointed out that authorities should not half-heartedly follow the market and should not be influenced by the fallacy that bond yields are an index to the credit standing of a nation.[48]

A Suggested Approach

The reversal of present trends will not be easy. For example, to approach the same percentage distribution in the maturities of the marketable debt that existed at the close of World War II, present debt maturities of ten years and more would have to be increased about $70 billion, and maturities of one year and less would have to be reduced about $40 billion. These data are not to be regarded as sacrosanct but they do suggest the magnitude of the task. Absolute and relative re-

---

* Since June 1967, the ceiling has applied to maturities of seven years or more. The ceiling limitation on the coupon rate on government bonds has had the following detrimental effects on the Government bond market: it has excluded government bonds from the capital market since 1965; it has forced the government to borrow in the short—and intermediate—term markets, where interest rates have exceeded long-term rates; and it has forced a decided shortening in the average maturity of the marketable debt. *Monthly Economic Letter* (First National City Bank of New York, May 1969).

duction in the short-term debt could come about through repayment from a Treasury cash surplus, refunding with longer-term marketable or non-marketable obligations, and financing of new fiscal deficits through the issue of long-term marketable and non-marketable obligations.

The goal that we suggest is, to be sure, arbitrary and not one readily to be achieved. But, unless efforts are made to reduce the short-term marketable debt, the average maturity of the total marketable debt will continue to decline. The Treasury will make more frequent trips to the market, and the Reserve System will be forced to maintain a policy of even keel at more frequent intervals and for longer periods. It will be stymied in its efforts to attain its basic policy objectives.[49]

The abhorrence with which many of our ancestors regarded the short-term public debt had its roots in experience. Floating debts, as they were called, were all too often closely linked with currency issues and inflationary expansion of central-bank credit. Their refinancing frequently required increases in one or the other or both. The long series of currency reforms that has been such an outstanding feature of economic developments in Western Europe over the past fifty years invariably began with reduction of the floating debt.

In answer to a question submitted by the Commission on Money and Credit about a desirable maturity structure of the debt, the Treasury replied:

> The undue and growing concentration of the public debt in the under-five-year area has important implications both for the money and capital markets and for the economy as a whole. If the composition of the debt is permitted to grow continuously shorter, Treasury refunding operations will occur more frequently and in larger amounts. The Treasury might often be forced to refund excessively large maturities under unfavorable conditions with unduly large repercussions on the structure of interest rates. This type of refunding would increase the cost to the Treasury and would tend to interfere with the orderly marketing of corporate and municipal bonds; it might also disrupt the market for real estate mortgages. Moreover, the emergence of a larger amount of highly liquid, short-term Government debt could create inflationary pressures. Excessive liquidity in the economy and frequent and large Treasury operations in the market can unduly complicate the flexible administration of Federal Reserve credit policies essential to sustainable growth. A balanced maturity structure of the debt, therefore, can make a major contribution toward sound financial policy by reducing the frequency, size and adverse consequences of Treasury financings, by helping to forestall potential inflationary pressures, and by enabling monetary policy to function more effectively.[50]

It is not to be expected that the program that we have proposed to achieve the Treasury objective of a balanced maturity structure will necessarily be implemented. Many unforeseen contingencies could block its complete fulfillment. What is important is to recognize the problem and to begin action that will over time reduce the amount of Federal debt and increase its average maturity.*

SOME IMMEDIATE PROBLEMS

The hazards of predicting future economic developments are many. In the short run the perils are great; in the long run they are devastating. If, even in the short-run, economic developments could with the assistance of sophisticated computers, be foretold, individuals might, to the extent that they believed the forecasts, take action to nullify their findings. Only to the extent that people did not believe the forecasts, might short-run predictions have a possibility of being realized.

Who could have foreseen twenty years ago the emergence of West Germany as a dominant and financial power, of Japan as a vigorous and successful competitor in international trade? Who, a decade ago, could have had the prescience to forecast interest rates exceeding all previous levels attained in American history, wholesale prices nearly 50 percent above the peak reached in the years following World War II? Who could have been so pessimistic as to predict the disappearance of the American foreign-trade surplus, the adoption by the United States of foreign-exchange controls, the skyrocketing of American short-term foreign debt, the abandonment of gold payments and a free market price of gold occasionally rising 40 percent above the mint level?

Rather than attempt the futile task of trying to penetrate the thick fog that obscures the future, we would do better in the few remaining paragraphs to set forth some of the immediate monetary problems facing the American economy. If these immediate problems can be successfully resolved, the long run may seem more promising. A journey of a thousand miles begins with a single step.

In our journey toward a successful economic future we must take two important and closely related steps: checking inflation and eliminating the deficit in the balance of payments. Otherwise the dollar will not command full confidence at home and abroad. Individuals will not be induced to amass savings that will be desperately needed in the 1970s to finance essential capital expenditures. Investors will not be willing to invest liquid funds in long-term bonds. "Hot-money" flows

---

*Following the Bank of England practice the Federal Reserve banks might be empowered on behalf of the Treasury to feed long-term bonds carrying attractive yields into the market at propitious times.

will continue to dominate and disrupt international currency relations. The mint price of gold will be subject to successive increases.

The basic problem is to make the dollar a dependable standard of deferred payments. Given popular determination, this can be done with a felicitous union of credit, fiscal and public debt maangement policies. The Federal Reserve System, in its discount rate and discount window policies, in its open-market operations, in its control over member-bank reserve requirements, in its selective credit control powers, in its influence over policies of individual banks through the bank examination department, has ample central banking powers to achieve this goal. Obviously these powers would be reduced to a mockery by political control over interest rates and the loans and investments of the Reserve banks.

A dependable standard of deferred payments will make a tremendous contribution to economic betterment by reducing the causes of social friction and by encouraging and rewarding savings. The great price rise since the end of World War II is symptomatic of a huge savings deficiency. The Federal government can itself make an important contribution to economic betterment and the reduction of structural unemployment by channeling expenditures into such areas as education, public transportation, medical care, the elimination of pollution and research and development. The importance of a constructive redirection of public expenditures is given ample proof in the case of post-war Germany and Japan.

The above policies, if history can be our guide, would, in combination with the elimination of foreign exchange and trade restrictions, of subsidies to particular economic groups, lay the basis for a rapid economic advance.

Building on this domestic base, the United States would be in a position to assist in the reconstruction of a viable international monetary system. The task, as indicated in Chapter 17, will not prove easy. Time, patience and sympathetic understanding of the aims and attitudes of other nations are required.

The American people may not be willing to endure the sacrifices necessary to achieve a stable consumer-price index. They may fail to realize that the sacrifices are minor relative to the cumulative economic chaos and distress that are brought about by the continued erosion of the purchasing power of money. They may not fully comprehend the economic and political results of efforts to camouflage the effects of inflation by adoption of totalitarian controls. They may not realize that to adopt such controls is to surrender basic political freedoms.

Whether subsequent decades in the country will be "the best of times" or "the worst of times," only the passing years will reveal. Whatever their character, they will call for the highest proficiency from Federal Reserve officials. The President must seek the best talent available for the Board of Governors; the Reserve banks must also seek men of ability, dedication, and independence—willing to develop and express their opinions in forthright fashion. Reserve officials and staff are not passive agents dependent upon machines for solutions to their problems. They must be men of competence, judgment, and purpose, endeavoring to make best use of the tools at hand to achieve the basic objectives of monetary and credit policy.

Notes

1. Hans Aufricht, with the assistance of Jane B. Evensen, *Central Banking Legislation,* Vol. II (Washington, D.C.: International Monetary Fund, 1967), p. 466.

2. *Federal Reserve Act.* Sections 14, 19, 12A; *Securities Exchange Act of 1934,* Section 7.

3. *Monetary Policy and the Management of the Public Debt,* Joint Committee on the Economic Report, 82nd Cong., 2nd sess. (Washington, D.C.: Government Printing Office, 1952), Document No. 123, Part I, p. 237.

4. *Ibid.,* p. 212.

5. *Committee on Finance and Industry, Report* (London: His Majesty's Stationery Office, 1931), p. 120.

6. *Ibid.,* p. 111.

7. Lyle E. Gramley, "Guidelines for Monetary Policy–The Case Against Simple Rules," address to the Financial Conference of the National Industrial Conference Board, New York City, February 21, 1969.

8. Frank R. Garfield, "Cycles and Cyclical Imbalances in a Changing World," *Federal Reserve Bulletin,* (November 1965), pp. 1518–1532.

9. *Ibid.,* p. 1519.

10. Geoffrey H. Moore, "The Quality of Credit in Booms and Depressions," *Journal of Finance,* Vol. XI, No. 2 (May 1956), p. 293.

11. Ilse Mintz, *Deterioration in the Quality of Foreign Bonds Issued in the United States 1920–1930* (New York: National Bureau of Economic Research, 1951).

12. *Ibid.,* pp. 46–49.

13. Martin H. Seiden, *The Quality of Trade Credit* (New York: National Bureau of Economic Research, 1964).

14. *Ibid.,* p. 5. For a further discussion of changes in credit quality in the postwar period see Chapter 13.

15. Geoffrey H. Moore and Philip A. Klein, *The Quality of Consumer Instalment Credit* (New York: National Bureau of Economic Research, 1967).

16. Robert E. Knight, "The Quality of Mortgage Credit," *Monthly Review* (Federal Reserve Bank of Kansas City, March and April 1969). See also George K. Brinegar and Lyle P. Fettig, *Some Measures of the Quality of Agricultural Credit* (New York: National Bureau of Economic Research, 1968); and Albert M. Wojnilower; *The Quality of Bank Loans* (New York: National Bureau of Economic Research, 1962).

17. Roy E. Moor, "Economic Liabilities," *Previews of the Economy,* Drexel, Harriman, Ripley, Incorporated, January 19, 1971. *Economic Report of the President.* Transmitted to The Congress February 1971 (Washington: Government Printing Office, 1971), pp. 165–179. *The Investment Outlook for 1970,* Economics Department, Bankers Trust Company of New York.

18. Roy L. Reierson, "Economic Prospects and Some Problems for Policy," Bankers Trust Company, New York. Remarks delivered before the Boston Economics Club, December 1970.

19. *1964 Report of the Royal Commission on Banking and Finance* (Ottawa: Queen's Printer), p. 400. Also see *Fiscal and Monetary Policies for Steady Economic Growth* (New York: Committee for Economic Development, January 1969).

20. D. H. Robertson, *Money* (New York: Pitman Publishing Corporation, Reprinted October 1948), Chapter 7.

21. Frank E. Morris, *Pax Americana and the U.S. Balance of Payments* (Federal Reserve Bank of Boston, January/February 1969), p. 43.

22. *Ibid*, p. 47.

23. *Federal Reserve Bulletin,* (April 1969), p. 306.

24. *International Monetary Arrangements: The Problem of Choice* ("International Finance Section, Department of Economics." [Princeton, N.J.: Princeton University Press, 1964]), p. 95.

25. *Report of the Royal Commission on Banking and Finance* (Ottawa: Queen's Printer), pp. 486–492; and *Quarterly Bulletin* (Bank of England "The Exchange Equalization Account: its origin and development," Vol. 8., No. 4, December 1968), 377–391.

26. Roy Harrod, "Problem of International Liquidity," lecture delivered at New York University, New York, April 12, 1966.

27. *Business Conditions* (Federal Reserve Bank of Chicago, July 1968).

28. *Ibid.,* p. 7. See also Sheldon W. Stahl "The Phillips Curve: A Dilemma for Public Policy. *Business Review* (Federal Reserve Bank of Philadelphia January, 1969). Also, see "The New Prices and Incomes Commission—Some Thoughts about its Task" (Bank of Nova Scotia, September 1969).

29. *Fiscal and Monetary Policies for Steady Economic Growth, op. cit.,* p. 26.

30. E. Victor Morgan, *Monetary Policy for Stable Growth* (Great Britain, Institute for Economic Affairs, 1966), p. 27.

31. *Business Review* (Federal Reserve Bank of Philadelphia, January 1969).

32. For a discussion of the effects of economic growth in industrial nations on destroying the basis for economic growth, see Wayne H. Davis, "Overpopulated America," *The New Republic,* January 10, 1970.

33. Morgan, *op. cit.,* pp. 24–25; and *The Economist* (London), January 16, 1971, pp. 58–59.

34. Richard G. Davis. "The Role of the Money Supply in Business Cycles," *Monthly Review* (Federal Reserve Bank of New York, April 1968), pp. 63–74.

35. *Ibid.,* p. 63.

36. *1969 Joint Economic Report.* Report of the Joint Economic Committee, Congress of the United States, on the January 1969 Economic Report of the President together with Minority Supplementary and Dissenting Views. (Washington: Government Printing Office, 1969), pp. 22, 23.

37. George K. Kaufman, "More on an Empirical Definition of Money," *The American Economic Review*, 59, No. 1. (March 1969); see also *New England Economic Review* (Federal Reserve Bank of Boston, March/April 1969); and George W. Mitchell, "Moni-

toring Monetary Policy," address to the New Hampshire Bankers Association, White-field, New Hampshire, October 14, 1966.

38. "Revision of Money Supply Figures," *Federal Reserve Bulletin* (October 1969), 787–789. See also *Federal Reserve Bulletin* (December 1970), pp. 887–909 for the effect of later revisions.

39. Daniel H. Brill, "Can the Government 'Fine-Tune' the Economy?" Address to the Washington Chapter of the American Statistical Association, Washington, D.C., February 28, 1968.

40. See J. Dewey Daane, "New Frontier for the Monetarists," address to Northern New England School of Banking, Dartmouth College, Hanover, New Hampshire, September 8, 1969.

41. *Monthly Review* (Federal Reserve Bank of Richmond, May 1969), p. 5. Also see "Treasury Balances and the Money Supply," *The Morgan Guaranty Survey* (March 1969); and Tilford C. Gaines, "Some Inadequacies of Financial Data and Theory," American Statistical Association Meeting, New York City, August 22, 1969.

42. "Open Market Operations and the Monetary and Credit Aggregates-1971," *Monthly Review* (Federal Reserve Bank of New York, April 1972).

43. Paul S. Anderson and Frank E. Morris, "Defining the Money Supply: The Case of Government Deposits," *New England Economic Review* (Federal Reserve Bank of Boston, March/April 1969), p. 29.

44. Stephen Colwell, *The Ways and Means of Payment: A Full Analysis of the Credit System, with its Various Modes of Adjustment* (Reprints of Economic Classics; New York: Augustus M. Kelly, Publisher, 1965).

45. To study this question in greater detail one should consult Milton Friedman and Anna Jackson Schwartz, *A Monetary History of the United States* (Princeton, N.J.; Princeton University Press, 1963); Friedman and Walter W. Heller, *Monetary vs. Fiscal Policy* (New York: Norton, 1969), pp. 83–87.

46. *Report of the Committee on National Debt and Taxation* (London: His Majesty's Stationery Office, 1927), pp. 341, 330.

47. *Ibid.*, pp. 35–36.

48. *Committee on the Working of the Monetary System, Report* (London: His Majesty's Stationery Office, August 1959), Chapter 7.

49. See Warren L. Smith, "Some Economic Policy Issues of the Coming Decade," address to the 11th Annual Forecasting Conference, New York Chapter of the American Statistical Association, New York City, April 25, 1969. Also see *A Stabilizing Fiscal and Monetary Policy for 1970,* statement by the Program Committee of the Committee for Economic Development, December 1969.

50. *The Federal Reserve and the Treasury,* Answers to questions from the Commission on Money and Credit (Englewood Cliffs, N.J.: Prentice-Hall Inc., 1963), p. 224.

Glossary

Accelerated depreciation. An increase in the rate of depreciation permitted by U.S. corporate income tax laws and regulations on corporate plant and equipment, often ordered to promote economic recovery.

Accord. An agreement entered into by the U.S. Treasury and the Federal Reserve System and announced on March 4, 1951, the purpose of which was to restore independence of action in the area of credit control to the Federal Reserve System.

Added value tax, or tax on value added. A relatively new technique for imposing taxes principally on business firms. Various methods have been suggested for computing the tax base. In one, the base equals sales of a business firm plus receipts from rent and interest minus purchases of all goods and services from outside firms minus expenditures on investment goods, on rent and interest. The difference is the value added to products and services through the operation of a business enterprise.

Agricultural Credits Act, March 4, 1923. An act which enlarged the types of agricultural paper eligible for discount by the Federal Reserve Banks and which established the Federal Intermediate Credit Banks, provided for the formation of the National Agricultural Credit Corporations and amended the Federal Farm Loan Act and the Federal Reserve Act. For text of the Act, see *Federal Reserve Bulletin,* Vol. 9, No. 3, March 1923, pp. 303-16.

Aldrich-Vreeland Currency. An "emergency" currency, permitted to be issued by national banks, by the Aldrich-Vreeland Act of May 30, 1908. Under the provisions of this Act, national banks were enabled, subject to various regulations, to issue bank notes secured by collateral, other than U.S. obligations. Such bank notes were not issued until the outbreak of World War I. The first issue was made on August 4, 1914 and the last on February 12, 1915. The total amount issued was $383 millions. By May 1, 1915, the entire amount had been retired and replaced by Federal Reserve notes.

Allied debts.   Debts owed to the U.S. for loans granted to its Allies in World War I.

All other loans.   An asset item on the books of member banks in the 1920s which included all loans other than those granted against securities and real estate. The amount was often taken as a measure of the business loan demand. Beginning on October 3, 1928, a more detailed classification was presented.

American Exchange Stabilization Fund.   A fund established by the Gold Reserve Act of January 30, 1934, from the "profits" of gold devaluation. The Fund, initially $2 billion, was placed under the exclusive control of the Secretary of the Treasury and was to be used for the purpose of stabilizing the exchange value of the dollar. Later on July 31, 1945, the Fund was reduced to $200 million when $1.8 billion were transferred to the IMF to cover part of the U.S. subscription. In the following 25 years the assets of the Fund increased rapidly and on September 30, 1970, totaled $2.6 billion. The assets consist mainly of cash, Special Drawing Rights, gold account of the Treasury with the Federal Reserve Bank of New York, foreign exchange due from foreign central banks and investments. Current transactions in the Fund appear monthly in the *Treasury Bulletin.*

Appreciation bonds.   A term applied to U.S. bonds which, sold at a discount, are redeemed at certain stated prices, rising over time until maturity. Thus in World War II the Series E bonds, which matured in ten years, were sold at $75 per $100 bond. If held until maturity, when they were redeemed at face value, they had an average annual yield of 2.9 percent.

Artificial clearings.   The clearing of goods and currencies against one another in international trade at prices which are determined by government fiat rather than by the demand and supply forces of the market place. Thus Germany in the 1930s purchased wheat from Rumania at prices which were slightly above the local prices and which seemed advantageous to the Rumanian farmer. The marks given in the purchase of the wheat were inconvertible and could be used for the sole purchase of certain goods in Germany, usually at prices above the international market. The marks themselves were, in terms of Rumanian currency, also given a value above the market level. The technique used was a form of economic exploitation of a weak nation by its dominating economic partner.

Balance of payments. The net debit or credit balance resulting from all the transactions of a nation in international trade, commerce and finance.

Bankers' acceptance. A bill of exchange accepted by a banking institution.

Bankers' balance. A deposit held by one bank with another financial institution.

Bank restricted debt. Obligations issued by the United States in World War II, which were not eligible for commercial bank purchase until after the lapse of a stipulated number of years.

Barter. The exchange of goods and services without the intermediation of money.

Basle credit. A lending arrangement among central banks, implemented by the Bank for International Settlements, for purposes of exchange stabilization.

Bill of exchange. Defined by the American Negotiable Instruments Law as "an unconditional order in writing, signed by the person giving it, requiring the person to whom it is addressed to pay on demand or at a fixed or determinable future time a sum certain in money to order or to bearer." Thus the one who writes the order is the "drawer," the one directed to make payment is the "drawee," the one named to receive payment is the "payee." To become obligated the drawee must "accept" the instrument. Bills of exchange include checks, drafts, trade acceptances (in which the acceptor is a merchant), and bankers' acceptances (in which the acceptor is a bank). A promissory note differs from a bill of exchange in that it is a promise to pay, not an order to pay.

Bond purchase fund. A fund established by the Treasury in 1918 for the purpose of supporting the prices of Liberty Bonds. By June 30, 1920, when it was superseded by the 2-½ percent Cumulative Sinking Fund, it had purchased $1.7 billion of bonds. Its activities were financed by the sale of Certificates of Indebtedness.

Bretton Woods Institutions. The two international institutions resulting from the Bretton Woods Conference of July 1-22, 1944: the International Monetary Fund and the International Bank for Reconstruction and Development.

Brokers' loans. In the 1920s, loans extended by banks (domestic and foreign), by individuals and corporations to finance stock exchange speculation.

Budget, cash basis. A record of or an estimate of the cash income and expenditures of the Federal or State governments.

Budget, federal. An estimate of receipts and expenditures for the forthcoming fiscal year (July 1–June 30) with recommendations for action, presented by the President of the U.S. to the Congress in January of each year.

Built-in stabilizers. An expression used particularly in the 1950s to describe certain fiscal operations of the U.S. government which have the effect of smoothing cyclical fluctuations in business activity. Thus social security and unemployment insurance payments increase in recession, and corporate and personal income tax payments decline. All in combination help to check a business recession; the opposite sequence occurs in a boom.

Central Rate. A rate selected by an IMF member (not presently maintaining exchange rates on a par value) at which its currency will be stabilized in terms of gold, SDRs or other currencies.

Certificate of deposit. A formal receipt for funds left with a bank. May be payable on demand or at a future date, may be negotiable or non-negotiable. May or may not be subject to Regualtion "Q" of the Board of Governors of the Federal Reserve System.

Certificate of indebtedness. Short-term coupon obligation issued by the United States Government.

Civilian Conservation Corps. A work stimulus project established in the Great Depression. Young men from the city and rural slums were put to work by the Federal government, mainly in clearing and replanting forests, building fire towers and trails for fire-fighters. The corps was modeled after the conservation camps set up by New York State while President Roosevelt was Governor.

Clearing-house loan certificate. An obligation issued against commercial bank assets during periods of acute monetary stringency by various clearing houses in the United States and used in the settlement of daily balances at the clearing house.

Clearinghouse run. A run on banks characterized by the shifting of deposits from banks considered unsound to institutions of better repute in the same or different city.

Commercial paper. Single-name promissory notes (short-term) issued in the open market by business firms in the U.S. for the purpose mainly of financing working capital needs.

Commercial paper, bank-related. Short-term promissory notes issued by affiliates of commercial banks, particularly through 1969 and the first half of 1970, when banks sought sources of lendable funds under pressure of increasing monetary restraint. The growth was halted in mid-1970 when the Board of Governors of the Federal Reserve System suspended Regulation Q ceilings on short-maturity large negotiable certificates of deposit and then placed reserve requirements on bank funds derived from commercial paper.

Commission on Money and Credit. A private group established by the Board of Trustees of the Committee for Economic Development and commissioned to make a study of the U.S. monetary and financial system. The report of the Commission appeared in *Money and Credit: Their Influence on Jobs, Prices and Growth* (Prentice-Hall, 1961).

Committee for Economic Development. Established by private business organizations in the United States during World War II to make plans for the rapid reconversion of plants which had been diverted to war production and for employment opportunities for returning servicemen.

Commodity rates. Preferential rates of discount established by the Federal Reserve Banks from 1915–17 on promissory notes secured by warehouse receipts for cotton, grain, and other staple, nonperishable agricultural products, of a readily marketable character. The purpose of the rates was to enable producers, in view of the decline in European demand, immediately following the out break of war, to withhold temporarily a portion of their crops from the market.

Common Market. Colloquialism for the European Economic Community, which came into effect on January 1, 1958, after Belgium, France, Italy, Luxembourg, the Netherlands and West Germany signed a treaty in Rome in March 1957. The purpose of the organization is to eliminate barriers to a free flow of goods and services and eventually to establish a common currency.

Confidence crisis. A sudden decline in confidence, in a banking system or in a currency. It may take the form of a run on banks, i.e., conversion of deposits into currency or a run on the gold and other reserves of a nation, i.e., the conversion of currency and deposits into gold, foreign currencies or Special Drawing Rights.

Consumer price index. A measure of changes in the retail prices of the goods and services bought by city wage earners and clerical workers.

Convertibility nonresident. The willingness of a nation to convert its currency into other currencies for nonresidents but not for its own citizens.

Cost push. An increase in costs and prices resulting principally from increases in wages brought about by trade union action. Cost push inflation is to be differentiated, although the two are closely related, from demand-pull inflation, resulting from an excess of money relative to available goods and services.

Crawling peg. A foreign exchange policy of government which progressively raises or lowers the value of its currency in terms of other currencies.

Credit crunch. The inability of financial institutions to meet pressing credit needs by reason of a serious impairment in their liquidity.

Cross rates. The exchange value of two currencies not in terms of each other but in terms of third currencies.

Council of Economic Advisors.   A three-member committee established by the Employment Act of 1946 and appointed by the President, with the advice and consent of the Senate, to study and advise the President on economic developments, appraise the economic programs and policies of the Federal government, make recommendations to the President for policies and action in the fields of economic growth and stability and assist in the preparation of the economic reports of the President to Congress.

Currency stabilization, de facto.   The stabilization of a currency in terms of other currencies or gold by action of the central bank or Treasury rather than by statute law.

Currency stabilization, de jure.   The stabilization of a currency in terms of other currencies or gold by statute law.

Current ratio.   On financial statements the ratio of total current assets to total current liabilities.

Dawes loan.   A loan of 800 million gold marks granted by investors in various foreign nations to Germany in 1924 in order to help rehabilitate its economy. The loan was named for Charles Gates Dawes, Vice President of the U.S., who played an active role in the reparation negotiations of which the loan was an essential feature.

Dealer in government securities.   A firm which buys and sells and makes a market in government obligations.

Debt management.   Policies followed by a government concerning the types, maturities and ownership distribution of the obligations it issues.

Debt monetization.   The extension of loans and the purchase of securities by commercial banks which in effect converts the obligations of the debtor into bank deposits.

Deposit, demand.   In the United States, one which is payable immediately or upon a notice of 29 days or less.

Deposit, time.   Savings deposits, time certificates of deposit, and time deposits open account.

Depression. A decline in business activity of such intensity that an index of production falls by 25 percent or more. The suggested dividing line between what constitutes a depression and a recession is of course an arbitrary one.

Devaluation. An increase in the price of gold in terms of a local currency, i.e., the local currency falls in value in terms of gold.

Discount rates. Rates of interest established by central banks for the discounting of eligible paper or for the granting of collateral loans.

Discipline of the balance of payments. The credit and fiscal policies which result from an imbalance in international accounts and which by their action rectify the imbalance.

Disintermediation. A term applied to action by creditors of savings institutions in shifting savings funds in periods of crisis into demand deposits, open-market obligations or currency.

Double liability. A characteristic at one time of the stock of national banks. In event of failure a stockholder stood to lose not only his original investment but could also be called upon to pay to the receivers of the bank an additional sum equal to the par value of the stock. The double liability of national bank stock was terminated by the Banking Acts of 1933 and 1935.

Economic growth. Conventionally measured by changes in Gross National Product. It is considered sustainable if underlying fiscal and monetary policies are such as to promote and not check growth over a period of time. In recent years attention has been directed to the effect of economic growth on the environment.

Economic stabilization. Policies followed by governments in an effort to reduce cyclical amplitudes in economic activity.

Eligible paper. Paper eligible for discount and purchase by central banks.

Employment. A person is considered employed if, during the week of reference, he did any work for pay or profit, on or off a farm, or worked at least 15 hours as an unpaid family worker in a business or on a farm operated by a member of the family or if he were temporarily absent from work by reason of illness, bad weather, vacation, labor management disputes. A person is considered unemployed if he has not been at work during the survey week but is actively seeking work, if he is not at work but waiting to be called back to a job from which he has been laid off or if he is waiting to report to a new wage or salary job in the next 30 days. The civilian labor force is the sum of the employed and the unemployed. It is confined to persons 14 years of age and over.

Equity debt ratio.   The ratio of total equity to total debt.

Eurodollars.   Broadly defined as dollars on deposit with banks located outside the United States.

European Monetary Agreement.   An agreement which came into effect on December 27, 1958, and which includes some sixteen European nations. The purpose of the Agreement is to encourage multilateralism in international trade and currency convertibility. Reviews of its operations are to be found in the *Annual Reports* of the Bank for International Settlements, which acts as agent.

Excess profits tax.   A tax usually levied during war time on what is defined as excess corporate earnings.

Exchange rates: spot, forward.   Spot rates apply to rates charged on immediate transactions, forward rates to those consummated at a future time.

Export-Import Bank of the United States.   Established as the Export-Import Bank of Washington in 1934, and, organized under the laws of the District of Columbia; it was made an independent agency of the government by the Export-Import Bank Act of 1945. The name was changed to the Export-Import Bank of the United States by Act of March 13, 1968. The purpose of the bank is to facilitate and finance the exports and imports of the United States.

Federal funds.   Surplus reserves of member banks on the books of the Federal Reserve Bank which are traded among member banks and others in the money markets.

Federal Home Loan Bank System.   Created by authority of the Federal Home
Loan Bank Act approved July 26, 1932. The twelve regional Federal Home
Loan Banks are under the supervision of the Federal Home Loan Bank Board
consisting of three members appointed by the President of the United States.
The function of the Banks is to make loans to member institutions, mainly
savings and loan associations, in order to enable them in turn to make mortgage loans or to meet deposit withdrawals.

Federal Housing Administration.   Established by the National Housing Act
June 27, 1934, it has undergone various reorganizations in subsequent years.
Now part of the Department of Housing and Urban Development. The pur-
pose of the agency is to insure mortgages on various types of housing.

Federal Intermediate Credit Banks.   Established by the Agricultural Credits
Act of 1923, which provided for twelve Federal Intermediate Credit Banks,
one in each farm credit district. All of the stock is owned by farmers through
some 452 local production credit associations. The banks make loans to, and
discount agricultural paper for production credit associations, State and national banks, agricultural credit corporations, livestock loan companies and
similar lending groups.

Federal National Mortgage Association.   Originally chartered on February 10,
1938, it later became a government-sponsored private corporation pursuant to
Title VIII of the Housing and Urban Development Act of 1968. Its purpose
is to provide a secondary market in real estate mortgages.

Federal Open-Market Committee.   A committee of the Federal Reserve System
which has complete charge of open-market operations. It includes the members of the Board of Governors of the Federal Reserve System and five representatives of the twelve Federal Reserve Banks.

Federal Reserve Agent.   An official of a Federal Reserve Bank (also serves as
chairman of the local Board of Directors), appointed by the Board of Governors of the Federal Reserve System who makes regular reports to the Board
of Governors and who has charge of the collateral against which Federal Reserve notes are issued. His duties may be assigned to one or more Assistant
Federal Reserve Agents.

Finance bills. Bills of exchange drawn mainly to finance general cash needs of business enterprise and hence are to be distinguished from self-liquidating bills which are drawn to finance short-term specific transactions.

Fiscal agent. An individual or firm which performs fiscal services for governmental or other borrowers.

Fiscal dividend. The rise in Federal tax receipts resulting from an upsurge in economic activity.

Fiscal drag. The surplus the Federal government enjoys by reason of revenue increases resulting from a rise in economic activity, which are thought by some economists to act as a check on economic growth.

Fiscal policy. Action taken by a government in the areas of government expenditures and revenues, and management of the public debt.

Float. The difference on the Federal Reserve statement between uncollected cash items on the asset side and deferred availability cash items on the liability side.

Floating debt. In the area of government finance, short-term government securities usually under one year in maturity.

Floating rate of exchange. A rate of exchange which is not tied to gold or to another currency, and which, in consequence, fluctuates in terms of other currencies.

Forward exchange transactions. Agreements to buy and sell foreign exchange at a future date.

Free gold. The amount of gold over and above the gold reserve requirements of the Federal Reserve Banks when these were in force.

Free silver. The action of governments in purchasing unlimited amounts of silver at a fixed price in terms of local currency.

Free Trade Association, European. A group of European nations including Austria, Denmark, Finland, Iceland, Norway, Portugal, Sweden, Switzerland

and the United Kingdom. The association was created by treaty dated January 4, 1960 for the purpose of gradually reducing customs duties and quantitative restrictions between the members on industrial but not agricultural products.

Full employment surplus. The revenue surplus of the Federal government which might be achieved when unemployment does not exceed, say, 4 percent of the labor force, a hypothetical concept.

German Gold Discount Bank, Berlin. Established on March 19, 1924, initially for the purpose of financing and facilitating export credits. Its functions were enlarged until the outbreak of World War II; operations have been quiescent since 1945.

Giro system. A clearing system used in the United Kingdom and by continental nations. A bank depositor pays debts by issuing an order to his bank to transfer the appropriate sums to his creditors.

Glass-Steagall Act. Adopted on February 27, 1932, it permitted the issuance of Federal Reserve notes directly against the Federal debt.

Gold earmarking. Gold held by one nation for the account of another.

Gold exchange standard. A type of standard used extensively in the 1920s under the terms of which a local currency is not redeemable in gold but in the currency of another nation which is itself redeemable in gold.

Gold Settlement Fund. Now the inter-District Settlement Fund, it is used to clear transactions between the Federal Reserve banks.

Gold tranche. The amount the U.S. or any other member nation borrow automatically from the IMF. It ordinarily equals a member's quota in the International Monetary Fund minus the Fund's holdings of its currency, if the amount is positive.

Greenbacks. Fiat paper money, i.e., irredeemable paper money issued by the U.S. government during the Civil War.

Gross National Product. A measure in dollars of the total volume of goods and services produced by a nation.

Group of Ten. Ten nations, including Belgium, Canada, France, Germany, Italy, Japan, Netherlands, Sweden, the United Kingdom and the United States, which since October 24, 1962, have stood ready, under what are termed the General Arrangements to Borrow, to make loans to the IMF for use in currency stabilization.

Hague Agreements on Reparations. Agreements signed by Germany on January 20, 1930, by which a final settlement of reparations and other financial claims arising from World War I was attempted. The Bank for International Settlements was organized to act as trustee for reparations payments and for interest payments on various bond issues.

Hoarded currency. Money removed from circulation by the owner, a widespread practice in the U.S. in the early 1930s, resulting from fear of bank failures.

Hot money. Short-term funds, in search of safety, moving from one money market to another in periods of crisis.

Implicit price deflators. Deflators used in the attempt to eliminate the effects of price changes on the components and the total value of Gross National Product.

Inflation alerts. Statements first issued by the Council of Economic Advisers in June 1970 for the purpose of calling attention to specific cases of exceptionally inflationary wage or price behavior.

Inter-District rediscounting. Loans extended in the early days of the Federal Reserve System among the Federal Reserve Banks.

Interest equalization tax. A tax imposed on the purchase of foreign securities by American investors designed to equalize foreign and domestic money rates.

Interest rate curve. The relationship of short-intermediate-and long-term interest rates.

International Financial Conference, Brussels, 1920. Called by the Council of the League of Nations, an international financial conference met in Brussels from September 24–October 8, 1920. Delegates were sent not only by members of the League of Nations but also by former enemy countries, with the exception of Turkey, and from certain of the newer countries, including Finland, Luxemburg, Esthonia, Latvia and Lithuania. Russia did not send a delegation and the United States was only unofficially represented. The work of the Conference consisted of the presentation of various statistical statements and of the reports of commissions assigned to specific problems in such fields as public finance, international trade, currency and exchange, and international credits. The Conference recommended the balancing of governmental budgets, the checking of inflation, a return to the gold standard, the establishment of central banks in nations in which they did not exist, the establishing of an international investment bank and an international system of export credit insurance.

Investment tax credit. A Federal tax credit permitted business corporations for investments in eligible machinery and equipment.

Joint Commission of Agricultural Inquiry. A commission consisting of U.S. Representatives and Senators, established in 1921, to inquire into the reasons for the then prevailing agricultural depression and the banking and financial and credit resources of the country, especially as affecting agricultural credits.

Leading indicators. Those economic series which on the upward thrust of the business cycle and the downward thrust lead other economic series. They include such series as the average work week of production workers in manufacturing; average weekly initial claims state unemployment insurance; new orders durable goods; contracts and orders for plant and equipment; index for net business formation; corporate profits, after taxes; ratio of price to unit labor cost; index of stock prices; index of industrial materials prices; index of new private housing units; changes in book value of manufacturing and trade inventories; and net change in consumer instalment debt. These indexes tend to move before such indexes as the unemployment rate, industrial production, personal income, and bank rate on short-term business loans.

Leads and lags in trade. Those leads and lags resulting from anticipated changes in currency values. Thus, if a devaluation of X's currency is anticipated, exporters of goods to X will demand quick payment and importers will delay payment.

Liquidity. The cash assets or assets quickly convertible into cash owned by a business corporation or bank in relation to its short-term liabilities.

Liquidity crisis. A condition in which the absence of an appropriate ratio of cash and cash assets to the short-term liabilities of a business firm or bank causes a creditor by reason of a growing lack of confidence to call loans, to refuse new credits and to demand redemption of deposits into currency or gold.

London Economic Conference. A world Monetary and Economic Conference, which, upon the initiative of President Hoover convened in London in June 1933, the purpose of which was to evolve cooperative action on world economic problems. Ended in failure by reason largely of the opposition of President Roosevelt to foreign exchange stabilization.

Macmillan Committee. Otherwise known as the Committee on Finance and Industry appointed by the British Chancellor of the Exchequer on November 5, 1929, "to inquire into banking finance and credit, paying regard to the factors both internal and international which govern their operation, and to make recommendations calculated to enable these agencies to promote the development of trade and commerce and the employment of labour." Report presented to Parliament, June 1931.

Maintenance margin. The margin which a purchaser of securities must maintain against his loan before the loan is called.

Margin. The amount of equity which the purchaser of securities on credit must himself provide to finance the transaction.

Margin debt, Stock-market credit. The total amount of debt incurred by stock purchasers when buying stocks on credit.

Market rates. Rates of interest resulting from the demand for and supply of funds in the money market.

Monetarists. Economists who maintain that fiscal and central bank policy should be directed toward increasing the money supply, variously defined, by a fixed invariable percentage.

Monetary aggregates. Include such series as adjusted credit proxy, (defined as including demand and time deposits, borrowings in the Eurodollar market and commercial paper issued by affiliated institutions) total reserve bank credit, total reserve deposits and cash held by member banks, currency in circulations plus demand deposits, currency in circulation plus demand and time deposits, total member bank borrowings, and member-bank borrowings minus excess member-bank reserves.

Money supply or stock. Currency in circulation (i.e. outside the Treasury, the Federal Reserve Banks and the vaults of commercial banks) plus demand deposits at all commercial banks other than those due to domestic commercial banks and the U.S. government, less cash items in the process of collection and Federal Reserve float, plus foreign demand deposists at the Federal Reserve Banks.

Moral suasion. Action by a central bank in dissuading commercial banks from making certain types of loans or investments; takes the form of admonitions, warnings and the like.

Mortgage debt. Debt secured by mortgages on one-family or multifamily homes or commercial buildings.

Multiple currency practices. Practices by nations, particularly in the 1930s, in establishing different foreign exchange rates on various types of international transactions, i.e. one rate for imports, another for exports, (each by classes of commodities), another for capital imports and exports, another for tourist expenditures, etc.

Multiplier. The multiple effect on personal income and GNP of increases in expenditures by government, business firms and individuals.

Municipal warrants. Short-term obligations issued by municipalities in anticipation of assured revenues.

New Economics. In the 1960's, the expansionist fiscal and monetary policies which were epitomized by "operation twist" and the revenue act of 1964.

New era. The economic attitudes and trends of the 1920s. The basic assumption was that cyclical declines would not again be experienced because wage payments would rise sufficiently fast to enable consumers to purchase the growing volume of goods and services being produced.

Official reserves.   Monetary reserves held by central banks and governments consisting of gold, convertible foreign exchange and Special Drawing Rights.

Open-market operations.   The purchase and sale of U.S. obligations, municipal obligations, acceptances and foreign exchange by the Federal Reserve Banks.

Operation twist.   Federal Reserve policy in the early 1960s which endeavored to keep short-term rates high while lowering long-term rates; thus the interest rate curve would be twisted.

Orderly market.   A security market in which prices move smoothly to lower or upper levels. A decline in prices evokes purchases and a rise in prices evokes sales, so that there is no sharp disequilibrium between demand and supply.

Other securities.   Securities other than U.S. obligations, U.S. agency obligations, and municipal obligations owned by member banks. These would include corporate and foreign obligations.

Par value.   That value of a currency expressed in terms of gold as a common denominator, or in terms of the U.S. dollar, of the weight and fineness in effect July 1, 1944. The present (1972) par value of the U.S. dollar is 0.818513 grams of fine gold.

Postal Savings Banks.   Savings banks established in 1910 as part of the U.S. post offices, to provide a safe depository for the savings of wage-earners particularly of emigrants. The low rates paid on savings, coupled with various restrictive regulations, checked the growth of the institutions excepting during the bank failure epidemic of the early 1930s. With the advent of deposit insurance there seemed little need for these banks and they were discontinued on April 27, 1966.

Preferential rates of discounts.   Rates of discount established on certain types of paper such as export bills, which are lower than the rates prevailing on other types of paper.

Production gap. The difference between actual production and estimated possible maximum production.

Progressive discount rates. Discount rates which were in effect at the Federal Reserve Banks of Atlanta, Dallas, Kansas City and St. Louis through much of 1920–21 and which, with deviations among these Reserve Banks, increased as the borrowings of a member-bank at its Reserve Bank rose in relation to its deposits at its Reserve Bank, its ownership of stock in its Reserve Bank, and its own capital funds.

Public debit. Conventionally, all obligations issued by a government.

Radcliffe Committee. A British Committee, otherwise known as Committee on the Working of the Monetary System. This committee, of which the Right Hon. Lord Radcliffe was Chairman, was appointed by Treasury Minute dated May 3, 1957, "to inquire into the working of the monetary and credit system, and to make recommendations." The report of the Committee was presented to Parliament by the Chancellor of the Exchequer by Command of Her Majesty, August 1959.

Recession. A decline in business activity often defined as one which causes a decline in the index of production of not more than 25 percent.

Reconstruction Finance Corporation. A government corporation established in January 1932, whose initial purpose was to assist in the financial reconstruction of banks, railways, agricultural institutions and business firms in the Great Depression. Later it financed the construction and operation of war plants. In 1948 the life of the R.F.C. was extended to 1956 but its lending powers were sharply curtailed.

Reflation. In the Great Depression, fiscal and monetary action which endeavored to raise prices (the wholesale and consumer price index) to some level, selected as highly desirable, existing prior to the business decline.

Regulation Q. A regulation issued by the Board of Governors of the Federal Reserve System establishing maximum interest rates on time and savings deposits of member banks.

Reichsbank. The central bank of Germany which was founded in 1876 and continued until 1945.

Reparations. Payments made in money or kind by a defeated nation in time of war. The reparations problem as it was called came to the fore after World War I, involving such questions as the amount of reparations Germany would be expected to pay, and the economic effect of those payments on Germany and the recipient nations. The payment of reparations ceased with the Hoover Moratorium of 1931.

Resale or Repurchase agreements. An agreement entered into by the Federal Reserve Banks, commercial banks, nonfinancial corporations and other customers on the one hand, and dealers in government securities and acceptances, on the other hand, under the terms of which the dealer buys or sells securities and simultaneously makes a commitment to sell or buy an equivalent amount at a later date. The purchase or sale is undertaken at prices or yields to provide a specific rate of return.

Reserves. The amount of gold, gold certificates and legal tender money which the Reserve Banks were once required to hold in certain definite proportions to deposit and note liabilities.

Secondary market. The market which develops for securities once the securities have been underwritten and the underwriters syndicate has dissolved.

Security affiliates. Corporations engaged in the underwriting, purchase and sale of securities which were closely affiliated with a commercial bank. Outlawed by the Banking Act of 1933.

Selective credit control. The control of the terms of loans (down payment, maturity, loan to value ratio) in certain selected credit areas such as consumer credit, real estate credit and security loan credit.

Self-liquidating paper. Promissory notes and bills of exchange which arise from a transaction, the consummation of which provides funds for the payment of the note or bill. Thus, a promissory note would be termed self-liquidating if the proceeds were used by a merchant to build up inventory for the Christmas trade which, when sold, would provide funds for the repayment of the loan. Self-liquidating paper, therefore, is short-term in form and finances a transaction which generates funds for the loan repayment.

Special Drawing Rights (SDRs). Certificates issued by the IMF to member nations which agree to abide by all prescribed rules and obligations. A means of increasing the reserves, within limits, of member nations.

Stabilization of currencies. The fixing of the value of currencies in terms of gold or in terms of each other; often one currency serves as a key currency in terms of which other currencies are stabilized.

Stock jobbers. In early American history, stock speculators, often engaging in illegal, illicit or unethical practices.

Street loans. In the 1920s, loans (usually call loans) extended to stock-brokers.

Tax and Loan Accounts. U.S. Government deposits held by commercial banks resulting from the purchase of government securities, and the deposit of income, social security and other taxes.

Technocracy. The theory developed in the Great Depression that the economy would be more productive if it were managed by engineers.

Tellers' runs. The encashment of deposits at a commercial bank thought to be approaching insolvency.

Tied loans. Loans granted by commercial banks or underwritten by investment banks or government with the stipulation that the proceeds are to be spent for goods and services produced in the lending nation.

Trade acceptance. A bill of exchange drawn by one merchant on another.

Trade credit. Credit granted by one nonfinancial corporation to another.

Treasury bills. Government obligations issued at a discount and sold on an auction basis with maximum maturities of about 360 days.

Treasury notes. By act of Congress signed by President Cleveland in July 1890, the Treasury was required to purchase 4 million ounces of silver each month at the market price as long as it did not exceed $1.29 an ounce, the price set in 1837. No silver dollars had actually to be coined, instead Treasury notes of full legal tender power were issued to the cost of the bullion, "redeemable on demand in coin." From a total of $40 million in June 30, 1891 they rose to $135 million in 1894, declining to a little more than $1 million in the early 1930s. Retirement of the Treasury notes of 1890 was finally ordered by Act of Congress on June 30, 1961.

Underwood Tariff Act of 1913. A tariff enactment sponsored by President Wilson which sharply reduced tariff rates on various imports.

Undistributed Profits Tax. Under the Revenue Act of 1936 corporations (excepting specified classes) were subject to a surtax on undistributed profits graduated from 7 to 27 percent. The act was based on the doctrine that corporations should go to the market to seek new funds and thus should undergo the tests of the market place. They would not be subject to these tests, it was argued, if they were to invest their own funds. Considerable opposition developed to the law which was finally eliminated for taxable years beginning after December 31, 1939.

Unemployment, structural. Unemployment resulting from racial discrimination, monopolistic power of trade unions, lack of universal educational opportunities and absence of free interplay of demand and supply.

Veterans Administration. Established as an independent agency on July 21, 1930 to coordinate and consolidate Federal agencies, especially created for or concerned in the administration of laws providing benefits for veterans.

Wider band. A suggestion that foreign exchange rates under the roles of the IMF be permitted to fluctuate within wider limits above and below par than now allowed.

Works Progress Administration. Authorized by the Federal government in April 1935 with an initial appropriation of $4.9 billion, it was designed to get 3,500,000 unemployed men and women off the relief rolls and into employment. Before it was terminated in 1943 it had provided employment for 8,000,000 persons. Total expenditures amounted to about $10 billion.

Index

D

N

T